Bureau of statistics

Wool and Manufactures of Wool

Vol. 2

Bureau of statistics

Wool and Manufactures of Wool
Vol. 2

ISBN/EAN: 9783337428020

Printed in Europe, USA, Canada, Australia, Japan

Cover: Foto ©Suzi / pixelio.de

More available books at **www.hansebooks.com**

TREASURY DEPARTMENT.

WOOL AND MANUFACTURES OF WOOL.

SPECIAL REPORT

RELATING TO

THE IMPORTS AND EXPORTS OF WOOL AND ITS MANUFACTURES IN
THE UNITED STATES AND THE PRINCIPAL FOREIGN COUNTRIES;
ALSO ITS PRODUCTION, CONSUMPTION, AND MANUFACTURE;
ALSO THE TARIFF DUTIES IMPOSED ON THE IMPORTS
OF WOOL AND THE MANUFACTURES OF WOOL,
FROM 1789 TO THE PRESENT TIME,
ETC., ETC., ETC.

PREPARED BY THE

CHIEF OF THE BUREAU OF STATISTICS,
TREASURY DEPARTMENT.

WASHINGTON:
GOVERNMENT PRINTING OFFICE.
1887.

5402 w

CONTENTS.

APPENDIX.

THE UNITED STATES.

LETTER OF TRANSMITTAL.

TREASURY DEPARTMENT,
BUREAU OF STATISTICS, *September* 6, 1887.

SIR: I have the honor herewith to transmit a special report on the imports, exports, &c., of wool and the manufactures of wool, in which will be found a brief history of the development of sheep husbandry, and of wool and woolen manufactures in the United States and other countries.

Among other interesting statistics are tables showing the production and consumption of wool, and the progress of our manufactures of wool and worsted, the number of machines and employés engaged in their manufacture, capital invested, wages paid, and the materials consumed in each State of the United States in 1880.

Tables are also presented showing the tariff duties on imports of wool and its manufactures into the United States from the first wool tariff of 1789 to the present time, together with synopses of all the decisions in customs cases made by the Treasury Department relating to wool and the manufactures of wool under the tariff act of 1883. The tariff duties imposed on imports of wool and the manufactures of wool in foreign countries are also exhibited.

I was induced to prepare this report on these great and growing industries of our country, and of other countries, because of very numerous calls for information in respect to them and of their prominence and increasing interest in the discussions of Congress and among the people.

Respectfully,

Chief of Bureau.

Hon. C. S. FAIRCHILD,
Secretary of the Treasury, Washington, D. C.

IX

SPECIAL REPORT ON WOOL AND THE MANUFACTURES OF WOOL.

INTRODUCTION.

The wool industry of the United States has assumed such proportions and importance, and the calls for information in respect to it are so numerous, as to justify a special report, more or less exhaustive, presenting the history of its development and disclosing its present condition and future possibilities.

It is not intended, of course, to enter upon a discussion of any of the phases of the economic problems involved in the past, present, or proposed tariff legislation of Congress in regard to raw wool or any of the various forms into which it has been or may be manufactured; the proper function of this Bureau being discharged by the collection and publication of full and accurate statistical and other information demanded by the current of public thought and the growing importance of the subject.

That it is of increasing interest and value to the people of the United States will be plainly seen by the following statistical totals of the progress of sheep-raising and of the manufactures of wool:

Number of sheep in the United States in 1875, 33,783,600; of which there were 4,683,200 in California; 4,592,600 in Ohio, and 3,416,500 in Michigan; seven other States containing on an average about 1,500,000 each. The remaining States had much less.

The total number of sheep in the United States and Territories in 1886, was 48,322,331; in 1887, 44,759,314, being a decrease in one year of 3,563,017. Considering, however, the period of the past twelve years, we find an increase of 10,975,914, or of 32 per cent., since 1875. In 1887 there were in California 6,069,698 head of sheep, in Ohio 4,562,913, in Michigan 2,156,127, and in Texas 4,761,831, showing since 1875 a decrease in Ohio and Michigan, while Texas more than tripled the number in the State in 1875. New Mexico in 1880 (we have no data for 1875), had 2,088,831 sheep, which number increased by 1887 to 4,025,742. Oregon, in 1875, had 634,400 sheep; in 1887, 2,593,029. Kansas, in 1875, had 118,000 sheep; in 1887, 1,106,852. Colorado, in 1875 (no returns for

1878), had 600,000; in 1887, 1,149,178.   Nebraska, in 1875, had 42,600 sheep; in 1887, 439,700.*

The quantities and value of wool produced in the United States and Territories, as estimated by the statistician of the Department of Agriculture, were: In 1865, 155,000,000 pounds; value not given; in 1875, 192,000,000 pounds, value, $94,320,652; in 1880, 240,000,000 pounds, value, $90,230,537; in 1886, 285,000,000 pounds, value, $68,400,000.

The value of the manufactures of worsted and woolen goods was: in 1850, $43,207,545; in 1860, $65,596,364; in 1870, $177,495,689; and in 1880, $267,252,913.

Respecting the quantities and values of imports and exports of raw wool into and from the United States for a long series of years, by principal foreign countries and geographical divisions, also the value of domestic

*Observing a remarkable decrease in the number of sheep in certain States in 1887 as compared with the number reported in other recent years, the Chief of the Bureau of Statistics addressed a letter of inquiry to the Agricultural Department as to the causes of the decrease. On July 16, 1887, Mr. J. R. Dodge, statistician of that Department, replied as follows:

The figures for four years as to sheep in Connecticut are:

	Numbers.
January, 1884	58,831
January, 1885	50,419
January, 1886	53,477
January, 1887	53,477

The number of sheep in Connecticut is very small at any time, and has been reduced slightly in consequence of low prices of two years past.

As to Ohio, the following figures give our estimate in January and the State enumeration in the following May:

Years.	Numbers by Department.	Numbers by State assessors.
1884	5,000,036	5,113,884
1885	4,900,035	4,823,922
1886	4,753,034	4,277,463
1887	4,562,913	Not yet issued.

The numbers of sheep of Ohio fluctuate, usually, within narrow limits, as the industry is as firmly founded in the rural economy of this State as it is in any district of the United States, according to prices obtained for wool. The decline in prices of wool always causes a decrease in the numbers of sheep in this State.

The sheep enumeration of Texas is more difficult to calculate. There evidently has been a recent increase in the numbers of cattle and a decline in the numbers of sheep, as is shown by our returns, and by those of the State authorities of Texas. But this does not account for the whole of the reduction of the present year. The State returns have only been made once since 1884, and they showed that our county estimates of increase for previous years had been too sanguine, requiring a correction. Therefore, while all returns indicate a reduction of numbers since 1884, the apparent decrease is partly due to the above-mentioned error. It has always been far more difficult to estimate accurately the changes occurring, sometimes rapid and sweeping, in ranch flocks than in farm stocks.

There is no kind of farm animals so sensitive to changes in prices as sheep—not even swine, which are cheap when corn is cheap—while the cost of caring for sheep is quite uniform and relatively inflexible.

manufactures of wool exported, and the values of manufactures of wool imported, the reader is referred to tables on pages 1 to 11 of the Appendix.

An examination of the totals above given, without reference to the more elaborate tables to be found in the Appendix of the report, will confirm the indications of the rapid development and the increasing interest of the people in the production of wool and in its manufacture.

CHARACTERISTICS OF WOOL, AND HOW IT DIFFERS FROM HAIR.

It is not improbable that a large number of those who will examine this report have a vague and indefinable, and in some respects a misleading idea of what wool in a commercial sense really is, and how it differs from hair or fur; hence it is deemed proper in this place to attempt to disentangle it from popular misconception.

While it is true wool is a variety of hair, which in ordinary language is accepted to mean a smooth, straight filament, growing from the skin of animals, like human or horse hair, and without serrations of any kind on its surface, wool is not hair, nor is hair wool.

Primarily the term wool is applied both to the fine hair, or fleece, of animals, as sheep, otter, beaver, rabbits, the alpaca, and the cashmere, some species of goats, and other animals, and to fine vegetable fibers, as cotton. But in this report the term wool refers only to the fleece of the sheep—an article which from the earliest periods of human history to the present time has been of primary importance, ranking next to cotton as a raw material for textile fabrics, and forming a very large part of the clothing of mankind in the temperate regions of the globe.

Hair is straight; wool is wavy. Hair is crisp and hard; wool is soft. Viewed under the microscope, hair presents a smooth surface, whereas each woolly filament is covered with scales underlying each other, and projecting wherever a bend occurs in the fiber. If each fiber were straight and smooth, as in the case of hair, it would not retain the twisted state given to it by spinning, but would rapidly untwist when relieved from the force of the spinning-wheel; but the wavy convolutions cause the fibers to become entangled with each other and hold the fibers in close contact. Moreover, the deeper these scales or teeth fit into each other, the closer becomes the structure of the thread and consequently the cloth made of it. This gives to wool the quality of *felting*, which with hair is impossible.

The New American Cyclopedia, page 535, says that, "placed under a lens of high magnifying power, each fiber of wool has the appearance of a continuous stem, showing along its margin minute serrations, like teeth of an extremely fine saw; and a closer inspection reveals the fact that these are severally continuous around the entire fiber, so that they may be compared to as many circular leaves, cups, or calyxes, set successively into each other, and all opening or pointing in the direction from the root toward the free extremity. It was by examination of a fiber of Merino wool that these cup like ridges were first discovered; but once recognized, it is very easy to detect them in the coarser sorts of fibers. * * * Upon holding up to the light a lock of wool, or a single fiber, it is further observed that the fibers have all permanently acquired in their growth a form more or less twisted or spiral, like that of a corkscrew; and by the two characteristics thus discovered the felting and thread-forming qualities of wool, and the valuable applications growing out of them, are at once explained. The contorted form of the fibers disposes them to embrace or interlace with, or to hook on to each other; and the serratures, when the fibers are brought close together in felt, thread, or cloth, present that resistance to slipping and separation which is indispensable to the strength of the fabric. In the long Merino and Saxon wools these scales or projections are very distinct and acutely pointed; in the Southdown, somewhat less distinct and sharp; in the Leicester, at least the ordinary variety, quite rounded off and indistinct. In fine Saxon wool, 2,720 of these imbrications are found to the inch; in the ordinary Merino, 2,400; in the Australian Merino, 1,920 to 2,400; in Southdown, 2,000 to 2,080; in Leicester wool, 1,850 to 1,860. So far as this single quality is concerned, the results are in strict accordance with the known relative values of the several wools for manufacture; since the felting of Saxon wool is superior to that of all others, that of the Southdown inferior to that of both Saxon and ordinary Merino, and that of the Leicester least of all. Either the Southdown or Leicester wool, alone, makes a fuzzy, hairy cloth, and neither is now used in England except for the poorest cloths, or when largely admixed with wool of a better quality of fiber. Of two varieties of wool in which the number of the imbrications is about equal, that in which they are at once smaller and more uniform will be the softer and more elastic."

KINDS AND SPECIES OF WOOL AND HOW IMPROVED BY DOMESTIC CULTURE.

[From Ure's Dictionary.]

"In reference to textile fabrics, sheep's wool is of two different sorts, the short and the long-stapled; each of which requires different modes of manufacture in the preparation and spinning processes, as also in the treatment of the cloth after it is woven, to fit it for the market. Each of these is, moreover, distinguished in commerce by the names of fleece wools and dead wools, according as they have been shorn at the usual annual period from the living animal, or are cut from its skin after death. The latter are comparatively harsh, weak, and incapable of imbibing the dyeing principles, more especially if the sheep has died of some malignant distemper.

"The wool of the sheep has been surprisingly improved by its domestic culture. The *mouflon* (*Ovis aries*), the parent stock from which our sheep is undoubtedly derived, and which is still found in a wild state upon the mountains of Sardinia, Corsica, Barbary, Greece, and Asia Minor, has a very short and coarse fleece, more like hair than wool. When this animal is brought under the fostering care of man, the rank fibers gradually disappear, while the soft wool round their roots, little conspicuous in the wild animal, becomes singularly developed. The male most speedily undergoes this change, and continues ever afterwards to possess far more power in modifying the fleece of the offspring than the female parent. The produce of a breed from a coarse-wooled ewe and a fine-wooled ram is of a mean quality between the two, but half-way nearer that of the sire. By coupling the female thus generated with such a male as the former, another improvement of one-half will be obtained, affording a staple three fourths finer than that of the grandam. By proceeding inversely, the wool would be as rapidly deteriorated. It is, therefore, a matter of the first consequence in wool husbandry to exclude from the flock all coarse-fleeced rams.

"Long wool is the produce of a peculiar variety of sheep, and varies in the length of its fibers from 3 to 8 inches. Such wool is not carded like cotton, but combed like flax, either by hand or appropriate machinery. Short wool is seldom longer than 3 or 4 inches; it is susceptible of carding and felting, by which processes the filaments become first convoluted, and then densly matted together. The shorter sorts of the combing wools are used principally for hosiery, though of late years the finer kinds have been extensively worked up into Merino and other useful fabrics. The longer wools of the Leicestershire breed are manufactured into hard yarns, for worsted pieces,such as waistcoats, carpets, bombazines, poplins, crapes, &c.

"The wool of which good broadcloth is made should be not only shorter, but, generally speaking, finer and softer than the worsted wools, in order to fit them for the fulling process. Some wool sorters and wool-staplers acquire by practice great nicety of discernment in judging of wools by the touch and traction of the fingers.

"There are four distinct qualities of wool upon every sheep, the finest being upon the spine, from the neck to within 6 inches of the tail, including one-third of the breadth of the back; the second covers the flanks, between the thighs and the shoulders; the third clothes the neck and rump; and the fourth extends upon the lower part of the neck and breast down to the feet, as also upon a part of the shoulders and the thighs to the bottom of the hind quarter. These should be torn asunder, and sorted, immediately after the shearing.

"The harshness of wools is dependent not solely upon the breed of the animal, or the climate, but is owing to certain peculiarities in the pasture derived from the soil. It is known that in sheep fed upon chalky districts wool is apt to get coarse; but in those upon a rich loamy soil it becomes soft and silky. The ardent sun of Spain renders the fleece of the Merino breed harsher than it is in the milder climate of Saxony. Smearing sheep with a mixture of tar and butter is deemed favorable to the softness of the wool.

"All wool, in its natural state, contains a quantity of a peculiar potash soap, secreted by the animal, called in this country the yolk (which possesses a peculiar odor), and which may be washed out by water alone, with which it forms a sort of lather. It constitutes from 25 to 50 per cent. of the wool, being most abundant in the Merino breed of sheep; and however favorable to the growth of the wool on the living animal, should be taken out soon after it is shorn, lest it injure the fibers by fermentation and cause them to become hard and brittle. After being washed in water, somewhat more than lukewarm, the wool should be well pressed and carefully dried."

[From McCulloch's Commercial Dictionary, vol. 2, ed. 1845.]

"It has been customary in this country to divide wool into two great classes—long and short wools; and these again into subordinate classes, according to the fineness of the fiber.

"Short wool is used in the cloth manufacture, and is therefore frequently called clothing wool. It may vary in length from 1 to 3 or 4 inches; if it be longer, it requires to be cut or broken to prepare it for the manufacture.

"The *felting* property of wool is known to every one. The process of hat-making, for example, depends entirely upon it. The wool of which hats are made is neither spun nor woven, but locks of it, being thoroughly intermixed and compressed in warm water, cohere and form a solid tenacious substance.

"Cloth and woolen goods are made from wool possessing this property; the wool is carded, spun, woven, and then, being put into the fulling mill, the process of felting takes place. The strokes of the mill make the fibers cohere; the piece subjected to the operation contracts in length and breadth, and its texture becomes more compact and uniform. This process is essential to the beauty and strength of woolen cloth. But the long wool of which stuffs and worsted goods are made is deprived of its felting properties. This is done by passing the wool through heated iron combs, which takes away the laminae or feathery part of the wool, and approximates it to the nature of silk or cotton.

"Long or combing wool may vary in length from 3 to 8 inches. The shorter combing wools are principally used for hose, and are spun softer than the long combing wools, the former being made into which is called hard, and the latter into soft worsted yarn.

"The fineness of the hair or fiber can rarely be estimated, at least for any useful purpose, except by the wool sorter or dealer, accustomed by long habit to discern those minute differences that are quite inappreciable by common observers. In sorting wools there are frequently eight or ten different species in a single fleece; and if the best wool of one fleece be not equal to the finest sort it is thrown to a second, third, or fourth, or to a still lower sort, of an equal degree of fineness with it. The best English short native fleeces, such as the fine Norfolk and Southdown, are generally divided by the worsted-sorter into the following sorts, all varying in fineness from each other, viz: 1, prime; 2, choice; 3, super; 4, head; 5, downrights; 6, seconds; 7, fine abb; 9, livery; 10, short coarse or breech wool. The relative value of each varies according to the greater demand for coarse, fine, or middle cloths.

"The softness of the fiber is a quality of great importance. It is not dependent on the fineness of the fiber, and consists of a peculiar feel approaching to that of silk or down. The difference in the value of two pieces of cloth made of two kinds of wool equally fine, but one distinguished for its softness and the other for the opposite quality, is such, that with the same process and expense of manufacture the one will be worth from 20 to 25 per cent. more than the other. The degree of softness depends principally on the nature of the soil on which sheep are fed; that sheep pastured on chalk districts, or light calcareous soils, usually produce hard wool; while the wool of those that are pastured on rich loamy, argillaceous soils, is always distinguished by its softness. Of the foreign wools the Saxon is generally softer than the Spanish. Hard wools are all defective in their *felting* properties.

"In clothing wool the color of the fleece should always approach as much as possible to the purest white, because such wool is not only necessary for cloths dressed white, but for all cloths that are to be dyed bright colors, for which a clear white ground is required to give a due degree of richness and luster. Some of the English fine wooled sheep, as the Norfolk and Southdown, have black or gray faces and legs. In all such sheep there is a tendency to grow gray wool on some part of the body, or to produce some gray fibers intermixed with the fleece, which renders the wool unfit for many kinds of white goods; for though the black hairs may be too few and minute to be detected by the wool-sorter, yet when the cloth is stoved they become visible, forming reddish spots, by which its color is much injured. The Herefordshire sheep, which have white faces, are entirely free from this defect, and yield a fleece without any admixture of gray hairs.

"The cleanness of the wool is an important consideration. The Spanish wool, for example, is always scoured after it is shorn; whereas the English wool is only imperfectly washed on the sheep previously to its being shorn. In consequence, it is said that while a pack of English clothing wool of 240 pounds weight will waste about 70 pounds in the manufacture, the same quantity of Spanish will not waste more than 48 pounds. Cleanness, therefore, is an object of much importance to the buyer.

"Before the recent improvements in the spinning of wool by machinery, great length and strength of staple was considered indispensable

in most combing wools. The fleeces of the long-wooled sheep fed in the
rich marshes of Kent and Lincoln used to be reckoned peculiarly suitable for the purposes of the wool-comber; but the improvements alluded
to have effected a very great change in this respect, and· have enabled
the manufacturer to substitute short wool of 3 inches staple, in the
place of long combing wool, in the preparation of most worsted articles.
A great alteration has, in consequence, taken place in the proportion of
long to short wool since 1800, there having been in the interim a considerable increase in the quantity of the latter.

"Whiteness of fleece is of less importance in the long combing than
in clothing wool, provided it be free from gray hairs. Sometimes, however, the fleece has a dingy brown color, called a *winter* stain, which is
a sure indication that the wool is not in a thoroughly sound state.
Such fleeces are carefully thrown out by the wool-sorter, being suitable
only for goods that are to be dyed black. The fineness of heavy combing wool is not of so much consequence as its other qualities.

"The Merino or Spanish breed of sheep was introduced into this country about the close of last century. George III was a great patron of
this breed, which was for several years a very great favorite. But it
has been ascertained that, though the fleece does not much degenerate
here, the carcass, which is naturally ill-formed, and affords comparatively little weight of meat, does not improve ; and as. the farmer, in
the kind of sheep which he keeps, must look not only to the produce of
wool, but also to the butcher market, he has found it his interest rather
to return to the native breeds of his own country, and to give up the
Spanish sheep. They have, however, been of considerable service to
the flocks of England, having been judiciously crossed with the Southdown, Ryeland, &c."

DIFFERENT BREEDS OF WOOL-PRODUCING SHEEP.

[From Chambers Encyclopedia.]

"As long-stapled wools are used for worsted goods, and short-stapled
for woolen goods, the various breeds which yield these two leading
kinds are naturally divided into the long-wooled and short-wooled classes
of sheep. The Lincoln, the Leicester, and the Cotswold breeds are considered good types of the former, and the Down, the Welsh, and the
Shetland breeds, of the latter.

"The following brief notice of the characteristic properties of the
various native wools is founded upon the description given of them in
the jury report of the International Exhibition of 1862, Class IV.

"Of the 'long wools' the Lincoln has greatly risen in value of late
years. It is coarse, of great length, and silky in appearance, so that it
is well adapted for 'luster' goods, in imitation of alpaca fabrics. Leicester wool is highly esteemed for combing. It is rather finer in the

hair, but not usually so soft and silky in the staple as the last. Cotswold wool is similar to the Leicester, but somewhat harsher. It is not suited for luster goods. Highland wool is long stapled, and of coarse quality, but known to be susceptible of great improvements. The practice of 'smearing' greatly depreciates its value. It is chiefly used for the coarsest kinds of woolen fabrics, as carpets, rugs, and similar articles. It is also used for Scotch blankets.

"Of the 'short wools,' the different breeds of Downs partake very much of the same characters, but soil and climate so far affect them· The Southdown is a short-stapled, small-haired wool, the longer qualities of which are put aside for combing purposes, and the shorter for the manufacture of light woolen goods, such as flannel. The Hampshire Down differs from it in being coarser, and in having the staple usually longer. The Oxford Down, again, exceeds the last in length and coarseness of staple. The Norfolk Down, on the other hand, when . clean, is of a very fine and valuable character. The Shropshire Down is a breed increasing in importance, and is longer in the staple, and has more luster than any of the other Down breeds. Ryeland's wool is fine and short, but the breed is nearly extinct. The Welsh and Shetland wools have a hair-like texture, deficient in the spiral form, upon which depends the relative value of high-class wools. They are only suited for goods where the properties of shrinking and felting are not required. Shetland wool is obtained of various natural tints, which enables it to be used for producing different patterns without dyeing.

"Of the intermediate wools, Dorset is clean, soft, and rather longer, and not quite so fine in the staple as the Down breeds. The Cheviot has increased very much of late years in public estimation. It is a small, fine-haired wool, of medium length, and is suitable for woolen and worsted purposes, for which it is largely used."

ENGLISH TERMS APPLIED TO SHEEP.

[From the American Sheep-Breeder and Wool-Grower, September, 1887.]

"The male is usually denominated a 'ram' or 'tup.' The term lamb is applied to the suckling young of both sexes; but the male, until weaned, is distinguished as a 'tup-lamb,' a 'ram-lamb,' a 'per-lamb,' or a 'heeder.' When weaned, until shorn (supposing him not shorn while a lamb) is called a 'hog,' a 'hogget,' a 'haggerel,' a ' teg,' a 'lamb-hog,' or a 'tup-hog;' and if castrated a 'wether-hog.' After shearing, say when a year and a half old, he is called a 'shearing' or ·shearling,' a 'shear-hog,' a 'diamond' or 'dinmont ram,' or 'tup;' and if castrated a 'shearing wether.'

"'Hogget-wool' is the wool of the first shearing, supposing the lamb was not shorn while it retained that title. After the second shearing, he is called a 'two-shear ram,' 'tup,' or 'wether;' next, a ·three-shear ram,' &c., the appellation indicating the number of shearings. In the north of England and in Scotland, he is called, until his first shearing, a 'tup-lamb,' then a 'tup-hog,' after that a 'tup;' or if castrated a 'din-mont' or a 'wedder.' The female while sucking is a 'ewe-lamb' or 'gimmer-lamb;' and when weaned a 'gimmer-hog,' a 'ewe-hog,' a 'teg,' a 'sheeder-ewe.' After the first shearing she is called a 'shearing-ewe' or 'gimmer;' sometimes a 'sheave' or a 'double-toothed ewe,' or 'teg.' After she is called a 'two-shear,' or a 'three-shear,' or a 'fourth-tooth, or a 'six-tooth ewe,' or 'sheave.' In some of the northern districts, ewes not in lamb, or that have weaned their lambs, are termed 'eild' or 'yeld' ewes. There are, besides these, other terms not in general use, but restricted in certain localities, which must be regarded in the sense of provincialisms. It is a singular fact that the age of a sheep is not calculated from the date of its birth, but from its first shearing, though at any time it may be, in reality, fifteen, sixteen or seventeen months old. How this custom arose is not known, but it is established."

COMMERCIAL WORDS AND PHRASES DEFINED.

"Woolens" and "Worsteds"—What is the difference between them?

There are two great classes of manufactures using wool as a raw material; in the one where carded wool is employed the goods are called " woolen fabrics"; in the other where combed wool is used the goods are called " worsted fabrics." To the uninitiated, and in popular concep-tion, there is no difference between the two fabrics. It is proper, therefore, that the distinctions of commerce in respect to them be clearly defined.

Worsted is the fiber of wool all laid exactly parallel. Woolen is crossed and uneven like a spider's web. They take all the long hairs and straighten them exactly parallel; and the shorter ones, or the noils, are used for woolen yarn. Only the long fiber can be made into " worsted."

The fibers of wool to be used in worsted are separated from the short by combing, and the fibers of woolen are crossed by carding. The former are *combing wools*. The latter, *card or clothing wools*, which formerly were the only wools used in cloths.

Mr. John L. Hayes, secretary of the National Association of Wool Manufacturers, in a paper submitted to the Senate Committee on Agri-culture, 1886, says:

Until the invention of combing by machinery or power, in the early part of the present century, the long-stapled wools, like those from the English mutton sheep, were regarded as combing wools exclusively. In England and in this country, which has always followed the English system, only the long-stapled wools were classified as combing wools until as late as 1867, the period of the tariff of that designation. Until after that time combed wools or yarns made of such wools had never been used in cloths, or the fabrics for the ordinary wear of men, but were used only in stuffs or thin unfelted fabrics, such as dress goods and linings.

Woolens, according to Simmond's Dictionary of Trade and Commerce, are textile fabrics made of wool, or of wool mixed with cotton, or some other similar material. *Worsted* is a thread spun of wool that has been combed, and which in the spinning is twisted harder than ordinary. It is chiefly used for knitting or weaving into carpets, stockings, caps, gloves, &c.

Chambers' Encyclopedia:

The difference between woolen and worsted fabrics is owing, in great part, to the way the yarn for each is spun. Yarn for woolen cloth is very slightly twisted, so as to leave the fibers as free as possible for the felting process. Worsted yarn, on the contrary, is hard spun, and made into a much stronger thread. On account of the feebleness of woolen yarn, it is more difficult to weave it by power-looms than either worsted, cotton, linen, or silk. " " " The term " worsted " is said to have derived its origin from a village of that name in Norfolk, England, where this manufacture was first carried on. Up to the end of the last century worsted goods were a staple trade of Norwich ; but the neglect of the factory system there led to its being transferred to Bradford, which has become renowned as the metropolis of the worsted manufacture. It is also extensively carried on at Halifax and other places in Yorkshire.

Messrs. Mauger & Avery, 105 Reade street, New York, in a letter to the former chief of the Bureau of Statistics, dated April 10, 1884, said:

Worsted yarn is made entirely of wool that has been combed. Strictly speaking, worsted goods are made entirely of worsted or combed yarns, but to cheapen the goods cotton yarn is frequently used for warp, and carded (woolen) and silk yarns are also frequently used for the same purpose. You are correct in your conclusion that the combing of the wool previous to spinning constitutes the basis of the distinction between " worsted " and " woolen " goods, but the processes are somewhat different all through. Woolen goods are generally "fulled," i. e., shrunk up in finishing, while worsted goods are generally finished without fulling. The peculiarity of most worsted goods is the silky or glossy finish which they have. The bulk of our fine wools go into ladies' dress goods, but knit goods, cassimere shawls, overcoatings, braids, bunting, in fact, a large variety of goods, are made now of worsted yarns. By the process of manufacture, which separates the short and weak staples, the fibers that are left are uniform in length and strength, and laid side by side ; the yarn can thus be drawn out farther, and is smooth and glossy. For any class of goods requiring to be light and strong, worsted yarns are especially suited.

Other words and phrases defined.

Donskoi wool.—A coarse carpet wool imported from Southern Russia. It is coming in direct competition with the coarse wools of New Mexico and Colorado.

Moquette.—A tapestry Brussel's carpet of a fine quality; a species of Wilton carpet. (Simmons' Commercial Dictionary.)

Waste.—Three kind of wool waste are quoted in the English wool markets: White stockings, pulled; colored stockings, pulled, and black, pulled.

Clippings.—The least valuable portion of wool clipped from the fleece and known as peddler's wool.

Territory.—The wool of the Western Territories, which has as yet no established character, but is from sheep of all grades, from the Mexican or Churro sheep of Spain to Merino. The wools of Texas and California are marked as shown, without washing.

Shoddy consists of cast-off woolen and worsted goods, reduced by powerful machinery to its original state, to be respun and woven alone or mixed with new wool.

Hard or superfine goods, reduced in the same way, makes a better class of goods than shoddy from soft or common goods, and is sometimes distinguished from it by the name of Mungo.

Mungo.—The appearance of Mungo is very deceptive, and the cheap Mungo broadcloths have considerably injured the woolen manufactures. Mungo cloth is, however, properly included with shoddy.

(We are indebted to Messrs. Justice, Bateman & Co., wool commission merchants, 122 South Front street, Philadelphia, Pa., for the following definitions:)

Ring waste.—Ring waste is so called only by exporters of the article to the United States. This name has been given to it within a few years, since the Treasury Department have promulgated the instructions to appraisers to admit articles for duty as they are commercially known. In France and Belgium, where this article is mostly manufactured, it is known as couronnes —crowns, or rings—is commercially dealt in under this name and bought and sold under this title by parties who are manufacturing it and selling it for export to the United States. It is a highly purified article of scoured wool, and is made from wool tops or combed wool, and the couronnes, when not made for export, is the tangled slubbing or wool top that, through accident, becomes disarranged in the process of spinning it into yarn. Before it was manufactured largely for export to the United States couronnes were carded over and recombed by the makers the same as other scoured wool.

A number of mills in the United States purchase it of importers, who have given it the name of ring waste for the purpose of avoiding the proper duties. It is in point of fact a very highly purified article of scoured wool, being made from wool top, which is the cream of the wool, by reason of having had the short and broken fibers or bottom combed from it by combing machinery.

American manufacturers treat it to a steam bath, which opens the crowns or rings ready for carding machines. This wool is principally used in the manufacture of cassimeres, the same as other scoured wools of merino blood. It is much more valuable than other scoured wool by reason of having been highly purified from noils, knots, and tangled fibers. •

Garnetted waste.—Garnetted waste is the product of a garnett machine, which tears and ravels out the twist in thread, thus reducing it back to the original purified wool by reason of taking out the twist which is originally given to the wool to make it yarn or thread. In the process of spinning yarn or thread from wool a percentage of this yarn becomes tangled and is called *thread waste*. By running it through a garnett machine the stock is restored to the original condition of wool, all the twist being taken out of the yarn, leaving the wool which com. poses it in a condition of unspun wool top. It is capable of being used for any purpose for which unmanufactured scoured wool can be used. It can be either combed or carded, and can be spun into worsted or woolen yarn. The garnett machine is only applied to tangled threads or yarn for the purpose of reducing them back to the original condition of purified wool. For purposes of making a saleable article noils and other scoured wools are frequently run through the garnett machine at the same time with the thread waste for the purpose of disguising the mixing. For instance, until recently garnetted waste was admitted at the same duty as waste, while scoured wools and noils made from scoured me. rino wools are subject to the duty of scoured wool, and to avoid this duty of 30 cents per pound on scoured wools, the latter were run through the garnett machine with thread waste for the purpose of mixing, and the material thus produced was a highly purified article of wool offered for sale as garnetted waste, but really scoured wool, noils, and garnetted waste, and by reason of the process of garnetting the scoured wool, noils were disguised. It was profitable to mix scoured wool with garnetted waste because of the large demand for the latter for export to the United States, where it was admitted at only the duty of waste. The demand for it for this purpose raised the price of it above the price of the scoured wool of which it is made, for the reason that scoured wool could not be sent to the United States because of the 30 cents per pound duty, while the same article under the name of garnetted waste could be admitted at only 10 cents per pound duty.

Wool tops.—Wool tops are highly purified scoured wool that have had the inferior particles, or so-called noils, removed by a process of combing. Unmanufactured scoured wool is fed to the combing machine, which combs out the short and broken fibers or bottom, and the long fibers are laid parallel with each other, and when drawn through the comb it becomes wool top and is capable of being manufactured into any kind of woolen goods, either worsted or woolen. In the original process of making worsteds practiced many years ago, only long coarse wools were combed and made into worsteds, but within a comparatively recent period wool of merino blood, after being carded, which is the first process in making woolen goods, is then combed and the long fibers laid parallel with each other, while the short fibers, knots, and bottom are called noils and are separated, but the long fibers so freed pass into what is called wool top, from which it is manufactured into yarn.

Garnetted thread waste.—Garnetted thread waste is a highly purified article of scoured wool restored to the original condition of manufact. ured wool by means of the garnett machine, and is fully described under the head of garnetted waste above.

Flocks.—Flocks is the nap sheared from the face of woolen cloth. Nap is the ends of the wool fibers teased up by teasles or gigging-machines. This furry appearance produced by the gigging-machine or teasel is sheared off by revolving knives to give the cloth a smooth-faced appearance, and the portion cut off is a short stapled wool fiber, and is called flocks, and is of such small value that in some cases manufacturers find it more profitable to throw it on the manure pile than to pay freight on it from one part of the United States to another. We have had flocks shipped to us from mills in the Western States which would not bring freight charges upon it to Eastern cities.

Noils.—Noils is the name given to the short fibers, knots, broken fleeces and tangled fibers combed from wool usually scoured. They are carded and mixed with longer fibers for clothing purposes. Sometimes long noils have been bought by worsted spinners to recomb, a percentage of top being obtained by the second process of combing, the first process having failed to remove all of the long fibers. This was more frequently the case with old-fashioned machinery.

Machinery for recombing ring waste.—The machinery used for recombing ring waste is the same machinery that produces ring waste. The couronnes, or ring waste, is carried back and treated to a steam bath or a bath in boiling water; the bubbling, boiling agitation of the water opens the rings, which are then dried and fed to the carding machine the same as the unmanufactured scoured wool. In point of fact it is more valuable than the original unmanufactured scoured wool, by reason of having been highly purified from noils in its previous process through the French combing machinery. Before couronnes became more valuable than the original scoured wool, of which it was made by reason of the demand for it in the United States, where it is admitted at the duty of waste, it was almost exclusively combed over again by the process described above by the manufacturers who made it. In fact they would not part with it except they could sell it for more money than they could get for the original scoured wool of which it was made. Owing to the demand for it by reason of the low duty placed upon it by the Treasury Department of the United States, it has become a valuable article of merchandise, and those manufacturers who know how to use it value it above the cost of the original scoured wool of which it is made.

Slubbing.—In the process of spinning yarn, wool-tops are sometimes called slubbing, or roving, in a process midway between wool-tops and yarn.

Slivver.—In the process of combing wool, the wool passes in a long stringy condition to its next process of manufacture and is called slivver. While under this name it is practically a highly purified article of scoured wool.

Combing wool.—Wool of the English blood, such as Cotswold, Leicester, and other bright-haired wools, and also all long-fibered wools that are used in the process of combing, the wool of which is prepared from what are called preparers in contradistinction from the wools which are prepared for the comb by carding machinery.

Delaine wool.—Delaine wools are wools of the merino blood prepared for combing-machinery by first subjecting them to the carding process the same as wools are carded which are prepared for clothing purposes. All combing wools which have a remote cross of merino blood are called delaine, and all wools which are carded before they are combed are called delaine wools.

Clothing wools.—Clothing wools are all short-fibered wools that are prepared for spinning into yarn by first being carded on a carding machine, and are the wools which formerly were not capable of being used for worsted purposes, but by the improvements in machinery by reason of first carding wool and afterwards of combing it, any class of wool whatever can be economically manufactured upon combing machinery as now constructed, so that practically any wool of any kind whatever having a more or less remote merino cross can be carded and then combed and used on worsted machinery.

How the terms combing, delaine, and clothing wools originated.—Originally nothing was made into wool-top except coarse long-haired wool, and the process of combing was done by hand, and the long wools suitable for this purpose were called combing wool. Subsequently improvements in machinery made it possible to use a shorter wool of finer quality having a more or less remote cross of merino blood, and to designate these wools from the long combing wools they were given the name of the class of fabrics into which they were made, viz, delaine, and wools which were too short for what was originally known as the combing process, but still long enough to be combed by modern processes, were named delaine wools and were manufactured into a class of goods called delaines, and the wools which were considered too short in staple for this purpose were called clothing wools. The recent improvements in combing machinery now make it possible to comb even the shortest of the clothing wools, and every class of wool grown in the world can now be used on worsted machinery by first carding the wool and then combing it. At the Antwerp Exposition in 1885 a combing machine was exhibited that made a very excellent article of wool-top out of a short-stapled burry Mestizo wool, the proportion of burs so far exceeding the proportion of wool that the raw material might with propriety have been called wooly burs. But the machine made of this article a very superior wool-top.

Washed wool.—Washed wool is wool washed on the back of the animal by a bath or by spout-washing, or washed upon the pelt or hide of the slaughtered animal.

Scoured wool.—All wools that are washed after they are shorn or pulled from the pelt or hide of the animal are called scoured wool. This term is generally applied where the use of warm or hot water is made.

Tub-washed.—Tub washing is a process of scouring wools that are washed after they are sheared or pulled from the pelt. It may be done either with cold or warm water, and is generally understood to signify an incomplete method of cleansing, although the bulk of the tub-washed wools are used by manufacturers without further cleansing.

Unmerchantable wool.—Unmerchantable wool is a term that describes wools which have been washed on the sheep's back, but so indifferently washed or left so long after washing and before shearing as to become almost, if not quite, as dirty as unwashed.

Pulled wool.—Pulled wool is the name given to wool that is pulled from the skin or pelt of the dead animal. *Dead-pulled* is a name given to unwashed wool pulled from the carcass of a dead animal.

Locks.—Broken pieces of wool, called locks, tags, and breech, are the names given to the soiled locks on the buttocks.

Fribbs.—Fribbs is the name given to the short locks of wool from the legs and face of the animal, as well as the short bits where the fiber is chopped up by the careless use of the shears.

Stuffing.—Stuffing is a name given to tags, fribbs, and breech-locks when they are rolled up and concealed inside of the fleece when the latter is tied up in its usual condition.

Sorts and matchings are names given to different qualities of the fleece when broken off and separated into grades. Some fleeces contain as many as five different qualities of wool. These qualities, when broken up and separated and divided, are called sorts or matchings.

Percentage of scoured wool.—Unwashed Merino wool shrinks from 50 to 80 per cent. in scouring. The lightest and choicest Australian medium, unwashed, will yield 50 per cent. less of scoured wool, and the heaviest Mestiza buck's fleeces will yield about 20 per cent. of pure scoured wool. Most unwashed wools yield less than 50 per cent. of scoured wool. The light, open, coarse, unwashed wools of the carpet class yield from 50 to 70 per cent. of scoured wool. Fine Ohio full-blood Merino unwashed wool, exclusive of buck's fleeces, yields from 35 to 40 per cent. of scoured wool. The merino fleeces grown in Texas and on the Western prairies of the United States yield from 20 to 35 per cent. of scoured wool. Unmerchantable Ohio fleeces yield from 37 to 40 per cent. of scoured wool. British and Canada wools yield from 70 to 85 per cent. of scoured wool. Cross-bred washed Ohio fleeces yield from 60 to 80 per cent. of scoured wool. Cross-bred Western American prairie fleeces yield from 30 to 50 per cent. of scoured wool. Tub-washed wools and cross-bred sheep generally yield from 80 to 90 per cent. of scoured wool. Scoured wools, as usually manufactured or as scoured for sale, yield from 85 to 90 per cent. of scoured wool in rewashing.

For the better understanding of the quotations of prices of wool, it may be well to explain the following marks and terms employed in designating the different kinds of wool :

"X and above" means wool of full Merino blood; the designation "X, XX, and XXX" indicates the variations in quality owing to the superior breeding, care, or local influences.

" No. 1 " means three-fourths-blood Merino.

"No. 2 " means half-blood Merino.

" No. 2 and coarse" one-fourth to half-blood.

(For the following we are indebted to Messrs. Sherman Hall & Co., Chicago, Ill.:)

American wools as they are received in Chicago and other distributing markets are described specifically as to condition, grade, and character, and more generally as to source of supply or region where produced.

Condition.—Refers to the amount of *yolk* (*animal* oil peculiar to the fleece), dust, soil, and other foreign matter appearing in the fleece as offered for sale. The fleece wool is marketed as unwashed, washed, tubwashed, and scoured. Lots not coming under these heads are sold as " unclassified," " rejections," &c.

Washed fleece.—Wool washed on the sheep in cold water before it is shorn. The alkaline portion of the yolk may thus be entirely removed, leaving only the free, colorless animal oil in the fleece. A fleece thus thoroughly washed should be free from the color of the yolk. Otherwise it passes as unmerchantable washed.

Tubwashed.—The fleeces broken and washed more or less by hand, formerly in a small way, in tubs with soap. Tubwashed varies in condition. If washed in cold water and without soap it is hardly as clean as good " washed fleece;" if in warm water and soap, much of the free oil is removed, and it approaches scoured wool in cleanness.

Scoured wool.—Is treated in a warm alkaline bath and subsequently thoroughly rinsed in clear water until nothing remains but the clean fiber, *absolutely* clean, and ready for manufacture.

Unwashed wool.—Is the fleece as shorn from the sheep.

Pulled wool.—Is wool pulled from pelts. The grades from fine to coarse are as follows: Extra, superfine, A super, B super, C pulled, or No. 1. These wools are partially washed in the process of pulling.

Dead pulled.—Wool pulled from the carcasses of dead sheep. Ranks in condition with unwashed fleeces.

Shrinkage, per cent.—The loss per hundred pounds in securing any variety of wool, and making it ready for manufacture.

Grades.—Designate the fineness of fiber. The full-blood wools of the West have for a standard the full-blooded French merino fleece. The fleece resulting from a straight cross between the Merino and Southdown or other coarse-wooled sheep of pure blood is termed half-blood, and in fineness of fiber is generally intermediate to the two stocks crossed. The inbreeding of a half-blood with a Southdown or other coarse-wooled sheep results in a still coarser fiber wool, designated as quarter-blood.

Following this theory of crossing well-defined coarse breeds with the fine breeds brings the full description of grades of fineness as quoted— full blood, one half blood, three-eighths blood, and quarter blood. The types of native or common sheep of the country are the Mexican, with a coarse hairy fleece little better than that of the goat; the New England sheep, brought over and crossed indiscriminately until all definite character was lost; and the Virginias, imported and carefully inbred for generations from the best English coarse-wooled flocks.

Fleeces from the first two named, and similar mongrel varieties throughout the country and from flocks carelessly and indiscriminately bred, furnish the coarse and low wools of the country, amounting in weight to perhaps an eighth of the clip, or, say, 40,000,000 pounds. The larger part in the west comes from New Mexico and adjacent States and Territories, and is known in grades as carpet, blanket, and western sorts. The coarse and low grades in the Eastern States come from indiscriminate breeding of small flockmen who change flocks and bucks as necessity or whim may compel or dictate.

Grades.—As commonly known and recognized in American markets with the blood designations, when applied, are as follows : Full-blood Saxony and Spanish merino (XX and XXX) very finest; French merino full blood (X, fine); half blood, fine medium, No. 1; three-eighths blood (intermediate grade) generally combing; low three-eights and high quarter, medium; quarter blood, low medium, common; coarse and native, (coarse, low, &c.)

Custom has brought the grades to nearly uniform standards as to fineness both East and West. In grading the actual character and fineness of the fiber determines the grade, the blood or breed not being considered by the grader.

Sorts.—The fleeces, broken into narrower and more accurate subdivisions as to fineness, there being several qualities or sorts of wool in the same fleece.

Western and Territory wools.—The wools as brought to the Chicago market are generally designated as follows : Western and Territory wools comprise wools raised in the far West, in the new States and Territories, where the pasturage consists of a broad average of wild grasses, which during the dry season become parched, leaving the dry, sandy soil underneath as a fine dust or sand, which permeates the fleece, adding much to its shrinkage and changing not only its appearance, but the strength of staple, more especially where the soil is alkaline.

Fairly bright wools.—Raised in the intermediate States more thickly settled, where the tame grasses have superseded the native, and the sward is thicker and more lasting. These wools have less dust in them than Western and Territory wools, but still retain in a measure the earthy color. Their character is also improved, and the shrinkage in scouring is less than that of wools from the ranches.

Bright wools.—Are raised in all the States from the Mississippi to the Atlantic with some slight local exceptions of territory which has been newly brought under cultivation and where the pasturage has not yet been brought to the thick, solid sward which generally characterizes the older settled regions. The wool is of a bright yellow color, the earthy matter not being sufficient to perceptibly modify the color. The western boundary for " bright wools" is gradually moving farther westward. Parts of Missouri and Iowa now furnish considerable, and occasional clips from States farther west show the improvement arising from cultivated pasturage and withdrawal of flocks from the wild range during the dry, dusty season.

The washed wool is almost entirely confined to bright wools raised east of the Mississippi. Not over one-fourth of the total bright wool clip is now washed before shearing. The practice of washing the sheep in the middle Western States is almost abandoned, excepting in the northern counties of Illinois and the southeastern counties of Wisconsin. About one-half of the wool from Michigan and other States farther east, including Ohio, still comes to market as washed wool.

The bulk of fairly bright wool and Western wools is sent to market unwashed, just as shorn from the sheep, except from the far Western States and Territories, more especially from the Pacific coast. The proportion being scoured before sending to eastern markets is increasing from year to year. It is estimated that nearly half the clip of the Pacific coast, amounting to over 30,000,000 pounds, was scoured the past year before being shipped to market. A large saving is thus made in the item of transportation, as the average shrinkage of these wools in the process of scouring would not be less than 60 per cent. The character of the wools, even under the general classification above noted, varies much with climate, soil, &c., which necessitates subdivisions, putting the wool from States and Territories having similar characteristics, well known to experts, in groups or subclasses, although this subclassification is by no means arbitrary, more than is the actual breed of the sheep in determining the grade. The Western wools we group as follows:

Kansas and Nebraska.—Better character than wools raised farther west and southwest ; some of it fairly bright.

Nevada, Oregon, Washington Territory, Utah, Wyoming, and Idaho.—Standard Territory wools running from [X] to coarse, but with little intermixture of the Mexican blood apparent.

Colorado and Arizona merino, inbred largely with Mexican sheep, the words " improved," " partly improved," and "native," showing the degree of improvements, if any.

New Mexico.—More native, coarse carpet wools, but " improved " in some sections.

Montana.—These wools stand at the head of Territory wools. The soil, climate, and parentage combine to produce wool of the best char-

acter possible on wild land. In addition, the sheep husbandry of the
Territory has been developed from the beginning by men of more than
ordinary intelligence, and usually with ample capital to carry on the
business with such system as to obtain the best results. Valley Oregon and the best Utah wools resemble them closely.

Texas.—These wools vary in quality, character, and condition from
the coarse Mexican and partly improved on the southern border, to
the finest and deepest grown merino; from red, sandy wool bearing
the heaviest shrinkage, to bright wools almost equal to the best unwashed Michigan and Ohio. In some parts of the State the wool is
shorn twice a year, as is the case on the Pacific slope; hence the terms
"spring clip," "fall clip," "twelve months wool," &c., as applied to
Texas and California wools.

The character of wool refers to the length of fiber, the strength, the
elasticity, the luster, felting properties, &c. The character of the wool
is largely determined by soil, climate, and the care given the flocks.
Alkaline soil, an unfavorable climate, insufficient food, and neglect
would result in an absolute change of the character of the wool.

Felting wools.—The felting properties of different wools depend on the
rough serrations on the face of the fiber, which give them the power of
adherence one to another, in cloth, under the process of fulling; in hats,
by felting machines, which reduce the wool to a solid mass of felt without any previous process of fabrication. These properties vary, the finer
wools being generally best adapted to felting and clothing purposes.

Combing and delaine.—Wools suitable for the manufacture of worsted
goods. For such goods the wool is first combed instead of carded, before being spun into yarn. Combing draws the fibers parallel to each
other, and, in this form, twists into a smooth, hard, lustrous yarn, with
few ends of the fiber appearing on the surface, as compared with the
clothing yarns which are made from carded wool. "Combing and delaine" wools require long, strong staple, of even strength throughout,
and for the best worsted goods it should be of bright lustrous color.

Clothing wools embrace the whole list of short staple wools not suited
to delaine and combing uses.

DEFINITIONS OF WOOL AS KNOWN IN   AGO MARKET.

(To the courtesy of Mr. Charles S. Fellows, assistant secretary of the
Board of Trade of Chicago, we are indebted for the following definitions of the commercial terms known to the Chicago wool market:)

Medium.—Refers to fineness of staple—neither the finest nor coarsest.

XXX.—The finest quality generally quoted.

Ohio and Pennsylvania No. 1 fleece.—Washed fleeces, raised in States
named, medium in quality.

Ohio and Pennsylvania X and above.—Fine wools from the States
named.

Ohio and Pennsylvania XX and above.—Finer than above.

Michigan X.—Fine Merino, from the State named *N. B.*—State always refers to place of production.

Michigan No. 1.—Medium quality; quotations for washed fleeces if not otherwise stated.

New York, New Hampshire, and Vermont X.—Fine Merino.

New York and New Hampshire No. 1.—Medium.

Combing, Kentucky ¾ blood.—Fine medium in quality. Staple long, strong, lustrous—suitable for combing purposes.

Combing, Kentucky ¼ blood.—Same as above—a grade coarser.

Combing, Indiana and Missouri ¼ blood.—Same as above, except States in which produced, and corresponding difference in character.

Combing, Indiana and Missouri ¾ blood.—One grade finer than above.

Combing, No. 1 Ohio.—Medium combing from said State.

Combing, No. 2 Ohio.—Low medium from said State.

Combing, No. 1 Michigan.—Medium combing from Michigan.

Delaine, Ohio.—Wool from Ohio of long staple, fit for the manufacture of delaine goods; properties like combing, but wool finer.

Delaine, Michigan fine.—From Michigan, same as above.

Montana fine.—Fine Montana wool.

Montana fine medium.—Same as above, grade coarser.

Montana medium.—Grade below fine medium.

Wyoming and Colorado fine.—From region named.

Wyoming and Colorado fine medium.—From region named.

Wyoming and Colorado medium.—From region named.

Georgia.—Wools raised in Georgia peculiar to that State.

Kentucky clothing, ¼ blood.—Clothing is of shorter staple, too short or too weak for combing purposes.

(*a*) *Texas spring medium, 12 months.*—Refers to time of shearing. Some shear twice a year, hence 12 months, 8 months, &c., refer to time since last previously shorn.

Texas spring, fine.—Shorn in the spring.

Texas spring, fine quality, 6 to 8 months.—Answered in (*a*).

*Texas spring, medium quality, 6 to 8 months—*Answered in (*a*).

Texas fall, fine quality.—Shorn in the fall.

Texas fall, medium quality.—Shorn in the fall.

Kansas and Nebraska carpet.—Very coarse, hairy wool, fit for manufacture of carpets, horse blankets, and other coarse goods.

Unwashed fine Ohio and Michigan.—Not washed on sheep before they are shorn.

Unmerchantable Ohio and Pennsylvania.—Partly washed, or otherwise unfit to go into merchantable piles or grades.

Unmerchantable Michigan.—Same as above.

Super pulled, Maine.—Medium from pelts in the State of Maine

Super medium.—Refers to quality of pulled wool.

Super A.—Refers to quality of pulled wool.

Super Western.—Refers to quality pulled in the West or from Western skins.

Extra pulled.—Finer than super.

California spring.—(See answers to "Texas" marked "(*a*)" and what follows).

California southern.—(Where raised) *Free,* not cotted, free from burrs or other foreign matter.

California southern, defective.—Poor staple, or otherwise unfit to be classed as free.

California fall.—(See Texas ("*a*").)

Oregon east.—Where raised.

Oregon east, fancy.—Above average in character or condition.

Oregon fine valley ; Oregon medium valley.—Raised west of mountains in Oregon.

Australian crossbred.—Coarser by inbreeding coarse English flocks with Merino.

Montevideo.—South American port from which the wools are exported.

HISTORY OF THE CONDITION, GROWTH, AND PROGRESS OF SHEEP-RAISING, WOOL-GROWING, AND WOOLEN MANUFACTURE IN THE AMERICAN COLONIES AND IN THE UNITED STATES.

(For much of the information presented in the following paper, we are indebted to Mr. Harold Snowden, of Alexandria, Va.)

ANTIQUITY OF SHEEP, WOOL, AND GARMENTS OF WOOL.

According to the New American Cyclopedia it appears that the rearing of sheep dates from the earliest times. The passages in the Bible alluding to sheep, wool, and woolen garments are well known, and it is a noticeable fact that distinct mention of the last two of these begins at a period much later than that in connection with which the first is named. In Leviticus, xiii, mention is made of garments having "the warp or woof of linen, or of woolen"; and these two materials appear to have been the staples of the primitive weavers of Syria, Palestine, Greece, Italy, and Spain. Pindar applies to Libya the epithet "flock-abounding." Attic wool was celebrated from an extremely early period, and at least down to the time of the Latin poet Laberius, in the first century before the Christian era ; and the woolen fabrics of both Greece and Italy attained special excellence. Strabo, however, living in the first century of our era, remarks that the fine cloths worn by the Romans in his time were manufactured from wool brought from Spain. Pliny, himself a governor of Spain, describes several fine-wooled varieties of sheep as having long been reared in that country. In view of these facts, further doubt is thrown upon the two attempts to account for the origin of the Merino sheep, neither of which in itself appears to wear the stamp of consistency.

At all events, when the Merinos of Spain first attracted the observation of other nations, they were found in nearly all parts of the country, and mainly in very large permanent flocks, which in separate districts appeared as different varieties; while so special were the management and lines of breeding, that the several flocks often constituted so many subvarieties. The flocks were of two general sorts, the traveling (*transhumantes*) and stationary (*estantes*). They were chiefly owned by the king and some of the nobles and clergy; and such was the importance attached to the products of these flocks, that the cultivators of vineyards and arable lands were by law required to leave broad roads through their estates for the passage of the flocks from the southerly to the northerly provinces in spring and their return in autumn, or for such other migrations as their owners might desire; and, in fact, all other agricultural interests were sacrificed to the convenience of their proprietors."

The myth of "The Golden Fleece," and the perilous adventures of the Argonauts attending its capture at the jaws of the fiery dragon, appear now to have been prophetic of the almost fabulous wealth which has attended the pursuit and capture of the rich-coated ram of the nineteenth century, and show that even prior to the days of Homer and Hesiod the golden qualities of the fleece of the ram were well known to the ancients.

The Romans brought with them to England at the time of their conquest of that country a knowledge of the use and manufacture of wool hitherto unknown there. Rude and imperfect as this knowledge was, it formed the basis of an industry which soon became the most valuable of all her industries, and as such it was guarded with jealous care until early in the nineteenth century, when English wool manufactures had attained such perfection that she threw down her woolen gauntlet and proclaimed free wool and free woolens to the world.

As early as the year 1261 England, by statute, prohibited the export from her borders of raw wool or the wearing within her borders of any foreign woolens, and from time to time afterwards she amended this prohibitory statute, and always in the direction of more stringent prohibition, until the year 1660, when she perfected it in that respect. This latter statute remained in force until 1824, except that in 1802 raw wool had for the first time to submit to a tariff of 6d. per pound. In 1824 she reduced the tariff on woolen goods from 6d. per pound to 1d. per pound and admitted raw wool free.

In the year 1331 the first great impulse was given in England to woolen manufactures by the importation by Edward III. of Flemish weavers, considered then the most expert weavers of Europe. Under their supervision the first blankets were manufactured in England in 1340.

The first record of any attempt to dye woolen cloths in England was in 1608; and six years later, in 1614, mixed yarns, "dyed in the wool," were first introduced in manufactures.*

*Dyed woolen cloths did not hold their colors as well as those cloths made from yarns previously dyed; hence, arose the now popular expression "Dyed in the wool," denoting deep convictions and unvarying opinions.

In the year 1678 England, by statute, enacted that all corpses should be buried in woolen shrouds, and this statute remained in force until the year 1808. Whether or not this law afforded any comfort or consolation to the English citizen, who thus secured for himself, in death, at least, if not before, one suit of woolen clothes, is not known, but the result of the law, it is said, was most beneficial to wool-growing and wool manufacture.

In the year 1684 the assembly of Virginia passed a law to encourage the manufacture of wool in that colony, but England annulled the law, and fifteen years later, viz, in 1699, becoming jealous of the colonies, prohibited under heavy penalties the exporting of wool or woolen manufactures from their borders.

As further evidence of the jealousy of England toward her colonies, in 1698 Governor Nicholson of Virginia suggested to the English Crown that cloth-making should be prohibited in the colonies, and the other royal governors soon followed the example of Governor Nicholson.

In 1731 the English Government " instituted inquiries to ascertain to what extent colonial manufactures were injuring English manufactures," and in 1750 the alarm became so great at the increase of American skill that a statute was enacted prohibiting the exporting from England of any tools or utensils used in woolen manufactures.

In the year 1700 the wool crop of England was only about 10,000,000 pounds per annum, and the value of her woolen manufactures about $40,000,000. In 1844 her woolen manufactures had increased to $120,-000,000 per annum in value, and her woolen exports to $40,000,000. In 1859 her woolen exports alone amounted to $75,000,000, while her wool crop in the United Kingdom was 250,000,000 pounds and her imports of raw wool 110,000,000 pounds. The average weight per fleece in the United Kingdom in 1860 was 5 pounds.

Woolen manufactures retained their supremacy as the first in importance of English industries until the close of the eighteenth century, when the wonderful increase in cotton production and manufacture sent cotton manufactures to the front.

WOOL, AND MANUFACTURES OF, IN THE AMERICAN COLONIES.

In the colonies wool production and manufacture were of slow growth, owing to the unfriendly attitude of the mother country; nevertheless considerable progress was made. Of course whatever of knowledge there was in the colonies as to the use or manufacture of wool was derived from England.

The first sheep introduced into the colonies were brought from England to Jamestown, Va., in the year 1609; the exact number is not known but probably only a few. There is but little subsequent information about these until 1649, when it is stated that they had increased to 3,000.

In 1633 a few sheep were brought from England to Massachusetts, and in the year 1640 they had increased to about three thousand. In 1625 the Dutch brought over some sheep to the New Netherlands, and again in 1630, but their efforts to raise sheep proved unsuccessful. In 1663 a Swedish colony in Delaware brought over 80 sheep.

No mention can be found of the names of these stocks of sheep introduced from Europe at this early period, but it is known that the wool was coarse and the sheep inferior, and there is no record of any effort to improve the stock by importing Merinos until after the Revolution.

In 1645 Massachusetts passed laws encouraging the raising of sheep, and in 1656 another statute was passed requiring each family to spin 3 pounds of wool, cotton, or flax per week for thirty weeks of each year.

In the same year, 1656, the first weaver who settled and commenced weaving at Lowell, Mass., was encouraged so to do by a grant of 30 acres of land.

In 1662 Virginia, by statute, prohibited the exporting of wool, and offered 5 pounds of tobacco [at that time Virginia currency] for every yard of woolen cloth made in the colony; and in 1664 the general assembly of Virginia established in each county looms and weavers.

Other colonies likewise encouraged wool raising and manufacture by various local statutes.

There are no means of ascertaining the number of sheep in the colonies prior to the Revolution, but it is known that before the close of the seventeenth century "spinning, carding, and weaving of wool, and the dressing of cloth were introduced in all of the old colonies by the successive arrivals of English and German artisans, and were encouraged by statutes, and it was said that New England then abounded in sheep."

Just prior to the Revolution it was deemed patriotic in all the colonies to use homespun cloth in preference to English goods, and in the year 1770 it is said that "the graduating class at Harvard College appeared clad in black cloth of New England manufacture," but this was probably of inferior grade.

ORIGIN AND DEVELOPEMENT OF WOOL GROWING IN THE UNITED STATES.

The first concerted action for the improvement of the stock of sheep seems to have come from the Society for the Promotion of Agriculture of South Carolina. In 1785 this society offered a medal for the first flock of Merino sheep kept in the State; but there were no importations of Merino sheep to any of the States until 1793.

Prior to Queen Elizabeth's reign, England raised the finest Merino sheep in the world; but during her reign Spain stepped to the front rank in raising sheep of fine grade, and she guarded her fine Merino stock with jealousy, forbidding the export of any Merino sheep from that country.

In 1793 Hon. William Foster, of Massachusetts, is said to have smuggled from Spain to a friend in Boston three fine Merinos, worth $1,500 each; but Foster's friend, in ignorance of the value of the gift, killed the sheep for mutton and thanked him for the delicious meat he had sent him.

The first full-blooded Merino stock ram kept in this country, so far as can be ascertained, was from 1801 to 1805, on the farms of M. Dupont de Nemours and M. de Lessert, on the Hudson River. This ram was imported from Spain at a cost of $1,000, and named Dom Pedro. In 1805 M. Dupont purchased Dom Pedro, and he became the sire of many fine-grade flocks, near Wilmington, Del.

In 1810 M. Dupont erected woolen mills on the Brandywine, and in his manufactures used the wool of these flocks.

In 1802 Hon. R. R. Livingston, United State minister at Paris, and afterwards chancellor, sent home to his New York farm two pairs of French Merinos from the French Government stock at Chalons; these he crossed with the Dom Pedro stock.

Col. David Humphreys, of Connecticut, United States minister to Spain, shipped to the United States in 1802 a flock of 20 Merino rams and 71 ewes.

In 1803 Dr. James Mease, of Philadelphia, imported 2 black Spanish Merinos.

In 1807 Dr. Muller imported several Merinos from Hesse-Cassel.

In 1809 William Jarvis, consul at Lisbon, purchased and shipped to the United States from Lisbon 3,850 sheep selected from the best Spanish breeds, which had been confiscated and ordered to be sold by the Spanish Junta, and it is estimated that up to 1810 there had been imported about 5,000 Merino sheep, which had been disseminated through New England and the Middle States, and as far west as Ohio.

At an exhibition of the Merino Society of the Middle States in October, 1811, there were specimens of the Irish, Tunisian or Barbary, New Leicester, Bakewell or Dishley, and Southdown breeds.

These 5,000 Merino sheep are the basis on which stands the American improved stock of the present day, although the stock has been, since 1810, kept up by numerous additions from the best flocks of Europe. In 1823 the Saxon Merinos were imported, and since then the French and Silesian Merinos have been introduced and distributed throughout the country, and the United States have for forty years past been raising as fine sheep and as fine wool as any country in the world, though not to the extent demanded by manufacturers.

It is the current popular opinion that English and Australian wool surpasses American in quality, but the reverse is true. The opinion referred to doubtless arises from the fact that England surpasses this country in fine broadcloths and cassimeres, but that is due to the *fine quality* and *length of fiber* of American wool, which renders it unsuitable for the short smooth nap of fine cloths. The American cloths, however, are more durable than the English, though not susceptible of so smooth a finish. In all goods where soft and fleecy finish is required, American wool and American manufactures excel those of the rest of the world.

In 1851, at the World's Exhibition in London, four prize medals were awarded to American sheep, and at the International Exhibition of 1863, at Hamburg, where all of the finest flocks of Europe were represented, two first-class prizes were awarded to Merino sheep from Vermont.

Since the year 1850, the Western States and Territories have taken the front rank as sheep and wool producing sections. In Texas, New Mexico, and California, there were 21 sheep ranches in 1880, aggregating 3,000,000 sheep, and averaging about 140,000 to the ranch; the greater portion of these (probably four-fifths of them) were in the hands of old Mexican families. The pasturage of these sheep, like the pasturage of a large part of the Western cattle, is supplied by the lands of the United States Government.*

Sheep, however, are not believed to injure lands; on the contrary, it is said that sheep-grazing produces a stronger grass, and it is estimated

---

* In the cases of the small flocks of sheep abounding principally in the Southern, Middle, and Eastern States, whose average size is small, probably not exceeding forty or fifty per flock, there is no rule of treatment with respect to their care, propagation, &c., which can be laid down. But among the large ranges of the West and Southwest, especially Texas, New Mexico, and California, the methods as to these vital matters are more uniform.

There the sheep are divided into flocks of from 1,200 to 2,500, with one shepherd in charge of each flock. The shepherd is generally assisted by one or more shepherd dogs. These dogs, together with the shepherd's wife, accompany him from pasture to pasture from the close of the sheep-shearing season until October or November, when he returns with his flock to their permanent winter abode.

As soon as he returns the weathers are separated from the ewes and the latter are corraled to receive the Merino rams.

These pure Merino rams have been fed for about a month previously on corn and oats mixed. They are admitted to the ewes at night and withdrawn at daybreak, when the ewes are driven to pasture and the rams fed with corn, oats, and alfalfa hay. This process is continued for about six weeks until all the ewes have been served.

Some ranchmen use 1 ram for 50 ewes, while most of them supply 1 ram to 100 ewes.

The rams are renewed every three years.

Ewes, if well treated, last for seven years.

The better grades of sheep now bear two lambs and not infrequently three, while the native and common stock never have over one. The period of gestation is from twenty to twenty-one weeks.

Just before the lambing season begins, three extra men are employed for each flock. These men care for the ewes during parturition. And within about ten days from the beginning of the season the important and delicate work of castrating, marking, and tailing the young lambs begin.

The lambing season, which lasts about the same length of time as the rutting season, say six weeks, being over, the shearing begins, and as soon as this is ended the extra hands are discharged and the shepherds, their wives and dogs, again depart with their flocks for the summer pastures.

that a Western sheep pasture, after five years' grazing, will support 40 per cent. more sheep than it did the first year.

Sheep raising has of late years superseded cattle raising to a great extent along the Mexican border. This revolution has been effected in consequence of the liability of cattle to the raids of cattle thieves who drive them across the border, while sheep cannot be made to travel rapidly or to any great distance.

Prior to 1850 the few sheep owned in Texas were of the old Spanish or Mexican breed, greatly degenerated, producing only about 1 pound to the fleece, and of inferior quality. From 1850 to 1860 greater attention was devoted to sheep-raising in Texas, and pure Merinos were imported and crossed on the native stock with the happiest results. In 1860 the number of sheep in Texas had increased 700 per cent. over that of the year 1850, and the wool clip was much better. From 1860 to 1870 there was no increase, but a slight decrease in numbers, the decrease being only for the years 1868–'69. In 1880 the number of sheep had doubled since 1870, and the wool clip had increased 300 per cent. In 1880 the native Mexican sheep, which in 1850 produced only 1 pound per fleece, produced on an average 2.17 pounds, while the half-breed Merinos produced 3.17 pounds, and the grades above half breeds produced 4.75 pounds per fleece. Here, as elsewhere in the United States, practical experience has demonstrated that the best sheep for the country generally is about three-fourths Merino, the grades above that proving less hardy and more liable to serious diseases, although during the last twenty years the long combing wool or mutton sheep, viz, the Leicesters or Lincolns and Cotswolds, have greatly increased and are still increasing, especially in localities convenient to the large fresh-meat markets of the country. This has been caused by the enhanced value of the long combing wools for worsted manufactures, and also by the superior quality of the mutton of these sheep; but the quality of their wool does not equal that of the Merinos, nor is the wool so valuable for general manufacturing purposes. Up to the present time, however, the long combing wools bring the highest prices, owing to their scarcity. It is now estimated that one-fourth of the stock of Michigan and a few other Western States is of the mutton or long combing wool stocks, while New York has to a great extent substituted the same stock for her Merinos. If the rest of the country should follow the example of New York, the prices of the combing wools would necessarily depreciate, while Merinos would enhance in value and the manufacturing interests would lose by the change.

Merinos are not only the hardiest sheep, but also produce the finest quality of wool, and sheep-growers have recently, in view of the dangers besetting the Merino stock from the rivalry of the mutton sheep, advocated and begun to practice the doctrine that the mutton qualities of the Merinos can be improved so that they will equal the best mutton sheep. Their theory is that Merinos are poorly fed, and, when young, kept lean, so that it is difficult to fatten the mature sheep, while the mutton stocks have been *fed* as well as *bred* to their superior capacity for taking on fat. In this way the Leicester breed was improved, and a concerted and determined effort has now begun to make the Merinos of the future mutton sheep. In a few years the experiment will be fully tested, and, if successful, will greatly increase their value to the farmer, as he can in times of wool depression find a market for his mutton.

The long combing wool sheep will, however, retain their value unless the production increases to so great an extent as to exceed the demand for that variety of wools.

It has already been definitely ascertained that crossing the Merino with the Cotswolds and Leicesters will, for the first generation, produce mutton equal to the Southdown, and wool superior in quality to the Cotswold, but further breeding in the same direction has always proved a failure.

It has, however, not yet been so definitely settled as to the result of crossing the Merinos with the downs, and the Messrs. Baechtel Brothers (large sheep raisers of California) have recently experimented success-fully, as they think, in that direction, and claim that they have secured a permanent cross stock, having larger carcass and more wool than the Merinos.

Texas, New Mexico, and the southern portion of California are well adapted to sheep-raising, and there the sheep are sheared twice a year.*

Prior to 1852 California had only a few sheep, and they were of the coarse-wool Mexican breeds. In 1852 New Mexico shipped, or rather drove, to California 40,000 sheep; in 1853, 135,000; in 1854, 27,000; in 1855, 19,000; in 1856, 200,000; in 1857, 130,000; but in 1858–'59 the Indians became so troublesome that the trade ceased; the war then came on, and the demand for the low grade of sheep seems to have ceased. From 1852 to 1858 California imported from Missouri, Illinois, and Ohio Spanish Merino rams and crossed them on the Mexican sheep, with the same results experienced in Texas. The severe storms of 1861–'62 and

---

* With respect to the raising in Texas, New Mexico, and Arizona of the valuable wool-producing alpaca of South America, Mr. E. L. Baker, U. S. Consul at Buenos Ayres, in his report of June, 1887, says:

"I merely make the suggestion that in these respects, if we had ransacked our inventiveness to describe an animal which should be pre-eminently adapted to some portions of our own country, we could hardly have imagined a breed more suited than these South American sheep. I refer particularly to the desert portions of Texas and of New Mexico and Arizona, whose arid soil and general scarcity of water are a great drawback to their proper development. Introduced under favorable circumstances, any or all these classes of animals might be able to fill an industrial gap in those regions which otherwise we can scarcely expect to find a filling for; and thus even the most unpromising portions of those Territories might in time attain to a development, through the valuable wools which these animals afford, that there else can be but little hope for, while in other parts of the country, wherever ordinary sheep may be produced, the introduction and acclimatization of these valuable wool-producing animals would give us a new source of national wealth."

the droughts of 1863–'64 proved disastrous to sheep-raising and almost stripped the State of her sheep, and it took several years to recover from these disasters. In 1876, 1877, 1878 California drove Merino sheep to New Mexico to the number of nearly 50,000 in the three years.

In New Mexico, as in Texas and California, the best results have followed from the crossing of breeds, and the agricultural reports since 1880 show a wonderful increase in the weight of the fleece there. In 1880 the average fleece in New Mexico only weighed about 2 pounds, while the most inferior in Texas and California was 2.17 pounds, the half-breeds 3.17 pounds, and those over half-breeds 4.75 pounds.

According to the official statistics of 1880, Ohio raised about one-seventh of the sheep and one-seventh of the wool of the United States; California about one-ninth of the sheep and one-ninth of the wool. Texas came next in number of sheep; Michigan next, but she produced nearly twice as much wool as Texas; New Mexico next in number of sheep, but behind Pennsylvania and New York in amount of wool; next in number of sheep came Pennsylvania, and next New York. The only other States that had as many as 1,000,000 sheep or produced as much as 5,000,000 pounds of wool in 1880 were Missouri, Illinois, Indiana, Kentucky, Oregon, and Wisconsin, in the order named. Colorado, however, shows wonderful improvement during the decade from 1870 to 1880, having in 1880, 746,443 sheep and raising 3,197,391 pounds of wool.

It will be observed that of the above-named thirteen States and one Territory, eight lie west of the Mississippi River, and prior to the year 1850 Missouri was the only one of the eight where sheep-raising had been considered of any importance.

LOCALITY OF PRODUCT AND RELATIVE AMOUNT OF CLOTHING, COMBING, AND CARPET WOOLS RAISED.

Mr. J. R. Dodge, statistician of the Department of Agriculture, in respect to the kinds of wool grown in the United States, has stated as follows:

The first of the three classes is clothing wool. This is the fleece of full-blood and grade Merino, of fine, short fiber, remarkable for its felting quality. These wools are prepared for manufacture by carding rather than combing. The highest type of this race, the registered thoroughbred, is found in Vermont, where breeding flocks are more numerous than elsewhere, and in considerable numbers in Western New York, Ohio, and Michigan, and scattered through the Western States.

The Merino type of wools prevails almost exclusively in the three States named, in Texas, and throughout the Rocky Mountain and Pacific coast areas. Few sheep of other blood are found west of the Missouri River.

Western Pennsylvania and West Virginia furnish wool of the Merino type mainly. The seaboard States of New England also furnish some grade wools of this type.

The second class, the combing wool of the tariff classification, includes the medium and long wools of the English breeds, the Cotswold, Leicester, Lincoln, several families of Downs, and other breeds of long and coarse wool, also popularly known as the mutton breeds. These are few in number compared with the Merino type. Nearly all the sheep of the South, exclusive of Texas, are of this class, mostly descendants of the less improved English sheep of a hundred years ago, with occasional infusions of better blood from England, Canada, or the Northern States. In Kentucky probably 99 per cent. are of the combing-wool class. A considerable portion, too, are highly improved, giving to this State the reputation of having a larger proportion of high-quality mutton than any other State.

In the vicinity of the Atlantic cities, from Maine to Virginia, sheep husbandry is principally lamb production, the males being Downs or other English breeds, and the ewes grades of both the Merino and the English types. This combination produces a mixed wool of a useful character. Then there are considerable numbers of the English breeds, though fewer than Merino, scattered through the Western States, from Ohio to Kansas, and a still smaller proportion on the Pacific coast and in the Territories.

As to the third class, the carpet wools, they are represented in the United States only by the Mexican sheep, which are the foundation of a large proportion of the ranch flocks, but so improved by repeated crosses as to furnish wool of the Merino type, much of it of high grade.

It is also stated that the carpet-wool product of the United States is almost exclusively the fleece of sheep of Mexican origin, which are raised chiefly in Texas, New Mexico, Arizona, and certain other Territories of the mountain region of the country situated between the Mississippi Valley and the Pacific slope.

The imports of combing wool into the United States are chiefly English long wool, which enters into competition with the delaine or combing merino wool produced in this country.

As to relative quantity of clothing, combing, and carpet wools, respectively, produced in the United States, Mr. James Lynch, of New York, a recognized authority upon wool statistics, states, under date of September 26, 1887, as follows:

You want estimates of the respective amounts of clothing, combing, and carpet wool in the United States clip of 1886. If you will refer to my last annual circular you will find my estimate of the total wool clip of the United States to be as follows in pounds, viz:

Iowa, Missouri, Minnesota, and States east of the Mississippi, except lower Southern	160,000,000
California	40,305,000
Oregon and other Western States and Territories	56,000,000
Colorado and New Mexico	24,000,000
Texas	26,000,000
Georgia, Lake, and Southern	16,000,000
Total	322,305,000

With the improved combing machinery now in use nearly all of the first mentioned 160,000,000 pounds could be passed through the combs; and so also could a small portion of the 40,305,000 pounds of California, and perhaps five-eighths of the 56,000,000 pounds of Oregon and other States and Territories. A good deal of the 24,000,000 pounds of the wool from Colorado and New Mexico can be combed, but very little use is made of it for that purpose. There is a small portion of the 26,000,-000 pounds of Texas and the 16,000,000 pounds of Southern that could be combed, but hardly any of it is used.

All the wool can be used for clothing purposes, barring a trifling quantity of hairy and kempy, which comes chiefly from Colorado, New Mexico, and Texas.

It may be said that the coarse wool from any section may be used for carpets. No one has ever embarked in the business of growing carpet wool by itself, nor is there any likelihood of its ever being done.

The classification of wools made by the tariff of March 2, 1867, is of very little account in reference to domestic wool now, twenty years later. The combing wool of to-day is, in my opinion, mostly taken from wool of the Merino blood, "immediate or remote." In old times the combs required a 4-inch staple of strong wool, while now 1½-inch staple is length enough, and the finest Merino can be spun into worsted yarn.

A considerable portion of the wool product of the country which, according to the terms of the tariff now in force, is classed as clothing wool has, by comparatively recent improvements in machinery, been rendered susceptible to the combing process, and thus has been utilized in the manufacture of worsted goods, embracing certain higher grades of wearing apparel, women's and children's dress goods, as well as fabrics for men's clothing. Such wools, though in the trade regarded as combing wools, under the terms of the revenue-law tariff would be classed as clothing wools.

NUMBER OF SHEEP AND WEIGHT OF CLIP.

There has been great difficulty in ascertaining the true amount of the wool product of the United States, especially prior to 1860, and even now some of these difficulties still exist, and all estimates are necessarily imperfect. There are several reasons for this state of uncertainty about the wool crop, the principal being (1) the imperfect census laws and the imperfect execution of those laws prior to 1860; (2) the raising of sheep in many localities in the South for meat alone, and the failure to shear the flocks or account for the wool on the hides; (3) the failure to report the wool sold to butchers on the sheep to be slaughtered; (4) the existence of small herds of from 1 to 25 sheep, which in the aggregate number many hundreds of thousands, and yet the wool clip from each herd being so small that the owners use it for domestic purposes, or, if they sell, fail to report the amount of the clip.

It is not surprising that with these difficulties in the way of ascertaining the true amount of wool raised annually there should be discrepancies between the agricultural and census reports on the one hand, and the commercial estimates on the other. In the following pages the official figures as shown by agricultural and census reports are given except where otherwise mentioned. The commercial estimates are higher and in some cases obviously too high, but it is believed that the official figures here given are on an average 15 per cent. below the actual wool product. As to the estimate of the number of sheep the same difficulties do not exist, and the official figures are believed to be accurate; the true average weight per fleece is therefore a little greater than the official estimates.

The estimate of the number of sheep and the wool product for 1810— admitted to be of doubtful accuracy—is about 10,000,000 sheep and 13,000,000 pounds of wool; in 1812 the number of sheep had increased about 15 per cent., but the wool clip was about 21,000,000 pounds, or over 50 per cent. increase, and of much finer quality than in 1810; in 1836 there were about 17,000,000 sheep, and in 1840, 19,311,374, producing 35,000,000 pounds of wool; in 1850 the number of sheep was

21,723,220, and the wool clip 52,516,959 pounds; in 1860 the number of sheep was 22,471,275, and the wool clip 60,511,343 pounds.

The increase in number of sheep from 1810 to 1860 was only a little over 100 per cent., and the increase in wool clip was about 350 per cent. during the same period of fifty years, while for the next twenty-five years, from 1860 to 1885, the increase was greater than for the former period of fifty years, viz, over 140 per cent. in number of sheep and over 375 per cent. in wool clip.

In 1870 the number of sheep was 28,477,951 and the wool clip 100,102,387 pounds. The most rapid increase ever attained in this country began in 1869 and continued until 1884, both in number of sheep and weight of clip. Since 1884, there has been an annual decrease in the number of sheep and an annual decrease in the wool clip.

Mr. Lynch, who is high authority as a statistician, put the wool clip of 1866 at 120,000,000 pounds in the old States and 17,000,000 pounds in the Territories and Pacific States, and for 1877 he puts the clip in the old States at 117,000,000 pounds (a loss of 3,000,000 pounds in ten years) and at 91,250,000 pounds in the Territories and Pacific States (a gain of 74,250,000 pounds in ten years), making the total clip for 1877 208,250,000 pounds, a net gain in the ten years in the United States of 71,250,000 pounds.

In 1880 the total wool product was 240,000,000 pounds and the number of sheep 40,765,900; in 1884 the number of sheep was 50,626,626; in 1885, 50,360,243; in 1886, 48,322,331; and in 1887, 44,759,314; showing losses in number of sheep since 1884. The weight of the wool clip has also, during the same period, decreased. In 1884 it was 308,000,000 pounds; in 1885 it was 302,000,000 pounds; in 1886 it was 285,000,000 pounds; and in 1887 it was 265,000,000 pounds, as estimated by J. R. Dodge, statistician.

Prior to the year 1885 some of the old States had for several years lost in the number of sheep and gained in the quantity of wool, but since 1885 the loss in numbers and weight has been general throughout the country, New Mexico and California decreasing in numbers and decreasing in weight, like the old States. The heavy decrease in Texas was phenomenal and due to local sheep diseases.

The present average weight of the fleece is only about 6 pounds, while the fleece of the best sheep is much greater; it can therefore be safely predicted that owing to the still imperfect quality of our average sheep, and the present overproduction of sheep caused by the high wool tariff, there may be little or no gain in numbers, if not an actual loss, in the near future; still the loss in numbers will be accompanied by a comparative gain in weight of the clip. The experience of the past, the increasing value of lands, the division of large farms and ranches, accompanied by greater personal care of farm stock, all point conclusively to a rapid improvement in the weight of fleeces, especially until the period arrives when mutton or long combing wools on account of their scarcity no longer sell higher than merinos.

In 1840 the average weight of the fleece was barely 1.85 pounds; in 1850 it was 2.42 pounds; in 1860, 2.68 pounds; in 1870, 3.52 pounds; in 1880, 4.79 pounds; and in 1887, about 6 pounds.

Since 1860 the population has not kept pace with the wool crop. In 1860 the country produced little over 2 pounds to each inhabitant; in 1880, over 4 pounds; and in 1885, over 5 pounds to each inhabitant.

INFORMATION IN REGARD TO THE QUALITIES OF WOOL.

From the report of the committee of the National Academy of Sciences, made in 1886 to the Secretary of the Treasury, it appears that "the different purposes to which wool is applied has produced the breeding of different stocks of sheep in the United States, so that we now produce wool from 1 inch to over 1 foot in length of fiber, and varying in fineness from $\frac{1}{1800}$ of an inch to $\frac{1}{400}$ of an inch in diameter.'

From the same authority it appears that " our wools differ in strength of fiber, elasticity under pulling strain, elasticity under bending strain, flexibility, softness, character, and amount of secretions, color, luster, and in many other ways; that the character of the wool varies as to its location on the hide, especially in the unimproved stock; that it also varies under different conditions of food, climate, soil, and water; that a flock which produces a certain quality of wool will not always produce the same quality in another pasture; that the same pasture varies greatly at different seasons of the year, and affects the quality of the wool by making fibers of unequal fineness in different portions of their length and decreasing their strength at certain points of their growth."

Dr. McMurtrie, formerly connected with the Agricultural Department, and now professor of chemistry at the University of Illinois (high scientific authority), furnishes the following information :

The merino sheep varies as to fineness of wool from 5 to 15 per cent., according to the condition of the animal as to health, nutrition, and care. The following is the result of tests made of merino wool selected from several States from the purest merinos, descended from the same parent stock in Vermont, first as to fineness of fiber which is measured in centimillimetres: Pennsylvania, 1.711; Texas, 1.837; California, 1.883; Illinois, 1.902; Vermont, 1.979; New York, 2.034; Wisconsin, 2.049—which shows that of the seven States named, Pennsylvania produced the finest and Wisconsin the coarsest fiber from pure merinos descended from the same stock.

As to elasticity, estimated in percentages, the following is the result from pure merinos from the same parent stock in Vermont: Illinois, 91.751; Texas, 90.292; Minnesota, 77.010; Vermont, 70.587; Pennsylvania, 63.795; California, 61.972; New York, 55.875; Wisconsin, 48.446—which shows that Illinois produced the most and Wisconsin the least elastic wool from the same stock of sheep.

Wool improves in elasticity to a maximum with the age of the sheep, to a certain age, and then deteriorates; the maximum point differing widely in the different breeds of sheep. The Cotswold and Lincoln or Leicester reaches its maximum at one year; the Downs at three years, and the Merino at four years. In strength of fiber the Southdown stands first; the Merino second; the Lincoln third, and the Cotswold is the weakest.

The fiber of wool is 1½ stronger than bone; nearly twice as strong as soft brass, iron, or steel wire rope; twice as strong as the hardest wood, and four times as strong as white pine.

The Merino wools are used for fine cassimeres and broadcloths and for felting purposes; the Lincoln and Cotswold sheep furnish the long combing wools used in manufacturing worsted and soft knit goods; the Merino and Down wools are called carding wools, while the Lincoln and Cotswold are denominated combing wools.

WOOL PRODUCT OF FOREIGN COUNTRIES.

While the United States, especially the western part of the country, has been steadily increasing its wool product, until 1884, the rest of the world has kept pace with us.

In the thickly-settled portions of Europe, where lands are valuable, there has been little or no increase in the wool product, but in the English dependencies and colonies the growth has been as rapid as in this country, and of late years the River Platte country of South America has also taken its place in the front rank of the wool growers of the world.

INDIA.

Prior to 1820 India exported no wool and raised very little. In 1840 her export was only about 2,500,000 pounds; in 1850 about 3,500,000 pounds; and in 1859 over 14,000,000 pounds; since which time her export of wool has greatly increased. India's wool clip of 1870 was estimated at about 30,000,000 pounds, and in 1880 at over 50,000,000 pounds.

AFRICAN COLONIES.

The English colonies in South Africa prior to 1820 produced no wool; in 1845 these colonies furnished England with 3,500,000 pounds of wool; in 1850, nearly 6,000,000 pounds; in 1855, over 11,000,000 pounds; and in 1859, over 14,000,000 pounds. In 1870 they produced 41,000,000 pounds; and in 1880, 46,000,000 pounds.

AUSTRALIA.

Capt. John McArthur, of the British Army, who settled in Australia, imported in 1797, 3 Merino rams, which were the first ever seen in that country. He crossed these on the native sheep. His experiment proved a success and he afterwards became a large sheep and wool raiser, but his example was not followed for many years, and in 1830 the wool crop was only about 1,000,000 pounds; in 1885 it was 3,776,191 pounds; in 1840, 6,215,329 pounds in New South Wales alone, and over 9,000,000 pounds in Australia; in 1845 it was 24,000,000 pounds; in 1850, 39,000,000 pounds; in 1855, 49,000,000 pounds; in 1860, 55,000,000 pounds; in 1870, 193,000,000 pounds; and in 1880, 392,000,000 pounds. In 1880 this immense wool clip was from 51,000,000 sheep, making the average of nearly 8 pounds per fleece. Since 1880 several years of severe drought in Australia destroyed 10,000,000 or 12,000,000 sheep, but at present her flocks and her wool clip are greater than in 1880. In 1885-'86 the exports from Australasia were 455,476,000 pounds.

THE ARGENTINE REPUBLIC.

Since 1860 wool growing has also increased very rapidly in the Argentine Republic or River Platte country, in South America, so that in 1880 the wool product amounted to 240,000,000 pounds.

Since 1880 this industry has continued to grow and it is now estimated that the number of sheep is 80,000,000, nearly, if not quite, equal to that of Australia and New Zealand.

RUSSIA.

Next after Australia, the Argentine Republic, and the United States comes Russia, as a wool-growing country. There is, however, little difference in the weight of the wool clip of Russia and this country. The number of sheep in Russia in 1882 was about 57,000,000 and the wool clip about 263,000,000 pounds.

ENGLAND, FRANCE, AND GERMANY.

These countries, in the order named, come next as wool growers, but none of them produce enough wool for home consumption, and they all are heavy importer of raw wool.

The countries that yield the largest surplus of wool for export are Russia, the Argentine Republic, South Africa, and Australasia. Their capacity for supplying the manufactures of the world seems to be ample. They have all improved their sheep by crossing with the merinos, and their wools, especially those of Australia and the Platte country, are among the finest in the world.

These two last-named countries are much alike in their peculiar fitness for sheep raising, and are as yet not taxed to anything like their capacity. Australia alone is as large in area as the United States.

In Australia the plains devoted to sheep-raising are in the hands of comparatively a few, who have perpetual leases of immense tracts of Government lands at low rates. Some of these tracts contain as much as 100,000 acres, so that the country bids fair to continue to be a sheep-raising section.

It is idle to talk about raising sheep in Europe or this country to compete with South Africa, the Platte country, or Australasia.

Our sheep farming must eventually be confined to small flocks of improved breeds, raised on farms where they require little or no extra labor. It has already come to this in Europe, and in the Eastern and Middle States, where lands are valuable, and will finally prevail in the West, as the large ranches are divided up and settled.

The conditions are entirely different in South Africa, Australia, and South America, where laborers are, at best, semi-barbarians or peons, and the immense plains of cheap lands and torrid climate seem better adapted to sheep raising than other industries.

The wools from South Africa are used chiefly in Scotland and the West of England for men's goods.

The Australasian clip varies from the long, bright, New Zealand cross-bred wools to the coarse carpet wools.

The River Platte wools also vary greatly, but are chiefly noted for their fine, short fiber, which fits them for fine broad cloths and cassimeres. The weight of the fleeces is therefore much less than in Australasia.

DEVELOPEMENT OF WOOLEN MANUFACTURES IN THE UNITED STATES.

The manufacture of wool in the Colonies properly began with the erection of fulling-mills in Massachusetts in 1648—or, as claimed by some, in 1643—by a society of Yorkshire people, supposed to be Non-conformists, who brought with them from England their looms and implements of trade.

The woolen webs of the hand-looms of the private families were carried to these fulling-mills to undergo a process which gave them greater body and thickness, adapted them to a better finish, and increased their durability; they increased very rapidly in number throughout the Colonies until every neighborhood seems to have had a fulling-mill, while every family had its loom and every woman was a weaver; there were also many weavers who wove on their hand-looms for the public, and some who traveled about from house to house plying their trade, but there is no record of any woolen factory or company organized for woolen manufacture prior to the year 1788.

The progress we made in thirty-five years of competition with English manufacturers is very well shown by the business experience of the late Mr. Thomas R. Hazard, one of the earliest woolen manufacturers in this country. Mr. Hazard said:

In 1816 and later I used to employ scores of women to spin at their homes at 4 cents a skein, by which they earned 12 cents a day at most. Inferior cotton shirtings *sold then at* 50 *cents a yard*, thus requiring four days' work of the woman to pay for 1 yard of cotton cloth, she boarding herself. The wool was carded into rolls at Peacedale and transported to and from on the backs of horses. Some time ago I stood in a manufactory in the same village, and took note of a stripling who tended two highly improved jennies, from which he was turning off daily as much yarn as *six or seven hundred* formerly spun on wheels in the same time. In the mean time the introduction of labor-saving machinery and perfected skill had so reduced the cost of goods that a superior article of cotton cloth was then sold in the village stores for 15 cents a yard, for what formerly cost 50 cents a yard. So that had this boy spinner been paid the same price per skein that was formerly paid to a woman for an equal amount of work, he would have received as much as could formerly have been earned by about *two thousand hand-spinners* in the same time.

The following is an extract from Wade's Fibre and Fabric in regard to the early condition and progress of our woolen manufacture:

Up to 1840 about the only woolen fabrics made in the United States were satinets, broadcloths, flannels, and blankets. Eighteen hundred and fifty saw the success of the Crompton loom at Lowell and Lawrence, on which were made a full line of Scotch plaids in all their beautiful colorings, as well as star twills, half-diamonds—basket weaving effects, all made from *scoured yarns*. The "Bay State shawl" was then being made in great abundance, and was universally worn. White flannels were then, as now, a staple product. There were also many mills making tweeds, used as water-proof cloaks for ladies. They were made on three harness, with cotton warp and wool filling, now substituted by the universally worn rubber water-proof. Up to that time fancy cassimeres had been largely made through the Blackstone Valley on the Crompton and Tappet looms, as made by William Crompton. These goods were woven in the grease, the same as at the present time. As early as 1846 the Jacquard was used at Woonsocket and Blackstone. From 1850 to 1860 fancy cassimeres made a rapid advance, and the styles ran to extremes far more than they ever have since. The Jacquard was again brought into use at Woonsocket, Blackstone, Millville, and at Rockville, the writer putting up some thirty machines at Warehouse Point, Conn. In 1854 very ultra styles were made, and sold well at large profit. When the war broke out almost every mill in the country was put on army goods and army flannels and blankets. The war brought its long stagnation; after which, with the revival of trade, came the demand for better-made goods. Ladies' worsted dress goods were also introduced, and following them the worsted industry for men's wear, which has grown to its present large proportions. With the downfall of worsted dress goods Bradford received a hard blow, and one of our largest corporations with difficulty weathered the storm. This fabric was followed by the "soft woolen" dress goods introduced by the French, and which have had such a long run and still remain popular. Wade's Fibre and Fabric, since the publication of its first number, has persistently advised the diversifying of cotton fabrics, and with the best results, as the close observer has noticed. The demand for better-made fabrics of all kinds has called for better made machinery, and the progress made in the past thirty-seven years has been wonderful, and the contest is still going on.

Fulling-mills of the present day are connected with and are a part of the woolen manufactories, except in remote and isolated localities in the West and South, where there are few factories, and the inhabitants still use their hand-looms in their families and wear their homespun cloths. They are, however, rapidly diminishing in number as separate establishments from woolen factories. In 1840 there were 2,585 fulling-mills in the United States, while in 1880 the number had become reduced to 991, and these combined wool carding with the fulling process.

In 1788 Jeremiah Wadsworth and others erected and put in operation at Hartford, Conn., the first woolen factory using more than one loom. This factory had the capacity of weaving 5,000 yards of cassimeres or broadcloth per annum, worth about $5 per yard. This was considered a stupendous undertaking at that time, and was deemed of such importance to the infant Republic that General Washington paid a special visit to it, and in 1791 Alexander Hamilton, Secretary of the Treasury, in his address to Congress, complimented the owners of the factory, and urged the importance of improving the breeds of sheep. When General Washington made his address to Congress he wore a suit of broadcloth manufactured and presented to him by the owners of the Hartford Woolen Factory.

About 1789 another woolen mill, with about the same capacity, commenced operations at Stockbridge, and in 1790 another at Watertown, so that in 1790 there were 3 woolen mills in operation, with a capacity of about 15,000 yards per annum, worth about $75,000.

In the year 1794 the first incorporated woolen company in the United States built a factory and commenced manufacturing at B yfield, Mass. with Arthur Schofield and other English operatives in charge. This, factory in the year 1804 made a little fine broadcloth from merino wool, the first made in the United States.

In 1809 another woolen company was formed at Pittsfield, Mass., and began manufacturing fine cloths.

It is believed that the above-named 5 mills were the only mills in the United States making fine cloth in 1810. There were, however, 9 other factories at work in 1810 making cloth of coarser grade and averaging over 10,000 yards each annually, besides 10 more smaller factories. The estimated factory product of cloth for that year (1810) was nearly 200,000 yards, worth in the market from $1 to $10 per yard. The estimate of woolen cloth manufactured in private families the same year was about 9,500,000 yards; so that the mills of that day only made about one-fiftieth of the whole woolen product of the country.

The total value of the manufactured product of 1810 was 825,608,788.

The principal mills were located at Byfield, Mass.; New Ipswich, N. H.; Warwick and Portsmouth, R. I.; Derby and Hartford, Conn.; Watertown and Poughkeepsie, N.Y.; Philadelphia, Pa.; Wilmington, Del.; and Baltimore, Elkton, and Frederick, Md.

In 1812 steam was first introduced in woolen mills in the United States at Providence and at Middletown, but no power-looms for broadcloth were used until 1825, when they were first used by the Pontoosac Manufacturing Company for making broadcloth, and also superior all-wool, cotton-warp, drab, and fancy cloths.

The first large woolen factory built in the United States was erected by Mr. L. Pomeroy, who, however, used hand-looms e ntirely.

The war of 1812 gave a great impetus to woolen manufactures, especially those of military and naval cloths, blankets, and negro cloths, and factories sprung up everywhere, but nearly all of these enterprises met with disaster when peace was established in 1815, and the superior English goods were imported, as at that day in this country there was not the skill or machinery required. In one year the foreign import of woolens amounted to $155,000,000 in value, and nearly all of our woolen mills failed, as all enterprises of sudden growth without a solid founda. tion are liable to do.

The extent of the disaster to our manufacturing interests is best ex-hibited by reference to the statistics of wool manufacture during the thirty years subsequent to 1810.

Value of manufactured wool product:

1810	$25,608,788
1820	4,413,060
1830	14,528,166
1840	20,696,699

Urgent appeals to Congress by the woolen manufacturers in the mean while resulted in several changes in the tariff.

In 1816 Congress laid a duty of 25 per cent. ad valorem for the next three years, and provided that after that time it should be reduced to 20 per cent.

In 1824 the tariff was again increased to 25 per cent. ad valorem ou goods costing as much as 33⅓ cents or less per square yard, and 33⅓ per cent. ad valorem on all goods costing over 33⅓ cents per square yard. Congress at the same time laid a duty of 30 per cent. ad valorem on raw wool costing over 10 cents per pound and 15 per cent. ad valorem on wool costing under 10 cents per pound.

The tariff law of 1824 did not, however, go into force fully until June, 1826.

England, in order to offset this statute, reduced her import duty on foreign wool in 1825, so as to enable her manufacturers to furnish woolen goods to America notwithstanding the tariff laws of 1824, and she competed successfully with our factories.

In 1828 Congress increased the duties on woolen goods costing 48 or less per square yard to 45 per cent. ad valorem, and on all costing over $4 per square yard to 50 per cent. ad valorem, and at the same time laid a higher duty on raw wool equal to 100 per cent. ad valorem on wool costing 8 cents per pound.

In 1846 raw wool was admitted free of duty if it cost 20 cents per pound or less, and the tariff was reduced to 30 per cent. ad valorem on raw wool costing over 20 cents per pound. In the same year the tariff on woolen manufactures was reduced to 30 per cent. ad valorem.

In 1850 the value of the manufactured wool product was $43,542,288, or an increase of between $17,000,000 and $18,000,000 over the product of 1810, in a period of forty years. The number of woolen mills of all kinds (exclusive of fulling-mills) in 1840 was 1,420. Four-fifths of these were located in Massachusetts, New York, Connecticut, Vermont, and Pennsylvania. In 1850 the number had increased to 1,559, and some of them were located in each of thirty-two States of the Union. The capital invested was $28,118,650, the number of hands employed was 39,252, the value of the product, $43,207,545, making the average annual value product for each mill less than $27,000.

After the year 1850 the worsted goods manufactures assumed such proportions that the statistics were made separate from the woolen manufactures. Carpet and hosiery required separate statistics also, and since 1870 felt goods, woolen hats, and shoddy are also put in separate tables.

The first decided advance towards perfection in woolen manufactures seems to have been in flannel goods. In 1821 flannels made in New York were equal to the best Welsh flannels: In 1823, 30,000 pieces of flannel were made near Boston; in 1827, three mills near Newburyport made flannel valued at $684,000. In 1829, Henry Stevens started a flannel mill with the capacity of 3,000 yards per week. In 1849, two flannel mills were in operation at Dover, N. H. In 1850, the Bay State and Ballard Vale mills and the mill of Gilbert and Stevens, at Ware, Mass., made flannels in every way equal to any imported, and the shawls, balmorals, fancy flannels, shirtings, and opera cloakings manufactured at Waterloo, N. Y., and Laconia, N. H., could not be excelled. Since 1860 our flannels have continued to maintain their high reputation.

The first large mill for blankets was established in 1831 in Pendleton District, S. C.; the blankets made there were of cotton warp and designed for negro use.

During the same year a large factory was built near Buffalo, N. Y., for the manufacture of Mackinaw or Indian blankets. From 1831 to 1860 blankets began to be made in nineteen different States, and in the year 1860, 616,400 were manufactured, principally in Maine, Massachusetts, New Hampshire, Pennsylvania, and California. Since that time blanket manufactures have steadily increased, and are equal to any imported blankets in beauty of texture and finish.

In the year 1860 there were in the United States 1,263 woolen establishments, with a capital of $30,922,654, consuming 83,608,468 pounds of wool, paying $10,153,938 wages to 43,738 employés, and yielding a product valued at $65,596,364; the average annual wages had increased from $205 in 1850 to $237 in 1860; the average value of the product per hand had increased from $1,248 in 1850 to $1,496 in 1860. New England produced in 1860 about 65 per cent. of the manufactured product of the United States. In 1870 the number of woolen mills had increased to 2,993 as against 1,263 in 1860; the amount of capital, $108,910,369; the number of pounds of wool consumed, 172,078,919; the number of hands employed, 92,973; the amount of wages paid, $31,246,432, and the value of manufactured product, $177,495,689.

In the year 1880 the number of woolen factories had increased to 2,689, but of these only 1,992 are properly woolen mills (the remainder, viz, 991, are simply fulling and carding mills); the number of hands employed in 1880 was 161,557; the amount of capital invested was $159,091,869; amount of wages paid, $47,389,087; the value of the annual product, $267,252,913.

In 1870 the following were the seven leading industries, yielding annual products of value in the order named: (1) flour and grist mills; (2) slaughter and meat packing; (3) iron and steel manufacture; (4) saw-mills; (5) foundries and machine-shops; (6) cotton goods manufactures; (7) woolen manufactures.

In 1880 woolen manufactures had outstripped numbers 4, 5, and 6, above named, and stood fourth of the seven named industries.

Mr. J. R. Dodge furnishes the following statistics, not yet published for circulation:

The annual requirement of wool for manufacture in 1840 was 3.4 pounds per capita for our population, and the annual requirement for 1860 was still only 3.4 pounds per capita, showing no increase of manufacture per capita for twenty years, while from 1860 to 1880 the annual requirement has increased to 6 pounds per capita. The proportion of this manufactured wool grown in this country has also increased greatly. The home-grown wool of 1840 amounted to 2.5 pounds per capita; in 1850, to 2.7 pounds; in 1860, to 2.3 pounds; in 1870, to 4.2 pounds; in 1880 to 4.2 pounds, and in 1885 to over 5 pounds.

The importation of woolens has relatively decreased, notwithstanding the enormous increase of wealth and the greatly enlarged rate of consumption. The average value per capita of woolens imported between 1850 and 1860 was $1.09. In the following decade, which included the war period with its immense waste of clothing and high cost of goods, the average importation for each individual was reduced to 91 cents, and between 1870 and 1880 it fell to 86 cents.

INCREASED PRODUCTIVE POWER OF WOOLEN MACHINERY.

Of late years the productive power of woolen machinery has greatly increased, so that the number of mills or number of sets of cards is no index of the condition of manufacture. For example, in 1870, 8,352 sets of cards used only 208,916 pounds of all materials, or 25,014 pounds per set; while in 1880, 5,961 sets used 276,949 pounds of all materials, or 46,460 pounds per set, thus nearly doubling in productive power. Again, in New England there was from 1870 to 1880 a reduction in the sets of cards from 3,358 to 2,922 (nearly 13 per cent. decrease); and during the same period the pounds of material used increased from 116,511,379 to 156,091,549 (an increase of about 33 per cent.).

In 1880 the great bulk of woolen manufacture was carried on in nine States, and in the order named: (1) Massachusetts; (2) Pennsylvania; (3) Connecticut; (4) Rhode Island; (5) New York; (6) New Hampshire; (7) Maine; (8) New Jersey; (9) Vermont.

The following were the seven leading cities in woolen manufacture in the order named, viz: (1) Philadelphia; (2) Lawrence; (3) Providence; (4) Lowell; (5) New York; (6) Manchester; (7) Boston.

In the same year (1880) 61 per cent. of the hands employed in woolen mills were natives and 39 per cent. were foreigners.

The statistics heretofore given include all branches of the woolen industries, but each demands a separate history.

WORSTED MANUFACTURES.

Under worsted manufactures are included all wool and cotton warp, delaines, challies, bareges, imitation bareges, all-wool and part-wool reps and worsted yarns for carpets and hosiery. In the year 1860 these goods were made in several States, but nearly all in value were made by three mills, viz: Manchester Print Works, Manchester, N. H.; Pacific Mills, Lawrence, Mass.; and Hamilton Woolen Company's Works, Southbridge, Mass. These three mills made in 1860 about 22,750,000 yards, valued at $3,701,378.

These mills employed 2,378 hands, and paid in wages $543,684; their capital was $3,230,000.

Prior to 1868 worsted manufacture was confined to the goods before named, but in 1868 diagonal and other worsteds for men's wear began to be made, and grew so rapidly in popularity that they created a revolution in worsted manufactures. In 1867 there were only a few combs running, but in 1880 there were 360 combs, and in 1886 there were 563 in active operation.

In 1870 the capital invested in worsted mills had increased to $10,085,000; the number of mills had increased to 102, employing 12,920 hands, paying $4,368,857 in wages, and producing annually in value $22,090,331.

In 1880 capital in worsted mills had increased to $20,374,043; there were 18,803 hands employed, receiving $5,683,027 in wages, and producing in value $33,549,942.

Since 1880 the worsted goods industry has continued to increase, and in 1885 Mr: Truitt, of the house of Dolan & Co., estimated that the combing-wool clip of the United States fell 80,000,000 pounds short of the amount necessary to run the machinery to its full capacity.

CARPET MANUFACTURES.

The first carpet seen in the United States, of which we have any knowledge, was a small Turkish rug, said to have been in the house of Kidd, the pirate, who was executed in 1701. As early as 1760 a few Scotch and other carpets were advertised by persons in New York, but prior to the Revolution they were very rare, and then only in the houses of wealthy Dutch merchants.

In 1791 William Peter Sprague started a carpet factory at Philadelphia, and wove a national pattern with a device representing the arms and achievements of the United States, and in the same year Secretary Hamilton recommended that Congress encourage the industry by increasing the duty on wool carpets.

Several years later John Dorsey started another factory at Philadelphia; but in 1810 there were only manufactured 9,984 yards of carpetings in the whole country, worth about $1 per yard. This industry increased very little, however, until 1827, when H. R. Knight & Co. established a factory in Hartford County, Connecticut. The next year the Thompsonville Company started another in the same county. The Lowell Manufacturing Company also started in 1828. Samuel Given put another in operation at Carlisle, Pa., in 1830, and in the year 1833 3 carpet factories were built in Columbia County, New York, and 1 at Rochester, N. Y. During the same year carpet factories were started in New Haven and New London Counties, Connecticut, Somersworth, N. H., Baltimore, Md., and Steubenville, Ohio.

In 1834 there were 18 or 20 carpet factories, running 511 looms, of which 18 looms were for Brussels, 21 for treble ingrained, 44 Venetian, 4 Damask Venetian, and 424 for ingrained carpets other than three-ply. They made 1,147,500 yards, worth about $1 per yard.

In 1838 quite a revolution occurred in carpet manufacture in consequence of the invention by Mr. Erastus B. Bigelow, of Massachusetts, of a carpet power loom for manufacturing Brussels carpets (manufactured by hand looms prior to that time). This invention was, however, not perfected for Brussel carpets until 1848. Since that time one female can easily weave from 20 to 25 yards per day, while the product of the hand looms did not exceed 4 yards per day. The cost of weaving Brussels carpets had hitherto been 30 cents per yard. This invention reduced the cost to about 4 cents per yard, and reduced the price of carpetings 20 per cent.

This invention surprised the manufacturing world, which up to that time considered the manufacture of Brussels carpets an impossibility except by use of the hand loom.

In 1857 American carpets, except the finest grades, had surpassed the rest of the world, and there were 5,000 power looms at work, and they could not supply the demand.

In 1860, 213 carpet factories used 8,843,691 pounds of wool; made 13,285,921 yards, worth about 60 cents per yard, or in all $7,857,636; employed 6,681 hands and paid $1,545,692 in wages; these 213 factories had a capital of $4,721,768.

In 1870 there were 215 factories (only two more than in 1860), employing 12,098 hands, paying $4,681,718 in wages, using 33,000,000 pounds of wool, making 22,000,000 yards, worth $21,761,573; the capital had increased to $12,540,750.

In 1880 the number of factories had decreased to 195, but the capital had increased to $21,468,587; amount of wages to $6,835,218; value of product to $31,792,802, and the number of employés to 20,371.

HOSIERY.

Woolen hosiery includes socks, stockings, gloves, drawers, undershirts, jackets, opera hoods, shawls, scarfs, comforters, and other knit goods, both all wool and mixed.

The hosiery mills use cotton, silk, flax, and wool; wool, however, is the greatest in value.

In 1850 there were 85 hosiery mills, with a capital of $544,735, yielding an annual product worth $1,028,102; more than one-half in value of these products were made in Pennsylvania.

In 1860 there were 197 factories, with a capital of $4,035,510, yielding an annual product of $7,280,606, exceeding the product of 1850 by 608 per cent.

In 1831 the only considerable hosiery establishment was that of the Newburyport Hose Manufacturing Company, of Massachusetts; they used hand looms, however; 2 pairs of drawers per day is the capacity of a hand loom, while the power looms can make 20 pairs, and have decreased the cost of manufacturing to nearly one-tenth of the former cost. Between 1835 and 1840 this industry received considerable impetus from the invention and use of the circular knitting machines, which make stocking legs without a seam, and recently many other new inventions have greatly stimulated this business.

In 1870 there were 248 hosiery mills, with a capital of $10,931,260, making a product worth $18,411,464, using 5,600,000 pounds of wool, and employing 14,788 hands.

In 1880 the hosiery product had increased to $29,167,227, the capital invested to $15,579,591, the number of hands to 28,885, and wages paid to $6,701,475.

WOOL HATS AND FELT GOODS.

In 1880, for the first time, the wool hat industry was separately noted. There was then invested in the business $3,615,830; 5,470 hands were employed, receiving in wages $1,893,215, and yielding a product of $8,516,569.

In the same year the capital invested in the manufacture of felt goods amounted to $1,958,254; 1,524 hands were employed, receiving in wages $439,760, and yielding a product of $3,619,652.

SHODDY.

Shoddy was originally used only for padding, but during the late war was much used for overcoats, army cloths, piano and table covers, &c.

White shoddy is used in white blankets, and dark shoddy in carpets and coarse cloths and dyed to cover the original colors. In 1842 a shoddy mill was projected at Woodstock, Vt., by Mr. Stearns, and in 1860 there were 5 small mills in New York employing 58 hands and producing manufactures valued at about $40,000; in 1870 the shoddy mills used about 19,372,002 pounds of raw shoddy, and in 1880 they used 52,136,926 pounds of raw shoddy on a scoured basis, which is equivalent to about 70,000,000 pounds on an unwashed basis.

MANUFACTURES OF ALPACA, ANGORA, AND CASHMERE WOOL.

Between 1855 and 1860 the Cashmere and Angora goats were introduced in this country, and mills were soon thereafter commenced at Lowell to manufacture their wool and the wool of the alpaca sheep; this industry is, however, still in its infancy.

In 1880 there were 3,351,701 yards of alpaca woolen goods, and 1,000,000 yards of alpaca worsted goods manufactured, and in the same year 2,919,050 yards of cashmere and 1,557,537 yards of cashmerettes.

THE DEVELOPMENT OF WOOL MANUFACTURES IN THE UNITED STATES.

[By Mr. Geo. Wm. Bond, of Boston, Mass.]

The early history of the woolen manufacture of the United States was given in the introduction to the census in 1860, volume "Manufactures." Therefore it is unnecessary to state more than some leading points bearing upon its influence upon the wool and woolen trade.

EARLY WOOL MACHINERY.

Great Britain was but a short time in advance of the United States in making wool by machinery. The first establishments were started there about 1785; the first carding machine here, at Byfield, Mass., in 1794, made by Arthur Scholfield. Shortly before 1785 there may have been some machines for carding wool used in England, as there had been for nearly forty years before the machine invented by Lewis Paul in 1848 for carding cotton. This machine was reported to have been purchased by a hat manufacturer and applied to the carding of wool for hats. The first that we find any record of, for the wool manufacture, was introduced by Benjamin Gott about 1785, together with the mule jenny and power loom, which were invented about that time.

ENGLISH PENAL LAWS AGAINST EXPORTING WOOL MACHINERY.

So in reality we were not much behind Great Britain in the use of such machinery, but we were materially behind her in the means of obtaining it. We had no knowledge of the machinery and no skilled artisans to make it. Great Britain, where alone such machinery was well known, had very stringent penal laws against exporting such machinery for textile manufacture, or even models or drawings of such machinery. Our people depended upon the descriptions which men who came over here from England, like the Scholfields, who represented themselves as woolen manufacturers, might give from recollection of what they had seen or perhaps worked on, and at the time these first came over there was hardly such a thing as a woolen factory in England.

PROCESSES OF MANUFACTURE.

The business was divided up. There were the staplers, who took the wool, sorted it according to its adaptation to various kinds of goods, perhaps scoured it, sold it to the spinners, who carded it and made it into yarn; the weavers, who bought the yarn and wove it into flannels; the finisher, who took these flannels and made them up into the styles of goods for which they were adapted. All these processes were formerly by hand, but this division of labor extended for a long time after the introduction of machinery, and, indeed, to a certain extent now exists. Here this system was not practicable. Our manufacturers were obliged to buy the fleeces entire, sort them, and generally make on the same set of machinery all the varieties of goods needed. This involved constant changes and consequently great delay in their work, thus materially increasing the cost of manufacture. Their means were generally limited. It was difficult in starting to estimate what would be the cost of their plant, and generally when it was completed their funds were exhausted and they had to put their goods into the hands of commission merchants in order to realize upon them at once, or to do simply a custom business for the farmers in their neighborhood, retaining a part of the wool as compensation therefor. They soon resorted to forming joint stock companies, and the stock for these, in many cases, was largely taken by commission merchants who looked quite as much to the profit from the sales as to that from the manufacture. Very few of these survived for any length of time.

The capital of the country was then small, and business was transacted with long credits.

EARLY IMPORTS OF WOOLEN GOODS.

Our imports of woolen goods continued heavy. The United States was the most important customer for British woolens.

In 1812 the exports of woolens from Great Britain were according to Bischoff on Wool, Woolens, and Sheep, vol. 2, page 34:

To—	Cloths of various kinds.	Stuffs.
	Pieces.	Pieces.
European countries	65, 974	336, 166
United States	145, 600	302, 944
Other countries	103, 378	253, 249

There was at that time in this country a duty of 20 per cent. on woolens, and wool was admitted free, while at the same time wool of foreign growth was in Great Britain subjected to a duty of 6d. per pound.

The manufacture of woolens had materially extended in this country, and the manufacturers were becoming disheartened by the difficulties they had to encounter at home and the heavy competition from abroad.

WOOL TARIFF OF 1824.

A protective tariff was deemed necessary, and in 1824 such was passed with a duty of 25 to 33⅓ per cent. on woolens, but also a duty of 20 per cent. on raw wool costing over 10 cents per pound and 15 per cent. on that costing under 10 cents. At that time our domestic product was insufficient for our manufacture, and little of it fitted for the manufacture of the finer classes of goods. We were obliged to import for such uses from Portugal, Spain, Germany, &c., the fine wools of those countries, and the wools for coarser fabrics from Turkey and elsewhere.

These importations, which had materially declined after the heavy importations of woolen goods, materially increased from 1826 to 1828.

Anticipating that in spite of the duty upon the raw material this protection would make the woolen manufacture remunerative, the erec-

tion of woolen mills steadily increased, but the protection thus gained
was checkmated by Great Britain, expressly to retain the business of
this country, which, as we have before shown, was her most important
customer. Professedly for this purpose she soon after reduced the
duty on raw wool from 6 pence to 1 penny, and later to half penny
per pound, while in this conutry foreign wool was subject to a duty of
20 per cent.

The increased demand for wool, consequent upon the increased number of mills, became so great that the manufacturers had to go into
the country at clip time to secure their supply for the year. This could
be bought only for cash. To enable them to do this many were obliged
to mortgage their mills and machinery to their selling agents to obtain
acceptances on which they could borrow the money. The clip of the
country was still insufficient. The importation of wool and woolens
continued under a tariff which was only nominally protective. Sooner
or later nearly all of them failed and their agents were obliged to take
possession under their mortgages—many of whom soon went through
the same experience.

In 1828 and 1829 the tariff was revised, but as the raw material was
subjected to a duty as high or higher than the manufactured goods,
this, like its predecessors, resulted only in a temporary relief, as the margin between the duties on the raw material and other articles which entered into the cost of manufacture and of the plant, nearly, if not quite,
neutralized the protection.

Besides carpets we imported various goods which required coarser
wools than those raised in this country, such as low blankets, goods
for negro wear, heavy kerseys for overcoating, &c. To enable the
manufacture of such in this country, these wools by the tariff of 1832
were made free, and continued virtually so until, in 1864, a duty was imposed upon them for revenue to meet the expenses of the war. This
duty was continued in the tariff of 1867, with an objectionable feature
which has led, in my opinion, to nearly all the attempts, or apparent
attempts, to defraud the revenue, namely, making the duty double on
all wools costing over 12 cents per pound. The product of such wools
the world over has not increased; and the rapid increase of our carpet
manufacture has created such a competition for this country that the
value of many such wools under 12 cents per pound has been kept up
to that price or near to it in the markets of production, while for no
country in Europe would they be worth that, as Europeans could supply themselves in consequence of that limit with wools which could be
bought much cheaper—at a little above 12 cents.

The tariff of 1832, known as " the compromise tariff," was abundantly
protective for the first five years, which were marked by general pros-

perity. Then came the great financial crash of 1837, in which the wool and woolen interests had their full share of suffering. They rallied, however, in 1839, only temporarily, for they soon declined, as the reduction of the duty was actually greater upon the manufactured wool than upon the raw, this declension being in sympathy with the extreme depression in the business of the country consequent upon the reduced protection to manufacturing interests in general.

The United States was practically out of the foreign markets for wool, the prices abroad, particularly of carpet wools, falling to a very low point.

WOOL TARIFFS OF 1842 AND 1857.

Under the impulse of the tariff of August 30, 1842, manufacturing slowly revived for a time, but woolen manufacturing was, as a whole, unprofitable until after the passage of the act of 1857. A little in anticipation of its passage it had a spasmodic revival, which about the time the law went into effect was followed by a most disastrous crisis, resulting in the bankruptcy of many of our largest corporations and some of the leading commission houses. For a time wool prices were nominal and many descriptions were absolutely unsalable at any price.

Two of our oldest manufacturers, practical men, who owned and ran their mills and controlled their own affairs, told me that 1857 was the first year in which the balance of their business results had been on the wrong side of the ledger, but one of them added, "The prices at which I bought wool in December for the coming year made it the most profitable of any."

It is thus seen that the wool manufacture has not been a universally unprofitable business. In almost every branch there were men who were eminently prosperous, for they had been brought up regularly to the business, begun within their means, and increased their operations without running in debt. Philadelphia and its vicinity have probably had a larger class of such men than any other part of the country.

Of the corporations, nearly all before this date failed disastrously. Their business in most cases was conducted by men who had no practical knowledge of its details. The purchasing of materials and the manufacturing were carried on by men with high salaries. When profits were made they were often distributed to stockholders without due regard to the great uncertainties which attend this business, perhaps more than most others.

The successful men who are above referred to were strictly economical, and all that was made beyond the expenses of a simple mode of life went to swell their means and tide over times of severe depression, which to such as survived were usually followed by a period of corresponding prosperity.

Such men survived the disasters of 1857, and many of the mills of those who succumbed at that time were bought by men of similar character, who carried them on prosperously under the tariff of that year, which made all classes of wool virtually free. The high prices for wool paid in anticipation of the passage of this law were not immediately realized upon its going into operation, owing to the financial crisis before referred to.

The anticipated advance of wool in this country had, however, its effect abroad, and put up the value of fine wools in all the markets of the world. Sample lots was sent to this market from Australia in 1856, costing 7½d. to 8d. per pound. The party receiving them sent a large ship to Melbourne for such wool to cost under 20 cents per pound. The market had so advanced that it could not be done. It was also soon found that with the limit of 20 cents, and afterwards of 18 cents, the best wools at the Cape of Good Hope could not be bought under said limits, and American buyers were obliged to take those of inferior quality and condition.

WOOL TARIFF OF 1864.

The tariff on wool was very little changed after this until the passage of the Morrill tariff in 1864, when for the first time duties were put on manufactured wool over and above the amount of protection required by the manufacturer, sufficient to compensate for the duty upon the raw materials.

The law of 1867 was imposed upon the wool manufacturers by the wool growers.

Contrary to the expectation of the framers of the law of 1864, it was found that under it large quantities of Buenos Ayrean wools, dirty and burry, could be bought at the Rio de la Plata under 12 cents per pound, and came in under the 3 cent duty, which was expected to cover only car, pet wools. An exaggerated statement of the influence of this led to a call from the wool growers for a revision. After the passage of the act of 1864 a convention was held at Syracuse at which it was agreed that the wool growers should have equal protection with the manufacturers. By simply adding to the clause "wools costing under 12 cents per pound, except such as are of merino blood, immediate or remote," their protection, it was claimed, would be *equal* to that of manufacturers. But they insisted on the form in which it was passed, which resulted well for the country but badly for the States that insisted upon it, as it led to such an extension of wool growing beyond the Mississippi as to give to those States a severer competition than they ever had from abroad.

PROPOSED TARIFF OF 1866.

Confident of the passage of the tariff introduced in 1866, and which had been passed by the House of Representatives, the farmers of the country increased their flocks, especially beyond the Mississippi, and the growth of wool rapidly increased in the expectation of a great rise in prices consequent upon the high rates of duty imposed. In this they were disappointed, for others as well as themselves anticipated improved values of wool, and both manufacturers and speculators had sent orders abroad. The long delay between the inception of the bill and its final passage resulted in large importations under the old tariff. Consequently when the tariff actually went into operation the market was overstocked.

In addition to this, large quantities of army clothing, accumulated during the war, were thrown upon the market at exceedingly low prices and added to the dullness of the demand for wool from the manufacturers.

It will be seen from the following table that while the wool clip increased one hundred and seventeen million pounds since 1867 or about 70 per cent., the imports more than tripled; but the prices, instead of increasing, declined.

Table showing the relation of imports to home production of wool, &c.

Calendar year.	Domestic product.	Imports entered for consumption fiscal year succeeding.	Total supply.	Average value. Ohio wool.			Classified entries of wool for consumption, fiscal year succeeding—		
				Fine.	Medium.	Coarse.	Clothing.	Combing.	Carpet.
	Pounds.	*Pounds.*	*Pounds.*	*Cents.*	*Cents.*	*Cents.*	*Pounds.*	*Pounds.*	*Pounds.*
1867	168,000,000	....	....	47½	43	39½	....	....	....
1868	180,000,000	34,695,939	214,695,939	36½	36	35	2,512,201	4,533,367	27,650,371
1869	162,000,000	38,634,067	200,634,166	36¾	35¼	30½	6,530,493	2,752,568	29,351,006
1870	160,000,000	50,174,056	210,174,055	35½	35½	33½	5,957,461	17,665,600	26,550,995
1871	150,000,000	94,315,933	244,315,964	43	42½	41	16,871,332	41,155,460	36,289,141
1872	158,000,000	84,212,581	242,212,581	64½	62	58	6,029,488	40,540,231	28,642,863
1873	170,000,000	56,793,738	226,793,816	64	56½	52	2,398,210	27,087,438	27,308,090
1874	181,000,000	51,686,294	233,686,540	49½	47	41½	13,117,679	7,769,157	30,799,458
1875	192,000,000	40,275,678	232,257,677	48¾	48	41¾	8,643,366	3,167,307	28,465,003
1876	200,000,000	40,114,394	240,114,394	42½	43½	37½	9,294,029	2,509,954	28,310,411
1877	208,250,000	39,801,161	248,052,163	40	37	30¾	9,916,012	3,028,869	26,856,280
1878	211,000,000	40,102,642	251,093,642	45¼	43½	31¾	5,229,987	1,709,601	33,163,054
1879	232,000,000	99,372,440	331,872,440	34¾	35½	31¾	26,785,172	13,266,856	59,320,412
1880	240,000,000	67,410,900	307,416,966	47	47¾	43	20,609,707	4,421,491	42,385,769
1881	272,000,000	63,016,769	335,016,763	45	46	38½	13,489,923	2,318,671	47,208,175
1882	290,000,000	53,049,967	343,049,964	42¾	44¾	35¼	11,546,530	1,373,114	40,130,323
1883	300,000,000	87,703,931	387,703,931	42¾	44¾	35	20,703,843	4,474,396	62,525,692
1884	308,000,000	68,146,652	376,146,652	37	34¼	30½	13,472,432	3,891,914	50,782,306
1885	302,000,000	107,910,549	409,910,549	34	32½	28½	23,321,758	4,872,739	79,716,052
1886	285,000,000	114,404,173	399,081,000	34	35	32	23,195,734	9,703,962	81,504,477

Year ending June 30—	Remaining in bond June 30.	Exports of domestic and foreign wool.	Total imports of wool.	Imports of woolen manufactures into Great Britain (at $5 per £1).	Imports of woolen manufactures into—	
					Great Britain.	United States.
	Pounds.	*Pounds.*	*Pounds.*	*Dollars.*	*Dollars.*	*Dollars.*
1868	6,235,098	3,360,287	24,124,803	....	32,469,342	97,468,026
1869	7,635,183	756,804	39,275,926	21,986,000	36,077,875	108,233,625
1870	8,309,789	1,862,945	49,230,199	23,417,000	37,004,001	111,192,003
1871	6,412,052	1,330,506	68,058,028	26,991,000	46,713,767	140,141,301
1872	33,761,434	2,406,908	122,256,499	31,577,000	55,561,850	166,685,550
1873	28,828,609	7,115,515	85,406,049	30,190,000	53,510,560	160,531,680
1874	6,536,317	7,135,757	42,939,541	29,354,000	48,826,816	146,480,448
1875	6,274,265	3,745,661	54,901,760	30,018,000	46,348,545	139,045,635
1876	11,424,948	1,623,194	44,642,836	31,903,000	34,859,506	104,578,518
1877	8,699,729	3,168,556	42,171,192	36,409,000	26,911,873	80,735,619
1878	10,386,604	6,300,075	48,449,079	38,634,000	26,505,573	79,516,719
1879	6,722,831	4,165,400	39,005,155	41,218,000	25,527,117	76,581,351
1880	31,184,022	3,840,071	128,131,747	38,494,000	35,356,992	106,070,976
1881	18,860,896	5,578,989	55,964,236	51,561,000	32,970,507	98,911,521
1882	14,382,748	3,918,015	67,861,744	40,506,000	38,726,975	116,180,925
1883	26,972,660	4,074,517	70,575,478	42,773,000	45,457,307	136,371,921
1884	15,226,416	2,315,094	78,350,651	45,059,000	41,157,583	123,472,749
1885	15,031,337	3,103,345	70,596,170	46,928,000	35,776,559	107,329,677
1886	28,318,952	6,680,849	129,084,958	49,763,000	41,421,319	124,263,957
1887	20,711,648	6,986,232	114,038,030	55,129,000	44,633,263	133,899,788

The depression of the wool market continued until 1871, when the production had fallen off 30,000,000 pounds since 1868. The surplus of woolens which had weighed upon the market had now been consumed, the manufacturing business which had been dull and unprofitable had now greatly improved, and the manufacturers looked forward to a season of prosperity. The machinery which had been idle or feebly running for three or four years was started, the wool market improved, and a short supply of wool carried prices up rapidly. At the same time prices in Europe, especially for fine wool, owing to the Franco-Prussian war, were exceedingly low, lower probably than ever before, and lower than they reached again until the latter part of 1885 and early part of 1886, when good average Port Phillip grease touched 8d. (Fine wools were similarly affected during the early period of our great war.) Wool dealers, manufacturers, and speculators sent their orders abroad freely, the result being a larger importation than had ever been in any one year. Notwithstanding this, prices were well maintained here, until the general depression in business of all kinds which followed the financial disasters of 1873, from which the country recovered slowly. Our heavy importations of 1871 and 1872 helped, with return of peace, to bring about a rapid reaction in the value of wool in Europe, and prices did not fall below paying rates until 1879. The large amount of wool in the raw and manufactured state consumed in the Boston fire of 1872, estimated at 31,000,000 pounds, had an influence to prevent a sudden decline in values, notwithstanding an increase of over 70,000,000 pounds in our home product since 1872, and this without a material increase in our woolen machinery. The machinery had been added to greatly during the war, and the country only now appeared to have grown to its capacity.

Prosperity generally reigned. While the machinery for general woolens had not increased, there had been a decided increase in that for carpets, and for worsted goods, particularly of the finer kinds, which required chiefly such wools of the first class as were suitable for this purpose and of which but a small quantity was then grown in the United States. Soon after 1879 opened, wool, particularly second-class wool, was in small demand abroad and had reached in Great Britain a value as low, comparatively, as did the fine wool in 1870, and lower than on record for the twenty years preceding.* Alpacas and other luster goods for women's wear had gone entirely out of fashion. Large quantities of these second-class wools were made into the coarse fabrics generally known as "cheviot goods," which were exceedingly good and cheap. As the men of this country must take their fashions from England, or I would rather say London, these goods were largely bought for America. At the same time large orders went abroad for wool for similar uses here. The prices

---

* The largest decrease in the clip of the country was in the States from which we get the most of this description of wool. The number of sheep in Ohio, the principal State, fell from 7,688,845 in 1868 to 4,302,904 in 1870.

in England were by this competition advanced from 10d. in August, 1879, to 18½d. in April, 1880. Thus an effectual check was put upon the shipment of these cheviot goods to this country, except such as the caprice of fashion demanded.

As cheviot goods were all the rage, it became necessary to make them for the masses; to do which, as we had but little suitable wool grown in this country, stock for this purpose was prepared by mixing some of the coarsest grades of native wools with the finer wools of the third class to give a feeling and character resembling that of an English cheviot. It was no doubt in part this use that swelled the consumption of third-class wool in 1880 to 59,320,112 pounds; but there was, as the census of 1880 shows, an unusually large consumption, not less than 45,000,000 pounds, in that year for carpets. The blanket manufacture, which always used largely third-class wool, was also a large consumer this year. The census of 1880 reported 34,008,252 pounds foreign, and 2,029,318 pounds domestic wool used in carpet manufactures ; also 8,985,162 pounds woolen yarn and 4,091,115 pounds worsted yarn purchased. Of these yarns 1,265,240 pounds woolen and 2,238,076 pounds worsted were among the marketable products reported by carpet mills, leaving 9,539,961 pounds yarn bought by carpet manufacturers. This would have required about 14,000,000 pounds, of which probably not less than 11,000,000 pounds was foreign, making 45,000,000 pounds for carpets, say for blankets, blanketing, &c., 4,000,000 pounds, leaving for 1880 only about 9,000,000 pounds unaccounted for. Of this a considerable portion was surplus in the hands of dealers and manufacturers, as is shown by the reduced quantity that went into consumption during the three succeeding years.

The imports of 1880, like those in 1872, were profitable in the beginning, and at its close there remained in the warehouses 31,184,022 pounds, while it was estimated that there were in the hands of manufacturers and dealers at least 25,000,000 pounds more. Nevertheless, domestic wool maintained a high average value until 1884, when there was again a considerable quantity of foreign entered for consumption, increased at this time by wools held back in bond until July, 1883, in order to get the benefit of reduction of duties by the act of that year. There were in warehouse 26,972,660 pounds.

Again, in 1886 the imports were large; and as again cheviot goods were ruling the market, undoubtedly some of the third-class wools were used for this purpose.

From 1880 to 1887 the machinery for making carpets in this country has increased in effective power at least two-thirds. Allowing that for the past year the product of this machinery has increased one-half, there would have been required for carpets 67,500,000 pounds; and allowing as before 4,000,000 pounds for blankets, there would remain to be accounted for only about 10,000,000 pounds with a general consumption of wool nearly 23 per cent. larger than in 1880. I may add that considerable quantities of these wools have been used for backing heavy coatings as well as for mixing with our wools for cheviots.

The imports of third class (carpet) entered for consumption during the fiscal year 1887 amounted to 81,504,477 pounds, the extreme amount of which I estimate could be used for clothing purposes would be about 8,800,000 pounds. My impression is that much less that this was thus used.

Many of the wools that were on hand when the demand suddenly stopped in 1880 were sold at severe loss, as were many that had been bought by manufacturers to make cheviots, and remained on hand when the fashion for this class of goods ceased. One lot of heavy, low-grade, first-class wool, on which duties had been paid, were sold at a price which resulted in an entire loss of the first cost abroad.

Without the occasional importation of wools of all classes when our home supply, for whatever reason, fails to meet the demands of our manufacturers, barring the excess imported by speculators, it is doubtful if these importations have lessened the value of our native product, as, if our manufacturers had been unable to obtain the wools requisite to make the goods demanded by fashion, such goods would have been imported from abroad, and our mills would have been obliged to stop for want of material to make the goods demanded by the market. It is certainly demonstrable that the advance in wools caused by American competition greatly checked the importation from England of coarse woolens in 1880.

COMPETITION IN WOOL RAISING WITH FOREIGN COUNTRIES.

In the foregoing pages I have endeavored to show, as requested by you, the relation which the product of wool in this country bears to the imported product.

You next ask me to state "whether any wool is imported which we cannot produce in this country, and the reasons why we cannot produce any particular grades of wool in competition with foreign countries."

In reply I would say there are none of the third-class wools that can be grown in this country to advantage. Most of them are from races adapted to entirely different climate and circumstances, whose yield of wool is so small that it would not pay for half their keeping. We could, I think, grow much more of the second-class wool than we do, because such wool is secondary in value, as the sheep could be raised profitably for mutton. This first-class mutton, if abundantly grown, would soon be appreciated and find a well-paying market at home and abroad.

It is more difficult to explain, so as to be readily understood, why we cannot produce any particular grades of first-class wools. We may grow wool in some places equally fine and apparently as good in other respects as wools that are imported, but they may not have the same working qualities. They will not produce the same effect when finished. Such is the influence of climate and soil upon wool that no two places can grow wool exactly alike. The descendants of the same flock raised in Vermont and Ohio, or even in Vermont and New Hampshire, will not yield the same wool.

I asked a correspondent in Australia what gave the superior luster to his neighbor's wool. The reply was, his was grown on a granite soil and mine on a limestone soil. In conversation once with one of the most distinguished wine merchants in Bordeaux upon this subject, he remarked that a friend in Crimea once wrote to him, saying that, if his patriotism did not prevent, he wished he would send him some grape cuttings with instructions for their propagation. He replied that his patriotism would not interfere; that he could send him the cuttings, but he could neither send him the climate nor the soil.

The wool from flocks bred of Vermont stock gains a character in every part of the country, modified in one way or another by the climate and soil of each locality.

We raise, comparatively to the demand, a small portion of first-class combing and delaine wool, and very little even of this has the characteristics required to make the finest goods which fashion demands from France and England.

Without the same wools that are used there these goods cannot be made here.

The bulletin of the Philadelphia Textile Association estimates the clip of 1886 at 282,331,026 pounds, of which it classes as combing 11,464,306 pounds, as combing X and above, 12,103,553 pounds medium, and 33,713,345 pounds quarter blood. It also estimates the decrease of the clip between 1884 and 1886 at 11,713,345 pounds, the decline from the States which yielded most of the combing wools being 10,000,000 pounds. To the quality of the clip must be added that of the wool pulled from the skins to give the entire product.

There are portions of the Western States and Territories, Montana in particular, where they are rapidly improving the character of their wools, and much will probably be had from these sections when they have been longer settled and provision made for better protecting and more uniform feeding of the sheep. A change of food or exposure often ruins the fiber for this purpose. Until this time comes, Australian or other fine combing wools must be imported or this branch of fine wool manufacture, now perhaps the most important, must to a great extent be abandoned.

We have also as yet been able to raise in this country very few wools fitted for the manufacture of fine broadcloths and similar finished goods.

In the early production of worsted goods, wools of English blood, combed by hand, were first used, but as machinery for combing was invented the long-stapled wools of other races began to be combed and the machinery was gradually improved, until now wools of any length of staple can be combed. As far back as 1860 I saw in Mr. Holden's establishment, at Rheims, a very handsome "top" made from miserable Cape of Good Hope bits and pieces. The process is now so far perfected that yarns made by the combing process are used for many classes of goods that at the time of the passage of the tariff of 1867 were only made by carding, and thus a fearful competition is set up with goods manufactured by the old process.

TARIFF DISCRIMINATIONS BETWEEN WORSTED AND WOOLENS.

This leads us to a consideration of the paper you sent to me written by Mr. A. D. Juillard on tariff discriminations between worsteds and woolens. These discriminations were made in the tariffs of 1867 and those preceding it, and the language of the tariff of 1867 was copied in the tariff of 1883.

Demands for change for duties now exacted upon worsted goods and wool waste are reasonable and equitable and should be heeded as promptly as possible, but, as I have more fully stated in correspondence with Mr. William Whitman, president of the National Association of Woolen Manufacturers, it seems to me clear that Congress alone has the power to make such changes, because these goods were described in the tariff of 1883 as in 1867, and under the administration of the tariff of 1867 the word "cloths" was understood to mean broadcloths, as they have been in the trade ever since I was first familiar with it, more than sixty years since. The headings for the census returns for 1870 and 1880 so indicated, and the late E. B. Bigelow, in his address upon the wool industry of the United States, delivered in New York, stated that the imports of woolen goods were as follows:

Cloths and cassimeres... $6,956,449
Shawls.. 1,559,999
Blankets 28,196
Carpets... 2,776,291
Dress goods... 15,196,233
Not specified... 5,902,591

Yarn waste of all kinds, fine and coarse, was imported under the tariff of 1867 and those which preceded it. Much more fine waste, and possibly some finer than before, has been imported within the last few years, but that does not change the character as described.

Therefore it seems as though Congress alone can remedy these evils, which are very serious for the wool grower and manufacturer, and to which, regardless of political bearings, they should immediately give their attention.

I have overlooked your inquiry, "Why there do not appear in the market quotations of wools the prices of foreign wools?" Such quotations are given as far as they are of any value, but the grades are so little known that few are interested in them.

DEVELOPMENT OF THE RAW WOOL TRADE.

Up to about 1825 the manufacturers bought of the farmers most of their wool or took it from them to work upon shares, but as the clip of the country increased the wool was received by the commission merchants in the leading cities, principally the dry goods commission merchants, either by purchase or on consignment. Wool was not made a distinct branch of trade until about 1830. In that year, or shortly before, distinct wool houses were opened in Boston, New York, and Philadelphia. Livermore & Kendall in that year started the first in Boston, and were the leading house in that market for some years. The factories increased so rapidly, that soon the clip of the country did not meet the demand, and, as before stated, in 1828 competition carried prices up so high and reduced the supply so low, that the larger manufacturers united and sent an agent to Europe to buy wool. On arrival the wool was sold at auction; each contributor had the privilege of buying what suited him, and the profit and loss account was divided *pro rata* among the subscribers. The result was satisfactory, and this course was repeated a few years afterwards, in 1831 or 1832.

With these exceptions, the importations were then generally made by merchants and ship owners engaged in foreign commerce, who bought wool in quantities larger or smaller, as they might obtain it for a part of their cargoes. The wool business increased very gradually. As late as 1841 there were in Boston but two wool houses and one wool broker. Others, of course, then dealt in wool, both home-grown and foreign—some to a considerable extent.

At that time Philadelphia probably did the largest business in domestic wool. The foreign, which had then attained considerable importance, especially in the low carpet-wools imported chiefly from South America and Turkey, was about equally divided between New York and Boston. Our business with Russia in wool did not begin to develop importance until after the passage of the law of 1857, although we did receive some Russian wools through other sources.

Since that time the importation of foreign wools has been chiefly through New York and Boston, with a small quantity to Philadelphia, which port within a few years has materially increased her imports. New York, owing to her extensive commerce, has been the heaviest port of entry, many of the imports for other markets having been made there on account of the greater facility of obtaining favorable freights.

I regret to add that recently there have been repeated attempts to enter wools under the third that should have paid duty as first or second class. I notice large quantities of wool imported as third class from Turkey in Europe, whence a very small percentage of wools of this class comes. Our advices from Liverpool have continually reported large quantities of noils from English wools shipped to this country, which, from the prices at which they have been sold, it is to be feared have been entered as third class.

The conferences of the appraisers of the several ports, it is hoped, will correct this; but these shipments from Liverpool still continue. Uniformity in the administration at the several ports should be carefully watched and absolutely demanded.

To secure this, it is of the first importance to have in each of the ports examiners who are thorough experts in wools of all descriptions.

[End of Mr. Bond's article.]

MANUFACTURES OF WOOLENS IN FOREIGN COUNTRIES.

England, France, and Germany enjoy practically a monopoly of the trade of the world in woolen manufactures. They are the only countries of the world that export woolen manufactures in excess of their imports of raw wool. The exact magnitude of their manufactures cannot, however, be adequately shown, as their governments do not collect periodically elaborate statistics of their products of industry, as does the United States by means of its decennial census.

Such information as has been obtained is fragmentary and lacking in desired details, rendering it impracticable to make a satisfactory comparison with the wool manufactures of the United States. These statistics will be found in table 64 of the Appendix.

COMMENTS ON APPENDIX TABLES.

In many respects the most valuable portion of this report will be found in the Appendix, consisting of seventy tables of statistics, twenty of which relate to the United States, and the remainder to the United Kingdom and to the more important states of continental Europe.

Within the limits at command we cannot summarize the tables; nevertheless, special attention is directed to the following as of peculiar value:

Table No. 1 presents the quantities and values of raw wool imported into the United States from the principal and other foreign countries, with the total quantities and values of foreign raw wool exported and the net imports of the same, from 1822 to 1887, inclusive.

Table No. 3 shows the quantities of wool produced, imported, exported, and retained for consumption in the United States from 1839 to 1886, inclusive.

Table No. 4 will be found one of peculiar interest, as it presents not only the quantities and values of imported wool, hair of the alpaca, goat, and other like animals, entered for consumption in the United States, including both entries for immediate consumption and withdrawals from warehouse for consumption, but also the rates of duty and amounts of accruing duty, during the years ending June 30 from 1867 to 1886, inclusive.

Table No. 6 shows the values of manufactures of wool imported into the United States from the principal and all other foreign countries, the total values of foreign manufactures of wool exported, and the net imports for each year from 1821 to 1887, inclusive.

Table No. 7 shows the quantities and values of the principal and all other manufactures of wool imported into the United States, and the estimated amounts of duty received on the same, for each year from 1821 to 1866, inclusive.

Table No. 8, in the first place, presents by itemized articles the rates of duty and amounts of accruing duties, followed by the quantities and values of imported manufactures of wool entered for consumption in the United States, including both entries for immediate consumption and withdrawals from warehouse for consumption, during the years ending June 30 from 1867 to 1886, inclusive.

Table No. 11 shows the quantity and value of domestic wool exported from the United States during each year from 1846 to 1887, the value of domestic manufactures of wool exported from 1864 to 1887, and the number and value of domestic sheep exported from 1821 to 1887, inclusive.

Table No. 12 will be consulted with peculiar interest, as it shows the price of wool during each year from 1824 to 1887, inclusive.

Table No. 13 exhibits the tariff rates of duty upon wool and manufactures of wool under all the acts of Congress imposing said duties from the first wool tariff of 1789 to 1883, inclusive.

Table No. 14 exhibits the statistics of number of establishments, capital invested, number of hands employed, wages paid, cost of material used, and value of products of the manufacture of worsted and woolen goods in each State and Territory of the United States for the years 1850, 1860, 1870, and 1880, according to the United States census of those years respectively.

Table No. 18 shows the weekly wages paid to employés in woolen factories in the United Kingdom of Great Britain and Ireland, and average wages paid daily in like factories in Massachusetts, New York, Ohio, and Kentucky, in 1885.

Tables Nos. 19 and 20 exhibit the number of sheep and the crop of wool in each State and Territory of the United States for each of the years 1840, 1850, 1860, 1870, 1880, and the number of sheep in each State and Territory from 1875 to 1887, inclusive.

Tables Nos. 21 to 63 comprise interesting data in regard to the imports into and the exports from the various foreign countries of wool and woolens, embracing in many cases all the information which could be procured in regard to the wool and woolen industries in those countries.

Table No. 45 is one of the many interesting tables having reference to the wool industries of foreign countries, and shows, by countries, the quantities and values of manufactures of wool imported into and exported from the United Kingdom in 1885; and Table No. 49 shows the quantities and values of wool and manufactures of wool exported from the United Kingdom for each year from 1861 to 1885, inclusive.

Table No. 65 is compiled from the United States consular reports, and possesses peculiar interest, for it shows the present tariff rates of foreign countries on importations of wool and manufactures of wool.

Table No. 68 exhibits the number of sheep and goats in the various countries of the world.

No. 1.—Diagram showing the Number of Sheep in the United States from 1875 to 1887. (See Appendix, Table No. 20.)

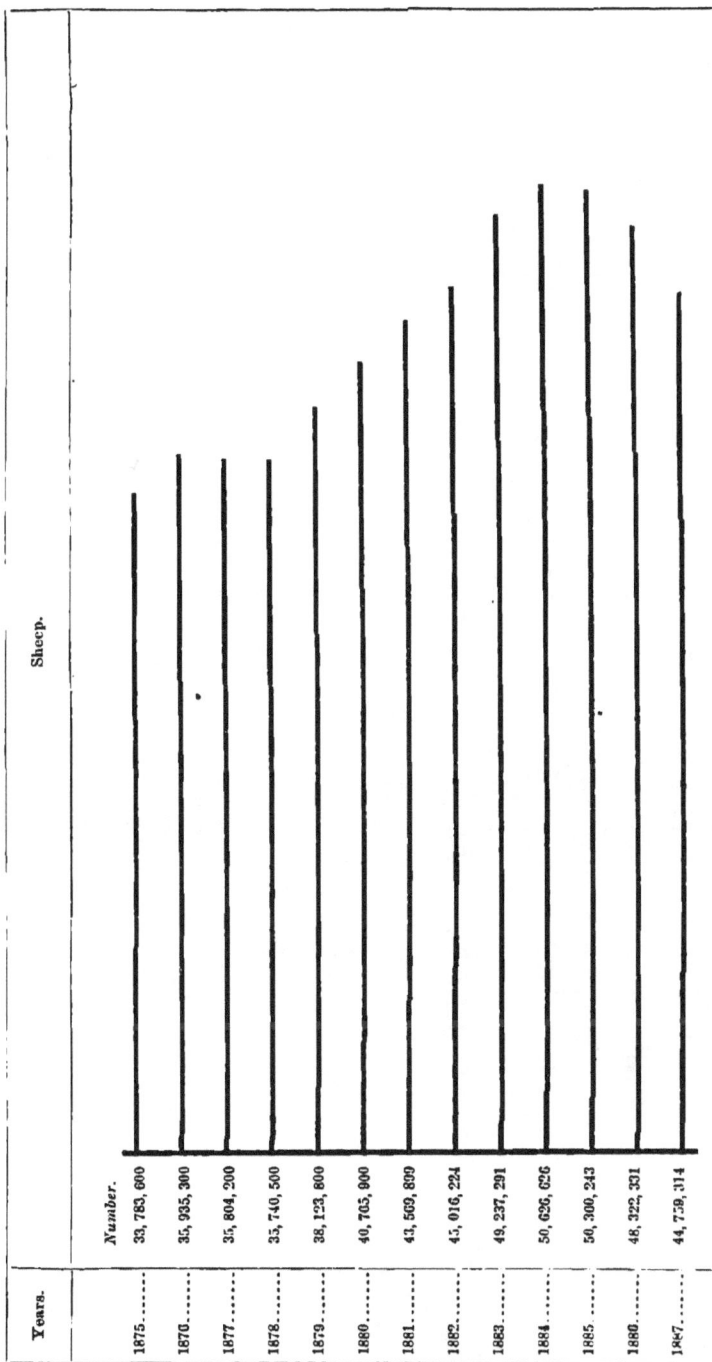

Sheep.

Scale: 1 inch = 10,000,000.

Years.	Number.
1875	33,783,600
1876	35,935,300
1877	35,804,200
1878	35,740,500
1879	38,123,800
1880	40,705,900
1881	43,569,899
1882	45,016,224
1883	49,237,291
1884	50,626,626
1885	50,360,243
1886	48,322,331
1887	44,759,314

No. 2.—Diagram showing the Quantities of Wool Produced, Imported, and Retained for Consumption in the United States from 1839 to 1887. (See Appendix, Table No. 3.)

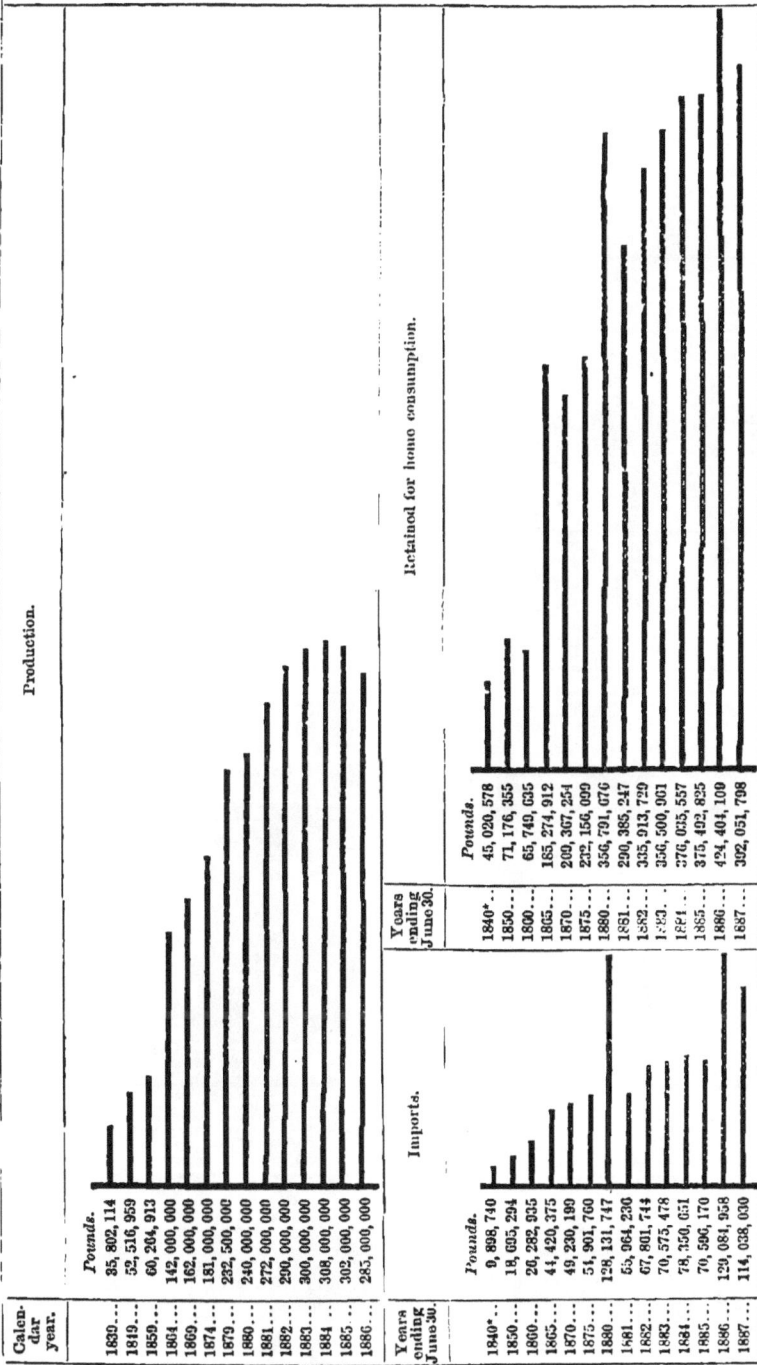

Production.

Retained for home consumption.

Imports.

Scale: 1 inch=100,000,000.

* Year ending September 30.

Calendar year.	Pounds.
1839...	35,802,114
1849...	52,516,959
1859...	60,264,913
1864...	142,000,000
1869...	162,000,000
1874...	181,000,000
1879...	232,500,000
1880...	240,000,000
1881...	272,000,000
1882...	290,000,000
1883...	300,000,000
1884...	308,000,000
1885...	302,000,000
1886...	285,000,000

Years ending June 30.	Pounds.
1840*...	9,898,740
1850...	18,695,294
1860...	26,282,935
1865...	44,420,375
1870...	49,230,190
1875...	51,901,760
1880...	128,131,747
1881...	55,964,230
1882...	67,801,744
1883...	70,575,478
1884...	78,150,651
1885...	70,596,170
1886...	129,084,958
1887...	114,038,030

Years ending June 30.	Pounds.
1840*...	45,020,578
1850...	71,176,355
1860...	65,749,635
1865...	165,274,912
1870...	209,367,254
1875...	232,156,099
1880...	356,791,676
1881...	290,385,247
1882...	335,913,729
1883...	356,500,901
1884...	376,035,557
1885...	375,492,825
1886...	424,404,109
1887...	392,051,798

THE YEARS ENDING JUNE 30, FROM 1872 TO 1886, INCLUSIVE. (See Appendix, Table No. 4.)

Class 1.—Clothing wools.

Years ending June 30.	Pounds.
1872	16,871,332
1873	6,029,488
1874	2,398,210
1875	13,117,679
1876	8,643,366
1877	9,294,029
1878	9,916,012
1879	5,229,987
1880	26,785,172
1881	20,609,707
1882	13,489,923
1883	11,546,530
1884	20,703,843
1885	13,472,432
1886	23,321,759

Class 2.—Combing wools.

Years ending June 30.	Pounds.
1872	41,155,460
1873	49,540,231
1874	27,087,438
1875	7,769,157
1876	3,167,307
1877	2,509,954
1878	3,028,869
1879	1,709,601
1880	13,266,858
1881	4,421,491
1882	2,318,671
1883	1,373,114
1884	4,474,390
1885	3,891,914
1886	4,872,739

Class 3.—Carpet wools and other similar wools.

Years ending June 30.	Pounds.
1872	30,289,141
1873	28,042,863
1874	27,308,090
1875	30,799,458
1876	28,465,005
1877	28,310,411
1878	26,850,280
1879	33,163,054
1880	69,320,412
1881	42,385,769
1882	47,208,175
1883	40,130,823
1884	62,625,692
1885	50,782,300
1886	79,710,952

Scale: 1 inch = 16,000,000.

No. 4.—Diagram showing the Value of Imported Wool entered for Consumption in the United States and the Amount of Duty Received during the Years ending June 30, from 1867 to 1885, inclusive. (See Appendix, Table No. 4.)

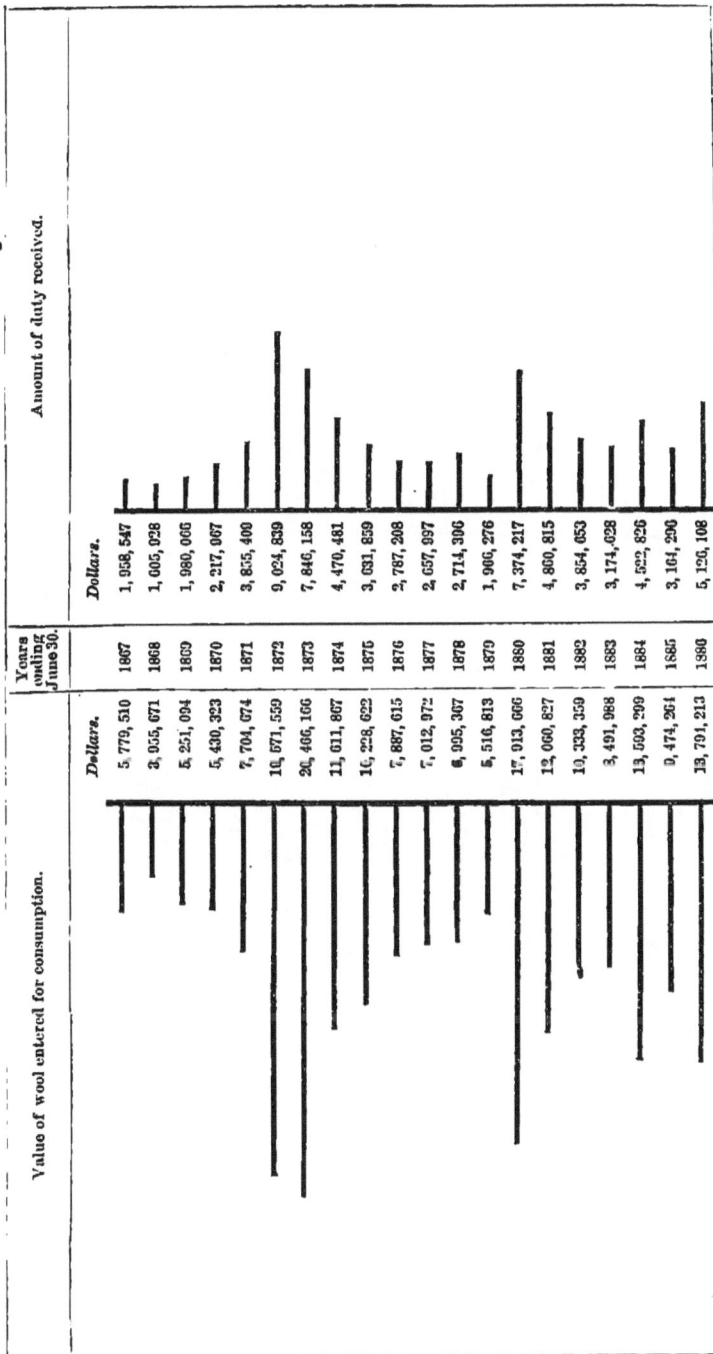

Value of wool entered for consumption.

Amount of duty received.

Dollars.	Years (ending June 30.)	Dollars.
5,779,510	1867	1,958,547
3,055,671	1868	1,005,028
5,251,094	1869	1,980,066
5,430,323	1870	2,217,067
7,704,074	1871	3,855,400
10,671,559	1872	9,024,839
20,466,166	1873	7,846,158
11,611,867	1874	4,470,481
16,228,622	1875	3,031,859
7,887,615	1876	2,787,208
7,012,972	1877	2,657,997
6,995,367	1878	2,714,306
5,516,813	1879	1,966,276
17,913,666	1880	7,374,217
12,060,827	1881	4,860,815
10,333,359	1882	3,854,053
3,491,988	1883	3,174,028
13,560,299	1884	4,522,826
9,474,261	1885	3,164,290
13,791,213	1880	5,120,108

Scale: 1 inch = $40,000,000.

No. 5.—DIAGRAM SHOWING THE VALUES OF MANUFACTURES OF WOOL IMPORTED INTO THE UNITED STATES. (See Appendix, Table No. 6.)

Manufactures of wool.

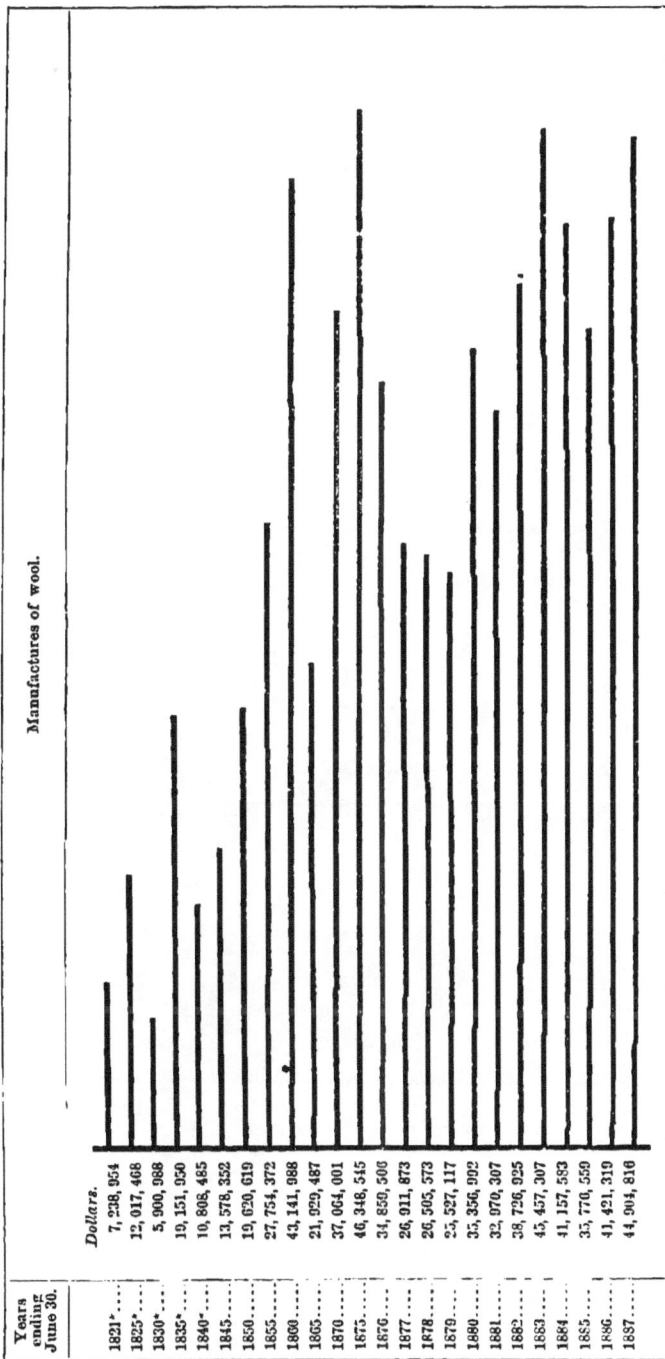

Years ending June 30.	Dollars.
1821*	7,238,954
1825*	12,017,468
1830*	5,900,988
1835*	19,151,950
1840*	10,806,485
1845	13,578,352
1850	19,630,619
1855	27,754,372
1860	43,141,988
1865	21,929,487
1870	37,064,001
1875	46,348,545
1876	31,859,506
1877	26,911,873
1878	26,505,573
1879	25,527,117
1880	35,356,992
1881	32,970,307
1882	38,726,025
1883	45,457,307
1884	41,157,583
1885	35,770,559
1886	41,421,319
1887	44,904,816

Scale: 1 inch = 8,000,000.

* Years ending September 30.

No. 6.—DIAGRAM SHOWING THE VALUE OF IMPORTED MANUFACTURES OF WOOL ENTERED FOR CONSUMPTION IN THE UNITED STATES AND THE AMOUNT OF DUTY RECEIVED DURING THE YEARS FROM 1867 TO 1886, INCLUSIVE. (See Appendix, Table No. 8.)

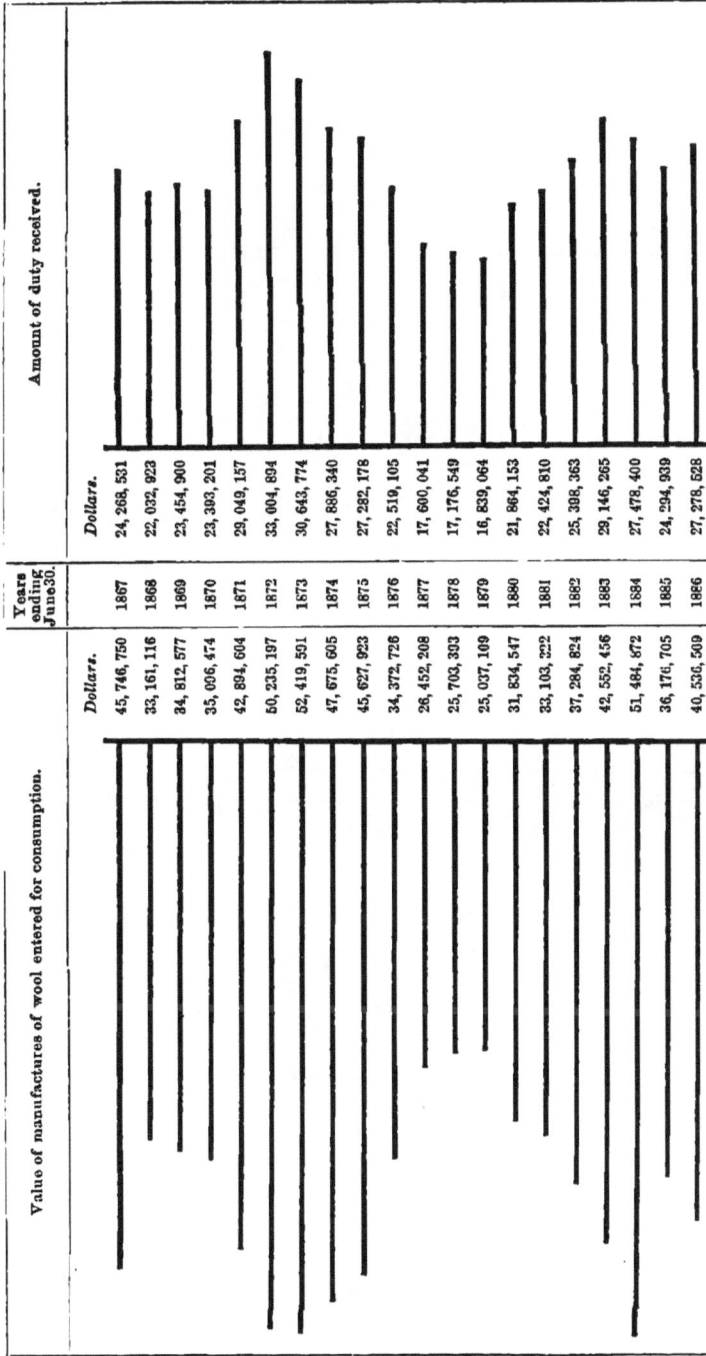

Amount of duty received.

Value of manufactures of wool entered for consumption.

Amount of duty received. Dollars.	Years ending June 30.	Value of manufactures. Dollars.
24,268,531	1867	45,746,750
22,032,923	1868	33,161,116
23,454,900	1869	34,812,577
23,393,201	1870	35,096,474
29,049,157	1871	42,894,604
33,004,894	1872	50,235,197
30,643,774	1873	52,419,591
27,886,340	1874	47,675,605
27,282,178	1875	45,627,923
22,519,105	1876	34,372,726
17,600,041	1877	26,452,208
17,176,549	1878	25,703,393
16,839,064	1879	25,037,109
21,864,153	1880	31,834,547
22,424,810	1881	33,103,222
25,398,363	1882	37,284,824
29,146,265	1883	42,552,456
27,478,400	1884	51,484,872
24,294,939	1885	36,176,705
27,278,628	1886	40,536,509

Scale: 1 inch = $16,000,000.

No. 7.—DIAGRAM SHOWING THE VALUE OF PRODUCTS OF THE PRINCIPAL MANUFACTURING INDUSTRIES OF THE UNITED STATES IN THE YEAR 1880, ACCORDING TO THE CENSUS.

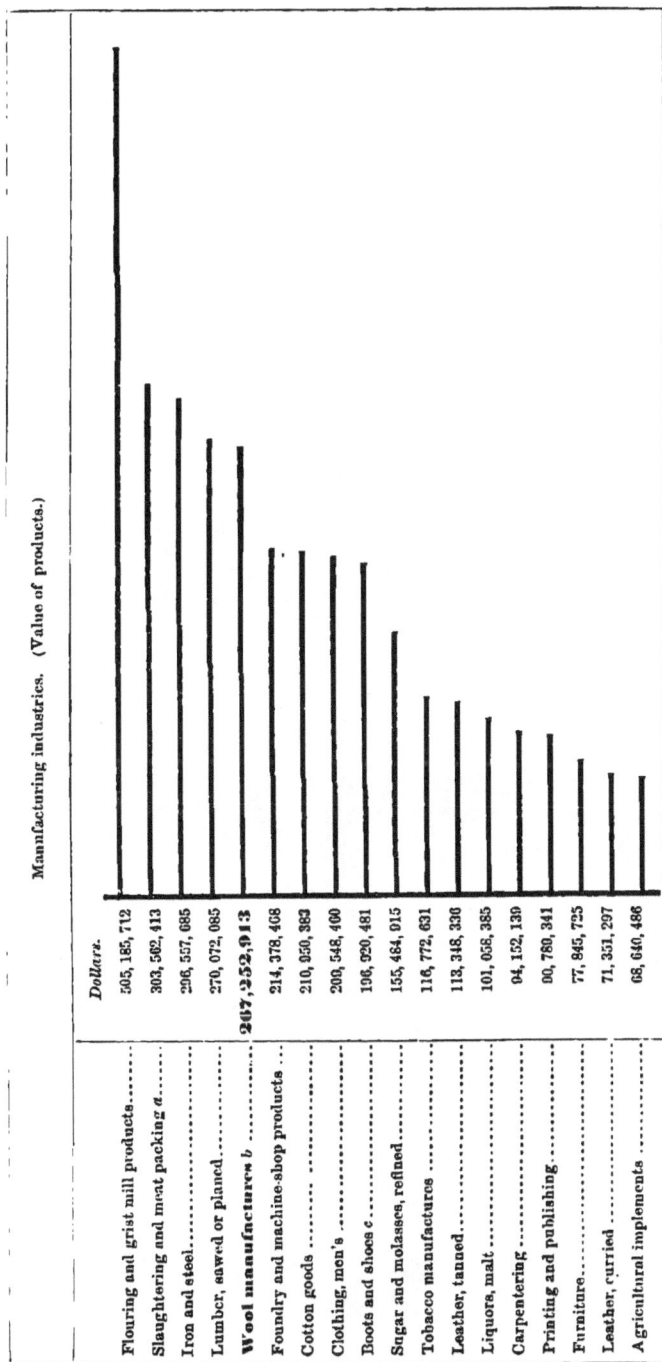

Manufacturing industries. (Value of products.)

Industry	Dollars.
Flouring and grist mill products	505,185,712
Slaughtering and meat packing a	303,562,413
Iron and steel	296,557,685
Lumber, sawed or planed	270,072,085
Wool manufactures b	267,252,913
Foundry and machine-shop products	214,378,468
Cotton goods	210,950,383
Clothing, men's	209,548,400
Boots and shoes c	196,920,481
Sugar and molasses, refined	155,464,015
Tobacco manufactures	116,772,631
Leather, tanned	113,348,330
Liquors, malt	101,058,385
Carpentering	94,152,139
Printing and publishing	90,780,341
Furniture	77,845,725
Leather, curried	71,351,297
Agricultural implements	68,640,486

a Not including retail butchering establishments.
b All classes, includes carpets, other than rag, felt goods, rag, felt goods, hosiery, and knit goods, wool hats, woolen goods, and worsted goods.
c Including custom work and repairing.

No. 6.—Diagram showing the Comparative Value of some of the Leading Agricultural and Mineral Products of the United States for 1885.

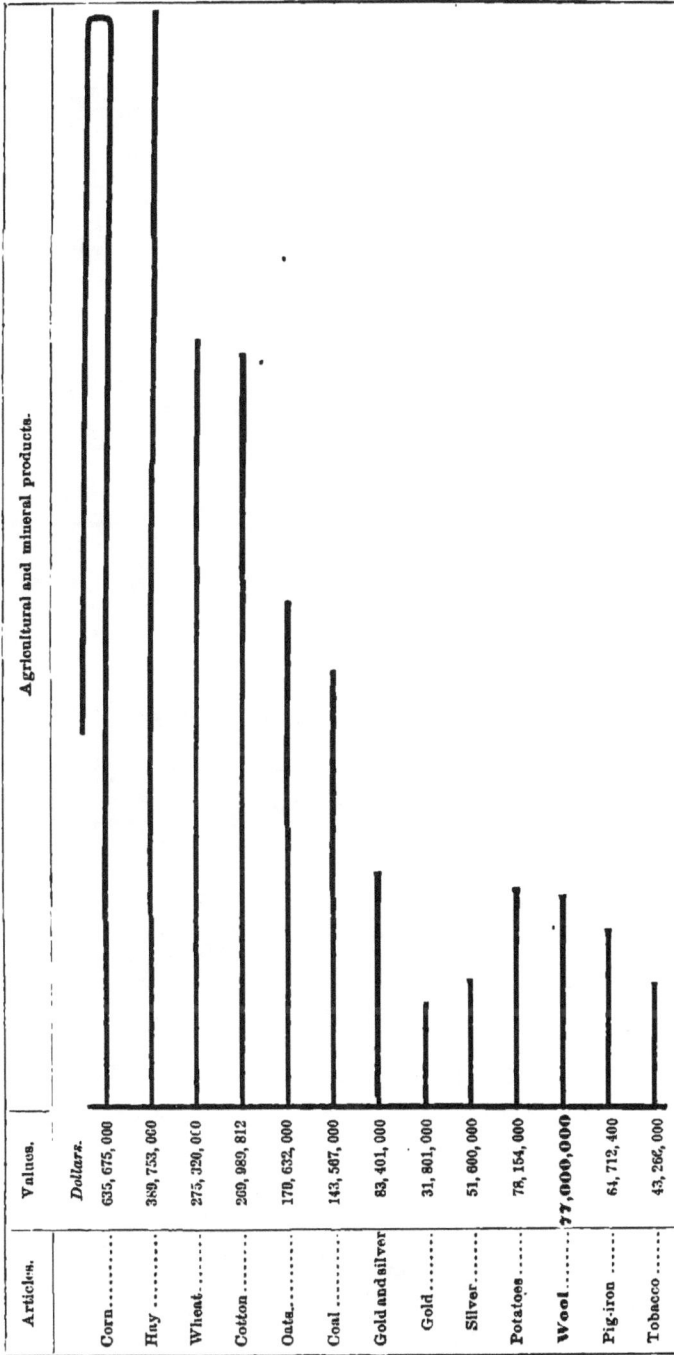

Agricultural and mineral products.

Articles.	Values.
	Dollars.
Corn.........	635,675,000
Hay	389,753,000
Wheat.......	275,320,000
Cotton	269,989,812
Oats.........	170,632,000
Coal	143,507,000
Gold and silver	83,401,000
Gold........	31,801,000
Silver.......	51,600,000
Potatoes	78,154,000
Wool......	**77,000,000**
Pig-iron	64,712,400
Tobacco......	43,266,000

No. 9.—Diagram showing the Number of Sheep and Lambs of the Principal Wool Producing Countries of the World. (See Appendix, Table No. 68.)

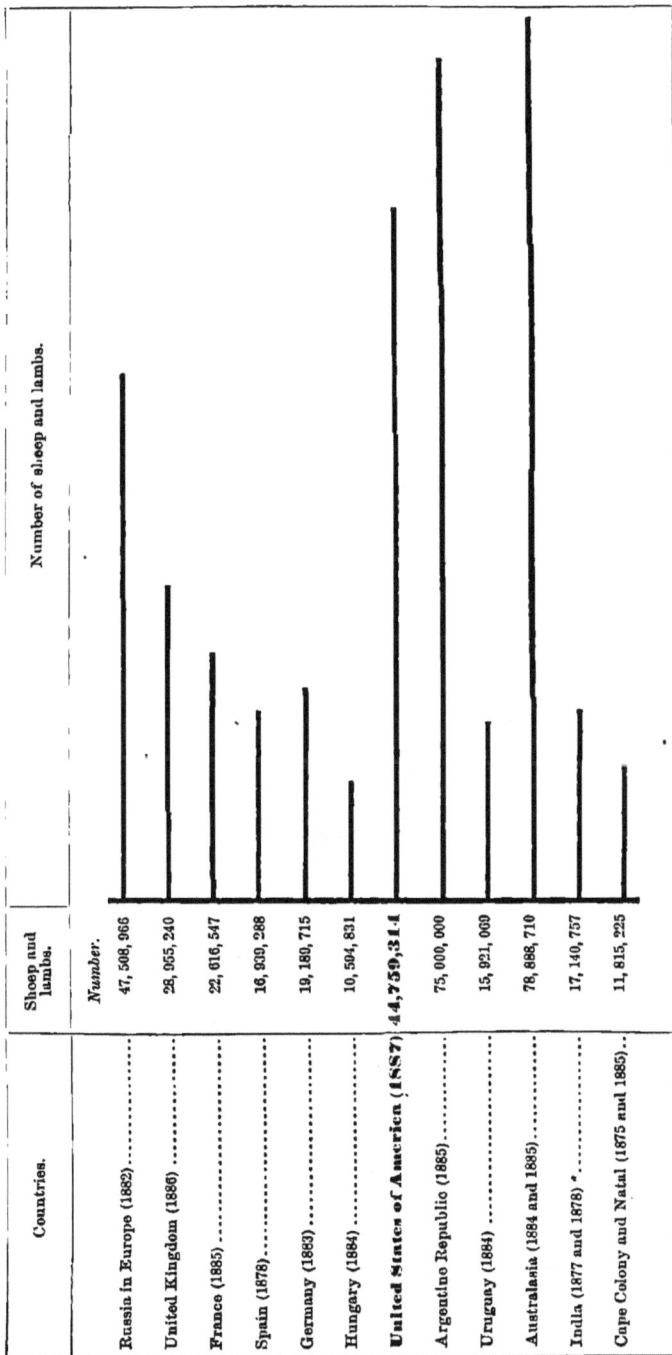

Countries.	Sheep and lambs.	Number of sheep and lambs.
	Number.	
Russia in Europe (1882)	47,508,966	
United Kingdom (1886)	28,965,240	
France (1885)	22,616,547	
Spain (1878)	16,939,288	
Germany (1883)	19,180,715	
Hungary (1884)	10,504,831	
United States of America (1887)	**44,759,314**	
Argentine Republic (1885)	75,000,000	
Uruguay (1884)	15,921,060	
Australasia (1884 and 1885)	78,888,710	
India (1877 and 1878) *	17,140,757	
Cape Colony and Natal (1875 and 1885)	11,815,225	

* Includes goats.

No. 10.—DIAGRAM SHOWING THE RAW WOOL PRODUCED IN EACH OF THE PRINCIPAL WOOL-PRODUCING COUNTRIES OF THE WORLD. (See Appendix, Table No. 67.)

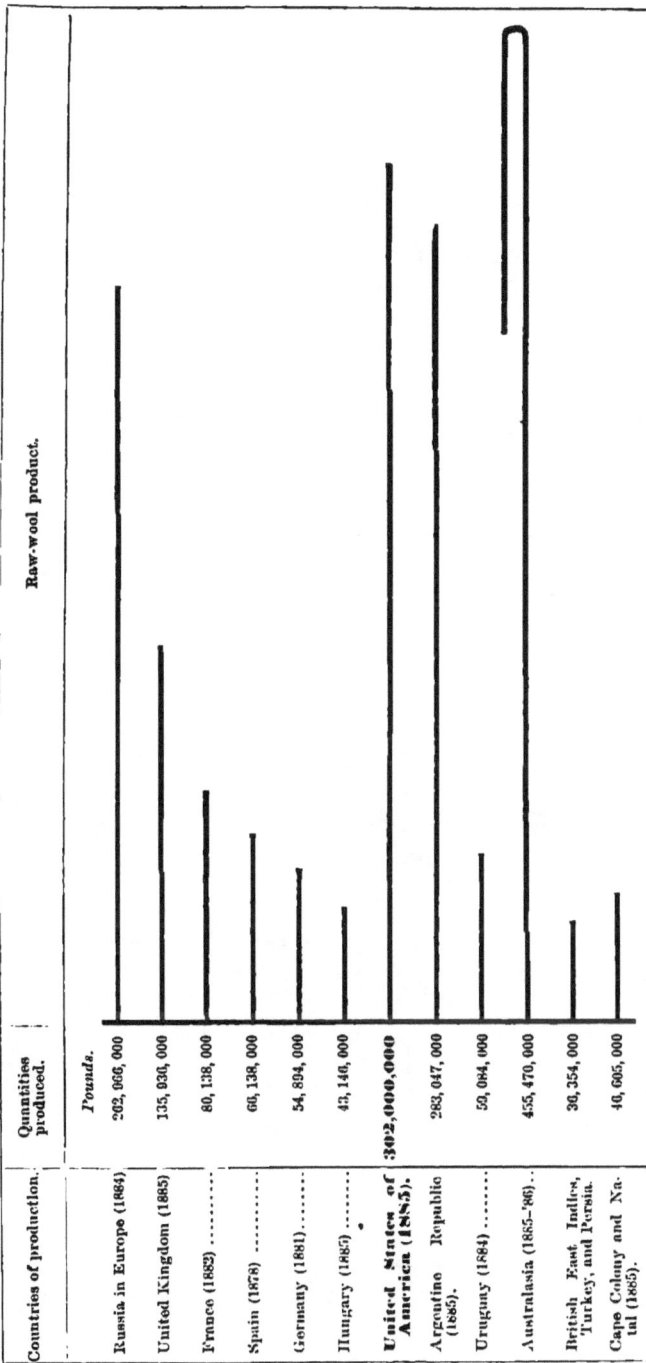

Countries of production.	Quantities produced.	Raw-wool product.
	Pounds.	
Russia in Europe (1864)	202,066,000	
United Kingdom (1885)	135,936,000	
France (1882)	80,138,000	
Spain (1878)	66,138,000	
Germany (1881)	54,894,000	
Hungary (1885)	43,146,000	
United States of America (1885).	302,000,000	
Argentine Republic (1885).	283,047,000	
Uruguay (1884)	59,084,000	
Australasia (1885–'86)..	455,470,000	
British East Indies, Turkey, and Persia.	30,354,000	
Cape Colony and Natal (1885).	40,605,000	

No. 11.—DIAGRAM SHOWING THE VALUE OF IMPORTS OF RAW WOOL AND MANUFACTURES OF WOOL INTO THE PRINCIPAL FOREIGN COUNTRIES FOR A RECENT YEAR. (See Appendix, Table No. 63.)

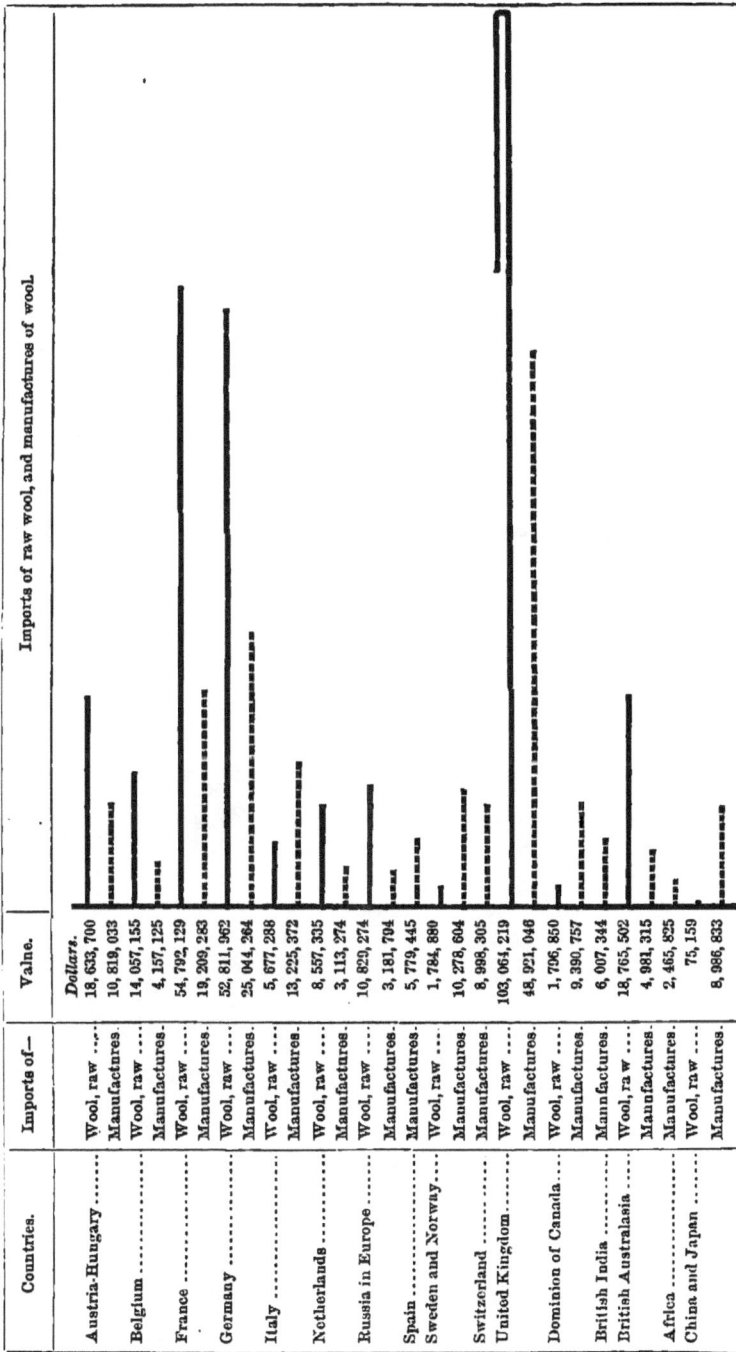

Countries.	Imports of—	Value.	Imports of raw wool, and manufactures of wool
		Dollars.	
Austria-Hungary	Wool, raw	18,633,700	
	Manufactures	10,819,033	
Belgium	Wool, raw	14,057,155	
	Manufactures	4,157,125	
France	Wool, raw	54,792,129	
	Manufactures	19,209,283	
Germany	Wool, raw	52,811,962	
	Manufactures	25,044,264	
Italy	Wool, raw	5,677,288	
	Manufactures	13,225,372	
Netherlands	Wool, raw	8,557,335	
	Manufactures	3,113,274	
Russia in Europe	Wool, raw	10,820,274	
	Manufactures	3,181,704	
Spain	Manufactures	5,779,445	
Sweden and Norway	Wool, raw	1,784,890	
	Manufactures	10,278,604	
Switzerland	Manufactures	8,998,305	
United Kingdom	Wool, raw	103,064,219	
	Manufactures	48,921,046	
Dominion of Canada	Wool, raw	1,796,850	
	Manufactures	9,390,757	
British India	Manufactures	6,007,344	
British Australasia	Wool, raw	18,765,502	
	Manufactures	4,981,315	
Africa	Manufactures	2,465,825	
China and Japan	Wool, raw	75,159	
	Manufactures	8,986,833	

No. 12.—Diagram showing the Value of Exports of Raw Wool and Manufactures of Wool from the Principal Foreign Countries for a recent year. (See Appendix, Table No. 63 *a.*)

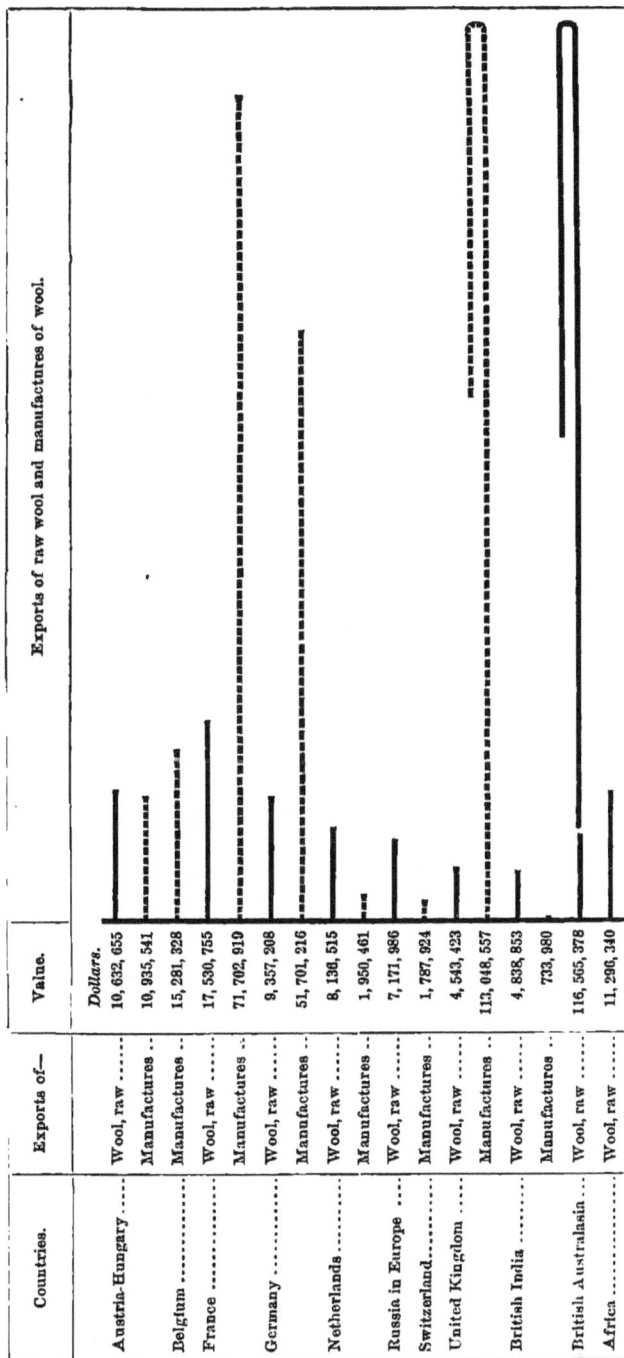

Countries.	Exports of—	Value.	Exports of raw wool and manufactures of wool.
		Dollars.	
Austria-Hungary	Wool, raw	10,632,655	
	Manufactures	10,935,541	
Belgium	Manufactures	15,281,328	
France	Wool, raw	17,530,755	
	Manufactures	71,702,919	
Germany	Wool, raw	9,357,208	
	Manufactures	51,701,216	
Netherlands	Wool, raw	8,136,515	
	Manufactures	1,950,461	
Russia in Europe	Wool, raw	7,171,986	
Switzerland	Manufactures	1,787,924	
United Kingdom	Wool, raw	4,543,423	
	Manufactures	113,048,557	
British India	Wool, raw	4,838,853	
	Manufactures	733,980	
British Australasia	Wool, raw	116,565,378	
Africa	Wool, raw	11,296,340	

APPENDIX

TO

REPORT ON WOOL AND MANUFACTURES OF WOOL.

No. 1.—Statement Showing, by Principal Foreign Countries and Geographical Divisions, the Quantity and Value of Raw Wool Imported into the United States, the Total Quantity and Value of Foreign Wool Exported, and the Net Imports of Wool During Each Year from 1822 to 1887, Inclusive.

Year ending—	From Europe.											
	Austria		Belgium		France		Germany		Great Britain		Italy	
	Pounds.	Dollars.	Pounds.	Dollars.	Pounds.	Dollars.	Pounds.	Dollars.	Pounds.	Dollars.	Pounds.	Dollars.
September 30—												
1822	15,375	1,845			56,937	9,583	137,375	32,635	59,493	13,683	350	91
1823	33,265	4,072			38,316	9,373	247,081	65,251	79,651	9,620	24,385	4,961
1824					3,773	2,040	108,405	55,708	72,655	27,271	21,638	1,461
1824a	c22,693	3,404			c10,050	5,427	c5,633	2,873	c209,058	79,442		
1825	c4,213	632			c45,630	23,565	c177,133	90,338	c427,950	102,621	c7,314	512
1826	c422	114			c19,883	10,737	c112,045	57,143	c174,013	66,125	c2,857	201
1827	c122	33			c50	67	c174,045	28,184	c423,519	131,291		
1828					c1,291		c680,536	79,066	c714,139	221,383	677	677
1829	13,376	3,570			14,308	7,823	c255,960	15,202	343,216	106,425		
1830	1,032	310			41,945	13,952	43,203	6,252	117,710	39,064		
1831					2	5	17,357	302,761	2,062,335	667,412	1,406	345
1832					516	319	779,708	68,772	332,515	80,856	34,502	2,019
1833			3,703	2,934	167,936	15,057	241,754	106,570	173,210	54,969	8	5
1834	1,124	346	17,441	5,956	436,424	33,779	217,135	41,731	79,173	47,630		
1835	130,253	12,778			51,015	6,705	94,850	204,022	2,154,888	516,033	124,914	9,197
1836	598,945	117,344			280,816	19,256	461,554	15,359	1,384,098	218,902	681,279	51,717
1837	183,745	13,931			200,210	24,993	24,988	2,151	334,969	25,299	527,270	40,704
1838	482,696	84,235	46,024	14,229	122,308	8,443	4,198	6,025	491,513	65,187	64,938	4,370
1839	75,456	5,405			216,507	16,515	29,908	21,325	342,479	74,920	297,873	20,331
1840	31,430	2,260			33,826	1,186	48,242	30,626	132,137	19,365	400,353	25,847
1841	44,564	3,390					146,635	40,253	505,781	96,534	104,414	13,301
1842	742	52					78,903	14,063	201,390	33,343		
June 30—												
1843a	1,422	345	11,882	5,025	1,321	758	17,060	9,002	51,920	18,593	98,100	6,532
1844	209,128	18,693	15,789	3,618	298,442	24,892	67,592	33,704	392,757	75,613	727,867	32,738
1845	111,081	8,151	8,564	1,023	638,759	48,107	88,297	44,987	995,328	87,579	61,156	4,720
1846			10,817	803	92,415	7,882	20,786	8,763	1,266,069	52,942		
1847	41,574	3,423	7,038	103	29,520	3,067	21,107	2,580	693,020	44,097	132,553	5,710
1848	43,303	5,511	13,423	6,650	257,669	24,730	4,410	1,846	1,324,823	180,367	34,106	3,464
1849	423,562	63,634	53,880	7,891	276,047	15,078	199,903	14,265	880,874	104,824	906,565	101,701
1850	44,236	7,241			1,018,921	103,348	14,992	6,429	1,952,123	274,923	280,468	19,390
1851	1,502	226	38,886	13,565	1,320,367	494,545	2,220	862	4,934,945	872,414	412,383	54,543
1852	826,273	56,167	6,380	1,595	1,240,163	118,715	8,510	633	804,982	117,202	517,126	78,558
1853	178,733	22,084	1,610	377	2,211,376	281,025	652	439	2,894,524	781,094	457,790	58,633
1854	33,285	4,999	44,764	6,790	1,642,044	101,531	54,889	15,914	1,397,756	281,973	351,600	37,026
1855					949,819	131,823	65,727	8,962	1,070,795	175,807		
1856					808,574	133,424	11,530	1,700	855,919	160,067		

Year										
1857	2,700	560			962	100,218	7,290	518,125	716	105,234	100,355	30,477
1858	c200,175	41,235			c1,031,559	175,365	c58,969	c4,335,910	7,066	807,182	c313,214	50,119
1859	c33,200	6,610			c2,453,983	417,178	c15,431	c5,827,245	2,006	1,105,440	c327,245	22,744
1860	c189,12o	28,368	c3,333	500	c1,703,193	345,479	c15,577	c3,052,544	2,648	1,003,458	c144,943	20,292
1861			c371,340	55,701	c229,880	34,482	c2,012	c2,718,822	155	489,388	c342,630	47,069
1862	112,610	16,083	c3,023,439	157,893	5,438,429	813,373	207,799	15,175,241	c35,450	2,741,170	429,793	50,433
1863			2,088,889	493,312	3,075,095	1,634,228	350,401	17,019,244	85,090	3,384,938	328,284	61,038
1864 d			1,511,347	343,941	1,011,877	1,774,628	391,138	13,099,825	106,833	2,710,041	1,261,078	65,400
1865 d	32,940	7,527	91,754	39,020	848,687	142,671	104,645	1,980,176	943	336,510	63,107	13,892
1866 d							c4,240	c6,175	13,411	2,408		
1867 d			1,923,495	324,204	535,010	87,417	325,714	8,642,100	1,650	1,559,740		
1868 d					c1,914	825	c6,135	c56,016	41,561	24,087		
1869			60,705	10,558	1,237,453	105,194	30,175	6,738,842	2,638	1,305,881		
1870	2,030	347			c4,500	810	c4,022	c44,150	3,385	947		38
1871					917,902	111,840	110	2,582,062	832	475,852	183	
1872					c4,511	812	c6,273	c111,994	1,129	20,159		
1873	12,494	1,284	435,088	40,649	1,134,056	110,235	18,992	8,593,299	2,887	2,153,118	40,171	4,401
1874	17,427	1,085	20,450	1,796	204,893	25,110		8,140,697		1,545,560	130,503	10,479
1875 b	101,045	9,334	320,984	42,045	706,071	77,968	30,989	15,593,106	5,767	3,244,755	36,012	5,952
1876	1,332,338	234,897	939,470	225,937	2,131,207	409,305	218,952	40,250,449	51,094	11,220,025	84,276	12,608
1877								366,343				
1878	109,165	15,379	495,955	118,570	265,098	62,747	146,137	19,040,920	40,245	6,459,138	535,482	110,388
1879			58,717	12,090	2,515,230	115,029	39,737	7,960,362	10,090	1,830,251	46,091	5,837
1880	1,017,850	120,597	664,510	165,187	2,972,589	326,430	91,127	11,882,212	21,774	1,753,649	75	14
1881	410,733	56,748	139,190	32,361	469,160	427,310	258,042	10,034,294	47,220	3,420,991	47	9
1882	240.8 5	48,530	93,198	17,343	913,602	52,786	90,100	14,270,595	20,833	2,833,198	59	5
1883	43,375	5,040	244,099	48,840	2,500,694	105,399	60,727	16,387,554	51,858	3,750,702		
1884	460,424	74,927	29,494	3,963	2,715,011	280,612	44,746	16,870,650	8,058	16,367,783	94,337	10,063
1885	302,412	73,180	4,408,568	942,210	3,311,775	420,717	691,498	58,009,641	94,060	12,447,235	83,759	12,392
1886	733,833	84,378	90,551	23,689	4,411,078	552,028	191,641	21,786,226	38,773	4,490,559	69,548	12,700
1887	44,432	64,188	340,963	00,013	5,798,993	706,857	17,827	20,642,887	11,169	3,835,142	33,029	15,239

a Nine months ended June 30.   b Three months ended September 30.   c Quantity estimated.   d Value of wool pelts and estimated quantity of wool thereon.

No. 1.—IMPORTS OF RAW WOOL, BY COUNTRIES, &C., FROM 1822 TO 1887, INCLUSIVE—Continued.

Year ending	Portugal Pounds	Portugal Dollars	Russia Pounds	Russia Dollars	Spain Pounds	Spain Dollars	Turkey Pounds	Turkey Dollars	All other countries in Europe Pounds	All other countries in Europe Dollars	Total Europe Pounds	Total Europe Dollars
September 30—												
1822	364,596	109,210	8,045	880	228,274	106,112	209,420	a0,653	280,842	59,002	1,369,707	353,374
1823	56,235	18,656	10,495	2,100	183,416	89,788	690,666	a67,966	174,635	35,407	1,536,145	307,254
1824 a	57,316	14,456	33,740	9,116	14,058	6,890	57,027	a4,364	193,110	38,250	562,328	159,562
1824 a	d183,172	43,799	d3,430	926	d21,071	10,325	d62,543	a4,378	d160,185	32,037	d674,405	183,679
1825	d234,524	58,631	d837	236	d201,584	95,770	d369,200	a25,704	d404,475	80,895	d1,873,462	542,690
1826	d491,853	100,463			d136,041	66,065	d1,199,729	a81,984	d219,815	43,963	d2,267,494	429,618
1827	d70,677	12,015	d121,800	9,728	d55,228	15,464	d1,224,890	a122,489	d71,033	10,655	d2,047,845	329,886
1828	d104,077	17,840	d38,650	3,092	d288,798	80,803	d504,840	a50,452	d35,753	5,363	d2,006,907	468,459
1829	43,461	7,705			112,149	31,408	647,941	a64,519	1,325	200	1,006,671	229,069
1830	71,455	8,591			68,684	13,032	223,773	a30,339	2,108	792	562,119	80,893
1831	254,914	55,536	35,918	2,981	227,295	73,183	942,536	a111,981	24,572	4,581	4,342,993	1,229,135
1832	158,615	37,919	131,351	11,977	335,393	109,743	2,000,983	a280,002	253,040	41,614	3,528,098	660,834
1833	67,844	19,996	38,992	3,027	67,112	16,804	266,319	a22,228	7,455	2,348	836,080	220,862
1834			19,265	10,374	121,360	64,917			17,653	2,994	333,967	158,313
1835			25,001	1,024	41,581	13,137	948,067	a70,524	158,372	13,480	4,191,808	857,171
1836			43,422	3,092	575,750	84,093	2,528,302	a183,510	1,243,577	90,543	7,515,808	801,135
1837			11,665	896	184,418	32,460	2,198,666	a220,152	1,533,556	119,327	5,041,268	463,875
1838					14,670	1,190	1,616,717	a129,819	111,670	7,720	3,110,563	290,108
1839							3,034,415	a297,112	41,260	3,030	4,123,841	399,130
1840	28,852	7,770	5,957	1,628	56,891	18,786	2,546,989	a377,306	309,089	22,850	6,280,275	505,520
1841		28					2,307,674	a180,010	72,460	4,138	3,730,693	3?2,708
1842	44,878	15,275	10,043	1,197	20,074	5,465		a155,744	6,916	138	2,684,799	206,613
June 30—												
1843 a							761,728	a46,415	4,682	276	831,959	75,668
1844			600,818	52,051	169,516	26,248	3,213,329	a163,884	680,735	46,682	4,008,200	309,291
1845			969,170	61,781	29,730	1,425	6,766,397	a466,895	207,176	12,432	11,182,634	828,498
1846			223,065	14,849			5,766,688	a406,676	8,761	600	8,545,355	565,795
1847					32,414	3,008	3,333,113	a240,491	22,359	1,913	4,338,429	313,090
1848							2,349,500	a160,598	25,784	4,320	4,172,456	382,690
1849					74,950	10,332	2,229,128	a140,828	129,177	14,000	6,330,301	2?8,899
1850			331,330	32,891	775,159	93,690	3,134,402	a229,684	478,516	60,582	10,977,534	650,751
1851	2,887	472	178,904	20,260	365,108	46,257	3,250,092	a442,192	1,074,990	145,967	7,353,001	2,210,402
1852	85,754	13,383	179,800	18,230	194,668	28,386	3,355,320	a289,656	678,725	55,477	12,001,438	765,793
1853	22,637	4,101	214,958	28,245	185,082	42,007	4,352,189	a372,211	415,381	73,193	9,090,692	1,617,570
1854	6,575	678	200,880	26,308	12,500	5,660	4,368,164	a402,630	491,154	45,620	3,961,659	1,217,912
1855					3,760	800	428,667	30,309	800,019	21,976	2,522,082	508,176
1856			291,054	43,626	5,460	1,040	332,455	5,135	d303,311	71,290	2,487,012	407,206
1857			d738,683	110,804	d75,058	14,261	91,032	105,959		54,596	d8,828,002	424,802
1858							d1,765,983					1,427,187

Year													
1859	d113,027	12,499	d12,540	1,881	d48,079	9,135	d573,425	45,874	d196,973	30,455	d9,419,991	1,719,361
1860	d27,557	3,858	d 269,955	48,592	d484,339	105,181	d216,439	20,959	d215,056	38,870	d6,690,063	1,273,406
1861	d59,264	8,298			d288,047	43,207	d 4,207	547	d179,462	23,330	d3,823,230	647,376
1862	129,275	e18,106	291,989	36,859	425,803	f 63,525	3,075,349	a394,378	24,730	3,255	26,334,457	4,340,434
1863	167,903	27,492	1,758,867	275,651	981,468	f 152,730	4,213,473	a618,776	686,860	78,034	38,776,044	6,802,789
1864	230,914	38,407	4,643,305	801,291	179,722	28,734	5,534,693	a805,115	260,728	39,854	38,124,627	6,720,146
1864 g									171	62	d3,768	1,005
1865	2,009	131	2,748,479	421,558	234,985	38,506	135,007	10,758	308,299	39,641	6,550,094	1,063,625
1865 g											d10,421	4,064
1866			1,607,699	275,809			3,981	253	133,101	21,835	13,071,706	2,310,825
1866 g											d64,065	27,550
1867			1,520,749	259,738			17,070	1,920	140	11	9,630,199	1,786,687
1867 g											d53,272	9,080
1868			4,294,064	806,194			168,602	10,746			7,964,973	1,413,585
1868 g											d122,778	22,100
1869			2,681,257	338,224			3,687,153	a441,721	160	h15	16,609,270	2,503,484
1870			4,533,656	543,627			3,069,755	a351,023	113	h17	16,116,500	2,485,409
1871			4,524,462	519,069			1,868,653	a203,820			23,183,382	4,108,710
1872	6,568	681	2,165,087	381,492			2,127,551	a311,928	181,454	22,480	49,437,351	12,871,107
1872 g					d40,517	9,319	d65	15			d1,633,334	375,667
1873			5,254,193	1,317,471	12,658	2,406	642,455	49,868	981,602	154,797	27,484,665	7,331,009
1874			3,118,930	545,088			12,295	1,141	881,505	91,819	12,838,351	2,641,167
1875			3,814,950	642,237			3,229	131	72,746	7,998	20,001,941	4,039,026
1876	49,347	4,609	1,972,624	320,822			6,023	519	11,241	937	22,754,603	4,317,869
1877			1,503,703	199,253			343	11	602,374	68,927	17,336,274	3,240,894
1878	3,168	810							289,489	29,974	20,149,674	3,992,680
1879			1,786,693	233,177					935	63	21,239,412	2,686,236
1880	3,601	395	3,322,700	375,053	1,680	227	1,350	524	7,212	564	79,716,031	15,896,911
1881			4,400,151	631,316	83,248	15,712	29,370	2,594	483,656	61,013	33,822,789	5,778,045
1882			10,983,587	1,465,765			211,308	25,417	29,546	3,260	37,390,577	6,008,412
1883	693	76	12,569,723	1,647,478			981,032	130,155	8,833	1,032	45,529,921	7,213,701
1884	1,323	307	12,588,840	1,422,020			332,055	31,152	266,150	45,002	50,604,318	8,026,027
1885			16,151,392	1,614,962			119,108	13,147			41,300,942	5,586,581
1886			17,663,056	1,746,657	71,659	8,175	514,889	69,406	72,635	8,908	77,075,786	10,888,475
1887	962	206	18,058,059	2,380,163			1,373,466	251,395	176,692	20,277	70,093,893	12,129,440

a Includes Levant, Egypt, Mocha, and Aden. b Nine months ending June 30. c Three months ending September 30. d Quantity estimated. e Includes Portuguese Possessions. f Includes the Canary Islands. g Value of wool pelts and estimated quantity of wool thereon. h Includes Dutch Guiana and British Honduras.

No. 1.—IMPORTS OF RAW WOOL, BY COUNTRIES, &C., FROM 1822 TO 1887, INCLUSIVE—Continued.

Year ending—	From North America						From West Indies		From South America			
	British North American Possessions		Mexico		From Central American States and British Honduras				Argentine Republic		Brazil	
	Pounds.	Dollars.	Pounds.	Dollars.	Pounds.	Dollars.	Pounds.	Dollars.	Pounds.	Dollars.	Pounds.	Dollars.
September 30—												
1822	5,300	1,430	(a)	(a)			2,100	147			9,287	064
1823	3,825	780	(a)	(a)			365	87			2,820	300
1824e	d15	3	d140	7								
1825	d8,605	1,721	d23,240	1,162			d18,844	1,690	d122,625	4,905	d10,518	1,157
1826	d8,905	1,781	d123,280	6,164			d1,555	140	d238,875	8,755	d136	15
1827	d13,175	1,581	d105,320	5,266			d180	17				
1828	d17,125	2,035	d62,040	3,102					63,250	120	30	5
1829	8,615	1,057	49,257	1,889			64	7	229,421	7,804		147
1830	17,692	2,790	1,013	30			683	96	114,397	2,079	4,705	7,063
1831	28,713	5,187	50,968	2,491			2,049	119	1,046,382	41,778	137,729	4,822
1832	32,697	5,413	42,288	2,671			478	74	348,894	18,594	85,547	2,378
1833	39,550	5,048					391	72	16,506	1,140	44,414	
1834	33,887	4,998	1,440	191	2,538	2,300	532	44	71,845	7,084		3,769
1835	42,791	5,417	364,328	20,996			57,968	4,355	1,425,824	78,194	54,490	14,824
1836	45,425	6,038	340,044	31,840			21,052	1,463	2,261,104	163,247	227,843	18,098
1837	40,082	6,426	445,432	32,054			296	45	2,113,512	134,684	232,150	3,090
1838	41,460	4,533	165,636	10,028					2,541,516	160,528	41,070	4,710
1839	94,320	7,997	384,634	27,261	600	450	31,389	1,873	601,339	4,517	63,020	20,609
1840	21,243	2,519	239,397	24,901			7,857	530	560,468	38,920	309,247	8,681
1841	25,878	2,498	287,164	21,834			157,071	12,467	8,878,665	531,783	121,021	15,530
1842	28,220	4,318	141,699	6,857			3,068	260	7,655,485	486,270	210,750	
June 30—												
1843e	20,597	1,912	43,542	2,465			6,754	414	2,327,904	128,381	129,151	8,048
1844	70,357	6,605	235,700	13,910			8,090	528	8,440,352	467,020	874,156	49,055
1845	140,827	15,772	272,840	10,885			14,875	725	11,775,488	798,794	191,819	12,644
1846	207,035	14,105	425,148	20,984			10,000	1,163	4,330,490	333,583	45,215	3,683
1847	177,848	14,652	551,909	31,396			18,292	1,041	792,062	48,458	137,945	11,300
1848	207,827	29,419	57,250	161			30,798	2,102	4,307,428	267,419	331,169	21,673
1849	290,400	31,557	3,100				35,817	2,329	12,003,094	769,106	133,591	9,390
1850	490,104	59,924			7,867	1,220	40,486	2,050	10,170,966	877,900	374,200	28,890
1851	621,020	92,018	270	21			44,042	3,305	12,100,530	1,328,337	400,844	40,834
1852	463,868	72,292	26,606	5,365			70,033	7,482	7,084,742	701,064	155,061	14,165
1853	410,639	53,630	40,630	14,898			88,393	7,466	5,745,837	586,633	64,654	5,184
1854	312,339	69,065	55,000	12,069			35,266	3,131	6,235,698	834,252	124,814	12,118
1855	280,622	65,958	86,432	6,305	34,723	4,481	39,671	2,837	5,900,969	637,718	60,345	4,735
1856	d104,448	24,023										
1856e	1,625,631	376,790	141,198	7,220			73,470	6,538	5,672,939	698,403	138,724	13,992
	d554,368	138,592										

(Table of wool imports, years 1857–1887, rotated on page)

Year													
1857	1,244,970	308,208	32,470	3,054	6,908	899	58,043	5,903	5,758,519	094,730	127,412	14,455
1857 e	d713,300	178,325	d45,968	4,137	6,048	504	d55,110	5,511	d7,210,675	866,001	d211,455	23,260
1858	d994,000	248,725	d109,600	9,864			160,160	16,916	d10,826,625	1,299,195	d228,227	25,105
1858 e	d407,635	81,527	d75,825	15,105			d22,165	4,433	d6,133,703	1,226,741	d247,465	49,493
1859 e	d2,007,436	524,359										
1859 e	d476,050	95,210										
1860 e	d1,137,290	241,177	d14,918	1,641			d58,418	6,426	d12,108,673	1,814,301	d727,750	101,885
1860 e	d758,849	151,768										
1861 e	d1,115,313	323,441										
1861 e	d563,400	112,680	31,209	3,560			130,450	f14,687	5,829,531	817,220	618,481	88,574
1862 e	d623,215	680,098										
1863 e	2,035,480	124,643	1,220,820	155,450			81,019	12,482	17,461,206	2,577,705	1,072,141	158,932
1863 e	d1,189,784	791,181										
1864 e	3,215,578	100,892	702,676	66,111	114	21	6,630	1,421	23,951,506	3,018,441	1,636,194	259,366
1864 e	d377,273	1,381,430	d1,080	392	d66	24	d2,094	760	d35,108	12,766	d1,537	658
1865 e	3,474,401	130,950	339,450	44,022			74,033	11,845	16,101,889	2,223,753	877,420	120,024
1865 e	d290,510	1,527,926	d3,764	1,468	d23	9	d2,795	1,090	d101,205	39,470		
1866	13,712	104,204	163,297	18,462			81,570	12,938	36,915,704	4,557,466	1,455,592	173,761
1866 e	d2,805,199	2,125										
1866 e	d355,507	1,206,234	d430	185	d116	50	d800	344	d93,139	40,050	d1,319	567
1867	593,834	152,868	0,300	352	27,334	3,469	54,009	12,087	12,666,274	1,049,107	1,880,804	301,431
1867 e	247,555	201,085	d139	25			21,617	651	d987,623	167,890	d4,271	728
1868	805,538	44,559	69,493	4,386			21,606	2,334	5,835,862	876,586	1,441,808	190,459
1868 e	d271,050	806,538					45,140	514		138,745		140
1869 e	d215,360	69,827	716,008	51,818			01,726	h10,392	8,249,659	1,020,736	2,055,259	264,007
1869 e	2,695,106	715,360	650,459	49,820			41,500	93,928	16,721,429	1,833,105	3,237,097	416,517
1870	2,488,094	819,764	865,909	68,007	203,836	29,880	21,680	93,967	23,333,237	2,605,956	2,538,313	357,607
1871	3,000,021	887,102	1,182,481	128,375			24,010	92,133	24,731,834	3,608,147	2,644,023	442,840
1872	4,734,299	1,722,068	404	93			d65	15	d1,636,787	390,261	d5,909	1,359
1872 e	d122,644	90,636	1,182,414	129,475			28,679	42,530	17,449,563	3,407,187	1,768,481	333,255
1873	4,369,728	1,940,204	1,173,099	112,228			10,049	A1,606	A8,602,627	1,276,451	1,430,141	211,935
1874	3,001,892	1,077,864	1,095,282	119,534			54,808	A0,905	8,999,693	1,241,916	1,142,750	154,717
1875	3,018,547	1,097,592	838,708	85,887			26,177	A2,376	7,376,249	1,030,278	937,158	128,960
1876	3,174,006	1,083,711	1,405,983	110,708			48,730	A4,081	8,166,025	1,056,262	960,520	114,209
1877	2,343,079	682,580	835,487	72,210			15,070	A1,443	6,489,121	1,191,429	708,998	97,127
1878	2,502,207	760,296	819,784	66,300			13,738		6,929,614	791,883	260,025	32,194
1879	2,546,270	570,003	1,009,870	90,470			33,798	2,735	12,278,776	1,025,378	839,424	113,645
1880	4,075,665	1,051,389	1,821,874	144,875			38,600	3,760	6,163,223	1,015,645	668,103	103,598
1881	502,407	602,407	191,666	18,037	2,020	205	41,122	3,638	9,821,234	1,431,772	493,505	65,336
1882	1,276,889	295,840	1,775	257			24,782	2,054	8,691,873	1,132,893	1,269,159	141,390
1883	1,347,627	282,503	438,401	37,648			33,685	2,728	5,316,983	623,371	526,910	55,409
1884	1,547,190	317,107	1,602,763	122,504			27,239	1,790	10,222,817	999,291	1,154,197	102,677
1885	1,011,111	202,534	2,884,054	186,277			16,783	1,061	12,109,844	1,183,727	1,565,132	151,074
1886	1,627,048	337,188	1,802,758	150,410			19,004	1,371	12,286,982	695,075	1,006,002	56,415
1887	1,010,123	357,142										

a Included under "all other South America." b Nine months ending June 30. c Three months ending September 30. d Quantity estimated. e Value of wool pelts and estimated quantity of wool thereon. f Includes British Possessions in Central and South America. g Includes Dutch Guiana. h Includes Dutch Guiana and British Honduras.

No. 1.—IMPORTS OF RAW WOOL, BY COUNTRIES, &C., FROM 1682 TO 1857, INCLUSIVE.—Continued.

Year ending—	From South America											From Asia	
	Chili		Uruguay		Venezuela		All other countries in South America		Total South America				
	Pounds.	Dollars.	Pounds.	Dollars.	Pounds.	Dollars.	Pounds.	Dollars.	Pounds.	Dollars.		Pounds.	Dollars.
September 30—													
1822							334,696	32,827	343,883	33,791			
1823							a118,123	a31,069	d118,123	31,309		10,595	810
1824c							a59,461	a11,003	d59,461	11,003			
1825	d966	145					d90,194	16,235	d223,337	22,297			
1826	d134,200	20,133					d217,261	3,107	d237,238	12,022			
1827							d1,027,360	51,888	d1,161,560	71,521			
1828							d363,980	18,199	d367,230	18,329			
1829									229,451	7,609			
1830									148,235	4,082			
1831	32	5					29,252	1,256	1,190,178	52,952			
1832	708	80					15,035	1,107	435,180	23,501		1,274	50
1833									72,091	5,008			
1834	12,429	1,870					11,171	1,481	95,474	17,898		123,616	134,153
1835	476,771	37,014					9,200	8,044	957,085	118,077		152,216	24,288
1836	129,257	12,651	5,983	460					2,618,204	190,726		66,396	12,735
1837	204,138	16,745	60,760	3,372			26,614	1,787	2,602,437	191,774		81,084	12,208
1838	65,475	5,352	764,588	65,035			219,464	15,139	2,930,275	187,481			
1839	133,505	9,940	645,893	49,372	2,421	170			1,660,893	118,262		68,744	5,432
1840	332,465	24,512	169,429	12,106			132,398	8,208	2,026,471	141,621		82,055	9,704
1841	456,846	31,124			684	50	87,430	5,491	10,212,525	612,242			
1842	322,220	29,920			704	23			8,387,687	543,849		22,210	1,828
June 30—													
1843b	84,227	7,058	11,184	640	227	10	3,250	180	2,555,725	144,307		29,416	2,025
1844	206,748	19,847			385	20			9,581,483	536,632		68,046	3,742
1845	220,365	29,003					90,730	4,071	12,278,767	816,136			
1846	1,819,772	130,837	306,803	11,631	1,158	47	122,686	8,568	6,327,163	476,001		248,126	53,047
1847	1,032,572	122,797	1,273,469	75,201			450	268	3,170,910	194,501		231,169	4,496
1848	767,034	62,822	43,066	4,563			86,229	13,019	6,708,239	439,634		46,153	3,512
1849	870,006	46,381			145,075	12,681	144,643	23,336	13,801,303	852,070		11,763	926
1850	1,031,260	47,049	306	20	8,569	614	43,100	5,410	11,770,607	973,339		191,911	2,804
1851	2,100,846	125,650			12,389	605	247	21	14,626,348	1,495,385		141,075	26,378
1852	1,864,509	160,820			7,180	330	655,372	84,442	14,772,073	973,190		3,349	28,212
1853	2,684,300	235,196	71,759	8,560	440,982	81,145	66,777	10,500	8,620,557	860,032			423
1854	1,857,447	161,066	847,825	42,385	15,348	913	628,071	103,057	9,654,837	1,254,003			15,699
1855	2,846,002	317,564	53,737	6,337			348,756	60,829	9,282,057	1,018,116		4,514,781	417,697
1856	2,523,632	299,145	137,554	19,333			130,026	19,949	8,603,075	860,822		3,143,428	336,720
1857	3,644,394	304,610	101,007	10,102	d1,860	118	81,417	7,112	9,014,609	1,091,133		3,503,600	416,077
1858	d3,290,736	361,981	d209,280	20,920	d1,200	84	d60,138	8,508	d10,995,464	1,280,850		d6,025,375	723,043

Year											
1859	d4,352,727	478,800	d234,460	34,134	d1,912	153	d301,554	30,202	d15,095,495	1,876,589	d2,321,700	278,604
1860	d1,763,050	352,610	d290,715	50,343			d246,710	40,342	d8,687,645	1,737,529	d2,627,609	525,536
1861	d4,756,400	523,204	d243,040	21,364	d5,718	620	d216,018	23,762	d18,058,199	2,490,145	d1,832,160	425,963
1862	2,943,501	319,816	14,061	207,421	e22,194		9,012,095	1,279,190	816,384	f119,177
1863	3,452,520	371,075	470,815	8,967	e1,359		22,481,651	3,164,528	137,984	f19,040
1864g	1,969,235	248,062	3,400,800	41,796	e5,256		31,134,035	4,729,014	927,017	181,875
1865g	d54,091	19,635		d99	36		d90,895	32,905		
1865g	3,362,473	376,193					21,579,203	2,919,720	1,234,411	216,782
1866g			1,161,260	197,001			d90,107,787	42,037		
1866g	2,277,746	233,351	0,582	2,507			42,882,421	5,280,483	3,389,407	374,954
1867			2,224,629	321,046			d94,497	40,806		
1867g	3,610,197	357,592				8,060	859	19,504,081	2,845,186	1,041,004	202,579
1868			1,434,504	236,777		d439	180	d1,000,012	170,002	d15,306	2,755
1868g	3,086,352	343,167	d5,618	955		2,212	279	10,831,010	498,465	2,276,473	256,436
1869			466,712	88,243	203	23	d2,500	425	d874,898	139,547		
1870	4,520,881	495,557	932,369	117,160		d3,894	662	16,579,207	1,985,371	29,983	3,278
1871	2,101,878	201,635	4,594,238	161,114		821,530	87,911	24,206,908	2,686,764	195,041	18,981
1872	2,986,030	267,297	7,110,871	637,308	25,947	3,215	699,400	64,413	33,887,624	3,807,980	43,667	3,996
1872g	3,849,473	397,829	d359,619	83,712	7,416	524	409,759	36,606	38,409,516	5,608,152	315,617	47,533
1873			6,110,911	1,137,560		65,890	13,053	d2,062,450	474,363		
1874	3,150,831	407,946	4,094,275	606,136	17,636	1,569	d135	31	28,624,753	5,312,875	2,670,769	458,100
1875	2,310,511	290,168	863,440	129,876	13,021	1,115	107,331	25,418	10,352,041	2,440,039	894,154	107,548
1876	3,616,299	433,501	750,219	105,888	7,212	658	1,463	209	14,034,199	1,961,320	103,148	12,939
1877	3,217,536	301,310	2,185,884	298,765	9,577	956	4,805		12,293,095	1,635,098	636,447	78,721
1878	2,600,613	294,586	5,273,092	758,212	22,069	1,902	4,356	1,562	14,536,554	1,843,300	4+0,659	68,479
1879	2,858,771	314,712	1,113,231	17,661	17,661	1,411	612,407	306	18,439,638	2,363,405	249,672	20,667
1880	3,773,604	305,645	9,577,300	108,673	10,656	881	4,015	73,636	12,047,042	1,329,281	713,298	112,508
1881	3,329,156	245,098	4,823,502	1,733,001	202,056	21,006	12	514	26,227,360	3,738,175	1,501,909	181,633
1882	3,352,721	175,522	6,894,985	882,600	17,330	1,822	539	5	13,500,996	3,184,811	954,500	117,616
1883	2,334,219	253,538	5,920,713	1,321,800	8,068	466	5,998	47	13,941,507	2,956,033	1,184,460	149,178
1884	1,090,260	110,879	2,599,301	868,403	8,160	511	189,596	575	10,989,247	2,234,095	2,346,364	276,041
1885	1,241,003	114,849	3,611,445	8,917	8,917	629	82	13,711	9,698,445	1,120,077	6,065,020	640,419
1886	1,740,605	170,542	2,955,287	14,386	14,386	677	5,325	8	16,675,122	1,686,881	6,626,963	646,124
1887	1,946,105	130,441	12,955,287	135,124	135,124	16,560	31,072	679	26,882,140	2,834,304	6,031,127	729,982
	2,528,676	217,688	2,891,481	15,070	15,070	729	1,635	321	12,329,906	1,400,447	13,765,850	1,234,874

a Includes Mexico. b Nine months ending June 30. c Three months ending September 30. d Quantity estimated. e Includes New Granada. f Includes New Granada. h Includes Australasia.

g Value of wool pelts and estimated quantity of wool thereon.

No. 1.—IMPORTS OF RAW WOOL, BY COUNTRIES, &C., FROM 1822 TO 1887, INCLUSIVE—Continued.

Year ending—	From Australasia		From Africa		From all other countries		Total imports		Foreign exports		Net imports	
	Pounds.	Dollars.	Pounds.	Dollars.	Pounds.	Dollars.	Pounds.	Dollars.	Pounds.	Dollars.	Pounds.	Dollars.
September 30—												
1822							1,715,690	387,312			1,715,690	387,312
1823							1,673,348	340,056			1,673,348	340,956
1824a							625,614	171,345			625,614	171,345
1824b							c674,560	183,689	c8,774	1,667	665,785	182,069
1825			3,657	256			c2,147,488	569,476	c91,721	17,407	2,055,767	552,069
1826							c2,638,472	449,725	c15,563	2,957	2,622,909	440,768
1827							c3,331,746	409,537	c150,979	28,680	3,180,767	379,641
1828			445	38	426	28	c2,453,302	401,045	c16,284	3,094	2,437,018	448,831
1829			660	30	1,252	104	1,494,439	239,882	198,672	35,234	1,295,767	204,648
1830							668,883	96,853	6,242	4,681	663,641	92,172
1831							5,622,900	1,288,900	3,607	1,389	5,619,353	1,287,540
1832							4,042,838	698,721	1,227,939	197,219	2,814,879	601,502
1833							950,205	240,892	676,574	146,935	273,631	93,957
1834							591,313	317,925	1,602,535	291,729		
1835			555,613	43,501	25,962	11,883	7,290,397	1,088,277	94,091	16,161	7,190,306	1,072,116
1836			1,853,136	141,307	184,640	78,970	12,687,021	1,270,126	391,372	66,189	12,296,243	1,203,937
1837	78,193	31,823	2,078,151	155,250			10,407,690	893,873	148,012	87,329	10,259,667	806,544
1838	76,946	23,158	641,167	46,718			6,966,363	532,971	162,659	23,668	6,785,704	509,283
1839	130,261	43,018	1,430,491	98,115	8,091	560	7,925,173	609,538	118,919	37,232	7,806,254	602,306
1840	300,468	100,356	841,983	60,357	8,310	22	9,498,740	846,076	85,528	28,246	9,813,212	819,830
1841	95,401	22,248	496,288	38,334	65,656	12,005	15,006,410	1,091,953	143,426	44,416	14,862,984	1,047,507
1842	58,350	15,750	28,333	2,896			11,420,952	797,382	571,179	80,614	10,849,773	716,768
June 30—												
1843a	124,010	35,881	437	85	11,942	819	3,612,440	262,757	114,903	d34,631	3,497,447	228,106
1844	2,420	122	5,106	294	331	21	14,077,936	672,143	71,222	24,171	14,077,936	672,143
1845			150,478	11,364			23,896,294	1,708,237	125,286	41,571	23,825,072	1,664,006
1846			57,512	3,230	20,485	1,300	16,630,165	1,134,549	239,350	37,302	16,504,279	1,112,978
1847			050	104			8,488,557	562,176	20,740	1,840	8,219,207	553,874
1848			1,123	313	2,440	176	11,400,223	864,515	46,752	6,491	11,379,483	862,673
1849			138,282	17,835			17,809,289	1,177,432	20,122		17,822,497	1,170,561
1850			489,021	77,080			18,695,294	1,090,380	350,572	10,861	18,095,294	1,690,389
1851	3,400	665	369,991	117,056	4,365	608	32,607,315	847,474	212,110	54,980	32,578,193	3,436,613
1852			985,966	261,154	6,500	877	18,343,218	1,931,516	193,143	52,845	18,992,646	1,876,556
1853			699,057	117,499			21,610,035	2,078,606	728,904	41,608	21,403,925	2,025,761
1854							20,228,635	2,884,226	105,938	131,442	20,033,492	2,792,578
1855							18,814,492	2,140,964	3,220	18,737	18,085,408	2,069,522
1856a							c104,448	23,023			104,448	24,023
1856b	51,204	18,030	206,049	39,408	14,810	1,879	16,280,047	2,032,642		1,203	16,175,009	2,037,845
1857a							c554,368	138,592			534,368	138,592
1857b	1,634	450	702,064	183,426	8,730	1,061	17,750,150	2,435,682			17,746,927	2,434,370
1858							c713,300	178,325			713,300	2,178,325
			c2,490,104	572,724	c87,700	10,524	c29,529,560	4,273,207	c4,374,726	531,198	25,134,843	3,442,069

No. 2.—STATEMENT SHOWING, BY PRINCIPAL AND ALL OTHER CUSTOMS DISTRICTS AND BY GEOGRAPHICAL DIVISIONS, THE QUANTITY AND VALUE OF RAW WOOL IMPORTED INTO THE UNITED STATES DURING EACH YEAR FROM 1856 TO 1887, INCLUSIVE.

Year ending June 30—	Atlantic ports.											
	Baltimore, Md.		Boston and Charlestown, Mass.		New York, N.Y.		Philadelphia, Pa.		All other Atlantic ports.		Total.	
	Pounds.	Dollars.	Pounds.	Dollars.	Pounds.	Dollars.	Pounds.	Dollars.	Pounds.	Dollars.	Pounds.	Dollars.
1856	358,062	50,830	8,607,268	895,380	5,516,800	710,358	830	55	131,152	11,980	14,614,118	1,668,023
1856a	305,216	45,808	9,351,024	1,144,943	6,503,428	893,590	61,309	9,236	265,099	31,481	16,486,076	2,125,067
1857	b965,829	135,218	b19,013,407	2,661,677	b8,314,543	1,178,036	b217,864	30,501	b11,323	8,214	b28,532,960	4,013,846
1857a	b675,031	114,240	b14,957,673	2,243,651	b14,458,676	2,096,488	b260,513	37,736	b34,879	4,683	b30,505,802	4,496,968
1858	b275,085	55,139	b10,634,091	2,233,150	b12,166,841	2,407,490	b194,542	63,963	b101,835	36,458	b23,763,624	4,828,210
1858a	b661,194	165,791	b18,086,233	2,669,450	b10,366,231	1,658,597	b139,838	22,374	b162,241	25,939	b30,015,740	4,682,201
1859			64,670	934	b143,129	50,095			b76,515	15,122	b61,185	16,056
1859a	509,857	63,826	13,407,116	2,089,847	24,530,302	3,763,650	102,314	18,534	2,932,752	593,195	41,508,341	6,528,652
1860			b686	124	b675,821	29,570	b3,174	2,408	b161,280	23,083	b162,142	23,207
1860a	584,029	57,961	20,591,794	3,342,621	40,932,898	8,232,891	632,894	112,127	142,574	39,891	71,027,180	11,785,301
1861	163,946	24,220	23,554,872	3,821,120	60,938,379	10,260,225	1,660,023	292,187	948,509	224,065	b406,077	43,471
1861a	678,192	26,667	b204,094	71,433	b143,129	50,095	b625,357	109,056	b121,063	40,710	87,272,629	14,021,846
1862	680,092	79,825	11,695,328	1,772,016	27,380,225	4,246,539	b3,174	2,408	33,698	13,109	b544,478	188,914
1862a			b194,911	76,015	b675,821	29,570	b9,174	8,414	b76,762	31,505	40,420,900	6,220,545
1863	243,394	30,201	22,873,030	3,118,882	44,242,058	6,156,737	47,937	16	363,905	64,847	b355,668	139,498
1863a			b132,502	19,300	b143,129	50,095			b10,351	4,451	67,890,301	9,378,721
1864			b44,884	58,301	b64,121	28,213			b80,998	35,639	b655,272	23,767
1864a			b132,145	2,030,717	b20,414,432	3,453,000			b345,698	101,650	b277,621	23,153
1865	918,934	98,382	13,677,145	2,030,717	20,414,432	3,453,000	387,932	52,080	660,641	10,300	33,744,141	5,741,811
1865a			b1,281,028	230,585	b391,694	67,008			196,430	57,774	61,736,363	307,902
1866	5,872	357	9,108,664	1,266,011	13,293,400	2,083,452	237,396	38,238	b100,659	17,112	22,829,762	3,445,852
1866a			b320,628	58,793	b696,964	118,480			074,180	274,007	b1,124,251	194,394
1867	272,307	20,062	14,354,005	1,999,069	21,105,709	2,807,744	470,923	75,325	224,199	26,131	37,177,814	5,185,818
1867a	242,736	25,763	16,5e2,175	2,303,687	28,805,700	3,497,284	207,790	33,669	275,160	47,810	40,152,620	5,496,534
1868	1,109	198	25,016,468	3,721,115	37,823,991	5,011,049	513,350	70,308	545,365	135,368	64,270,027	8,850,396
1868a	30,017	4,877	52,545,362	10,651,232	59,869,356	12,786,160	668,366	143,130	b133	32	13,658,466	23,720,776
1869	52,635	583	63,490,204	800,447	b637,725	160,254			889,692	244,410	b1,120,597	961,310
1870	25,684	3,803	30,974,345	8,539,873	39,828,678	8,874,743	1,164,578	310,215	153,652	41,622	78,882,077	17,973,191
1871	12,798	1,624	10,234,553	2,922,903	21,691,025	3,965,458	317,011	65,906	219,540	61,312	38,429,934	6,907,803
1872	28,619	3,906	24,384,420	2,988,370	24,902,918	4,570,011	1,250,613	201,321	147,567	39,511	50,748,016	9,885,219
1872a	13,681	2,257	14,040,812	2,522,941	24,421,680	4,240,334	1,302,290	277,222	147,567	39,511	40,502,048	7,081,245
1873	30,442	4,945	10,640,763	3,508,670	17,174,545	2,518,511	1,421,200	272,258	64,681	13,320	38,286,631	6,317,704

Year													
1878	8,606	816	22,148,747	4,006,403	21,918,155	3,338,398	757,099	147,136	37,136	8,461	44,860,803	7,501,214
1879			16,778,786	2,102,300	17,660,397	2,150,824	1,077,860	118,545	32,098	7,612	35,548,741	4,386,181
1880	83,693	15,612	67,474,670	12,611,450	57,916,683	9,318,806	6,997,063	1,160,036	127,339	32,401	22,600,017	22,538,858
1881	40,874	5,915	18,811,058	3,586,299	30,319,866	4,842,153	3,169,702	435,455	106,987	29,410	52,457,577	8,902,232
1882			27,111,894	4,488,187	35,128,624	4,482,841	2,443,003	398,286	214,108	34,242	64,895,778	10,403,536
1883	110,480	10,399	31,429,249	4,976,028	22,031,876	4,714,456	4,076,228	508,670	14,451	3,460	67,652,284	10,279,013
1884			31,435,318	5,688,712	77,160,111	5,101,870	5,515,282	819,827	11,056	2,525	74,111,767	11,515,934
1885			27,890,301	3,885,009	34,330,390	3,939,803	5,527,837	650,850	67,013	16,257	67,816,471	8,532,009
1886			48,398,810	7,407,511	59,980,836	6,617,451	14,059,851	1,709,893	1,990,878	400,676	125,060,414	16,225,471
1887	7,522	7,522	40,924,821	6,535,803	55,752,888	7,325,121	13,517,801	1,778,456	1,289,473	274,738	110,568,942	15,941,639

a Value of wool pelts and estimated quantity of wool thereon.　　*b* Quantity estimated.

No. 2.—Imports of Raw Wool by Customs Districts, &c., from 1856 to 1857, inclusive—Continued.

Year ending June 30—	Gulf ports.								Pacific ports.		Lake and Northern border ports.		Total imports.	
	Brazos de Santiago, Tex.		Corpus Christi, Tex.		All other Gulf ports.		Total.							
	Pounds.	Dollars.	Pounds.	Dollars.	Pounds.	Dollars.	Pounds.	Dollars.	Pounds.	Dollars.	Pounds.	Dollars.	Pounds.	Dollars.
1856	140,908	7,204			200	16	141,198	7,220			1,525,631	a376,799	16,280,917	2,052,642
1856c											b554,368	138,592	554,368	c138,592
1857											1,244,970	a209,268	17,730,156	2,435,382
1857c					13,750	690	13,750	696			b713,300	178,325	713,300	c170,325
1858					b19,150	4,213	b19,150	4,213	5,360	551	926,753	248,701	29,529,569	4,273,297
1858c											b407,635	81,527	407,635	c81,527
1859					b2,473	544	b2,473	644	b30,700	6,417	2,126,367	a524,224	32,725,383	5,021,003
1859c	660,809	13,830							b721	137	b176,030	93,291	476,050	c65,210
1860					b10,831	2,275	b77,641	16,103	b4,653	1,070	1,678,786	a340,873	25,524,106	5,184,250
1860c											b758,819	151,768	758,819	c151,768
1861					b4,463	848	b4,463	818	b24,832	5,217	b1,449,042	a218,787	31,494,057	5,007,653
1861c											b382,215	96,624	563,400	c112,680
1862									13,893	1,750	1,883,642	563,849	43,407,876	7,094,451
1862c											b461,073	101,436	625,215	c124,643
1863									71,748	10,617	1,931,047	759,525	73,931,944	12,555,583
1863c											b782,807	117,421	1,189,781	c160,892
1864					12,376	4,321	12,376	4,321	82,951	15,920	b4,464,002	1,335,519	90,464,002	15,977,400
1864c					b1,530	392	b1,530	392	12,947	1,639	3,096,016	96,131	786,112	c285,437
1865					41,537	6,660	41,537	6,660			b310,328	1,505,502	43,877,408	7,734,346
1865c					b1,528	581	b1,528	581	22,701	2,692	3,402,024	72,718	542,907	c212,797
1866					1,230	101	1,230	101			b185,771	1,281	67,918,253	9,382,795
1866c											4,021	4	2,805,196	d1,206,234
1867					8,936	1,604	8,936	1,604	6,150	237	b2,749,924	b1,182,467	564,539	c248,408
1867c					b206	35	b206	35	b147	25	b286,918	1,126,255	36,240,201	6,905,708
1868	57,002	3,002			11,564	691	68,626	4,293	6,708	3,776	480,954	101,950	1,918,181	c341,010
1868c									63,679	699	b181,405	32,958	24,125,197	3,703,365
1869	321,288	21,772	295,349	23,571	75,020	4,596	691,657	49,930	19,587	2,291	1,220,101	339,444	1,312,139	c237,589
1870	290,393	22,814	310,754	21,320	49,588	4,370	652,735	49,516	31,303	3,035	b214,209	42,406	39,275,921	5,600,058
1871	210,475	16,135	590,002	48,694	45,723	3,518	862,099	68,347	59,078	8,500	1,386,868	363,000	49,280,199	6,743,350
1872	139,340	14,256	870,306	96,937	150,823	16,135	1,172,559	127,348	3,083,961	763,233	2,392,541	794,365	68,038,028	8,760,443
1872c			b383	88	b22		b405	93			2,866,624	853,290	122,256,490	26,214,195
1873	402,520	49,075	496,724	49,591	197,427	27,674	1,156,671	126,340	1,063,609	552,213	3,832,702	1,782,191	4,250,910	c991,878
1874	504,003	60,224	540,831	46,379	34,437	2,835	1,146,251	100,438	654,024	116,215	2,807,332	1,026,810	85,496,049	20,433,938
1875	525,357	57,965	448,516	46,032	5,272	448	970,145	104,465	402,823	59,707	2,733,776	1,021,968	42,939,611	8,250,300
1876	354,650	39,068	429,156	40,781	8,621	839	792,427	81,298	262,563	40,710	2,993,796	1,636,365	54,901,760	11,071,259
1877	454,474	40,035	870,700	72,017	20,392	2,373	1,300,632	115,945	258,208	55,150	2,265,631	608,139	42,171,192	7,156,944

1878	303,997	28,363	496,451	34,250	14,969	1,262	755,417	63,877	405,956	63,329	2,417,903	734,595	46,440,079
1879	278,054	24,388	521,300	40,489	15,597	1,109	615,620	65,980	129,654	12,768	2,510,240	567,610	39,005,155
1880	406,487	46,103	870,005	94,510	32,244	3,459	1,314,736	144,072	392,484	48,753	3,824,530	695,970	128,131,747
1881	301,077	30,138	588,401	55,673	117,007	13,504	1,007,985	99,315	963,257	231,290	1,535,417	471,131	65,964,236
1882	128,103	11,072	41,815	4,149	20,400	1,784	190,324	17,905	1,713,358	412,851	1,062,284	261,738	67,801,714
1883	1,402	146	270	100			1,732	252	1,622,624	395,133	1,298,838	274,033	70,575,478
1884	65,320	5,157	146,407	12,503	226,674	19,026	438,401	37,648	2,290,314	521,031	1,510,169	310,098	79,350,651
1885	205,449	17,048	890,810	71,239	500,495	33,297	1,602,763	122,504	92,630	16,674	1,024,297	308,836	79,596,170
1886	451,450	30,843	778,141	61,723	1,146,233	93,823	2,375,824	145,380	129,958	12,876	1,518,762	322,345	129,084,958
1887	346,818	29,200	845,125	60,714	610,044	47,008	1,804,883	145,922	255,713	21,987	1,408,403	314,931	111,038,030

a Includes total wool free of duty under reciprocity treaty, which cannot be distributed by districts.
b Quantity estimated.
c Value of wool pelts and estimated quantity of wool thereon.

No. 3—Statement showing the Quantities of Wool Produced, Imported, Exported, and Retained for Consumption in the United States, from 1839 to 1886, inclusive.

Calendar year.	Production.	Year ending June 30—	Imports.	Total production and imports.	Exports. Domestic.	Exports. Foreign.	Exports. Total.	Retained for home consumption.	Imports.
	Pounds.		Pounds.	Pounds.	Pounds.	Pounds.	Pounds.	Pounds.	Pr. ct.
1839...	35,802,114	1840 a	9,898,740	45,700,854	....	85,528	85,528	45,020,578	21.7
1849...	52,516,959	1850...	18,695,294	71,212,253	35,898	....	35,898	71,176,355	20.3
1859...	60,264,913	1860...	26,282,935	86,547,848	389,512	133,493	523,005	65,749,035	30.4
1862...	106,000,000	1863...	75,121,728	181,121,728	355,722	708,850	1,064,572	180,057,156	41.1
1863...	123,000,000	1864...	91,250,114	214,250,114	155,482	223,475	378,957	213,871,137	42.4
1864...	142,000,000	1865...	44,420,375	186,420,375	466,182	679,261	1,145,463	185,274,912	23.6
1865...	155,000,000	1866...	71,287,988	226,287,988	073,075	851,645	1,824,720	224,463,268	33.1
1866...	160,000,000	1867...	38,158,382	198,158,382	307,418	619,550	926,968	197,231,414	9.4
1867..	163,000,000	1868 ..	25,462,197	193,462,197	558,435	2,801,852	3,360,287	190,101,910	12.6
1868...	180,000,000	1869...	39,275,026	219,275,926	444,387	342,417	786,804	218,489,122	17.9
1869...	162,000,000	1870...	49,230,199	211,230,199	152,892	1,710,053	1,862,945	209,367,254	23.3
1870...	160,000,000	1871...	68,058,028	228,058,028	205,311	1,305,311	1,330,506	226,727,552	29.9
1871...	150,000,000	1872...	126,507,409	276,507,409	140,515	2,266,393	2,406,908	274,100,501	44.9
1872...	158,000,000	1873...	85,496,049	243,496,049	75,129	7,040,386	7,115,515	236,380,531	35.1
1873...	170,000,600	1874...	42,939,541	212,939,541	319,600	6,816,157	7,135,757	205,803,784	20.2
1874...	181,000,000	1875 ..	54,901,760	235,991,760	178,034	3,567,627	3,745,661	232,150,099	23.3
1875...	192,000,000	1876...	44,642,836	236,692,836	104,768	1,518,426	1,623,194	235,019,612	18.9
1876...	200,000,000	1877...	42,171,192	242,171,192	79,590	3,088,957	3,168,556	239,002,636	17.4
1877...	208,250,000	1878...	48,449,079	256,699,079	347,854	5,952,221	6,300,075	250,399,004	18.9
1878...	211,000,000	1879...	39,005,155	250,005,155	60,784	4,104,616	4,165,400	245,839,755	15.6
1879...	232,500,000	1880...	128,131,747	360,631,747	191,551	3,648,520	3,840,071	356,791,676	35.5
1880...	240,000,000	1881...	55,964,236	295,964,236	71,455	5,507,534	5,578,989	290,385,247	18.9
1881...	272,000,000	1882...	67,861,744	339,861,744	116,179	3,831,836	3,948,015	335,913,729	20.0
1882...	290,000,000	1883...	70,575,478	360,575,478	64,474	4,010,043	4,074,517	356,500,961	19.6
1883...	300,000,000	1884...	78,350,651	378,350,651	10,393	2,304,701	2,315,094	376,035,557	20.7
1884...	308,000,000	1885...	70,596,170	378,596,170	88,006	3,015,339	3,103,345	375,492,825	18.7
1885...	302,000,000	1886...	129,084,958	431,084,958	146,423	6,534,426	6,680,849	424,404,109	29.0
1886...	285,000,000	1887...	114,038,030	399,038,030	257,940	6,728,292	6,986,232	392,051,798	29.1

a Year ended September 30, 1840.

Note.—The data as to the production have been furnished by Mr. J. R. Dodge, statistician of the Department of Agriculture.

No. 4.—STATEMENT SHOWING THE QUANTITIES AND VALUES OF IMPORTED WOOLS, HAIR OF THE ALPACA, GOAT, AND OTHER LIKE ANIMALS ENTERED FOR CONSUMPTION IN THE UNITED STATES, INCLUDING BOTH ENTRIES FOR IMMEDIATE CONSUMPTION AND WITHDRAWALS FROM WAREHOUSE FOR CONSUMPTION; ALSO SHOWING THE RATES OF DUTY AND AMOUNTS OF ACCRUING DUTIES, DURING THE YEARS ENDING JUNE 30, FROM 1867 TO 1886, INCLUSIVE.

NOTE.—The kinds of wool embraced in each of the classes of wool are prescribed by the tariff as follows:

Class 1, clothing wools: That is to say, merino, mestiga, metz, or metis wools, or other wools of merino blood, immediate or remote, Down clothing wools, and wools of like character with any of the preceding, including such as have been heretofore usually imported into the United States from Buenos Ayres, New Zealand, Australia, Cape of Good Hope, Russia, Great Britain, Canada, and elsewhere, and also including all wools not hereinafter described or designated in classes 2 and 3.

Class 2, combing wools: That is to say, Leicester, Cotswold, Lincolnshire, Down combing wools, Canada long wools, or other like combing wools of English blood, and usually known by the terms herein used, and also hair of the alpaca, goat, and other like animals.

Class 3, carpet wools and other similar wools: Such as Donskoi, native South American, Cordova, Valparaiso, native Smyrna, and including all such wools of like character as have been heretofore usually imported into the United States from Turkey, Greece, Egypt, Syria, and elsewhere.

1867.

Wools, hair of the alpaca, goat, and other like animals.	Rates of duty.	Quantities.	Values.	Amount of duty received.
		Pounds.	*Dollars.*	*Dollars.*
Class No. 1.—Clothing wools:				
Value 32 cents or less p. lb.....	10c. p. lb. & 11 p. c.	567, 010	149, 663 74	73, 164 01
Value over 32 cents p. lb........	12c. p. lb. & 10 p. c.	703, 346	265, 945 67	110, 996 09
Total class 1	....	1, 270, 356	415, 609 41	184, 160 10
Class No. 2.—Combing wools:				
Value 32 cents or less p. lb......	10c. p. lb. & 10 p. c.	150, 302	31, 827 10	18, 212 91
Class No. 3.—Carpet and other similar wools:				
* Value 12 cents or less p. lb......	3c. p. lb	13, 986, 817	1, 440, 745 92	419, 604 51
Value over 12 cents p. lb........	6c. p. lb	22, 276, 072	3, 891, 290 43	1, 336, 564 32
Value 12 cents or less p. lb. (Sec. 2908, Rev. Stat.)	4c. p. lb	128	38 00	5 12
Total class 3	....	36, 263, 017	5, 332, 074 35	1, 756, 173 95
Total unmanufactured wools.................	....	37, 683, 675	5, 779, 510 86	1, 958, 546 96
Sheep-skins and Angora goat-skins, with the wool or hair on, washed or unwashed	20 p. c	....	324, 967 56	64, 993 51
Do................	30 p. c.............	....	16, 964 27	5, 089 28

5402 WOOL——2

No. 4.—Imported Wools, &c., entered for Consumption, &c., 1867 to 1886—
Continued.

1868.

Wools, hair of the alpaca, goat, and other like animals.	Rates of duty.	Quantities.	Values.	Amount of duty received.
		Pounds.	Dollars.	Dollars.
Class No. 1.—Clothing wools:				
Value 32 cents or less p. lb......	10c. p. lb. & 11 p. c.	4,461,512	833,083,68	537,790 40
Value over 32 cents p. lb........	12c. p. lb. & 10 p. c.	219,916	85,363 74	37,252 62
Scoured—				
Value (before scouring) over 32 cents p. lb.....................	36c. p. lb. & 30 p. c.	251	141 00	132 66
Total class 1............	....	4,681,679	918,588 42	575,175 68
Class No. 2.—Combing wools:				
Value 32 cents or less p. lb......	10c. p. lb. & 11 p. c.	1,801,358	331,961 81	216,651 60
Value over 32 cents p. lb........	12c. p. lb. & 22 p. c.	2,914	353 00	427 34
Total class 2............		1,804,272	332,314 81	217,078 94
Class No. 3.—Carpet and other similar wools:				
Value 12 cents or less p. lb.....	3c. p. lb	9,020,818	966.594 00	270,624 54
Value over 12 cents p. lb........	6c. p. lb	9,000,893	1,728,526 60	540,053 58
Value 12 cents or less p. lb. (Sec. 2908, Rev. Stat.)	4c. p. lb	74,889	9,647 00	2,905 56
Total class 3............		18,096,600	2,704,767 60	813,673 68
Total unmanufactured wools...............		24,582,551	3,955,670 83	1,605,928 30
Sheep-skins and Angora goat-skins, with the wool or hair on, washed or unwashed................	20 p. c............		777 00	155 40
Do...............	30 p. c............		129,982 45	38,904 74

1869.

Class No. 1.—Clothing wools:				
Value 32 cents or less p. lb.....	10c. p. lb & 11 p. c.	2,435,202.50	477,222 64	296,014 74
Value over 32 cents p. lb........	12c. p. lb. & 10 p. c.	76,999	28,492,00	12,089 08
Total class 1	....	2,512,201.50	505,714 64	308,103 82
Class No. 2.—Combing wools:				
Value 32 cents or less p. lb......	10c. p. lb. & 11 p. c.	3,956,048.50	893,157 83	493,852 21
Value over 32 cents p. lb........	12c. p. lb. & 10 p. c.	577,318	199,139 28	89,192 09
Total class 2............	....	4,533,366.50	1,092,297 11	583,044 30
Class No. 3.—Carpet and other similar wools:				
Value 12 cents or less p. lb.....	3c. p. lb	19,003,481	2,038,131 05	570,104 43
Value over 12 cents p. lb........	6c. p. lb	8,646,890	1,614,951 00	518,813 40
Total class 3	....	27,650,371	3,653,082 05	1,088,917 83
Total unmanufactured wools.............		34,695,939	5,251,093,80	1,980,005 05
Sheep-skins and Angora goat-skins, with the wool or hair on, washed or unwashed................	30 p. c............		561,986 43	168,580 98

No. 4.—IMPORTED WOOLS, &c., ENTERED FOR CONSUMPTION, &c., 1867 TO 1886—
Continued.

1870.

Wools, hair of the alpaca, goat, and other like animals.	Rates of duty.	Quantities.	Values.	Amount of duty received.
		Pounds.	*Dollars.*	*Dollars.*
Class No. 1.—Clothing wools;				
Value 32 cents or less p. lb......	10c. p. lb. & 11 p. c.	5, 835, 879	997, 692 08	693, 334 03
Value over 32 cents p. lb........	12c. p. lb. & 10 p. c.	694, 614	251, 460 00	108, 499 68
Total class 1............		6, 530, 493	1, 249, 152 08	801, 833 71
Class No. 2.—Combing wools:				
Value 32 cents or less p. lb......	10c. p. lb. & 11 p. c.	1, 973, 194	479, 265 55	250, 038 61
Value over 32 cents p. lb........	12c. p. lb. & 10 p. c.	779, 374. 50	285, 881 76	122, 113 12
Total class 2............		2, 752, 568. 50	765, 147 31	372, 151 73
Class No. 3.—Carpet and other similar wools :				
Value 12 cents or less p. lb......	3c. p. lb............	23, 902, 621. 50	2. 505, 413 00	717, 078 65
Value over 12 cents p. lb........	6c. p. lb............	5, 448, 384	910, 611 00	326, 903 04
Total class 3............		29, 351, 005. 50	3, 416, 024 00	1, 043, 981 69
Total unmanufactured wools................		38, 634, 067. 00	5, 430, 323 39	2, 217, 967 13
Sheep-skins and Angora goat-skins, with the wool or hair on, washed or unwashed	30 p. c............		1, 577, 110 14	473, 133 04

1871.

Class No. 1.—Clothing wools :				
Value 32 cents or less p. lb....	10c. p. lb. & 11 p. c.	5, 848, 203. 25	1, 162, 087 85	712, 650 00
Value over 32 cents p. lb......	12c. p. lb. & 10 p. c.	82, 494	30, 829 00	12, 982 18
Scoured—				
Value 32 cents or less p. lb. (before being scoured).	30c. p, lb. & 33 p. c.	3, 334	1, 216 00	1, 401 48
Washed—				
Value 32 cents or less p. lb. (before being washed).	20c. p. lb. & 22 p. c.	23, 430	7, 068 00	6, 240 96
Total class 1............		5, 937, 461. 25	1, 201, 200 85	733, 274 62
Class No. 2.—Combing wools:				
Value 32 cents or less p. lb......	10c. p. lb. & 11 p. c.	17, 431, 746. 50	3, 081, 672 82	2, 082, 158 66
Value over 32 cents p. lb........	12c. p. lb. & 10 p.c.	233, 853	86, 162 00	36, 678 56
Total class 2............		17, 665, 599. 50	3, 167, 834 82	2, 118, 837 22
Class No. 3.—Carpet and other similar wools :				
Value 12 cents or less p. lb......	3c. p. lb............	19, 658, 743	2, 072, 516 46	589, 762 29
Value over 12 cents p. lb........	6c. p. lb............	6, 892, 252	1, 263, 122 00	413, 535 12
Total class 3............		26, 550, 995	3, 335, 638 46	1, 003, 297 41
Total unmanufactured wools......		50, 174, 055. 75	7, 704, 074 13	3, 855, 409 25
Wool noils and pickings............	10 p. c............		3, 563 00	356 30
Sheep-skins and Angora goat-skins, with the wool or hair on, washed or unwashed................	30 p. c............		2, 197, 793 90	659, 338 17

No. 4.—IMPORTED WOOLS, &C., ENTERED FOR CONSUMPTION, &C., 1867 TO 1886—
Continued.

1872.

Wools, bair of the alpaca, goat, and other like animals.	Rates of duty.	Quantities.	Values.	Amount of duty received.
Class No. 1.—Clothing wools:		*Pounds.*	*Dollars.*	*Dollars.*
Value 32 cents or less p. lb......	10c. p. lb. & 11 p. c.	14,733,970	3,342,687 58	1,841,092 04
Value over 32 cents p. lb........	12c. p. lb. & 10 p. c.	1,983,186.50	703,011 31	317,283 51
Scoured—				
Value over 32 cents p. lb. (before being scoured).	36c. p. lb. & 30 p. c.	679	250 00	322 14
Washed—				
Value 32 cents or less p. lb. (before being washed).	20c. p. lb. & 22 p. c.	122,049	33,795 00	32,024 70
Value over 32 cents p. lb. (before being washed).	24c. p. lb. & 20 p. c.	30,547	14,207 00	10,172 68
Total class 1...............		16,871,331.50	4,163,959 89	2,200,895 67
Class No. 2.—Combing wools:				
Value 32 cents or less p. lb..	10c. p. lb. & 11 p. c.	35,873,654.50	6,648,434 96	4,318,693 30
Value over 32 cents p. lb....	12c. p. lb. & 10 p. c.	5,280,738.75	2,303,289 19	864,017 57
Scoured—				
Value 32 cents or less p. lb. (before being scoured).	30c. p. lb. & 33 p. c.	694	265 00	295 65
Value over 32 cents p. lb. (before being scoured).	36c. p. lb. & 30 p. c.	373	142 00	176 88
Total class 2...............		41,155,460.25	8,952,131 15	5,183,183 40
Class No. 3.—Carpet and other similar wools:				
Value 12 cents or less p. lb	3c. p. lb	17,887,464	1,934,673 30	536,623 92
Value over 12 cents p. lb.......	6c. p. lb	18,401,364	4,500,674 00	1,104,083 04
Scoured—				
Value over 12 cents p. lb. (before being scoured).	18c. p. lb	293	121 00	52 74
Total class 3...............		36,289,141	6,435,468 30	1,640,759 70
Total unmanufactured wools...............		94,315,932.75	19,571,559 34	9,024,838 77
Wool noils and pickings...............	10c. p. lb. & 10 p. c.	33	17 00	5 00
Sheep-skins and Angora goat-skins, with the wool or hair on, washed or unwashed...............	30 p. c		4,466 00	1,339 80

1873.

Class No. 1.—Clothing wools:				
Value 32 cents or less p. lb......	10c. p. lb. & 11 p. c.	272,718	67,759 27	34,725 32
Do...............	10c. p. lb. & 11 p. c. less 10 p. c.	4,738,486.50	1,183,443 61	543,624 80
Value over 32 cents p. lb......	12c. p. lb. & 10 p. c.	14,030	8,686 20	2,552 15
Do...............	12c. p. lb. & 10 p. c. less 10 p. c.	708,517.50	339,739 88	107,096 56
Scoured—				
Value over 32 cents p. lb. (before being scoured).	36c. p. lb. & 30 p. c. less 10 p. c.	3,332	1,901 00	1,593 65
Washed—				
Value 32 cents or less p. lb. (before being washed).	20c. p. lb. & 22 p. c. less 10 p. c.	258,336	124,767 00	71,204 37
Value over 32 cents p. lb. (before being washed).	24c. p. lb. & 20 p. c. less 10 p. c.	34,068	17,900 00	10,580 70
Total class 1...............		6,029,488.00	1,744,199 94	771,377 55
Class No. 2.—Combing wools:				
Value 32 cents or less p. lb.....	10c. p. lb. & 11 p. c.	1,566,377	350,961 00	195,243 41
Do...............	10c. p. lb. & 11 p. c. less 10 p. c.	42,278,227	9,597,768 00	4,755,219 56
Value over 32 cents p. lb.......	12c. p. lb. & 10 p. c.	135,306	67,824 00	23,019 12
Do...............	12c. p. lb. & 10 p. c. less 10 p. c.	5,558,537	2,705,681 00	843,833 35
Scoured—				
Value over 32 cents p. lb. (before being scoured).	30c. p. lb. & 30 p. c. less 10 p. c.	1,784	1,267 00	920 11
Total class 2.........		49,540,231	12,723,501 00	5,818,235 55

No. 4.—IMPORTED WOOLS, &C., ENTERED FOR CONSUMPTION, &C., 1867 TO 1886— Continued.

1873—Continued.

Wools, hair of the alpaca, goat, and other like animals.	Rates of duty.	Quantities.	Values.	Amount of duty received.
Class No. 3.—Carpet and other similar wools:		Pounds.	Dollars.	Dollars.
Value 12 cents or less p. lb......	3c. p. lb	447, 758	50, 482 78	13, 432 74
Do...................	3c.p lb. less 10 p. c.	10, 475, 613	1, 247, 781 70	282, 841 66
Value over 12 cents p. lb........	6c. p. lb.	569, 727. 50	120, 632 13	34, 183 65
Do...................	6c. p. lb. less 10 p.c.	17, 149, 764	4, 579, 568 00	926, 087 31
Total class 3.............	....	28, 642, 862. 50	5, 998, 464 61	1, 256, 545 36
Total unmanufactured wools.................	....	84, 212, 581. 50	20, 466, 165 55	7, 846, 158 46
Wool noils and pickings............	10 p. c. less 10 p. c.	....	192 00	17 28

1874.

Class No. 1.—Clothing wools:				
Value 32 cents or less p. lb......	10c. p. lb. & 11 p. c. less 10 p. c.	1, 264, 904. 50	362, 292 55	149, 708 42
Value over 32 cents p. lb........	12c. p. lb. & 10 p. c. less 10 p. c.	1, 087, 391	431, 752 00	156, 295 94
Scoured—				
Value 32 cents or less p. lb. (before being scoured).	30c. p. lb. & 33 p. c. less 10 p. c.	8, 116	1, 674 00	2, 688 50
Value over 32 cents p. lb. (before being scoured).	36c. p. lb & 30 p. c. less 10 p. c.	1, 908	880 00	855 79
Washed—				
Value 32 cents or less p. lb. (before being washed).	20c. p. lb. & 22 p. c. less 10 p. c.	31, 218	16, 062 00	8, 799 54
Value over 32 cents p. lb. (before being washed).	24c. p. lb. & 20 p. c. less 10 p. c.	4, 672	2, 646 00	1, 485 45
Total class 1.............	....	2, 398, 209. 50	815, 306 55	319, 833 64
Class No. 2.—Combing wools:				
Value 32 cents or less p. lb......	10c. p. lb. & 11 p. c. less 10 p. c.	25, 560, 382. 50	5, 595, 347 00	2, 854, 373 80
Value over 32 cents p. lb........	12c. p. lb. & 10 p. c. less 10 p. c.	1, 525, 055	596, 614 00	218, 401 26
Scoured—				
Value over 32 cents p. lb. (before being scoured).	36c. p. lb. & 30 p. c. less 10 p. c.	2, 000	1, 189 00	969 03
Total class 2.............	....	27, 087, 437. 50	6, 193, 150 00	3, 073, 744 09
Class No. 3.—Carpet and other similar wools:				
Value 12 cents or less p. lb	3c. p. lb. less 10 p. c.	14, 730, 863	1, 774, 327 01	397, 733 35
Value over 12 cents p. lb........	6c. p. lb. less 10 p. c.	12, 577, 227	2, 829, 083 00	679, 170 30
Total class 3	....	27, 308, 090 ●	4, 603, 410 01	1, 076, 903 65
Total unmanufactured wools.................	....	56, 793, 737	11, 611, 866 56	4, 470, 481 38
Wool noils and pickings............	10 p. c. less 10 p. c.	....	460 00	41 40

No. 4.—IMPORTED WOOLS, &c., ENTERED FOR CONSUMPTION, &c., 1867 TO 1886—
Continued.

1875.

Wools, hair of the alpaca, goat, and other like animals.	Rates of duty.	Quantities.	Values.	Amount of duty received.
		Pounds.	*Dollars.*	*Dollars.*
Class No. 1.—Clothing wools:				
Value 32 cents or less p. lb......	10c. p. lb. & 11 p. c.	1,470,850	378,570 53	189,607 76
Do..............................	10c. p. lb. &11 p. c. less 10 p. c.	9,975,654	2,564,249 51	1,151,669 52
Value over 32 cents p. lb........	12c. p. lb. & 10 p. c.	65,376	27,045 07	10,549 63
Do..............................	12c. p. lb. & 10 p. c. less 10 p. c.	1,582,453	625,248 00	227,177 30
Washed—				
Value 32 cents or less p. lb. (before being washed).	20c. p. lb. & 22 p. c.	648	315 00	198 50
Do..............................	20c. p. lb. & 22 p. c. less 10 p. c.	13,585	6,848 00	3,801 22
Value over 32 cents p. lb. (before being washed).	24c. p. lb. & 20 p. c. less 10 p. c.	315	259 00	114 66
Total class 1	....	13,117,679	3,602,535 11	1,583,118 59
Class No. 2.—Combing wools:				
Value 32 cents or less p. lb......	10c. p. lb. & 11 p. c.	172,262	55,531 00	23,334 61
Do..............................	10c. p. lb. & 11 p. c. less 10 p. c.	5,308,266	1,183,501 00	594,910 48
Value over 32 cents p. lb	12c. p. lb. & 10 p. c.	266,963	111,689 00	43,204 46
Do..............................	12c. p. lb. & 10 p. c. less 10 p. c.	2,021,666	802,450 00	290,560 44
Total class 2	....	7,769,157	2,153,261 00	952,018 90
Class No. 3.—Carpet and other similar wools:				
Value 12 cents or less p. lb......	3c. p. lb	4,606,453	569,179 00	138,193 59
Do..............................	3c. p. lb. less 10 p. c.	17,207,295	2,129,832 70	464,597 07
Value over 12 cents p. lb........	6c. p. lb	1,450,322	314,984 00	87,019 32
Do..............................	6c. p. lb. less 10 p. c.	7,535,388	1,458,830 00	406,910 98
Total class 3	....	30,799,458	4,472,825 70	1,096,720 96
Total unmanufactured wools............	....	51,686,294	10,228,621 81	3,631,858 54

1876.

Class No. 1.—Clothing wools:				
Value 32 cents or less p. lb......	10c. p. lb. & 11 p. c.	4,756,911.50	1,109,456 33	597,731 36
Do..............................	10c. p. lb. & 11 p. c. less 10 p. c.	3,093,767.50	784,738 00	356,128 15
Value over 32 cents p. lb........	12c. p. lb. & 10 p. c.	779,286.50	286,617 00	122,176 10
Do..............................	12c. p. lb. & 10 p. c. less 10 p. c.	3,816	1,843 00	560 00
Scoured—				
Value 32 cents or less p. lb. (before being scoured).	30c. p. lb. & 33 p. c.	2,332	1,598 00	1,226 94
Washed—				
Value 32 cents or less p. lb. (before being washed).	20c. p. lb. & 22 p. c.	7,248	3,659 00	2,254 58
Value over 32 cents p. lb. (before being washed).	24c. p. lb. & 20 p. c.	4	2 00	1 36
Total class 1	....	8,643,365.50	2,187,713 33	1,080,078 49
Class No. 2.—Combing wools:				
Value 32 cents or less p. lb......	10c. p. lb. & 11 p. c.	449,262	131,562 00	59,398 02
Do..............................	10c. p. lb. & 11 p. c. less 10 p. c.	86,656	21,947 00	8,351 79
Value over 32 cents p. lb........	12c. p. lb. & 10 p. c.	2,631,333	999,952 00	415,735 16
Scoured—				
Value over 32 cents p. lb. (before being scoured).	36c. p. lb. & 30 p. c.	56	43 00	30 99
Total class 2	....	3,167,307	1,153,504 00	483,535 96

No. 4.—IMPORTED WOOLS, &C., ENTERED FOR CONSUMPTION, &C., 1867 TO 1886—
Continued.

1876—Continued.

Wools, hair of the alpaca, goat, and other like animals.	Rates of duty.	Quantities.	Values.	Amount of duty received.
Class No. 3.—Carpet and other similar wools :		*Pounds.*	*Dollars.*	*Dollars.*
Value 12 cents or less p. lb......	3c. p. lb	14,431,527	1,747,976 45	432,945 81
Do......................	3c. p. lb. less 10 p. c.	675,291	80,651 00	18,232 87
Value over 12 cents p. lb........	6c. p. lb	11,903,130	2,501,185 00	714,187 80
Do......................	6c. p. lb. less 10 p. c.	1,806	144 00	97 52
Value 12 cents or less p. lb. (Sec. 2908, Rev. Stat.)	4c. p. lb	1,453,251	207,442 00	58,130 04
Total class 3	....	28,465,005	4,546,398 45	1,223,594 04
Total unmanufactured wools.............	....	40,275,677.50	7,887,615 78	2,787,208 49

1877.

Class No. 1.—Clothing wools :				
Value 32 cents or less p. lb......	10c. p. lb. & 11 p. c.	9,175,219.50	2,160,119 32	1,155,135 07
Do...........................	10c. p. lb. & 11 p. c. less 10 p. c.	58,442	15,220 00	6,766 56
Value over 32 cents p. lb........	12c. p. lb. & 10 p. c.	49,981.25	22,173 00	8,215 05
Scoured—				
Value over 32 cents p. lb. (before being scoured).	36c. p. lb. & 30 p. c.	130	67 00	66 90
Washed—				
Value 32 cents or less p. lb. (before being washed).	20c. p. lb. & 22 p. c.	9,777	4,806 00	3,012 72
Value over 32 cents p. lb. (before being washed).	24c. p. lb. & 20 p. c.	479.50	254 00	165 88
Total class 1............	....	9,294,029.25	2,202,639 32	1,173,362 18
Class No. 2.—Combing wools :				
Value 32 cents or less p. lb......	10c. p. lb. & 10 p. c.	1,083,513.50	385,310 00	168,552 62
Do...........................	10c. p. lb. & 11 p. c.	1,426,440.50	445,405 00	191,638 60
Total class 2.............	....	2,509,954	830,715 00	360,191 22
Class No. 3.—Carpet and other similar wools :				
Value 12 cents or less p. lb......	3c. p. lb	18,952,776	2,182,817 26	568,583 28
Value over 12 cents p. lb........	6c. p. lb	9,077,737	1,753,990 00	544,664 22
Value 12 cents or less p. lb. (Sec. 2908, Rev. Stat.)	4c. p. lb	279,898	42,810 00	11,195 92
Total class 3.............	....	28,310,411	3,979,617 26	1,124,443 42
Total unmanufactured wools.............	....	40,114,394.25	7,012,971 58	2,657,996 82

No. 4.—IMPORTED WOOLS, &c., ENTERED FOR CONSUMPTION, &c., 1867 TO 1886—
Continued.

1878.

Wools, hair of the alpaca, goat, and other like animals.	Rates of duty.	Quantities.	Values.	Amount of duty received.
		Pounds.	*Dollars.*	*Dollars.*
Class No. 1.—Clothing wools:				
Value 32 cents or less p. lb......	10c. p. lb. & 11 p. c.	9,338,199. 25	2,214,233 40	1,177,383 61
Do	10c. p. lb. & 11 p. c. less 10 p. c.	49,345	14,097 00	5,836 65
Value over 32 cents p. lb........	12c. p. lb. & 10 p. c.	483,842	182,810 00	76,342 04
Scoured—				
Value 32 cents or less p. lb. (before being scoured).	30c. p. lb. & 33 p. c.	4,037	1,863 00	1,825 89
Washed—				
Value 32 cents or less p. lb. (before being washed).	20c. p. lb. & 22 p. c.	40,488	17,000 00	12,048 80
Value over 32 cents p. lb. (before being washed).	24c. p. lb. & 20 p. c.	101	80 00	40 24
Total class 1............	....	9,916,012. 25	2,431,043 40	1,273,479 23
Class No. 2.—Combing wools:				
Value 32 cents or less p. lb......	10c. p. lb. & 10 p. c.	951,487	336,219 00	147,800 34
Do............................	10c. p. lb. & 11 p. c.	2,077,382	633,464 40	277,419 29
Total class 2..............	....	3,028,869	969,683 40	425,219 63
Class No. 3.—Carpet and other similar wools:				
Value 12 cents or less p. lb......	3c. p. lb	19,855,982	2,233,597 89	595,679 46
Value over 12 cents p. lb........	6c. p. lb............	7,000,298	1,361,042 00	420,017 88
Total class 3..............	....	26,856,280	3,594,639 89	1,015,697 34
Total unmanufactured wools................	....	39,801,161. 25	6,995,366 69	2,714,396 20

1879.

	Rates of duty.	Quantities.	Values.	Amount of duty received.
Class No. 1.—Clothing wools:				
Value 32 cents or less p. lb......	10c. p. lb. & 11 p. c.	5,173,616. 20	$1,091,135 01	637,386 48
Value over 32 cents p. lb........	12c. p. lb. & 10 p. c.	50,714	20,031 00	8,088 78
Scoured—				
Value 32 cents or less p. lb. (before being scoured).	30c. p. lb. & 33 p. c.	229	166 00	123 48
Washed—				
Value 32 cents or less p. lb. (before being washed).	20c. p. lb. & 22 p. c.	5,328	2,013 00	1,706 46
Value over 32 cents p. lb. (before being washed).	24c. p. lb. & 20 p. c.	100	56 00	35 20
Total class 1............	....	5,229,987. 20	1,114,301 01	647,340 40
Class No. 2.—Combing wools:				
Value 32 cents or less p. lb......	10c. p. lb. & 10 p. c.	89,438. 25	34,727 00	14,205 29
Do....	10c. p. lb. & 11 p. c.	1,618,587	378,207 71	203,461 56
Scoured—				
Value 32 cents or less p. lb. (before being scoured).	30c. p. lb. & 33 p. c.	1,576	826 00	745 38
Total class 2............	....	1,709,601. 25	413,760 71	218,412 23
Class No. 3.—Carpet and other similar wools:				
Value 12 cents or less p. lb......	3c. p. lb............	29,641,993	3,350,109 71	889,259 79
Value over 12 cents p. lb........	6c. p. lb............	3,521,061	638,642 00	211,263 66
Total class 3..............	....	33,163,054	3,988,751 71	1,100,523 45
Total unmanufactured wools................	....	40,102,642. 45	5,516,813 43	1,966,276 08

No. 4.—IMPORTED WOOLS, &C., ENTERED FOR CONSUMPTION, &C., 1867 TO 1836—
Continued.

1880.

Wools, hair of the alpaca, goat, and other like animals.	Rates of duty.	Quantities.	Values.	Amount of duty received.
		Pounds.	*Dollars.*	*Dollars.*
Class No. 1.—Clothing wools:				
Value 32 cents or less p. lb	10c. p. lb. & 11 p. c.	24,907,049.83	5,644,976 13	3,111,652 36
Value over 32 cents p. lb.........	12c. p. lb. & 10 p. c.	1,166,056.75	435,947 00	163,521 51
Scoured—				
Value 32 cents or less p. lb. (before being scoured).	30c. p. lb. & 33 p. c.	13,661	8,757 00	6,988 11
Washed—				
Value 32 cents or less p. lb. (before being washed).	20c. p. lb. & 23 p. c.	695,525	320,992 00	209,723 24
Value over 32 cents p. lb. (before being washed).	24c. p. lb. & 20 p. c.	2,879	1,601 00	1,011 16
Total class 1..............		26,785,171 58	6,412,273 13	3,512,896 38
Class No. 2.—Combing wools:*b*				
Value 32 cents or less p. lb......	10c. p. lb. & 10 p. c.	2,346,036.42	875,596 00	369,083 97
Do........................	10c. p. lb. & 11 p. c.	10,920,005·	2,925,417 00	1,413,796 38
Scoured—				
Value 32 cents or less p. lb. (before being scoured).	30c p. lb. & 33 p. c.	815	717 00	481 11
Total class 2.............		13,266,856.42	3,801,730 00	1,783,361 46
Class No. 3.—Carpet and other similar wools:				
Value 12 cents or less p. lb	3c. p. lb	49,301,443.50	5,524,952 05	1,479,043 31
Value over 12 cents p. lb.........	6c. p. lb	9,907,849.50	2,161,250 00	594,470 97
Value 12 cents or less p. lb. (Sec. 2908, Rev. Stat.).	4c. p. lb	111,119	13,461 00	4,444 76
Total class 3.............		59,320,412	7,699,663 05	2,077,959 04
Total unmanufactured wools.................		99,372,440,00	17,913,666 18	7,374,216 88

1881.

Class No. 1.—Clothing wools:				
Value 32 cents or less p. lb......	10c. p. lb. & 11 p. c.	19,944,040.30	4,792,839 79	2,488,616 40
Value over 32 cents p. lb........	12c. p. lb. & 10 p. c.	643,832	244,435 00	101,703 35
Scoured—				
Value 32 cents or less p. lb. (before being scoured).	30c. p. lb. & 33 p. c.	9,099	8,544 00	5,546 52
Washed—				
Value 32 cents or less p. lb. (before being washed).	20c. p. lb. & 23 p. c.	11,765	5,218 00	3,500 96
Value over 32 cents p. lb. (before being washed).	24c. p. lb. & 20 p. c.	980	417 00	318 00
Total class 1..............		20,609,707.30	4,751,453 79	2,599,685 83
Class No. 2—Combing wools:				
Value 32 cents or less p. lb......	10c. p. lb. & 10 p. c.	213,932	77,432 00	33,415 04
Do....................	10c. p. lb. & 11 p. c	4,207,558.50	1,193,900 39	552,084 89
Total class 2.............		4,421,490.50	1,271,332 39	585,499 93
Class No. 3.—Carpet and other similar wools:				
Value 12 cents or less p. lb......	3c. p. lb	28,917,217.33	3,384,423 97	867,516 52
Value over 12 cents p. lb........	6c. p. lb	13,468,552	2,653,616 73	808,113 12
Total class 3............		42,385,769.33	6,038,040 72	1,675,629 64
Total unmanufactured wools.................		97,416,967.13	12,060,826 90	4,860,815,40

No. 4.—IMPORTED WOOLS, &c., ENTERED FOR CONSUMPTION, &c., 1867 TO 1886—Continued.

1882.

Wools, hair of the alpaca, goat, and other like animals.	Rates of duty.	Quantities.	Values.	Amount of duty received.
Class No. 1.—Clothing wools:		*Pounds.*	*Dollars.*	*Dollars.*
Value 32 cents or less p. lb......	10c. p. lb. & 11 p. o.	13, 378, 362. 50	2, 990, 173. 30	1, 666, 755. 31
Value over 32 cents p. lb........	12c. p. lb. & 10 p. c.	73, 136	30, 079 00	11, 784. 22
Scoured—				
Value 32 cents or less p. lb. (before being scoured).	30c. p. lb. & 33 p. c.	9, 498	8, 700 00	5, 750 10
Washed—				
Value 32 cents or less p. lb. (before being washed).	20c. p. lb. & 22 p. c.	26, 748	12, 169 00	8, 026 78
Value over 32 cents p. lb. (before.being washed).	24c. p. lb. & 20 p. c.	2, 178	1, 106 00	761 92
Total class 1..........		13, 489, 922. 50	3, 042, 407 30	1, 693, 078 83
Class No. 2.—Combing wools:				
Value 32 cents or less p. lb......	10c. p. lb. & 10 p. c.	58, 821	21, 831 00	9, 241 62
Do................	10c. p. lb. & 11 p. o.	2, 259, 850	626, 421 14	294, 891 33
Total class 2..........		2, 318, 671	648, 252 14	304, 132 95
Class No. 3.—Carpet and other similar wools;				
Value 12 cents or less p. lb......	3c. p. lb	32, 501, 620	3, 825, 762 10	975, 048 60
Value over 12 cents p. lb........	6c. p. lb	14, 706, 555	2, 816, 937 00	882, 393 30
Total class 3..........		47, 208, 175	6, 642, 699 10	1, 857, 441 90
Total unmanufactured wools..........		63, 016, 769	10, 333, 358 54	3, 854, 653 18

1883.

Wools, hair of the alpaca, goat, and other like animals.	Rates of duty.	Quantities.	Values.	Amount of duty received.
Class No. 1.—Clothing wools:				
Value 32 cents or less p. lb......	10c. p. lb. & 11 p. c.	11, 466. 637. 50	2, 526, 477 00	1, 424, 576 19
Value over 32 cents p. lb	12c. p. lb. & 10 p. c.	57, 478	25, 960 40	9, 493 40
Scoured—				
Value 32 cents or less p. lb. (before being scoured).	30c. p. lb. & 33 p. c.	10, 916. 80	9, 515 00	6, 414 99
Value over 32 cents p. lb. (before being scoured).	36c. p. lb. & 30 p. c.	4, 792	2, 332 00	2, 424 72
Washed—				
Value 32 cents or less p. lb. (before being washed).	20c. p. lb. & 22 p. c.	6, 563	3, 029 00	1, 078 98
Value over 32 cents p. lb. (before being washed).	24c. p. lb. & 20 p. c.	143	130 00	60 32
Total class 1..........		11, 546, 530. 30	2, 567, 443 40	1, 444, 948 60
Class No. 2.—Combing wools:				
Value 32 cents or less p. lb......	10c. p. lb. & 10 p. c.	66, 362. 90	29, 506 00	10, 923 12
Do................	10c. p. lb. & 11 p. c.	1, 306, 751	314, 391 10	165, 258 12
Total class 2..........		1, 373, 113. 90	343, 897 10	176, 181 24
Class No. 3.—Carpet and other similar wools:				
Value 12 cents or less p. lb......	3c. p. lb	28, 477, 503	3, 436, 786 73	854, 327 79
Value over 12 cents p. lb........	6c. p. lb	11, 632, 509. 83	2, 143, 730 00	699, 150 59
Scoured—				
Value 12 cents or less p. lb. (before being scoured).	9c. p. lb	220	21 00	19 80
Total class 3..........		40, 130, 322. 83	5, 580, 537 73	1, 553, 498 18
Total unmanufactured wools		53, 049, 966. 50	8, 491, 988 23	3, 174, 628 02

No. 4.—IMPORTED WOOLS, &c:, ENTERED FOR CONSUMPTION, &c., 1867 TO 1886—
Continued.

1884.

Wools, hair of the alapaca. goat, and other like animals.	Rates of duty.	Quantities.	Values.	Amount of duty received.
Class No. 1.—Clothing wools:		Pounds.	Dollars.	Dollars.
Value 30 cents or less per pound	10c. p. 1b ...	19, 007, 978. 75	4, 419, 611 40	1, 990, 797 88
Value over 30 cents per pound	12c. p. 1b ...	569, 339. 72	178, 109 00	68, 320 79
Washed—				
Value (before washing) 30 cents or less per pound.	20c. p. 1b ...	139, 419	61. 078 00	27, 883 80
Value (before washing) over 30 cents per pound.	24c. p. 1b ...	43, 062	16, 467 00	10, 334 88
Scoured—				
Value (before scouring) 30 cents or less per pound.	30c. p. 1b ...	31, 895	17, 479 00	9, 568 50
Value (before scouring) over 30 cents per pound.	36c. p. 1b ..	12, 149	7, 861 00	4, 373 64
Total class 1		20, 703, 843. 47	4, 700, 605 40	2, 111, 279 49
Class No. 2.—Combing wools:				
Value 30 cents or less per pound	10c. p. 1b ...	4, 270, 310. 20	976, 732 15	427, 031 02
Value over 30 cents per pound	12c. p. 1b ...	204, 085. 50	82, 026 00	24, 490 26
Scoured—				
Value (before scouring) 30 cents or less per pound.	30c. p. 1b ...	....	....	....
Value (before scouring) over 30 cents per pound.	36c. p. 1b ...	....	....	....
Total class 2		4, 474, 395. 70	1, 058, 758 15	451, 521 28
Class No. 3.—Carpet wools and other similar wools:				
Value 12 cents or less per pound	2½c. p. 1b ...	46, 654, 102. 20	5, 153, 586 50	1, 166, 352 55
Value over 12 cents per pound	5c. p. 1b ...	15, 870, 660	2, 680, 214 00	793, 533 00
Scoured—				
Value (before scouring) 12 cents or less per pound.	7½ c· p. 1b ...	....	....	....
Value (before scouring) over 12 cents per pound.	15c. p. 1b ...	930	135 00	139 50
Total class 3		62, 525, 692. 20	7, 833, 935 50	1, 960, 025 05
Total unmanufactured wools		87, 703, 931. 37	13, 593, 299 05	4, 522, 825 92

1885.

Class No. 1.—Clothing wools:				
Value 30 cents or less per pound	10c. p. 1b ...	13, 379, 118	2, 950, 500 10	1, 387, 911 80
Value over 30 cents per pound	12c. p. 1b ...	36, 173	15, 449 00	4, 340 76
Washed—				
Value (before washing) 30 cents or less per pound.	20c. p. 1b ...	20, 852	10, 916 00	4, 170 40
Value (before washing) over 30 cents per pound.	24c. p. 1b ...	5, 405	2, 417 00	1, 297 20
Scoured—				
Value (before scouring) 30 cents or less per pound.	30c. p. 1b ...	28, 938	14, 596 00	8, 681 40
Value (before scouring) over 30 cents per pound.	36c. p. 1b ...	1, 946	655 00	700 56
Total class 1		13, 472, 432	2, 994, 533 10	1, 357, 102 12
Class No. 2.—Combing wools:				
Value 30 cents or less per pound	10c. p. 1b ...	3, 607, 512	796, 482 00	360, 751 20
Value over 30 cents per pound	12c. p. :b ...	284, 281	124, 567 00	34, 113 72
Scoured—				
Value (before scouring) 30 cents or less per pound.	30c. p. 1b ...	....	....	....
Value (before scouring) over 30 cents per pound.	36c. p. 1b ...	121	203 00	43 56
Total class 2		3, 891, 914	921, 252 00	394, 908 48

No. 4.—IMPORTED WOOLS, &C., ENTERED FOR CONSUMPTION, &C., 1867 TO 1886—
Continued.

1885—Continued.

Wools, hair of the alapaca, goat, and other like animals.	Rates of duty.	Quantities.	Values.	Amount of duty received.
Class No. 3.—Carpet wools and other similar wools :		*Pounds.*	*Dollars.*	*Dollars.*
Value 12 cents or less per pound.........	2½c. p. lb ...	45, 073, 356	4, 572, 971 77	1, 126, 833 90
Value over 12 cents per pound	5c. p. lb	5, 708, 792	985, 478 00	285, 439 60
Scoured—				
Value (before scouring) 12 cents or less per pound.	7½c. p. lb ...	158	29 00	11 86
Value (before scouring) over 12 cents per pound.	15c. p. lb ..	....	....	....
Total class 3	....	50, 782, 306	5, 558, 478 77	1. 412, 285 36
Total unmanufactured wools	....	68, 146, 052	9, 474, 263 87	3, 164, 295 96

1886.

Class	Rates of duty.	Quantities.	Values.	Amount of duty received.
Class No. 1.—Clothing wools :				
Value 30 cents or less per pound.........	10c. p. lb ..	22, 317, 623	4, 021, 398 60	2, 231, 762 30
Value over 30 cents per pound	12c. p. lb ...	84, 677. 50	41, 701 00	10, 161 30
Washed—				
Value (before washing) 30 cents or less per pound.	20c. p. lb ...	804, 520	244, 060 00	160, 904 00
Value (before washing) 30 cents per pound.	24c. p. lb ...	13, 669	4, 376 00	3, 280 56
Scoured—				
Value (before scouring) 30 cents or less per pound.	30c. p. lb ...	91, 937. 10	29, 820 00	27, 581 13
Value (before scouring) over 30 cents per pound.	36c. p. lb ...	9, 332	2, 813 00	3, 359 52
Total class 1......................	....	23, 321, 758. 60	4, 344, 183 60	2, 437, 048 81
Class No. 2.—Combing wools:				
Value 30 cents or less per pound.........	10c. p. lb ..	4, 695, 358	1, 036, 001 40	469, 535 80
Value over 30 cents per pound...........	12c. p. lb ...	176, 858	69, 914 00	21, 226 56
Scoured—				
Value (before scouring) 30 cents or less per pound.	30c. p. lb ...	493	201 00	147 90
Value (before scouring) over 30 cents per pound.	36c. p. lb ...	....	....	....
Total class 2	....	4, 872, 739	1, 106, 116 40	490, 910 26
Class No 3.—Carpet wools and other similar wools:				
Value 12 cents or less per pound.........	2½c. p. lb ...	71, 550, 877. 70	6. 944, 333 73	1, 788, 771 95
Value over 12 cents per pound...........	5c. p. lb	8, 121, 089	1, 393, 414 24	406, 054 45
Scoured—				
Value (before scouring) 12 cents or less per pound.	7½c. p. lb ...	43. 865	6, 087 00	3, 289 88
Value (before scouring) over 12 cents per pound.	15c. p. lb ...	220	73 00	33 00
Total class 3......................	....	79, 716, 051. 70	8, 343, 907 97	2, 198, 149 28
Total unmanufactured wools.....	....	107, 910, 549. 30	13, 794, 212 07	5, 126, 108 35

No. 5.—STATEMENT SHOWING, BY COUNTRIES OF PRODUCTION AND OF IMMEDIATE SHIPMENT TO THE UNITED STATES, THE QUANTITIES AND KINDS OF RAW WOOL IMPORTED INTO THE PORTS OF NEW YORK, BOSTON, AND PHILADELPHIA DURING EACH YEAR ENDING JUNE 30, FROM 1882 TO 1887, INCLUSIVE.

Note.—The imports of raw wool into the ports of New York, Boston, and Philadelphia comprise about 95 per cent. of the total imports of wool into the United States.

1882.

Countries of production.	Countries of immediate shipment.	Class 1, clothing wools.	Class 2, combing wools.	Class 3, carpet wools.	Total.
		Pounds.	*Pounds.*	*Pounds.*	*Pounds.*
Argentine Republic	Argentine Republic	936,106		8,888,128	} 9,834,392
	England	10,158			
Austria	Austria			351,728	} 634,543
	England			282,815	
Chili	Chili	4,383		2,529,836	} 2,566,264
	England			20,406	
	France	2,203		9,436	
China	China			141,240	} 283,840
	England			142,600	
Belgium	Belgium	166,552		11,617	} 193,393
	France			15,224	
Brazil	Brazil	62,354		431,151	} 512,317
	England			18,812	
Denmark	Denmark			19,786	19,786
Greenland	England			156,270	156,270
France	France	100,739		1,370,966	1,471,705
French Possessions in Africa.	French Possessions in Africa.			228	228
Germany	Germany	8,770		6,216	} 52,597
	England	2,841	4,719	30,051	
England	England	483,152	1,939,357	1,760,129	4,191,638
Scotland	Scotland	18,768	38,130	1,671,642	} 2,254,975
	England		48,044	478,391	
Ireland	England		295,239	46,334	341,573
Nova Scotia	Nova Scotia		406		406
British West Indies	British West Indies	513		2,697	} 3,466
	England			256	
British East Indies	England			3,645,174	} 3,669,981
	British West Indies			18,040	
	France			6,767	
British Possessions in Africa.	British Possessions in Africa.	1,064,660			} 3,864,088
	Germany	48,757			
	England	1,849,349			
	British West Indies	1,322			
British Possessions in Australasia.	British Possessions in Australasia.	1,515,132			} 4,611,989
	England	3,096,857			
British Possessions, all other.	England			85,097	85,097
Greece	England			4,674	} 31,689
	France			27,015	
Italy	Italy			67,017	} 71,212
	France			4,195	
Mexico	Mexico	29			29
Dutch West Indies	Dutch West Indies			35,504	} 37,692
	Italy			2,188	
Peru	Peru			183,896	} 189,219
	England		5,323		
Portugal	England			607,697	607,697
Azores	Azores			3,331	3,331
Russia on the Baltic and White Seas.	England			1,406,332	} 2,584,941
	France			50,661	
	Belgium			157,371	
	Denmark			970,577	
Russia on the Black Sea.	Russia on the Black Sea			141,429	
	Austria			103,724	
	Denmark			65,127	} 10,119,596
	Italy			2,331	
	England			9,195,412	
	France			611,373	
Turkey in Europe	Turkey in Europe			46,858	} 708,971
	Italy			140,475	
	England		7,639	513,999	
Turkey in Asia	England		9,456	4,003,519	} 6,052,246
	France			2,039,271	
Turkey in Africa	England			358,324	358,324

No. 5.—KINDS OF RAW WOOL, BY COUNTRIES OF PRODUCTION AND OF IMMEDIATE SHIPMENT, IMPORTED INTO NEW YORK, BOSTON, AND PHILADELPHIA, &C., 1882-1887—Continued.

1882—Continued.

Countries of production.	Countries of immediate shipment.	Class 1, clothing wools.	Class 2, combing wools.	Class 3, carpet wools.	Total.
		Pounds.	*Pounds*	*Pounds.*	*Pounds.*
United States of Colombia.	United States of Colombia.	....	....	5,700	5,700
Uruguay	Uruguay	5,158,685	....	1,249,583	} 6,914,212
	England	505,944	....	....	
Venezuela	Venezuela	....	....	8,068	8,068
Asia, all other	England	....	....	2,127,343	} 2,311,424
	France	....	....	164,081	
Africa, all other	Africa, all other	....	....	325	325
Total		15,937,274	2,348,313	46,467,646	64,753,233

1883.

Countries of production.	Countries of immediate shipment.	Class 1, clothing wools.	Class 2, combing wools.	Class 3, carpet wools.	Total.
Argentine Republic	Argentine Republic	457,789	....	8,234,101	} 8,775,653
	England	83,743	....	....	
Austria	France	....	....	15,953	} 46,177
	England	....	....	30,224	
Belgium	Belgium	....	....	1,694	1,694
Brazil	Brazil	288,863	....	980,296	1,269,159
Chili	Chili	117,552	....	891,788	
	France	....	....	2,015	} 1,140,634
	England	....	....	129,279	
China	China	....	....	389,958	} 699,364
	England	....	....	309,406	
Denmark	Denmark	50	....	50	} 16,264
	England	....	....	16,164	
Greenland and Iceland	England	....	....	284,132	284,132
France	France	14,001	....	1,908,633	} 1,923,824
	England	....	....	1,190	
French Africa	France	....	....	12,689	12,689
Germany	Germany	8,798	1,798	75	} 41,514
	England	....	....	30,843	
England	England	897,589	1,950,815	1,776,413	4,633,817
Scotland	Scotland	68,388	314	1,197,984	} 2,351,190
	England	....	19,043	1,065,461	
Ireland	Ireland	....	20,327	....	} 306,699
	England	....	125,828	160,544	
Nova Scotia	Nova Scotia	52	....	....	52
British West Indies	British West Indies	822	1,280	....	} 194,900
	England	....	....	192,798	
British Guiana	British Guiana	82	....	....	82
British East Indies	British East Indies	....	18,544	318,926	} 4,509,371
	England	....	....	4,105,408	
	Scotland	....	....	60,493	
British Africa	British Africa	746,260	....	13,943	} 2,056,134
	Germany	49,320	....	....	
	England	1,246,611	....	....	
British Australasia	British Australasia	1,087,079	....	....	} 5,095,987
	England	4,008,908	....	....	
Greece	Austria	....	....	44,432	} 71,596
	France	....	....	27,164	
Italy	Italy	....	....	28,692	} 46,721
	France	....	....	5,262	
	England	....	....	12,767	
Dutch West Indies	Dutch West Indies	....	....	22,600	22,600
Portugal	Portugal	693	....	....	} 839,484
	England	....	....	838,791	
Azores	Azores	....	....	5,483	5,483
Russia on the Baltic and White Seas	Denmark	....	....	266,627	} 2,403,059
	England	....	....	2,136,432	
Russia on the Black Sea	France	....	....	503,570	
	England	....	....	10,349,597	
	Ireland	....	....	23,953	} 11,815,588
	Italy	....	....	857,564	
	Netherlands	....	....	20,904	
Cuba	Cuba	....	....	80	80
Turkey in Europe	Turkey in Europe	....	....	268,101	
	France	....	....	6,645	
	England	....	5,807	1,045,560	} 1,026,148
	Italy	....	....	600,035	
Turkey in Asia	Turkey in Asia	....	....	575,162	
	France	....	....	3,097,688	
	England	12,424	90,348	6,485,860	} 10,290,571
	Nova Scotia	....	....	29,209	
Turkey in Africa	England	....	....	239,987	239,987

No. 5.—Kinds of Raw Wool, By Countries of Production and of Immediate Shipment, Imported into New York, Boston, and Philadelphia, &c., 1882–1887—Continued.

1883—Continued.

Countries of production.	Countries of immediate shipment.	Class 1, clothing wools.	Class 2, combing wools.	Class 3, carpet wools.	Total.
		Pounds.	*Pounds.*	*Pounds.*	*Pounds.*
Uruguay	Uruguay	4,748,446		1,172,267	} 5,932,608
	England			11,895	
Venezuela	Venezuela			8,160	8,160
South America, other	South America, other	251			} 14,619
	England			12,339	
	Central American States.	2,029			
Asia, all other	France			217,218	} 617,633
	England			400,415	
Total		13,839,770	2,243,104	51,510,799	67,593,673

1884.

Countries of production.	Countries of immediate shipment.	Class 1, clothing wools.	Class 2, combing wools.	Class 3, carpet wools.	Total.
Argentine Republic	Argentine Republic	37,693		5,279,290	} 5,365,888
	England	30,360		18,543	
Austria	Austria			152,815	
	France			96,871	} 630,574
	England			377,688	
	Belgium	3,200			
Belgium	Belgium	42,995		48,235	} 121,507
	England		1,214	29,063	
Brazil ?	Brazil	341,858		185,058	} 527,698
	Belgium	782			
Chili	Chili	77,949		868,879	} 1,389,559
	England	3,605		439,126	
China	China		4,556	691,415	} 1,200,655 •
	England			504,684	
Denmark	Denmark			252,679	} 288,425
	England			35,746	
Greenland	England			310,054	
	Ireland			19,505	} 341,692
	Denmark			12,043	
France	France	57,958	60	1,380,900	} 1,439,168
	Belgium	350			
Germany	Germany	7,394	2,011	82,643	
	England			34,131	} 149,854
	Belgium			23,476	
England	England	728,679	3,474,003	1,285,500	} 5,506,836
	Scotland		18,654		
Scotland	Scotland			3,988,329	} 6,427,314
	England	2,209	30,761	2,406,015	
Ireland	England	41,534	507,011		} 553,498
	Scotland		4,953		
Nova Scotia	Nova Scotia	393	709		1,102
British West Indies	British West Indies	722		200	} 1,122
	England			200	
British East Indies	England		16,154	6,107,612	} 6,126,146
	Germany		2,580		
British Australasia	British Australasia	3,905,490			} 13,131,693
	England	8,784,136	240,702	201,365	
British Africa	British Africa	725,001			
	England	830,768	21,290	42,088	1,653,247
	Germany	34,100			
Greece	Austria			35,009	} 57,868
	France			22,859	
Italy	Italy	1,113		111,015	112,128
Dutch West Indies	Dutch West Indies			32,374	} 32,774
	England			400	
Peru	Peru	1,231		4,094	5,325
Portugal	England			904,363	} 905,686
	France			1,323	
Azore Islands	Azore Islands			1,399	1,399
Russia on the Baltic Sea.	Belgium			117,106	
	England			1,575,680	
	Scotland			3,003	} 2,169,524
	France			31,781	
	Denmark			441,954	
Russia on the Black Sea.	Russia on the Black Sea.			1,326,581	
	Belgium			75,070	
	England			10,028,408	
	Germany			21,273	} 12,644,467
	France			1,179,127	
	Denmark			1,733	
	Italy			12,275	
Spain	England			21,164	21,164

No. 5.—KINDS OF RAW WOOL, BY COUNTRIES OF PRODUCTION AND OF IMMEDIATE SHIPMENT, IMPORTED INTO NEW YORK, BOSTON, AND PHILADELPHIA, &C., 1882–1887—Continued.

1884—Continued.

Countries of production.	Countries of immediate shipment.	Class 1, clothing wools.	Class 2, combing wools.	Class 3, carpet wools.	Total.
		Pounds.	*Pounds.*	*Pounds.*	*Pounds.*
Turkey in Europe......	Turkey in Europe........	....	....	24,044	}
	France ...			37,701	682,106
	England...	2,337	18,782	403,028	
	Italy ...			196,214	
Turkey in Asia...	Turkey in Asia ...			1,112,447	}
	England ...	2,669	42,744	4,453,561	
	France ...			729,294	6,379,844
	Italy ...			39,129	
Turkey in Africa...	England ...		5,157	911,507	916,664
Uruguay ...	Uruguay ...	1,438,569		1,160,732	} 2,673,812
	England ...	74,511			
Venezuela ...	Venezuela ...			8,917	8,917
Asia, all other...	England ...			2,062,661	} 2,603,616
	France ...			540,955	
Total ...		**17,177,706**	**4,391,141**	**52,502,425**	**74,071,272**

1885.

Countries of production.	Countries of immediate shipment.	Class 1, clothing wools.	Class 2, combing wools.	Class 3, carpet wools.	Total.
Argentine Republic......	Argentine Republic......	371,696		9,851,121	}
	Belgium...	45,865			} 10,499,380
	Brazil ...			208,440	
	England...	22,208			
Austria...	England...			96,740	} 141,325
	Germany...			44,585	
Belgium ...	Belgium...	129,493		20,931	150,424
Brazil ...	Brazil ...	263,437		532,165	}
	England...			150,153	} 953,857
	Germany...	8,100			
Chili...	Chili ...			1,702,697	1,738,793
	England...	36,096			
China...	China ...			855,008	1,256,132
	England...	993	19,315	380,216	
Greenland...	England...			58,387	58,387
France ...	France ...	11,236		1,032,677	}
	Belgium ...			8,257	} 1,121,366
	England...			21,709	
	Scotland ...			47,487	
Germany ...	Germany...	9,027	4	130,541	}
	England...	28,584	61,456	121,781	} 355,970
	France ...			4,577	
England...	England...	272,669	2,281,572	1,448,496	4,002,737
Scotland...	Scotland...	1,272	5,440	4,009,624	} 5,840,993
	England...			1,324,639	
Ireland ...	England...		144,827	27,969	172,796
Nova Scotia...	Nova Scotia ...		169		169
British West Indies ...	British West Indies ...		709	280	909
British East Indies ...	British East Indies...			21,455	} 4,682,823
	England...		6,605	4,604,763	
Hong-Kong...	Hong-Kong ...	7,697			7,697
British Australasia......	British Australasia...	2,032,329			}
	England...	3,592,482	33,312		} 5,666,210
	Scotland ...	3,087			
British Africa...	British Africa...	786,852			}
	England...	187,742	9,338	3,295	} 987,227
British Possessions, all other.	England...	30,729		113,388	144,117
Italy ...	Italy ...			488	488
Dutch West Indies...	Dutch West Indies ...			26,201	26,201
Peru...	Peru ...			31,672	31,672
Portugal ...	England...			494,595	494,595
Russia on the Baltic Sea.	Russia on the Baltic Sea..			207,642	}
	England...			2,890,114	
	Denmark...			548,771	} 3,963,018
	Germany...			166,704	
	Belgium ...			149,787	
Russia on the Black Sea.	Russia on the Black Sea...			1,105,377	}
	England...			10,587,811	
	Belgium ...			824,009	} 12,797,472
	Denmark...			77,878	
	France ...			112,397	
Spain...	England...			54,785	} 84,661
	France ...			29,876	
Porto Rice...	Porto Rico...		40		40
Turkey in Europe......	England...	170	84,450	345,319	}
	Italy ...			92,424	} 531,007
	France ...			8,638	

No. 5.—KINDS OF RAW WOOL, BY COUNTRIES OF PRODUCTION AND OF IMMEDIATE SHIPMENT, IMPORTED INTO NEW YORK, BOSTON, AND PHILADELPHIA, &C., 1882-1887—Continued.

1885—Continued.

Countries of production.	Countries of immediate shipment.	Class 1, clothing wools.	Class 2, combing wools.	Class 3, carpet wools.	Total.
		Pounds.	*Pounds.*	*Pounds.*	*Pounds.*
Turkey in Asia	Turkey in Asia			500,009	
	England		166,264	5,942,722	
	France			733,760	} 7,495,355
	Italy			149,147	
	Scotland			3,453	
Turkey in Africa	England		1,567	499,594	501,161
Uruguay	Uruguay	2,305,402		1,250,693	
	Belgium	39,898			
	England	260,909			} 3,756,962
Venezuela	Venezuela			14,396	14,396
Asia, all other	England			841,858	841,858
Total		10,348,033	2,820,074	54,611,122	67,779,229

1886.

Countries of production.	Countries of immediate shipment.	Class 1, clothing wools.	Class 2, combing wools.	Class 3, carpet wools.	Total.
Argentine Republic	Argentine Republic	1,641,918		10,329,595	
	Belgium	327,699	2,056	16,571	
	Brazil	11,370		171,477	} 13,906,165
	France	326,757	31,748		
	England	979,068		67,906	
Austria	Austria			394,895	
	Germany			5,432	} 541,378
	England	11,763		129,288	
Belgium	Belgium	364,769	441	133,592	498,802
Brazil	Brazil	1,056,306		467,474	} 1,524,233
	England	453			
Chili	Chili	170,917		1,785,198	
	England			102,650	} 2,208,903
	Peru			150,138	
China	China		350	1,872,889	} 3,530,764
	England		33	1,657,492	
Denmark	Denmark			26,951	} 28,537
	England			1,586	
Greenland, &c	England			504,184	} 521,496
	Scotland			17,312	
France	France	20,583	296	2,924,560	
	Germany			4,273	
	England	862		314,594	} 3,436,224
	Scotland			85,385	
	Italy			87,671	
French Possessions in Africa.	France	507			507
Germany	Germany	12,850		209,287	} 729,299
	England			507,162	
England	England	407,409	4,318,150	3,724,637	
	France		28,334		
	Scotland		8,922	144,013	} 8,631,465
Scotland	Scotland		141,895	5,284,807	
	England	2,693	145,967	1,696,023	} 7,271,385
Ireland	England	4	1,457,517	24,708	} 1,484,869
	Scotland			2,640	
Nova Scotia, &c	Nova Scotia, &c	81	353		434
British West Indies	British West Indies	1,230	248	1,957	3,435
British East Indies	France			69,265	
	England		45,811	11,493,184	} 11,055,385
	Scotland			47,125	
British Possessions in Africa.	British Possessions in Africa.	1,164,768	472		
	France			91,732	} 2,750,413
	Germany		1,306		
	England	1,377,421	43,364	67,225	
	Scotland	4,125			
British Possessions in Australasia.	British Possessions in Australasia.	5,384,624	44,184		} 16,577,074
	Belgium	946			
	England	10,811,464	287,563	49,193	
Italy	Italy			1,158	
	France	1,577			} 19,876
	England			17,141	
Mexico	Mexico	158		306	464
Dutch West Indies	Dutch West Indies	1,296		12,052	13,348
Peru	Peru	300			} 510
	United States of Colombia.	210			

No. 5.—KINDS OF RAW WOOL, BY COUNTRIES OF PRODUCTION AND OF IMMEDIATE SHIPMENT, IMPORTED INTO NEW YORK, BOSTON, AND PHILADELPHIA, &c., 1882–1887—Continued.

1886—Continued.

Countries of production.	Countries of immediate shipment.	Class 1, clothing wools.	Class 2, combing wools.	Class 3, carpet wools.	Total.
		Pounds.	Pounds.	Pounds.	Pounds.
Portugal	England		9,585	594,519	604,104
Azore, Madeira, &c., Islands.	Azore, Madeira, &c., Islands.	521			521
Roumania	England			14,524	} 43,577
	Italy			29,033	
Russia on the Baltic and White Seas.	Russia on the Baltic and White Seas.			192,965	
	Belgium			106,290	
	Denmark			140,100	} 6,643,738
	France			565,334	
	Germany			197,689	
	England			5,441,301	
Russia on the Black Sea.	Russia on the Black Sea.			1,578,675	
	Belgium			45,762	
	France			1,161,057	} 13,329,470
	England	8,955		10,533,021	
Spain	Spain			71,659	} 132,264
	England			60,605	
Turkey in Europe	Turkey in Europe			13,314	
	Belgium			6,332	
	France			46,537	} 749,136
	England	22,339	122,252	538,362	
Turkey in Asia	Turkey in Asia			791,830	
	Belgium			45,852	
	France			1,553,423	} 10,244,228
	England		928,392	6,895,995	
	Italy			28,736	
Turkey in Africa	England			588,236	588,236
Uruguay	Uruguay	12,222,290		492,958	
	Argentine Republic	58,288			
	Belgium	454,689			} 13,378,272
	Brazil	168			
	England	149,879			
Venezuela	Venezuela	141,968		13,136	155,124
Asia, all other	Asia, all other			419,066	
	France			263,939	} 1,916,395
	England		7,266	1,226,104	
Total		37,143,575	7,626,155	78,353,201	123,122,931

1887.

Countries of production.	Countries of immediate shipment.	Class 1, clothing wools.	Class 2, combing wools.	Class 3, carpet wools.	Total.
Argentine Republic	Argentine Republic	58,682		6,214,685	
	England	232,007		30,744	} 6,559,588
	Brazil			23,470	
Austria	Austria			81,745	} 502,374
	England			420,629	
Belgium	Belgium	72,358		8,753	} 87,709
	France			6,598	
Brazil	Brazil	235,028		295,969	530,997
Chili	Chili	520,059		2,008,617	
	England	25,113		112,675	} 2,666,464
China	China			2,047,067	
	England	5,012	1,011	393,363	
	France			59,933	
	Germany			500,585	} 3,611,892
	Hong-Kong			556,018	
	Italy			48,903	
Denmark	England			5,380	5,380
Greenland, Iceland, and the Faroe Islands.	England			608,012	608,012
France	France	6,131	13,281	1,211,461	
	England	6,729		436,419	
	Scotland			170,660	} 1,931,334
	Germany		10,818		
	Belgium			69,835	
Germany	Germany	15,218	2,107	92,079	} 492,361
	England			362,957	
England	England	60,310	6,815,421	4,373,868	
	Scotland			139,976	
	Belgium			7,245	} 11,393,791
	Nova Scotia			5,923	
Scotland	Scotland		8,613	2,832,875	} 5,324,385
	England		5,428	2,477,469	

No. 5.—KINDS OF RAW WOOL, BY COUNTRIES OF PRODUCTION AND OF IMMEDIATE SHIPMENT, IMPORTED INTO NEW YORK, BOSTON, AND PHILADELPHIA, &C., 1882–1887—Continued.

1887—Continued.

Countries of production.	Countries of immediate shipment.	Class 1, clothing wools.	Class 2, combing wools.	Class 3, carpet wools.	Total.
		Pounds.	*Pounds.*	*Pounds.*	*Pounds.*
Ireland	England..................	....	1,551,062	....	1,551,062
Nova Scotia.............	Nova Scotia.............	....	491	....	491
British West Indies	British West Indies......	1,574	439	....	} 19,625
	England.................	....	....	191	
British East Indies	British East Indies.......	....	....	17,421	
		....	....	75,268	
	England.................	....	58,450	12,738,506	} 13,082,465
	Scotland	....	....	157,320	
	France	....	....	52,921	
British Australasia	British Australasia.......	3,382,684	....	....	} 9,328,467
	England.................	5,920,076	....	21,525	
	Belgium.................	4,182	....	....	
British Africa	British Africa.............	1,552,281	75	....	} 2,188,966
	England.................	335,807	9,482	248,417	
	France	....	....	27,958	
	Denmark................	....	14,946	....	
British Possessions, all other.	England.................	....	170	....	170
Greece.	Austria	....	....	10,070	10,070
Italy....................	Italy	....	....	2,873	} 13,938
	England.................	....	....	11,065	
Hawaiian Islands........	Germany................	5,776	....	....	5,776
Mexico	Mexico	....	....	57,876	57,876
Netherlands	Netherlands	....	20,456	62	} 65,702
	England.................	....	....	45,184	
Dutch West Indies	Dutch West Indies.......	....	....	13,372	} 17,634
	Venezuela...............	....	....	4,262	
Peru....................	United States of Colombia.	....	1,635	....	1,635
Portugal.................	England.................	....	2,292	684,313	} 687,531
	Spain...................	....	....	926	
Roumania	England.................	....	....	6,104	} 49,261
	Italy...................	....	....	43,157	
Russia on the Baltic	Russia on the Baltic......	....	....	139,432	
	England.................	....	....	3,180,180	
	Denmark................	....	....	253,444	
	France	....	....	592,556	} 4,665,034
	Germany................	....	....	410,205	
	Netherlands.............	....	....	39,460	
	Sweden and Norway	....	....	46,757	
Russia on the Black Sea..	England.................	....	2,932	14,521,307	
	Scotland	....	....	15,626	
	France	....	....	463,465	} 15,364,720
	Belgium.................	....	....	306,391	
	Germany................	....	....	44,258	
	Austria	....	....	10,741	
Russia, Asiatic...........	France	....	....	44,439	44,439
Spain	England.................	....	....	28,378	28,378
Turkey in Europe	Turkey in Europe........	....	162,394	360,657	
	England.................	17,750	698,690	602,966	
	France	....	....	288,636	} 2,253,111
	Belgium	....	441	17,128	
	Germany................	....	128	10,843	
	Scotland	....	441	....	
	Italy	....	....	93,037	
Turkey in Asia	Turkey in Asia	....	4,367	1,448,312	
	Turkey in Europe........	....	3,908	33,471	
	England.................	14,875	754,570	12,881,486	
	Scotland	....	....	176,634	} 19,518,851
	France	4,224	....	4,179,848	
	Belgium.................	....	6,427	....	
	Italy	....	....	10,642	
Turkey in Africa	England.................	....	....	47,346	
	Italy	....	....	200	} 502,142
	Spain...................	....	....	4,596	
Uruguay	Uruguay	2,585,292	....	312,743	
	England.................	1,618	....	....	} 2,937,056
	Belgium.................	1,562	....	....	
	Brazil	....	....	35,841	
Venezuela	Venezuela...............	....	....	13,817	13,817
Asia, all other	England.................	305	17,782	2,197,414	
	France	....	....	321,750	} 2,579,812
	Russia on the Black Sea..	....	....	42,551	
Africa, all other	England.................	....	....	3,186	3,186
Total	....	15,064,659	10,168,344	83,472,499	108,705,502

No. 6.—STATEMENT SHOWING THE VALUES OF MANUFACTURES OF WOOL IMPORTED INTO THE UNITED STATES FROM THE PRINCIPAL AND ALL OTHER FOREIGN COUNTRIES; THE TOTAL VALUES OF FOREIGN MANUFACTURES OF WOOL EXPORTED, AND OF THE NET IMPORTS, FOR EACH YEAR FROM 1821 TO 1887, INCLUSIVE.

Years ending	From Europe							From British North American Provinces	From Mexico	From West Indies	From South America	From Asia and Oceanica	From Africa	From all other countries	Total imports	Total foreign exports	Net imports
	Great Britain and Ireland	France	Germany	Netherlands	Belgium	All other	Total										
Sept. 30—	*Dollars*	*Dollars*	*Dollars*	*Dollars*	*Dollars*	*Dollars*	*Dollars*	*Dollars*	*Dollars*	*Dollars*	*Dollars*	*Dollars*	*Dolls*	*Dolls*	*Dollars*	*Dollars*	*Dollars*
1821	6,936,403	89,335	81,061	57,315		313	7,174,427	10,108	(a)	6,405	719	31,276	150	487	7,238,161	379,252	6,859,702
1822	11,384,903	291,418	43,009	83,091		23,210	11,737,628	7,409	(a)	5,469	212	226	282		11,762,505	199,563	11,502,032
1823	7,711,311	90,230	65,313	56,712		1,544	7,920,098	2,098	(a)	24,642	1,647	1,682		164	7,053,433	461,071	7,490,362
1824	7,778,873	136,303	117,730	74,027		807	8,468,400	2,248		20,9-3	4,430	160		259	8,124,667	555,973	7,568,714
1825	11,336,884	341,448	151,622	97,860		14,783	11,943,499	6,523	7,500	34,366		20,055		66	12,017,468	696,905	11,320,563
1826	7,780,272	464,817	230,137	63,674		20,311	8,590,641	22,138	22,138	17,319	10,465	7,825	12	2,618	8,657,424	408,314	8,191,110
1827	8,146,332	490,102	84,623	43,115		1,910	8,778,112	3,210	49,544	9,797	11,465	7,333	120	6,815	8,466,226	252,173	8,614,053
1828	8,025,677	502,014	107,157	49,976		7,932	8,782,7-6	8,030	28,019	18,455	1,984	2,090	37		8,842,380	194,658	8,647,731
1829	8,360,844	608,018	125,356	61,637		410	7,176,-65	7,085	336	5,231	691	3,635		486	7,193,653	212,748	6,980,905
1830	5,218,283	522,511	97,307	49,185		1,119	5,688,405	4,440	320	4,914	1,984	506	43	543	5,900,088	235,545	5,665,443
1831	11,050,322	1,214,628	249,080	44,880		8,122	12,173,047	14,308	25	7,802	2,112	831	63	1,077	13,197,364	307,2-0	12,890,155
1832	9,434,176	790,481	140,965	25,715		1,141	10,401,090	9,098	330	10,068	7,465	10,873	61	646	10,410,490	391,160	10,187,258
1833	12,291,725	1,148,119	179,748	76,517		1,111	13,676,331	14,877		13,421	1,782	6,234	245	205	13,713,141	525,883	13,187,258
1834	9,940,935	346,804	82,515	18,512	29,052	1,594	7,407,859	20,892	346	1,817		3,517	450	145	7,441,035	818,042	6,625,993
1835	16,667,993	1,996,782	318,512	108,007	10,170	1,421	19,112,928	24,913		8,657	272	2,943	567	1,670	19,151,950	382,655	18,768,295
1836	20,255,060	3,541,060	590,897	87,651	22,120	16,657	30,393,528	22,408	1,955	8,971	1,18-	852	297	70	24,122,517	515,590	24,122,517
1837	7,668,569	2,251,331	372,293	31,074	85,382	1,102	10,393,524	5,317		3,184		446		2,307	10,410,782	534,737	9,832,104
1838	10,101,732	2,412,303	417,850	21,133	58,703	8,817	13,974,063	21,800	431	20,054	107		140	14,415	10,415,427	296,952	8,864,904
1839	13,460,634	2,438,125	668,084	11,470	26,817	8,572	20,981,255	14,613	5,306	10,498		985	8	7,640	21,024,427	242,303	20,782,091
1840	7,851,329	2,683,227	208,082	11,476	37,308	3,752	10,701,807	10,147		3,5-4	274	701		174	10,608,485	431,393	10,365,092
1841	9,240,231	3,337,001	148,931	14,924	141,740	12,071	12,914,785	21,339	258	3,102		205		4,104	12,943,882	187,626	12,756,257
1842	6,430,478	2,836,067	108,596	21,842	205,906	7,062	9,081,509	4,831	142	2,065	463	109		668	9,680,644	140,534	9,543,124
June 30—																	
1843 b	1,903,670	842,594	30,197	903	66,797	1,216	2,943,783	6,852		463	1,705	18,474		109	2,971,456	71,172	2,900,284
1844	7,801,001	3,228,040	184,064	9,800	350,435	6,501	11,646,537	6,396		3,254	1,385	97,516	28-	111	11,721,951	71,888	11,640,063
1845	8,318,614	4,498,378	203,505	5,601	279,308	3,331	13,308,910	10,010	12	2,097	1,34-	164,791			13,578,352	237,546	13,340,806
1846	6,408,713	5,430,553	406,814	26,069	311,323	11,038	12,751,414	8,067	1,129	4,964	4,409	10,535		12	12,778,854	350,270	12,428,024
1847	7,220,471	5,257,105	708,600	9,210	350,775	4,418	13,620,570	5,763	440	2,996		23,3-8	18		13,664,102	349,551	13,314,551
1848	10,222,459	6,360,305	1,321,045	22,152	410,874	5,5-7	18,369,042	12,839	34	4,357	2,256	18,033			18,405,401	235,102	18,170,250
1849	9,755,531	4,542,006	1,491,041	24,022	930,975	9,336	16,746,917	9,61	135	3,042	353	8,813			10,179,501	247,942	18,531,559
1850	12,229,011	4,666,404	681,676	75,249	944,750	8,939	19,605,827	9,157	60	4,237	1,219	4,072	14	23	10,179,561	227,748	19,392,871
1851	13,511,351	4,374,494	1,474,806	12,736	496,089	8,757	22,282,432	3,115	131	7,354	3,060	30,914	2,597	354	22,358,878	331,669	22,027,210
1852	14,303,266	4,098,860	1,096,299	10,643	476,464	2,837	20,508,640	3,711	28	1,247	300	300		15	20,611,286	285,375	20,325,911
1853	22,012,051	6,848,663	3,494,752	13,504	610,745	6,044	31,780,017	3,285	142	4,10K	1,190	22,530	33		31,810,771	434,589	31,384,685
1854	26,127,308	5,732,374	4,086,209	21,842	611,668	7,501	37,506,403	14,420	3,911	4,636	50,733	320,933	2,024	1,333	37,001,473	1,407,711	36,430,762

No. 7.—Statement showing the Quantities and Values of the Principal and all other Manufactures of Wool Imported into the United States, and the Estimated Amounts of Duties Received on the same, for each Year from 1821 to 1866, inclusive.

Note.—Most of the classes of goods named in the various tariffs are enumerated in this table. The blanks under many of the classes do not indicate that there were no importations of such goods, but that, under the different phraseology of the several acts, on importation they were described and returned under some more general head, as "all other manufactures of wool," &c.

Year ending—	Balmorals and skirting of wool, worsted, or other material.			Blankets.								Total.		Bunting.	
				Blankets, value per pound not stated.	Valued at not over 28 cents per pound.		Valued at over 28 cents and not over 40 cents per pound.		Valued at over 40 cents per pound.					
	Pounds.	Values.	Duties.	Values.	Pounds.	Values.	Pounds.	Values.	Pounds.	Values.	Values.	Duties.	Values.	Duties.
		Dollars.	Dollars.	Dollars.		Dollars.		Dollars.		Dollars.	Dollars.	Dollars.	Dollars.	Dollars.
Sept. 30—														
1821				434,256							434,256 00	100,064 00		
1822				891,147							991,147 00	247,780 75		
1823				604,896							604,896 00	151,224 00		
1824				526,023							526,023 00	131,505 75		
1825				891,197							891,197 00	222,784 25		
1826				527,781							527,784 00	131,940 00		
1827				703,477							703,477 00	175,869 25		
1828				624,239							624,239 00	156,050 75		
1829				455,407							455,467 00	159,413 45		
1830				594,044							594,044 00	207,915 40		
1831				1,180,478							1,180,478 00	413,167 36		
1832				602,796							602,796 00	210,978 00		
1833				1,165,360							1,165,360 00	407,841 00		
1834				1,068,063							1,068,065 00	181,933 01		
1835				1,865,344							1,865,344 00	263,405 85		
1836				2,397,822							2,397,822 00	368,549 20		
1837				939,814							939,814 00	141,242 42		
1838				946,546							946,546 00	148,183 94		
1839				1,356,046							1,356,046 00	186,630 75		
1840				570,417							570,417 00	88,039 65		
1841				691,895							691,895 00	68,507 45		
1842				566,233							566,233 00	78,235 83		
June 30—														
1843a				201,454							201,454 00	47,363 90		
1844				1,004,826							1,004,826 00	214,178 10		
1845				998,914							996,914 00	219,361 00		
1846				633,745							633,745 00	141,806 65		
1847				803,914							803,914 00	166,172 63		
1848				1,146,587							1,146,687 00	220,317 40		
1849				1,101,429							1,101,429 00	232,285 80		

Year												
1850				1,244,335							1,244,335 00	248,867 00
1851				1,506,409							1,508,469 00	301,253 80
1852				1,016,361							1,046,361 00	209,272 20
1853				1,455,650							1,455,650 00	201,151 80
1854				1,790,590							1,790,590 00	358,118 40
1855				1,170,642							1,170,642 00	234,128 40
1856				1,205,300							1,205,300 00	241,080 00
1857				1,630,973							1,630,973 00	320,104 60
1858				1,574,716							1,574,716 00	236,207 40
1859				1,097,386							1,097,380 00	254,C07 00
1860				1,005,181							1,005,181 00	240,777 15
1861				1,251,628							1,341,049 00	223,518 35
1862				1,945,707							1,945,747 00	635,392 55
1863				1,297,864							1,297,864 00	412,431 07
1864				749,703	430,428	86,904	10,344	2,301	219	*115	749,793 00	287,160 48
1865	283,117	232,864	161,093 08	676,008							678,008 00	582,386 71
1866	394,637	359,040	238,352 48		1,808,956	308,317	158,030	57,545	218,390	113,209	539,121 00	428,247 31

41,734   7,928 56

a Nine months.

No. 7.—IMPORTED MANUFACTURES OF WOOL ENTERED FOR CONSUMPTION, &c., 1821-1863—Continued.

Carpets and carpeting.

Year ending—	Brussels, Turkey, Wilton, and treble ingrain. Sq. yards.	Values.	Venetian and ingrain. Sq. yds.	Values.	Wilton, Saxony, Aubusson, Brussels, Turkey, treble ingrain, Venetian and other ingrain. Sq. yards.	Values.	Baizes, bindings, bockings, and druggets. Sq. yds.	Values.	Brussels carpets, wrought on the Jacquard machine, and all medallion or whole carpets. Valued at $1.25 or under per square yard. Sq. yds.	Values.	Valued at over $1.25 per square yard. Sq. yds.	Values.	Brussels and tapestry Brussels carpet, and carpeting printed on the warp or otherwise. Sq. yds.	Values.	Treble ingrain and worsted chain Venetian carpets and carpeting. Sq. yds.	Values.
		Dollars.		*Dollars.*		*Dollars.*		*Dollars.*		*Dollars.*		*Dollars.*		*Dollars.*		*Dollars.*
Sept. 30—																
1821																
1822																
1823																
1824	29,299		93,339													
1825	85,700		502,378													
1826	71,201		601,452													
1827	60,750		630,871													
1828	60,634		763,360													
1829	64,570		341,593													
1830	64,885	77,502	162,870	123,850												
1831	127,746	170,713	385,839	240,080												
1832	144,066	210,335	512,793	346,560												
1833	104,108	147,820	240,668	171,606			89,427	28,319								
1834	118,008	197,037	257,022	199,631			108,194	40,063								
1835	205,666	321,812	395,441	261,272			329,980	129,434								
1836	335,680	614,712	614,974	449,043			436,071	168,760								
1837	223,064	369,046	333,321	253,195			63,457	27,137								
1838	130,034	101,301	101,213	121,032			179,603	61,968								
1839	282,052	414,869	272,086	197,798			287,351	119,620								
1840	107,650	246,068	127,583	92,433			144,082	51,025								
1841	297,562	293,048	77,768	52,440			256,634	95,863								
1842	161,425	208,835	50,772	33,414			157,769	59,909								
June 30—																
1843a	125,218	170,188	17,550	11,622			58,018	10,670								
1844	194,172	272,195	23,949	17,280			125,040	40,214								
1845	230,088	300,963	46,778	34,951			278,450	100,332								
1846	139,496	220,913	33,230	23,570			265,480	88,075								
1847	270,644	273,805	19,241	14,059			109,933	60,427								
1848	621,159	695,465	74,175	38,895			(b)	(b)								
1849	397,818	367,975	144,558	96,433			122,485	51,518								

1850	685,328	626,813	148,172	93,091			237,689	101,256								
1851	812,404	835,174	142,540	88,655			190,492	110,600								
1852	555,088	559,000	129,821	75,573			184,973	111,051								
1853	800,281	844,038	239,157	142,817			298,166	118,203								
1854	2,200,895	1,404,337	353,725	165,391			380,073	113,048								
1855					1,492,952	1,327,707	376,457	97,578								
1856					2,000,586	1,920,196	502,244	117,561								
1857					1,714,093	1,784,106	491,405	119,835								
1858						1,542,600		124,008								
1859						2,200,164		136,174								
1860						2,542,523		200,683	867	1,113	3,731	7,250	1,911	1,446	5,340	400
1861						1,746,649		138,781								
1862					539,928	466,596		68,4x5								
1863					1,092,498	1,016,562		102,510								
1864					1,504,370	1,058,389		20,725								
1865							51,537				105,786	156,194	317,500	290,641	10,055	7,520
1866							170,148	74,473	220,536	213,791	503,671	865,878	1,566,207	1,424,650	45,044	36,642

a Nine months.   b Included in flannels.

No. 7.—Imported Manufactures of Wool Entered for Consumption, &c., 1821-1866—Continued.

Year ending	Carpets and carpeting—Continued								Clothing						Cloths and cassimeres		
	Two-ply, ingrain, and yarn venetian		Mats, screens, rugs, all other mats of wool and other material		Of wool, flax, or whatever material not otherwise provided for		Total		Ready made		Articles of wear		Total				
	Sq. yds.	Values	Sq. yds.	Values	Sq. yds.	Values	Values	Duties	Pounds	Values	Pounds	Values	Values	Duties	Pounds	Values	Duties
Sept. 30—																	
1821																5,038,255	1,097,651 00
1822																3,491,935	1,658,387 00
1823																5,844,608	1,168,613 00
1824						358	37,831	38,055 85								5,045,159	1,169,237 00
1825						3,091	515,391	169,092 70								5,264,562	1,993,627 10
1826						5,570	545,148	167,077 60								4,546,714	1,375,296 69
1827						14,628	511,186	221,373 35								4,285,413	1,427,041 62
1828						5,179	581,948	222,192 80		79,136			79,136	39,568 00		4,315,691	1,437,132 70
1829				137		26,678	323,251	190,373 16		46,789			46,789	23,394 50		3,333,991	1,334,883 00
1830				401		184	201,649	118,601 75		108,242			108,242	54,121 00		2,834,339	1,284,753 30
1831				851		471	421,094	243,858 05		120,443			120,443	60,221 50		6,131,442	2,755,074 80
1832				166		814	537,775	300,176 15								5,101,841	2,200,443 05
1833						137	347,011	164,171 66								6,128,194	3,064,097 00
1834							436,931	172,192 00								4,364,340	2,051,239 80
1835							732,516	303,314 84								7,046,755	3,311,975 30
1836							1,135,415	412,529 12								8,939,362	3,023,606 00
1837							650,234	239,847 00								3,013,460	1,325,923 40
1838							377,321	130,019 38								5,195,965	2,139,346 00
1839							731,227	267,500 18								4,696,629	2,002,350 40
1840							789,556	185,318 04								4,941,867	1,784,681 40
1841							441,351	154,734 66								878,289 60	878,289 60
1842							302,218	102,577 29								3,995,577	1,398,452 00
June 30—																	
1843							201,480	83,054 92		60,591		114,493	175,084	76,092 70		1,386,628	542,651 20
1844							329,646	133,388 50		66,175		864,886	931,061	379,041 90		4,777,940	1,911,176 00
1845							532,246	189,014 04		67,232		1,105,706	1,173,028	473,034 40		5,411,850	2,104,740 00
1846							311,61?	125,893 09		64,397		783,345	847,742	345,610 50		4,192,310	1,676,924 00
1847						2,017	850,305	90,346 85		71,435		605,027	676,462	277,724 30		4,527,742	1,258,322 00
1848						8,827	643,187	192,650 10		99,283		553,939	653,222	195,960 60		6,364,145	1,909,243 50

Year											
1849		544,570	163,373 80		87,283		580,307	587,500	176,277 00		4,905,067	1,408,787 19
1850	28,050	991,860	267,558 00		74,803		734,268	813,281	243,978 30		6,184,100	1,855,257 00
1851	70,700	1,107,381	332,214 30		113,700		945,294	1,058,994	317,698 20		7,669,520	2,300,856 00
1852	72,932	642,018	232,005 40		115,070		1,253,742	1,308,812	410,643 60		6,009,742	2,072,022 60
1853	86,783	1,335,442	400,644 00		107,350		2,100,776	2,307,135	692,140 50		11,071,906	3,321,671 80
1854	229,404	2,381,803	714,558 00		330,497		3,570,644	3,927,141	1,178,142 30		13,159,083	3,947,874 90
1855	697,087	1,004,155	481,240 50		388,410		1,687,252	1,975,062	592,698 60		9,144,861	2,743,458 30
1856	178,870	2,329,879	608,963 70		404,133		1,574,211	1,974,344	593,503 20		11,083,476	3,505,042 80
1857	263,122	2,101,125	690,317 50		347,471		1,571,517	1,918,988	575,696 40		11,009,605	3,302,881 60
1858	307,064	1,646,608	399,985 02		322,024		961,514	1,283,538	308,049 12		7,626,810	1,830,430 20
1859		2,336,838	560,721 12		284,649		1,252,435	1,537,284	368,048 16		11,259,693	2,702,320 32
1860		2,743,200	658,360 44		340,030		1,750,237	2,102,296	504,551 64		12,787,754	3,069,060 96
1861		1,895,048	466,340 30	1,890	291,389 / 1,367		1,109,666 / 9,302	1,411,726	423,248 81	245,517	299,043	104,222 70
1862		535,081	100,624 30		52,320		62,330	52,472	620,160 00	4,432,392	5,441,710	1,802,316 70
1863		1,116,562	400,624 90		73,472		73,472	48,206	640,736 00	4,303,008	5,147,404	1,810,530 18
1864		1,701,290	704,516 00		48,206		48,206	52,839	624,103 00	9,853,327	10,608,085	6,283,369 36
1865	157 / 64,047	603,703	312,231 30	23,430	50,679	2,150		52,839	27,026 72	4,700,021	5,411,043	3,292,472 24
1866	19,611 / 247,907	2,077,607	1,003,702 35	59,664	130,880	1,133		130,880	66,671 36	13,656,472	16,676,963	9,031,810 14

No. 7.—IMPORTED MANUFACTURES OF WOOL ENTERED FOR CONSUMPTION, &c., 1821-1886—Continued

Year ending—	Worsted stuff goods. Values.	Silk and worsted goods. Values.	De-laines and dress goods. Pounds.	De-laines Values.	Dress and piece goods — Of wool or worsted, wholly or in part. Gray or uncolored. Sq. yards.	Gray Values.	Printed or colored. Sq. yards.	Printed Values.	Total. Values.	Total. Duties.	Endless belts for paper and blanketing for printing machines. Pounds.	Endless Values.	Endless Duties.
	Dollars.	Dollars.		Dollars.		Dollars.		Dollars.	Dollars.	Dollars.		Dollars.	Dollars.
September 30—													
1821	1,766,443								1,766,413	441,610 73			
1822	2,269,513								2,269,513	667,378 25			
1823	1,504,460								1,504,469	376,117 25			
1824	2,158,680								2,158,680	530,670 00			
1825	2,277,468	625,294							2,092,672	756,028 20			
1826	1,143,160	225,450							1,386,610	333,426 50			
1827	1,382,875	123,525							1,500,400	382,776 25			
1828	1,440,146	162,884							1,609,030	410,401 70			
1829	1,000,622	233,028							1,883,650	470,063 00			
1830	1,397,545	53,910							1,431,461	365,561 05			
1831	3,392,037								3,392,037	848,000 25			
1832	2,615,124								2,615,124	653,781 00			
1833	4,201,300	339,824							4,621,133	462,113 30			
1834	555,121	51,760							606,867	60,688 70			
1835	a6,540,278	a660,377							7,542,653				
1836	3,340,266	3,171,023							5,840,335				
1837	3,033,455	1,410,047							5,161,213				
1838	7,025,898	1,823,272							5,455,727				
1839	2,387,336	2,310,884							9,345,782				
1840	3,712,206	1,729,792							4,117,130				
1841	2,366,122	1,931,826							5,643,534	735,578 40			
1842		1,311,770							3,677,802				
June 30—													
1843a	450,051	318,685							774,736	232,450 80			
1844	1,895,875	1,292,484							3,129,363	938,508 90			
1845	1,995,109	1,510,310							3,448,419	1,031,525 70			
1846	2,658,023	774,202							4,436,225	1,330,867 50			
1847	2,124,002	1,065,403							4,980,097	1,330,278 41			
1848	3,824,416	2,456,632							6,313,068	1,578,767 00			
1849	4,070,185	2,492,290							6,522,474	1,630,018 50			
1850	5,604,250	1,653,800							6,658,050	1,664,514 75			
1851	5,419,171	1,780,076							6,202,250	1,800,565 00			
1852	6,296,677	1,697,513							7,963,570	1,990,892 50			
1853	9,799,387	1,860,918							11,677,305	2,010,329 25			

Year										
1854	10,875,870	1,594,638		240,722			11,969,917	2,992,470 25		
1855	8,590,606	1,133,639		307,328			9,065,067	2,491,268 75		
1856	12,230,275	1,335,247		503,093			13,878,850	3,469,712 50		
1857	11,365,609	1,680,246		515,641			13,449,008	3,362,477 00		
1858	10,780,879	1,240,385		613,248			12,545,405	2,383,620 95		
1859	12,289,574	1,022,106		909,371			14,525,028	2,769,920 32		
1860	15,018,351	2,108,376		641,890			18,121,098	3,443,008 03		
1861	20,944,727			201,903	5,025	1,135	21,487,762	4,140,046 29	11,473	2,868 25
1862			23,183	17,229	7,672,087	1,744,639	279,192	84,478 11		
1863				458,471	39,777,032	10,060,708	2,213,110	596,024 60		
1864				840,646	289,476	84,697	10,610,414	3,563,324 98		
1865				220,670	430,885	97,414	8,461,908	4,743,299 41	87,213	47,177 95
1866				677,193	37,589	10,124	21,985,253	10,603,441 05	140,706	78,490 30

a Free.   b Nine months.

No. 7.—IMPORTED MANUFACTURES OF WOOL ENTERED FOR CONSUMPTION, &C., 1821-1866—Continued.

Year ending.	Flannels									Hats and hat bodies.							Hosiery, shirts, and other knit goods of wool or mixed.		
	Flannels, not otherwise specified.		Valued 30 cents or less per square yard.		Valued above 30 cents per square yard.		Composed in part of silk.	Total.		Hats of wool.		Felts or hat bodies wholly or chiefly of wool.		Total.		Hosiery		
	Sq. yds.	Values.	Pounds.	Values.	Pounds.	Values.	Values.	Values.	Duties.	Pounds.	Values.	No.	Values.	Values.	Duties.	Pounds.	Values.	Duties.
		Dollars.		Dollars.		Dollars.	Dollars.	Dollars.	Dollars.	Pounds.	Dollars.		Dollars.	Dollars.	Dollars.	Pounds.	Dollars.	Dollars.
Sept. 30—																		
1821																		
1822																	55,86*	16,760 40
1823																	302,747	110,024 10
1824		156,850						156,850	47,055 00								199,893	56,997 90
1825		1,085,609						1,065,609	319,682 70								376,927	113,618 10
1826		586,823						586,823	176,046 90								365,330	100,601 70
1827		587,250						587,250	176,175 00								230,046	80,845 10
1828		521,177						521,177	156,353 10								134,453	46,708 55
1829		95,034						95,034	28,510 20								325,856	114,049 6*
1830																	260,963	91,197 05
1831																	463,348	115,837 00
1832		118,151						118,151	46,206 08			12	2*	28	2 16		383,977	17,278 07
1833	288,788	200,580						200,580	62,661 85			147	219	240	26 46		652,080	29,370 60
1834	407,433	270,351						270,351	91,470 9*			326	57	57	53 95			28,021 20
1835	597,660	300,052						300,052	93,598 53			1,750	405	405	260 50		700,330	
1836	635,316	84,112						84,112	24,636 21			576	400	400	98 94		177,002	7,083 68
1837	166,188	9*,011						98,011	2*,251 54			700	512	512	118 9*		356,665	12,493 78
1838	199,740	172,753						172,753	52,198 52			426	260	269	60 22		1,017,096	30,298 36
1839	373,512	67,690						67,690	20,130 1*			513	269	269	76 9*		506,432	15,193 50
1840	153,281	89,046						89,046	27,496 86			178	87	87	20 1*		471,877	14,156 31
1841	212,319	30,380						30,380	9,102 25			63	31	31	7 *7		375,207	9,382 43
1842	75,805																	
June 30—																		
1843 a	35,596	17,779						17,779	4,955 44	228	95			95	40 04		61,073	18,321 90
1844	93,635	37,705						37,705	13,136 90	91	20	101	69	69	34 56		962,903	193,198,*71
1845	205,130	70,055						76,055	2*,718 20								741,242	122,372 00
1846	163,974	68,776						68,776	22,956 36								804,486	251,059 *0
1847	117,122	50,210						50,210	14,847 91								621,640	188,504 00
1848	514,121	206,895						206,895	61,723 75								731,069	219,302 70
1849	170,396	52,330						52,330	13,064 75								718,704	215,638 20
1850	281,770	88,593						88,593	22,148 25								716,135	215,440 50
1851	334,117	130,489						130,4*9	32,622 25								1,211,048	363,311 *0
1852	231,048	87,492						87,492	21,873 00								860,907	258,200 10
1853	296,218	106,381						106,381	2*,707 75								1,047,686	314,305 *0

1854	487,230	143,079			143,079	85,769 75					1,272,857	381,857 10
1855	356,545	134,811			134,811	33,703 75					1,043,057	325,187 10
1856	360,991	100,248			100,248	25,063 00					1,173,094	351,928 20
1857	304,539	105,779			105,779	26,444 75					1,740,829	522,248 70
1858		137,087			137,067	26,160 53					1,837,501	441,014 04
1859		101,011			101,011	19,363 09					710,415	172,659 60
1860		178,890			178,890	33,989 10					831,627	219,590 48
1861	1,050	186,445 327	yds. 7	6	186,778	35,524 45	223	223	44 60	701,942	168,466 08
1862	92,642	30,798			30,708	9,239 40					
1863											
1864	1,208,606	457,410			157,410	100,093 50					
1865	10,630		12,956	39,773	52,210	18,154	83,329	43,984 97	615	307 00	615	321,889 129,344 10	163,887
1866	32,883		25,976	105,660	123,088	551	149,615	85,688 22	35,772	17,856 00	35,772	603,808 246,039 20	324,464

₰ Nine months.

No. 7.—Imported Manufactures of Wool Entered for Consumption, &c., 1821-1866—Continued.

Year ending—	Flocks, waste, or shoddy.			Shawls.					Total.		Yarns.							
	Pounds.	Values.	Duties.	Camlets of goat's hair, &c.	Merino shawls.	Of wool, and cotton, silk, and silk and cotton.	Shawls, not otherwise specified.				Woolen.		Worsted.		Exceeding No. 14.		Valued under 50 cents per pound and not exceeding in fineness No. 14.	
				Values.	Values.	Values.	Pounds.	Values.	Values.	Duties.	Pounds.	Values.	Pounds.	Values.	Pounds.	Values.	Pounds.	Values.
		Dollars.	*Dollars.*	*Dollars.*	*Dollars.*	*Dollars.*		*Dollars.*	*Dollars.*	*Dollars.*		*Dollars.*		*Dollars.*		*Dollars.*		*Dollars.*
Sept. 30—																		
1821																		
1822																		
1823																		
1824																		
1825																		
1826																		
1827																		
1828																		
1829																		
1830																		
1831																		
1832																		
1833				110,789	5,249				116,029	58,014 50		4,640		98,079				
1834				12,092					12,692	6,346 00		298		166,299				
1835				a324,002	1,579				335,671	742 13		869		261,626				
1836				a380,450	19,127				403,577	9,215 88	462	812		211,804				
1837				a 90,143	2,323				101,466	1,022 12	686	334		172,128				
1838				a95,252	152,963				248,215	62,714 82	282			126,603				
1839				a128,389	282,467				410,836	115,811 47	313	86		368,602				
1840				a7,240	126,600				133,849	48,111 42	156	156		103,911				
1841				a10,529	99,178				109,707	37,687 64	1,547	807		157,564				
1842				2,122	185,298				187,420	61,854 30	1,758	660		216,558				
June 30—																		
1843b				5,438	41,436				46,874	18,749 60	2,670	1,053		60,961				
1844				52,571	271,534				324,105	129,642 00				159,020				
1845				a28,838	226,317				455,155	182,052 00				187,975				
1846				60,091	296,124				385,215	146,086 00				206,330				
1847				23,732	740,715				764,447	245,907 90				128,833				
1848				54,704	1,357,120				1,411,833	423,519 90				143,407				
1849				35,016	1,190,270				1,231,392	392,309 17				113,463				
1850				2,040	935,314				937,308	284,291 216 49				170,630				
1851				0,501	1,008,635				1,013,036	305,410 80				210,876				
1852				1,267	715,814				717,087	215,124 30				220,259				

Year			a Free.				b Nine months.					
1853			9,807	1,402,589			1,412,389	423,716 70			280,896	
1854			700	1,476,072			1,476,772	443,031 00			359,341	
1855							2,240,104	560,026 00			160,699	
1856				2,240,104			2,529,771	632,412 75			108,746	
1857				2,529,771			2,246,351	561,687 75			192,147	
1858				2,246,351			2,002,653	580,604 07			190,285	
1859				2,002,653			2,877,352	516,696 88			386,824	
1860				2,877,352			2,806,087	533,327 53			589,371	
1861		47,182	35,590	2,806,087		66,637	2,032,746	491,605 81	470,558		461,656	5,441
1862	4,718 20	442,370	49,882	1,066,149		105,925	105,925	32,407 09	337,967		372,533	
1863	44,237 60	581,234									383,011	
1864	116,246 80	621,514	28,596			34,205	34,296	20,580 04	413,028		434,549	4,017
1865	244,001 73	410,795	17,474			32,901	32,901	17,354 16	365,333		395,689	2,223
1866	214,413 24	589,490										7,499

430

3,086

No. 7.—IMPORTED MANUFACTURES OF WOOL ENTERED FOR CONSUMPTION, &C., 1821–1866—Continued.

Years ending—	Yarns—Continued. Total (Values)	Total (Duties)	All other manufactures of wool (Values)	Valued at not exceeding 33½ cents per square yard (Sq. yds.)	(Values)	All other manufactures Total (Values)	Total (Duties)	Grand total (Values)	Grand total (Duties)
September 30—									
1821	102,719	21,471 80						7,234,954	1,555,325 75
1822	166,507	33,355 04						11,752,595	2,513,562 00
1823	262,515	52,063 02						7,953,433	1,696,154 85
1824	212,706	42,685 91	144,273			144,273	43,281 90	12,124,687	1,985,066 80
1825	172,462	34,567 76	1,008,272			1,008,272	302,441 60	8,057,424	3,475,430 65
1826	136,680	27,337 71	892,340			892,340	267,703 80	8,466,226	2,548,495 20
1827	368,938	73,622 21	895,573			895,573	294,223 80	8,842,369	2,704,539 27
1828	104,738	21,081 57	678,399	367,322	146,545	824,914	262,543 11	7,193,653	2,754,224 92
1829	158,224	31,766 20	551,958	1,002,643	268,174	840,132	287,572 03	5,900,968	2,501,229 71
1830	217,611	43,680 90	353,193	1,034,780	260,000	619,233	280,147 66	13,197,364	2,333,082 21
1831			932,509	2,59N,621	695,696	744,2x6		10,440,490	5,172,566 82
1832			078,755	1,866,544	503,193	1,181,948	553,098 10	13,713,141	4,151,896 41
1833			510,539	479,417	139,829	630,368	332,367 88	7,444,035	4,662,142 38
1834			203,787			203,787	95,779 89	a10,151,950	2,641,520 65
1835			453,404			453,404	213,089 88	a24,637,881	2,266,176 03
1836			713,757			713,757	314,073 08	a10,4 0,782	5,242,550 43
1837			90,525			90,525	39,831 00	a13,130,956	1,817,292 66
1838			315,065			315,065	129,152 05	a21,034,427	2,677,638 18
1839			522,554			522,554	214,247 14	a10,804,455	3,828,925 25
1840			221,985			221,85	81,310 30	a12,943,843	2,196,949 08
1841			395,293			395,293	130,211 34	a12,943,84+	2,382,876 24
1842			336,989			336,989	117,946 15	9,089,614	2,559,817 42
June 30—									
1843	60,961	18,288 39	75,292			75,292	30,116 80	2,971,456	1,072,035 60
1844	159,020	47,706 00	390,176			396,178	158,471 20	11,751,971	4,124,155 56
1845	187,975	56,392 50	553,468			553,468	221,387 20	13,578,352	4,701,477 94
1846	266,330	70,899 00	788,027			788,027	315,210 80	12,778,834	4,436,930 71
1847	128,833	31,692 05	845,409			845,409	298,552 10	13,064,102	3,903,352 77
1848	143,407	35,851 73	790,108			790,108	227,032 40	18,495,461	5,073,711 10
1849	113,463	28,385 75	851,487			851,487	255,446 10	16,779,561	4,583,293 80
1850	170,039	42,659 75	1,014,150			1,014,159	574,247 70	19,620,619	5,415,687 65
1851	216,878	54,219 00	1,237,810			1,237,816	371,344 60	22,358,679	6,179,538 55
1852	220,259	55,064 75	591,014			591,054	178,460 20	20,611,286	5,665,183 05
1853	280,896	70,224 00	1,124,932			1,124,932	337,479 60	31,819,771	8,707,248 80

Year										
1854			359,341	80,835 25	1,423,330			426,989 00	37,994,473	10,568,666 05
1855			160,599	40,109 75	274,514			82,354 20	27,754,372	7,584,260 35
1856			198,746	49,686 50	505,004			151,501 20	35,582,712	9,718,002 85
1857			192,147	48,036 75	693,640			208,002 00	35,289,315	9,623,906 05
1858			196,285	37,294 15	663,372			159,200 28	29,534,655	6,202,491 26
1859			386,824	73,406 56	1,853,463			444,831 12	37,395,594	7,903,577 07
1860			593,371	112,740 49	1,311,578			314,778 72	43,141,068	9,139,103 58
1861	6,289		485,430	95,652 22	472,811	12,337	15,164	118,746 08	30,430,140	6,282,930 70
1862	5,075		372,533	122,231 10	6,434,262			1,929,678 60	15,639,813	4,936,725 54
1863	12,829		383,011	150,175 74	10,822,145			806,750 75	21,524,802	7,368,120 62
1864	14,232		434,549	163,443 76	7,968,491			788,971 85	33,346,702	13,238,984 64
1865	45,081 28,616		305,589	188,943 03	4,964,907			482,453 50	21,929,487	12,177,142 57
1866	404,848 517,965		559,667 273,194 56	13,639,793	132,351 143,161		7,006,925 14	13,982,954	58,719,736	30,813,761 51

a During these years dress and piece goods and camlets of goat's hair, &c., were free of duty.

b Nine months.

No. 8.—STATEMENT SHOWING THE QUANTITIES AND VALUES OF IMPORTED MANUFACTURES OF WOOL ENTERED FOR CONSUMPTION IN THE UNITED STATES, INCLUDING BOTH ENTRIES FOR IMMEDIATE CONSUMPTION AND WITHDRAWALS FROM WAREHOUSE FOR CONSUMPTION; ALSO SHOWING THE RATES OF DUTY AND AMOUNTS OF ACCRUING DUTIES, DURING THE YEARS ENDING JUNE 30, FROM 1867 TO 1886, INCLUSIVE.

ARTICLES.	Rates of duty.	1867. Quantities.	1867. Values.	1867. Duties.	1868. Quantities.	1868. Values.	1868. Duties.	1869. Quantities.	1869. Values.	1869. Duties.
			Dollars.	Dollars.		Dollars.	Dollars.		Dollars.	Dollars.
Balmorals:										
Composed wholly or in part of wool ......pounds.	50c. p. lb. & 35 p.c	467	476 00	189 05						
Do ......pounds.	24c. p. lb. & 35 p.c.	322,085	308,407 00	185,456 85	28,592	23,659 00	15,142 73			
Valued at not exceeding 40 cents per pound .. pounds.	20c. p. lb. & 35 p.c.				39	59 00	28 45	10	4 00	3 40
Valued at above 40 and not exceeding 60 cents per pound ...pounds.	30c. p. lb. & 35 p.c.				5,516	3,214 00	2,779 70	5	3 00	2 55
Valued at above 60 and not exceeding 80 cents per pound, ...pounds.	40c. p. lb. & 35 p.c.				13,867	10,415 05	9,192 05	11,836	8,368 00	7,664 00
Valued at above 80 cents per pound ...pounds	50c. p. lb. & 35 p.c.				27,721.50	41,210 48	28,284 41	152,351	195,086 00	144,065 60
Total balmorals......		323,452	308,883 00	185,048 80	75,735.50	78,557 53	55,427	34 164,204	204,061 0?	152,335 55
Belts or felts, endless, for paper or printing machines...pounds.	20c. p. lb. & 35 p.c.	130,755	110,368 00	75,279 80	91,882	92,465 37	50,739 28	102,593	97,221 00	54,545 05
Blankets:										
Valued at not exceeding 28 cents per pound .. pounds.	12c. p. lb. & 20 p.c.	740,727	156,329 78	120,151 40	316	167 00	71 32			
Valued at over 28 and not exceeding 40 cents per pound, ..pounds.	24c. p. lb. & 25 p.c.	58,562	21,272 00	19,372 88	1,473	551 00	491 27			
Valued at above 40 cents per pound .. pounds.	24c. p. lb. & 30 p.c.	130,912.25	85,451 02	58,494 25	2,063	1,333 00	1,039 07			
Valued at not exceeding 40 cents per pound ...pounds.	20c. p. lb. & 35 p.c.				27,800	12,866 25	10,082 00	1,135.50	316 34	338 82
Valued at above 40 and not exceeding 60 cents per pound, ...pounds.	30c. p. lb. & 35 p.c.	1,170	616 25	566 69	12,752.50	6,412 00	6,000 96	11,157	5,730 55	5,352 79
Valued at above 60 and not exceeding 80 cents per pound, ...pounds.	40c. p. lb. & 35p.c.	8,034.50	13,792 38	8,401 13	2,530	1,841 75	1,650 61	3,704	2,661 45	2,413 11

Description	Rate of duty									
Valued at above 60 cents per pound...........pounds..	50c. p. lb. & 35 p. c.	2,043.50	2,846 40	2,017 99	7,372.25	6,089 00	5,817 28	3,231.50	3,466 00	2,828 85
Total blankets...........		948,349.25	260,298 83	209,004 34	55,005.75	29,260 00	25,228 44	19,228	12,174 34	10,933 57
Bunting: And all stained, colored, or printed goods.	50 p. c.		7,043,759.25	3,521,879 62		238,644 00	119,322 00		8,978 00	4,489 00
Bunting...........sq. yards.	6c. p. sq. yd. & 30 p. c.			7,800		3,010 00	1,371 54			
Do...........do.	20c. p. sq. yd. & 35 p. c.			31,049		9,555 00	9,554 05	43,038	9,429 00	11,907 75
Carpets and carpeting of all kinds: Brussels and tapestry Brussels, printed on the warp, square...........yards.	50c. p. sq. yd	1,558,567.23	1,571,135.25	779,283 62	13,819	16,287 00	6,909 50			
Do...........sq. yards.	50c. p. sq. yd. & 50 p. c.				279	930 00	604 50			
Wilton, Saxony, Aubusson, velvet, and all Jacquard woven— Value $1.25 or less per sq. yd...........sq. yards.	70c. p. sq. yd.	62,531.70	74,990.33	43,772 20						
Value over $1.25 per sq. yd...........sq. yards.	80c. p. sq. yd.	376,260.12	555,959.00	301,008 10	12,741.50	19,298 00	10,194 80	1,819.25	2,781 00	1,455 40
Aubusson, Axminster, and Chenille carpets and carpets woven whole for rooms.			39,272 00	19,030 00		227 00	181 60			
Do...........sq. yards.	80 p. c.									
Do...........do.	50 p. c.					313,863 18	156,931 59			
Brussels carpets...........do.	44c. p. sq. yd. & 35 p. c.	152,664.50	240,966.00	154,150 48	547,976.75	735,704 97	498,627 51	687,820.75	1,100,453 00	706,799 68
Druggets and bockings, printed, colored, or otherwise.	25c. p. sq. yd.	269,934.50	129,297.00	66,483 63	1,857	696 00	464 38	675 00		108 75
Do...........sq. yards.	25c. p. sq. yd. & 35 p. c.	9,447	4,945.00	4,092 50	65,772.73	29,298 00	26,697 48	43,294	19,700 61	17,718 71
Mats, screens, hassocks, and rugs, not exclusively vegetable material	50 p. c.		139,050.00	62,572 50		55,972 00	25,187 40		2,008 00	1,004 00
Do...........	45 p. c.								70,386 40	31,673 88
Of wool, flax, or cotton, or parts of either, or other material not specially enumerated or provided for...........	do	132,525.98		53,010 30		155,609 00	62,243 00		135,338 00	54,135 20
Patent velvet and tapestry velvet carpets, printed on the warp, or otherwise...........sq. yards.	40c. p. sq. yd. & 35 p. c.	52,399	86,841.00	51,353 95	245,248.50	380,782 00	231,373 10	285,217	462,000 00	275,096 80

No. 8.—STATEMENT SHOWING THE QUANTITIES AND VALUES OF IMPORTED MANUFACTURES OF WOOL ENTERED FOR CONSUMPTION IN THE UNITED STATES, &c., DURING THE YEARS ENDING JUNE 30, FROM 1867 TO 1866, INCLUSIVE—Continued.

ARTICLES.	Rates of duty.	1867 Quantities.	1867 Values.	1867 Duties.	1868 Quantities.	1868 Values.	1868 Duties.	1869 Quantities.	1869 Values.	1869 Duties.
Carpets and carpeting of all kinds—Continued.										
Saxony, Wilton, and Tournay velvet carpets ...sq. yards.	70c. p. sq. yd. & 35 p. c	13,355	*Dollars.* 31,086 00	*Dollars.* 20,543 00	61,080 25	*Dollars.* 126,030 00	*Dollars.* 80,869 83	99,330 25	*Dollars.* 197,127 00	*Dollars.* 138,522 10
Tapestry Brussels, printed on the warp, or otherwise. ...sq. yards.	28c. p. sq. yd. & 35 p. c	568,334 87	551,927 77	352,308 27	1,839,478 75	1,001,039 13	1,075,420 27	2,053,737	1,667,002 37	1,160,337 19
Treble ingrain, three-ply, and worsted chain, Venetian carpets....sq. yards.	40c. p. sq. yd	54,035 75	41,428 50	21,622 30	2,808	717 00	1,123 20			
Do ...do.	17c. p. sq. yd. & 35 p. c	14,346	13,951 00	7,321 67	29,153 50	28,010 31	14,760 56	21,050 50	19,717 54	10,032 72
Yarn, Venetian, and two-ply ingrain carpets..sq. yards.	30c. p. sq. yd	207		62 10						
Do ...do.	35c. p. sq. yd	158,377 75	111,754 00	55,432 21	75,895 50	51,930 38	27,285 19	56,761	38,404 75	20,252 98
Do ...do.	12c. p. sq. yd. & 35 p. c	25,191	18,005 82	9,356 48						
Total carpets........			3,743,124 63	2,002,009 98		3,516,468 00	2,224,874 61		4,085,557 67	2,659,379 41
Clothing, ready-made, and wearing apparel (except knit goods), not especially enumerated or provided for, composed wholly or in part of wool, worsted, the hair of the alpaca, goat, or other like animals, made up or manufactured wholly or in part by the tailor, seamstress, or manufacturer: Cloaks, dolmans, jackets, talmas, ulsters, or other outside garments for ladies' and children's apparel, and goods of similar description, or used for like purposes, ... pounds..	50c. p. lb. & 40 p. c.	611 13	1,198 01	784 77	161,030	646,101 00	339,255 40	804,874 75	1,549,295 50	1,067,155 58

Description	Rate of duty	(1)	(2)	(3)	(4)	(5)	(6)	(7)	(8)	(9)
Clothing, ready-made, and wearing apparel of every description not specially enumerated or provided for, and balmoral skirts and skirting, and goods of similar description or used for like purposes......pounds.	24c. p. lb. & 40 p. e.	60,560	113,803 90	62,216 96	4,170 00	2,617	2,272 08	530	1,050 00	547 20
Do......do.	50c. p. lb. & 35 p. c.	.....	.....	.....	6,010 00	3,231	4,034 00	.....	313,831 93	160,232 52
Do......do.	50c. p. lb. & 40 p. c.	32,550	91,977 68	53,006 07	889,126 10	253,663.75	482,427 32	69,399.50		
Total clothing......		102,721.13	206,979 59	116,066 80	1,546,307 10	420,931.75	827,988 80	904,804.25	1,804,177 43	1,227,095 30
Cloths, woolen: Value less than $2 per square yard......pounds.	24c. p. lb. & 40 p. e.	8,040,505.50	9,186,084 09	5,603,754 96	400,490 00	339,849	241,759 70	50,692	50,090 06	34,722 46
Value over $2 per square yard......pounds.	24c. p. lb. & 45 p. e.	26,882.00	68,145 44	32,017 27	4,213 00	1,849	2,339 61			
Cloths......do.	50c. p. lb. & 35 p. c.	816,138.45	1,301,866 18	863,722 38	6,479,254 14	4,181,678.50	4,358,078 20	4,275,679.25	6,171,933 17	4,298,016 36
Total cloths......		8,883,636.55	10,545,096 71	6,500,004 61	6,883,957 14	4,623,376.60	4,602,677 57	4,345,371.25	6,222,034 12	4,332,738 82
Dress goods, women's and children's, coat linings, Italian cloths, and goods of like description: Gray or uncolored— Valued not over 30 cents per sq. yard..sq. yards.	4c. p. sq. yd. & 25 p. c.	511,223.75	105,751 96	46,886 94	8,895 00	57,342	4,517 43	996	156 00	62 88
Do......do.	5½c. p. sq. yd. & 30 p. c.									
Valued over 30 cents per sq. yard......sq. yards.	6c. p. sq. yd. & 30 p. c.	155,950.50	70,215 75	30,421 76	1 00	2	42			
Printed or colored— Valued at not over 30 cents per square yard......sq. yards.	4c. p. sq. yd. & 30 p. c.	42,902,805	10,208,535 66	4,778,069 90	218,723 57	1,138,231	111,146 31	9,031	2,316 00	1,092 04
Valued over 30 cents per sq. yard......sq. yards.	6c. p. sq. yd. & 35 p. c.	19,342,307.50	8,090,058 28	3,994,162 44	6,510 00	30,925	4,134 00			
Composed in part of wool, worsted, the hair of the alpaca, goat, or other animals— Valued at not exceeding 20 cents per square yard......sq. yards.	6c. p. sq. yd. & 35 p. c.					24,681,603.50				
Valued at above 20 cents per sq. yard..sq. yards.	8c. p. sq. yd. & 40 p. c.	5,639,183.50	1,737,707 08	1,188,217 75	4,382,630 91		3,008,817 03	31,621,006.35	5,614,011 02	3,821,205 79
					10,642,759 05	37,156,202.50	7,229,510 82	33,060,705.10	10,542,042 52	6,862,753 42

No. 8.—Statement showing the Quantities and Values of Imported Manufactures of Wool entered for Consumption in the United States, &c., during the years ending June 30, from 1867 to 1886, inclusive—Continued.

ARTICLES.	Rates of duty.	1867 Quantities.	1867 Values.	1867 Duties.	1868 Quantities.	1868 Values.	1868 Duties.	1869 Quantities.	1869 Values.	1869 Duties.
Dress goods, &c.—Continued. Composed wholly of wool, worsted, the hair of the alpaca, goat, or other animal, or of a mixture of them, and all such goods of like description, with selvedges made wholly or in part of other materials, or with threads of other materials introduced for the purpose of changing the classification— All weighing over 4 oz. per sq. yard ...pounds..	50c. p. lb. & 35 p. c.	110,873	*Dollars.* 138,376 00	*Dollars.* 160,868 10	864,152.75	*Dollars.* 1,608,842 52	*Dollars.* 995,171 20	1,220,510.50	*Dollars.* 2,221,063 53	*Dollars.* 1,387,637 48
Total dress goods....			20,356,635 33	10,092,226 89		16,868,362 03	11,353,306 27		18,240,469 67	12,072,771 61
Flannels: Colored, printed, or part silk.	50 p. c		186,067 00	93,033 50						
Unbleached, valued 30 cents or less per square yard, ...pounds.	24c. p. lb. & 30 p. c.	18,656.12	16,026 65	8,865 46						
Colored, value over 30 cents per square yard ...pounds.	24c. p. lb. & 33 p. c.	73,411.75	104,838 18	54,312 18	4,276	6,686 00	3,366 34	264	338 00	181 66
Valued at not exceeding 40 cents per pound...pounds.	20c. p. lb. & 35 p. c.	1,820	610 00	577 50	11,745.50	4,092 40	3,991 44	1,371	412 00	418 40
Valued at above 40 and not exceeding 60 cents per pound, ...pounds	30c. p. lb. & 35 p. c.	10,002	5,737 00	5,029 55	4,417.50	4,427 50	2,877 84	74	45 03	37 06
Valued at above 60 and not exceeding 80 cents per pound, ...pounds	40c. p. lb. & 35 p. c.	322	237 00	211 75	3,523	2,739 08	2,367 88	948.50	660 00	610 40
Valued at above 80 cents per pound...pounds.	50c. p. lb. & 35 p. c	2,181.50	2,697 47	2,034 86	751	1,154 00	779 40	7,970.25	17,603 45	10,146 34
Total flannels....			316,273 30	164,004 80	24,713	19,698 98	13,382 04	10,627.75	19,058 50	11,304 76

Description	Rate	Quantity	Value	Duty	Quantity	Value	Duty	Quantity	Value	Duty
Hats of wool:										
Valued at above 40 and not exceeding 60 cents per pound, ... pounds.	24c. p. lb. & 35 p. c.	13,022	12,773 15	8,075 88	1,778	1,523 00	1,066 45	142	69 30	06 82
Do ...... do.	30c. p. lb. & 35 p. c.									
Valued at above 60 and not exceeding 80 cents per pound, ...pounds.	40c. p. lb. & 35 p. c.	31,955	38,085 00	29,989 75	1,569	1,112 00	1,016 80	433	308 00	281 00
Valued at over 80 cents per pound ......pounds.	50c. p. lb. & 35 p. c.				60,414	125,565 24	74,154 83	55,515.50	97,631 77	01,935 87
Flat roundings or trimmings.	30 p. c.								56 00	10 80
Do.	10 p. c.								101 00	10 10
Total hats of wool		46,977	50,808 15	37,365 63	63,761	128,200 24	76,238 08		98,186 07	03,310 59
Knit goods:										
Hosiery:—										
Valued at not over 40 cents per pound ......pounds.	20c. p. lb. & 35 p. c.							24	15 00	10 05
Valued at above 40 and not exceeding 60 cents per pound ...... pounds.	30c. p. lb. & 35 p. c.							11,015	5,636 00	5,277 10
Valued at above 60 and not exceeding 80 cents per pound ......pounds.	40c. p. lb. & 35 p. c.							4,307	3,129 00	2,817 95
Valued at above 80 cents per pound ...... pounds.	50c. p. lb. & 35 p. c.							223,685.50	515,559 95	202,288 73
Total hosiery								239,031.50	524,339 95	300,393 83
Shirts, drawers, and other knit goods—										
Valued at not over 40 cents per pound ......pounds.	20c. p. lb. & 35 p. c.				3	369	1 80	272	1,058 00	371 80
Valued at above 40 and not exceeding 60 cents per pound ......pounds.	30c. p. lb. & 35 p. c.							33,325	17,184 00	16,011 90
Valued at above 60 and not exceeding 80 cents per pound ...... pounds.	40c. p. lb. & 35 p. c.				2,081	1,133 00	1,020 85	10,160	6,647 00	6,390 45
Valued at above 80 cents per pound	50c. p. lb. & 35 p. c.							12,304.26	19,271 15	12,897 03
Knit goods, and all goods made on knitting frames—All not specified	35 p. c.		896 00	313 60						
Do ...... pounds.	20c. p. lb. & 30 p. c.	370,504.75	841,423 50	326,628 00	10,341	46,182 00	17,722 80			
Total knit goods, except hosiery			842,310 50	326,841 00	21,425	47,318 09	18,745 54	56,001.25	44,160 15	35,071 18

No. 8.—Statement showing the Quantities and Values of Imported Manufactures of Wool entered for Consumption in the United States, &c., during the years ending June 30, from 1867 to 1886, inclusive—Continued.

ARTICLES.	Rates of duty.	1867. Quantities.	1867. Values.	1867. Duties.	1868. Quantities.	1868. Values.	1868. Duties.	1869. Quantities.	1869. Values.	1869. Duties.
			Dollars.	*Dollars.*		*Dollars.*	*Dollars.*		*Dollars.*	*Dollars.*
Rags, shoddy, mungo, waste, and flocks, woolen ....pounds	10 p.c.	5,313,786	33,251 63	3,325 16		9,823 00	982 30			
Do ...... do	3c. p. lb		482,526 00	159,413 58						
Do ...... do	12c. p. lb	248,003	19,628 00	29,760 36	619,916	89,767 00	74,389 92	574,579	63,334 00	63,049 48
Shawls:										
Woolen ....pounds	24c. p. lb. & 40 p. c.	56,956	82,321 48	46,598 09						
Do ..... do	24c. p. lb. & 45 p. c.	45,158	84,219 90	48,736 87						
Do ..... do	35c. p. lb. & 50 p. c.				4,679	6,083 00	4,679 15			
Do ..... do	50c. p. lb. & 35 p. c.				104,081.50	305,873 17	159,098 36	41,637.50	139,001 47	69,895 31
Worsted—										
Not otherwise specified. ...pounds	50c. p. lb. & 45 p. c.	200	3,558 00	1,701 10	7.50	25 40	15 18			
Do ...... pounds	50c. p. lb. & 40 p. c.	46,702	157,040 35	86,127 14	882.25	1,669 00	967 40			
Total shawls.....		149,016	327,139 73	183,163 20	109,150.25	313,650 57	164,778 09	41,857.50	139,901 47	69,895 31
Webbings, gorings, suspenders, braces, beltings, bindings, braids, galloons, fringes, gimps, cords, cords and tassels, dress trimmings, head nets, buttons or barrel buttons, or buttons of other forms for tassels or ornaments, wrought by hand or braided by machinery, made of wool or of which wool, worsted, the hair of the alpaca, goat, or other animals is a component material ....pounds	50c. p. lb. & 50 p. c.	98,892	166,616 00	129,754 00	376,003.75	742,113 00	559,058 98	182,714.25	356,918 00	269,816 13
Yarns, woolen and worsted:										
Valued less than 50 cents per pound not exceeding No. 14 ......pounds	16c. p. lb. & 25 p. c	1,508	1,766 85	682 99						
Valued over 50 cents and not over $1 per pound pounds	20c. p. lb. & 25 p. c.	37,174 25	31,403 12	15,286 03	2.50	1 00	75			
Valued over $1 per lb ...lbs	24c. p. lb. & 30 p. c.	325,239 50	400,731 29	200,978 66	9,242	4,150 00	3,464 88			
Do .... do	24c. p. lb. & 40 p. c.				633	803 00	473 12			

Item	Rate	C1	C2	C3	C4	C5	C6	C7	C8	C9
Valued at not exceeding 40 cents per pound ....pounds.	20c. p. lb. & 35 p. c.	7,503.75	3,549 77	2,743 57	2,646.50	1,935 00	1,206 55	1,335.50	449 00	424 25
Valued at above 40 and not exceeding 60 cents per pound ......pounds.	30c. p. lb. & 35 p. c.	407	231 02	202 96	4,951.25	2,839 65	2,479 26	14,202	7,376 00	6,842 20
Valued at above 60 and not exceeding 80 cents per pound ....pounds	40c. p. lb. & 35 p. c.	49	40 00	33 60	12,577.75	9,142 00	8,223 80	6,458.75	4,527 00	4,167 95
Valued at above 80 cents per pound ......pounds.	50c. p. lb. & 35 p. c.	60,515	80,844 00	58,566 90	499,423.75	638,930 89	472,637 69	450,441.25	531,016 22	411,076 31
Total yarns......		432,398.56	527,566 05	278,492 70	520,476.75	655,807 54	488,485 05	472,437.50	543,368 22	422,510 71
All manufactures of every description, not specially enumerated or provided for, made wholly or in part of wool: Manufactures not otherwise specified......pounds.	50c. p. lb. & 35 p.c.	228,639.25	287,864 72	215,072 28	1,079,481.50	1,212,725 85	964,109 80	235,364.75	329,909 97	233,150 86
Worsted, the hair of the alpaca, goat, or other animals (except such as are composed in part of wool)— Valued at not exceeding 40 cts. per pound, pounds	20c. p. lb. & 35 p. c.	14,865	6,188 00	5,137 05	5,754	2,883 00	2,136 65	15,401	5,491 05	5,002 07
Valued at above 40 and not exceeding 60 cents per pound....pounds.	30c. p. lb. & 35 p. c.	60	147 00	68 10	33,398	16,141 00	15,668 75	3,444	1,793.00	1,660 75
Valued at above 60 and not exceeding 80 cents per pound....pounds.	40c. p. lb. & 35 p. c.	a884	715 00	603 85	105,848.50	80,563 76	70,536 72	5,409.50	4,153 00	3,617 35
Do ......do.	24c. p. lb. & 35 p. c.				34	38 00	21 46			
Valued at above 80 cents per pound......pounds.	50c. p. lb. & 35 p. c.				203	212 00	175 70			
Total manufactures not elsewhere specified......		244,448.25	294,909 72	220,881 28	1,224,660	1,312,563 61	1,052,709 68	1,559,117.25	1,696,948 00	1,443,490 42
								1,818,736 50	2,238,295 02	1,666,921 40
Grand total......			45,746,750 44	24,268,531 45		33,161,116 42	22,032,922 62		34,812,576.61	23,454,900 45

a 40 cents per pound and 30 per cent.

No. 8.—STATEMENT SHOWING THE QUANTITIES AND VALUES OF IMPORTED MANUFACTURES OF WOOL, ENTERED FOR CONSUMPTION IN THE UNITED STATES, &C., DURING THE YEARS ENDING JUNE 30, FROM 1867 TO 1886, INCLUSIVE.—Continued.

ARTICLES.	Rate of duty.	1870.			1871.			1872.		
		Quantities.	Values.	Duties.	Quantities.	Values.	Duties.	Quantities.	Values.	Duties.
			Dollars.	Dollars.		Dollars.	Dollars.		Dollars.	Dollars.
Balmorals:										
Valued at not exceeding 40 cents per pound...pounds	20c. p. lb. & 35 p. c.				9	6 75	4 16	57		11 40
Valued at above 40 and not exceeding 60 cents per pound...pounds	30c. p. lb. & 35 p. c	5	3 00	2 55	982	508 00	471 70	9,251	4,707 00	4,422 75
Valued at above 60 and not exceeding 80 cents per pound...pounds	40c. p. lb. & 35 p. c.	1,382	966 00	690 90	437	274 00	270 70	7,152	5,351 00	4,733 65
Valued at above 80 cents per pound...pounds	50c. p. lb. & 35 p. c.	3	4 00	2 90	2,012	2,679 00	1,943 65	324,592.50	491,303 81	334,252 58
Total balmorals		1,390	973 00	696 35	3,440	3,465 75	2,690 21	341,052.50	501,361 81	343,420 38
Belts or felts, endless, for paper or printing machines...pounds	20c. p. lb. & 35 p. c.	101,045	95,891 00	63,739 35	100,028	65,572 00	53,635 80	115,080.25	114,348 00	63,037 85
Blankets:										
Valued at not exceeding 40 cents per pound...pounds	20c. p. lb. & 35 p. c.	434	178 07	149 12	2,937.50	789 00	863 65	1,156	384 10	365 63
Valued at above 40 and not exceeding 60 cents per pound...pounds	30c. p. lb. & 35 p. c.	750	400 25	365 09	2,005	922 00	924 30	6,341.50	3,299 80	3,057 28
Valued at above 60 and not exceeding 80 cents per pound...pounds	40c. p. lb. & 35 p. c.	432	273 00	268 35				743.50	569 20	490 62
Valued at above 80 cents per pound...pounds	50c. p. lb. & 35 p. c.	354.25	409 05	341 30	3,642.50	2,730 60	2,412 71	24,807	24,209 26	20,897 74
Weighing 4 ounces and over per square yard...pounds	50c. p. lb. & 35 p. c. less 10 p. c.				15,695	14,985 35	12,092 37	50	91 00	56 85
Total blankets		1,970.25	1,320 37	1,123 86	24,280	19,426 05	17,292 03	33,098	28,613 36	24,874 22
Bunting:										
And all stained, colored, or printed goods	50 p. c.		261 00	130 50						
Bunting...sq. yards	20c. p. sq. yd. & 35	12,101	2,084 30	3,371 71	17,199 75	4,167 00	4,898 40	24,897 40	7,043 25	7,444 62

Article	Rate	Col 1	Col 2	Col 3	Col 4	Col 5	Col 6	Col 7	Col 8	Col 9
Carpets and carpeting of all kinds: Brussels and tapestry Brussels, printed on the warp....sq. yards.	50c. p. sq. yd	11 25	36 00	22 50	34 13	94 57	68 25			
Aubusson, Aixminster, and chenille carpets and carpets woven whole for rooms, sq. yards.	50 p. c.	259,013 50	518,027 00	341,860	162,428 75	324,857 50	209,290	155,400 92	310,801 85	203,704
Brussels carpets....do...	44c. p. sq. yd. & 35 p. c.	1,081,388 08	1,626,767 58	1,163,680 50	1,135,879 82	1,604,956 98	1,204,850 87	878,077 04	1,276,122 00	961,896 25
Druggets and bockings, printed, colored, or otherwise....sq. yards.	25c. p. sq. yd. & 35 p. c.	17,030 06	19,273 73	41,137	25,344 72	28,453 00	61,544 67	18,849 51	20,815 00	46,257
Mats, screens, hassocks, and rugs, not exclusively vegetable material	50 p. c.	49,935 60	110,968 00		46,536 13	103,413 61		11 50	23 00	
Do.	45 p. c.							30,717 05	68,260 11	
Of wool, flax, or cotton, or parts of either, or other material not specially enumerated or provided for.	40 p. c.	53,737 88	134,344 70		45,121 13	112,802 83		40,719 90	101,799 74	
Patent velvet and tapestry velvet carpets, printed on the warp, or otherwise, sq. yards.	40c. p. sq. yd. & 35 p. c.	246,652 88	404,790 00	262,441	276,823 30	436,834 26	300,828 25	215,587 55	363,707 00	220,735 25
Saxony, Wilton, and Tournay velvet carpets...sq. yards.	70c. p. sq. yd. & 35 p. c.	200,638 01	291,140 00	141,055 70	188,488 47	260,208 00	138,165 25	125,439 65	180,272 00	89,063 50
Tapestry Brussels printed on the warp, or otherwise, sq. yards.	28c. p. sq. yd. & 35 p. c.	1,591,468 78	2,339,780 91	2,759,090 75	1,400,769 66	1,986,026 06	2,517,716 25	1,181,599 61	1,753,017 49	2,027,976 75
Treble ingrain, three-ply, and worsted chain Venetian carpets...sq. yards.	17c. p. sq. yd. & 35 p. c.	10,043 45	18,818 00	20,336 16	11,329 76	21,008 40	23,393	6,937 65	12,791 12	14,104 50
Yarn, Venetian, and two-ply ingrain carpets ...sq. yards.	12c. p. sq. yd. & 35 p. c.	25,771 25	50,333 00	67,655 75	27,528 42	51,404 14	79,474 75	22,055 15	40,817 39	64,742 25
Total carpets		3,535,690 74	5,514,278 92		3,320,284 29	4,932,089 35		2,675,093 53	4,129,206 70	

Clothing, ready-made, and wearing apparel (except knit goods), not specially enumerated or provided for, composed wholly or in part of wool, worsted, the hair of the alpaca, goat, or other like animals, made up or man-

No. 8.—Statement showing the Quantities and Values of Imported Manufactures of Wool entered for Consumption in the United States, &c., during the years ending June 30, from 1867 to 1886, inclusive—Continued.

ARTICLES.	Rates of duty.	1870. Quantities.	1870. Values.	1870. Duties.	1871. Quantities.	1871. Values.	1871. Duties.	1872. Quantities.	1872. Values.	1872. Duties.
Clothing, &c.—Continued. ufactured wholly or in part by the tailor, seamstress, or manufacturer:			*Dollars.*	*Dollars.*		*Dollars.*	*Dollars.*		*Dollars.*	*Dollars.*
Cloaks, dolmans, jackets, talmas, ulsters, or other outside garments for ladies' and children's apparel, and goods of similar description, or used for like purposes, ...pounds.	50c. p. lb. & 40 p. c.	495,167	1,841,147 00	984,042 30	582,545 67	2,116,220 25	1,137,760 90	75,031.63	276,506 00	148,154 25
Clothing, ready-made, and wearing apparel of every description not specially enumerated or provided for, and balmoral skirts and skirting, and goods of similar description or used for like purposes......pounds. ....do.....	24c. p. lb. & 40 p. c. 50c. p. lb. & 40 p. c.	362 39,946 00	560 00 154,163 00	314 48 81,638 53	34,010.75	133,370 73	70,807 26	113,268.80	564,824 29	262,574 11
Total clothing ...		535,475 00	1,993,679 00	1,065,995 31	617,456.42	2,249,600 00	1,298,568 22	188,320.43	841,420 20	430,728 36
Cloths, woolen: Value less than 80 per square yard..........pounds. Cloths	24c. p. lb. & 40 p. c 50c. p. lb. & 35 p. c.	4,796 4,369,298.50	5,200 00 6,407,296 86	3,233 44 4,427,203 22	6,429,297.12	9,167,365 28	6,430,226 41	8,958,511.87	12,887,288 45	8,989,806 90
Total cloths		4,374,094.50	6,412,502 86	4,430,430 06	6,429,297.12	9,187,365 28	6,430,226 41	8,958,511.87	12,887,288 45	8,989,806 90
Dress goods, women's and children's, coat linings, Italian cloths, and goods of like description: Composed in part of wool, worsted, the hair of the alpaca, goat, or other animals—Valued at not exceeding 20 cents per square yard..........sq. yards.	6c. p. sq. yd. & 35 p. c.	28,335,800 70	4,965,311 80	3,457,017 16	36,735,561	6,421,148 30	4,451,535 71	28,789,674 25	5,278,653 00	3,574,979 01

Article / classification	Rate									
Valued at above 20 cents per sq. yd....sq. yards..	8c. p. sq. yd. & 40 p. c.	34,496,138.50	10,639,551 60	6,975,611 73	35,978,009.63	11,458,083 77	7,461,522 28	42,664,533	14,312,290 96	9,138,060 62
Composed wholly of wool, worsted, the hair of the alpaca, goat, or other animals, or of a mixture of them, and all such goods of like description, with selvedges made wholly or in part of other materials, or with threads of other materials introduced for the purpose of changing the classification— All weighing over 4 oz. per sq. yard..pounds..	50c. p. lb. & 35 p. c.	1,233,365	2,520,118 08	1,488,724 05	2,290,259 25	3,772,190 37	2,465,399 26	2,744,760.25	4,480,668 00	2,940,620 65
Total dress goods......			18,044,962 06	11,891,262 94		21,651,422 64	14,378,451 25		24,071,831 96	16,053,080 58
Flannels: Valued at not exceeding 40 cents per pound...pounds..	20c. p. lb. & 35 p. c.	8	16 20	7 27	719	182 76	207 77	50	19 00	16 65
Valued at above 40 and not exceeding 60 cents per pound, ..pounds..	30c. p. lb. & 35 p. c.	382.25	210 00	188 18	50	23 00	23 03	600	266 00	243 10
Valued at above 60 and not exceeding 80 cents per pound, ...pounds..	40c. p. lb. & 35 p. c.	1,531.73	1,039 00	980 20	2,021.50	1,014 00	1,373 50	903.25	585 48	566 32
Valued at above 80 cents per pound ....pounds..	50c. p. lb. & 35 p. c.	8,007	10,728 00	7,758 31	8,290.12	5,300 73	3,470 33	3,761.50	6,467 75	4,144 46
Total flannels......		9,029	12,004 20	8,933 96	6,020.62	7,120 49	5,074 65	5,211.75	7,338 23	4,970 03
Hats of wool: Valued at above 40 and not exceeding 60 cents per pound, ..pounds..	30c. p. lb. & 35 p. c.				725	330 00	333 00			
Valued at above 60 and not exceeding 80 cents per pound, ...pounds..	40c. p. lb. & 35 p. c.	1,164	805 00	747 35	80	51 00	49 85	20	15 00	13 25
Valued at over 60 cents per pound ....pounds..	50c. p. lb. & 35 p. c.									
Hat roundings or trimmings..	10 p. c.									
Total hats of wool......		49,126.50	83,644 00	63,838 00	60,620.12	130,899 00	60,624 72	53,656	90,878 46 / 278 00	60,735 46 / 27 80
Knit goods:— Hosiery:— Valued at above 40 and not exceeding 60 cents per pound..... pounds..	30c. p. lb. & 35 p. c.	50,290.50	84,449 00	54,566 01	70,425.12	131,280 00	81,007 57	867	470 00	427 75

No. 8.—STATEMENT SHOWING THE QUANTITIES AND VALUES OF IMPORTED MANUFACTURES OF WOOL ENTERED FOR CONSUMPTION IN THE UNITED STATES, &c., DURING THE YEARS ENDING JUNE 30, FROM 1867 TO 1886, INCLUSIVE—Continued.

ARTICLES.	Rates of duty.	1870. Quantities.	1870. Values.	1870. Duties.	1871. Quantities.	1871. Values.	1871. Duties.	1872. Quantities.	1872. Values.	1872. Duties.
			Dollars.	Dollars.		Dollars.	Dollars.		Dollars.	Dollars.
Knit goods:										
Hosiery—										
Valued at above 60 cents per pound .... pounds.	40c. p. lb. & 35 p. c.	3	2 00	1 00	677.50	444 00	426 40	425	333 00	286 57
Valued at above 80 cents per pound ...... pounds.	50c. p. lb. & 35 p. c.	188,866.50	453,031 00	253,300 11	241,009.50	536,612 50	308,769 14	251,702.62	570,206 70	325,468 65
Total hosiery		188,860.50	453,933 00	253,311 01	242,587	537,056 50	309,195 54	253,084.62	571,018 70	326,182 07
Shirts, drawers, and other knit goods—										
Valued at not over 40 cents per pound, pounds.	20c. p. lb. & 35 p.c.	1,100	147 00	273 25	512	307 00	269 85	814	435 50	403 45
Valued at above 40 and not exceeding 60 cents per pound ...... pounds.	30c. p. lb. & 35 p. c.	11,195	5,049 00	5,440 65	1,303	753 00	654 45	1,180	895 00	788 85
Valued at above 60 and not exceeding 80 cents per pound ...... pounds.	40c. p. lb. & 35 p. o.	7,948	5,434 00	6,081 10						
Valued at above 80 cents per pound ...... pounds.	50c. p. lb. & 35 p. c.	191,834.25	254,364 00	184,900 63	8,801.60	20,069 00	11,634 97	12,304.50	25,133 00	14,948 85
Total shirts, drawers, &c		212,086.25	265,784 00	195,704 53	10,916.60	21,729 00	12,559 27	14,307.60	26,483 00	16,141 15
Other manufactures of mohair, and goat's hair, not otherwise specified	30 p. c								1,013 15	463 05
Rags, shoddy, mungo, waste, and flocks, woolen ...... pounds	12c. p. lb	738,541	68,357 00	88,624 92	1,375,505	81,249 00	165,060 60	2,092,057	243,576 07	251,046 84
Shawls:										
Woolen ...... pounds	50c. p. lb. & 35 p c	66,301.75	220,610 28	112,509 45	104,036.75	281,669 00	161,052 53	139,997.25	397,372 00	208,578 81
Worsted—										
Not otherwise specified, ... pounds.	50c. p. lb. & 40 p c.							734,764.66	2,072,363 00	1,436,338 20
Total shawls		66,301.75	220,610 28	112,509 45	104,936.75	281,669 00	151,052 53	873,781.01	3,060,737 00	1,644,917 01
Webbings, gorings, suspenders, braces, beltings, binding, braids, galloons, fringes, gimps, cords, cords and tassels, dress										

	Rate									
trimmings, bead-nets, buttons or barrel buttons, or buttons of other forms for tassels or ornaments, wrought by hand or braided by machinery, made of wool, or of which wool, worsted, the hair of the alpaca, goat, or other animals is a component material ...... pounds.	50c. p. lb. & 50 p. o.	144,141.25	227,333 49	185,737 38	174,153.50	282,941 75	296,547 63	120,119.25	304,150 70	212,134 90
Yarns, woolen, and worsted: Valued at not exceeding 40 cents per pound ...pounds.	20c. p. lb. & 35 p. c.	1,282.63	396 02	395 13	.60	20 50	19 18	71.00	25 00	22 95
Valued at above 40 and not exceeding 60 cents per pound ......pounds.	30c. p. lb. & 35 p. c.	2,328.50	1,234 00	1,131 85	3,563.75	1,822 40	1,712 97	4,479.25	2,436 00	2,196 38
Valued at above 60 and not exceeding 80 cents per pound ......pounds.	40c. p. lb. & 35 p. c.	917	625 00	585 55	4,470.75	3,298 60	2,942 81	7,103.75	5,051 00	4,609 35
Valued at above 80 cents per pound ......pounds.	50c. p. lb. & 35 p. c.	224,097	240,236 04	196,131 82	258,641.19	279,651 40	227,198 50	243,853	274,387 40	217,962 13
Total yarns..........		228,625.13	242,497 06	198,244 35	266,755.60	284,792 90	231,873 55	255,507.00	281,899 40	224,790 81
All manufactures of every description not specially enumerated or provided for, made wholly or in part of wool: Manufactures not otherwise specified ......pounds.	50c. p. lb. & 35 p. c.	291,336.50	429,404 38	295,959 80	184,211.25	289,710 03	193,504 42	130,044.87	222,836 76	143,015 33
Worsted, the hair of the alpaca, goat, or other animals (except such as are composed in part of wool)—Valued at not exceeding 40 cts. per pound, pounds.	20c. p. lb. & 35 p. c.	5,793	2,216 00	1,934 20	17,926	6,861 00	5,986 55	7,676	2,325 00	2,348 95
Valued at above 40 and not exceeding 60 cents per pound ......pounds.	30c. p. lb. & 35 p. c.	44,188	21,884 00	20,898 30	39,883	19,756 00	18,879,50	19,246	9,925 00	9,247 55
Valued at above 60 and not exceeding 80 cents per pound ...... pounds.	40c. p. lb. & 35 p. c.a	16,692	11,067 00	10,805 25	271,495.75	207,204 00	181,119 70	157,628.75	122,015 00	105,756 75
Valued at above 80 cents per pound ...... pounds.	50c. p. lb. & 35 p. c.	1,949,373.50	2,366,464 35	1,802,949 31	2,285,408	2,500,125 85	2,049,248 09	902,548.50	1,308,920 87	954,396 56
Total manufactures not elsewhere specified..........		2,307,383	2,831,885 73	2,132,606 86	2,798,024	3,113,656 88	2,448,738 26	1,307,144.12	1,666,022 63	1,214,765 13
Grand total..........		....	35,096,174 07	23,393,200 71	....	42,894,604 49	29,049,157 11	....	50,235,197 28	33,004,893 64

a 40c. p. lb. and 30 p. o.

5402 WOOL——5

No. 8.—Statement showing the Quantities and Values of Imported Manufactures of Wool entered for Consumption in the United States, &c., during the years ending June 30, from 1867 to 1886, inclusive—Continued.

ARTICLES.	Rates of duty.	1873 Quantities.	1873 Values.	1873 Duties.	1874 Quantities.	1874 Values.	1874 Duties.	1875 Quantities.	1875 Values.	1875 Duties.
			Dollars.	*Dollars.*		*Dollars.*	*Dollars.*		*Dollars.*	*Dollars.*
Balmorals:										
Valued at not exceeding 40 cents per pound ...pounds..	20c. p. lb. & 35 p. c.	5	2 00	1 70						
Do ......do..	20c. p. lb. & 35 p. c. less 10 p. c.	680	270 00	207 46						
Valued at above 40 and not exceeding 60 cents per pound, ...pounds.	30c. p. lb. & 35 p. c.	716	380 00	347 80						
Do ......do..	30c. p. lb. & 35 p. c. less 10 p. c.	3,566	1,918 00	1,566 90	1,594	864 00	702 54	245	133 00	108 05
Valued at above 60 cents per pound, ...pounds.	40c. p. lb. & 35 p. c. less 10 p. c.	7,486	5,742 00	4,503 70	10,572	7,422 00	6,143 86	3,734	2,710 00	2,197 90
Do ......pounds.	50c. p. lb. & 35 p. c.									
Do ......do..	50c. p. lb. & 35 p. c. less 10 p. c.	3,363	5,430 00	3,225 70	840	1,018 05	717 59	10	28 49	14 98
Do ......pounds.	50c. p. lb. & 35 p. c. less 10 p. c.							671.50	1,142 78	662 17
Weighing 4 ounces and over per square yard...pounds.	50c. p. lb. & 35 p. c. less 10 p. c.	254	238 00	189 27	20	35 00	20 03			
Total balmorals.		10,070	13,086 00	10,042 02	13,026	9,399 05	7,584 02	4,060.50	4,014 27	2,983 10
Belts or felts, endless, for paper or printing machines ...pounds.	20c. p. lb. & 35 p. c.	2,002.50	7,669 00	4,096 05	129,261.25	134,883 00	65,755 18	23,690.50	24,050 00	13,155 60
Do ......do..	20c. p. lb. & 35 p. c. less 10 p. c.	133,684	139,920 00	64,137 95				102,719.50	102,344 00	50,727 90
Blankets:										
Valued at not exceeding 40 cents per pound ...pounds..	20c. p. lb. & 35 p. c.	10	3 00	3 05	511.50	165 95	144 36	65	21 50	20 52
Do ......pounds..	20c. p. lb. & 35 p. c. less 10 p. c.	230.75	71 50	64 07				240.50	96 00	73 53
Valued at above 40 and not exceeding 60 cents per pound, ...pounds.	30c. p. lb. & 35 p. c.	40	21 00	19 35	5	3 00	2 55	296	151 00	138 65
Do ......pounds.	30c. p. lb. & 35 p. c. less 10 p. c.	800	439 00	353 92	704	381 00	310 15	560	301 96	246 33
Valued at above 60 and not exceeding 80 cents per pound, ...pounds.	40c. p. lb. & 35 p. c	41	29 00	20 55				106	76 00	69 00

Article	Rate									
Do ..... pounds	40c. p. lb. & 35 p. c. less 10 p. c.	58 01	68 00	101 50	742 20	867 00	1,303	138 12	163 00	241
Valued at above 80 cents per pound ..... pounds	50c. p. lb. & 35 p. c. less 10 p. c.	7,591 10	9,736 00	8,367	2,559 47	3,098 70	3,098.50	169 46	308 47	163
Do ..... pounds	50c. p. lb. & 35 p. c. less 10 p. c.	211 73	352 08	224				5,329 85	9,028 56	5,524
Weighing 4 ounces and over per square yard .. pounds	50c. p. lb. & 35 p. c. less 10 p. c.	42 35	73 00	43	106 04	275 50	42.75	241 02	309 40	319
Total blankets		8,451 22	10,875 00	9,993	3,864 77	5,391 15	5,664.75	6,367 39	10,372 03	7,374.75
Bunting: Bunting ..... sq. yards	20c. p. sq. yd. & 35 p. c.	744 40	634 00	2,612.50						16,464.25
Do ..... do	20c. p. sq. yd. & 35 p. c. less 10 p. c.	1,122 31	1,228 00	4,088	3,477 90	3,672 00	12,895.50	4,009 00	5,223 50	
Carpets and carpeting of all kinds: Brussels and tapestry Brussels, printed on the warp, ... sq. yards	50c. p. sq. yd				134 39	476 05	298.62	39 81	126 00	78.02
Do ..... sq. yards	50c. p. sq. yd., less 10 p. c.							319 02	1,096 00	710.25
Aubusson, Axminster, and Chenille carpets and carpets woven whole for rooms, ... sq. yards	50 per cent.	29,087 00	68,174 00	21,754.25	3 50	7 00	2	3,331 50	6,663 00	3,806
Do ..... sq. yards	50 p. c. less 10 p. o.	125,471 25	278,825 00	129,416.50	148,789 84	330,644 07	162,358	188,096 25	419,325 00	229,012
Brussels carpets ..... do	44c. p. sq. yd. & 35 p. c.	42,100 00	64,633 00	44,271.25				7,008 35	10,766 00	7,577.60
Do ..... do	44c. p. sq. yd. less 10 p. c.	312,515 45	531,382 51	366,489.75	546,749 70	939,008 73	638,746.90	744,137 10	1,279,736 70	861,361.38
Druggets and bockings, printed, colored, or otherwise, ... sq. yards	25c. p. sq. yd. & 35 p. c.	393 05	408 00	1,001	6,842 25	8,868 25	17,904.25	12,319 41	16,322 00	33,302
Do ..... do	25c. p. sq. yd. & 35 p. c. less 10 p. c.	7,012 04	9,379 00	18,034						
Mats, screens, hassocks, and rugs, not exclusively vegetable material	45 per cent.	6,538 46	14,529 90		38,625 48	95,371 40		2,720 25	6,045 00	
Do ..... do	45 p. c. less 10 p. o.	35,311 02	87,187 50					36,829 84	90,937 70	
Of wool, flax, or cotton, or parts of either, or other material not specially enumerated or provided for, ... sq. yards	40 per cent.	3,356 00	8,390 00		35 00	89 00		749 20	1,873 00	
Do ..... do	40 p. c. less 10 p. o.	32,110 56	89,171 00		39,217 79	108,938 29		51,560 68	143,224 11	

No. 8.—Statement showing the Quantities and Values of Imported Manufactures of Wool entered for Consumption in the United States, &c., during the years ending June 30, from 1867 to 1886, inclusive—Continued.

Articles.	Rates of duty.	1873.			1874.			1875.		
		Quantities.	Values.	Duties.	Quantities.	Values.	Duties.	Quantities.	Values.	Duties.
			Dollars.	Dollars.		Dollars.	Dollars.		Dollars.	Dollars.
Carpets and carpeting of all kinds—Continued.										
Patent velvet and tapestry velvet carpets, printed on the warp, or otherwise, ...sq. yards.	40c. p. sq. yd. & 35 p. c.	4,307	5,846 00	3,804 90				22,943.50	36,734 00	22,034 30
Do ......do....	40c. p. sq. yd. & 35 p. c. loss 10 p. c.	205,774.25	341,690 00	181,711 17	214,645.50	356,837 00	189,676 12	200,401.50	322,338 00	173,681 03
Saxony, Wilton, and Tournay velvet carpets...sq. yards.	70c. p. sq. yd. & 35 p. c.	1.362	2,406 00	1,795 50				5,212	10,692 00	7,390 61
Do ......do....	70c. p. sq. yd. & 35 p. c. loss 10 p. c.	106,348.12	234,278 00	142,057 00	95,695	210,155 00	126,480 78	60,160.50	130,042 00	78,864 41
Tapestry Brussels, printed on the warp, or otherwise, ...sq. yards.	28c. p. sq. yd. & 35 p. c.	21,751.50	10,531 00	12,926 27				85,924	76,107 40	50,696 13
Do ......do....	28c. p. sq. yd. & 35 p. c. loss 10 p. c.	2,570,731	2,338,550 00	1,385,979 63	2,099,300.87	1,890,958 85	1,124,676 01	1,368,786.50	1,206,605 72	725,033 90
Treble ingrain, three-ply, and worsted chain Venetian carpets ...... sq. yards.	17c. p. sq. yd. & 35 p. c.	85	67 00	37 00						
Do ......do....	17c. p. sq. yd. & 35 p. c. loss 10 p. c.	8,331.75	8,024 57	3,802 53	2,534	2,294 67	1,110 55	169	137 74	60.25
Yarn, Venetian, and two-ply ingrain carpets...sq. yards.	12c. p. sq. yd. & 35 p. c.	73	47 00	25 21				108	81 00	41 31
Do ......do....	12c. p. sq. yd. & 35 p. c. loss 10 p. c.	29,350	22,780 45	10,349 51	5,682	4,532 50	2,041 45	4,008.50	3,624 81	1,671 96
Total carpets			4,048,334 53	2,790,291 72		3,948,175 81	2,224,389 46		2,928,602 68	1,653,369 00
Clothing, ready-made, and wearing apparel (except knit goods), not especially enumerated or provided for, composed wholly or in part of wool, worsted, the hair of the alpaca, goat, or other										

Article	Rate									
like animals, made up or manufactured wholly or in part by the tailor, seamstress, or manufacturer:										
Cloaks, dolmans, jackets, talmas, ulsters, or other outside garments for ladies' and children's apparel, and goods of similar description, or used for like purposes......pounds	50c. p. lb. & 40 p. c.	1,655	6,116 00	8,274 70				8,630.43	44,306 00	22,010 65
Do......do	50c. p. lb. & 40 p. c. less 10 p. c.	53,303 87	243,586 39	111,718 38	51,309.80	228,609 45	105,421 25	50,058 25	217,177 53	104,980 18
Clothing, ready-made, and wearing apparel of every description not specially enumerated or provided for, and balmoral skirts and skirting, and goods of similar description or used for like purposes......pounds	50c. p. lb. & 40 p. o.	2,390.75	11,621 00	5,843 78				17,003.75	93,500 47	45,902 07
Do......do	50c. p. lb. & 40 p. c. less 10 p. c.	129,896.30	638,248 00	288,223 09	159,006.87	641,145 11	302,500 41	133,346.75	453,974 07	223,436 04
Total clothing......		187,336.98	899,673 39	409,059 95	210,816.67	869,844 56	408,011 66	209,548.18	809,018 07	302,335 24
Cloths, woolen: Cloths......pounds	50c. p. lb. & 35 p. c.	176,049	243,947 00	173,055 95	51.12	29 47	35 80	886,960.25	1,342,801 71	913,451 70
Do......do	50c. p. lb. & 35 p. c. less 10 p. c.	10,845,856.38	16,392,731 73	10,044,346 39	8,928,234.25	13,598,416 71	8,301,206 80	6,640,888.75	10,353,229 14	6,249,607 38
Total cloths......		11,021,905.38	16,635,679 73	10,217,402 34	8,928,285.37	13,598,446 18	8,301,242 66	7,627,780.00	11,696,090 85	7,163,119 08
Dress goods, women's and children's, coat linings, Italian cloths, and goods of like description: Composed in part of wool, worsted, the hair of the alpaca, goat, or other animals— Valued at not exceeding 20 cents per square yard......sq. yds.	6c. p. sq. yd. & 35 p. c.	253,395.75	47,249 49	31,741 07		3,943,352 54	2,000,703 44	5,697,660	1,005,777 00	693,881 60
Do......do	6c. p. sq. yd. & 35 p. c. less 10 p. c.	20,775,708	3,912,095 85	2,354,487 00	17,713,889		18,512,155		3,318,220 40	2,044,895 83
Valued at above 20 cents per sq. yard...sq. yards.	8c. p. sq. yd. & 40 p. c.	653,401.75	109,860 35	132,212 28	121	50 34	29 84	7,481,886.43	2,000,848 50	1,638,890 31
Do......do	8c. p. sq. yd. & 40 p. c. less 10 p. c.	47,928,338	15,916,332 13	9,180,576 10	51,720,634	17,132,903 84	9,802,400 72	41,844,299	13,229,494 62	7,775,407 70

No. 2.—STATEMENT SHOWING THE QUANTITIES AND VALUES OF IMPORTED MANUFACTURES OF WOOL ENTERED FOR CONSUMPTION IN THE UNITED STATES, &C., DURING THE YEARS ENDING JUNE 30, FROM 1867 TO 1886, INCLUSIVE—Continued.

ARTICLES.	Rates of duty.	1873. Quantities.	Values.	Duties.	1874. Quantities.	Values.	Duties.	1875. Quantities.	Values.	Duties.
Dress goods, &c.—Continued. Composed wholly of wool, worsted, the hair of the alpaca, goat, or other animals, or of a mixture of them, and all such goods of like description, with selvedges made wholly or in part of other materials, or with threads of other materials introduced for the purpose of changing the classification—										
All weighing over 4 oz. per sq. yard......pounds..	50c. p. lb. & 35 p. c.	40,476.50	60,409 00	41,381 40				190,026.80	357,231 14	220,344 31
Do...............do...	50c. p. lb. & 35 p. c. less 10 p. c.	1,071,511	2,982,596 08	1,691,697 78	1,137,814.25	1,887,392 65	1,106,545 13	1,044,198 37	1,818,446 00	1,042,699 76
Total dress goods......			23,119,432 90	13,432,095 75		22,363,759 37	13,008,679 13		22,330,017 72	13,416,119 51
Flannels:										
Valued at not exceeding 40 cents per pound ...pounds..	20c. p. lb. & 35 p. c. less 10 p. c.	240	85 00	71 06	78	58 00	32 21	121	63 80	42 43
Valued at above 40 and not exceeding 60 cents per pound, ...pounds..	30c. p. lb. & 35 p. c.	710	351 00	302 27	17	11 48	9 12	48	24 00	20 53
Do.................do...	30c. p. lb. & 35 p. c. less 10 p. c.				43.50	25 00	19 63			
Valued at above 60 and not exceeding 80 cents per pound, ...pounds..	40c. p. lb. & 35 p. c.	550	437 00	376 55				340	250 00	227 10
Do.................do...	44c. p. lb. & 35 p. c. less 10 p. c.	1,214	939 00	732 83	39.25	29 00	23 27	1,516.75	1,112 00	896 33
Valued at above 80 cents per pound ......pounds..	50c. p. lb. & 35 p. c.	551	922 00	508 20				539	689 00	510 65
Do.................do...	50c. p. lb. & 35 p. c. less 10 p. c.	13,736.75	23,729 70	13,656 44	12,790.75	25,093 20	13,924 85	6,734.38	13,909 66	7,412 90
Weighing 4 ounces and over per square yard ...pounds..	50c. p. lb. & 35 p. c							344.75	827 00	461 83

Article	Rate									
Do ......do....	50c. p. lb. & 35 p. c. less 10 p. c.	761	1,123 00	696 20	84	101 00	60 62	2,301.75	5,372 00	2,727 97
Total flannels......		17,777.75	27,588 70	16,433 57	13,082 50	26,157 68	14,060 70	11,957.03	22,247 48	12,308 93
Hats of wool:										
Valued at not exceeding 40 cents per pound....pounds..	20c. p. lb. & 35 p. c.	8.50	5 00	4 30				.25	2 00	76
Valued at above 40 and not exceeding 60 cents per pound, ...pounds..	30c. p. lb. & 35 p. c.				857	480 00	384 48	722	351 00	305 51
Do ......do....	30c. p. lb. & 35 p. c. less 10 p. c.								26 00	25 10
Valued at above 60 and not exceeding 80 cents per pound, ...pounds..	40c. p. lb. & 35 p. o.				240	179 00	142 70	40	179 00	150 83
Do ......do....	40c. p. lb. & 35 p. c. less 10 p. c.							279	2 00	83
Valued at over 80 cents per pound ....pounds..	50c. p. lb. & 35 p. c.	309	813 00	484 05					21,674 00	12,045 05
Do ......do....	50c. p. lb. & 35 p. o. less 10 p. c.	35,598.62	66,164 25	36,807 49	22,448 40	43,820 00	23,005 10	11,506.25		
Hat roundings or trimmings..	10 p. o.		2,529 00	252 90		1,307 00	130 70		114 00	11 40
Total hats			69,531 25	37,008 74		45,792 00	24,563 07		22,348 00	12,516 07
Knit goods:										
Hosiery—										
Valued at not over 40 cents per pound ....pounds..	20c. p. lb. & 35 p. c. less 10 p. c.	2,418	1,380 00	1,087 56	79	24 62	21 99	1,062	624 00	483 30
Valued at above 40 and not exceeding 60 cents per pound ....pounds..	30c. p. lb. & 35 p. e.		40 45	35 61	138	76 00	01 21	1,290	979 00	776 03
Valued at above 60 and not exceeding 80 cents per pound ....pounds..	40c. p. lb. & 35 p. c.	3,078.	9,236 20	4,771 67	007	487 00	365 03	10,257.80	49,305 34	25,406 77
Valued at above 80 cents per pound ....pounds..	50c. p. lb. & 36 p. c.	220,028.87	544,739 75	270,604 11	218,100 25	509,218 38	258,548 04	227,545.50	554,366 00	277,020 82
Do ......do....	50c. p. lb. & 35 p. c. less 10 p. c.									
Total hosiery......		225,588.37	555,398 40	270,500 95	218,024 25	509,786 00	258,907 77	246,164.30	605,334 34	303,686 92
Shirts, drawers, and other knit goods—										
Valued at not over 40 cents per pound ....pounds..	20 c. p. lb. & 35 p. c. less 10 p. c.		5 00	4 01	170	55 00	47 93	321	144 00	132 03
Valued at above 40 and not exceeding 60 cents per pound....pounds..	30c. p. lb. & 25 p. c. less 10 p. c.	9			1,941	938 00	790 08			

No. 8.—STATEMENT SHOWING THE QUANTITIES AND VALUES OF IMPORTED MANUFACTURES OF WOOL ENTERED FOR CONSUMPTION IN THE UNITED STATES, &c., DURING THE YEARS ENDING JUNE 30, FROM 1867 TO 1886, INCLUSIVE—Continued.

ARTICLES.	Rates of duty.	1873. Quantities.	1873. Values.	1873. Duties.	1874. Quantities.	1874. Values.	1874. Duties.	1875. Quantities.	1875. Values.	1875. Duties.
Knit goods—Continued. Shirts, drawers, and other knit goods—Continued.			*Dollars.*	*Dollars.*		*Dollars.*	*Dollars.*		*Dollars.*	*Dollars.*
Valued at above 60 cents and not exceeding 80 cents per pound .... pounds.	40 c. p. lb. & 35 p. c. less 10 p. c.	4	3 00	2 30				1,225	818 00	708 12
Valued at above 80 cents per pound ......pounds.	50 c. p. lb. & 35 p. c. less 10 p. c.	1,440	2,450 00	1,577 50	1,768.50	1,183 50	1,009 48	2,186.50	6,207 00	3,265 71
Do.......do....	50 c. p. lb. & 35 p. c. less 10 p. c.	29,100.38	44,209 25	22,971 15	28,543.63	57,378 61	30,918 91	40,139.25	72,935 98	41,037 58
Total shirts, drawers, &c.		21,553.38	46,667 25	24,555 07	32,323.13	59,550 11	32,767 33	43,871.75	80,134 98	45,143 44
Other manufactures of mohair, and goat's hair, not otherwise specified.	30 p. c.		1,690 14	507 04		58 00	15 12		62 00	18 60
Do	30 p. c. less 10 p. c.		44 00	11 88						
Rags, shoddy, mungo, waste, and flocks, woollen ......pounds.	12 c. p. lb.	110,674	10,223 80	13,280 88	1,920,098	165,993 00	207,370 63	77,248	11,336 00	9,269 76
Do ....do....	12 c. p. lb. less 10 p. c.	1,912,164	202,383 00	206,515 93				1,381,974	146,990 00	149,253 24
Shawls: Woollen......pounds.	50 c. p. lb. & 35 p. c.	1,867.25	5,609 60	2,890 77	78,188.25	264,571 10	118,324 71	14,200.75	46,007 12	23,202 87
Do.......do....	50 c. p. lb. & 35 p. c. less 10 p. c.	100,781.50	320,698 34	146,371 79				74,570.25	231,368 75	106,406 43
Worsted— Not otherwise specified, ...pounds.	50 c. p. lb. & 40 p. c.	7,259	22,022 00	12,438 30	604,339	1,996,091 70	991,825 00	70,176.33	257,677 00	138,278 97
Do .....do....	50 c. p. lb. & 40 p. c. less 10 p. c.	695,059.50	2,407,589 00	1,170,508 87				503,944.50	1,654,595 00	822,438 2
Total shawls		804,967.25	2,755,918 34	1,341,215 73	682,527.25	2,363,662 89	1,110,150 31	662,911.83	2,180,817 87	1,090,326 50
Webbings, gorings, suspenders, braces, beltings, bindings, braids, galloons, fringe, gimps, cords, cords and tassels, dress trimmings, head-nets, buttons or barrel buttons, or buttons of										

Article									
other forms for tassels or ornaments, wrought by hand or braided by machinery, made of wool, or of which wool, worsted, or other animals is a component material ......pounds. — 50c. p. lb. & 50 p. c.	5,719.75	17,887 00	11,803 38	2.50	2 82	2 66	199,779 33	530,375 97	362,077 65
Do ....do.... — 50c. p. lb. & 50 p. c. less 10 p. c.	149,635.84	505,500 58	294,811 23	303,809.38	1,056,237 54	642,021 22	358,266 25	1,157,237 00	681,976 51
Yarns, woolen and worsted: Valued at not exceeding 40 cents per pound...pounds. — 20c. p. lb. & 35 p. c.	524	120 00	132 12	4.00	2 00	1 50	3.50	1 00	1 05
Do ....do.. — 20c. p. lb. & 35 p. c. less 10 p. c.				87.00	28 00	24 49	38	14 60	11 45
Valued at above 40 and not exceeding 60 cents per pound...pounds. — 30c. p. lb. & 35 p. c.	2	1 00	95				2.50	1 60	1 31
Do ....do.... — 30c. p. lb. & 35 p. c. less 10 p. c.	172.50	161 00	78 40	353.00	206 10	160 25	5	3 60	2 17
Valued at above 60 and not exceeding 80 cents per pound ......pounds. — 40c. p. lb. & 35 p. c.	75	61 00	51 33				124	78 00	76 90
Do ....do.... — 40c. p. lb. & 35 p. c. less 10 p. c.	3,031	2,475 00	2,080 80	5,671	3,920 00	3,276 39	3,685	2,743 00	2,190 84
Valued at above 80 cents per pound ......pounds. — 50c. p. lb. & 35 p. c.	1,950	2,932 00	2,004 20				22,223	27,703 00	20,897 55
Do ....do.... — 50c. p. lb. & 35 p. c. less 10 p. c.	311,472	408,265 08	268,765 99	2*4,467.25	368,486 88	244,083 72	309,379.50	366,279 88	250,899 03
Total yarns........	317,832.50	413,935 08	273,119 79	290,582.25	372,642 98	247,546 35	335,460.50	416,824 28	283,090 30
All manufactures of every description not specially enumerated or provided for, made wholly or in part of wool: Manufactures not otherwise specified, pounds...pounds. — 50c. p. lb. & 35 p. c.	8,660	24,754 00	12,993 90	385,212.63	1 00	60	50,845.75	92,715 00	57,873 15
Do ....do.... — 50c. p. lb. & 35 p. c. less 10 p. c.	244,160.50	459,929 70	254,750 30		741,598 37	406,949 28	297,705.38	630,667 00	329,477 71
Of worsted, the hair of the alpaca, goat, or other animals (except such goods as are composed in part of wool)— Valued at not exceeding 40 cts. per pound, pounds. — 20c. p. lb. & 35 p. c.	31	11 44	10 20	471	153 00	132 98	326.50	130 00	99 72
Do ....do.... — 20c. p. lb. & 35 p. c. less 10 p. c.	2,423.75	1,630 00	949 73						
Valued at above 40 and not exceeding 60 cents per pound ......pounds. — 30c. p. lb. & 35 p. c.	1,401	670 00	654 80	21,021	12,024 00	9,463 25	14,871	8,434 00	7,413 20
Do ....do.... — 30c. p. lb. & 35 p. c. less 10 p. c.	12,239	6,815 00	5,451 27				26,401	14,707 00	11,701 01

No. 8.—STATEMENT SHOWING THE QUANTITIES AND VALUES OF IMPORTED MANUFACTURES OF WOOL ENTERED FOR CONSUMPTION IN THE UNITED STATES, &c., DURING THE YEARS ENDING JUNE 30, FROM 1867 TO 1885, INCLUSIVE—Continued.

ARTICLES.	Rates of duty.	1873. Quantities.	1873. Values.	1873. Duties.	1874. Quantities.	1874. Values.	1874. Duties.	1875. Quantities.	1875. Values.	1875. Duties.
All manufactures of every description not specially enumerated or provided for, made wholly or in part of wool.—Continued.										
Valued at above 60 and not exceeding 80 cents per pound .... pounds.	40c. p. lb. & 35 p. c.	555	Dollars. 436 00	Dollars. 374 00		Dollars. 6,789 00	Dollars. 5,417 27	30,941.50	Dollars. 23,734 00	Dollars. 20,653 50
Do ....do	40c. p. lb. & 35 p. c. less 10 p. c.	14,771	10,785 00	8,718 02	9,125			32,434.50	24,400 00	10,362 47
Valued at above 80 cents per pound ....pounds.	50c. p. lb. & 35 p. c.	9,134	11,254 54	8,506 10	971,469.31	1,481,607 58	903,867 68	275,690.59	354,995 00	262,078 50
Do ....do	50c. p. lb. & 35 p. c. less 10 p. c.	1,067,235.50	1,510,320 89	912,897 12				1,067,129.25	1,398,427 20	920,712 78
Total manufactures not elsewhere specified		1,260 610.75	2,032,616 57	1,205,306 04	1,387,299.14	2,242,159 95	1,325,831 00	1,796,315.38	2,538,209 20	1,629,462 05
Grand total			52,419,591 09	30,643,773 60		47,675,605 09	27,886,340 00		45,627,922 31	27,282,178 23

No. 8.—STATEMENT SHOWING THE QUANTITIES AND VALUES OF IMPORTED MANUFACTURES OF WOOL ENTERED FOR CONSUMPTION IN THE UNITED STATES, &C., DURING THE YEARS ENDING JUNE 30, FROM 1867 TO 1885, INCLUSIVE—Continued.

		1876			1877			1878		
		Quantities.	Values.	Duties.	Quantities.	Values.	Duties.	Quantities.	Values.	Duties.
			Dollars.	Dollars.		Dollars.	Dollars.		Dollars.	Dollars.
Balmorals:										
Valued at not exceeding 40 cents per pound .. pounds..	20c. p. lb. & 35 p. c.				2.50	1 00	85			
Valued at above 40 and not exceeding 60 cents per pound, ... pounds..	30c. p. lb. & 35 p. c.							1,429	844 00	724 10
Valued at above 60 and not exceeding 80 cents per pound, ... pounds..	40c. p. lb. & 35 p. c.							1,800	1,238 00	1,153 30
Valued at above 80 cents per pound .... pounds..	50c. p. lb. & 35 p. c.	1,309	1,626 50	1,223 78	21,426.50	33,147 00	23,314 70			
Total balmorals.......		1,309	1,626 50	1,223 78	23,429	33,148 00	23,315 55	3,229	2,082 00	1,877 40
Belts or felts, endless, for paper or printing machines..pounds..	50c. p. lb. & 35 p. c.	97,284.25	100,249 90	56,644 00	97,430	90,566 00	51,185 90	103,204.75	93,839 00	53,484 60
Blankets:										
Valued at not exceeding 40 cents per pound ..pounds..	20c. p. lb. & 35 p. c.	1,101.50	413 61	365 06	2,369.00	869 25	778 03	117.50	43 00	38 55
Valued at above 40 and not exceeding 60 cents per pound, ... pounds..	30c. p. lb. & 35 p. c.	1,768.75	921 74	853 24	8,423.13	4,339 75	4,045 84	753.00	438 00	379 30
Valued at above 60 and not exceeding 80 cents per pound, ... pounds..	40c. p. lb. & 35 p. c.	4,795.50	3,296 00	3,071 80	319.00	209 00	200 75	56.00	38 20	35 77
Valued at above 80 cents per pound .... pounds..	50c. p. lb. & 35 p. c.	758.75	880 76	887 64	684.00	804 00	623 40	198.25	240 67	183 37
Do .... do....	50c. p. lb. & 35 p. c. less 10 p. c.	45.70	70 00	42 30						
Weighing 4 ounces and over per square yard ...pounds..	50c. p. lb. & 35 p. c.	17.50	16 00	14 35	112.00	219 00	132 65	62.00	78 00	58 30
Total blankets		8,487.70	5,598 11	5,034 99	11,907.13	6,441 00	5,780 67	1,186.75	837 87	695 19
Bunting:										
Bunting ....sq. yards..	20c. p. sq. yd. & 35 p. c.	10,840.00	2,640 00	3,094 10	8,946.50	2,159 20	2,545 02	2,066.25	425 00	562 00

No. 8.—STATEMENT SHOWING THE QUANTITIES AND VALUES OF IMPORTED MANUFACTURES OF WOOL ENTERED FOR CONSUMPTION IN THE UNITED STATES, &c., DURING THE YEARS ENDING JUNE 30, FROM 1867 TO 1886, INCLUSIVE—Continued.

ARTICLES.	Rates of duty.	1876.			1877.			1878.		
		Quantities.	Values.	Duties.	Quantities.	Values.	Duties.	Quantities.	Values.	Duties.
Carpets and carpeting of all kind: Axminster, and Chenille carpets, and carpets woven whole for rooms. ...sq. yards.	50 p. c. less 10 p. c.	122,550	*Dollars.* 291,816 50	*Dollars.* 145,908 25	100,123.25	*Dollars.* 235,886 90	*Dollars.* 117,848 00	76,664.16	*Dollars.* 172,408 00	*Dollars.* 86,203 00
Do .... do	50 p. c. less 10 p. c.	3,451	7,415 00	3,336 75	948	2,130 00	958 50	....	....	....
Brussels carpets .... do	44c. p. sq. yd. & 35 p. c.	244,367.75	347,271 00	229,066 68	132,213	178,507 00	120,651 28	93,507.50	123,253 00	84,281 85
Do .... do	44c. p. sq. yd. & 35 p. c. less 10 p. c.	12,137	17,685 00	10,377 04	427	658 00	376 36	285	421 00	245 48
Druggets and bockings, printed, colored, or otherwise, ...sq. yards.	25c. p. sq. yd. & 35 p. c.	15,128	7,994 00	6,579 00	12,099.50	6,407 00	5,492 33	3,360	1,396 00	1,330 85
Do .... do	25c. p. sq. yd. & 35 p. c. less 10 p. c.	787	396 00	301 82	....	....	....	....	....	....
Mats, screens, hassocks, and rugs, not exclusively vegetable material ... Do.	45 p. c.	....	112,115 00	50,451 75	....	122,463 00	55,108 35	....	128,706 00	57,917 70
Do.	45 p. c. less 10 p. c.	....	808 00	363 69	....	14 00	5 67	....	....	....
Of wool, flax, or cotton, or parts of either, or other material not specially enumerated or provided for, ...sq. yards.	40 p. c.	....	86,066 00	34,426 40	....	63,292 35	25,316 94	....	55,714 00	22,295 60
Do.	40 p. c. less 10 p. c.	....	2,254 00	811 44	....	....	....	....	....	....
Patent velvet and tapestry velvet carpets, printed on the warp, or otherwise, sq. yards.	40c. p. sq. yd. & 35 p. c.	134,305	210,168 00	127,280 80	104,459.25	156,067 00	96,407 15	37,820.75	51,948 00	33,309 40
Do .... do	40c. p. sq. yd. & 35 p. c. less 10 p. c.	15,197	24,303 00	13,126 38	2,136	3,392 00	1,837 44	1,893	2,098 00	1,625 82
Saxony, Wilton, and Tournay velvet carpets ... sq. yards.	70c. p. sq. yd. & 35 p. c.	40,318.75	83,174 00	57,334 03	23,603	45,885 00	32,581 88	11,032	21,470 00	15,236 91
Do .... do	70c. p. sq. yd. & 35 p. c. less 10 p. c.	1,462	3,123 00	1,904 81	....	....	....	....	....	....
Tapestry Brussels, printed on the warp, or otherwise, ...sq. yards.	28c. p. sq. yd. & 35 p. c.	438,094.33	394,993 20	260,914 06	269,217.25	222,786 50	153,356 11	87,732.63	79,612 89	52,429 64

Article	Rate of duty									
Do................do.....	28c. p. sq. yd. & 35 p. c. less 10 p. c.	108,864	97,587 00	68,176 81	10,132	9,351 00	5,408 82	6,520	6,982 00	3,527 37
Treble ingrain, three-ply, and worsted chain Venetian carpets ....sq. yards..	17c. p. sq. yd. & 35 p. c.	1,231.25	1,425 00	708 07	1,250.50	1,345 00	683 34	911	1,043 00	519 02
Yarn, Venetian, and two-ply ingrain carpets...sq. yards..	12c. p. sq. yd. & 35 p. c.	916	585 00	282 17	2,952	1,863 50	1,006 47	12,759.87	9,276 00	4,777 78
Do................do......	12c. p. sq. yd. & 35 p. c. less 10 p. c.	742	621 00	275 75						
Total carpets.........			1,689,909 80	1,001,626 58		1,050,057 35	617,228 04		654,223 89	303,601 32
Clothing, ready-made and wearing apparel (except knit goods), not specially enumerated or provided for, composed wholly or in part of wool, worsted, the hair of the alpaca, goat, or other like animals, made up or manufactured wholly or in part by the tailor, seamstress, or manufacturer:										
Cloaks, dolmans, jackets, talmas, ulsters, or other outside garments for ladies' and children's apparel, and goods of similar description, or used for like purposes......pounds.. / ....do.....	50c. p. lb. & 40 p. c. / 50c. p. lb. & 40 p. c. less 10 p. c.	101,639.10 / 4	370,657 97 / 80 00	199,074 75 / 30 60	125,545.66	894,999 31	220,772 63	165,936.15	576,439 48	313,543 93
Clothing, ready-made and wearing apparel of every description not specially enumerated or provided for, and balmoral skirts and skirting, and goods of similar description or used for like purposes......pounds.. / ....do.....	50c. p. lb. & 40 p. c. / 50c. p. lb. & 40 p. c. less 10 p. c.	153,879.70 / 123.50	444,146 17 / 394 00	254,509 11 / 197 42	40,553.17	133,953 22	73,857 87	39,901.68	114,811 11	65,905 33
Total clothing.........		255,646.30	815,269 14	453,001 88	160,098 83	526,962 53	204,630 50	205,807 83	691,250 59	379,449 26
Cloths, woolen: Cloths......pounds.. / Do......do....	50c. p. lb. & 35 p. c. / 50c. p. lb. & 35 p. c. less 10 p. c.	5,568,357.47 / 197,442.50	8,636,761 72 / 267,672 00	5,807,045 30 / 173,165 83	3,863,410.11 / 1,301	5,735,037 12 / 2,534 00	3,938,972 55 / 1,383.07	4,003,575.28 / 198	5,657,394 31 / 388 00	3,982,675 76 / 211 32
Total cloths		5,765,799.97	8,904,433 72	5,980,211 13	3,864,720 11	5,737,571 12	3,040,356 22	4,005,773.28	4,657,782 31	3,983,087 08

No. 8.—Statement showing the Quantities and Values of Imported Manufactures of Wool entered for Consumption in the United States, &c., during the years ending June 30, from 1867 to 1886, inclusive—Continued.

ARTICLES.	Rates of duty.	1876. Quantities.	1876. Values.	1876. Duties.	1877. Quantities.	1877. Values.	1877. Duties.	1878. Quantities.	1878. Values.	1878. Duties.
			Dollars.	*Dollars.*		*Dollars.*	*Dollars.*		*Dollars.*	*Dollars.*
Dress goods, women's and children's, coat linings, Italian cloths, and goods of like description: Composed in part of wool, worsted, the hair of the alpaca, goat, or other animals— Valued at not exceeding 20 cents per square yard, ...sq. yards.	6c. p. sq. yd. & 35 p. c.	20,781,790.58	3,655,851 37	2,526,455 28	19,290,310.58	3,307,147 91	2,314,920 47	22,133,465.25	3,745,160 09	2,636,813 96
Do......do.	6c. p. sq. yd. & 35 p. c. less 10 p. c.	771,999	138,277 00	85,245 26						
Valued at above 20 cents per sq. yd....sq. yards.	8c. p. sq. yd. & 40 p. c.	32,541,035.74	10,364,039 19	6,749,256 51	30,951,302.30	9,588,504 46	6,311,500 49	28,162,128.67	8,728,460 77	6,744,334 56
Do......do.	8c. p. sq. yd. & 40 p. c. less 10 p. c.	2,124,506	658,371 00	389,984 51	6,098	2,124 00	1,311 68			
Composed wholly of wool, worsted, the hair of the alpaca, goat, or other animals, or of a mixture of thread, and all such goods of like description, with selvedges, made wholly or in part of other materials, or with threads of other materials introduced for the purpose of changing the classification— All weighing over 4 oz. per sq. yd......pounds.	50c. p. lb. & 35 p. c	1,103,701	1,698,488 00	1,146,222 13	749,346.73	1,213,447 00	799,379 83	1,014,341.34	1,690,509 00	1,088,848 83
Do......do.	50c. p. lb. & 35 p. c. less 10 p. c.	25,651	30,175 00	23,863 08	180	320 00	185 85			
Total dress goods ...			16,555,090 56	10,921,048 77		14,111,643 37	9,427,304 32		24,164,129 98	9,482,017 35
Flannels: Valued at not exceeding 40 cents per pound ..pounds.	20c. p. lb. & 35 p. c				10	5 60	4 03	18	15 00	8 85

Article	Rate of duty									
Valued at above 40 and not exceeding 60 cents per pound, ... pounds.	30c. p. lb. & 35 p. o.	97	61 60	50 66	28	13 00	12 35	70	38 00	34 30
Valued at above 60 and not exceeding 80 cents per pound, ...pounds.	40. p. lb. & 35 p. c.	356	234 00	224 30	2	1 40	1 20	77	47 00	47 25
Valued at above 80 cents per pound ....do......	50c. p. lb. & 35 p. o. / 50c. p. lb. & 35 p. c. less 10 p. c.	935.25 / 4	1,272 97 / 5 00	913 17 / 3 38	1,468.88	2,057 00	1,454 40	1,303.25	2,596 00	1,560 23
Weighing 4 ounces and over per square yard ...pounds..	50c. p. lb. & 35 p. c.	175	278 00	184 86	26.50	28 00	23 05			
Total flannels		1,567.25	1,851 57	1,376 31	1,533.38	2,105 20	1,495 12	1,468.25	2,696 00	1,650 63
Hats of wool:										
Valued at not exceeding 40 cents per pound ...pounds.	20c. p. lb. & 35 p c	316	134 00	110 10	45	35 88	21 56	8.25	3 30	2 80
Valued at above 40 and not exceeding 60 cents per pound, ...pounds.	30c. p. lb. & 35 p. c.	250	122 00	117 70				100	52 00	48 20
Valued at above 60 and not exceeding 80 cents per pound, ...pounds.	40c. p. lb. & 35 p. c.	569	447 00	384 05	3,125	2,437 00	2,102 95	3,128.50	2,342 12	2,071 14
Valued at over 80 cents per pound ....pounds.	50c. p. lb. & 35 p. o.	5,276.50	8,674 41	5,674 29	5,031.56	7,752 66	5,229 22	3,344.56	5,794 00	3,700 15
Do ....do.......	50c. p. lb. & 35 p.c. less 10 p. c.	2,437	4,265 00	2,440 13						
Hat roundings or trimmings ...	10 p. e.								1,151 00	115 10
Total hats		8,848.50	13,642 41	8,726 27	8,201 56	10,225 54	7,353 73		9,342 42	5,937 39
Knit goods:										
Hosiery—										
Valued at not over 40 cents per pound ...pounds.	20c. p. lb. & 35 p. c.	28	15 00	10 45						
Valued at above 40 and not exceeding 60 cents per pound ...pounds.	30c. p. lb. & 35 p. c.	41	23 00	20 35						
Valued at above 60 and not exceeding 80 cents per pound ...pounds.	40c. p. lb. & 35 p. c.	61	44 40	39 94	138	59 00	62 05	2	1 00	95
Valued at above 80 cents per pound ....pounds.	50c. p. lb. & 35 p. c.	216,176.99	556,099 38	302,723 25	198,062.37	505,128 00	275,826 00	178,840.27	464,598 00	252,029 46
Do ....pounds.	50c.p. lb. & 35 p. c. less 10 p. c.	916	2,656 00	1,248 84	1	1 00	75	1.50	1 00	95
Total hosiery		217,220.99	558,887 78	304,042 83	198,201.37	565,188 00	275,888 80	178,843.77	464,600 00	252,031 36

No. 8.—STATEMENT SHOWING THE QUANTITIES AND VALUES OF IMPORTED MANUFACTURES OF WOOL ENTERED FOR CONSUMPTION IN THE UNITED STATES, &c., DURING THE YEARS ENDING JUNE 30, FROM 1867 TO 1886, INCLUSIVE.—Continued.

ARTICLES.	Rates of duty.	1876.			1877.			1878.		
		Quantities.	Values.	Duties.	Quantities.	Values.	Duties.	Quantities.	Values.	Duties.
Knit goods—Continued.			*Dollars.*	*Dollars.*		*Dollars.*	*Dollars.*		*Dollars.*	*Dollars.*
Shirts, drawers, and other knit goods—										
Valued at not over 40 cents per pound, pounds.	20c. p. lb. & 35 p. c.	306	113 00	100 75						
Valued at above 40 and not exceeding 60 cents per pound..... pounds.	30c. p. lb. & 35 p. c.									
Valued at above 60 and not exceeding 80 cents per pound..... pounds.	40c. p. lb. & 35 p. c.	18	13 50	11 93	186.50	113 00	114 15	.80	43 00	40 65
Valued at above 80 cents per pound.... pounds.	50c. p. lb. & 35 p. c.	56,709.18	117,306 00	69,411 71	51,865.06	106,686 51	63,272 84	28,417.63	62,472 00	30,074 27
Total shirts, drawers, &c..		57,033.18	117,432 50	69,524 39	52,051.56	100,799 51	63,386 99	28,503.63	62,515 00	30,113 12
Other manufactures of mohair, and goat's hair, not otherwise specified....	30 p. c.					102 00	30 60			
Rags, shoddy, mungo, waste, and flocks, woolen.....pounds.	12c. p. lb.....	250,810	50,804 00	30,097 20	200,302	35,902 00	24,036 24	133,926	23,831 00	16,071 12
Do.....do....	12c. p. lb. less 10 p. c.	31,819	2,699 00	3,436 46	1,188	124 00	128 31			
Shawls:										
Woolen.....pounds..	50c. p. lb. & 35 p. c.	70,550.31	203,888 33	106,676 10	62,396.69	161,145 00	87,599 11	86,568.87	198,153 80	112,647 30
Do.....do....	50c. p. lb. & 35 p. c. less 10 p. c.	2,482	4,740 00	2,610 02						
Worsted—										
Not otherwise specified, pounds..	50c. p. lb. & 40 p. c.	466,005.14	1,272,235 00	712,196 57	358,248.13	1,099,303 00	618,805 29	380,268.17	1,102,873 50	631,263 51
Do......do..	50c. p. lb. & 40 p. c. less 10 p. c.	8,862	29,858 00	14,749 38						
Total shawls....		448,519.46	1,510,731 33	830,102 07	420,644.82	1,260,348 00	706,404 40	466,855.04	1,301,027 30	743,930 81
Webbings, gorings, suspenders braces, beltings, bindings, braids, gallons, fringes, gimpe, cords, cords and tassels, dress										

Description	Rate									
trimmings, lead nets, buttons or barrel buttons, or buttons of other forms for tassels or ornaments, wrought by hand or braided by machinery, made of wool, or of which wool, worsted, the hair of the alpaca, goat, or other animals is a component material.........pounds.. Do.........do...	50c. p. lb. & 50 p.c. 50c. p. lb. & 50 p.c. less 10 p. c.	452,283 42 896	1,385,092 95 3,284 00	918,088 20 1,881 00	352,851 24	883,115 00	617,983 12	333,206 06	605,693 00	569,549 56
Yarns, woolen and worsted:										
Valued at not exceeding 40 cents per pound..pounds.	20c. p. lb. & 35 p.c.	80.75	24 00	24 55	96.75	35 00	31 60	79.50	23 40	24 00
Valued at above 40 and not exceeding 60 cents per pound..........pounds.	30c. p. lb. & 35 p.c.	520.25	305 00	262 83	72.25	34 00	33 58	1,012	567 50	502 23
Valued at above 60 and not exceeding 80 cents per pound.......pounds	40c. p. lb. & 35 p.c.	429	271 00	266 45	49.50	35 00	32 05	3,854.25	2,874 00	2,547 60
Valued at above 80 cents per pound.........pounds Do.............pounds	50c. p. lb. & 35 p.c. 50c. p. lb. & 35 p.c. less. 10 p. c.	321,919 10,516	415,309 50 23,351 00	306,364 35 10,137 77	336,450.08	390,940 00	308,204 05	458,296.44	543,163 00	410,220 29
Total yarns.........		342,495	430,359 50	323,035 05	336,668.08	400,044 00	303,301 28	463,172.19	546,627 00	422,294 21
All manufactures of every description not specially enumerated or provided for, made wholly or in part of wool:										
Manufactures not otherwise specified.......pounds. Do........do..	50c. p. lb. & 35 p.c. 50c. p. lb. & 35 p. less 10 p. c.	185,871.04 3,177.50	314,009 40 5,111 00	202,835 60 3,019 86	145,262.53 2,726.50	233,803 11 4,193 00	154,462 35 2,528 01	126,725.68 274	209,203 86 362 00	117,684 25 237 33
(Of worsted, the hair of the alpaca, goat, or other animals (except such as are composed in part of wool)—										
Valued at not exceeding 40 cts.per pound..pounds.	20c. p. lb. & 35 p.c.	861	233 00	253 75	3,178.75	894 00	948 05	1,034	300 00	343 36
Valued at above 40 and not exceeding 60 cents per pound ......pounds. Do.........do..	30c. p. lb. & 35 p.c. 30c. p.lb. & 35 p.c. less 10 p. c.	45,040 120	25,309 00 71 83	22,661 15 55 03	44,208	24,452 00	21,820 60	70,601.50	38,153 00	34,561 00
Valued at above 60 and not exceeding 80 cents per pound......pounds. Do........do..	40c. p. lb. & 35 p.c. 40c. p. lb. & 35 p.c. less 10 p. c.	138,244.75 1,249	107,383 00 940 00	92,563 00 748 54	138,260	109,671 00	91,553 85	159,662.75	91,222 00	80,192 79

No. 8.—STATEMENT SHOWING THE QUANTITIES AND VALUES OF IMPORTED MANUFACTURES OF WOOL ENTERED FOR CONSUMPTION IN THE UNITED STATES, &C., DURING THE YEARS ENDING JUNE 30, FROM 1867 TO 1886, INCLUSIVE—Continued.

ARTICLES.	Rates of duty.	1876.			1877.			1878.		
		Quantities.	Values.	Duties.	Quantities.	Values.	Duties.	Quantities.	Values.	Duties.
All manufactures of every description not specially enumerated or provided for, made wholly or in part of wool.—Continued. Of worsted, &c.—Continued. Valued at above 80 cents per pound ....pounds..	50c. p. lb. & 35 p. c.	1,290,166.25	*Dollars.* 1,701,709 00	*Dollars.* 1,240,681 82	998,279.69	*Dollars.* 1,320,662 80	*Dollars.* 961,371 85	604,300.01	*Dollars.* 882,958 00	*Dollars.* 611,185 77
Do ....pounds..	50c. p. lb. & 35 p. c. less 10 p. c.	42,965	53,356 89	30,141 07						
Total manufactures, not elsewhere specified		1,708,594.54	2,208,186 12	1,690,300 05	1,331,015.47	1,687,515 91	1,232,665 91	925,668.84	1,222,288 80	864,104 44
Grand total			34,872,725 90	22,519,105 36		26,452,207 73	17,600,041 92		25,703,392 60	17,176,648 84

No. 8.—STATEMENT SHOWING THE QUANTITIES AND VALUES OF IMPORTED MANUFACTURES OF WOOL ENTERED FOR CONSUMPTION IN THE UNITED STATES, &C., DURING THE YEARS ENDING JUNE 30, FROM 1867 TO 1886, INCLUSIVE—Continued.

ARTICLES.	Rates of duty.	1872. Quantities.	1872. Values.	1872. Duties.	1880. Quantities.	1880. Values.	1880. Duties.	1881. Quantities.	1881. Values.	1881. Duties.
			Dollars.	*Dollars.*		*Dollars.*	*Dollars.*		*Dollars.*	*Dollars.*
Balmorals:										
Valued at above 40 and not exceeding 60 cents per pound ....pounds.	30c. p. lb. & 35 p. c.				1,105	584 00	553 00			
Valued at above 60 cents per pound ......pounds.	40c. p. lb. & 35 p. c.				8,126	6,041 00	5,364 75	16,611	13,153 00	11,247 95
Valued at above 80 cents per pound ......pounds.	50c. p. lb. & 35 p. c.	1	3 46	1 71	2,727	3,964 00	2,750 90	7,389.50	11,691 00	7,856 10
Weighing 4 ounces and over per square yard ...pounds.	50c. p. lb. & 35 p. c.	8.75	22 50	8 75						
Total balmorals		9.75	25 96	10 46	11,958	10,589 00	8,651 65	24,000.50	25,044 00	19,104 05
Belts or felts, endless, for paper or printing machines..pounds..	20c. p. lb. & 35 p. c.	103,110.50	90,690 00	52,365 70	183,063.75	144,872 00	87,317 95	145,239.50	123,085 00	72,120 65
Blankets:										
Valued at not exceeding 40 cents per pound..pounds.	20c. p. lb. & 35 p. c.	366.50	166 59	111 00	163.25	50 80	53 60	618	328 45	238 56
Valued at above 40 and not exceeding 60 cents per pound..pounds.	30c. p. lb. & 35 p. c.	1,834.25	1,082 43	929 11	1,350.75	715 00	658 16	163	88 12	79 74
Valued at above 60 and not exceeding 80 cents per pound.......pounds.	40c. p. lb. & 35, p. c.	59.50	39 00	37 45	238	165 19	153 02	417	281 00	258 15
Valued at above 80 cents per pound.......pounds.	50c. p. lb. & 35 p. c.	150.50	220 70	162 40	221.75	280 00	208 88	917.50	1,256 87	898 05
Weighing 4 ounces and over per square yard..pounds.	50c. p. lb. & 35 p. c.	4	5 00	3 75	18.50	10 00	15 90	20	20 00	17 00
Total blankets		2,416.75	1,453 72	1,233 83	2,001.25	1,239 08	1,089 68	2,135.50	1,954 44	1,492 10
Bunting.............sq. yards..	20c. p. sq. yd. & 35 p. c.	818	193 00	232 00	586	136 00	164 00	60	28 40	21 94
Carpets and carpeting of all kinds: Aubusson, Axminster, and Chenille carpets and carpets woven whole for rooms, ...sq. yards.	50 p. c.	68,703.53	168,865 00	83,432 50	95,983.83	237,292 00	118,601 00	165,748	371,081 00	185,840 50

No. 8.—STATEMENT SHOWING THE QUANTITIES AND VALUES OF IMPORTED MANUFACTURES OF WOOL ENTERED FOR CONSUMPTION IN THE UNITED STATES, &C., DURING THE YEARS ENDING JUNE 30, FROM 1867 TO 1886, INCLUSIVE.—Continued.

ARTICLES.	Rate of duty.	1879.			1880.			1881.		
		Quantities.	Values.	Duties.	Quantities.	Values.	Duties.	Quantities.	Values.	Duties.
Carpets and carpeting of all kinds—Continued.			*Dollars.*	*Dollars.*		*Dollars.*	*Dollars.*		*Dollars.*	*Dollars.*
Brussels carpets...sq. yards..	4c. p. sq. yd. & 35 p. c.	76,706.00	100,678 00	68,988 23	118,871.69	142,955 00	102,337 70	102,100.33	213,724 00	146,130 19
Druggets and bockings, printed, colored, or otherwise...sq. yards..	25c. p. sq. yd. & 35 p. c.	3,102	1,124 00	1,168 90	12,007	5,069 00	4,985 00	6,870	2,802 00	2,698 20
Mats, screens, hassocks, and rugs, not exclusively vegetable material	45 p. c........		179,547 00	80,706 15		232,073 99	104,433 29		287,425 16	123,341 32
Of wool, flax, or cotton, or parts of either, or other material not specially enumerated or provided for...sq. yards.	40 p. c........		46,757 10	18,702 84		58,743 10	23,497 23		77,333 63	30,933 45
Patent, velvet and tapestry velvet carpets, printed on the warp or otherwise...sq. yards.	40c. p. sq. yd. & 35 p. c.	32,788.75	45,245 00	28,951 25	66,037.50	83,900 00	55,783 15	53,710.75	66,721 00	44,836 65
Saxony, Wilton and Tournay velvet carpets...sq. yards.	70c. p. sq. yd. & 35 p. c.	6,091.14	11,621 00	6,331 15	16,442.44	31,540 00	22,548 72	33,919.71	71,674 00	48,829 70
Tapestry Brussels, printed on the warp or otherwise...sq. yards.	28c. p. sq. yd. & 35 p. c.	44,518.25	41,544 55	27,005 70	789,259.50	504,361 00	397,498 02	415,447.29	284,258 00	215,815 54
Treble ingrain, three-ply, and worsted chain Venetian carpets ....sq. yards.	17c. p. sq. yd. & 35 p. c.	841	903 00	450 02	8,501.60	7,238 00	3,076 82	9,601.06	9,454 00	4,941 08
Yarn, Venetian, and two-ply ingrain carpets...sq. yards.	12c. p. sq. yd. & 35 p. c.	1,352.50	957 00	497 25	14,492.23	9,726 00	5,143 17	20,462	14,969 80	7,701 87
Total carpets			595,241 65	318,392 99		1,313,353 09	638,805 00		1,400,062 50	817,068 50

	Rate of duty									
Clothing, ready-made, and wearing apparel (except knit goods), not specially enumerated or provided for, composed wholly or in part of wool, worsted, the hair of the alpaca, goat, or other like animals, made up or manufactured wholly or in part by the tailor, seamstress, or manufacturer:										
Cloaks, dolmans, jackets, talmas, ulsters, or other outside garments for ladies' and children's apparel, and goods of similar description, or used for like purposes,........pounds.	50c. p. lb. & 40 p. c.	55,625.01	172,562 00	96,813 58	57,803.93	163,051 07	94,512 62	50,556.10	174,155 74	97,940 38
Clothing, ready-made, and wearing apparel of every description not specially enumerated or provided for, and balmoral skirts and skirting, and goods of similar description or used for like purposes......pounds.	50c. p. lb. & 40 p. c.	159,257.62	441,469 84	256,224 72	201,079.52	615,054 07	346,501 40	810,859.19	834,054 17	489,051 31
Total clothing		214,882.63	613,092 44	353,038 30	258,943.45	779,005 74	441,074 02	367,415.38	1,008,209 91	588,991 09
Cloths, woolen: Cloths ....pounds.	50c. p. lb. & 35 p. c.	4,054,199.21	5,623,806 50	3,995,431 95	6,362,234.84	8,415,214 68	6,126,442 58	7,056,921.38	9,376,097 72	6,810,073 89
Dress goods, women's and children's, and Italian cloths, and goods of like description:										
Composed in part of wool, worsted, the hair of the alpaca, goat, or other animals—										
Valued at not exceeding 20 cents per square yard, ...sq. yards.	6c. p. sq. yd. & 35 p. c.	21,846,272.17	3,735,597 85	2,618,235 01	30,705,622.08	5,195,735 00	3,080,844 52	26,385,238.75	4,556,833 02	3,178,005 86
Valued at above 20 cents per sq. yd. . sq. yards.	8c. p. sq. yd. & 40 p. c.	29,721,032.90	9,074,508 80	6,007,736 20	33,338,100.38	9,057,107 86	6,529,895 98	31,540,809.33	9,395,887 38	6,281,624 47

No. 8.—Statement showing the Quantities and Values of Imported Manufactures of Wool entered for Consumption in the United States, &c., during the years ending June 30, from 1867 to 1886, inclusive—Continued.

ARTICLES.	Rates of duty.	1879.			1880.			1881.		
		Quantities.	Values.	Duties.	Quantities.	Values.	Duties.	Quantities.	Values.	Duties.
Dress goods, &c.—Continued. Composed wholly of wool, worsted, the hair of the alpaca, goat, or other animals, or of a mixture of them, and all such goods of like description, with selvedges, made wholly or in part of other materials, or with threads of other materials introduced for the purpose of changing the classification—			*Dollars.*	*Dollars.*		*Dollars.*	*Dollars.*		*Dollars.*	*Dollars.*
All weighing over 4 oz. per sq. yd......pounds.	50c. p. lb. & 35 p. c.	960,522.88	1,555,148 00	1,024,063 29	1,108,810.58	1,899,224 67	1,219,138 45	1,143,021 06	2,008,345 44	1,274,431 48
Total dress goods...			14,365,254 05	9,660,025 10		16,752,067 53	11,409,878 05		15,901,065 74	10,734,061 81
Flannels: Valued at not exceeding 40 cents per pound...pounds.	20c. p. lb. & 35 p. c.	3	1 00	92	7.09	2 84	2 53	3	1 00	05
Valued at above 40 and not exceeding 60 cents per pound, pounds.	30c. p. lb. & 35 p. c.	6,783.25	3,428 00	3,234 78	0	4 74	4 35	2,479.50	1,100 30	1,128 96
Valued at above 60 and not exceeding 80 cents per pound, pounds.	40c. p. lb. & 35 p. c.	4,507.00	3,402.	3,017 50	2,489	1,754 00	1,609 50	21,607	14,243 85	12,028 15
Valued at above 80 cents per pound...pounds.	50c. p. lb. & 35 p. c.	953.50	1,596.00	1,035 35	705.38	1,308 40	810 62	1,211.50	1,989 51	1,302 08
Weighing 4 ounces and over per square yard...pounds.	50c. p. lb. & 35 p. c.				7	13 00	8 05	155.50	294 00	180 65
Total flannels...		12,306.75	8,427 00	7,288 58	3,218.07	3,082 98	2,435 05	25,456.50	17,628 06	10,240 79
Hats of wool: Valued at above 40 and not exceeding 60 cents per pound, ... pounds.	30c. p. lb. & 35 p. c.							9	4 50	4 31

Article	Rate	(1)	(2)	(3)	(4)	(5)	(6)	(7)	(8)	(9)
Valued at above 60 and not exceeding 80 cents per pound, ...pounds.	40c. p. lb. & 35 p.c.	4,231.63	6,754 80	4,470 99	351	261 00	231 75	75	49 16	47 21
Valued at over 80 cents per pound .....pounds.	50c. p. lb. & 35 p.c.		1,702 00	170 20		863 00	85 30	437	940 88	547 82
Hat roundings or trimmings..	10 p.c.									
Total hats			8,456 80	4,650 19	4,017.45	7,272 50	4,481 23	521	904 63	599 34
Knit goods:										
Hosiery—										
Valued at not over 40 cents per pound .....pounds.	20c. p. lb. & 35 p.c.	465	183 00	157 05	20.50	10 00	9 65	49	27 00	24 15
Valued at above 40 and not exceeding 60 cents per pound .....pounds.	30c. p. lb. & 35 p.c.	3,327	1,598 00	1,557 40	61	42 83	39 39	30	22 45	10 80
Valued at above 60 and not exceeding 80 cents per pound .....pounds.	40c. p. lb. & 35 p.c.	2,250	1,651 00	1,480 25						
Valued at above 80 cents per pound .....pounds.	50c. p. lb. & 35 p.c.									
Total hosiery		131,136.10	322,706 04	178,530 17	190,007.50	468,114 00	256,843 71	343,882 85	827,508 11	401,569 30
			326,198 04	181,730 87	190,089.06	468,166 83	256,892 75	342,961 85	827,657 56	461,613 31
Shirts, drawers, and other knit goods—										
Valued at not over 40 cents per pound. .....pounds.	20c. p. lb. & 35 p.c.				2.50	2 60	1 41			
Valued at above 40 and not exceeding 60 cents per pound .....pounds.	30c. p. lb. & 35 p.c.				15	10 00	8 00			
Valued at above 60 and not exceeding 80 cents per pound .....pounds.	40c. p. lb. & 35 p.c.	1,668	989 00	843 40	1,746	1,003 00	1,079 45			
Valued at above 80 cents per pound .....pounds.	50c. p. lb. & 35 p.c.									
Total shirts, drawers, &c		33,459.45	60,570 00	40,032 40	85,186.03	138,121 69	87,435 58	117,805 84	176,685 50	121,442 91
		35,127.45	67,559 00	40,675 80	86,949.53	129,197 29	88,515 44	117,805 84	176,685 50	121,443 01
Rags, shoddy, mungo, waste, and flocks, woolen .....pounds.	12c. p. lb. less 10 p.c.	111,840	25,781 00	13,420 80	1,289,140	260,902 65	154,097 52	513,110 75	160,498 00	65,174 01
Shawls:										
Woolen .....pounds.	50c. p. lb. & 35 p.c.	61,733.31	134,923 05	78,069 77	52,400.05	114,771 75	66,370 44	54,156 71	112,083 06	66,307 31
Worsted— Not otherwise specified, ...pounds.	50c. p. lb. & 40 p.o.	417,573.12	1,157,555 07	671,808 82	440,588.54	1,157,755 55	683,390 50	383,928 66	1,064,115 00	017,010 86
Total shawls		470,306.43	1,292,473 72	749,898 50	492,089.10	1,272,527 30	749,766 94	438,085 37	1,176,198 00	683,917 07

No. 8.—STATEMENT SHOWING THE QUANTITIES AND VALUES OF IMPORTED MANUFACTURES OF WOOL ENTERED FOR CONSUMPTION IN THE UNITED STATES, &C., DURING THE YEARS ENDING JUNE 30, FROM 1867 TO 1886, INCLUSIVE—Continued.

ARTICLES.	Rates of duty.	1879.			1880.			1881.		
		Quantities.	Values.	Duties.	Quantities.	Values.	Duties.	Quantities.	Values.	Duties.
Webbings, gorings, suspenders, braces, beltings, bindings, braids, galloons, fringes, gimps, cords, cords and tassels, dress trimmings, head nets, buttons or barrel buttons, or buttons of other forms for tassels or ornaments, wrought by hand or braided by machinery, made of wool, or of which wool, worsted, the hair of the alpaca, goat, or other animals is a component material............pounds.	50c. p. lb. & 60 p. c.	173,301.78	*Dollars.* 450,103 00	*Dollars.* 311,747 42	184,720.81	*Dollars.* 455,813 56	*Dollars.* 320,267 21	119,560.24	*Dollars.* 327,321 00	*Dollars.* 223,443 61
Yarns, woolen and worsted:										
Valued at not exceeding 40 cents per pound ...pounds..	20c. p. lb. & 35 p. o.	142	44 00	43 80	18,210.39	7,024 35	6,100 50	3,644	1,501 82	1,254 44
Valued at above 40 and not exceeding 60 cents per pound.......pounds.	30c. p. lb. & 35 p. o.	211.25	103 00	99 43	3,476.50	1,833 00	1,685 40	3,741.16	2,237 19	1,965 97
Valued at above 60 and not exceeding 80 cents per pound.......pounds.	40c. p. lb. & 35 p. o.	2,815	2,035 00	1,838 25	11,028.50	8,390 00	7,310 40	6,832	5,165 57	4,540 76
Valued at above 80 cents per pound.......pounds.	50c. p. lb. & 35 p. o.	505,929.71	587,042 00	458,744 57	603,030.13	687,904 43	542,284 05	462,565.92	531,192 25	417,200 28
Total yarns.		509,097.96	590,124 00	460,726 05	635,754.52	705,061 78	507,367 04	476,783.08	640,090 83	434,900 85
All manufactures of every description not specially enumerated or provided for, made wholly or in part of wool: Manufactures, not otherwise specified.......pounds.	50c. p lb. & 35 p. c.	124,913.97	209,751 00	135,809 88	183,878.17	282,016 60	190,644 01	278,257.50	425,837 71	288,178 96
Worsted, the hair of the alpaca, goat, or other animals, (except such as are composed in part of wool)— Valued at not exceeding 40 cents per pound.......pounds.	20c. p. lb. & 35 p. c.	314	105 08	99 57	10,170	3,424 00	3,232 40	50,162	20,283 00	17,124 45

Valued at above 40 and not exceeding 60 cents per pound....pounds..	30c. p. lb. & 35 p. o.	53,097	29,243 00	20,344 15	86,892	45,595 00	42,025 85	42,076	21,755 00	20,237 05
Valued at above 60 and not exceeding 80 cents per pound....pounds..	40c. p. lb. & 35 p. o.	127,773.76	97,102 00	85,126 70	103,573.50	142,010 00	127,447 90	110,286.26	90,174 42	79,275 55
Valued at above 80 cents per pound....pounds..	50c. p. lb. & 35 p. o.	452,569.54	640,04_ 88	450,014 45	466,399.11	022,100 00	450,094 59	968,875.99	1,420,824 00	981,720 22
Total manufactures not elsewhere specified......		759,208.26	077,22_ 00	098,054 75	940,012.78	1,000,045 00	814,285 05	1,458,057.14	1,978,874 13	1,360,542 23
Grand total......			25,087,10_ 44	10,839,064 28		31,834,546 01	21,864,153 16		33,103,322 11	22,424,809 58

No. 8.—STATEMENT SHOWING THE QUANTITIES AND VALUES OF IMPORTED MANUFACTURES OF WOOL ENTERED FOR CONSUMPTION IN THE UNITED STATES, &C., DURING THE YEARS ENDING JUNE 30, FROM 1867 TO 1886, INCLUSIVE—Continued.

ARTICLES.	Rates of duty.	1862.			1863.			1864.		
		Quantities.	Values.	Duties.	Quantities.	Values.	Duties.	Quantities.	Values.	Duties.
			Dollars.	Dollars.		Dollars.	Dollars.		Dollars.	Dollars.
Balmorals:										
Valued at not exceeding 40 cents per pound ...pounds.	20c. p.lb. & 35 p.c.				31	9 00	9 35			
Valued at above 40 and not exceeding 60 cents per pound ...pounds.	30c. p.lb. & 35 p.c.	4,660	2,479 00	2,265 65	20	13 00	12 35	9,471	5,466 00	3,617 88
Do. ...do.	18 c. p. lb. & 35 p.c.									
Valued at above 60 and not exceeding 80 cents per pound, ...pounds.	40 c. p. lb. & 35 p. c.	1,113	839 00	738 85	1,150.50	811 00	741 05	4,168	2,777 00	1,977 07
Do. ...do.	24 c. p. lb. & 35 p. c.									
Valued at above 80 cents per pound ...pounds.	50 c. p. lb. & 35 p. c.	417	453 00	367 05	1,657	2,010 00	1,532 00	127	144 00	102 05
Do. ...do.	35 c. p. lb. & 40 p. c.									
Total balmorals ...		6,190	3,771 00	3,371 53	2,864.50	2,843 00	2,297 75	13,766	8,387 00	5,097 00
Bolts or felts, endless, for paper or printing machines ...pounds.	20 c. p.lb. & 35 p. c.	141,771.88	127,060 00	73,143 53	151,254.75	139,749 00	79,163 10	150,029.49	150,211 00	70,660 20
Do. ...do.	20c. p. lb. & 30 p.c.									
Blankets:										
Valued at not exceeding 40 cents per pound ...pounds.	20c. p. lb. & 35 p. c.	8,924	3,539 45	3,023 61	1,666	459 97	494 20			
Valued at not exceeding 30 cents per pound ...pounds.	10c. p. lb. & 35 p. c.							539	148 00	103 80
Valued at above 30 and not exceeding 40 cents per pound, ...pounds.	12c. p. lb. & 35 p. c.							590	194 00	138 70
Valued at above 40 and not exceeding 60 cents per pound, ...pounds.	30c. p. lb. & 35 p.c.	451	228 26	215 19	1,428	745 00	689 36	541.50	286 18	198 17
Do. ...do.	18c. p. lb. & 35 p.c.									
Valued at above 60 and not exceeding 80 cents per pound, ...pounds.	40c. p. lb. & 35 p.c.	197	131 00	124 65	520.75	345 22	329 12	333.25	234 00	161 88
Do. ...do.	24c. p. lb. & 33 p.c.									

Article	Rate	1	2	3	4	5	6	7	8	9
Valued at above 80 cents per pound.........pounds..	50c. p. lb. & 35 p. c.	3,517.13	4,978 08	3,501 09	1,012.50	1,334 20	973 24	98,186.06	118,145 63	81,623 40
Do.........do..	35c. p. lb. & 40 p. c.	13,089.18	8,877 30	6,864 54	4,627.25	2,855 02	2,485 92	100,173.81	119,007 83	82,225 95
Total blankets........										
Bunting: Bunting.........sq. yards	20c. p. sq. yd. & 35	528.25	110 25	144 24	106	39 00	34 85			
Carpets and carpeting of all kinds: Aubusson, Axminster, and Chenille carpets and carpets woven whole for rooms, ...sq. yards	50 p. c.	214,749.37	469,961 00	234,980 50	269,174	474,575 53	237,287 77	130,752.05	395,256 92	177,415 54
Do.........do..	45c. p. sq. yd. & 30 p. c.	109,540	134,320 00	95,200 61	130,505.05	165,630 30	118,034 94			
Brussels carpets.........sq. yards	44c. p. sq. yd. & 35 p. c.							212,524.36	239,080 64	135,481 54
Do.........do..	30c. p. sq. yd. & 30 p. c.									
Druggets and bockings, printed, colored, or otherwise, ...sq. yards	25c. p. sq. yd. & 35 p. c.	5,331	2,080 00	2,046 40	7,766.25	2,763 00	2,908 26	5,629	1,655 00	1,334 65
Do.........do..	15c. p. sq. yd. & 30 p. c.									
Mats, screens, hassocks, and rugs, not exclusively vegetable material.....	45 p. c.		370,785 65	160,853 54		296,897 87	133,604 04		400,076 00	160,030 40
Do.....	40 p. c.									
Of wool, flax, or cotton, or parts of either, or other material, not specially enumerated or provided for, ...do..		172,461	72,328 75	28,929 90	120,293	77,058 96	30,823 58	60,569.25	33,221 50	13,238 60
Patent velvet and tapestry velvet carpets, printed on the warp or otherwise, ...sq. yards	40c. p. sq. yd. & 35 p. c.	54,780.50	62,818 00	43,808 50	38,508.75	42,545 50	30,294 43	80,464.50	90,605 00	48,824 05
Do.........sq. yards	25c. p. sq. yd. & 30 p. c.									
Saxony, Wilton, and Tournay velvet carpets.........sq. yards	70c. p. sq. yd. & 35 p. c.	19,162	37,659 00	26,559 06	37,956.80	75,470 32	52,087 52			
Do.........do..	45c. p. sq. yd. & 30 p. c.									
Tapestry Brussels, printed on the warp or otherwise, ...sq. yards	28c. p. sq. yd. & 35 p. c.	113,552.75	83,242 07	60,929 50	43,636.75	30,189 00	24,884 44	79,121.95	149,272 90	80,386 49

No. 4.—STATEMENT SHOWING THE QUANTITIES AND VALUES OF IMPORTED MANUFACTURES OF WOOL ENTERED FOR CONSUMPTION IN THE UNITED STATES, &C., DURING THE YEARS ENDING JUNE 30, FROM 1867 TO 1866, INCLUSIVE—Continued.

ARTICLES.	Rates of duty.	1882.			1883.			1884.		
		Quantities.	Values.	Duties.	Quantities.	Values.	Duties.	Quantities.	Values.	Duties.
			Dollars.	Dollars.		Dollars.	Dollars.		Dollars.	Dollars.
Carpets, &c.—Continued.										
Tapestry Brussels, printed on the warp or otherwise, ...sq. yards.	20c. p. sq. yd. & 30 p. c.							237,141.87	134,346 12	87,732 21
Treble ingrain, three-ply, and worsted chain, Venetian carpets ...sq. yards.	17c. p. sq. yd. & 35 p. c.	13,993	13,554 00	7,122 73	7,352.50	7,204 00	3,771 33	8,109.66	7,696 00	3,281 90
Do ...... do	12c. p. sq. yd. & 30 p. c.									
Yarn, Venetian, and two-ply ingrain carpets ...sq. yards.	12c. p. sq. yd. & 35 p. c.	15,556	10,631 00	5,587 57	67,791.83	46,808 00	24,517 87	106,537.50	65,802 00	28,263 60
Do ...... do	80c. p. sq. yd. & 30 p. c.									
Total carpets......			1,257,234 47	672,117 31	....	1,225,156 48	650,114 18	....	1,517,081 18	736,039 84
Clothing, ready-made, and wearing apparel (except knit goods), not specially enumerated or provided for, composed wholly or in part of wool, worsted, the hair of the alpaca, goat, or other like animals, made up or manufactured wholly or in part by the tailor, seamstress, or manufacturer:										
Cloaks, dolmans, jackets, talmas, ulsters, or other outside garments for ladies' and children's apparel, and goods of similar description, or used for like purposes, ...pounds.	50c. p. lb. & 40 p. c.	55,668 42	177,382 36	98,772 19	218,714	490,084 72	305,890 88	942,788 30	1,395,467 18	982,441 46
Do ...... do	45c. p. lb. & 40 p. o.									
Clothing, ready-made, and wearing apparel of every description, not specially enumerated or provided for,										

Description	Duty									
and balmoral skirts and skirting, and goods of similar description or used for like purposes......pounds..	50c. p. lb. & 40 p. c.	466,536.33	982,485.02	626,262.21	403,649.66	937,372.43	621,773.81	426,025.63	972,792.17	510,887.50
Do.............do...	40c. p. lb. & 35 p. c.									
Total clothing		522,174.76	1,159,867.38	725,054.40	712,363.66	1,427,457.15	927,164.60	1,368,813.93	2,368,259.35	1,493,320.14
Cloths, woolen: Cloths........pounds..	50c. p. lb. & 35 p. c.	8,053,891.92	10,487,059.97	7,697,416.96	8,220,025.38	10,806,324.01	7,892,226.12	10,246,906.09	12,973,683.15	8,775,890.41
Valued at not exceeding 80 cents per pound	35c. p. lb. & 35 p. c.									
Valued at above 80 cents per pound......pounds..	35c. p. lb. & 40 p. c.							383,055.83	242,975.17	219,110.83
Total cloths		8,053,891.92	10,487,059.97	7,697,416.96	8,220,025.38	10,806,324.01	7,692,226.12	10,629,961.92	13,216,658.32	8,995,001.24
Dress goods, women's and children's, coat linings, Italian cloths, and goods of like description:										
Composed in part of wool, worsted, the hair of the alpaca, goat, or other animals—Valued at not exceeding 20 cents per square yard. ....sq. yards..	6c. p. sq. yd. & 35 p. c.	30,984,710	5,507,852.37	3,786,830.93	44,581,580	7,830,094.00	5,415,427.65	23,126,509.04	3,557,185.20	2,401,340.28
Do.........do...	5c. p. sq. yd. & 35 p. c.									
Valued at above 20 cents per sq. yd ... sq. yards..	8c. p. sq. yd. & 40 p. c.	36,297,705	10,733,297.40	7,197,125.38	42,582,940.25	11,959,028.68	8,186,246.70	6,971,078	2,151,470.20	1,348,563.55
Do.........do...	7c. p. sq. yd. & 40 p. c.									
Composed wholly of wool, worsted, the hair of the alpaca, goat, or other animals, or of a mixture of them, and all such goods of like description, with selvedges made wholly or in part of other materials, or with threads of other materials introduced for the purpose of changing the classification—										
Weighing 4 ounces or less per sq. yd ......sq. yards..	9c. p. sq. yd. & 40 p. c.							26,023,083.47	6,649,294.84	5,001,842.28

No. 8.—STATEMENT SHOWING THE QUANTITIES AND VALUES OF IMPORTED MANUFACTURES OF WOOL ENTERED FOR CONSUMPTION IN THE UNITED STATES, &C., DURING THE YEARS ENDING JUNE 30, FROM 1867 TO 1886, INCLUSIVE—Continued.

ARTICLES.	Rates of duty.	1882. Quantities.	Values.	Duties.	1883. Quantities.	Values.	Duties.	1884. Quantities.	Values.	Duties.
			Dollars.	Dollars.		Dollars.	Dollars.		Dollars.	Dollars.
Dress goods, &c.—Continued. Composed wholly of wool, &c.—Continued. All weighing over 4 oz. per sq. yd ....pounds.	50c. p. lb. & 35 p. c.	1,872,656.25	2,829,667 00	1,926,711 64	1,914,088.23	2,829,083 31	1,947,538 20	2,168,522.08	2,991,147 11	1,935,441 59
Do ....do....	35c. p. lb. & 40 p. c.									
Total dress goods...			19,070,816 77	12,910,677 05		22,619,105 99	15,540,212 63		15,349,097 35	10,707,187 70
Flannels: Valued at not exceeding 40 cents per pound ...pounds.	20c. p. lb. & 35 p. o.	3,724	1,291 00	1,196 65	31	11 30	10 13			
Valued at not exceeding 30 cents per pound ...pounds.	10c. p. lb. & 35 p. o.							2,050	529 00	411 15
Valued at above 30 and not exceeding 40 cents per pound, pounds.	12c. p. lb. & 35 p. c.							7,730	2,676 00	1,864 20
Valued at above 40 and not exceeding 60 cents per pound, pounds.	30c. p. lb. & 35 p. e.	1,235.50	687 00	611 10	46	22 00	21 50	25,578.50	14,933 00	9,831 38
Do ....do.......	18c. p. lb. & 33 p. o.									
Valued at above 60 and not exceeding 80 cents per pound, pounds.	40c. p. lb. & 35 p. c.	4,319.50	2,706 00	2,700 40	9,382	6,580 70	6,056 05	21,222.75	15,227 30	10,423 01
Do ....do.......	24c. p. lb. & 35 p. o.									
Valued at above 80 cents per pound ....pounds.	50c. p. lb. & 35 p. o.	7,109.75	9,650 12	6,932 41	132,085.83	171,931 42	126,218 92	214,409.39	272,397 05	184,002 50
Do ....do.......	35c. p. lb. & 40 p. o.									
Total flannels...		16,388.75	14,424 12	11,446 59	141,544.83	178,545 42	132,306 62	270,090.64	303,825 25	206,532 24
Hats of wool: Valued at not exceeding 40 cents per pound ...pounds.	20c. p. lb. & 33 p. c.	901.50	352 00	303 50						
Valued at above 30 and not exceeding 40 cents per pound, pounds.	12c. p. lb. & 25 p. o.	180	104 00	90 40				540	164 00	122 20
Valued at above 40 and not exceeding 60 cents per pound, pounds.	30c. p. lb. & 35 p. c.									

Description	Rate									
Valued at above 60 and not exceeding 80 cents per pound, pounds.	40c. p. lb. & 35 p. c.	611	362 00	371 10	1,819 13	4,018 56	2,316 06	3,596	2,580 00	1,766 04
Do .... do.	24c. p. lb. & 35 p. c.									
Valued at over 80 cents per pound, pounds.	50c. p. lb. & 35 p. c.	1,386.13	2,735 62	1,657 54				7,073 25	11,576 46	7,106 25
Do .... do.	35c. p. lb. & 40 p. c.									
Total hats		3,078.63	8,573 02	2,422 54	1,819.13	4,018 56	2,316 06	11,200 25	14,320 46	8,994 49
Knit goods: Hosiery:—										
Valued at not over 40 cents per pound, pounds.	20c. p. lb. & 35 p. c.	1.50	1 00	65						
Valued at above 40 and not exceeding 60 cents per pound, pounds.	30c. p. lb. & 35 p. c.	339.25	169 00	160 93	43	22 00	20 60			
Valued at above 60 and not exceding 80 cents per pound, pounds.	40c. p. lb. & 35 p. c.	556.25	400 84	362 79	63.25	46 12	41 44			
Valued at above 80 cents per pound, pounds.	50c. p. lb. & 35 p. c.	333,206.11	736,601 35	425,494 03	302,088.90	677,418 26	388,140 80			
Total hosiery		330,103.11	737,402 10	426,018 40	302,195.15	677,486 38	388,202 84			
Shirts, drawers, and other knit goods—										
Valued at not over 40 cents per pound, pounds.	20c. p. lb. & 35 p. c.	5.50	3 00	2 70	7.50	3 00	2 55			
Valued at above 40 and not exceeding 60 cents per pound, pounds.	30c. p. lb. & 35 p. c.				5	3 00	2 55			
Valued at above 60 and not exceding 80 cents per pound, pounds.	40c. p. lb. & 35 p. c.				11.50	8 20	7 47			
Valued at above 80 cents per pound, pounds.	50c. p. lb. & 35 p. c.	114,772.26	180,686 40	120,591 41	94,501.09	224,966 30	125,989 04			
Knit goods, and all goods made on knitting frames— All not specified	35 p. o.		84,327 00	12,017 95		100,003 00	66,532 55			
Valued at not exceeding 30 cents per pound, 30 cents per pound	35 p. o.									
Valued at above 30 and not exceeding 40 cents per pound, pounds.	10c. p. lb. & 35 p. c.							3,021	799 00	581 75
Valued at above 40 and not exceeding 60 cents per pound, pounds.	12c. p. lb. & 35 p. c.							51	18 00	12 42
Valued at above 60 cents per pound, pounds.	18c. p. lb. & 35 p. c.							3,666	2,034 00	1,375 74
Valued at above 80 cents per pound, pounds.	24c. p. lb. & 35 p. c.							87,339.75	64,232 92	43,443 07

No. 8.—Statement showing the Quantities and Values of Imported Manufactures of Wool entered for Consumption in the United States, &c., during the Years ending June 30, from 1867 to 1886, inclusive—Continued.

ARTICLES	Rates of duty	1882			1883			1884		
		Quantities	Values	Duties	Quantities	Values	Duties	Quantities	Values	Duties
			Dollars.	*Dollars.*		*Dollars.*	*Dollars.*		*Dollars.*	*Dollars.*
Knit goods—Continued.										
Knit goods, and all goods made on knitting-frames—Cont'd. Valued at above 80 cents per pound......pounds.	35c. p. lb. & 35 p. c.							997,007.26	2,028,029 81	1,160,188 51
Total knit goods, except hosiery.....			214,928 40	132,612 06		415,073 50	102,534 16	1,091,107.01	2,095,173 73	1,205,601 49
Rags, shoddy, mungo, waste, and flocks, woolen......pounds.	12c. p. lb	917,621.50	342,071 00	110,114 68	871,401.50	423,120 00	110,568 78	1,225,360.50	533,730 00	122,536 03
Do......do.	10c. p. lb									
Shawls:										
Woolen......pounds. Valued at not exceeding 80 cents per pound......pounds	50c. p. lb. & 35 p. c.	71,815.75	140,364 75	85,035 54	238,763.72	569,421 50	297,670 44			
Valued at above 80 cents per pound......pounds	35c. p. lb. & 35 p. c.							4,293	2,652 00	2,430 70
Worsted— cents per pound......pounds	35c. p. lb. & 40 p. c.							394,764.30	745,206 75	436,250 12
Not otherwise specified......pounds	50c. p. lb. & 40 p. c.	340,776.46	631,302 09	542,909 10	282,015.78	636,267 00	415,514 72			
Total shawls......		412,592.21	1,071,660 84	627,944 64	520,779.50	1,195,688 50	713,194 16	399,057.30	747,858 53	438,680 88
Webbings, gorings, suspenders, braces, beltings, bindings, braids, galloons, fringes, gimps, cords, cords and tassels, dress trimmings, head nets, buttons or barrel buttons, or buttons of other forms for tassels or ornaments wrought by hand or braided by machinery, made of wool, or of which wool, worsted, the hair of the alpaca, goat, or other animals is a component material......pounds	50c. p. lb. & 50 p. c.	169,388.74	462,711 00	316,049 87	228,560.15	639,523 00	434,041 60	184,609.25	469,207 29	284,998 40
Do......do.	30c. p. lb. & 50 p. c.									

Article	Rate									
Yarns, woolen and worsted:										
Valued at not exceeding 40 cents per pound...pounds.	20c. p. lb. & 35 p. c.	321	215 50	104 63	2,400.33	629 51	701 66	8,897.25	2,069 70	1,803 12
Valued at not exceeding 30 cents per pound...pounds.	10c. p. lb. & 35 p. c.									
Valued at above 30 and not exceeding 40 cents per pound...pounds.	12c. p. lb. & 35 p. c.	1,288.75	824 08	675:12	1,958	999 35	037 17	235,646.41	89,158 50	59,111 03
Valued at above 40 and not exceeding 60 cents per pound...pounds.	30c. p. lb. & 35 p. c.									
Do......do...	18c. p. lb. & 35 p. c.	16,503.25	12,226 70	10,860 07	87,407.25	64,750 15	67,652 00	194,702.02	98,275 90	60,459 86
Valued at above 60 and not exceeding 80 cents per pound...pounds.	40c. p. lb. & 35 p. c.									
Do......do...	24c. p. lb. & 35 p. c.									
Valued at above 80 cents per pound...pounds.	50c. p. lb. & 35 p. c.	344,591.50	402,840 33	314,289 89	320,408.03	300,975 05	291,675 70	670,430.63	502,181 84	338,827 02
Do......do...	35c. p. lb. & 40 p. c.							324,420.39	350,517 44	250,156 23
Total yarns		364,704.50	416,007 51	325,930 41	418,300.51	433,363 06	350,907 13	1,440,063.82	1,048,743 38	725,331 27
All manufactures of every description not specially enumerated or provided for, made wholly or in part of wool:										
Manufactures not otherwise specified...pounds	50c. p. lb. & 35 p. c.	726,501.84	1,107,291 97	750,603 17	926,080.31	1,308,388 92	953,479 29			
Wool—										
Valued at not exceeding 80cts. per pound, pounds.	35c. p. lb. & 35 p. o.							98,101.25	41,307 17	38,202 98
Valued at above 80 cts. per pound...pounds.	35c. p. lb. & 40 p. c.							748,212.08	1,089,902 95	697,850 67
Worsted, the hair of the alpaca, goat, or other animals, (except such as are composed in part of wool)—										
Valued at not exceeding 40cts. per pound, pounds.	20c. p. lb. & 35 p. c.	150,472	55,565 00	50,742 15	41,146.50	14,977 00	13,471 25	40,358.50	11,110 00	7,024 35
Valued at not exceeding 30 cts. per pound, pounds.	10c. p. lb. & 35 p. c.									
Valued at above 30 and not exceeding 40 cents per pound...pounds.	12c. p. lb. & 35 p. c.	85,072	46,023 00	41,809 03	124,090.50	66,860 00	60,601 40	34,017.50	12,151 00	8,334 95
Valued at above 40 and not exceeding 60 cents per pound...pounds.	30c. p. lb. & 35 p. c.									
Do......pounds.	18c. p. lb. & 35 p. c.	114,928.88	107,079 00	95,050 20	374,543.25	272,050 00	245,852 95	577,513.25	327,828 00	218,698 81
Valued at above 60 and not exceeding 80 cents per pound...pounds.	40c. p. lb. & 35 p. c.							777,337.25	500,219 08	382,035 23
Do......do...	24c. p. lb. & 36 p. c.									

No. 8.—Statement showing the Quantities and Values of Imported Manufactures of Wool entered for Consumption in the United States, &c., during the years ending June 30, from 1867 to 1886, inclusive.—Continued.

ARTICLES.	Rates of duty.	1882.			1883.			1884.		
		Quantities.	Values.	Duties.	Quantities.	Values.	Duties.	Quantities.	Values.	Duties.
All manufactures of every description not specially enumerated or provided for, made wholly or in part of wool—Continued. Worsted, &c.—Continued.			*Dollars.*	*Dollars.*		*Dollars.*	*Dollars.*		*Dollars.*	*Dollars.*
Valued at above 80 cents per pound ...... pounds..	50c. p. lb. & 35 p.c..	423,193.11	589,776 00	418,019 16	438,775.77	608,603 00	432,468 94	1,234,677.25	1,508,724 00	1,035,636 67
Do ...... do..	35c. p. lb. & 40 p.c..									
Total manufactures, not elsewhere specified		1,506,769.83	1,906,334 07	1,357,033 33	1,904,048.33	2,302,677 92	1,704,433 89	3,490,213.68	3,551,302 20	2,380,307 16
Grand total			37,284,823,68	25,398,362 90		42,552,435 99	29,140,264 50		41,484,671 80	27,478,400 05

No. 8.—Statement showing the Quantities and Values of Imported Manufactures of Wool entered for Consumption in the United States, &c., during the years ending June 30, from 1857 to 1866, inclusive—Continued.

ARTICLES.	Rates of duty.	1865 Quantities.	1865 Values.	1865 Duties.	1866 Quantities.	1866 Values.	1866 Duties.
			Dollars.	*Dollars.*		*Dollars.*	*Dollars.*
Balmorals:							
Valued at above 40 and not exceeding 60 cents per pound ....pounds	40c. p. lb. & 35 p. c	21.50	11 30	7 82			
Valued at above 60 cents per pound ....do	35c. p. lb. & 40 p. c	70.50	66 00	51 07	;002	3,853 00	2,238 40
Total balmorals		92	77 30	58 69	1,003	3,853 00	2,238 40
Belts or felts, endless, for paper or printing machines, ...pounds	20c. p. lb. & 30 p. c	151,004.25	139,697 00	72,262 05	144,412.25	127,050 00	67,260 25
Blankets:							
Valued at not exceeding 30 cents per pound..pounds	10c. p. lb. & 35 p. c	3,757.50	1,011 66	740 31	5,102	1,328 97	975 35
Valued at above 30 and not exceeding 40 cents per pound.....pounds	12c. p. lb. & 35 p. c	606	221 00	157 27	1,535.25	539 00	379 87
Valued at above 40 and not exceeding 60 cents per pound.....pounds	18c. p. lb. & 35 p. c	638.01	331 25	230 88	4,770.75	2,570 92	1,760 16
Valued at above 60 and not exceeding 80 cents per pound.....pounds	24c. p. lb. & 35 p. c	310	214 18	149 37	1,363	896 00	641 92
Valued at above 80 cents per pound ....do	35c. p. lb. & 40 p. c	813.70	1,061 19	709 27	872.22	1,202 02	766 45
Total blankets		6,185.81	7,860 22	1,087 10	13,637.32	6,557 81	4,543 75
Bunting............square yards	10c. p. sq. yd. & 35 p. c	13	8 00	4 10	220	52 00	40 20
Carpets and carpeting of all kinds:							
Aubusson, Axminster, and Chenille carpets and carpets woven whole for rooms.........sq. yards	50 p. c. less 10 p. c.	125,288	317,032 00	160,489 21	143,034.60	371,861 00	178,173 87
Brussels carpets.........do	30c. p. sq. yd. & 30 p. c.	222,175.85	237,837 58	138,004 03	180,950.06	186,850 74	110,343 15
Druggets and bockings, printed, colored, or otherwise.........sq. yards	15c. p. sq. yd. & 30 p. c.	3,160	842 00	727 95	5,256	1,905 00	1,360 20
Mats, screens, hassocks, and rugs, not exclusively vegetable material	40 p. c		274,569 14	169,835 66		313,627 35	125,450 04
Of wool, flax, or cotton, or parts of either, or other material not specially enumerated or provided for,.........sq. yards	.........do	20,176.34	19,210 62	7,684 25	57,261.50	47,197 61	18,879 04
Patent velvet and tapestry velvet carpets, printed on the warp, or otherwise.........sq. yards	25c. p. sq. yd. & 30 p. c.	75,667.07	78,090 92	42,344 20	111,188.80	108,992 36	60,467 02
Saxony, Wilton, and Tournay velvet carpets.....do	45c. p. sq. yd. & 30 p. c.	47,772.40	91,551 34	48,062 08	72,649.10	130,766 57	71,922 11
Tapestry Brussels, printed on the warp, or otherwise.........sq. yards	20c. p. sq. yd. & 30 p. c.	122,516.06	80,090 20	48,806 27	186,350.72	126,082 13	75,351 00

No. 8.—STATEMENT SHOWING THE QUANTITIES AND VALUES OF IMPORTED MANUFACTURES OF WOOL ENTERED FOR CONSUMPTION IN THE UNITED STATES, &C., DURING THE YEARS ENDING JUNE 30, FROM 1867 TO 1886, INCLUSIVE—Continued.

ARTICLES.	Rates of duty.	1885. Quantities.	1885. Values.	1885. Duties.	1886. Quantities.	1886. Values.	1886. Duties.
			Dollars.	Dollars.		Dollars.	Dollars.
Carpets and carpeting of all kinds—Continued.							
Treble ingrain, three-ply, and worsted chain, Venetian carpets......sq. yards.	12c. p. sq. yd. & 30 p. c	2,752	2,200 00	992 94	2,804	2,205 00	997 06
Yarn, Venetian, and two-ply ingrain carpets..do...	8c. p. sq. yd. & 30 p. o	66,346 25	40,899 00	17,817 42	63,042 25	39,084 00	16,828 68
Total carpets ...		....	1,173,251 80	575,664 91	....	1,329,340 76	659,874 79
Clothing, ready-made, and wearing apparel (except knit goods), not specially enumerated or provided for, composed wholly or in part of wool, worsted, the hair of the alpaca, goat, or other like animals, made up or manufactured wholly or in part by the tailor, seamstress, or manufacturer:							
Cloaks, dolmans, jackets, talmas, ulsters, or other outside garments for ladies' and children's apparel, and goods of similar description, or used for like purposes......pounds.	45c. p. lb. & 40 p. c	903,272 81	1,167,103 50	849,314 18	561,545 25	793,098 93	510,174 97
Clothing, ready-made, and wearing apparel of every description not specially enumerated or provided for, and balmoral skirts and skirting, and goods of similar description, or used for like purposes......pounds.	40c. p. lb. & 35 p. c	333,715 54	696,597 72	377,295 41	297,341 95	628,060 87	339,073 11
Total clothing ...		1,236,988 35	1,863,701 22	1,226,009 59	858,887 20	1,422,659 80	909,248 08
Cloths, woolen:							
Valued at not exceeding 80 cents per pound......pounds.	35c. p. lb. & 35 p. c	330,371	213,840 75	190,474 11	510,377 80	313,078 81	288,419 83
Valued at above 80 cents per pound......do.	35c. p. lb. & 40 p. c	7,683,834 46	9,867,139 94	6,636,196 03	7,470,638 51	9,150,678 70	6,274,994 99
Total cloths...		8,014,205 40	10,080,980 69	6,829,672 14	7,981,016 31	9,464,357 51	6,563,414 82
Dress goods, women's and children's, coat linings, Italian cloths, and goods of like description:							
Composed in part of wool, worsted, the hair of the alpaca, goat, or other animals—							
Valued at not exceeding 20 cents per square yard......sq. yards.	5c. p. sq. yd. & 35 p. c	23,232,962 52	8,418,313 30	2,813,058 78	25,654,460	8,005,136 50	2,649,521 27
Valued at above 20 cents per sq. yd....do.	7c. p. sq. yd. & 40 p. c	4,955,726 50	1,615,883 56	993,254 28	7,851,111	2,067,999 72	1,616,777 65

Article	Rate						
Composed wholly of wool, worsted, the hair of the alpaca, goat, or other animals, or of a mixture of them, and all such goods of like description, with selvedges made wholly or in part of other materials, or with threads of other materials introduced for the purpose of changing the classification—							
Weighing 4 ounces or less per sq. yd......sq. yds..	9c. p. sq. yd. & 40 p. c..	27,006,379	6,479,491 09	5,021,830 74	25,200,570	5,377,093 28	4,418,888 21
All weighing over 4 oz. per sq. yd......pounds..	35c. p. lb. & 40 p. c.	2,025,680 50	2,684,298 78	1,782,707 69	25,430,019 80	3,021,049 05	2,056,926 55
Total dress goods................			14,197,986 72	14,110,851 49		14,971,277 01	10,744,113 08
Flannels:							
Valued at not exceeding 30 cents per pound..pounds..	10c. p. lb. & 35 p. c	300	85 00	63 75	659	185 00	130 65
Valued at above 30 and not exceeding 40 cents per pound.........pounds.	12c. p. lb. & 35 p. c	666	256 00	169 52	5	2 00	1 30
Valued at above 40 and not exceeding 60 cents per pound.........pounds.	18c. p. lb. & 35 p. c	15,865 75	9,280 00	6,103 84	3,890 63	1,939 00	1,378 96
Valued at above 60 and not exceeding 80 cents per pound.........pounds.	24c. p. lb. & 35 p. c	21,493	15,016 91	10,414 00	8,985	6,216 30	4,332 10
Valued at above 80 cents per pound..........do.	35c. p. lb. & 40 p. c	39,383 50	42,465 20	30,778 32	36,920 44	39,560 31	28,746 29
Total flannels................		77,707 25	67,123 11	47,531 43	50,460 67	47,903 61	34,589 30
Hats of wool:							
Valued at above 30 and not exceeding 40 cents per pound.........pounds.	12c. p. lb. & 35 p. c				1	32	24
Valued at above 40 and not exceeding 60 cents per pound.........pounds.	18c. p. lb. & 35 p. c	601	208 00	301 98	652	406 00	264 86
Valued at above 60 and not exceeding 80 cents per pound.........pounds.	24c. p. lb. & 35 p. c						
Valued at over 80 cents per pound............do.	35c. p. lb. & 40 p. c	471	1,926 70	935 62	5,640 50	3,936 00	2,731 82
Hat roundings or trimmings................	10 p c		169 00	16 90	4,746 63	7,080 10	4,856 98
Total hats			2,363 76	1,154 40	11,070 13	12,351 42	7,853 40
Knit goods, and all goods made on knitting frames—							
Valued at not exceeding 30 cents per pound..pounds	10c. p. lb. & 35 p. c	236	68 50	47 57	626	175 81	124 13
Valued at above 30 and not exceeding 40 cents per pound.........pounds.	12c. p. lb. & 35 p. c	33.50	12 00	8 22	97	34 45	23 70
Valued at above 40 and not exceeding 60 cents per pound.........pounds.	18c. p. lb. & 35 p. c	7,178 87	4,200 00	2,797 22	24,338 75	12,785 99	8,856 08
Valued at above 60 and not exceeding 80 cents per pound.........pounds.	24c. p. lb. & 35 p. c.	75,112 70	54,323 60	37,040 31	57,442 25	40,710 66	28,034 85
Valued at above 80 cents per pound..........do.	35c. p. lb. & 35 p. c.	1,084,963 43	2,035,247 46	1,201,856 16	1,092,348 70	1,876,682 34	1,132,004 08
Total knit goods................		1,107,524 50	2,113,951 65	1,241,729 46	1,174,852 70	1,930,369 19	1,170,033 74
Rags, shoddy, mungo, waste, and flocks, woolen, pounds..	10c. p. lb.	789,040 50	323,522 00	78,904 05	2,696,617	919,771 00	200,654 70

No. 8.—STATEMENT SHOWING THE QUANTITIES AND VALUES OF IMPORTED MANUFACTURES OF WOOL ENTERED FOR CONSUMPTION IN THE UNITED STATES, &C., DURING THE YEARS ENDING JUNE 30, FROM 1867 TO 1886, INCLUSIVE—Continued.

ARTICLES.	Rates of duty.	1885.			1886.		
		Quantities.	Values.	Duties.	Quantities.	Values.	Duties.
Shawls:				*Dollars.*		*Dollars.*	*Dollars.*
Woolen—			*Dollars.*			*Dollars.*	
Valued at not exceeding 80 cents per pound..........pounds..	35c. p. lb. & 35 p. c	5, 608. 25	3, 831 56	3, 303 92	12, 763	8, 610 75	7, 441 52
Valued at above 80 cents per pound ....do....	35c. p. lb. & 40 p. c	302, 083. 25	542, 052 64	322, 553 72	228, 570	345, 252 40	218, 100 50
Worsted—							
Composed wholly or in part of worsted, the hair of the alpaca, goat, or other animals ..pounds..	40c. p. lb. & 35 p. c	270, 058	511, 081 00	290, 816 55	452, 699. 75	690, 061 00	422, 602 30
Total shawls		586, 750. 50	1, 057, 865 11	616, 674 19	691, 034. 75	1, 043, 927 15	648, 184 32
Webbings, gorings, suspenders, braces, beltings, bindings, braids, galloons, fringes, gimps, cords, cords and tassels, dress trimmings, head nets, buttons or barrel buttons, or buttons of other forms for tassels or ornaments, wrought by hand or braided by machinery, made of wool, or of which wool, worsted, the hair of the alpaca, goat, or other animals is a component material, ...pounds..	30c. p. lb. & 50 p. c	298, 315. 20	470, 897 00	315, 343 09	308, 128. 54	616, 674 00	427, 875 57
Yarns, woolen, and worsted:							
Valued at not exceeding 30 cents per pound, pounds..	10c. p. lb. & 33 p. c	11, 166. 50	3, 501 65	2, 237 30	102, 360. 50	29, 900 00	20, 691 63
Valued at above 30 and not exceeding 40 cents per pound ....pounds..	12c. p. lb. & 35 p. c	72, 200. 25	27, 725 58	18, 367 96	1, 258, 468. 36	471, 863 05	316, 108 03
Valued at above 40 and not exceeding 60 cents per pound .... pounds..	18c. p. lb. & 35 p. c	164, 538. 50	83, 918 68	56, 088 47	1, 353, 836. 75	733, 584 41	509, 445 20
Valued at above 60 and not exceeding 80 cents per pound ....pounds..	24c. p. lb. & 35 p. c	430, 251. 36	360, 123 84	211, 453 67	1, 190, 262. 56	819, 258 82	573, 829 19
Valued at above 80 cents per pound ....do....	35c. p. lb. & 40 p. c	218, 278. 46	254, 542 65	177, 414 52	1, 180, 020. 85	228, 569 05	154, 435 83
Total yarns		896, 435. 00	676, 512 30	404, 461 82	4, 090, 767. 01	2, 283, 176 23	1, 565, 508 80
All manufactures of every description not specially enumerated or provided for, made wholly or in part of wool:							
Wool—							
Valued at not exceeding 80cts. per pound..pounds..	35c. p. lb. & 35 p. c	20, 766. 25	17, 088 00	16, 812 49	90, 540. 50	61, 091 78	50, 431 30
Valued at above 80 cts. per pound ....do....	35c. p. lb. & 40 p. c	545, 402	840, 401 67	527, 081 00	571, 713. 39	908, 955 80	600, 732 02
Worsted—the hair of the alpaca, goat, or other animals, (except such as are composed in part of wool)—							
Valued at not exceeding 40 cts. per pound..pounds..	10c. p. lb. & 35 p. c	60, 868	16, 027 00	11, 698 25	105, 674. 50	27, 219 12	20, 094 15

Valued at above 30 and not exceeding 40 cents per pound .... pounds..	12c. p. lb. & 35 p. c.	35,445 25	12,245 00	8,539 18	144,840	51,379 00	35,384 17
Valued at above 40 and not exceeding 60 cents per pound .... pounds..	18c. p. lb. & 35 p. c.	937,164 08	524,885 00	352,399 33	2,057,730 50	1,125,444 00	764,297 97
Valued at above 60 and not exceeding 80 cents per pound .... pounds..	24c. p. lb. & 35 p. c.	1,407,051 38	1,020,910 38	695,013 05	2,795,244 00	1,092,840 53	1,308,352 89
Valued at above 80 cents per pound .... do	35c. p. lb. & 40 p. c.	1,274,730 84	1,633,813 50	1,099,632 01	1,483,811 38	2,098,553 03	1,358,705 24
Total manufactures, not elsewhere specified..		4,290,643 80	4,065,088 53	2,711,029 27	7,252,560 87	6,350,983 20	4,294,027 74
Grand total.......................		....	36,170,705 44	24,294,038 90	....	40,636,600 38	37,278,527 54

No. 9.—Summary Statement showing the Quantities and Values of Wool, and the Values of the Manufactures of Wool Imported into the United States, with the Estimated Amounts of Duties Received on the same, for each Year from 1822 to 1866, inclusive.

Year ending—		Unmanufactured wool			Manufactures of wool					
		Net imports		Estimated amount of duties	Carpets	Cloths	Dress goods	All other manufactures	Total	Estimated amount of duties
	Free/Dutiable	Quantity	Value		Value	Value	Value	Value	Value	
		Pounds.	*Dollars.*	*Dollars.*	*Dollars.*	*Dollars.*	*Dollars.*	*Dollars.*	*Dollars.*	*Dollars.*
September 30—										
1822		1,715,690	387,312	58,097		8,491,935	2,308,513	991,147	11,752,595	2,513,552
1823		1,673,348	340,936	51,143		5,843,068	2,501,469	604,896	7,951,433	1,606,155
1824		1,291,400	353,367	62,110		6,047,150	2,168,680	683,014	8,124,687	1,963,667
1825		2,035,707	552,069	107,936	37,634	5,261,562	2,902,672	3,331,813	12,017,468	3,473,441
1826		2,622,949	410,768	101,182	515,391	4,546,714	1,368,616	2,196,946	8,657,424	2,544,495
1827		3,180,767	379,811	87,774	545,148	4,285,413	1,506,400	2,563,227	8,866,229	2,794,539
1828		2,437,019	458,831	133,080	511,186	4,315,714	1,609,030	2,335,699	8,842,389	2,734,283
1829		1,295,767	204,643	131,690	581,916	3,335,994	1,833,650	1,700,755	7,193,653	2,501,230
1830		663,611	92,172	68,273	323,251	2,654,339	1,451,461	1,393,519	5,939,988	2,343,062
1831		5,019,353	1,257,540	663,544	201,649	6,121,442	3,392,027	3,262,791	13,197,364	5,172,467
1832		2,814,879	501,562	370,048	421,094	5,101,841	2,615,124	2,163,750	10,440,490	5,151,806
1833		273,631	93,937	49,641	557,775	6,128,194	2,621,133	2,615,903	13,713,141	4,662,112
1834		(a) 543,626	384,830	319,205	436,931	4,364,340	606,887	2,035,837	7,444,035	2,681,321
1835	Free	1,632,640	683,286	217,993	732,518	7,046,755	7,542,655	3,830,022	19,151,950	4,264,176
	Dutiable	10,905,571	785,493							
1836	Free	1,390,678	418,412	65,256	1,133,415	8,926,382	9,840,335	4,737,749	24,637,881	5,242,550
	Dutiable	0,460,195	703,270							
1837	Free	770,492	100,268	34,525	630,238	3,013,460	5,161,213	1,565,871	10,410,782	1,817,293
	Dutiable	6,453,250	438,669							
1838	Free	332,418	70,614	58,264	37,321	5,195,065	5,455,727	2,101,943	13,130,056	2,677,638
	Dutiable	7,388,719	520,899							
1839	Free	417,535	135,407	38,564	731,227	7,078,906	9,315,782	3,868,512	21,024,427	3,828,925
	Dutiable	9,303,092	675,009							
1840	Free	509,220	144,421	52,308	389,526	4,096,529	4,117,130	1,605,300	10,808,483	2,196,940
	Dutiable	11,400,929	918,061							
1841	Free	456,055	122,416	10,403	441,351	4,942,807	5,643,534	1,910,131	12,943,863	2,382,576
	Dutiable	10,637,231	653,649							
1842	Free	212,522	31,119		302,218	3,095,577	3,677,892	1,713,901	9,689,648	2,559,817
	Dutiable									
June 30—										
1843b	Free	51,039	3,612	18,221	201,480	1,356,028	774,736	638,612	2,971,456	1,072,036
	Dutiable	3,414,569	223,674							
1844	Free	14,077,938		73,510	329,640	4,777,940	3,128,363	3,515,970	11,751,071	4,124,150
	Dutiable	572,143	572,143							

Year									
1845	23,825,072	1,094,006	124,004	512,216	5,411,859	3,449,419	4,185,837	13,578,352	4,704,478
1846	16,504,870	1,112,918	55,539	341,618	5,192,310	4,430,225	3,808,701	12,778,854	4,436,931
1847	8,249,207	521,874	90,207	356,308	4,527,742	4,889,037	3,590,953	13,661,102	3,007,353
1848	11,379,463	862,675	256,054	633,187	6,364,145	6,315,163	5,083,061	18,403,461	5,073,721
1849	17,822,497	1,170,561	333,103	514,576	4,903,557	6,622,474	4,710,494	16,779,561	4,583,291
1850	18,695,294	1,690,380	506,245	891,860	6,181,190	6,658,050	5,886,510	19,620,619	5,415,888
1851	32,578,193	3,836,613	1,150,496	1,107,381	7,660,520	7,292,250	6,379,728	22,358,879	6,179,539
1852	17,992,646	1,876,536	570,034	842,018	6,969,742	7,963,570	4,895,936	20,611,260	5,665,184
1853	21,403,925	2,615,761	802,693	1,335,483	11,071,906	11,677,303	7,735,078	31,810,771	8,797,240
1854	29,033,492	2,793,558	837,043	2,381,863	13,159,583	11,969,917	10,393,110	37,904,473	10,568,000
1855	18,189,946	2,033,545	585,575	1,604,153	9,144,861	9,965,067	7,016,280	27,754,372	7,584,269
1856	16,729,377	2,172,477	497,257	2,329,479	11,653,476	13,678,850	7,690,507	35,582,713	9,718,003
1857	18,460,227	2,612,704	637,007	2,301,123	1?,009,605	13,440,908	8,628,707	35,289,345	9,623,007
1858	23,563,478	3,523,530		1,666,608	7,626,830	12,543,405	7,695,813	29,334,655	6,202,491
1859 Free	31,674,337	4,877,848	27,563	2,336,338	11,259,693	14,525,928	9,173,603	37,295,594	7,903,577
1859 Dutiable	1,355,775	206,714							
1860 Free	23,730,520	4,791,517	93,785	2,743,200	12,787,754	18,121,093	9,469,930	43,141,988	9,139,194
1860 Dutiable	2,403,363	503,215							
1861 Free	30,534,578	4,824,416	26,265	1,895,048	290,043	21,467,753	6,748,207	30,430,140	6,282,931
1861 Dutiable	1,104,255	190,586							
1862 Free	3,836,675	625,378	453,079	535,081	5,441,710	279,192	9,363,921	15,630,913	4,906,726
1862 Dutiable	30,861,463	6,514,736							
1863	74,412,878	12,529,600	810,199	1,016,562	5,147,404	2,203,110	13,157,726	21,524,802	7,368,121
1864	91,026,639	16,128,209	1,001,683	1,761,290	10,098,035	10,610,414	10,270,983	33,349,703	13,238,985
1865	43,741,094	7,634,422	1,949,852	593,703	5,411,013	8,461,908	7,462,833	21,929,487	12,177,143
1866	70,435,943	10,082,257	3,159,484	2,977,507	16,656,963	21,193,253	17,129,973	58,719,756	30,813,762

a The exports of foreign wool exceed the gross imports for 1854.   b Nine months.

No. 10.—SUMMARY STATEMENT SHOWING THE TOTAL QUANTITIES AND VALUES OF IMPORTED WOOLS AND MANUFACTURES OF WOOL ENTERED FOR CONSUMPTION IN THE UNITED STATES, INCLUDING BOTH ENTRIES FOR IMMEDIATE CONSUMPTION AND WITHDRAWALS FROM WAREHOUSE FOR CONSUMPTION; ALSO SHOWING THE AMOUNTS OF DUTY COLLECTED DURING THE YEARS ENDING JUNE 30, FROM 1867 TO 1886, INCLUSIVE.

Year ending June 30—	Class No. 1.—Clothing wools.			Class No. 2.—Combing wools.		
	Quantity.	Value.	Amount of duty received.	Quantity.	Value.	Amount of duty received.
	Pounds.	Dollars.	Dollars.	Pounds.	Dollars.	Dollars.
1867	1,270,356	415,609	184,160	150,302	31,827	18,213
1868	4,681,679	918,588	573,176	1,804,272	332,315	217,079
1869	2,512,201	505,715	308,104	4,533,367	1,092,297	583,044
1870	6,530,403	1,240,152	801,834	2,752,568	765,147	372,152
1871	5,957,461	1,201,201	733,275	17,665,600	3,167,835	2,118,837
1872	16,871,332	4,187,960	2,200,806	41,155,460	8,952,131	5,183,183
1873	6,029,488	1,744,200	771,378	40,540,231	12,723,504	5,818,236
1874	2,398,210	815,307	319,834	27,087,438	6,103,150	3,073,744
1875	13,117,679	3,602,535	1,583,110	7,769,157	2,153,261	952,019
1876	8,643,366	2,187,713	1,080,078	3,167,307	1,153,504	483,536
1877	9,294,029	2,202,639	1,173,363	2,509,954	830,715	360,191
1878	9,916,012	2,431,043	1,273,479	3,028,809	900,663	425,220
1879	5,229,987	1,114,301	647,340	1,709,601	413,761	218,412
1880	26,785,172	6,412,273	3,512,806	13,266,856	3,801,730	1,783,302
1881	20,609,707	4,751,454	2,599,686	4,421,401	1,271,332	585,500
1882	13,489,923	3,042,407	1,693,078	2,318,671	648,252	304,133
1883	11,546,530	2,567,443	1,444,949	1,373,114	343,987	176,181
1884	20,703,813	4,700,605	2,111,279	4,474,300	1,058,758	451,521
1885	13,472,432	2,994,533	1,357,102	3,891,014	921,252	394,004
1886	23,321,758	4,344,189	2,437,049	4,872,739	1,106,116	490,910

Year ending June 30—	Class No. 3.—Carpet wools and other similar wools.			Total wools.		
	Quantity.	Value.	Amount of duty received.	Quantity.	Value.	Amount of duty received.
	Pounds.	Dollars.	Dollars.	Pounds.	Dollars.	Dollars.
1867	36,203,017	5,332,074	1,756,174	37,683,675	5,779,510	1,058,547
1868	18,096,600	2,704,768	813,673	24,582,551	3,955,671	1,005,028
1869	27,650,371	3,653,082	1,088,918	34,695,939	5,251,004	1,080,066
1870	29,351,006	3,416,024	1,043,981	38,634,067	5,430,323	2,217,967
1871	26,550,095	3,335,628	1,003,297	50,174,050	7,704,674	3,855,409
1872	36,289,141	6,435,463	1,640,760	94,315,933	19,575,559	9,024,839
1873	28,642,863	5,098,465	1,256,545	84,212,542	20,466,106	7,846,158
1874	27,308,090	4,603,410	1,076,904	56,703,737	11,011,867	4,470,482
1875	30,790,458	4,472,826	1,096,721	51,680,294	10,228,622	3,031,859
1876	28,465,005	4,546,308	1,223,594	40,275,678	7,887,615	2,787,208
1877	28,310,411	3,979,617	1,124,443	40,114,304	7,012,971	2,657,996
1878	26,856,280	3,594,640	1,015,697	39,801,101	6,995,366	2,714,396
1879	33,163,054	3,088,752	1,100,524	40,102,642	5,516,814	1,966,276
1880	59,320,412	7,690,603	2,077,950	99,372,440	17,913,606	7,374,217
1881	42,385,769	6,038,041	1,675,630	67,416,967	12,000,827	4,860,816
1882	47,208,175	6,642,690	1,837,442	63,016,760	10,333,358	3,854,633
1883	40,130,323	5,580,558	1,553,498	53,049,967	8,491,988	3,174,028
1884	62,525,692	7,833,996	1,960,025	87,703,931	13,593,290	4,522,825
1885	50,782,306	5,558,479	1,412,285	68,140,632	9,474,264	3,164,206
1886	79,716,052	8,343,908	2,198,149	107,910,549	13,794,213	5,126,108

No. 10.—SUMMARY STATEMENT SHOWING THE TOTAL QUANTITIES AND VALUES OF IMPORTED WOOLS AND MANUFACTURES OF WOOL ENTERED FOR CONSUMPTION IN THE UNITED STATES, INCLUDING BOTH ENTRIES FOR IMMEDIATE CONSUMPTION AND WITHDRAWALS FROM WAREHOUSE FOR CONSUMPTION; ALSO SHOWING THE AMOUNTS OF DUTY COLLECTED DURING THE YEARS ENDING JUNE 30, FROM 1867 TO 1886, INCLUSIVE—Continued.

Year ending June 30—	Carpets and carpeting of all kinds.	Cloths.	Dress goods.	All other manufactures.	Total.	
					Value.	Amount of duty received.
	Dollars.	Dollars.	Dollars.	Dollars.	Dollars.	Dollars.
1867	3,743,125	10,545,096	20,356,635	11,101,894	45,746,750	24,268,531
1868	3,516,460	6,883,957	16,868,362	5,892,329	33,161,117	22,032,923
1869	4,085,558	6,222,924	18,280,490	6,223,605	34,812,577	23,454,900
1870	4,129,207	6,412,503	18,044,982	6,509,782	35,096,474	23,393,201
1871	4,932,089	9,187,365	21,651,423	7,123,727	42,894,604	29,049,157
1872	5,514,279	12,887,288	24,071,832	7,761,798	50,235,197	33,004,894
1873	4,948,335	16,635,679	23,119,433	7,716,144	52,419,591	30,643,774
1874	3,948,176	13,598,446	22,363,750	7,765,224	47,675,605	27,886,340
1875	2,928,503	11,696,091	22,330,018	8,673,311	45,627,923	27,282,178
1876	1,689,910	8,904,434	16,255,100	7,523,282	34,372,726	22,519,105
1877	1,050,057	5,737,571	14,111,843	5,552,737	26,452,208	17,660,041
1878	654,224	5,657,782	14,164,130	5,227,257	25,703,393	17,176,549
1879	505,242	5,623,807	14,365,255	4,452,805	25,037,109	16,839,064
1880	1,313,352	8,415,215	16,752,068	5,353,912	31,834,547	21,864,153
1881	1,400,063	9,376,038	15,961,066	6,366,155	33,103,322	22,424,809
1882	1,257,234	10,457,060	19,070,817	6,469,713	37,284,824	25,398,363
1883	1,225,156	10,806,324	22,619,106	7,901,870	42,552,456	29,146,265
1884	1,517,081	13,216,658	15,349,007	11,402,036	51,484,872	27,473,400
1885	1,173,252	10,080,981	14,197,987	10,724,485	36,176,705	24,294,939
1886	1,320,341	9,464,358	14,971,278	14,771,532	40,536,509	27,278,528

NOTE.—For fuller details of the data contained in this table see tables Nos. 4 and 8.

No. 11.—Statement showing the Quantity and Value of Domestic Wool Exported from the United States During each Year from 1846 to 1887; the Value of Domestic Manufactures of Wool Exported from 1864 to 1887, and the Number and Value of Domestic Sheep Exported from 1821 to 1887, inclusive.

Years ending—	Unmanufactured wool.		Manufactures of wool.	Sheep.	
	Pounds.	Dollars.	Dollars.	Number.	Dollars.
September 30—					
1821				11,117	22,175
1822				6,308	12,276
1823				6,880	15,028
1824				7,421	14,938
1825				9,681	20,027
1826				8,695	17,603
1827				8,745	13,580
1828				5,545	7,499
1829				6,846	10,644
1830				15,460	22,110
1831				8,262	14,499
1832				12,260	22,385
1833				11,821	21,464
1834				16,654	20,002
1835				19,145	36,566
1836				6,342	18,548
1837				3,460	16,852
1838				6,698	20,462
1839				6,084	15,960
1840				14,558	30,698
1841				14,039	35,767
1842				19,557	38,892
June 30—					
1843 (9 months)				13,609	29,061
1844				12,980	27,824
1845				6,464	23,948
1846	668,380	203,906		9,254	30,303
1847	378,440	80,400		10,533	29,100
1848	781,102	57,497		6,231	20,823
1849	159,925	81,015		4,195	16,305
1850	35,898	22,778		3,945	15,733
1851				4,357	18,875
1852	55,550	14,308		2,968	16,201
1853	216,472	20,567		3,669	17,808
1854	114,268	33,895		2,642	15,194
1855	88,886	27,802		4,233	18,637
1856	145,115	27,453		3,520	18,802
1857	50,202	19,097		4,373	22,758
1858	884,807	211,861		(a)	40,319
1859	1,706,536	355,563		(a)	41,182
1860	1,055,928	389,512		(a)	33,613
1861	847,301	237,840		(a)	28,417
1862	1,153,388	296,225		(a)	34,600
1863	355,722	178,434		(a)	39,504
1864	155,482	66,358	81,943	9,301	30,185
1865	466,182	254,721	139,628	15,182	74,388
1866	973,075	264,306	139,462	12,478	87,214
1867	307,418	130,857	94,698	7,882	60,842
1868	558,435	191,119	206,870	17,902	83,936
1869	441,387	152,443	164,438	(a)	(a)
1870	152,892	54,028	124,159	30,570	95,193
1871	23,195	8,762	218,403	43,465	90,888
1872	140,515	36,434	212,669	35,218	79,562
1873	75,129	17,624	200,897	66,717	107,608
1874	319,600	72,109	121,099	124,248	159,735
1875	178,034	62,754	154,401	124,416	183,898
1876	104,768	13,845	336,389	110,312	171,101
1877	79,509	26,446	201,837	179,017	244,480
1878	347,854	93,358	448,984	183,905	333,499
1879	60,784	17,644	346,743	215,680	1,082,938
1880	191,551	71,987	216,576	209,137	892,647
1881	71,455	19,217	331,083	179,919	762,932
1882	110,179	37,327	408,104	139,676	642,778
1883	64,474	22,114	366,214	337,251	1,154,856
1884	10,393	3,073	704,108	273,874	850,146
1885	88,006	16,739	775,962	234,500	512,568
1886	146,423	19,625	653,633	177,594	320,844
1887	257,940	78,002	539,342	121,701	254,725

a Not stated.

Note.—Prior to 1864 manufactures of wool were not stated separately, but were included under the head of "wearing apparel."

No. 12.—PRICES OF WOOL IN THE MARKETS OF NEW YORK (1824–1887) AND PHILA-
DELPHIA (1865–1887).

(See also Appendixes Nos. 69 and 70.)

(a) *Price of Fine, Medium, and Coarse Washed Clothing Fleece Wool in the New York Market, for the Months of January, April, July, and October, during each year from 1824 to 1887, inclusive.*

[From Mauger & Avery's Annual Wool Circular.]

Year.	January.			April.			July.			October.		
	Fine.	Medium.	Coarse.	Fine.	Medium.	Coarse.	Fine.	Medium.	Coarse.	Fine.	Medium.	Coarse.
	Cts.	Cts.	Cts.	Cts.	Cts.	Cts.	Cts.	Cts.	Cts.	Cts.	Cts.	Cts.
1824	68	53	40	70	46	31	55	40	30	60	40	30
1825	60	43	32	60	42	33	50	41	32	50	42	36
1826	55	43	38	52	46	41	37	30	26	43	37	32
1827	36	32	28	45	34	30	37	31	25	43	32	25
1828	42	30	25	44	36	28	48	38	33	48	40	32
1829	54	45	35	45	35	32	46	36	32	37	30	27
1830	40	35	30	50	38	32	60	50	40	70	60	48
1831	70	60	48	70	60	50	75	65	50	70	60	50
1832	65	55	44	60	52	42	50	42	30	50	40	30
1833	55	41	38	63	53	38	61	54	40	65	55	45
1834	70	60	48	67	56	44	60	50	40	62	50	40
1835	63	50	40	65	60	45	63	56	42	65	60	45
1836	65	60	45	68	62	47	70	60	50	70	60	50
1837	72	63	48	68	56	46	52	52	36	49	48	31
1838	50	42	35	56	42	35	46	36	30	56	48	37
1839	56	48	38	56	48	38	57	48	40	60	55	44
1840	50	45	38	49	43	36	45	39	33	46	38	33
1841	52	45	35	53	46	37	50	44	34	48	42	32
1842	48	42	35	46	40	32	43	37	30	38	31	25
1843	35	30	25	33	28	25	35	30	26	36	32	26
1844	37	30	26	43	36	30	45	37	32	50	40	33
1845	47	40	31	45	38	32	40	36	30	38	35	28
1846	40	35	30	38	33	28	38	32	27	36	30	22
1847	45	40	30	47	40	31	46	40	31	47	40	30
1848	45	38	30	43	37	30	38	32	28	33	30	24
1849	33	30	22	40	36	30	40	35	28	42	36	30
1850	47	40	33	45	37	30	45	37	30	46	40	35
1851	46	40	33	50	44	36	47	42	37	45	40	35
1852	43	38	34	42	36	33	45	38	33	50	42	37
1853	58	56	50	62	56	50	60	53	48	55	50	48
1854	53	47	42	57	52	46	45	37	30	42	36	30
1855	40	35	32	43	35	32	50	40	33	52	41	36
1856	50	38	35	57	45	38	55	42	36	60	55	45
1857	58	50	42	60	56	45	56	50	40	38	30	25
1858	40	33	27	42	35	30	43	37	30	56	41	30
1859	60	52	45	60	46	37	56	40	35	60	50	42
1860	60	50	42	52	45	40	55	50	40	50	45	40
1861	45	40	37	45	37	32	38	30	22	47	48	50
1862	48	50	50	46	45	43	48	47	45	60	60	63
1863	75	68	70	80	85	80	75	70	65	85	80	76
1864	80	78	76	78	77	72	100	100	90	103	95	100
1865	102	100	96	80	80	75	75	73	65	75	75	65
1866	70	65	50	65	60	48	70	67	60	63	60	56
1867	68	53	50	60	55	50	55	49	45	48	46	40
1868	48	43	38	50	48	45	46	45	43	48	48	45
1869	50	50	48	50	50	48	48	48	47	48	48	46
1870	48	46	44	48	47	46	46	45	43	48	49	44
1871	47	46	43	50	52	47	62	60	55	63	62	58
1872	70	72	66	80	80	76	72	70	65	66	60	57
1873	70	68	65	56	53	48	50	48	44	54	53	47
1874	58	54	47	56	56	47	53	53	46	54	54	47
1875	55	56	47	54	52	46	52	49	46	48	50	42
1876	48	52	42	46	49	40	38	35	31	45	40	33
1877	46	43	36	45	40	33	50	44	37	48	44	36
1878	41	40	38	40	40	35	36	36	32	35	37	32
1879	34	35	32	34	34	31	37	38	31	41	43	38
1880	50	55	48	55	60	52	46	48	42	46	48	42
1881	47	49	43	40	44	37	42	44	36	43	46	36
1882	44	46	47	42	45	34	42	45	34	42	45	34
1883	40	43	33	44	44	34	39	41	37	39	40	34
1884	40	40	34	48	38	34	35	34	30	35	34	30
1885	34	33	29	32	32	28	32	31	28	33	35	32
1886	35	36	32	33	34	30	33	33	29	35	38	34
1887	33	38	33	33	37	33	34	38	35			

No. 12.—Prices of Wool in the Markets of New York (1824-1887) and Philadelphia (1865-1887)—Continued.

(b) Prices of the different kinds of Wool in the Philadelphia Market for each Year from 1865 to 1884, inclusive, for each Month of 1884 and 1885, and from May, 1886, to May, 1887, inclusive.

[From Coates Brothers' Wool Circulars.]

On July 1—

Kinds of wool.	1865	1866	1867	1868	1869	1870	1871	1872	1873	1874	1875	1876	1877	1878	1879	1880	1881	1882	1883	1884
OHIO, PENNSYLVANIA, AND WEST VIRGINIA FLEECE, WASHED.																				
XX and above	65-70	65-70	58-62	50-55	52-55	48-55	63-65	70-75	48-52	52-58	50-55	34-40	46-50	34-37	40-42	44-46	42-45	41-43	37-40	33-35
X	65-68	63-67	53-58	47-49	50-52	46-48	59-60	70-72	46-49	51-54	60-52	35-35	43-46	34-36	38-40	44-46	41-42	40-42	36-37	32-33
Half blood	61-68	62-65	52-54	52-54	50-52	47-48	60-62	72-74	47-49	52-54	60-52	35-37	41-40	35-37	40-42	48-50	45-46	41-46	40-42	34-35
Quarter blood	60-65	59-62	48-50	44-46	48-50	45-47	58-60	72-75	45-17	48-50	48-60	33-35	37-40	32-34	36-38	43-45	37-39	35-38	33-36	30-32
Common and cotted	58-60	50-55	44-46	40-42	46-48	41-46	55-58	65-70	38-42	43-46	45-44	25-30	33-36	30-32	33-35	40-42	30-42	28-32	26-29	22-25
NEW YORK, MICHIGAN, INDIANA, AND WISCONSIN FLEECE, WASHED.																				
XX	60-65	61-65	52-55	46-50	45-48	46-50	55-56	65-68	43-46	47-50	46-48	30-33	42-43	33-34	33-38	42-44	38-41	38-40	35-37	30-32
X	60-62	60-62	50-52	45-46	44-46	43-45	55-58	65-68	43-46	47-50	40-48	30-33	40-43	29-34	35-35	42-44	38-40	38-40	35-36	30-31
Half blood	60-63	59-60	50-51	44-45	44-46	43-45	56-59	68-70	45-48	48-52	48-50	33-35	33-38	37-40	47-49	43-45	41-44	41-46	40-40	31-34
Quarter blood	60-63	60-62	48-50	43-47	41-46	43-48	55-58	68-70	34-46	42-45	40-44	30-35	33-38	32-33	34-36	42-14	36-38	35-38	34-35	30-31
Common and cotted	58-60	50-52	40-43	38-40	41-46	42-43	50-55	60-65	34-40	42-45	41-40	25-28	32-35	28-32	32-34	28-40	28-30	28-30	26-29	22-25
COMBING AND DELAINE FLEECE.																				
Washed, fine delaine																				
Washed, medium																				
Washed, low					53-60	58-60	63-67	82-83	55-60	55-62	60-65	40-43	50-52	38-42	43-45	48-50	44-45	45-47	40-42	35-36
Washed, coarse a														35-38	38-42	44-46	38-42	45-46	42-43	35-37
Unwashed, medium							41-46	60-62	37-42	38-43	40-44	31-35	37-40	28-31	32-34	34-37	30-35	30-33	30-31	26-28
Unwashed, low and coarse	70-75	65-70	55-60	70-72	70-72	68-70	63-84	85-90	55-60	56-62	62-65	40-45	52-55	26-28	29-30	30-33	25-28	25-27	22-27	22-25
Canada													37-40	37-40	40-42	41-46	40-43	35-38	32-33	28-30
UNWASHED. Light and bright.																				
Fine									28-32	32-35	33-35	20-22	22-32	23-25	24-27	25-28	26-30	24-27	22-25	20-22
Medium									30-33	34-37	37-39	23-28	30-33	26-30	26-30	30-33	30-35	30-33	28-33	25-27
Low medium									28-32	31-33	34-37	21-23	26-28	24-26	28-30	30-32	25-28	25-27	23-25	21-23
Coarse, or burry																18-23	16-22	18-20	16-20	16-18
Heavy or dark colored.																				
Fine																20-23	18-23	19-23	16-18	15-17
Medium																23-28	25-30	23-30	23-23	19-21

COLORADO. c																					
Low																					
Coarse carpet																					
Heavy, or faulty b																					
Medium and fine, choice	40-50	33-38	43-40	30-32	33-35	30-31	40-46	50-55	25-28	28-30	30-35		25-30	22-25		28-32	25-28	23-25	24-26	25-28	22-25	20-23
Medium and fine, average	35-40	28-35	30-33	28-30	33-34	28-30	38-44	45-50	21-24	25-27	26-28		20-25	17-22		20-25	20-21	19-22	21-24	20-21	20-20	17-19
Common and quarter blood	28-35	22-30	25-30	21-26	30-32	25-28	36-40	40-45	18-22	22-25	23-27	18-25	19-20	17-18		18-22	19-20	18-22	21-23	18-20	18-20	17-18
Coarse carpet	22-28	16-20	20-25	21-23	23-23	18-20	30-40	30-40	16-19	17-20	20-21	18-10	14-16	15-17		17-20	16-17	15-16	19-20	17-17	15-16	15-16
NEW MEXICAN. c																					
Choice improved	33-38	33-40	30-32	33-35	30-31	40-46	50-55	25-28	28-30	30-35	20-25	22-27	22-25	28-32	25-30	19-20	23-25	22-24	22-25	17-20		
Average improved	24-35	30-33	28-30	33-34	28-30	38-40	45-50	21-24	25-27	26-28	18-20	20-21	17-22	23-27	19-20	20-22	20-22	18-20	18-20	16-17		
Coarse, carpet, light, long, staple	22-30	25-30	21-26	30-32	25-28	36-40	40-45	18-22	22-25	23-27	17-18	19-20	17-18	22-25	18-19	18-20	18-22	17-17	15-17	15-15		
Coarse, carpet, heavy, sandy or very short	16-20	20-25	21-23	23-23	18-20	30-40	30-40	16-19	17-20	20-21	17-18	18-20	15-16	20-21	17-18	16-16	17-18	16-16	14-14	14-14		
Black											14-16	15-17	13-16		16-17	16-17	15-16	14-14				
TEXAS.																						
Fine northern and eastern	28-32	30-36	27-31	35-40	43-48					25-27	26-30	27-32	25-33	22-25								
Medium northern and eastern	27-30	30-34	27-30	35-40	45-50					27-35	20-32	20-25	18-22	20-25								
Coarse northern and eastern	20-25	25-28	20-22	20-35	30-40					22-25	18-25	23-28	16-18									
Improved western and southern										23-27		23-28										
Coarse western and southern										18-20		16-18										
IOWA, NEBRASKA, AND MONTANA. d																						
Unwashed, fine, bright										23-26	26-30	24-27	28-32									
Unwashed, medium, bright										33-35	26-30	24-27	28-32									
Unwashed, coarse, bright										27-30	18-25	17-23	25-28									
Dark colored or heavy b																						
UTAH AND WYOMING.																						
Unwashed, choice fine, light										20-23	22-24					25-28	20-23	18-20				
Unwashed, fine, heavy										20-23					20-25	20-25	15-17					
Unwashed, choice selected medium										25-28					27-30	23-25	20-22					
Unwashed, low medium										20-28					24-25	23-21	16-18					
Unwashed, coarse, carpet															18-22	17-17	15-15					
TUB WASHED.																						
Choice selected	68-70	63-66	55-58	48-50	55-58	50-52	66-69	78-80	52-52	55-58	55-58	38-42	42-45	42-44	38-42	48-50	45-47	41-43	41-42	40-42	34-36	
Good	65-70	60-62	50-55	46-48	52-55	48-50	65-66	76-78	50-52	52-55	35-37	40-42	35-37	40-42	40-42	36-38	40-40	36-38	32-33			
Fair ordinary	55-65	45-55	45-48	43-46	45-48	45-48	62-65	65-75	47-50	50-53	32-35	36-38	33-40	35-40	43-4	38-40	35-38	30-31				
PULLED.																						
City merino	58-60	55-60	49-52	42-44	42-45	37-38	50-53	63-66	42-46	45-48	38-44	28-30	35-38	35-38	32-35	35-38	34-36	33-37	30-33	26-30		
City super and lambs	55-58	50-55	40-44	40-44	42-44	37-39	50-54	60-68	40-41	43-44	38-44	28-32	33-35	33-37	30-34	40-42	35-37	34-37	30-35	26-28		
Western super and lambs	50-55	45-50	35-40	38-40	38-40	35-37	50-52	63-65	37-43	38-42	38-42	25-30	30-34	33-36	30-34	35-38	35-38	35-38	28-32	23-26		

a Not quoted prior to August, 1884.
b Not quoted prior to June, 1885.
c Colorado and New Mexican not separately stated prior to 1881.
d Montana only for 1886 and 1887.

No. 12.—Prices of Wool in the Markets of New York (1824-1887) and Philadelphia (1865-1887)—Continued.

(b) *Prices of the different kinds of Wool in the Philadelphia Market for each year from 1865 to 1884, inclusive, for each month of 1884 and 1885, and from May, 1886, to May, 1887, inclusive—Continued.*

[From Coates Brothers' Wool Circulars.]

1884.

Kinds of wool.	January. Quiet but firm.	February. Quiet and weak.	March. Dull and lower.	April. Dull and depressed.	May. New York money panic.	June. Stagnant.	July. Some demand at lower prices.	August. Active and strong.	September. Less active.	October. Very quiet.	November. Nominal.	December. Quiet.
OHIO, PENNSYLVANIA, AND WEST VIRGINIA FLEECE, WASHED.	*Cents.*	*Cents.*	*Cents.*	*Cents.*	*Cents.*	*Cents.*	*Cents.*	*Cents.*	*Cents.*	*Cents.*	*Cents.*	*Cents.*
XX and above	39-42	39-41	38-40	37-40	37-40	36-38	33-35	32-35	34-36	34-36	34-35	34-35
X	36-38	35-37	35-36	35-36	35-36	34-35	32-33	31-33	33-34	33-34	32-33	31-33
Half blood	39-40	38-40	38-39	37-38	36-37	36-36	34-35	33-34	33-34	33-34	33-34	32-34
Quarter blood	33-34	32-31	34-36	34-36	33-35	32-34	30-32	28-30	30-31	30-31	28-30	28-30
Common and cotted	23-27	25-27	25-27	27-28	27-28	25-27	22-25	22-25	24-26	24-26	23-25	23-25
NEW YORK, MICHIGAN, INDIANA, AND WISCONSIN FLEECE, WASHED.												
XX	35-37	33-36	34-36	33-35	33-35	32-34	30-32	30-31	30-31	30-31	30-31	29-30
X	34-35	33-35	32-34	32-33	32-33	30-33	30-31	29-30	30-31	30-31	26-33	28-30
Half blood	36-39	38-39	37-38	36-37	35-36	33-36	33-34	33-33	33-31	33-31	32-33	31-32
Quarter blood	32-33	32-33	33-35	33-35	32-34	31-33	30-31	27-30	30-30	29-30	27-29	28-30
Common and cotted	25-26	25-26	25-26	26-27	26-27	25-27	22-25	22-25	23-25	23-25	23-24	23-24
COMBING AND DELAINE FLEECE.												
Washed, fine delaine	40-41	39-41	39-41	38-40	37-39	36-38	35-38	35-36	35-37	36-38	35-37	35-37
Washed, medium	42-45	42-45	41-43	42-43	40-42	38-40	35-37	35-37	35-37	36-38	36-38	36-37
Washed, low	33-38	33-38	37-40	38-40	35-38	33-36	32-33	32-33	32-33	32-33	30-33	30-32
Washed, coarse												
Unwashed, medium	28-32	28-32	28-32	26-32	28-30	27-29	26-28	26-28	28-30	28-30	28-30	27-29
Unwashed, low and coarse	25-27	25-27	26-28	27-30	26-28	23-26	22-25	25-27	26-28	26-25	26-24	26-24
Canada	32-33	32-33	32-33	32-35	32-35	31-33	26-30	30-32	31-33	31-33	31-33	31-33
UNWASHED. *Light and bright.*												
Fine	23-28	23-25	23-25	23-25	23-24	22-24	20-22	20-21	21-22	21-22	21-22	20-22
Medium	27-32	27-32	27-32	27-32	27-30	27-30	25-27	24-29	25-27	25-27	25-27	25-27

Description												
Low medium	20-22	20-22	20-23	20-23	20-22	21-23	23-25	25-26	26-28	25-27	25-28	24-26
Coarse, or burry	15-17	15-17	15-18	15-18	15-17	16-18	17-18	17-20	18-20	18-20	18-20	18-20
Heavy or dark colored.												
Fine	16-17	16-17	16-18	16-18	15-17	15-17	16-18	15-17	15-18	15-18	15-18	16-18
Medium	17-19	17-19	17-20	17-20	18-20	19-21	20-22	20-22	22-23	22-23	22-23	22-23
Low	17-17	17-17	17-18	17-18	16-18	17-18	18-20	18-19	19-20	19-20	18-20	18-20
Coarse, carpet	15-16	15-16	15-16	14-16	15-15	15-15	15-16	15-16	15-16	15-16	16-16	16-17
Heavy, or faulty												
COLORADO.												
Medium and fine, choice	18-20	18-20	18-20	18-20	19-20	19-20	20-22	20-22	20-23	20-23	21-23	21-23
Medium and fine, average	17-18	17-18	17-18	17-18	17-19	17-19	17-20	17-20	18-20	18-20	20-21	20-21
Common and quarter blood	16-17	16-17	16-17	16-17	17-18	17-18	18-19	18-19	19-20	19-20	18-20	18-20
Coarse, carpet	15-15	15-15	15-16	15-16	15-15	15-16	15-16	15-16	15-16	15-16	16-17	16-17
NEW MEXICAN.												
Choice improved	Fall clip	Fall clip	Spr'g clip	Spr'g clip	Spr'g clip	Spr'g clip	Spr'g clip	Spr'g clip	Fall clip	Fall clip	Fall clip	Fall clip
Average improved	17-18	17-18	17-20	17-20	17-20	18-22	18-22	17-20	17-20	17-20	18-20	18-20
Coarse, carpet, light, long staple	15-16	15-16	16-17	16-17	16-17	17-18	17-18	16-17	16-17	16-17	16-17	16-17
Coarse, carpet, heavy, sandy, or very short	14-15	14-15	15-16	15-16	14-14	13-16	14-15	14-15	14-15	14-15	15-16	15-16
Black	13-13	13-13	13-14	13-14	14-14	14-14	14-15	15-15	15-16	15-16	15-16	15-16
TEXAS.												
Fine northern and eastern	Fall clip	Fall clip	Spr'g clip	Spr'g clip	Spr'g clip	Spr'g clip	Spr'g clip	Spr'g clip	Fall clip	Fall clip	Fall clip	Fall clip
Medium northern and eastern	16-18	16-19	20-24	20-23	20-23	20-25	22-26	23-27	20-24	20-24	20-22	20-22
Coarse northern and eastern	13-14	13-14	15-15	15-15	15-15	15-15	16-17	16-17	16-16	16-16	16-17	16-17
Improved western and southern	14-17	14-17	15-20	15-20	15-20	15-20	17-22	17-22	17-20	17-20	17-20	17-20
Coarse western and southern	13-14	13-14	14-15	14-15	14-15	14-14	15-15	15-15	15-15	15-15	15-16	15-16
IOWA, NEBRASKA, AND MONTANA.												
Unwashed, fine bright	18-20	18-20	18-20	18-20	17-20	17-20	20-22	20-22	20-22	20-22	20-22	20-22
Unwashed, medium bright	18-20	18-20	20-22	20-22	20-22	20-23	23-27	23-27	20-24	20-24	25-28	25-28
Unwashed, coarse bright	15-17	15-17	15-18	15-18	15-18	15-17	16-20	16-20	17-20	17-20	18-19	18-19
Dark colored or heavy												
UTAH AND WYOMING.												
Unwashed, choice fine, light	18-20	18-20	18-20	18-20	18-20	18-20	20-21	20-21	20-22	20-22	20-22	20-22
Unwashed, fine, heavy	16-17	16-17	16-17	16-17	15-16	15-16	16-17	16-17	16-17	16-17	16-17	16-17
Unwashed, choice selected, medium	20-21	20-21	20-22	20-22	20-22	20-23	18-20	22-23	23-24	23-24	23-21	24-21
Unwashed, low medium	17-17	17-17	17-18	17-18	16-18	16-18	18-18	18-18	18-20	18-20	20-21	20-17
Unwashed, coarse, carpet	15-15	15-15	15-16	15-16	15-15	15-15	15-16	15-16	15-16	15-16	16-17	16-17
TUB WASHED.												
Choice selected	33-35	33-35	34-35	34-35	34-35	34-36	37-38	37-39	39-40	39-40	3P-40	38-40
Good	30-32	30-32	32-33	32-33	32-33	32-38	31-33	34-36	35-37	35-37	33-37	35-37
Fair ordinary	26-30	26-30	30-31	30-31	30-31	30-31	32-33	32-34	31-35	32-35	32-35	32-35
PULLED.												
City merino	25-26	25-26	25-28	25-28	25-28	24-30	28-30	29-30	29-30	29-32	29-32	20-32
City super and lambs	25-26	25-26	25-28	25-28	25-28	26-28	28-30	28-30	29-30	29-32	29-32	29-12
Western super and lambs	20-23	20-23	22-25	22-25	2-25	23-20	25-27	25-27	25-27	25-27	25-27	25-27

No. 12.—PRICES OF WOOL IN THE MARKETS OF NEW YORK (1824–1867) AND PHILADELPHIA (1865–1887)—Continued.

(b) *Prices of the different kinds of Wool in Philadelphia each year from 1865 to 1884, inclusive, and for each month of 1881 and 1855, and from May, 1856, to May, 1887, inclusive—Continued.*

[From Coates Brothers' Wool Circulars.]

1885.

Kinds of wool.	January. Steady.	February. Quiet.	March. Quiet, slight decline.	April. More active.	May. Between seasons.	June. Demand moderate.	July. Active on low and medium.	August. Active and firm.	September. Active and higher.	October. Strong and advancing.	November. Less demand.	December. Quiet and firm.
OHIO, PENNSYLVANIA, AND WEST VIRGINIA FLEECE, WASHED.	*Cents.*	*Cents.*	*Cents.*	*Cents.*	*Cents.*	*Cents.*	*Cents.*	*Cents.*	*Cents.*	*Cents.*	*Cents.*	*Cents.*
XX and above	34–38	34–38	33–35	32–35	32–35	32–35	32–35	32–35	33–35	34–36	34–38	34–37
X	31–33	31–33	31–32	30–31	30–31	30–31	30–31	30–32	31–32	31–32	32–34	32–33
Half blood	32–34	32–33	31–32	30–32	30–31	30–31	30–31	30–32	32–34	35–37	36–38	36–38
Quarter blood	28–30	28–30	28–30	28–30	28–30	28–30	28–29	28–29	29–31	32–33	34–35	35–35
Common and cotted	22–25	22–25	22–25	22–25	22–25	22–25	22–25	22–25	24–28	25–30	27–30	27–30
NEW YORK, MICHIGAN, INDIANA, AND WISCONSIN FLEECE, WASHED.												
XX	30–30	30–30	29–30	28–29	28–29	28–29	28–29	28–30	29–30	31–33	32–33	31–32
X	29–30	29–32	28–30	28–28	27–28	27–30	27–28	27–30	29–30	31–32	31–32	30–31
Half blood	31–32	30–32	30–31	30–30	28–30	28–30	30–28	30–30	31–30	31–32	34–36	35–36
Quarter blood	27–29	27–29	27–29	27–29	27–28	27–28	27–28	27–28	28–29	31–32	33–34	34–35
Common and cotted	22–23	22–23	22–23	22–23	22–23	22–23	22–23	22–23	24–26	25–28	27–30	27–30
COMBING AND DELAINE FLEECE.												
Washed, fine delaine	36–38	36–38	35–38	34–36	34–36	34–35	33–35	33–35	34–36	35–38	36–38	36–38
Washed, medium	36–37	36–37	35–37	35–36	30–31	34–36	33–33	33–32	34–39	36–39	38–40	38–40
Washed, low	30–32	30–32	31–32	30–32	30–31	30–31	30–31	30–31	31–33	33–36	37–38	37–38
Washed, coarse	27–29	28–29	29–30	28–29	28–29	28–29	27–29	28–30	28–30	30–33	33–35	35–35
Unwashed, medium	26–28	24–26	24–26	24–25	24–25	24–25	24–26	24–26	21–24	26–28	28–30	29–30
Unwashed, low and coarse	21–24	22–24	22–25	22–25	24–24	22–24	21–24	21–24	21–24	24–29	25–28	27–29
Canada	31–33	31–33	31–33	31–33	31–33	31–33	31–33	31–33	31–33	32–34	34–35	35–36
UNWASHED. *Light and bright.*												
Fine	20–22	20–22	20–22	20–21	20–21	20–21	20–21	20–21	20–22	21–23	22–23	22–23
Medium	24–26	22–24	22–24	20–24	20–22	22–24	20–24	22–25	23–25	25–26	26–28	27–30
Low medium	20–20	20–22	20–22	20–22	20–22	20–22	20–22	20–22	21–23	23–23	25–26	26–27
Coarse, or burry	15–17	15–17	15–17	15–17	15–17	15–17	15–17	16–18	16–18	18–20	18–22	18–22

Heavy or dark colored.

	Fall clip.			Spr'g clip.	Spr'g clip.	Spr'g clip.	Spr'g clip.	Fall clip.	Fall clip.	Fall clip.		
Fine	16–18	16–18	16–18	16–18	16–18	16–18	17–20	17–20	17–20	17–20	18–21	19–21
Medium	17–20	17–20	17–20	17–20	17–20	17–19	18–20	18–20	18–21	18–22	21–24	24–25
Low	17–17	17–17	17–17	17–17	16–17	17–17	16–18	16–18	16–18	18–20	21–23	21–23
Coarse, carpet	15–16	15–16	15–16	14–15	14–15	14–15	15–16	15–16	15–16	16–18	18–20	18–20
Heavy, or faulty	15–16	15–16	15–16	14–15	14–15	14–15	15–16	15–16	15–16	16–18	17–18	17–18

COLORADO.

	Fall clip.		Spr'g clip.					Fall clip.				
Medium and fine, choice	18–20	18–20	18–20	18–20	18–20	18–22	19–21	18–22	20–24	20–24	22–27	23–27
Medium and fine, average	17–18	17–18	17–18	17–17	16–18	17–18	17–18	18–18	18–20	18–20	20–22	21–22
Common and quarter blood	16–17	17–17	16–17	16–17	17–18	17–17	17–19	17–20	19–21	19–21	20–21	20–21
Coarse, carpet	14–15	14–15	14–15	14–15	15–16	15–16	15–16	15–16	16–17	16–17	17–18	17–19

NEW MEXICAN.

	Fall clip.		Fall clip.		Spr'g clip.							
Choice improved	17–18	17–18	15–18	15–18	16–20	16–20	16–20	18–22	20–23	20–23	20–23	21–24
Average improved	15–17	15–16	14–15	14–15	15–15	15–15	15–15	20–25	16–18	17–19	19–20	20–20
Coarse, carpet, light, long staple	13–14	13–14	13–13½	13–13½	14–15	14–15	14–15	14–15	16–17	16–17	17–18	17–18
Coarse, carpet, heavy, sandy, or very short	12–13	12–13	12–13	12–13	12–13	12–13	14–17	17–20	14–17	15–16	15–17	15–17
Black	12–13	12–13	12–12	12–12	12–13	12–13	13–14	13–14	13–14	13–14	15–16	15–15

TEXAS.

	Fall clip.		Fall clip.		Spr'g clip.							
Fine northern and eastern	18–20	18–20	15–18	15–18	18–22	18–22	18–22	18–22	20–25	20–25	20–25	20–25
Medium northern and eastern	18–21	18–21	15–17	15–17	22–25	22–25	20–25	20–25	20–25	22–26	22–25	22–25
Coarse northern and eastern	15–17	15–17	13–15	12–13	14–15	14–15	14–15	14–15	14–15	16–18	16–18	16–18
Improved western and southern	17–20	17–20	13–15	13–13½	17–20	17–20	17–20	17–20	17–20	20–22	18–22	18–22
Coarse western and southern	15–16	15–16	13–13	12–12	12–14	12–14	13–14	13–14	13–14	15–17	15–16	15–16

IOWA, NEBRASKA, AND MONTANA.

Unwashed, fine, bright	18–20	18–20	18–22	18–22	18–22	20–22	20–22	20–22	20–23	21–24	21–23	21–23
Unwashed, medium, bright	18–21	18–21	18–21	18–21	18–18	20–22	20–22	20–22	22–25	24–26	24–26	25–27
Unwashed, coarse, bright	15–17	15–17	15–17	15–17	15–17	16–18	16–18	16–18	18–19	20–20	20–21	20–20
Unwashed, dark colored or heavy												

UTAH AND WYOMING.

Unwashed, choice fine, light	18–20	18–20	18–19	18–19	18–19	18–19	18–19	18–19	19–20	20–22	19–20	20–22
Unwashed, fine, heavy	16–17	16–17	16–17	16–17	16–17	16–17	16–17	17–18	16–17	18–20	19–20	19–20
Unwashed, choice selected medium	20–21	20–21	18–19	18–19	17–17	20–22	20–22	18–20	18–20	20–22	23–25	24–26
Unwashed, low medium	17–18	17–18	17–17	17–17	14–15	15–16	15–16	15–16	15–16	17–18	20–22	21–23
Unwashed, coarse, carpet	15–15	15–15	14–15	14–15	15–16	15–16	15–16	15–16	15–16	17–18	18–20	18–20

TUB WASHED.

Choice selected	33–35	33–35	33–35	33–35	33–35	33–36	32–33	32–33	32–33	33–35	35–38	36–38
Good	30–32	30–32	30–32	30–32	30–32	30–32	30–32	30–32	30–32	30–33	33–35	35–35
Fair ordinary	28–30	28–30	28–30	28–30	28–28	28–28	27–29	27–29	28–29	28–30	30–33	32–34

PULLED.

City merino	24–25	24–25	24–25	24–25	24–25	24–25	24–25	24–25	25–27	27–30	28–30	28–30
City super and lambs	24–28	24–28	24–26	14–26	24–26	24–26	24–26	24–25	25–28	28–32	30–32	32–33
Western super and lambs	20–23	20–23	20–23	20–23	20–23	22–24	22–24	23–25	23–25	25–28	28–30	30–32

No. 12.—PRICES OF WOOL IN THE MARKETS OF NEW YORK (1824–1887) AND PHILADELPHIA (1865–1887)—Continued.

(b) Prices of the different kinds of Wool in Philadelphia each year from 1865 to 1884, inclusive, and each month of 1884 and 1885, and from May, 1886, to May, 1887, inclusive.—Continued.

[From Coates Brothers' Wool Circulars.]

Kinds of wool.	1886								1887				
	May.	June.	July.	August.	September.	October.	November.	December.	January.	February.	March.	April.	May.
	Between seasons; quiet.	Active; foreign ma'els advancing.	Active and higher.	Firm but quiet.	Increased demand.	Firm; less demand.	Slight decline.	Dull.	Improved demand.	Weakening.	Quiet and declining.	Depressed.	Stocks light.
OHIO, PENNSYLVANIA, AND WEST VIRGINIA FLEECE, WASHED.	*Cents*	*Cents*	*Cents*	*Cents*	*Cents*	*Cents*	*Cents*	*Cents*	*Cents*	*Cents.*	*Cents.*	*Cents.*	*Cents.*
XX and above	32–45	31–33	34–35	34–36	34–36	35–38	31–37	35–36	35–36	35–36	34–36	33–15	33–15
X	30–31	30–31	30–31	33–34	32–34	33–35	33–35	33–34	33–34	32–33	32–33	31–32	31–32
Half blood	33–34	33–34	34–35	37–38	37–38	37–38	38–39	38–39	38–39	39–40	38–39	37–38	37–38
Quarter blood	33–33	31–32	33–34	36–37	36–37	37–38	38–39	37–38	37–38	39–40	38–40	37–38	37–38
Common and cotted	27–28	26–27	27–30	30–32	30–32	30–32	30–32	30–32	30–32	30–32	30–32	30–31	30–31
NEW YORK, MICHIGAN, INDIANA, AND WISCONSIN FLEECE, WASHED.													
XX	30–32	29–30	31–33	32–34	32–33	31–34	33–34	32–34	32–33	32–33	32–33	30–32	30–32
X	29–30	27–29	30–31	31–32	31–32	32–33	32–33	32–33	32–32	32–32	31–32	30–32	30–31
Half blood	32–33	32–33	33–35	34–37	36–37	36–38	37–38	37–38	37–38	38–39	38–38	37–37	36–37
Quarter blood	32–33	30–32	32–33	35–30	35–36	30–37	37–38	36–37	36–37	38–39	38–39	37–37	37–37
Common and cotted	26–27	26–27	27–29	30–31	30–31	30–31	30–31	30–31	30–31	30–31	30–31	30–30	30–30
COMBING AND DELAINE FLEECE.													
Washed, fine delaine	33–35	32–34	33–35	35–36	35–37	37–40	37–40	37–38	36–38	36–38	35–37	34–37	34–37
Washed, medium	35–36	34–35	35–36	38–39	38–40	38–40	38–40	39–40	39–40	39–40	38–40	38–39	34–39
Washed, low	34–35	34–35	34–36	37–38	37–38	37–38	38–40	38–39	38–39	39–40	39–40	38–39	38–30
Washed, coarse	33–34	30–32	32–34	34–35	34–35	34–35	35–36	35–36	35–36	35–36	35–37	34–38	34–36
Unwashed, medium	26–27	24–26	27–28	30–32	30–32	30–32	30–32	30–31	30–31	30–31	30–31	28–31	28–31
Unwashed, low and coarse	25–26	22–24	26–27	28–30	28–30	28–30	28–30	27–29	27–29	28–30	29–30	28–30	28–30
Canada	32–33	30–32	31–34	35–37	35–37	35–37	35–37	35–37	35–37	37–38	37–38	36–37	36–37

	C1	C2	C3	C4	C5	C6	C7	C8	C9	C10	C11	C12	C13	C14
UNWASHED.														
Light and bright.														
Fine	18-21	18-21	21-22	22-23	23-24	23-24	23-24	22-25	22-23	22-24	22-24	22-23	21-22	20-22
Medium	25-28	24-26	27-28	30-32	30-31	30-31	30-31	30-33	30-32	30-31	30-31	30-32	29-30	28-30
Low medium	23-25	22-23	25-26	28-29	28-30	28-30	27-29	28-29	28-29	28-30	28-30	28-29	28-29	27-28
Coarse, or burry	17-20	17-20	20-22	20-25	20-25	20-25	20-25	20-25	20-25	20-25	20-25	20-25	20-23	20-23
Heavy or dark colored.														
Fine	17-19	17-19	19-21	20-21	20-21	20-21	20-21	21-22	21-22	20-21	20-21	20-21	19-20	19-20
Medium	21-23	21-23	22-23	23-25	23-25	23-25	23-25	25-26	25-26	24-25	23-25	23-25	23-24	23-24
Low	19-21	19-21	22-23	23-24	22-24	22-24	23-25	23-26	23-24	23-24	23-24	22-24	22-23	22-23
Coarse, carpet	17-18	17-18	17-19	18-20	18-20	18-20	16-20	16-20	18-20	18-20	18-20	17-20	16-18	17-19
Heavy, or faulty	15-16	15-16	15-18	17-20	17-20	17-20	17-20	17-20	17-20	17-20	17-20	17-20	17-19	17-19
COLORADO.														
Medium and fine, choice	22-25	22-24	23-26	23-25	26-28	26-27	25-27	25-27	26-27	24-26	24-26	23-25	22-23	22-23
Medium and fine, average	20-21	20-21	21-23	21-23	23-24	23-24	22-23	22-23	23-24	21-22	21-22	21-22	20-21	20-21
Common and quarter blood	18-19	18-19	20-21	22-24	22-23	22-23	22-23	22-23	22-23	20-21	20-21	20-21	18-21	18-21
Coarse, carpet	16-17	16-17	17-18	18-20	18-20	16-20	18-20	18-20	18-20	18-21	17-19	17-19	16-17	16-17
NEW MEXICAN.	Fall clip.	Spr'g clip	Spr'g clip	Spr'g clip	Spr'g clip	Fall clip.	Fall clip.	Fall clip.	Fall clip.	Fall clip.	Fall clip.	Fall clip.	Fall clip.	Fall clip.
Choice improved	20-21	20-23	22-25	25-27	25-26	22-24	22-24	25-27	26-27	25-27	20-22	20-22	20-22	22-23
Average improved		18-19	19-21	21-24	21-24	18-19	20-22	22-23	24-25	23-25	16-20	18-20	18-19	20-21
Coarse, carpet, light	15-16	15-16	17-18	18-19	18-19	18-18	18-18	18-19	18-20	18-20	17-17	17-17	15-16	15-16
Coarse, carpet, heavy, sandy, or very short	14-15	14-15	15-17	17-18	17-18	17-17	16-17	16-20	17-18	17-17	15-16	15-16	15-16	14-15
Black	14-14	14-14	15-16	16-17	16-17	16-17	16-16	16-17	16-17	16-16	15-15	15-15	14-15	14-15
TEXAS	Fall clip.	Spr'g clip	Spr'g clip	Spr'g clip	Spr'g clip	Fall clip.	Fall clip.	Fall clip.	Fall clip.	Fall clip.	Fall clip.	Fall clip.	Fall clip.	Fall clip.
Fine northern and eastern	19-22	20-22	21-24	23-25	23-25	22-22	21-22	25-27	26-27	25-25	20-22	20-22	20-21	20-21
Medium northern and eastern	21-24	22-25	25-27	26-30	26-30	25-26	25-27	25-26	27-28	27-28	23-25	23-25	23-24	22-24
Coarse northern and eastern	15-15	16-16	17-18	20-20	20-20	18-20	18-20	18-23	20-25	20-26	17-18	17-18	16-17	17-0
Improved western and southern	16-20	16-19	20-23	22-26	22-26	18-21	18-21	16-17	20-23	22-26	18-21	18-21	17-20	14-15
Coarse western and southern	14-14	14-15	15-17	17-18	17-18	16-18	16-17	16-17	17-18	16-18	15-16	15-16	14-15	14-15
MONTANA.														
Unwashed, fine, bright	19-20	19-20	20-23	23-25	22-24	22-24	22-24	22-24	22-24	21-22	21-22	21-22	20-21	20-21
Unwashed, medium, bright	23-25	23-25	24-27	26-30	26-26	26-28	26-28	26-28	26-28	24-26	24-26	24-26	23-26	23-25
Unwashed, coarse, bright	20-22	20-22	20-23	24-26	23-25	23-25	22-25	20-23	22-23	22-23	22-23	22-23	20-22	20-22
Unwashed, dark colored or heavy	16-17	16-17	18-20	20-24	20-23	20-23	20-23	18-20	19-21	19-21	19-21	19-21	18-21	18-20
UTAH AND WYOMING.														
Unwashed, choice, fine, light	19-20	19-20	20-22	21-22	21-22	21-22	21-22	21-22	21-22	20-21	20-21	20-21	20-21	20-21
Unwashed, fine, heavy	16-18	16-18	18-20	19-20	19-20	19-20	10-20	18-19	16-19	18-19	18-19	16-19	17-19	17-19
Unwashed, choice selected medium	23-24	22-24	24-26	25-27	25-27	25-27	24-26	23-25	24-26	22-25	22-25	22-25	22-25	22-25
Unwashed, low medium	20-21	20-21	21-23	25-27	25-26	25-26	24-25	24-26	22-23	22-23	22-23	22-23	22-23	20-22
Unwashed, coarse, carpet	16-17	16-17	17-19	18-20	18-20	18-20	18-20	17-19	17-19	17-19	17-19	17-19	16-18	16-18

No. 12.—Prices of Wool in the Markets of New York (1824-1887) and Philadelphia (1865-1887)—Continued.

(b) Prices of the different kinds of Wools in Philadelphia each year from 1-65 to 1884, inclusive, and each month of 1884 and 1885, and from May, 1886, to May inclusive, 1887—Continued.

[From Coates Brothers' Wool Circulars.]

Kinds of wool.	1886.								1887.				
	May.	June.	July.	August.	September.	October.	November.	December.	January.	February.	March.	April.	May.
	Between seasons; quiet.	Active; foreign markets advancing.	Active and higher.	Firm but quiet.	Increased demand.	Firm; less demand.	Slight decline.	Dull.	Improved demand.	Weakening.	Quiet and declining.	Depressed.	Stocks light.
TUB WASHED.	Cents.	Cents.	Cents.	Cents.	Cents.	Cents.	Cents.	Cents.	Cents.	Cents.	Cents.	Cents.	Cents.
Choice selected	35-37	35-37	36-38	39-40	39-40	40-42	40-42	40-42	40-42	41-42	40-42	40-40	40-40
Good	33-35	33-35	31-36	37-38	37-38	38-40	38-40	38-40	38-40	38-40	38-40	38-38	38-38
Fair ordinary	31-33	30-33	32-34	35-36	35-38	36-37	36-37	36-37	30-37	36-37	36-37	35-37	35-37
PULLED.													
City merino	25-28	25-28	27-30	28-31	28-31	28-31	28-31	28-31	28-31	28-31	28-31	27-29	27-29
City super and lambs	30-32	30-32	32-33	33-35	33-35	31-35	33-35	33-35	32-34	32-34	31-33	32-34	32-34
Western super and lambs	27-29	27-29	30-32	32-35	32-35	32-33	30-35	30-33	30-32	30-32	28-32	26-30	26-30

NOTE.—From our circulars, issued during the past wool year, we show the course of the market. At the beginning of the season foreign wools were lower than for very many years, and our prices were crowded down by the competition from abroad. The strong advance at the Antwerp May auctions, followed by the London June sales, was soon felt here, and through the summer prices ruled firm, and holders were confident. With winter came the feeling that woolen goods would not command higher values, so that wool markets became more quiet, and with the exception of a slight improvement in January, they have since been weak and declining. Good wools are, however, now closely sold up, and the small stock left consists mostly of undesirable lots. It is hoped that this yearly summary may be useful for comparison with the course of the market during the coming season.

No. 13.—STATEMENT SHOWING THE RATES OF DUTY UPON WOOL AND MANUFACTURES OF WOOL, UNDER THE SEVERAL TARIFF ACTS RELATING TO MERCHANDISE IMPORTED INTO THE UNITED STATES, FROM 1789 TO 1883, INCLUSIVE.

[Where no rates are given to articles in any column, such articles are regarded as unenumerated and subject to the duty levied on unenumerated.]

Wool, and manufactures of.	July 4, 1789. (Aug. 2, 1789.)	Aug. 10, 1790. (Jan. 1, 1791.)	May 2, 1792. (July 1, 1792.)	June 7, 1794. (July 1, 1794.)	May 13, 1800. (July 1, 1800.a)	May 28, 1804. (July 1, 1804.)	July 1, 1812. (July 1, 1812.)	Apr. 27, 1816. (July 1, 1816.)	May 22, 1824. (July 1, 1824.)	May 19, 1828. (Sept. 2, 1828.)	July 14, 1832. (Mar. 4, 1833.)	Mar. 2, 1833. (Jan. 1, 1834.b)
Raw or unmanufactured:												
Wool (all)	Free	Free	Free	Free	Free	Free	Free	15 p. c. (n. o.)	15 p. o. (d)			
Valued at 10 cents or less per pound..										4c. lb. & 40 p. c.		
Other (valued over 10 cents per pound)										(c)		
Valued at not exceeding 8 cents per pound.											Free	
Valued at exceeding 8 cents per pound [Wool on the skin shall be estimated as to weight and value as other wool.]											4c. lb. & 40 p. o.	
Manufactures of:												
Blankets—												
Blankets (all other)									25 p. c.	35 p. c.	25 p. c.	
Valued not above 75 cents each											5 p. c.	
Carpets—												
Carpets and carpeting (of all kinds)		7½ p. c.	10 p. c.	15 p. c.		17½ p. c.	35 p. c.					
Brussels, Turkey, and Wilton.....										50c. sq. yd.	63c. sq. yd.	
Venetian and ingrain..........										25c. sq. yd.	40c. sq. yd. 35c. sq. yd.	

a "Increase rates on certain articles named (wool not included)," "upon goods, wares, and merchandise now paying a duty of ten per centum ad valorem, two and one-half per centum ad valorem.

b Sec. 1. That from and after the 31 December, 1833, in all cases where duties are imposed on foreign imports by the act of the 14th day of July, 1832, entitled "An act to alter and amend the several acts imposing duties on imports " or by any other act, shall exceed twenty per centum on the value thereof, one-tenth part of such excess shall be deducted ; from and after the 31 of December, 1837, another tenth part thereof shall be deducted ; from and after the 31 of December, 1839, another tenth part thereof shall be deducted ; and from and after the 31 of December, 1841, one half of the residue of such excess shall be deducted ; and from and after the 30 of June, 1842, the other half thereof shall be deducted.

c 4 cents per pound and 45 per cent. ; after June 30, 1829, 4 cents per pound and 50 per cent.

d 20 per cent. until June 1, 1825; 25 per cent. until June 1, 1826; 30 per cent. afterwards.

No. 12.—STATEMENT SHOWING THE RATES OF DUTY UPON WOOL AND MANUFACTURES OF WOOL, FROM 1789 TO 1883, INCLUSIVE.—Continued.

Wool, and manufactures of.	Acts of— July 4, 1789. / Went into effect— Aug. 2, 1789.	Aug. 10, 1790. / Jan. 1, 1791.	May 2, 1792. / July 1, 1792.	June 7, 1794. / July 1, 1794.	May 13, 1800. / July 1, 1800.a	May 20, 1804. / July 1, 1804.	July 1, 1812. / July 1, 1812.	Apr. 27, 1816. / July 1, 1816.	May 22, 1824. / July 1, 1824.	May 19, 1828. / Sept. 2, 1828.	July 1, 1829.	July 14, 1832. / Mar. 4, 1833.	Mar. 2, 1833. / Jan. 1, 1834.b
Manufactures of—Continued.													
Carpets—Continued.													
All other.													
Clothing, ready made	7½ p.c.	7½ p.c.	10 p.c.	15 p.c.		17½ p.c.	35 p.c.	30 p.c.	20c. sq. yd.	32c. sq. yd.		25 p.c.	
Flannels and bockings and baizes										50 p.c.		50 p.c.	
Hats—													
Wool, or mixture of	7½ p.c.	7½ p.c.	10 p.c.	15 p.c.		17½ p.c.	35 p.c.	30 p.c.				16c. sq. yd.	
Wool or felt, or mixture of												30 p.c.	
Wool or felt bodies.												18c each	Free.
Knit goods—													
Caps, gloves, mits or mittens and bindings			10 p.c.	15 p.c.		17½ p.c.	25 p.c.	20 p.c.		35 p.c.		25 p.c.	
Socks and stockings				15 p.c.		17½ p.c.	35 p.c.			35 p.c.		25 p.c.	
Hosiery, woolen or worsted													
Rags of whatever kind					Free	Free	Free	Free	Free	Free		Free	
Shawls—													
Merino												50 p.c.	
Worsted												10 p.c.	
Yarns—													
Worsted												4c. lb. & 50 p.c.	
Wool												20 p.c.	
Worsted													Free.
All manufactures of every description, not specially enumerated or provided for, made wholly or in part of—												50 p.c.	
Wool—													
Manufacture of, not otherwise provided for								(c)	(d)			50 p.c.	
Valued at not exceeding 33⅓ cents per square yard									25 p. c	14c. sq. yd			
Valued at not exceeding 50 cents per square yard										40 p. c	45 p. c		

Article								
Valued exceeding 50 cts. and not exceeding $1 per square yard							40 p. c	45 p. c
Valued exceeding $1 and not exceeding $2.50 per square yard							40 p. c	45 p. c
Valued exceeding $2.50 and not exceeding $4 per square yard							40 p. c	45 p. c
Valued exceeding $4 per square yard							45 p. c	45 p. c
Worsteds—							45 p. c	50 p. c
Worsted stuff goods						25 p. c		10 p. c
Manufactures of, not otherwise provided for								10 p. c
Laces, fringes, tassels, and trimmings, commonly used by upholsterers and coach-makers								Free.
Silk and worsted	15 p. c	15 p. c	17½ p. c	35 p. c	35 p. c	35 p. c		35 p. c / 10 p. c
Milled and fulled cloth, known by the name of plain kerseys, or Kendal cottons, of which wool shall be the only material, the value whereof shall not exceed 35 cents square yard								Free.
Unenumerated articles	5 p. c	5 p. c	7½ p. c	12½ p. c	15 p. c	30 p. c		5 p. c
Discriminating duty in addition to regular duty on merchandise imported in foreign vessels	10 p. c	10 p. c	10 p. c	10 p. c	10 p. c	10 p. c	10 p. c	10 p. c
Articles, &c. (other than tea), from China or India, in ships not built or owned in the United States (additional duty)	12½ p. c	12½ p. c	10 p. c	20 p. c				10 p. c

a "Increases rates on certain articles named (wool not included)," upon goods, wares, and merchandise now paying a duty of ten per centum ad valorem, two and one-half per centum ad valorem.

b Sec. 1. That from and after the 31 December, 1833, in all cases where duties are imposed on foreign imports by the act of the 14th day of July, 1832, entitled "An act to alter and amend the several acts imposing duties on imports," or by any other act, shall exceed twenty per centum on the value thereof, one-tenth part of such excess shall be deducted; from and after the 31 of December, 1837, another tenth part thereof shall be deducted; from and after the 31 of December, 1839, another tenth part thereof shall be deducted; and from and after the 31 of December, 1841, one-half, one-half of the residue of such excess shall be deducted; and from and after the 30 of June, 1842, the other half thereof shall be deducted.

c 25 per cent.; after June 30, 1819, 20 per cent.

d 30 per cent.; after June 30, 1825, 33⅓ per cent.

No. 13.—Statement showing the Rates of Duty upon Wool and Manufactures of Wool, from 1789 to 1883, inclusive—Continued.

Wool, and manufactures of.	Aug. 30, 1842.	July 30, 1846.	Mar. 3, 1857.	Mar. 2, 1861.	July 14, 1862.	June 30, 1864.	Mar. 2, 1867.	June 6, 1872.	Mar. 3, 1875.	Mar. 3, 1883.
Went into effect—	Aug. 30, 1842.	Dec. 1, 1846.	July 1, 1857.	Apr. 2, 1861.	Aug. 2, 1862.	July 1, 1864.	Mar. 2, 1867.	Aug. 1, 1872.	Mar. 3, 1875.	July 1, 1883.
Raw or unmanufactured:										
Value 7 cents or less per pound	5 p. c									
All other (1842)	3 c. lb. & 30 p.c	30 p. c								
Valued 20 cents or less per pound		20 p. c	24 p. c							
Thibet, Angora, and all other goats' hair or mohair, unmanufactured.	1 c. p		Free							
Also hair of the alpaca, goat, and other like animals—			15 p. c							
Value less than 18 cents per pound				5 p. c		3 c. lb.				
Value less than 12 cents per pound				3 c. lb		6 c. lb.				
Value exceeding 18 cents and not exceeding 24 cents per pound.										
Value exceeding 24 cents and not exceeding 30 cents per pound.				9 c. lb		10 c. lb & 10 p. c				
Value exceeding 32 cents per pound.						12 c. lb. & 10 p. c				
Mixed to reduce value to evade duty	(a)		(a)		(a)	(a)	Double duty.	Double duty.	Double duty.	Double duty.
Class I.—Clothing wools—										
Value 32 cents or less per pound							10 c. lb. & 11 p. c	9 c. lb. & 9 9/10 p. c	10 c. lb. & 11 p. c	10 c. lb.
Value exceeding 32 cents per pound							12 c. lb. & 10 p. c	10 8/10 c. lb. & 9 p. c	12 c. lb. & 10 p. c	12 c. lb.
Value 30 cents or less per pound.										
Value over 30 cents per pound.										
Class II —Combing wool—										
Value 32 cents or less per pound.							10 c. lb. & 11 p. c	9 c. lb. & 9 9/10 p. c	10 c. lb. & 11 p. c	10 c. lb.
Value exceeding 32 cents per pound							12 c. lb. & 10 p. c	10 8/10 c. lb. & 9 p. c	12 c. lb. & 10 p. c	12 c. lb.
Class III.—Carpet wools—										
Value 30 cents or less per pound.										
Value over 30 cents per pound.										
Value 12 cents or less per pound.							3 c. lb.	2 7/10 c. lb.	3 c. lb.	2¼ c. lb.

Article				Treble duty	6 c. lb. Double duty. Treble duty	5.4 c. lb. Double duty. Treble duty	6 c. lb. Double duty Treble duty	5 c. lb. Double duty. Treble duty
Value over 12 cents per pound								
Of Class I, washed								
Of all classes, scoured								
(Wool on the skin shall pay the same rate of duty as that not on the skin.)								
Sheepskins, raw or unmanufactured, with the wool on, washed or unwashed	15 p. c.	15 p. c.		20 p. c.	30 p. c.	27 p. c.	30 p. c.	
[Manufactures								
Balmorals—								
Balmoral skirts and skirtings, and goods of similar description, or used for like purposes, composed wholly or in part of wool, worsted, the hair of the alpaca, goat, or other like animals, made up or manufactured, except knit goods			18 c. lb. & 30 p. c.	24 c. lb. & 35 p. c.				
Valued at not exceeding 40 cents per pound					20 c. lb. & 35 p. c.	18 c. lb. & 31.5 p. c.	20 c. lb. & 35 p. c.	10 c. lb. & 35 p. c.
Valued at not exceeding 30 cents per pound					35 p. c.	31.5 p. c.	35 p. c.	35 p. c.
Valued at above 30 and not exceeding 40 cents per pound					30 c. lb. & 35 p. c.	27 c. lb. & 31.5 p. c.	30 c. lb. & 35 p. c.	12 c. lb. & 35 p. c.
Valued at above 40 and not exceeding 60 cents per pound					40 c. lb. & 35 p. c.	36 c. lb. & 31.5 p. c.	40 c. lb. & 35 p. c.	18 c. lb. & 35 p. c.
Valued at above 60 and not exceeding 80 cents per pound					35 p. c.	31.5 p. c.	35 p. c.	24 c. lb. & 35 p. c.
Valued at over 80 cents per pound					50 c. lb. & 35 p. c.	45 c. lb. & 31.5 p. c.	50 c. lb. & 35 p. c.	35 c. lb. & 35 p. c.
Belts or felts, endless, for paper or printing machines			30 p. c.		35 p. c.	31.5 p. c.	35 p. c.	40 p. c.
Blankets—								
Valued not above 75 cents each, not beyond 72 by 52 inches, nor less than 45 by 60 inches.	15 p. c.	0 c. Th. & 10 p. c.	6 c. lb. & 25 p. c.		20 c. lb. & 35 p. c.	18 c. lb. & 31.5 p. c.	20 c. lb. & 35 p. c.	20 c. lb. & 35 p. c.
Of goats' hair or mohair	20 p. c.		12 c. lb. & 20 p. c.					
All other	25 p. c.							
Of all kinds		0 c. Th. & 15 p. c.						
Value not exceeding 28 cents per pound		6 c. lb. & 25 p. c.		12 c. p. & 20 p. c.				30 p. c.
Value exceeding 28 cents, and not exceeding 40 cents per pound		12 c. lb. & 20 p. c.	6 c. lb. & 30 p. c.	24 c. lb. & 25 p. c.				
Value exceeding 40 cents per pound		20 p. c.	12 c. lb. & 25 p. c.	24 c. lb. & 30 p. c.	25 p. c.			
Value at not exceeding 40 cents per pound					20 c. lb. & 35 p. c.	18 c. lb. & 31.5 p. c.	20 c. lb. & 35 p. c.	10 c. lb. & 35 p. c.
Value at not exceeding 30 cents per pound					35 p. c.	31.5 p. c.	35 p. c.	35 p. c.

a To pay the highest rate of duty.

No. 13.—STATEMENT SHOWING THE RATES OF DUTY UPON WOOL AND MANUFACTURES OF WOOL, FROM 1789 TO 1883, INCLUSIVE.—Continued.

Wool, and manufactures of.	Aug. 30, 1842.	July 30, 1846.	Mar. 3, 1857.	Mar. 2, 1861.	July 14, 1862.	June 30, 1864.	Mar. 2, 1867.	June 6, 1872.	Mar. 3, 1875.	Mar. 3, 1883.
Went into effect—	Aug. 30, 1842.	Dec. 1, 1846.	July 1, 1857.	Apr. 2, 1861.	Aug. 2, 1862.	July 1, 1864.	Mar. 2, 1867.	Aug. 1, 1872.	Mar. 3, 1875.	July 1, 1883.
Manufactures—Continued.										
Blankets—Continued.										
Value at above 30 and not exceeding 40 cents per pound.							30 c. lb. & 35 p. c.	27 c. lb. & 31.5 p. c.	30 c. lb. & 35 p. c.	12 c. lb. & 35 p. c.
Value at above 40 and not exceeding 60 cents per pound.							40 c. lb. & 35 p. c.	36 c. lb. & 31.5 p. c.	40 c. lb. & 35 p. c.	18 c. lb. & 35 p. c.
Value at above 60 and not exceeding 80 cents per pound.							50 c. lb. & 35 p. c.	45 c. lb. & 31.5 p. c.	50 c. lb. & 35 p. c.	24 c. lb. & 35 p. c.
Value at over 80 cents per pound										35 c. lb. & 35 p. c.
Bunting				30 p. c.	35 p. c.	50 p. c.	35 p. c.	31.5 p. c.	35 p. c.	40 p. c.
Carpets and carpetings—										
Carpets and carpetings of all kinds	14 c. sq. yd.	30 p. c.	24 p. c.				20 c. sq. yd. & 35 p. c.	14 c. sq. yd. & 31.5 p. c.	20 c. sq. yd. & 35 p. c.	10 c. sq. yd. & 35 p. c.
Baizes and beckings		25 p. c.	19 p. c.							
Wilton, Saxony, and Aubusson, Axminster, patent velvet, Tournay velvet, and tapestry velvet carpets and carpeting, Brussels carpets wrought by the Jacquard machine, and all medallion or whole carpets—										
Valued at $1.25 or under per square yard				40 c. sq. yd.	45 c. sq. yd.	70 c. sq. yd.	28 c. sq. yd. & 35 p. c.	25.2 c. sq. yd. & 31.5 p. c.	28 c. sq. yd. & 35 p. c.	
Valued at over $1.25 per square yard				50 c. sq. yd.	55 c. sq. yd.	80 c. sq. yd.				
Brussels and Turkey	55 c. sq. yd.									
Brussels and tapestry Brussels carpets and carpeting, printed on the warp or otherwise				30 c. sq. yd.	33 c. sq. yd.	50 c. sq. yd.	44 c. sq. yd. & 35 p. c.	39.6 c. sq. yd. & 31.5 p. c.	41 c. sq. yd. & 35 p. c.	30 c. sq. yd. & 30 p. c.
Aubusson and Saxony	63 c. sq. yd.									
Aubusson, Axminster, and chenille carpets, and carpets woven whole for rooms							50 p. c.	45 p. c.	50 p. c.	45 c. sq. yd. & 30 p. c.
Brussels carpets							44 c. sq. yd. & 35 p. c.	39.6 c. sq. yd. & 31.5 p. c.	41 c. sq. yd. & 35 p. c.	30 c. sq. yd. & 30 p. c.

Article										
Druggets and bockings, printed, colored, or otherwise				20 c. sq. yd.	25 c. sq. yd.	25 c. sq. yd. & 35 p.c	22.5 c. sq. yd. & 31.5 p.c	25 c. sq. yd. & 35 p.c	25 c. sq. yd. & 35 p.c	15 c. sq. yd. & 30 p.c
Mats, screens, hassocks, and rugs, not exclusively of vegetable material (only rugs up to 1864)	40 p. c	30 p. c	24 p. c	30 p. c	35 p. c	45 p. c	45 p. c	40.5 p. c	45 p. c	40 p. c
Of wool, flax, or cotton, or parts of either, or other material not specially enumerated or provided for	30 p. c.	30 p. c	24 p. c	30 p. c	35 p. c	40 p. c	40 p. c	36 p. c	40 p. c	40 p. c
Patent velvet and tapestry velvet, carpets, printed on the warp or otherwise					50 c. sq. yd.		40 c. sq. yd. & 35 p.c	36 c. sq. yd. & 31.5 p. o.	40 c. sq. yd. & 35 p.c	25 c. sq. yd. & 30 p.c
Wilton and treble ingrain	65 c. sq. yd.				40 c. sq. yd					45 c. sq. yd. & 30 p.c
Saxony, Wilton, and Tournay velvet carpets							70 c. sq. yd. & 35 p.o.	63 c. sq. yd. & 31.5 p. o.	70 c. sq. yd. & 35 p.o	45 c. sq. yd. & 30 p.c
Tapestry Brussels, printed on the warp or otherwise		30 p. c	24 p. c	25 c. sq. yd.						20 c. sq. yd. & 30 p.c
Treble ingrain, three-ply and worsted chain Venetian carpets	30 c. sq. yd				28 c. sq. yd.	35 c. sq. yd.	17 c. sq. yd. & 35 p.c	15.3 c. sq. yd. & 31.5 p.o.	17 c. sq. yd. & 35 p.o.	12 c. sq. yd. & 30 p.c.
Venetian and ingrain	30 c. sq. yd									
Yarn, Venetian, and two-ply ingrain carpets [Hassocks, rugs, screens, mats, bedsides, covers, &c., pay duty as carpetings of all description.]							12 c. sq. yd. & 35 p.c	10.8 c. sq. yd. & 31.5 p.o.	12 c. sq. yd. & 35 p.c	8 c. sx. yd. & 30 p.c
Clothing:										
Ready made	50 p. c.									
Other articles made by hand	40 p. c.									
Embroidered, gold, &c.	50 p. c.		24 p. c							
Clothing, ready-made, and wearing apparel (except knit goods), not specially enumerated or provided for, composed wholly or in part of wool, worsted, the hair of the alpaca, goat, or other (like) animals, made up or manufactured wholly by the tailor, or seamstress, or manufacturer		30 p. c		30 p. c		30 p. c				
Clothing, ready-made, and wearing apparel of every description, not specially enumerated or provided for, and balmoral skirts and skirting and goods of similar description, or used for like purposes						24 c. lb. & 40 p. c.	50 c. lb. & 40 p. c.	45 c. lb. & 36 p. c.	50 c. lb. & 40 p. c.	40 c. lb. & 35 p. c.
Cloaks, dolmans, jackets, talmas, ulsters, or other out-side garments for ladies and children's apparel, and goods of similar description, or used for like purposes										
Cloths, woolen: Cloth not otherwise provided for		12 c. lb. & 25 p. c.		12 c. lb. & 25 p. c.	18 c. lb. & 30 p. c.	24 c. lb. & 40 p. c.	50 c. lb. & 35 p. c.	45 c. lb. & 31.5 p. c.	50 c. lb. & 35 p. c.	45 c. lb. & 40 p. o.

NO. 13.—STATEMENT SHOWING THE RATES OF DUTY UPON WOOL AND MANUFACTURES OF WOOL, FROM 1789 TO 1883, INCLUSIVE—Continued.

Column headers show **Acts of—** (top date in each cell) and **Went into effect—** (bottom date in each cell).

Wool, and manufactures of.	Aug. 30, 1842. / Aug. 30, 1842.	July 30, 1846. / Dec. 1, 1846.	Mar. 3, 1857. / July 1, 1857.	Mar. 2, 1861. / Apr. 2, 1861.	July 14, 1862. / Aug. 2, 1862.	June 30, 1864. / July 1, 1864.	Mar. 2, 1867. / Mar. 2, 1867.	June 6, 1872. / Aug. 1, 1872.	Mar. 3, 1875. / Mar. 3, 1875.	Mar. 3, 1883. / July 1, 1883.
Manufactures—Continued.										
Cloths, woolen—Continued.										
Valued over $2 per square yard						24 c. lb. & 45 p. c.				35 c. lb. & 35 p. c.
Valued at not exceeding 80 cents per pound										
Valued at above 80 cents per pound										35 c. lb. & 40 p. c.
Valued at over $1 per square yard, or weighing less than 12 ounces per square yard					18 c. lb. & 35 p. c.					
Dress goods, women's and children's, coat linings, Italian cloths, and goods of like description—				25 p. c.						
Delaines, cashmere delaines, muslin delaines, barége delaines, and goods of similar description—										
Gray or uncolored—										
Valued not exceeding 40 cents per square yard					2 c. sq. yd. & 25 p. c.					
Valued exceeding 40 cents per square yard					30 p. c.					
Stained, colored, or printed—										
Valued not exceeding 40 cents per square yard					2 c. sq. yd. & 30 p. c.					
Valued exceeding 40 cents per square yard					35 p. c.					
Gray or uncolored—										
Valued not over 30 cents per square yard						4 c. sq. yd. & 25 p. c.				
Valued over 30 cents per square yard						6 c. sq. yd. & 30 p. c.				
Stained, colored, or printed—										
Valued not over 30 cents per square yard						4 c. sq. yd. & 30 p. c.				
Valued over 30 cents per square yard						6 c. sq. yd. & 35 p. c.				

Description									
Composed in part of wool, worsted, the hair of the alpaca, goat, or other animals—									
Valued at not exceeding 20 cents per square yard.....									
Valued at above 20 cents per square yard...	5 c. sq.yd & 35 p.c.	6 c. sq.yd & 35 p.c.	6 c. sq.yd & 35 p.c.	6 c. sq.yd. & 35 p.c.					
All weighing over 4 ounces per square yard...	7 c. sq.yd. & 40 p.c.	8 c. sq.yd. & 40 p.c.	5.4 c. sq.yd. & 31.5 p.c. / 7.2 c. sq.yd. & 31.5 p.c.	8 c. sq.yd. & 40 p.c.					
Composed wholly of wool, worsted, the hair of the alpaca, goat, or other animals, or of a mixture of them—									
Weighing 4 ounces or less per square yard	35 c. lb. & 40 p.c.	50 c. lb. & 35 p.c.	45 c. lb. & 31.5 p.c.	50 c. lb. & 35 p.c.					
Weighing over 4 ounces per square yard.	9 c. sq.yd. & 40 p.c. / 35 c. lb. & 40 p.c.	35 p.c.	31.5 p.c.	35 p.c.					
Flannels:									
Of whatever material (except cotton).........									14 c. sq.yd. / 25 p.c.
Unbleached—									
Valued 30 cents or less per square yard....						30 p.c.	25 p.c.		
Valued above 30 cents per square yard...						35 p.c.	30 p.c.	19 p.o.	
All colored, printed, or part of silk.					24 c. lb. & 30 p.c.				
Valued at not exceeding 40 cents per pound...	40 p.c.				24 c. lb. & 35 p.c.	35 p.c.	30 p.c.		
Valued at not exceeding 30 cents per pound...	10 c. lb. & 35 p.c.	20 c. lb. & 35 p.c.	18 c. lb. & 31.5 p.c.	20 c. lb. & 35 p.c.	50 p.c.				
Valued at above 30, and not exceeding 40 cents per pound	12 c. lb. & 35 p.c.	30 c. lb. & 35 p.c.	27 c. lb. & 31.5 p.c.	30 c. lb. & 35 p.c.					
Valued at above 40, and not exceeding 60 cents per pound	18 c. lb. & 35 p.c.	35 p.c.	36 c. lb. & 31.5 p.c.	35 p.c.					
Valued at above 60, and not exceeding 80 cents per pound	24 c. lb. & 35 p.c.	40 c. lb. & 35 p.c.	45 c. lb. & 31.5 p.c.	40 c. lb. & 35 p.c.					
Valued at above 80 cents per pound	35 c. lb. & 35 p.c. / 40 p.c.	50 c. lb. & 35 p.c. / 35 p.c.	31.5 p.c.	50 c. lb. & 35 p.c. / 35 p.c.					
Hats:									
Felt or hat bodies.............					24 c. lb. & 35 p.c.	25 p.c.	20 p.c.	15 p.c.	18 c. each / 30 p.c.
Hats............						30 p.c.	20 p.c.	15 p.c.	
Valued at not exceeding 40 cents per pound.....	10 c. lb. & 35 p.c.	20 c. lb. & 35 p.c.	18 c. lb. & 31.5 p.c.	20 c. lb. & 35 p.c.					20 p.c. / 20 p.c.
Valued at not exceeding 30 cents per pound.	35 p.c.	35 p.c.	35 p.c.	35 p.c.					
Valued at above 30, and not exceeding 40 cents per pound	12 c. lb. & 35 p.c.	30 c. lb. & 35 p.c.	27 c. lb. & 31.5 p.c.	30 c. lb. & 35 p.c.					
Valued at above 40, and not exceeding 60 cents per pound	18 c. lb. & 35 p.c.	35 p.c.	31.5 p.c.	35 p.c.					
Valued at above 60, and not exceeding 80 cents per pound	24 c. lb. & 35 p.c.	40 c. lb. & 35 p.c.	30 c. lb. & 31.5 p.c.	40 c. lb. & 35 p.c.					
Valued at above 80 cents per pound......	35 c. lb. & 35 p.c. / 40 p.c.	50 c. lb. & 35 p.c. / 35 p.c.	45 c. lb. & 31.5 p.c. / 31.5 p.c.	50 c. lb. & 35 p.c. / 35 p.c.					

No. 13.—STATEMENT SHOWING THE RATES OF DUTY UPON WOOL AND MANUFACTURES OF WOOL, FROM 1789 TO 1883, INCLUSIVE—Continued.

Acts of—

Wool, and manufactures of.	Aug. 30, 1842.	July 30, 1846.	Mar. 3, 1857.	Mar. 2, 1861.	July 14, 1862.	June 30, 1864.	Mar. 2, 1867.	June 6, 1872.	Mar. 3, 1875.	Mar. 3, 1883.
Went into effect—	Aug. 30, 1842.	Dec. 1, 1846.	July 1, 1857.	Apr. 2, 1861.	Aug. 2, 1862.	July 1, 1864.	Mar. 2, 1867.	Aug. 1, 1872.	Mar. 3, 1875.	July 1, 1883.
Manufactures—Continued.										
Knit goods:										
Caps, gloves, leggins, mits, socks, stockings, wove-shirts and drawers, and all similar articles made on frames	30 p. c.	30 p. c.	24 p. c.	30 p. c.	35 p. c.	20 c. lb. & 30 p. c.	20 c. lb. & 35 p. c.	18 c. lb. & 31.5 p. c.	20 c. lb. & 35 p. c.	10 c. lb. & 35 p. c.
Shirts, drawers, and hosiery										
Valued at not exceeding 40 cents per pound							30 c. lb. & 35 p. c.	27 c. lb. & 31.5 p. c.	30 c. lb. & 35 p. c.	
Valued at not exceeding 30 cents per pound										12 c. lb. & 35 p. c.
Valued at above 30 and not exceeding 40 cents per pound										16 c. lb. & 35 p. c.
Valued at above 40 and not exceeding 60 cents per pound							40 c. lb. & 35 p. c.	36 c. lb. & 31.5 p. c.	40 c. lb. & 35 p. c.	24 c. lb. & 35 p. c.
Valued at above 60 and not exceeding 80 cents per pound							35 c. lb. & 35 p. c.	31.5 c. lb. & 31.5 p. c.	35 c. lb. & 35 p. c.	35 c. lb. & 35 p. c.
Valued at above 80 cents per pound							50 c. lb. & 35 p. c.	45 c. lb. & 31.5 p. c.	50 c. lb. & 35 p. c.	35 c. lb. & 40 p. c.
Laces, fringes, tassels, and trimmings commonly used by upholsterers and coach-makers	35 p. c.									
Lastings, mohair cloth cut in strips or patterns of the size and shape for shoes, boots, bootees, or buttons exclusively. (From and after 1867, buttons exclusively.)		5 p. o.	4 p. c.	Free	10 p. c.	10 p. c.	10 p. c.	9 p. c.	10 p. c.	10 p. c.
Rags (1842), shoddy, mungo, waste, and flocks	½ c. lb.	5 p. c.	4 p. c.	10 p. o.	10 p. c.	3 c. lb.	12 c. lb.	10.8 c. lb.	12 c. lb.	10 c. lb.
Shawls:										
Wool or in part of wool					18 c. lb. & 30 p. c.	24 c. lb. & 40 p. c.	50 c. lb. & 35 p. c.			
Valued at over $1 per square yard, or weighing less than 12 ounces per square yard				12 c. lb. & 25 p. c.	18 c. lb. & 35 p. a.					

Item										
Valued at over $2 per square yard	35 c. lb. & 35 p. c.									
Valued at not exceeding 80 cents per pound										
Valued at above 80 cents per pound	35 c. lb. & 40 p. c.									
Composed wholly or in part of worsted, the hair of the alpaca, goat, or other animals	40 c. lb. & 35 p. c.				24 c. lb. & 45 p. c.		16 c. lb. & 20 p. c.			
Webbings, gorings, suspenders, braces, beltings, bindings, braids, galloons, fringes, gimps, cords, cords and tassels, dress trimmings, head nets, buttons or barrel buttons, or buttons of other forms for tassels or ornaments, wrought by hand or braided by machinery, made of wool, worsted, the hair of the alpaca, goat, or other animals, or of which wool, worsted, the hair of the alpaca, goat, or other animals is a component material										
Yarns, woolen and worsted:										
Woolen and worsted	30 c. lb. & 50 p. c.	50 c. lb. & 50 p. c.	45 c. lb. & 45 p. c.	50 c. lb. & 50 p. c.		35 p. c.	30 p. c.	10 p. c.	25 p. c.	30 p. c.
Value less than 50 cents per pound, not exceeding No. 14					16 c. lb. & 25 p. c.	30 p. c.	25 p. c.			
Value less than 50 cents per pound, exceeding No. 14						35 p. c. / 12 c. lb. & 20 p. c.	30 p. c. / 12 c. lb. & 15 p. c.			
Valued over 50 cents and not over $1 per pound					20 c. lb. & 25 p. c. / 24 c. lb. & 30 p. c.					
Valued over $1 per pound	10 c. lb. & 35 p. c.	20 c. lb. & 35 p. c.	18 c. lb. & 31.5 p. c.	20 c. lb. & 35 p. c.						
Valued at not exceeding 40 cents per pound	12 c. lb. & 35 p. c.									
Valued at not exceeding 30 cents per pound	18 c. lb. & 35 p. c.	30 c. lb. & 35 p. c.	27 c. lb. & 31.5 p. c.	30 c. lb. & 35 p. c.						
Valued at above 30 and not exceeding 40 cents per pound	24 c. lb. & 35 p. c.	35 c. lb. & 35 p. c.	36 c. lb. & 31.5 p. c.	35 c. lb. & 35 p. c.						
Valued at above 40 and not exceeding 60 cents per pound	35 c. lb. & 35 p. c.	40 c. lb. & 35 p. c.	45 c. lb. & 31.5 p. c.	40 c. lb. & 35 p. c.						
Valued at above 60 and not exceeding 80 cents per pound	36 c. lb. & 40 p. c.	50 c. lb. & 35 p. c.		50 c. lb. & 35 p. c.						
Valued at above 80 cents per pound										
Manufactures of every description, not specially enumerated or provided for, made wholly or in part of...	30 c. lb. & 60 p. c.					35 p. c.	30 p. c.	19 p. c.	25 p. c.	20 p. c.
(Goat's hair or mohair)										
Camlets, coatings, and all other manufactures of...						35 p. c.	30 p. c.	19 p. c.	25 p. c.	20 p. c.

No. 13.—Statement showing the Rates of Duty upon Wool and Manufactures of Wool from 1789 to 1883, inclusive.—Continued.

Wool and manufactures of.	Aug. 30, 1842.	July 30, 1846.	Mar. 3, 1857.	Mar. 2, 1861.	July 14, 1862.	June 30, 1864.	Mar. 2, 1867.	June 6, 1872.	Mar. 3, 1875.	Mar. 3, 1883.
Acts of—										
Went into effect—	Aug. 30, 1842.	Dec. 1, 1846.	July 1, 1856.	Apr. 2, 1861.	Aug. 2, 1862.	July 1, 1864.	Mar. 2, 1867.	Aug. 1, 1872.	Mar. 3, 1875.	July 1, 1883.
Manufactures—Continued.										
Wool—										
Manufactures of wool, or of which wool shall be the component material of chief value, not otherwise provided for	40 p. c	30 p. o	24 p. o	12 c. lb. & 25 p. o	18 c. lb. & 30 p. o	24 c. lb. & 40 p. c	50 c. lb. & 35 p. c	45 c. lb. & 31.5 p. c	50 c. lb. & 35 p. c	
Valued at $1 per square yard, or weighing less than 12 ounces per square yard					18 c. lb. & 35 p. c					
Valued over $2 per square yard						24 c. lb. & 45 p. c				
Valued at not exceeding 80 cents per pound										35 c. lb. & 35 p. c.
Valued at above 80 cents per pound										35 c. lb. & 40 p. c.
Listings		20 p. o	15 p. o	20 p. c	30 p. o					
Worsted a (except such as are composed in part of wool)—										
Manufactures of, not otherwise provided for	30 p. o	25 p. c	19 p. o	30 p. o	35 p. c	50 p. o				
Valued at not exceeding 40 cents per pound							20 c. lb. & 35 p. o	18 c. lb. & 31.5 p. d	20 c. lb. & 35 p. c	
Valued at not exceeding 30 cents per pound										10 c. lb. & 35 p. c.
Valued at above 30 and not exceeding 40 cents per pound										12 c. lb. & 35 p. c.
Valued at above 40 and not exceeding 60 cents per pound							30 c. lb. & 35 p. c	27 c. lb. & 31.5 p. c	30 c. lb. & 35 p. c	18 c. lb. & 35 p. c.
Valued at above 60 and not exceeding 80 cents per pound							40 c. lb. & 35 p. c	36 c. lb. & 31.5 p. c	35 c. lb. & 35 p. c	24 c. lb. & 35 p. c.
Valued at above 80 cents per pound							50 c. lb. & 35 p. o	45 c. lb. & 31.5 p. c	50 c. lb. & 35 p. c	35 c. lb. & 35 p. c. / 35 c. lb. & 40 p. c.

Additional duty on goods, wares, and merchandise (except new cotton and raw silk reeled from the cocoon, 1865) of the growth or produce of countries beyond the Cape of Good Hope, when imported from places this side of Cape of Good Hope, in addition to the duties imposed on any such articles, when imported directly from the place or places of their growth or production b ...... | 10 p. o .... | 10 p. o .... | 10 p. o .... | 10 p. o .... | 10 p. o .... | 10 p. o .... | 10 p. o .... | (*)

a Additional duty by acts of April 29 and June 27, 1864, 10 por cent.
b Act May 6, 1882, to take effect January 1, 1883, repealed discriminating duties.
Reciprocity treaty, act of June 5, 1854, approved August 5, 1854. Treaty with Great Britain and the provincial parliaments of Canada, New Brunswick, Nova Scotia, and Prince Edward's Island, admits free of duty raw wool from the said provinces. (Expiration of treaty, March 17, 1866.)
Joint resolution of April 29, 1864.— *Resolved* * * * that until the end of 60 days from the passage of this resolution 50 per cent. of the rates of duties and imposts now imposed by law on all goods, wares, merchandise, and articles imported shall be added to the present duties and imposts now charged on the importation of such articles.
Joint resolution of June 27, 1864.— *Be it resolved* * * * that the joint resolution increasing the duties on imports, approved April 29 1864, be, and is hereby, continued in force until the first day of July next.

No. 13a.—SYNOPSES OF DECISIONS IN CUSTOMS CASES BY THE TREASURY DEPART-
MENT RELATING TO WOOL AND THE MANUFACTURES OF WOOL, UNDER THE TARIFF
ACT OF MARCH 3, 1883, WHICH WENT INTO EFFECT JULY 1, 1883.

[Department No. 15, January 26, 1884.]

(1) Matelassé cloth, composed of silk and wool, of which silk is chief value. Held
to be dutiable at 50 per cent. ad valorem, under paragraph 383 and section 2499 of
the Revised Statutes. (Letter to collector of customs at Philadelphia, Pa.)

(2) Wool noils held to be dutiable as washed wools, and not as scoured wools, and
to be assigned to the class of wools from which the noils are taken. (Letter to collector of customs at Boston, Mass.)

(3) Merino trousers, shirts, hose, &c., composed mainly of cotton, having an inte-
gral part of wool, claimed to be dutiable under paragraph 323, for stockings, &c.,
composed wholly of cotton. Held to be dutiable under paragraph 362, for goods
made in part of wool. (Letter to collector of customs at Chicago, Ill.)

[Department No. 38, March 1, 1884.]

(4) Zephyr yarns, packed in paper wrappers having labels thereon. Held to be
dutiable at a valuation which included that of the labels and paper wrappers. (Letter to collector of customs at Philadelphia, Pa.)

[Department No. 46, March 15, 1884.]

(5) Woolen bands which are intended for use as badges of mourning on men's hats
are not commercially known as "trimmings" for hats, nor are they the materials
which are used in the manufacture of hats. They are not, therefore, entitled to ad-
mission at the rate of 30 per cent. ad valorem, as "trimmings for hats." (Letter to
collector of customs at Philadelphia.)

[Department No. 59, April 19, 1884.]

(6) Hats made of Tweed cloth, being composed in part of wool, held not to be dutiable as hats of wool, but to be charged with 30 per cent., under paragraph 400, in accordance with the Department's ruling of September 1, 1860. (Letter to collector of
customs at Boston.)

[Department No. 63, April 26, 1884.]

(7) Worsted laces, held not to be dutiable as dress trimmings under paragraph
368, but to be dutiable under the provision of paragraph 362, for all manufactures of
every description, composed wholly or in part of worsted. (Letter to collector of customs at New York.)

[Department No. 72, May 10, 1884.]

(8) The concluding proviso of paragraph 365, relating to women's and children's
dress-goods, &c., that all such goods weighing over 4 ounces to the square yard shall
pay a duty of 35 cents per pound and 40 per cent. ad valorem, held to apply only to
goods composed wholly of wool, worsted, &c., or of a mixture of them, and not to
those described in the first part of said paragraph, which are composed in part of
wool, worsted, &c. (Letter to collector of customs at New York.)

[Department No. 90, June 21, 1884.]

(9) So-called waste, which is obtained from the thread waste of scoured wool by
what is known as the garneting process, held to be dutiable as wool and not as wool
waste. (Letter to collector of customs at New York.)

[Department No. 136, August 9, 1884.]

(10) Decision No. 6428, of June 28, 1884, does not apply to all hosiery and gloves, but only to such gloves as are composed of a cotton exterior and wool lining, the wool portion being quite an important feature. Knit goods and all goods made on knitting-frames are to be classified under paragraph 363, T. I., new. (Letter to collector of customs at Philadelphia.)

(11) The dutiable value of Italian cloths includes the value of the tillots. (Letter to collector of customs at New York.)

[Department No. 143, August 23, 1884.]

(12) Woolen carpets woven in same manner as Brussels carpets and of the same materials, with the exception that a metal thread is introduced at irregular intervals, are dutiable under paragraph 371 as Brussels carpets. (Letter to surveyor of customs at Cincinnati, Ohio.)

[Department No. 146, August 30, 1884.]

(13) The value of "rollings," which is a process of making up dress-goods in merchantable condition, is part of the dutiable value of the goods. (Letter to collector of customs at Boston.)

[Department No. 171, November 22, 1884.]

(14) Woolen or worsted yarns, cut in lengths for the purpose of knitting into mats, are dutiable under the provision for yarns in schedule K. The fact that they are cut in unusual lengths does not remove them from the category of yarns. (Letter to collector of customs at Philadelphia.)

(15) Silk-and-worsted cloaks, matelassé cloth, which is a fabric composed of silk, wool or worsted, and cotton, are dutiable under the provision for woolen cloaks, at the rate of 45 cents per pound and 40 per cent. ad valorem. (Letter to collector of customs at New York.)

[Department No. 5, January 3, 1885.]

(16) Mohair noils, fit only for use as carpet-stock, are to be classified under class 3 of schedule K; when fit for any other purpose they are to be placed in class 2. (Letter to collector of customs at Boston.)

[Department No. 10, January 17, 1885.]

(17) So-called "Scotch bonnets," consisting of woolen caps, which are partly woven and partly knitted, are dutiable at compound rate, under schedule K and not under schedule N, T. I, new, 400. (Letter to collector of customs at New York.)

[Department No. 25, February 14, 1885.]

(18) Silk and worsted shawls of which silk is a component of chief value, are dutiable as manufactures of silk under schedule L, when that rate of duty is higher than that imposed by the wool tariff, section 2499, prescribing that when two rates of duty are applicable the highest rate shall be exacted.

[Department No. 28, February 24, 1885.]

(19) So-called "turbans," made wholly or in part of wool, are dutiable, under schedule K, paragraph 363, and not under paragraph 400, at a duty of 30 per cent. ad valorem. (Letter to collector of customs at New York.)

[Department No. 51, April 18, 1885.]

(20) Cloaks made of worsted cloth, lined with fur, are dutiable under paragraph 367, schedule K, and are not dutiable as fur cloaks, as claimed by the appellant. (Letter to collector of customs at New York.)

134 WOOL AND MANUFACTURES OF WOOL.

[Department No. 54, April 25, 1885.]

(21) Textile fabrics, composed of goat's-hair, cotton, and silk, silk being the component of chief value, are dutiable, under schedule K, as manufactures composed wholly or in part of the hair of the alpaca, goat, or other animals, where the duties imposed by that schedule are higher than those imposed by schedule L, relating to manufactures of which silk is the component of chief value. (Letter to collector of customs at New York.)

[Department No. 58, May 2, 1885.]

(22) So called "wool-waste," composed of about 50 per cent. of broken tops, laps, and slubbings, the balance being fine rovings with a very small percentage of spinners' waste, the noil having all been combed out, is dutiable according to the character of the wool from which it is taken. This case embraces stock from Australian wool, dutiable at 10 cents per pound, when scoured, is liable to a duty of three times that rate. (Letter to collector of customs at Boston.)

[Department No. 71, May 23, 1885.]

(23) The proviso in schedule K, T. I., new, 365, does not cover "women's and children's dress-goods, coat-linings, Italian cloths, and goods of like description, composed in part of wool, worsted, the hair of the alpaca, goat, or other animals," specified in the first portion of the paragraph, and decision 6429 is revoked. (Letter to collector of customs at Philadelphia.)

[Department No. 79, June 6, 1885.]

(24) Certain wool and worsted panels or screens, with paintings thereon for the purpose of ornamentation, are not paintings within the meaning of the law, but are dutiable at the rate of 35 cents per pound and 40 per cent. ad valorem, being valued at over 80 cents per pound, under schedule K, T. I., new, 362. (Letter to collector of customs at New York.)

(25) Certain umbrella-cloths, composed of a mixture of worsted and cotton, with stripes or borders woven at the sides, which render them fit exclusively for the manufacture of umbrellas, are dutiable according to value per pound, under schedule K, T. I., new, 363. (Letter to collector of customs at Boston.)

[Department No. 113, July 25, 1885.]

(26) Certain so-called "gray China wool," which was returned by the appraiser as "China cashmere goat hair," and is known commercially by the latter name, is dutiable at the rate prescribed by T. I., new, 358, for "all hair of the alpaca, goat, and other like animals." Decision 5743 and any other rulings to the contrary are revoked. (Letter to collector of customs at Philadelphia.)

(27) Certain mohair or goat's hair noils are held to be dutiable under the provision of T. I., new, 358, for "all hair of the alpaca, goat, and other like animals." (Letter to collector of customs at Philadelphia.)

(28) Certain "Cheviot britch" wool, erroneously invoiced and entered as carpet britch, the product of sheep of mixed English blood, is dutiable under the provision of T. I., new, 358, for ' wools of the second class." (Letter to collector of customs at Philadelphia.)

(29) Dress-goods composed of silk and wool, which are provided for under T. I., new, 365, for "women's and children's dress-goods, * * * composed in part of wool, worsted, the hair of the alpaca, goat, or other animals," are dutiable thereunder, notwithstanding the fact that silk may be the component of chief value. (Letter to collector of customs at New York.)

[Department No. 124, August 7, 1885.]

(30) In fixing the value for classification of imported carpet-wools, the cost of bags in the foreign country should not be added. (Letter to collector of customs at Philadelphia, Pa.)

[Department No. 129, August 29, 1885.]

(31) Certain so-called "wool waste," which was found to consist of China cashmere goat's hair, from which the long hairs had been combed and which was imported apparently in a carded condition, is dutiable under paragraph 358, T. I., new, schedule K, which provides for "all hair of the alpaca, goat, and other like animals." (Letter to collector of customs at New York.)

(32) Certain black cattle-hair yarn is dutiable at the rate of 10 cents per pound and 35 per cent. ad valorem, under the provisions in schedule K, T. I., 363. (Letter to collector of customs at New York.)

(33) Certain so-called moquette, a fabric of worsted and cotton, made of the same materials, and by the same process as patent velvet carpets, but which is used.for covering seats in railway cars, barbers' chairs, &c., is dutiable at the rate of 35 cents per pound and 40 per cent. ad valorem, under the provision in schedule K, T. I., new, 363, for "all manufactures of every description, composed wholly or in part of worsted." (Letter to collector of customs at Philadelphia.)

[Department No. 164, October 31, 1885.]

(34) Certain wool and rubber water-proof cloaks are held to be dutiable at the rate of 40 per cent. ad valorem and 45 cents per pound, under the special provision in schedule K, T. I., new, 367, for * * * "cloaks composed wholly or in part of wool." (Letter to collector of customs at Philadelphia.)

(35) Certain wool or hair taken from Angora goat skins, imported from the Cape of Good Hope, which was found to consist of a fine quality of combing-wool, was held to be dutiable at the rate of 10 cents per pound, being valued at 30 cents per pound or less, under the provisions of schedule K, T. I., new, 358; for class two, combing wools, including "hair of the alpaca, goat, and other like animals." This wool or hair, being imported on Angora goat skins, is not entitled to exemption from duty, inasmuch as under T. I., new, 719, Angora goat skins are only entitled to free entry when imported without the wool. (Letter to collector of customs at Philadelphia.)

[Department No. 167, November 21, 1885.]

(36) The wool or hair on Angora goat skins from the Cape of Good Hope, when of superior character and fineness, cannot be exempted from the payment of duty. (Letter to Keen & Coates, Philadelphia.)

(37) Wool-tweed caps are not provided for under the clause in Schedule N. T. I., new, 400, for "bonnets, hats, and hoods, for men, women, and children," &c., but are dutiable at the rate of 40 cents per pound and 5 per cent. ad valorem, under the provisions in schedule K, T. I., new, 366, for "wearing apparel of every description * * * composed wholly or in part of wool, worsted," &c. (Letter to collector of customs at Boston.)

(38) Wool tops, the product of clothing-wool, which are produced by scouring the wool and then passing it in the usual manner through the combing or carding machine, are not comprised under the clause for manufactures of worsted, &c., but are dutiable at twice the rate prescribed for scoured wools of the clothing class, which, in this instance, is 60 cents per pound. (Letter to collector of customs at Boston.)

[Department No. 170, November 28, 1885.]

(39) Shoes or slippers made of woolen or worsted felt are not outside garments within the meaning of that term as used in schedule K, T. I., new, 267, but come with-

in the purview of the provision in the same schedule, T. I., new, 366, for "wearing-apparel of every description * * * composed wholly or in part of wool, worsted," &c., and are dutiable at the rate of 40 cents per pound and 35 per cent. ad valorem. (Letter to collector of customs, Toledo, Ohio.)

[Department No. 179, December 19, 1885.]

(40) Imported wools which, under the statue, pay duty according to their value per pound, are subject to the imposition of the additional (penal) duty prescribed by section 2900 of the Revised Statutes, provided the appraiser, on appraisement, returns their value at a sum greater by 10 per cent. than the invoice and entered value. (Letter to collector of customs at New York.)

[Department No. 3, January 2, 1886.]

(41) Fabrics composed in part of wool, hair of the alpaca, goat, or other animal, which are not covered by the special provision in schedule K for women's and children's dress-goods, coat-linings, Italian cloths, and goods of like description, are subject to the duty prescribed for such manufactures in paragraphs 362 and 363 of said schedule, and not under paragraph 365, as erroneously stated in Department's decision of April 24, 1885, synopsis, 6875. (Letter to collector of customs at Philadelphia, January 2, 1886.)

[Department No. 4, January 9, 1886.]

(42) Certain carriage-robes or traveling-rugs, manufactured partly of wool and partly of hair, are not known commercially by the term "blankets," and are, therefore, not liable to the duties imposed on blankets by schedule K, T. I., new, 363, but, being otherwise unenumerated, are dutiable, according to the value per pound, at the rates prescribed in the siad schedule T. I., new, 362, for "all manufactures * * * made wholly or in part of wool." Letter to collector of customs at New York, January 4, 1886.)

[Department No. 5, January 16, 1886.]

(43) Certain skin jackets, lined throughout with wool flannel, are held to be dutiable at the rate of 40 cents per pound and 35 per cent. ad valorem, under the provision in schedule K, T. I., new, 366, for "wearing apparel of every description * * * composed wholly or in part of wool. (Letter to collector of customs at Baltimore, January 15, 1886.)

[Department No. 11, January 30, 1886.]

(44) Certain so-called "flannels," which, upon examination, were found to consist of a fabric known as "muslin delaines," manufactured of worsted, and to be women's and children's dress goods, are dutiable under the provisions therefor in schedule K, T. I., new, 365. (Letter to collector of customs at New York, January 27, 1886.)

[Department No. 26, February 27, 1886.]

(45) Certain Mexican wool, which, although of very poor quality, was found to consist of a mixture of 24 per cent. of merino or first-class wool, the remaining portion being carpet or third-class wool, was held to be dutiable, in the condition in which imported, as wool of the first class, the statute (schedule K, T. I., new, 353) requiring all merino wools or other wools of merino blood, immediate or remote, to be classified as such. Where, however, the different classes of wools can be separated for the purpose of classification, the merino portion may be classified as such, and the third class, or carpet wools, subjected to the rate of duty prescribed by law therefor. (Letter to collector of customs at Corpus Christi, February 27, 1886.)

[Department No. 30, March 18, 1886.]

(46) Worsted "coatings," so called, which, upon examination, are found to be composed of wool, worsted, and cotton, cannot be classified under paragraph 363, in schedule K, act of March 3, 1883, inasmuch as goods composed in part of wool are expressly excluded from such classification. (Letter to collector of customs at New York, March 10, 1886.)

[Department No. 40, April 3, 1886.]

(47) Certain Donskoi wools, which for more than twenty years have been classified as washed wools, upon a thorough investigation are held to be entitled to that classification. (Letter to collector of customs at New York, March 29, 1886.)

[Department No. 46, April 24, 1886.]

(48) Noils (wool or mohair) should be classified the same as the wools from which they are made; so that, if the noils come from class one wool, they should be classed as clothing wool, either washed or scoured, as the case may be. If the noils are made from class two wool, or hair of the alpaca, goat, or other like animals, they should be classed as combing wools, and, if scoured, pay three times the rate to which the wool or hair is dutiable in the unwashed condition. If these class-two wools are simply washed and not scoured, they pay but a single rate of duty. Decision synopsis 1404 will be considered as modified to accord with these views. (Letter to collector of customs at Boston, April 20, 1886.

(49) Weardale carpets, so called, which are not carpets woven whole for rooms, but simply ingrain carpets, intended to be placed as crumb-cloths over carpets for their preservation, are dutiable at the rate of 8 cents per square yard and 30 per cent. ad valorem, as two-ply ingrain carpets, under the provision therefor in schedule K, T. I., new, 375. (Letter to surveyor of customs at Cincinnati, April 21, 1886.)

[Department No. 61, May 22, 1886.]

(50) The cost of boards on which woolen dress goods are rolled should be excluded in estimating the dutiable value of such goods, inasmuch as such cost is incurred after the goods are finished and in putting them up for shipment. (Letter to the collector of customs at Baltimore, May 19, 1886.)

(51) The cost of skeining worsted yarns, imported in skeins weighing less than one ounce each, is a part of the finishing process of the goods, and cannot be deducted in ascertaining the dutiable value of such merchandise. (Letter to collector of customs at Boston, May 21, 1886.)

[Department No. 66, June 5, 1886.]

(52) Certain wax figures dressed in wool clothing, which latter is firmly fastened to the figures so that it cannot be removed without taking the whole to pieces, the legs and arms also being stuffed with wool and cotton, and the feet covered with wool socks and shoes, are held to be dutiable at the rate of 35 cents per pound and 35 per cent. ad valorem, under the provision in schedule K, T. I., new, 362, for "all manufactures of wool of every description, made wholly or in part of wool, not specially enumerated or provided for in this act." (Letter to collector of customs at Philadelphia, June 5, 1886.)

[Department No. 74, June 19, 1886.]

(53) Snow-white cape wool is admitted on all hands to be scoured wool of the first class, and is, therefore, dutiable at the rate of 30 cents per pound. (Letter to collector of customs at Boston, June 19, 1886.)

138 WOOL AND MANUFACTURES OF WOOL.

[Department No. 88, July 3, 1886.]

(54) Goat's hair, imported as such, is liable to a duty of 10 cents per pound, without regard to quality or use for which it may be intended, under the provision in schedule K, for "all hair of the * * * goat." (Letter to Henry Schmidt, Philadelphia, July 2, 1886.)

[Department No. 93, July 17, 1886.]

(55) Wool-lace dress goods, 41 inches wide, used for women's and children's dresses are dutiable, under the provision in T. I., new, 365, for women's and children's dress-goods. (Letter to collector of customs at New York, July 8, 1886.)

(56) Chinese shoes, composed of cotton, leather, pith, &c., having soles about one inch in thickness, which are composed largely of hair are dutiable under the provision in T. I., new, 366, for wearing apparel of every description, composed wholly or in part of wool, worsted, the hair of the alapaca, goat, or other animals. (Letter to collector of customs at Chicago, July 8, 1886.

(57) So-called " fancy zephyrs," or cloth, the body of which is cotton, and which is ornamented by being partly covered with tufts of worsted, the worsted adding largely to the value of the goods, and which is manufactured for women's and children's dress-goods, is dutiable under the provision for such goods in T. I., new, 365. (Letter to collector of customs at Boston, July 14, 1886.)

[Department No. 133, September 25, 1886.]

(58) Certain Saxolaine hosiery, found to consist of stockings manufactured partly of cotton, but with merino soles, which gives them the distinctive name of "Saxo laine," that word being printed on the foot, and the label being marked " medicated merino," are held to be dutiable at the rate of 35 cents per pound and 40 per cent. ad valorem, under the provision in schedule K, T. I., new, 363, for "goods * * * composed wholly or in part of worsted, the hair of the alapaca goat, or other animals, * * * not specially enumerated or provided for." Such merchandise is excluded from classification as cotton hosiery, inasmuch as the provisions for cotton hosiery, T. I., new, 322 and 323, relate to stockings, &c., "composed wholly of cotton. (Letter to collector of customs at New York, September 20, 1886.)

[Department No. 159, November 20, 1886.]

(59) Certain so-called wool "sweepings" and "tags," which consisted of clothing-wool which had been picked up on ranges after the winter was over, and from sheep which perished during snow-storms, the same being in a very rotten and dirty condition, was held to be dutiable at the rate of 10 cents per pound, either as wool-waste, under the provisions of schedule K, T. I., new, 361, or as first-class wool, valued at less than 30 cents per pound. (Letter to collector of customs at Portland, Oreg., November 11, 1886.)

(60) Wools of different classes, though contained in the same bale or package, may be subjected to the rates of duty respectively prescribed for each class, the Department holding that the provisions of section 2912 of the Revised Statutes relate to different qualities and values of the same class of wool, and not to different classes when contained in the same package. (Letter to collector of customs at New York, November 12, 1886.)

[Department No. 164, December 4, 1886.]

(61) Certain Broché carpets, which are found to consist, in fact, of Brussels carpets, in which a portion of the threads have been cut to bring out certain figures in imitation of the figures in Wilton carpets, are held to be dutiable at the rate of 30 cents per square yard and 30 per cent. ad valorem, under the provision in schedule K, T. I., new, 371, for " Brussels carpets." (Letter to collector of customs at Chicago, December 3, 1886.)

[Department No. 168, December 11, 1886.]

(62) Certain so-called hair-felt, which, upon an analysis of samples, was found to be composed of wool and hair, felted, was held to be dutiable at the rate of 35 cents per pound and 35 per cent. ad valorem, under the provision in schedule K, T. I., new, 362, for "all manufactures of wool of every description, made wholly or in part of wool." (Letter to collector of customs at Chicago, December 9, 1886.)

(63) Ring-waste of wool, so called, which consists of refuse from the spindles that cannot be utilized without being broken by machinery, whereby the fiber of the wool and the use of the article for other purposes than that of waste are destroyed, is held to be dutiable at the rate of 10 cents per pound, under the provision in schedule K, T. I., new, 361, for "woolen * * * waste." (Letter to collector of customs, Burlington, Vt., December 10, 1886.)

[Department No. 8, January 22, 1887.]

(64) Saddle-bags manufactured in part of Brussels carpet are held to be dutiable at the rate of 35 per cent. ad valorem, under the provision in schedule N, T. I., new, 415, for "saddlery." (Letter to collector of customs at Portland, Oreg., January 18, 1887.)

[Department No. 12, February 5, 1887.]

(65) Certain so-called "croises," which consist of fabrics composed wholly of worsted 40 inches wide and weighing about 3 ounces to the yard, and which are commercially known as women's and children's dress goods, are held to be dutiable according to the value per square yard, under the provision in schedule K, T. I., new, 365. (Letter to collector of customs at San Francisco, February 1, 1887.)

[Department No. 15, February 12, 1887.]

(66) Certain so-called "gloria" cloth, a fabric composed of silk in the warp and worsted in the weft, and intended to be used in the manufacture of women's and children's dresses, is held to be dutiable according to value per square yard, under the provision in schedule K, T. I., 365. (Letter to collector of customs at New York, February 11, 1887.)

[Department No. 23, February 26, 1887.]

(67) Imported wool noils should be classified either as washed or scoured, in accordance with the report of the United States appraiser as to the character of each particular importation—that is to say, a careful examination should be made of each importation, and if, thereupon, the noils are found to consist of what are commercially known as scoured wools, they should be classified as scoured; but if they consist of wools which are ordinarily and commercially considered as washed, they should be subjected to duty as washed. (Letter to collector of customs at Boston, February 25, 1887.)

[Department No. 40, March 26, 1887.]

(68) Bath robes and slippers, composed of cotton and Turkish toweling, elaborately and expensively embroidered with worsted, are dutiable as wearing apparel in part of worsted, under T. I., 366. (Letter to collector of customs at Boston, March 22, 1887.)

(69) So-called "horse-clothing," consisting of hoods and bandages for the legs, composed of wool, is dutiable, under T. I., 362, as "manufactures * * * made wholly or in part of wool," not being otherwise specially enumerated or provided for. (Letter to collector of customs at Chicago, March 24, 1887.)

[Department No. 43, April 2, 1887.]

(70) Certain fabrics called "worsted veilings", which upon investigation were found to be manufactured exclusively of wool and known and used almost exclusively

for women's and children's dress goods, were held to be dutiable according to value per square yard, under the provision in schedule K, T. I., 365, for "women's and children's dress-goods, * * * and goods of like description, composed in part of wool, worsted, the hair of the alpaca, goat, or other animals." (Letter to collector of customs at New York, March 28, 1887.)

[Department No. 52, April 30, 1887.]

(71) Where different classes of wools are imported in the same package, no necessity exists for an actual assorting of such classes unless a correct classification of the different classes cannot be determined except by a separation and assortment of each class.

(72) Certain woolen fabric known as "saddle-felt," which may be used to a certain extent in the manufacture of saddles, is not entitled to classification under the provision in schedule N, T. I., 415, for "saddlery," but is dutiable (inasmuch as it is valued at over 80 cents per pound) at the rate of 35 cents per pound and 35 per cent. ad valorem, under the provision in schedule K, T. I., 362, for "all manufactures of wool of every description, made wholly or in part of wool." (Letter to collector of customs at Chicago, April 22, 1887.)

[Department No. 54, May 7, 1887.]

(73) Charges on invoices for shrinkage on wool tidies and coatings form an element of dutiable value of the goods, inasmuch as it is ascertained that shrinking is essential to the purpose of preparing the goods for use. (Letter to surveyor of customs at Louisville, Ky., May 2, 1887.)

[Department No. 67, June 4, 1887.]

(74) Webbings composed wholly or in part of wool, worsted, the hair of the alpaca, &c., although intended for use as saddle-girths, are held not to be covered by the term "saddlery," in schedule N, T. I., 45, but to be dutiable at the rates prescribed by schedule K, T. I., 368, for "webbing" composed of the materials mentioned. (Letter to collector of customs at Chicago, May 27, 1887.)

(75) Merino hose composed in part of wool, the wool having been sifted in during the process of knitting the threads, which are composed of cotton, are held to be dutiable under the provisions in schedule K, T. I., 362, for all manufactures made wholly or in part of wool, according to value per pound. (Letter to collector of customs at Chicago, June 2, 1887.)

(76) Certain fabrics, commonly known as "Novelty Scotch Flannels," composed of cotton warp and wool filling, which are generally known to the trade, both in this country and in Scotland, where manufactured, as flannels, are held to be dutiable at the rates specially prescribed for "flannels" composed wholly or in part of worsted, in schedule K, T. I., 363, and not as women's and children's dress-goods, under the further provision in the same schedule, T. I., 365. (Letter to collector of customs at Boston, June 3, 1887.)

(77) Following the decision of March 29, 1886 (synopsis 7438), it is held that Russian (Donskoi) wool of the third class, which has been subjected to no other or different process of cleaning than the wool covered by said decision, is not liable to the duty prescribed by the tariff act for scoured wool, but is dutiable as washed wool of the class mentioned. (Letter to collector of customs at New York, June 3, 1887.)

[Department No. 85, July 16, 1887.]

(78) Certain so-called " thread waste," which consists of a waste of worsted in the condition in which it is dropped from or is broken on the machine, and which, when broken up and put through the garneting machine, becomes practically wool, and, as such, is used in adulterating other wools in making cloths, dress-goods, &c., is held

WOOL AND MANUFACTURES OF WOOL.

to be dutiable at the rate of 10 cents per pound, under the provision in schedule K, T. I., 361, for "woolen rags, shoddy, mungo, *waste*, and flocks." (Letter to collector of customs at Philadelphia, July 13, 1887.)

[Department No. 95, August 20, 1887.]

(79) Certain so-called "dentelle" goods, composed of woolen lace, certain threads of which have been wrapped with silk, are dutiable under the provision in the first class of T. I., 365, for "women's and children's dress-goods," composed in part of wool, &c. (Letter to collector of customs at Philadelphia, August 16, 1887.)

[Department No. 100, September 3, 1887.]

(80) Certain so-called "sliped" wool, which is ascertained to consist of "cross-bred lamb's wool—that is, coming from sheep which are a cross between English and Merino blood—is held to be in a condition not advanced beyond washed wool, and, consequently, is liable to the duty imposed by law on wools of that class. (Letter to collector of customs at San Francisco, September 1, 1887.)

(81) Where wools are purchased in a foreign country by regular commission merchants at the order of merchants in the United States, which purchase was made by the commission merchants in the due and ordinary course of their business, the invoices therefor may be declared to by the said commission merchants, who, in the opinion of the Department, are, under such circumstances, the shippers of the wool, and as such entitled under the law to declare the invoices before the United States consular officers. (Letter to the Secretary of State, September 2, 1887.)

[Department No. 102, September 10, 1887.]

(82) Certain cork soles, which, upon inspection of samples, are found to consist of manufactures of cork and wool, wool being a leading and important feature thereof, were held to be dutiable at the rate of 35 cents per pound and 35 per cent. ad valorem under the provision in schedule K, T. I., 362, for "all manufactures of wool of every description, made wholly or in part of wool," &c. (Letter to collector of customs at New York, September 7, 1887.)

No. 14.—Statement showing the Number of Establishments, Capital Invested, Number of Hands Employed, Wages Paid, Cost of Materials Used, and Value of Products of the Manufacture of Worsted and Woolen Goods in each State and Territory of the United States for the years 1850, 1860, 1870, and 1880.

[From the official Reports of the United States Census.]

States.	Establishments.				Capital invested.			
	1850.	1860.	1870.	1880.	1850.	1860.	1870.	1880.
	No.	No.	No.	No.	Dollars.	Dollars.	Dollars.	Dollars.
Alabama	......	6	14	14	....	140, 000	22, 375	28, 900
Arkansas	......	......	13	25	....	....	32, 500	85, 550
California	......	1	5	9	....	100, 000	1, 785, 000	1, 676, 500
Connecticut	149	84	114	102	3, 773, 950	2, 491, 000	12, 901, 000	14, 221, 637
Delaware	8	4	11	5	148, 500	117, 000	384, 500	352, 559
Florida	......	......	1	......	....	....	500	....
Georgia	3	11	46	32	68, 000	242, 500	936, 585	180, 733
Illinois	16	21	109	67	154, 500	207, 600	2, 962, 443	1, 433, 353
Indiana	33	79	175	86	171, 545	264, 341	3, 821, 913	2, 318, 705
Iowa	1	12	85	37	10, 000	82, 500	1, 440, 484	555, 700
Kansas	......	......	9	5	....	....	96, 000	131, 925
Kentucky	25	37	125	98	249, 820	408, 500	700, 440	890, 750
Louisiana	......	1	2	......	....	75, 000	34, 000	....
Maine	36	26	108	97	467, 600	932, 400	4, 187, 745	4, 016, 828
Maryland	38	27	31	16	244, 000	318, 200	205, 245	344, 010
Massachusetts	110	136	220	271	9, 089, 342	11, 023, 953	23, 472, 900	38, 231, 375
Michigan	15	16	54	14	94, 000	103, 950	1, 011, 050	706, 189
Minnesota	......	......	10	14	....	....	246, 600	198, 500
Mississippi	......	4	11	8	....	75, 500	195, 250	331, 500
Missouri	1	11	156	102	20, 000	103, 750	716, 524	755, 550
New Hampshire	61	52	79	85	2, 437, 700	2, 621, 300	5, 316, 600	8, 374, 855
New Jersey	41	35	34	45	494, 274	583, 400	1, 369, 200	3, 795, 605
New Mexico	......	......	1	......	....	....	65, 000	....
New York	249	140	259	264	4, 459, 570	3, 115, 700	10, 199, 482	23, 583, 574
North Carolina	1	7	52	49	18, 000	223, 000	237, 800	203, 100
Ohio	130	115	235	146	870, 220	658, 750	3, 066, 069	1, 570, 340
Oregon	......	1	9	10	....	70, 000	389, 200	566, 800
Pennsylvania	380	270	488	654	3, 005, 064	4, 339, 310	17, 588, 913	35, 642, 016
Rhode Island	45	57	76	62	1, 013, 000	3, 188, 500	10, 467, 500	13, 022, 116
South Carolina	......	1	15	11	....	50, 000	25, 900	7, 900
Tennessee	4	1	148	106	10, 900	6, 000	373, 868	418, 664
Texas	1	2	20	1	8, 000	60, 000	97, 250	97, 500
Utah	......	......	15	11	....	....	223, 400	382, 000
Vermont	72	46	66	50	836, 300	1, 746, 300	2, 330, 900	2, 812, 161
Virginia	121	45	68	48	392, 640	463, 600	435, 375	436, 750
West Virginia	......	......	74	56	....	....	236, 100	298, 170
Wisconsin	9	15	65	52	31, 225	100, 600	1, 244, 280	1, 359, 964
Washington	......	......	......	1	....	....	....	40, 000
District of Columbia	1	......	......	......	700	....	....	....
Total	1, 559	1, 263	2, 993	2, 689	28, 118, 656	34, 093, 654	108, 910, 369	159, 091, 869

Note.—The statistics for 1870 do not include the manufacture of hats. This industry comprised, in 1880, 43 establishments, a capital of $3,615,830; employed 5,470 hands and paid $1,893,215 for wages; used materials valued at $4,785,774, and produced hats to the value of $8,516,569.

No. 14.—STATEMENT SHOWING THE NUMBER OF ESTABLISHMENTS, CAPITAL INVESTED, NUMBER OF HANDS EMPLOYED, WAGES PAID, COST OF MATERIALS USED, AND VALUE OF PRODUCTS OF THE MANUFACTURE OF WORSTED AND WOOLEN GOODS IN EACH STATE AND TERRITORY OF THE UNITED STATES FOR THE YEARS 1850, 1860, 1870, AND 1880.—Continued

[From the official Reports of the United States Census.]

States.	Hands employed.				Wages paid.			
	1850.	1860.	1870.	1880.	1850.	1860.	1870.	1880.
	No.	No.	No.	No.	Dollars.	Dollars.	Dollars.	Dollars.
Alabama		198	41	18		34,116	4,881	3,037
Arkansas			31	90			6,870	13,226
California		60	659	835		33,600	230,200	334,318
Connecticut	5,488	3,767	7,667	12,024	1,239,702	949,020	2,981,070	3,986,965
Delaware	140	114	399	261	31,251	27,564	115,137	108,504
Florida			1					
Georgia	78	383	563	142	19,615	63,348	122,138	25,070
Illinois	178	162	1,763	1,749	40,849	44,044	535,185	388,610
Indiana	246	533	2,469	2,025	57,035	150,276	726,113	487,381
Iowa	7	120	1,088	505	936	23,652	269,432	118,252
Kansas			91	124			30,682	25,825
Kentucky	318	437	683	823	55,267	103,284	159,373	166,189
Louisiana		60	29			6,720	8,900	
Maine	624	1,027	3,104	3,265	128,310	263,216	1,065,151	1,091,329
Maryland	362	381	327	389	72,746	86,712	82,019	60,491
Massachusetts	11,130	14,277	25,825	38,128	2,545,350	3,324,405	8,976,764	11,635,889
Michigan	129	126	667	1,309	27,284	30,672	202,813	168,564
Minnesota			146	241			45,592	48,927
Mississippi		235	116	218		22,620	28,800	53,100
Missouri	25	70	718	807	6,540	19,728	137,408	129,177
New Hampshire	2,127	2,588	4,911	7,352	463,427	670,142	1,733,164	2,237,736
New Jersey	898	835	1,375	5,142	174,643	203,136	432,642	1,392,515
New Mexico			20				2,000	
New York	6,674	4,220	9,063	24,286	1,361,727	992,975	2,891,926	7,225,256
North Carolina	30	253	249	185	4,500	60,036	39,101	23,195
Ohio	1,201	728	2,320	2,177	257,215	179,160	574,164	374,472
Oregon		30	179	216		16,200	112,213	86,088
Pennsylvania	5,726	6,088	16,632	42,261	1,084,674	1,410,324	5,736,962	12,338,157
Rhode Island	1,758	4,229	7,894	12,164	385,616	1,069,176	2,862,492	3,711,657
South Carolina		92	53	13		11,400	3,815	1,173
Tennessee	17	10	428	402	3,323	2,472	62,780	67,063
Texas	8	43	100	36	1,920	7,680	20,278	25,700
Utah			106	277			48,040	68,108
Vermont	1,393	2,073	1,895	2,467	301,095	214,572	649,628	645,175
Virginia	668	494	278	365	126,818	106,692	58,765	71,720
West Virginia			316	357			59,828	44,861
Wisconsin	25	105	785	875	6,744	27,036	230,106	218,357
Washington				29				4,000
District of Columbia	2					720		
Totals	39,252	43,738	92,973	161,557	8,397,307	10,153,935	31,246,432	47,389,087

NOTE.—The statistics for 1870 do not include the manufacture of hats. This industry comprised, in 1880, 43 establishments, a capital of $3,615,830; employed 5,470 hands and paid $1,893,215 for wages; used materials valued at $4,785,774, and produced hats to the value of $8,516,569.

No. 14.—STATEMENT SHOWING THE NUMBER OF ESTABLISHMENTS, CAPITAL INVESTED, NUMBER OF HANDS EMPLOYED, WAGES PAID, COST OF MATERIALS USED, AND VALUE OF PRODUCTS OF THE MANUFACTURE OF WORSTED AND WOOLEN GOODS IN EACH STATE AND TERRITORY OF THE UNITED STATES FOR THE YEARS 1850, 1860, 1870, AND 1880—Continued.

[From the official Reports of the United States Census.]

States.	Cost of materials used.				Value of products.			
	1850.	1860.	1870.	1880.	1850.	1860.	1870.	1880.
	Dollars.	Dollars.	Dollars.	Dollars.	Dollars.	Dollars.	Dollars.	Dollars.
Alabama		80,790	57,338	49,361		191,474	89,998	63,745
Arkansas			55,082	85,972			78,690	127,430
California		50,000	608,141	997,539		150,000	1,102,754	1,634,858
Connecticut	3,325,709	4,043,124	11,351,425	14,742,091	6,465,216	6,840,220	17,962,048	24,855,729
Delaware	204,172	75,807	392,614	448,285	251,000	153,035	576,067	665,253
Florida				150				500
Georgia	30,392	260,475	268,176	165,065	88,750	464,420	471,523	239,300
Illinois	115,307	110,462	1,701,323	1,623,693	200,572	187,613	2,849,249	2,380,584
Indiana	120,486	352,362	2,684,315	1,926,670	235,802	649,771	4,329,711	2,887,547
Iowa	3,500	67,293	998,073	437,301	13,000	127,640	1,647,606	682,812
Kansas			86,105	107,251			158,150	211,525
Kentucky	205,287	510,902	831,628	852,405	318,819	845,226	1,312,458	1,264,988
Louisiana		31,300	10,047			45,200	30,795	
Maine	405,940	1,003,366	4,013,759	4,444,990	753,300	1,717,007	6,483,881	6,962,003
Maryland	165,568	267,353	233,924	382,224	295,140	605,992	427,590	539,028
Massachusetts	8,671,671	13,886,475	30,539,366	41,677,919	12,770,565	21,657,165	47,783,083	67,451,805
Michigan	43,402	69,010	659,700	583,241	90,242	139,246	1,204,868	838,766
Minnesota			108,540	160,867			211,323	263,378
Mississippi		119,849	79,566			211,646	147,323	299,605
Missouri	16,000	56,745	849,313	723,286	56,000	143,025	1,256,213	1,015,901
N. Hampshire	1,267,329	2,739,553	6,342,740	7,854,955	2,127,745	4,301,653	10,213,526	13,220,850
New Jersey	548,367	548,578	1,507,250	4,117,035	1,164,446	1,085,104	2,422,805	6,820,074
New Mexico			12,775					21,000
New York	3,838,292	3,424,614	8,629,516	19,550,793	7,030,004	5,870,117	14,633,186	34,978,287
North Carolina	13,950	151,005	166,497	255,707	23,750	291,000	298,638	303,160
Ohio	578,423	476,833	2,119,869	1,395,512	1,111,027	825,000	3,467,699	2,198,264
Oregon			27,000	227,595		85,000	505,857	549,030
Pennsylvania	3,282,718	4,427,138	22,390,853	43,664,468	5,321,866	8,191,675	35,463,624	67,821,307
Rhode Island	1,463,900	4,070,224	9,826,158	13,094,650	2,381,825	6,015,205	15,394,067	21,624,204
South Carolina		60,000	22,238	19,455		80,000	34,459	24,075
Tennessee	1,675	5,225	500,737	423,054	6,310	8,100	696,844	620,724
Texas	10,000	25,980	86,817	44,435	15,000	38,796	152,968	80,500
Utah			98,272	147,226			190,600	279,424
Vermont	830,684	1,662,650	1,935,972	2,372,428	1,579,161	2,938,626	3,644,459	3,813,077
Virginia	488,899	389,204	317,800	383,080	841,013	717,827	488,352	577,068
West Virginia			307,051	247,543			475,763	350,586
Wisconsin	32,630	85,743	687,368	901,918	87,992	172,720	1,256,467	1,498,886
Washington				52,000				70,000
Dist. Columbia	1,630				2,400			
Total	25,755,991	39,029,062	110,740,799	164,371,551	43,207,545	65,596,364	177,495,689	267,252,913

NOTE.—The statistics for 1870 do not include the manufacture of hats. This industry comprised, in 1880, 43 establishments, a capital of $3,615,830; employed 5,470 hands and paid $1,893,215 for wages; used materials valued at $4,785,774, and produced hats to the value of $8,510,569.

No. 15.—STATEMENT SHOWING THE NUMBER OF MACHINES, LOOMS, AND SPINDLES USED IN THE MANUFACTURE OF WOOLEN AND WORSTED GOODS, IN EACH STATE AND TERRITORY OF THE UNITED STATES, IN 1870 AND 1880.

[From the official Reports of the United States Census.]

1870.

States and Territories.	Woolen goods.					Worsted goods.						
	Cards.		Looms.		Spindles.	Cards.	Braiders.	Combing-machines.		Knitting-machines.	Looms.	Spindles.
	Sets.	Daily capacity in carded wool.	Broad.	Narrow.		Sets.		Ameri-can.	Foreign.			
		Pounds.	No.	No.	No.	Sets.	No.	No.	No.	No.	No.	No.
Alabama	24	1,836		2	530							
Arkansas	17	1,448										
California	46	8,000	163	22	3,880						104	
Connecticut	660	70,045	1,190	1,703	178,410		1,069		3			
Delaware	30	2,475	53	174	8,750							3,680
District of Columbia												
Florida	1	50										
Georgia	72	5,454	6	389	14,465							
Illinois	250	21,302	210	423	30,888							
Indiana	346	32,467	252	948	57,063							
Iowa	199	19,483	133	241	31,462							
Kansas	24	1,270	9	20	1,616							
Kentucky	208	17,768	34	288	10,509							
Louisiana	12	800	20	80	4,000							
Maine	331	33,020	962	199	65,249	4	500					1,400
Maryland	60	4,158	57	91	12,348							
Massachusetts	1,367	159,484	4,469	3,374	470,785		1,080	64	54	14	3,341	96,826
Michigan	116	11,430	74	158	15,650							
Minnesota	19	2,103	17	22	2,664							
Mississippi	17	1,495		30	314							
Missouri	258	21,102	68	115	10,371							
New Hampshire	351	44,550	909	699	117,017			4			46	8,022
New Jersey	81	10,700	183	421	23,457		300	6	2		119	3,312
New Mexico	1	100	4	1	210							
New York	845	84,470	1,314	1,127	163,540	8			1		74	3,720
North Carolina	78	5,698	11	86	2,800		47					
Ohio	334	28,376	300	752	52,748		300					
Oregon	21	3,935	65	25	4,320							

No. 15.—NUMBER OF MACHINES, LOOMS, AND SPINDLES USED IN THE MANUFACTURE OF WOOLEN AND WORSTED GOODS, &c.—Continued.

1870.

States and Territories	Woolen goods						Worsted goods					
	Cards.		Looms.				Cards.	Combing-machines.		Knitting-machines.	Looms.	Spindles.
	Sets.	Daily capacity in carded wool.	Broad.	Narrow.	Spindles.	Braiders.	Sets.	American.	Foreign.			
		Pounds.	No.	No.	No.	No.	Sets.	No.	No.	No.	No.	No.
Pennsylvania	1,317	140,362	2,296	6,394	310,877	977	74	17	3	133	1,423	23,237
Rhode Island	474	61,639	652	1,710	157,089	2,161	10	4	3	29	1,021	58,884
South Carolina	25	1,458	2	7	330							
Tennessee	177	10,307	20	60	3,614							
Texas	29	1,855	14	10	1,070							
Utah	19	1,475	11	20	1,430							
Vermont	175	18,070	379	291	47,719		2					
Virginia	118	8,011	61	76	6,230							1,536
Washington												
West Virginia	132	10,152	50	70	6,387							
Wisconsin	134	11,013	112	110	10,445							
Total	8,306	857,392	14,039	20,144	1,845,496	7,334	98	95	66	176	6,128	200,617

No. 15.—NUMBER OF MACHINES, LOOMS, AND SPINDLES USED IN THE MANUFACTURE OF WOOLEN AND WORSTED GOODS, &c.—Continued.

1880.

States and Territories	Machines — Cards: Sets	Machines — Cards: Daily capacity in scoured wool (Pounds)	Combing-machines — Foreign: Number	Combing-machines — Foreign: Daily capacity in scoured wool (Pounds)	Combing-machines — American: Number	Combing-machines — American: Daily capacity in scoured wool (Pounds)	Looms — Broad: On woolen goods (No.)	Looms — Broad: On worsted goods (No.)	Looms — Narrow: On woolen goods (No.)	Looms — Narrow: On worsted goods (No.)	Looms — Hand-looms (No.)	Power-looms — Brussels (No.)	Power-looms — Ingrain (No.)	Knitting-looms (No.)
Alabama	15	1,200					7		10					
Arkansas	29	2,860							34					
California	60	7,240					201		26		3			
Connecticut	435	59,055					1,384	50	1,228					
Delaware	13	1,700					20		99		1			
District of Columbia														
Florida														
Georgia	42	3,713					181		88		4			
Illinois	106	10,078			1	75	150		193		7			
Indiana	100	18,445							660		2			
Iowa	50	4,420							108		5			
Kansas	9	802					24		15					
Kentucky	154	14,737					15		493					
Louisiana														
Maine	261	30,530					1,045		58		13			
Maryland	30	2,870					20		91					
Massachusetts	1,250	175,839	20	6,600	20	5,500	5,292	162	2,377	1,765				
Michigan	51	4,680					41		126					
Minnesota	21	2,230					40		13					
Mississippi	15	1,635					6		116					
Missouri	126	12,275					42		149		2			
New Hampshire	293	37,304					1,180		320		28			
New Jersey	136	27,065					609		444		98			
New Mexico														

No. 15.—Number of Machines, Looms, and Spindles used in the Manufacture of Woolen and Worsted Goods, &c.—Continued.

1860.

States and Territories	Cards		Combing-machines				Broad		Narrow		Hand-looms	Power-looms		Knitting-looms
			Foreign		American							Brussels	Ingrain	
	Sets	Daily capacity in scoured wool (Pounds)	Number	Daily capacity in scoured wool (Pounds)	Number	Daily capacity in scoured wool (Pounds)	On woolen goods (No.)	On worsted goods (No.)	On woolen goods (No.)	On worsted goods (No.)	(No.)	(No.)	(No.)	(No.)
New York	483	50,735	2	600	3	600	1,158	68	591	2	39		26	
North Carolina	57	5,329					7		23		34			
Ohio	162	14,000					126		412					
Oregon	21	2,225					63		3					
Pennsylvania	638	172,468	10	4,300			1,495	88	7,895		205	2	22	34
Rhode Island	433	54,028	16	2,000			1,100	261	1,313					
South Carolina	11	4,790												
Tennessee	93	8,450					17		150					
Texas	2	250					10		2					
Utah	21	1,560					22		91		1			
Vermont	115	10,708					583		163					
Virginia	51	5,035					69		75		11		1	
Washington	2	250					8		4					
West Virginia	72	5,313					30		134		15			
Wisconsin	75	6,390					143		77					
Total	5,901	764,000	48	13,500	24	6,175	15,040	620	17,679	1,767	528	2	49	34

No. 15.—NUMBER OF MACHINES, LOOMS, AND SPINDLES USED IN THE MANUFACTURE OF WOOLEN AND WORSTED GOODS, &c.—Continued.

1880.

States and Territories.	Woolen goods—Continued.				Worsted goods.									
					Machines.						Looms.			
					Cards.		Combing-machines.				Broad.		Narrow.	
							Foreign.		American.					
	Knitting-machines.	Sewing-machines.	Woolen spindles.	Worsted spindles.	Sets.	Daily capacity in scoured wool.	Number.	Daily capacity in scoured wool.	Number.	Daily capacity in scoured wool.	On woolen goods	On worsted goods	On woolen goods	On worsted goods
	No.	No.	No.	No.		Pounds.		Pounds.		Pounds.	No.	No.	No.	No.
Alabama	1		100											
Arkansas		10	1,300											
California	138	11	18,740											
Connecticut	8		152,004		22	2,700	6	1,275			30		58	
Delaware			4,300											
District of Columbia														
Florida														
Georgia	2		2,224											
Illinois	22		26,092											
Indiana	12	1	36,480											
Iowa	4		11,025											
Kansas			2,630											
Kentucky	3	2	14,110											
Louisiana	1													
Maine	7	22	68,193											
Maryland			6,580											
Massachusetts	15	110	461,770	11,696	96	22,764	75	31,850	11	2,550	12	1,296		3,103
Michigan	1	7	10,088											
Minnesota		2	3,852											
Mississippi		2	3,734											
Missouri	15	49	12,022											
New Hampshire	24	14	126,071		23	8,400	17	7,000	4	1,800				1,850
New Jersey	2		31,710		5	1,500	4	1,200						
New Mexico														
New York	2	30	131,020	1,068	6	700	30	6,130	1	400		24		902

No. 15.—NUMBER OF MACHINES, LOOMS, AND SPINDLES USED IN THE MANUFACTURE OF WOOLEN AND WORSTED GOODS, &c.—Continued.

States and Territories.	Woolen goods—Continued.				1880. Worsted goods.									
					Machines.						Looms.			
					Cards.		Combing-machines.				Broad.		Narrow.	
							Foreign.		American.					
	Knitting-machines.	Sewing-machines.	Woolen spindles.	Worsted spindles.	Sets.	Daily capacity in scoured wool.	Number.	Daily capacity in scoured wool.	Number.	Daily capacity in scoured wool.	On woolen goods.	On worsted goods.	On woolen goods.	On worsted goods.
	No.	No.	No.	No.		Pounds.		Pounds.		Pounds.	No.	No.	No.	No.
North Carolina	1	2	2,374											66
Ohio	55	7	33,950				2	500						
Oregon	9	2	4,248											
Pennsylvania	45	54	293,625	7,142	44	11,316	83	24,406	1	200		486		650
Rhode Island	2	4	100,524	15,120	63	12,725	52	14,400	2	700	5	157		1,100
South Carolina														
Tennessee			6,860											
Texas			600											
Utah		2	5,422											
Vermont		1	46,264											
Virginia			8,488											
Washington			400											
West Virginia	10		8,081											
Wisconsin		4	16,689											
Total	279	348	1,720,820	35,926	250	55,105	269	86,761	19	5,650	47	1,963	68	7,231

No. 15.—NUMBER OF MACHINES LOOMS, AND SPINDLES USED IN THE MANUFACTURE OF WOOLEN AND WORSTED GOODS, &c.—Continued.

1880.

States and Territories.	Worsted goods—Continued.						Felt goods.		Wool hats.		Sewing-machines.
	Looms—Continued.			Sewing-machines.	Woolen spindles.	Worsted spindles.	Machines. Cards.		Cards.		
	Hand-looms.	Power-looms. Brussels.	Knitting-looms.				Sets.	Daily capacity in scoured wool.	Sets.	Daily capacity in scoured wool.	
	No.	No.	No.	No.	No.	No.		Pounds.		Pounds.	No.
Alabama											
Arkansas											
California											
Connecticut					2,600	5,000	30	8,500	31	2,226	18
Delaware											
District of Columbia											
Florida											
Georgia											
Illinois											
Indiana											
Iowa											
Kansas											
Kentucky											
Louisiana											
Maine							3	1,000	10	700	7
Maryland		1,200									
Massachusetts				12	4,044	76,647	53	14,650	43	8,600	22
New Hampshire				6	672	10,980	1	230			
New Jersey	30	150		8		2,000	15	5,310			
New York						20,092	12	1,950	197	8,100	215
Ohio						1,250					
Pennsylvania	159	650	2	21	6,080	58,235	8	2,500	81	4,518	63
Rhode Island		3,005	16	15	7,208	45,350					
Total	189	4,905	18	57	20,604	210,454	122	20,160	362	19,144	325

No. 15.—NUMBER OF MACHINES, LOOMS, AND SPINDLES USED IN THE MANUFACTURE OF WOOLEN AND WORSTED GOODS, &c.—Continued.

1880.

States and Territories.	Cards.		Combing-machines.				Carpets, other than rags.							Spindles.	
			Foreign.		American.		Broad looms on woolen goods.	Narrow looms on worsted goods.	Hand-looms.	Power-looms.		Tapestry looms.	Sewing-machines.		
	Sets.	Daily capacity in scoured wool.	No.	Pounds.	No.	Pounds.	No.	No.	No.	Brussels. No.	Ingrain. No.	No.	No.	Woolen. No.	Worsted. No.
Alabama															
Arkansas															
California															
Connecticut	25	7,500	14	6,000	1	200			10	84	295			4,256	12,858
Delaware															
District of Columbia															
Florida															
Georgia															
Illinois															
Indiana															
Iowa															
Kansas															
Kentucky															
Louisiana															
Maine															
Maryland															
Massachusetts	74	16,900	18	10,550	46	9,000		75	12	250	260	161		7,860	20,918
Minnesota															
Mississippi															
Missouri							0								
New Jersey	5	1,000			5	400			80	0	33			840	1,232
New York	132	32,440	10	3,500	34	9,350			149	68	273	26	8	8,592	26,748
Pennsylvania	40	15,375	22	10,800	5	1,000			3,794	345	1,012	360	3	11,305	15,000
Rhode Island															
Total	285	73,275	64	30,850	91	10,950	0	75	3,995	750	1,873	547	11	32,853	82,256

No. 15.—Number of Machines, Looms, and Spindles used in the Manufacture of Woolen and Worsted Goods, &c.—Continued.

1880.

Hosiery and knit goods.

States and Territories.	Cards. Sets.	Combing-machines. Daily capacity in scoured wool. (Pounds)	Combing-machines. Foreign. (No.)	Combing-machines. Daily capacity in scoured wool. (Pounds)	Broad looms on woolen goods. (No.)	Broad looms on worsted goods. (No.)	Narrow looms on woolen goods. (No.)	Hand-looms. (No.)	Patent power-frames. (No.)	Seaming and crocheting machines. (No.)	Knitting-looms. (No.)	Knitting. (No.)	Sewing. (No.)	Spindles. Woolen. (No.)	Spindles. Worsted. (No.)
Alabama															
Arkansas															
California	79	9,590									317	720	340	15,674	
Connecticut							1		16	55					
Delaware															
Florida							4								
Illinois	3	450			1							433	48	680	
Indiana											6	183	5		
Iowa												7			
Maine															
Maryland								6			539	818	257	9,028	
Massachusetts	38	3,500									1	521	9	920	
Michigan	4	600										10	2		
Minnesota												2			
Missouri					1		18				128	992	118		
New Hampshire	68	7,830										343	75	17,540	
New Jersey	23	4,170									103	1,311	1,933	6,048	
New York	320	59,975									30	368	4	71,008	
Ohio	35	5,600	3	1,100	87	20	73	58			492	6,769	1,653	15,970	
Pennsylvania												32	7	60	
Rhode Island	22	2,925										69	94	3,805	2,290
Vermont												1			
West Virginia															
Wisconsin											4	19	4		
Total	592	94,640	3	1,100	89	20	96	64	16	55	1,624	12,659	4,560	140,733	2,290

No. 16.—STATEMENT SHOWING THE NUMBER OF ESTABLISHMENTS, CARDS, MACHINES, LOOMS, SPINDLES, AND EMPLOYÉS, ALSO THE AMOUNTS OF CAPITAL INVESTED AND WAGES PAID, AND THE TOTAL VALUES OF MATERIAL USED, AND OF PRODUCTS OF THE MANUFACTURE OF WOOLEN AND WORSTED GOODS, CARPETS, FELT GOODS, AND HOSIERY IN EACH STATE AND TERRITORY OF THE UNITED STATES IN 1890.

[From the official Report of the United States Census.]

a. WOOLEN GOODS.

States and Territories	Establishments	Cards	Machines	Looms	Spindles	Operatives	All other	Capital	Wages	Total value of all materials	Value of production at wholesale
	No.	No.	No.	No.	No.	No.	No.	Dollars.	Dollars.	Dollars.	Dollars.
Pennsylvania	324	938	10	9,791	302,767	17,020	669	18,780,604	5,231,328	21,185,804	32,341,291
Massachusetts	167	1,356	40	9,500	473,472	22,390	1,231	24,640,782	7,457,115	27,839,583	45,099,203
New York	159	483	5	1,884	142,948	5,763	367	8,266,878	1,774,143	6,212,835	9,874,973
Ohio	122	182		572	33,930	1,238	58	1,316,340	256,214	1,084,323	1,678,140
Tennessee	100	98		167	6,810	363	30	416,664	67,063	422,054	620,724
Kentucky	98	154		513	14,110	776	47	890,750	166,189	852,405	1,264,968
Missouri	98	126		193	12,623	659	60	726,130	100,877	681,711	930,961
Maine	93	261	1	1,103	63,192	2,902	163	3,870,038	1,044,606	4,294,042	6,886,073
Indiana	61	100		814	36,888	1,650	91	2,273,705	462,681	1,823,390	2,723,347
Connecticut	78	435		2,662	152,004	6,600	290	4,510,271	2,342,035	10,176,987	10,892,284
New Hampshire	58	293		1,534	126,671	3,705	232	7,907,452	1,181,738	4,993,709	8,113,830
West Virginia	55	72		179	8,081	321	32	293,170	44,161	245,843	356,946
Illinois	53	100		374	20,992	969	73	1,327,563	296,225	1,332,798	1,806,460
Rhode Island	50	432	10	2,674	175,644	7,699	422	8,448,700	2,480,907	9,138,429	15,410,450
North Carolina	49	57		30	2,374	171	14	23,100	23,195	255,707	303,160
All other	390	803		3,638	179,133	9,548	738	12,175,417	2,875,015	10,304,691	16,407,793
Total	1,990	5,961	72	35,634	1,758,746	81,914	4,590	90,095,564	25,836,392	100,645,611	100,006,721

b. WORSTED GOODS.

States and Territories	Establishments	Cards	Machines	Looms	Spindles	Operatives	All other	Capital	Wages	Total value of all materials	Value of production at wholesale
Pennsylvania	28	44	84	1,847	84,315	4,819	181	$4,959,639	1,473,958	7,277,469	10,072,473
Massachusetts	23	96	80	5,611	80,691	5,501	282	6,195,247	1,670,030	6,465,476	10,466,016
Rhode Island	11	63	54	4,283	52,618	3,757	247	4,567,410	1,222,350	3,041,383	6,177,754
New York	6	6	31	1,136	20,092	1,633	74	1,670,157	385,152	1,348,376	2,321,990
Connecticut	3	22	6	88	7,600	462	28	232,000	172,256	1,258,655	1,597,227
New Hampshire	2	23	21	1,350	11,552	1,369	162	2,628,584	512,881	1,582,226	2,604,232
New Jersey	2	5	4	30	2,900	100	20	45,000	22,200	70,417	119,000
Ohio	1		2	66	1,250	101	7	67,000	23,400	60,606	101,250
Total	76	259	298	14,411	240,118	17,802	1,001	20,374,043	5,682,027	22,013,628	33,549,942

c. CARPETS.

States.							Dollars.	Dollars.	Dollars.	Dollars.
Pennsylvania	172	49	27	4,151	20,305	8,682	7,210,483	3,035,071	8,892,385	14,304,600
New York	10	133	44	850	35,340	5,200	6,422,158	1,952,391	4,435,410	8,419,254
Massachusetts	7	74	64	746	34,778	3,617	4,637,646	1,223,302	3,950,673	8,337,629
Connecticut	2	25	15	389	16,614	1,546	3,085,000	565,654	1,440,199	2,500,559
New Jersey	3	5	5	104	2,072	219	103,000	48,000	109,425	179,500
Maryland	1			12		75	10,000	9,900	32,000	50,000
Maine	1						300		785	1,200
Total	195	285	155	7,252	115,109	19,439	21,468,587	6,835,218	18,984,877	31,792,802

d. FELT GOODS.

States.	Establishments.	Cards.	Employees.		Capital.	Wages.	Total value of all materials.	Total value of production at wholesale.
	No.	No.	Operatives. No.	All other. No.	Dollars.	Dollars.	Dollars.	Dollars.
Massachusetts	11	53	468	44	820,000	161,440	1,194,339	1,627,320
New Jersey	6	15	235	31	316,000	80,170	510,195	685,386
New York	4	12	167	28	157,500	35,289	155,893	257,450
Connecticut	2	30	155	19	405,734	53,515	313,325	439,496
Pennsylvania	1	8	250	12	150,000	80,000	250,000	450,000
Maine	1	3	46	8	100,000	14,320	67,538	120,000
New Hampshire	1	1	41		12,000	7,000	20,420	50,000
Total	26	122	1,382	142	1,958,254	430,780	2,530,710	3,619,652

No. 16.—Establishments, Machines, Capital, Wages, Products, &c., of the Manufactures of Woolens, 1860, &c.—Continued.

e. HOSIERY.

States.	Establishments.	Cards.	Looms.	Spindles.	Employés.		Capital.	Wages.	Total value of all materials.	Value of production at wholesale.
					Operatives.	All other.				
	No.	No.	No.	No.	No.	No.	Dollars.	Dollars.	Dollars.	Dollars.
Pennsylvania	106	35	730	18,260	9,108	164	3,743,790	2,175,913	4,924,138	8,935,147
New York	75	3?0	103	71,008	7,461	397	5,334,876	2,036,076	5,072,058	9,899,540
Massachusetts	57	38	545	9,028	3,341	70	1,467,375	608,067	1,394,748	2,483,590
New Hampshire	24	68	147	17,540	1,714	39	1,224,000	536,117	1,249,600	2,362,779
Ohio	23		30	60	742	3	187,000	94,658	211,583	418,825
Connecticut	14	70	389	15,674	2,105	106	1,966,431	664,93	1,013,949	2,432,271
Illinois	14	3	11	680	697	10	105,900	92,385	290,895	484,124
Michigan	11			920	933	29	147,380	92,324	226,677	377,249
New Jersey	8	28		6,048	1,059	11	804,570	239,761	258,043	661,181
Vermont	6	22		3,805	375	8	492,000	101,037	350,938	593,270
Indiana	5				278	6	45,600	24,700	103,280	156,200
Missouri	4				118		29,400	10,300	41,575	85,000
Wisconsin	4				28		10,610	3,364	9,125	18,817
All other	8		9		76	7	21,950	13,280	25,392	65,228
Total	359	592	1,964	143,023	28,035	850	15,579,591	6,701,475	15,210,951	29,167,227

No. 17.—STATEMENT SHOWING THE QUANTITIES AND VALUES OF THE MATERIALS
USED IN, AND THE QUANTITIES OF THE VARIOUS PRODUCTS, WITH THEIR TOTAL
VALUES, OF THE MANUFACTURE OF WOOLEN GOODS, WORSTED GOODS, FELT
GOODS, HATS, CARPETS, HOSIERY AND KNIT GOODS, IN THE UNITED STATES DUR-
ING THE YEAR ENDING MAY 31, 1880.

[From the official Report of the United States Census.]

WOOLEN GOODS.

Materials used in manufacture.	Quantity.	Value.
		Dollars.
Foreign wool, in the condition purchased..................pounds..	20,482,667	⎫
Domestic wool, in the condition purchased ....do....	177,042,288	⎬ 67,380,250
Scoured wool (not including waste purchased and shoddy).......do....	109,724,213	⎭
Camels' hair and noils.....................................do....	1,234,064	332,419
Mohair and noils ....do....	84,080	50,837
Buffalo hair and noils ....do....	556,601	25,284
Hair of other animals......................................do....	3,040,923	212,762
Cotton used on cards.......................................do....	24,744,964	3,395,569
Shoddy used, or waste, not including that made in mill......do....	46,583,983	7,014,100
Cotton warp used on woolen goods..........................do....	17,550,212	4,374,985
Cotton warp used on worsted goods.........................do....	8,517,580	897,211
Woolen yarn used, not made in mill ....do....	1,485,009	872,023
Worsted yarn used, not made in mill......................do....	2,495,050	8,139,746
Value of chemicals and dyestuffs............................		4,758,498
Cords of wood...number..	142,250	371,236
Coal..tons..	350,769	1,461,467
Value of all other materials used............................		6,559,224
Total value of all materials		100,645,611

Products.	Quantities.	Products.	Quantities.
Blankets.....................pairs..	1,083,671	Woolen rolls................pounds..	8,541,429
Horse blankets ....number..	1,114,827	Cottonades..................yards..	1,821,600
Carriage robes ....do....	58,485	Dress goods ....do....	4,771,140
Cloths, cassimeres, doeskins, diagonal,		Cashmere ....do....	2,919,050
and suitings ....yards..	78,440,525	Worsted coatings ....do....	1,082,236
Beavers and overcoating ....do....	7,095,924	Worsted overcoatings ....do....	492,331
Horse clothing ....do....	616,157	Worsted dress goods ....do....	11,275,884
Blanketing ....do....	22,393	Alpaca ....do....	8,851,701
Cloaking ....do....	1,359,296	Bunting.......................do....	355,000
Felted cloth...................do....	129,904	Worsted suitings ....do....	914,587
Coverlets ....number..	1,330,066	Worsted shawls............number..	83,612
Flannels ....yards..	70,923,196	Binding ....yards..	63,520
Jeans.........................do....	29,538,959	Worsted yarn ....pounds..	2,238,076
Kersey ....do....	2,579,374	Reps ....yards..	1,957,050
Linsey ....do....	4,781,007	Lining.........................do....	50,000
Waterproof cloaking and repellants,		Ingrain carpets, 2-ply........do....	169,555
yards....................................	5,838,297	Ingrain carpets, 3-ply ....do....	700
Satinets ....yards..	16,629,116	Rag carpets ....do....	6,800
Tweeds........................do....	2,035,015	Girthen carpets ....do....	820
Shawls ....number..	1,242,979		
Cashmerettes ....yards..	1,557,537	Value of all products not heretofore	
Balmorals ....dozen..	144,900	named	$3,058,616
Cotton yarn ....pounds..	1,420,968	Value of production at wholesale....	160,606,721
Woolen yarn ....do....	25,581,217		

WORSTED GOODS.

Materials used in manufacture.	Quantities.	Values.
		Dollars.
Foreign goods, in the condition purchased ....pounds..	15,687,811	⎫
Domestic wool, in the condition purchased.................do...	25,461,515	⎬ 15,235,878
Scoured wool (not including waste purchased and shoddy)...........do...	26,834,685	⎭
Camel's hair and noils.......................................do...	207,065	40,341
Mohair and noils..do...	31,598	19,458
Hair of other animals.......................................do...	319	237
Cotton used on cards ....do...	1,757,842	211,293
Shoddy used, or waste, not including that made in mill ....do...	190,800	31,300
Cotton warp used on woolen goods ....do...	262,000	80,062
Cotton warp used on worsted goods ....do...	5,086,952	1,505,980

No. 17.—QUANTITIES AND VALUES OF MATERIALS USED IN MANUFACTURE, &c., IN
1880—Continued.

WOORSTED GOODS—Continued.

Materials used in manufacture.	Quantities.	Values.
Woolen yarn used, not made in mill..pounds..	416, 574	271, 25.̈
Worsted yarn used, not made in mill....................................... do....	2, 100, 532	2, 418, 086
Value of chemicals and dyestuffs		565, 660
Cords of wood ....number..	2, 132	6, 497
Coal........... ... . tons..	72, 779	308, 421
Value of all other materials useda..		1, 319, 151
Total value of all materials......................................		22, 013, 628

Products.	Quantities.	Products.	Quantities.
Coatings .... yards..	2, 875, 672	Rep.........................yards..	9, 000
Dress goods.....................do...	63, 833, 341	Tapestry.........................do...	329, 000
Upholstery goods ....do...	205, 000	Elastic frills .. ..do...	105, 000
Alpaca ....do...	1, 000, 000	Worsted yarn made and sold, not	
Serges ....do...	530, 741	used at mill ....pounds..	9, 650, 000
Picture cord ....pieces..	250, 000	Lastings.....................yards..	910, 553
Terry.........................yards..	214, 000	Noils, shorts, &c ....pounds..	4, 238, 295
Bunting.........................do...	2, 230, 221	Cloakings.....................yards..	16, 107
Snitings.........................do...	362, 168		
Worsted shawls ....number..	574, 257	Value of all products not heretofore	
Italian cloths.................yards..	1, 357, 444	named	$965, 512
Braiding or braids...........dozen..	2, 612, 691	Value of production at wholesale ..	33, 549, 942

a Including 5,000 pounds silk yarn, value $23,500 ; 20,000 pounds shoddy yarn, value $10,000.

FELT GOODS.

Materials used in manufacture.	Quantities.	Values.
		Dollars.
Foreign wool. in the condition purchased.............................pounds..	709, 067	⎱ 1, 624, 871
Domestic wool, in the condition purchased ....do....	4, 294, 806	⎰
Scoured wool (not including waste purchased and shoddy)..............do ...	2, 733, 796	
Camel's hair and noils..do ...	70, 000	7, 500
Buffalo hair and noils ....do...	71, 000	5, 840
Hair of other animals ....do...,	1, 657, 0.0	40, 010
Cotton used on cards ....do...,	1, 181, 500	114, 660
Shoddy used, or waste, not including that made in mill................do...,	2, 406, 849	383, 267
Value of chemicals and dyestuffs..		150, 921
Cords of wood ....number..	4, 624	13, 878
Coal ....tons..	14, 915	63, 559
Value of all other materials used..		126, 204
Total value of all material		2, 530, 710

Products.	Quanti- ties.	Products.	Quanti- ties.
Cloths, cassimeres, and docskins ..yds..	275, 000	Trimming and lining felts...........yds..	205, 208
Beavers and overcoatings..........do...	336, 160	Table and piano covers ....do ...	60, 979
Felt skirtings......................do...	3, 093, 600	Hair felting ....feet..	1, 262, 950
Rubber shoe linings ....,......do...	1, 688, 880		
Felt cloths......................do...	1, 642, 485	Value of all products not heretofore	
Felt for ladies' hats...............do...	65, 800	named	$258, 084
Saddle felts.......................do...	23, 500	Value of production at wholesale	3, 619, 352

No. 17.—QUANTITIES AND VALUES OF MATERIALS USED IN MANUFACTURE, &C., IN 1880—Continued.

WOOL HATS.

Materials used in manufacture.	Quantities.	Values.
		Dollars.
Foreign wool in the condition purchased......................pounds..	1, 864, 139	⎫
Domestic wool in the condition purchased.......................do....	6, 107, 471	⎬ 2, 644, 298
Scoured wool (not including waste purchased and shoddy)..........do....	3, 597, 279	⎭
Camels' hair and noils ....do....	3, 911	1, 875
Buffalo hair and noils ....do....	7, 436	3, 615
Cotton used on cards.................. ....do....	185, 400	21, 870
Shoddy used, or waste, not including that made in mill.............do....	1, 368, 562	370, 963
Value of chemicals and dyestuffs...................................		173, 040
Cords of wood ....number..	296	1, 478
Coal ... .tons..	30, 227	109, 507
Value of all other materials used		1, 459, 133
Total value of all materials.......................		4, 785, 774

Products.	Quantities.	Products.	Quantities.
Cloths, cassimeres, and doe-skins, ...yards..	699, 428	Straw hats................dozens..	9, 358
Wool hats.................dozen..	1, 391, 863	Value of all products not hereto-	
Felt linings.................yards..	8, 194	fore named	$153, 218
Saddle felt....................do....	109	Value of production at wholesale..	8, 516, 569
Felt skirts....................do....	3, 176		

CARPETS OTHER THAN RAG.

Materials used in manufacture.	Quantities.	Values.
		Dollars.
Foreign wool in the condition purchased......................pounds..	34, 008, 252	⎫
Domestic wool in the condition purchased.........................do....	2, 029, 318	⎬ 6, 975, 129
Scoured wool (not including waste purchased and shoddy).........do....	23, 500, 216	⎭
Camels' hair and noils ....do....	46, 300	8, 808
Mohair and noils. .... do ..	4, 000	700
Buffalo hair and noils ....do ..	30, 840	2, 352
Hair of other animals..do....	65, 700	5, 250
Shoddy used, or waste, not including that made in mill.............do....	90, 469	12, 442
Cotton warp used..... ....do....	9, 544 214	1, 799, 646
Woolen yarn used, not made in mill....................................do....	8, 985, 162	2, 597, 182
Worsted yarn used, not made in mill..................................do....	4, 091, 115	2, 858, 199
Value of chemicals and dyestuffs		1, 369, 439
Cords of wood ....number..	767	3, 899
Coal ... .tons..	60, 641	259, 581
Value of all other materials used (a)................................		3, 092, 248
Total value of all materials		18, 984, 877

Products.	Quantities.	Products.	Quantities.
Brussels carpet ....yards..	4, 077, 190	Rugs ....number..	47, 530
Ingrain carpet, 2-ply ....do....	21, 986, 434	Noils, shorts, &c..........pounds..	288, 614
Ingrain carpet, 3-ply.........do....	862, 394	Lastings ....yards..	107, 452
Venetian carpet ....do....	1, 984, 201	Serges .... do	55, 748
Tapestry carpet..............do....	9, 441, 195	Worsted yarn made and sold, not	
Velvet carpet.................do....	60, 000	used at mill . .. pounds..	1, 134, 143
Wilton carpet.................do....	157, 629	Woolen yarn made and sold, not	
Axminster carpet..............do....	303, 366	used at mill............. pounds..	1, 265, 240
Cottage carpet..............do....	241, 220		
Dutch carpet..................do....	12, 060	Value of all products not heretofore	
Rag carpet..................do....	157, 005	named.........................	$334, 181
Druggets ....number..	40, 000	Value of production at wholesale ..	31, 692, 802

a Including 6,559,550 pounds shoddy yarn, value $559,133.

No. 17.—Quantities and Values of Materials used in Manufacture, &c., in 1880—Continued.

HOSIERY AND KNIT GOODS.

Materials used in manufacture.	Quantities.	Values.
		Dollars.
Foreign wool in the condition purchased ....pounds..	448,758	
Domestic wool in the condition purchased............................do...	8,146.137	3,821,183
Scoured wool (not including waste purchased and shoddy) ....do....	5,927,692	
Camels' hair and noils...do....	21,779	10,848
Mohair and noils ....do....	40,000	18,040
Buffalo hair and noils...do....	5,150	518
Merino yarn used ....do....	67,561	22,970
Cotton used on cards...do....	20,131,151	2,469,783
Shoddy used, or waste, not including that made in mill.............do....	1,523,263	233,823
Cotton warp used..do....	270,950	66,025
Cotton yarn used...do....	8,074,137	1,991,749
Woolen yarn used, not made in mill..................................do....	3,753,566	2,853,722
Worsted yarn used, not made in mill.................................do....	750,255	758,803
Value of chemicals and dyestuffs.......................................		631,060
Cords of wood...number..	8,344	28,416
Coal ....tons..	42,980	181,253
Value of all other materials used..		2,104,800
Total value of all materials...		15,210,951

Products.	Quantities.	Products.	Quantities.
Woolen half-hose ....dozens..	288,111	Nubias ....dozens..	72,050
Woolen hose ....do....	1,216,274	Ulsters........................do....	12,389
Mixed half-hose.................do....	637,234	Shawls.........................do....	49,545
Mixed hose......................do....	2,653,099	Fancy knit goods............do ..	19,868
Cotton hosiery ....do....	2,491,243	Yarn, worsted and woolen..pounds..'	25,000
Shirts and drawers.............. do....	2,671,712	Yarn, woolen..................do....	195,000
Leggins ....do....	41,683	Sacques.....................dozens..	925
Gloves ....do....	48,462	Boot and shoe lining.........yards..	451,350
Mittens.....................do....	199,889	Waists.....................dozens..	2,800
Gaiters..........................do....	43,310	Coverlets ....number..	1,550
Hoods...........................do....	64,830	Skirts ....dozens..	62
Scarfs ....do....	47,178		
Wristers ....do....	20,745	Value of all products not heretofore	
Cardigan jackets................do....	105,321	named	$1,546,713
Fancy jackets...................do....	58,522	Value of production at wholesale	20,107,227

No. 18.—Statement showing the Weekly and Daily Wages Paid to Employés in Woolen Factories in the United Kingdom, and average rates of Daily Wages Paid in like Factories in the States of Massachusetts, New York, Ohio, and Kentucky, in 1885.

[From the Annual Report of the U. S. Commissioner of Labor, 1886.]

Occupations	Great Britain				Massachusetts		New York		Ohio		Kentucky	
	Weekly wages		Daily wages. a		Daily wages.		Daily wages.		Daily wages.		Daily wages.	
	Male	Female	Male	Female	Male	Female	Male	Female	Male	Female	Male	Female
	Dolls.	Dolls.	Dolls.	Dolls.	Dolls.	Dolls.	Dolls.	Dolls.	Dolls.	Dolls.	Dolls.	Dolls.
Burlers	b5 32	b2 66	97	48			1 15					
Carders					1 15	85	1 08	1 40	c2 00		1 75	1 10
Drawers-in	b8 47		1 54		1 14		1 50					
Dressers	b5 32		97		1 47	85	1 53					
Driers	b5 32		97		1 00		1 09					
Dyers	92		17		1 12		1 16		c1 50		1 39	
Engineers	b9 68		1 76		1 94		2 47		c1 75		2 98	
Finishers	87		16		99	82	1 25		c2 00		1 43	
Firemen	b4 36		79				1 29				1 60	
Fullers	b6 05		1 10		1 03		1 00		c1 25			
Giggers	b5 32		97		97		1 11		c1 25			
Laborers	b4 84		88		98		1 03		c1 50		1 32	
Loom fixers	1 33		24		1 90		2 16		c2 00		1 75	
Machinists					1 96		2 18					
Overseers					2 66		2 90				3 09	
Pickers					1 14		1 14				1 13	
Pressers					1 02		1 30					
Scourers	80		15		1 30		1 15		c1 50			
Second hands					1 54		2 31					
Shearers					93		1 15		c1 50			
Spinners, mule	68		16		1 31		1 45		c1 25			
Spinners, other	b2 90	b2 90	53	53		98		1 00				
Teamsters					1 59		1 36		c1 00			
Twisters					1 38							
Weavers	83	50	15	09	1 28	1 16	1 08	1 11	c1 00			79
Wool sorters	1 20		22		1 81		1 65		c1 50		1 56	

a The weekly wages paid in Great Britain have been reduced to daily wages at the rate of five and one-half days to the week.

b Wages per week, Vol. XX, census 1880, p. 376, &c.

c Wages paid by L. Rambo & Co., Dresden, and New Lisbon Woolen Manufacturing Company, New Lisbon, Ohio, Vol. XX, p. 400, &c., census 1880.

No. 19.—Statement Showing the Number of Sheep on Farms and the Crop of Wool in each State and Territory of the United States for each of the Years 1840, 1850, 1860, 1870, and 1880.

[From the Official Reports of the United States Census.]

States and Territories.	Number of sheep.					Production of wool.				
	1840.	1850.	1860.	1870.	1880.	1840.	1850.	1860.	1870.	1880.
						Pounds.	Pounds.	Pounds.	Pounds.	Pounds.
Maine	649,264	451,577	452,472	434,666	565,918	1,465,551	1,364,034	1,493,060	1,774,168	2,778,407
New Hampshire	617,390	384,756	310,534	248,760	211,825	1,260,517	1,108,476	1,160,122	1,124,442	1,059,589
Vermont	1,681,819	1,014,122	752,201	580,347	430,570	3,699,235	3,400,717	3,118,950	3,102,137	2,551,113
Massachusetts	378,226	188,651	114,829	78,560	67,079	941,906	585,136	377,267	306,039	359,089
Rhode Island	90,146	44,290	32,624	23,938	17,211	163,830	129,692	90,699	77,328	65,680
Connecticut	403,462	174,181	117,107	83,884	59,431	889,670	497,454	335,896	254,129	230,133
Total New England States	3,820,307	2,257,563	1,779,767	1,450,155	1,302,234	8,440,969	7,085,509	6,578,094	6,043,863	6,983,011
New York	5,118,777	3,453,241	2,617,855	2,181,578	1,715,180	9,845,295	10,071,301	9,454,474	10,599,225	8,527,195
New Jersey	219,285	160,488	135,228	120,067	117,020	397,207	375,396	349,250	330,609	441,110
Pennsylvania	1,767,620	1,822,357	1,631,540	1,794,301	1,776,598	3,048,564	4,481,570	4,752,522	6,561,722	8,470,273
Delaware	35,247	27,503	18,857	22,714	21,967	61,404	57,768	56,201	58,316	97,940
Maryland	257,922	177,902	153,765	120,697	171,184	488,201	477,425	491,511	435,213	850,684
District of Columbia	706	150	40	604		707	100	100		
Total Middle States	7,403,557	5,641,641	4,550,285	4,218,901	3,801,949	13,844,378	15,463,098	15,008,058	17,991,085	18,666,008
Virginia	1,293,772	1,310,004	1,043,269	370,145	497,280	2,538,374	2,860,765	2,510,019	877,110	1,896,673
North Carolina	538,279	595,249	546,749	463,435	461,038	625,044	970,738	883,473	700,607	917,756
South Carolina	232,981	285,551	233,509	124,594	118,849	299,170	487,233	427,102	156,314	272,758
Georgia	267,107	560,435	512,618	419,465	527,549	371,303	990,019	946,427	846,947	1,280,500
Florida	7,198	23,311	30,158	26,599	56,081	7,285	23,247	59,171	37,562	162,810
Alabama	163,243	371,880	370,156	241,934	347,838	220,353	657,118	775,117	381,233	702,297
Mississippi	128,367	304,929	352,632	232,732	287,694	175,196	559,619	662,059	284,285	734,643
Louisiana	98,072	110,333	181,253	118,002	135,631	49,283	109,897	290,847	140,428	406,678
Texas		100,530	753,363	714,351	2,411,633		131,917	1,493,738	1,251,328	6,928,019
Arkansas	42,151	91,256	202,753	161,077	240,737	64,943	182,595	410,382	214,784	557,364
Tennessee	711,593	811,591	773,317	826,783	672,789	1,060,332	1,364,378	1,405,230	1,339,762	1,918,295
West Virginia				552,327	674,760				1,593,511	2,641,444
Kentucky	1,008,240	1,102,091	938,990	936,765	1,000,269	1,786,847	2,297,433	2,329,105	2,234,430	4,592,576
Total Southern States	4,521,003	5,667,160	6,038,767	5,188,809	7,430,166	7,198,130	10,634,959	12,196,976	10,211,431	23,061,787
Ohio	2,028,401	3,942,929	3,546,767	1,924,635	4,902,486	3,685,315	10,196,371	10,608,927	20,539,643	25,003,756
Michigan	99,618	746,435	1,271,743	1,085,996	2,189,389	153,375	2,043,283	3,960,888	8,726,145	11,458,497
Indiana	675,982	1,122,493	991,175	1,012,040	1,100,511	1,237,019	2,610,287	2,552,318	5,029,023	6,167,498

										Pounds.
Illinois	305,672	894,043	709,135	1,568,286	1,037,073	659,007	2,150,113	1,089,507	5,730,240	6,003,096
Wisconsin	3,402	124,896	332,954	1,008,282	1,336,807	6,777	253,903	1,011,533	4,960,670	7,016,491
Minnesota		80	18,044	132,343	267,508		85	20,388	401,186	1,362,124
Iowa	15,354	149,960	269,041	855,408	455,369	23,039	373,898	660,858	2,307,043	2,971,075
Missouri	348,018	762,511	937,445	1,352,001	1,411,298	562,205	1,027,164	2,060,778	8,640,390	7,313,924
Kansas			17,669	109,088	400,071			24,740	335,005	2,855,832
Nebraska			2,355	22,725	109,453			3,302	74,655	1,282,656
Colorado				120,928	740,448				204,925	3,197,391
Total Western States	3,566,507	7,743,347	8,141,228	13,757,367	14,146,088	6,318,697	19,255,164	22,902,706	51,756,083	76,113,210
California		17,574	1,088,002	2,708,187	4,152,340		5,620	2,088,190	11,301,743	16,798,030
Nevada			370	11,018	131,695			330	27,029	655,012
Oregon	15,382		86,052	318,123	1,083,162		29,680	219,012	1,090,638	5,718,524
Washington Territory			10,157	44,063	292,883			18,810	162,713	1,380,123
Total Pacific coast	32,956	1,184,587	3,141,391	5,662,080			35,296	2,922,270	12,082,123	24,560,695
Dakota		103	1,001	30,244					8,810	157,025
Idaho			1,021	27,320					3,415	127,149
Montana			2,024	184,277					100	905,484
New Mexico	377,271	880,116	610,438	2,088,831		32,901	492,045	684,640	4,010,188
Arizona			903	70,624					079	313,008
Utah	3,202	37,332	60,072	233,121		9,222	74,705	109,018	973,246
Wyoming			6,409	140,225					30,000	691,650
Total Territories not elsewhere specified	380,533	807,641	691,268	2,780,548		42,123	567,410		836,052	7,277,440

Recapitulation by groups.

New England States	3,820,307	2,357,563	1,779,767	1,450,155	1,362,234	8,440,900	7,085,500	6,578,094	6,043,963	6,983,011
Middle States	7,403,657	5,641,641	4,550,285	4,248,901	3,801,949	13,844,376	15,403,908	15,098,638	17,981,045	18,086,008
Southern States	4,621,603	5,667,160	5,938,707	5,188,800	7,439,166	7,198,130	10,634,939	12,196,376	10,211,431	23,060,787
Western States	3,566,507	7,743,347	8,141,228	13,757,307	14,146,088	6,318,697	19,255,164	22,902,705	51,756,083	75,113,210
Pacific coast	32,956	1,184,587	3,141,391	5,662,080			35,200	2,922,270	12,082,123	24,560,695
Territories not elsewhere specified	380,533	807,641	691,268	2,780,548		42,123	567,410		836,052	7,277,440
Total United States	19,311,374	21,723,220	22,471,275	28,477,951	35,192,074	35,802,114	52,516,039	60,284,913	100,102,387	a155,681,751

a This table of the wool crop for 1880 has been supplemented as follows:

	Pounds.
Spring clip of 1880 on farms	155,081,751
Fall clip in California and Texas	13,000,000
Wool of ranch sheep	34,000,000
Pulled wool and fleece of slaughtered sheep	38,000,000
Total number	240,081,751

No. 20.—STATEMENT SHOWING THE NUMBER OF SHEEP IN EACH STATE AND TERRITORY OF THE UNITED STATES FROM 1875 TO 1897, INCLUSIVE.

[From the Official Reports of the Department of Agriculture.]

States and Territories.	1875.	1876.	1877.	1878.	1879.	1880.	1881.	1882.	1883.	1884.	1885.	1886.	1887.
Maine	401,500	525,900	520,600	525,800	557,300	506,300	632,078	577,236	677,236	577,236	548,374	637,407	526,650
New Hampshire	212,100	242,400	242,400	230,900	335,100	242,100	240,942	213,043	211,804	209,686	201,299	195,260	195,260
Vermont	516,400	490,500	475,700	461,400	466,000	498,600	598,572	444,289	448,712	448,712	385,892	378,174	378,174
Massachusetts	70,300	76,300	61,000	60,300	60,900	61,300	65,109	68,650	69,346	69,346	67,050	64,561	63,270
Rhode Island	23,300	25,300	25,000	24,500	24,500	28,200	28,200	21,514	21,729	21,077	20,466	20,449	20,245
Connecticut	88,100	92,500	92,500	92,500	96,200	97,100	98,071	60,025	58,831	58,831	59,419	63,477	53,477
Total New England States	1,440,000	1,452,000	1,417,200	1,404,400	1,440,000	1,525,600	1,570,052	1,385,640	1,338,252	1,384,988	1,293,809	1,249,328	1,237,085
New York	1,996,400	1,936,500	1,897,700	1,518,100	2,121,000	2,205,800	2,338,148	1,732,335	1,732,332	1,782,332	1,697,685	1,593,824	1,570,866
New Jersey	127,100	125,800	125,800	128,300	127,000	127,400	129,748	118,190	117,008	117,008	110,348	107,413	106,330
Pennsylvania	1,674,000	1,640,500	1,607,600	1,607,600	1,666,000	1,640,300	1,632,807	1,783,481	1,803,336	1,749,236	1,486,857	1,189,481	1,001,323
Delaware	23,200	23,600	23,600	35,000	37,400	38,800	36,800	22,077	22,077	22,077	22,510	22,291	22,294
Maryland	138,500	141,200	144,000	151,200	152,700	152,700	152,700	172,890	173,760	172,022	172,020	168,582	165,210
Total Middle States	3,030,200	3,667,600	3,798,700	3,440,200	4,104,100	4,174,000	4,292,203	3,830,976	3,848,513	3,792,675	3,494,425	3,081,594	2,968,032
Virginia	207,500	336,400	307,000	422,000	417,800	428,100	447,403	502,202	502,262	487,194	477,450	463,127	449,213
North Carolina	275,500	243,900	281,000	490,000	425,000	425,000	385,000	430,871	466,162	432,176	488,350	468,816	450,963
South Carolina	147,200	142,700	144,100	175,000	182,000	170,500	187,000	120,078	120,078	116,476	117,641	112,035	105,418
Georgia	375,000	371,200	378,000	382,300	374,400	374,400	378,144	638,141	532,700	541,415	532,547	500,594	465,553
Florida	31,500	37,800	40,400	56,500	50,900	59,900	70,083	58,382	102,000	98,940	97,951	91,004	90,183
Alabama	182,300	185,800	195,100	270,000	204,000	214,200	224,010	354,480	330,914	343,9.5	343,025	337,047	323,565
Mississippi	147,400	151,800	163,300	250,000	192,600	200,300	202,303	290,571	293,477	203,477	281,738	276,103	242,971
Louisiana	62,600	68,800	71,500	125,000	127,500	135,100	100,094	135,631	128,849	124,084	121,234	110,385	111,730
Texas	1,445,700	1,601,400	2,836,700	3,674,700	4,560,000	5,149,400	6,021,628	6,830,000	7,877,500	7,943,275	7,558,461	6,802,015	4,761,831
Arkansas	183,300	102,400	190,400	285,000	203,500	393,500	290,435	219,225	239,256	227,293	225,020	231,021	224,660
Tennessee	225,500	341,700	345,100	650,000	858,500	858,500	85?,500	675,478	675,478	635,214	635,558	603,760	561,515
West Virginia	510,200	544,300	544,300	540,900	571,900	600,500	860,530	981,266	684,925	671,226	637,665	624,012	593,646
Kentucky	739,600	683,600	690,400	900,000	1,020,000	1,040,800	1,020,000	1,000,160	1,000,160	980,166	950,761	903,221	858,062
Total Southern States	4,842,500	5,052,100	6,238,700	8,430,400	9,287,100	9,022,300	10,872,936	11,916,911	12,073,860	12,050,761	12,468,301	11,534,65x	9,241,449
Ohio	4,592,600	4,546,600	3,900,000	3,783,010	4,040,000	4,040,400	4,243,617	4,061,511	5,050,641	5,000,03x	4,900,015	4,733,034	4,562,913
Michigan	3,416,500	3,450,400	2,100,000	1,750,600	1,820,000	1,854,400	1,930,046	2,320,752	2,436,790	2,412,42x	2,361,174	2,269,607	2,156,127
Indiana	1,360,400	1,250,400	2,175,000	1,002,700	1,050,500	1,010,000	1,029,570	1,111,516	1,122,631	1,145,081	1,122,182	1,088,517	1,034,091
Illinois	1,380,900	1,311,000	1,258,500	1,258,500	1,089,000	1,110,800	1,155,232	1,029,702	1,149,900	1,128,908	1,053,101	1,005,033	925,201
Wisconsin	1,211,300	1,211,600	1,151,100	1,333,700	1,313,000	1,316,100	1,329,203	1,303,173	1,363,677	1,336,403	1,063,677	1,218,890	1,072,544
Minnesota	174,300	190,300	260,200	300,000	307,500	307,500	313,630	278,30	291,085	275,463	272,708	278,102	278,162
Iowa	607,900	663,800	649,300	560,000	445,600	454,400	461,484	461,681	497,161	497,161	472,303	407,580	425,408
Missouri	1,364,200	1,284,200	1,297,500	1,271,000	1,296,400	1,523,300	1,619,911	1,425,411	1,454,910	1,430,360	1,38,623	1,285,078	1,182,272
Kansas	118,000	123,900	142,400	150,600	312,500	371,900	448,909	649,572	747,008	821,706	838,143	1,190,103	1,106,852

Nebraska	42,000	48,900	60,600	62,400	144,000	172,800	193,536	249,316	324,111	333,834	373,894	448,673	439,700
Colorado				600,000					1,212,000	1,248,360	1,185,942	1,126,645	1,149,178
Total Western States	15,301,300	15,032,100	12,874,300	12,157,900	11,807,400	12,212,600	12,728,939	13,845,038	5,638,829	15,636,760	15,214,052	15,131,912	14,332,538
California	4,683,200	6,750,000	7,290,000	6,661,003	6,889,000	7,646,200	7,493,864	6,352,344	5,907,680	6,203,064	5,892,911	6,469,098	6,069,699
Nevada	10,000	20,000	24,000	72,000					367,000	385,350	423,985	661,281	674,446
Oregon	634,400	710,500	859,700	1,074,600	1,160,600	1,265,100	1,176,433	2,333,162	2,403,157	2,571,378	2,519,950	2,469,551	2,503,029
Washington Territory									390,000	456,300	533,871	544,548	555,439
Total Pacific coast	5,336,600	7,481,400	8,173,700	7,707,600	8,049,600	8,911,900	8,670,297	8,685,506	9,067,837	9,616,092	9,370,617	9,745,058	9,892,052
Dakota									140,000	182,000	183,850	253,672	256,209
Idaho									125,000	187,500	191,250	210,375	231,413
Montana									405,000	465,750	625,000	718,750	754,668
New Mexico									3,960,000	4,435,200	5,410,944	4,328,755	4,025,742
Arizona									602,000	812,700	853,335	890,002	627,201
Utah									513,000	564,300	620,730	651,767	658,285
Wyoming									a 575,000	598,000	609,960	518,466	534,020
Total Territories not elsewhere specified	2,904,000	3,049,200	3,201,600	2,600,000	3,435,600	4,019,600	5,426,460	5,351,247	6,320,000	7,245,450	8,495,039	7,577,787	7,087,558
Recapitulation by groups:													
New England States	1,440,000	1,452,900	1,417,200	1,404,400	1,440,000	1,525,600	1,579,062	1,385,646	1,368,252	1,384,888	1,283,809	1,240,329	1,237,085
Middle States	3,059,200	3,867,600	3,798,700	3,440,200	4,104,100	4,174,000	4,292,203	3,830,076	3,848,513	3,793,675	3,498,425	3,083,594	2,968,032
Southern States	4,842,500	5,052,100	6,238,700	8,430,400	9,287,100	9,922,200	10,872,938	11,916,011	10,872,973	12,860,760	12,468,901	11,534,632	9,211,449
Western States	15,301,300	15,032,100	12,974,300	12,157,900	11,817,400	12,212,600	12,728,939	13,845,038	12,973,829	12,636,760	12,244,052	15,131,912	14,332,538
Pacific coast	5,336,600	7,481,400	8,173,700	7,707,600	8,049,600	8,911,900	8,670,297	8,685,506	9,067,837	9,616,092	9,370,617	9,745,058	9,892,052
Territories	2,904,000	3,049,200	3,201,600	2,600,000	3,435,600	4,019,600	5,426,460	5,351,247	6,320,000	7,245,450	8,495,039	7,577,787	7,087,558
Total United States	33,783,600	33,935,300	35,804,200	35,740,500	38,123,800	40,765,900	43,569,899	45,016,224	49,237,291	50,626,626	50,360,243	48,322,331	44,759,314

a Includes Indian Territory.   b Includes Nevada and Colorado.

The following tables, unless otherwise specified, have been compiled from official data.

IMPORTS AND EXPORTS.

No. 21.—Statement showing, by Countries, the Quantities of Manufactures of Wool, and their Total Values, Imported into and Exported from Austria-Hungary in 1885.

Countries from and through which imported and to and through which imported.	Yarns of all kinds.		Wool and hair tablets, hat felts and hat wadding.		Shaggy cloths, Halina and pressed cloths, cloths cuttings, &c.	
	Imports.	Exports.	Imports.	Exports.	Imports.	Exports.
	Pounds.	*Pounds.*	*Pounds.*	*Pounds.*	*Pounds.*	*Pounds.*
Germany	10,421,124	2,450,452	180,998	6,173	21,164	77,161
Russia		474,190		661	2,205	2,205
Roumania	661	119,209			2,866	348,146
Servia		59,965			18,960	85,979
Turkey		441			14,330	
Italy	1,764	21,385	221	441	661	17,196
Switzerland	35,715		441			5,291
Via Trieste	3,307	52,249			441	47,619
Via Fiume and other ports	7,716				7,716	221
Total	10,470,287	3,177,891	181,660	7,275	68,343	583,818
Total value	$4,555,154	$1,500,375	$53,804	$2,155	$15,309	$94,317

Countries from and through which imported and to and through which exported.	Carpets and girths.		Woolen woven goods.		Shawls and shawl-like textures.	
	Imports.	Exports.	Imports.	Exports.	Imports.	Exports.
	Pounds.	*Pounds.*	*Pounds.*	*Pounds.*	*Pounds.*	*Pounds.*
Germany	631,818	102,293	3,220,038	1,484,838	80,027	21,605
Russia	2,646	1,102	2,205	61,049		1,984
Roumania	441	30,864	221	1,242,292		3,748
Servia	5,952	6,834	5,732	604,261		1,102
Turkey	221		882			
Italy	221	7,716	8,378	581,333		10,582
Switzerland	882	882	8,818	14,991		
Via Trieste	99,428	18,078	37,919	3,603,238	1,323	221
Via Fiume and other ports	3,527	1,985	13,448	177,470		
Total	745,136	169,754	3,306,641	7,770,372	81,350	39,242
Total value	$357,369	$77,131	$3,570,304	$6,537,948	$244,007	$48,107

166

No. 21.—STATEMENT SHOWING, BY COUNTRIES, THE QUANTITIES OF MANUFACTURES OF WOOL, AND THEIR TOTAL VALUES, IMPORTED INTO AND EXPORTED FROM AUSTRIA-HUNGARY IN 1885—Continued.

Countries from and through which imported and to and through which exported.	Felt and felt goods.		Velvet, fringes, ribbons, buttons, and knit goods.		Felt hats.		Wearing apparel.	
	Imports.	Exports.	Imports.	Exports.	Imports.	Exports.	Imports.	Exports.
	Pounds.	*Pounds.*	*Pounds.*	*Pounds.*	*Pounds.*	*Pounds.*	*Pounds.*	*Pounds.*
Germany	64,154	87,302	598,088	188,934	49,604	93,034	209,878	87,964
Russia	7,275	19,621	221	16,755		11,464	221	5,071
Roumania		6,614		127,867		52,029	441	522,691
Servia		661	5,291	29,101		16,535	8,157	308,904
Turkey	661		6,834				221	
Italy	882	1,323	221	22,928	1,323	13,228	1,764	13,448
Switzerland	1,323	5,291	1,102	13,448			441	5,952
Via Trieste		1,102	4,630	1,193,130		16,535	6,173	352,115
Via Fiume and other ports	6,393		3,527	221	661	661	5,071	3,527
Total	80,688	121,914	619,914	1,592,384	51,588	203,486	232,367	1,299,672
Total value	$32,353	$69,755	$975,455	$1,249,385	$115,900	$306,576	$899,378	$1,049,792

No. 22.—STATEMENT SHOWING THE QUANTITIES AND VALUES OF WOOL AND MANUFACTURES OF WOOL IMPORTED INTO AND EXPORTED FROM AUSTRIA-HUNGARY DURING EACH YEAR FROM 1875 TO 1884 INCLUSIVE.

[One metric centner equals 123.4615 pounds. One gulden equals 48.5 cents.]

	Imports.						Exports.			
Years.	Wool, raw.		Woolen yarn.		Other manufactures.		Wool, raw.		Manufactures of wool.	
	Quantity.	Value.	Quantity.	Value.	Quantity.	Value.	Quantity.	Value.	Quantity.	Value.
	Met. ctr.	*Gulden.*	*Met. ctr.*	*Guldvn.*	*Met. ctr.*	*Gulden.*	*Met. ctr.*	*Gulden.*	*Met. ctr.*	*Gulden.*
1875	(a)	(a)	34,062	14,090,000	41,557	26,696,000	(a)	(a)	37,921	20,718,000
1876	(a)	(a)	27,642	9,898,000	35,212	21,963,000	(a)	(a)	37,675	21,314,000
1877	(a)	(a)	34,249	11,769,000	26,412	15,844,000	(a)	(a)	38,643	20,883,000
1878	(a)	(a)	35,646	11,225,000	37,358	20,131,000	(a)	(a)	43,587	25,114,000
1879	192,959	34,482,000	38,497	13,623,000	31,811	19,579,000	76,251	15,009,000	49,338	27,616,000
1880	189,478	35,934,000	36,764	13,692,000	33,103	21,043,000	120,469	26,267,000	43,676	24,401,000
1881	210,902	40,181,000	38,763	14,161,000	34,052	21,411,000	94,631	19,768,000	53,637	30,335,000
1882	238,585	38,863,000	42,924	14,913,000	34,726	22,350,000	96,997	20,379,000	52,840	30,025,000
1883	244,856	37,075,000	42,343	13,029,000	32,519	19,263,000	122,901	24,605,000	46,680	26,235,0:0
1884	255,856	38,420,000	28,100	18,017,000	49,548	14,708,000	113,748	21,923,000	50,822	26,615,000

a Not stated.

No. 23.—STATEMENT SHOWING, BY COUNTRIES, THE QUANTITIES AND VALUES OF MANUFACTURES OF WOOL IMPORTED INTO AND EXPORTED FROM BELGIUM IN 1885.

Countries from which imported and to which exported.	Yarns of all kinds Imports Lbs.	Yarns Imports Dolls.	Yarns Exports Lbs.	Yarns Exports Dolls.	Shawls and scarfs of Indian cashmere Imports Dolls.	Shawls Exports Dolls.	Cloths, cassimeres, and other like Imports Dolls.	Cloths Exports Lbs.	Cloths Exports Dolls.	Coatings, duffels, malmouks, and other heavy Imports Dolls.	Coatings Exports Lbs.	Coatings Exports Dolls.	All other light Imports Dolls.	All other light Exports Lbs.	All other light Exports Dolls.
Austria-Hungary	112	79	94,370	37,502				71,230	63,476	696	126	91	21	11,590	13,190
Denmark	1,601,016	1,098,474	3,797,708	1,458,224				9,673	8,892		3,294	2,370		4,755	5,412
France	40,195	31,291	4,497,490	1,723,585	502		63,202	1,092,040	1,003,819	50,946	17,443	12,599	1,259,178	379,464	431,859
Germany							61,742	218,722	201,633	22,049	5,564	4,010	707,273	24,445	27,820
Bremen	6,850	4,797	5,428	2,613				2,747	2,525					2,011	2,288
Hamburg								23,891	21,961				190	40,104	45,709
Lubeck	7,245	4,688	101,599	40,626			5,140	7,950	7,308		8,779	6,340		939	1,000
Luxemburg											1,310	947	6,884	11,975	13,629
Great Britain and Ireland	431,297	301,261	23,311,266	9,923,668	213		445,185	249,807	229,682	135,089	115,177	83,160	1,273,873	42,438	46,298
Greece								2,787	2,561		884	638		59,513	67,728
Italy	9,294	6,163	4,925,657	1,813,963			3,491	26,255	24,132	153,549	127,300	91,948	40,780	1,200,293	1,306,025
Netherlands			10,498,081	3,873,912		5		310,450	285,376		5,926	4,240		5,154	5,866
Portugal								37,835	34,779		2,090	1,509		225	256
Roumania								541	563					4,387	4,993
Russia								2,503	2,300					937	5,643
Spain			166,668	68,448				12,485	11,476		16,074	11,009		2,339	2,662
Sweden and Norway			6,118,251	2,259,368				4,000	4,513		716	517		31,018	35,312
Switzerland			102,135	92,512			386	179,733	165,212	2,682	12,301	8,028	77	1,353	1,541
Turkey								1,836	1,088		2,974	2,148		46,039	52,385
United States of America			20,434	7,513				173,707	159,674		43,410	31,350		21,451	24,413
Brazil			1,649	794				172,380	156,462		7,879	5,601		14,919	16,978
Uruguay								30,344	27,893		993	717		41,586	47,327
Argentine Republic								242,100	222,542		83,181	60,041			
Peru								25,302	23,313		8,869	6,406			
Chili								142,187	130,701		3,517	2,540			
British East Indies								94,800	88,040		1,140	823		16,949	19,289
China								3,915	3,599		650	432			
Japan								9,082	8,900					6,733	7,663
Australasia								20,068	18,447		657	474			
Other countries			41,492	16,473			420	2,876	2,273	1,992	2,497	1,747	104	395	447
Total	2,162,009	1,446,753	53,773,868	21,319,301	715	6	578,560	3,174,896	2,918,042	367,005	472,680	341,388	3,280,386	1,975,092	2,247,803

No. 24.—STATEMENT SHOWING THE QUANTITIES AND VALUES OF WOOL AND MAN-
UFACTURES OF WOOL IMPORTED INTO AND EXPORTED FROM BELGIUM FOR EACH
YEAR, FROM 1874 TO 1884, INCLUSIVE.

[One kilogram equals 2.20462 pounds; one franc equals 19.3 cents.]

Years.	Imports.			Exports.			
	Wool, raw.		Manufactures of wool.	Manufactures of wool.			
				Yarn.		Other manufactures.	
	Quantity.	Value.	Value.	Quantity.	Value.	Quantity.	Value.
	Kilograms.	*Francs.*	*Francs.*	*Kilograms.*	*Francs.*	*Kilograms.*	*Francs.*
1874	51,054,000	114,871,000	26,318,000	4,949,000	49,309,000	2,792,000	43,390,000
1875	45,825,000	114,562,000	28,765,000	4,571,000	47,854,000	2,608,000	41,628,000
1876	51,905,000	153,714,000	25,710,000	3,689,000	39,527,000	2,318,000	38,953,000
1877	48,954,000	150,099,000	22,081,000	4,880,000	48,890,000	2,256,000	34,195,000
1878	46,541,000	146,604,000	21,946,000	6,392,000	67,511,000	2,723,000	38,960,000
1879	43,287,000	140,683,000	19,266,000	6,541,000	63,551,000	1,938,000	25,754,000
1880	49,265,000	184,743,000	23,494,000	7,699,000	78,516,000	1,948,000	27,903,000
1881	45,509,000	177,485,000	22,746,000	7,790,000	73,987,000	2,180,000	31,365,000
1882	57,005,000	114,010,000	23,210,000	6,864,000	41,961,000	2,356,000	30,380,000
1883	48,358,000	96,716,000	20,817,000	8,966,000	55,240,000	1,982,000	25,168,000
1884	36,417,000	72,835,000	21,025,000	8,911,000	53,227,000	2,219,000	26,469,000

No. 25.—STATEMENT SHOWING BY COUNTRIES THE QUANTITIES OF MANUFACTURES
OF WOOL IMPORTED INTO AND EXPORTED FROM DENMARK IN 1884.

Countries from which imported and to which exported.	Felt for ships' sheathing.		Yarns.			
			Uncolored.		Colored.	
	Imports.	Exports.	Imports.	Exports.	Imports.	Exports.
	Pounds.	*Pounds.*	*Pounds.*	*Pounds.*	*Pounds.*	*Pounds.*
Danish Possessions:						
Faroe Islands		248	7			
Iceland		860			5	
West Indies					2	
Norway			4	413	10	532
Sweden	796	7,468	268	971	125	11,033
Germany:						
Hamburg	93		69,820	6	108,513	270
Luebeck	73		5,448		24,888	106
Schleswig-Holstein	16,250		17,802	1,163	77,378	
All other Germany	2,778		60,450		23,693	902
Great Britain and Ireland	49,972		744,603		274,354	1,022
Netherlands					188	
Belgium			21,257	22	6,375	
France			3,246		724	
All other countries			375	4,309	1,349	7,955
Total	69,962	8,576	923,280	6,884	517,594	21,820
Total entered into consumption	66,173		854,392		495,335	

No. 25.—STATEMENT SHOWING BY COUNTRIES THE QUANTITIES OF MANUFACTURES OF WOOL IMPORTED INTO AND EXPORTED FROM DENMARK IN 1884—Continued.

| Countries from which imported and to which exported. | Other woolen merchandise. | | | | | |
| | Carpet stuffs. | | Open and loose. | | All other. | |
	Imports.	Exports.	Imports.	Exports.	Imports.	Exports.
	Pounds.	Pounds.	Pounds.	Pounds.	Pounds.	Pounds.
Danish Possessions:						
Faroe Islands	90				123,708	1,623
Iceland	234	141			30,118	20,326
Greenland		21				1,464
West Indies		55				6
Norway	246	1,917	10	6	1,291	167,654
Sweden	2,184	18,342	102	1,070	8,529	474,811
Russia	154	13			3	1,253
Germany:						
Hamburg	5,523	1,449	5,910	103	491,660	7,625
Luebeck	43,026	1,130	25,537		675,105	12,934
Schleswig-Holstein	9,186	112	3,456	176	938,661	41,094
All other Germany	32,041	445	5,726	17	457,517	9,770
Great Britain and Ireland	249,646	2,220			973,895	14,771
Netherlands	178				39,241	2,049
Belgium	43,366	141	118		87,188	61
France	239	17			56,974	1,058
Spain	263				10	
Italy	42				57	
Austria					49	99
United States of America	90				1,118	
All other countries	3,511	834	6,199	1,675	519,948	27,639
Total	390,019	26,837	47,058	3,047	4,405,072	785,136
Total entered into consumption	330,254		44,097		3,713,639	

No. 26.—STATEMENT SHOWING THE QUANTITIES OF WOOL AND MANUFACTURES OF WOOL IMPORTED INTO, AND OF WOOL EXPORTED FROM, DENMARK FOR EACH YEAR FROM 1874 TO 1884.

[One pund equals 1.1025 pounds.]

| Years. | Imports. | | Exports. |
	Wool, raw.	Manufactures of wool.	Wool, raw.
	Pund.	Pund.	Pund.
1874	1,392,091	4,100,930	3,967,986
1875	1,376,399	4,449,805	3,582,602
1876	1,292,834	4,118,877	3,869,789
1877	1,638,146	3,573,974	4,231,661
1878	1,939,641	3,589,007	3,417,483
1879	1,572,275	4,145,125	4,004,440
1880	1,669,408	4,775,031	4,372,171
1881	1,961,046	4,960,478	4,513,293
1882	2,867,862	5,227,864	4,103,886
1883	2,233,953	5,524,364	4,625,936
1884	2,348,541	5,699,830	3,333,405

No. 27.—STATEMENT SHOWING BY COUNTRIES THE QUANTITY, KINDS, AND TOTAL VALUE OF MANUFACTURES OF WOOL IMPORTED INTO AND EXPORTED FROM FRANCE IN 1885.

IMPORTS.

Countries from which imported.	Blankets.	Carpets.	Uphol- stery.	Cloths.	Bolting cloth, seam- less.	Slippers of list.
	Pounds.	*Pounds.*	*Pounds.*	*Pounds.*	*Pounds.*	*Pounds.*
Austria....................	....	....	898	12,358	....	809
Belgium	842	38,215	....	515,309	....	....
Germany	1,658	88,079	2,308	1,156,599	138	484,310
Great Britain and Ireland..	28,239	1,586,046	....	6,403,163	....	....
Italy.....................	....	....	....	8,245	....	....
Netherlands..............	....	....	....	16,352	....	....
Spain	....	....	....	1,168	....	....
Switzerland	340	....	....	5,249	....	....
Turkey...................	....	230,680	....	....	....	....
Other countries...........	2,498	37,403	403	3,777	....	889
Total........	33,777	1,980,423	3,609	8,122,220	138	486,008
Total value...........	$18,224	$815,799	$18,956	$6,221,718	$182	$297,835

Countries from which imported.	Stuffs.		Shawls.	Laces.	Hosiery, trimmings, and ribbons.	Fez, or red caps.	Listing.
	For up- holstery.	Other.					
	Pounds.	*Pounds.*	*Pounds.*	*Pounds.*	*Pounds.*	*Number.*	*Pounds.*
Austria..................	....	17,075	....	....	3,980	22,061	....
Belgium..................	587	81,222	2,235	4,826	35,971	....	15,505
Germany.................	3,186	476,840	680	22,895	350,524	....	72,538
Great Britain and Ireland	2,853	626,194	28,075	4,351	172,376	....	20,329
Italy....................	3,396	279	....	....	1,554	....	54,165
Netherlands..............	....	7,080	....	....	....	....	....
Spain	....	....	....	....	273	....	33,160
Switzerland..............	....	2,380	11	....	16,437	27,540	....
Turkey	21,088	....	....	....	....	2,102	....
Egypt	260	....	....	....	....	....	....
Other countries	200	101	136	114	423	1,365	8,603
Total...............	31,570	1,211,171	31,137	32,186	581,538	53,068	204,300
Total value	$24,874	$1,086,819	$32,711	$54,809	$1,046,894	$15,363	$18,885

Countries from which imported.	Mixed stuffs.		Tissues of alpaca, la- ma, and vicuna.	Yarns.	Felt and hats of felt.	Hats of wool.
	For up- holstery.	Other.				
	Pounds.	*Pounds.*	*Pounds.*	*Pounds.*	*Pounds.*	*Number.*
Austria...................	....	....	....	....	10,236	....
Belgium	45	108,676	....	1,186,203	41,282	31,184
Germany..............	5,976	231,566	....	729,279	181,828	20,563
Great Britain and Ireland ..	....	5,772,876	89,807	7,481,416	621,365	465,483
Italy.....................	....	1,300	....	....	5,469	1,352
Switzerland	....	1,840	....	1,131	13,472	....
Turkey	....	1,696	....	....	....	....
Other countries...........	83	417	1,483	2,745	1,314	638
Total...............	6,104	6,118,371	91,290	9,400,713	874,966	519,220
Total value...........	$8,551	$4,713,681	$191,826	$6,229,953	$358,837	$175,367

No. 27.—STATEMENT SHOWING BY COUNTRIES THE QUANTITY, KINDS, AND TOTAL VALUE OF MANUFACTURES OF WOOL IMPORTED INTO AND EXPORTED FROM FRANCE IN 1885—Continued.

EXPORTS.

Countries from which exported.	Blankets.	Carpets.	Uphol-stery.	Merinos.	Cloths.	Stuffs. For up-holstery.	Stuffs. Other.
	Pounds.	*Pounds.*	*Pounds.*	*Pounds.*	*Pounds.*	*Pounds.*	*Pounds.*
Austria	53,898	259,765	8,045	12,324	107,406		
Belgium	15,742	44,189	4,592	237,486	1,973,587	89,855	743,964
Germany	29,683	74,083	1,069	29,220	767,176	55,609	375,245
Great Britain and Ireland	18,316			5,672,668	3,964,397	45,139	5,732,866
Greece	21,245	23,074		29,802	147,796		
Italy				223,271	541,655		1,276,809
Netherlands						21,364	125,180
Portugal					240,927		105,038
Spain		17,500		165,892	1,712,886		911,809
Switzerland	106,931	33,221		1,766	1,059,546		
Turkey	61,446	5,133		207,525	297,929		
Egypt	81,812			127,218	84,558		
Tunis		24,855			77,046		
Algeria	118,176	28,794		16,927	599,779		102,426
United States of America		8,673	3,148	34,929	436,182	90,632	1,732,549
Mexico					173,286		143,947
West Indies							69,622
Brazil	69,996			81,213	250,252		160,874
Uruguay	51,934			13,080	57,612		
Argentine Republic	85,345			79,758	1,330,659		228,183
Chili					81,096		74,022
Peru	15,134				98,497		
United States of Colombia					101,409		
Dutch East Indies					3,058		
British East Indies				17,511			
Japan				13,294			174,672
Australasia				6,572			56,169
Other countries	118,504	71,906	112	52,241	436,074	109,083	480,159
Total	848,102	591,188	16,966	7,022,697	14,548,813	401,682	12,493,334
Total value	$542,032	$414,041	$89,020	$6,086,313	$16,557,184	$316,485	$11,210,622

Countries from which exported.	Slippers of list.	Shawls.	Laces.	Hosiery.	Trimmings and ribbons.	Mixed stuffs. For up-holstery.	Mixed stuffs. Other.
	Pounds.	*Pounds.*	*Pounds.*	*Pounds.*	*Pounds.*	*Pounds.*	*Pounds.*
Austria				26,367			72,344
Belgium	7,108	32,610	97,443	134,873	81,136	128,793	742,349
Germany	9,125	15,115	25,966	204,163	138,453	1,993	614,825
Great Britain and Ireland		29,846	50,344	178,829	499,464	12,196	1,795,424
Italy		57,823		43,593	60,459		348,060
Netherlands							89,048
Portugal				17,950	14,332		152,844
Spain		64,696		70,909	105,197		753,865
Switzerland	13,757			103,409	22,476		242,662
Turkey				18,583	41,971		47,302
Egypt					17,306		23,063
Algeria		593		133,669			16,481
British North America							54,607
United States of America		105,805	124,095	126,678	154,683	43,236	2,311,291
Mexico		46,061		11,374			15,133
West Indies				67,778	24,187	641	141,222
Brazil	43,141	9,503		41,097			15,130
Uruguay				113,930	719,427		124,704
Argentine Republic		7,430		7,813			11,186
Chili				16,032			
Peru							2,293
Dutch East Indies							
Other countries	10,696	15,641	31,684	60,082	145,235	2,564	76,270
Total	83,830	385,123	329,532	1,378,029	2,024,326	189,423	7,651,092
Total value	$70,672	$876,599	$1,298,190	$2,412,770	$4,391,988	$291,860	$19,089,056

No. 27.—STATEMENT SHOWING BY COUNTRIES THE QUANTITY, KINDS, AND TOTAL VALUE OF MANUFACTURES OF WOOL IMPORTED INTO AND EXPORTED FROM FRANCE IN 1885—Continued.

EXPORTS—Continued.

Countries from which exported.	Tissues of goat's hair.	Other tissues of hair or mixed materials.	Yarns.	Felt.	Hats of felt and wool.
	Dollars.	Pounds.	Pounds.	Pounds.	Number.
Belgium			5,821,184	100,456	27,088
Germany	5,234		1,677,374	30,693	64,472
Great Britain and Ireland	50,425		2,736,299	111,392	124,574
Italy			280,264	37,906	7,114
Portugal					14,013
Spain			59,636	31,250	60,654
Switzerland			246,534		107,025
Turkey					16,180
Egypt				17,147	9,789
Tunis					9,616
Algeria				22,465	173,430
United States of America			3,822		31,854
Mexico					36,352
West Indies					230,598
Brazil					115,120
Uruguay					18,592
Argentine Republic	710				176,355
Chili					93,216
Peru					51,156
United States of Colombia					61,652
Other countries	531	a94,637	188,180	49,817	65,048
Total		94,637	11,013,293	410,126	1,506,907
Total value	56,900	a$25,845	b$10,872,899	$260,305	$1,146,871

a Of this; bolting cloths 6,453 pounds, value $8,474.
b Of this, $40,269 without specified quantities.

No. 28. — STATEMENT SHOWING THE QUANTITIES AND VALUES OF WOOL AND MANUFACTURES OF WOOL IMPORTED INTO AND EXPORTED FROM FRANCE FOR EACH YEAR FROM 1861 to 1885, INCLUSIVE.

[One kilogram equals 2.20462 pounds. One franc equals 19.3 cents.]

Years.	Imports.			Exports.			
	Wool, raw.		Value of wool manufactures.	Wool, raw.		Value of wool manufactures.	
	Quantity.	Value.		Quantity.	Value.	Yarn.	Other manufactures.
	Kilograms.	Francs.	Francs.	Kilograms.	Francs.	Francs.	Francs.
1861	55,359,000	166,100,000	20,600,000	6,448,000	21,000,000		188,000,000
1862	48,826,000	180,700,000	41,000,000	12,177,000	45,100,000	12,500,000	221,700,000
1863	63,792,000	218,600,000	33,400,000	11,006,000	48,200,000	15,200,000	293,600,000
1864	63,028,000	214,300,000	32,000,000	12,141,500	51,100,000	19,100,000	355,900,000
1865	72,663,000	236,200,000	38,100,000	7,913,000	33,000,000	21,200,000	302,800,000
1866	86,261,000	245,800,000	42,800,000	10,080,000	33,500,000	23,600,000	301,700,000
1867	93,205,000	223,700,000	42,100,000	13,611,683	43,200,000	30,800,000	236,800,000
1868	110,700,000	237,900,000	54,500,000	12,067,000	36,500,000	25,000,000	224,900,000
1869	108,600,000	206,300,000	64,300,000	17,147,000	44,700,000	27,800,000	268,300,000
1870	88,147,000	189,500,000	57,900,000	21,300,000	50,100,000	24,700,000	231,600,000
1871	101,958,000	193,700,000	76,500,000	29,881,000	75,300,000	40,600,000	254,400,000
1872	107,862,000	324,000,000	99,900,000	22,504,000	102,200,000	31,100,000	314,500,000
1873	120,545,000	325,600,000	59,700,000	19,445,000	86,600,000	31,300,000	325,900,000
1874	117,353,000	310,987,000	66,600,000	21,413,000	104,200,000	36,900,000	328,000,000
1875	128,010,000	326,522,000	78,100,000	21,617,000	84,100,000	39,720,000	346,400,000
1876	123,178,000	277,200,000	79,000,000	21,077,000	74,800,000	28,600,000	316,500,000
1877	134,235,000	315,500,000	68,000,000	21,443,000	77,100,000	26,800,000	325,100,000
1878	144,100,000	334,017,000	68,700,000	27,072,000	89,725,000	37,200,000	312,800,000
1879	134,214,000	288,728,000	63,170,000	34,996,000	117,222,000	43,692,000	309,297,000
1880	151,067,000	370,224,000	79,100,000	35,062,000	132,450,000	49,300,000	370,200,000
1881	138,332,000	304,333,000	76,991,000	29,470,000	105,618,000	38,147,000	360,717,000
1882	140,983,000	303,126,000	84,200,000	29,555,000	95,360,000	39,849,000	401,900,000
1883	157,112,000	330,087,000	91,858,000	31,448,000	95,139,000	34,602,000	370,106,000
1884	165,956,000	332,105,000	88,799,000	32,917,000	95,999,000	32,337,000	334,291,000
1885	172,446,627	283,897,043	99,529,962	36,980,833	90,832,927	35,398,776	336,118,938

No. 29.— STATEMENT SHOWING, BY COUNTRIES, THE QUANTITIES OF IMPORTED WOOL ENTERED FOR CONSUMPTION IN FRANCE, AND THE TOTAL VALUE AND AMOUNT OF DUTY COLLECTED, FOR EACH YEAR FROM 1820 TO 1840, INCLUSIVE.

[From Macgregor's Commercial Statistics, Vol. I.]

Years	Quantities imported from—					Total.	Value.	Duty collected.
	Belgium.	Spain.	Germany.	The United States, Barbary and Algiers	Other countries.			
	Kilograms.	*Kilograms.*	*Kilograms.*	*Kilograms.*	*Kilograms.*	*Kilograms.*	*Francs.*	*Francs.*
1820..	178,000	1,531,000	165,000	1,513,000	1,493,000	4,912,000	8,351,000	297,000
1821..	967,000	1,782,000	508,000	862,000	2,758,000	6,877,000	11,690,000	935,000
1822..	964,000	1,922,000	565,000	3,608,000	1,989,000	9,118,000	15,500,000	1,430,000
1823..	815,000	822,000	347,000	2,244,000	1,251,000	5,482,000	9,319,000	1,341,000
1824..	1,316,000	882,000	566,000	778,000	868,000	4,410,000	7,497,000	2,602,000
1825..	942,000	1,200,000	778,000	909,000	804,000	4,639,000	7,880,000	8,100,000
1826..	1,486,000	1,772,000	858,000	1,581,000	732,000	6,435,000	10,940,000	3,147,000
1827..	1,437,000	1,932,000	829,000	1,977,000	1,207,000	7,382,000	11,131,000	3,67,000
1828..	1,32,000	2,148,000	1,104,000	1,507,000	1,516,000	7,687,000	13,391,000	4,417,000
1829..	930,000	1,820,000	809,000	1,224,000	066,000	5,749,000	9,276,000	3,030,000
1830..	929,000	2,276,000	1,064,000	1,705,000	1,240,000	7,214,000	12,872,000	4,246,000
1831..	549,000	826,000	157,000	1,740,000	524,000	3,850,000	5,253,000	1,733,000
1832..	1,398,000	1,202,000	178,000	984,000	870,000	4,622,000	7,862,000	2,504,000
1833..	1,715,000	3,220,000	540,000	2,140,000	1,682,000	9,306,000	19,140,000	6,314,000
1834..	1,219,000	2,637,000	654,000	3,271,000	1,440,000	9,221,000	17,915,000	4,752,000
1835..	2,221,000	3,818,000	1,719,000	4,660,000	2,427,000	14,845,000	34,219,000	7,550,000
1836..	2,691,000	4,365,000	1,420,000	3,676,000	2,014,000	14,166,000	31,891,000	7,116,000
1837..	2,126,000	3,290,000	1,011,000	1,941,000	1,632,000	10,000,000	18,997,000	4,220,000
1838..	3,637,000	3,557,000	2,609,000	3,030,000	2,093,000	14,926,000	34,178,000	7,554,000
1839..	3,035,000	3,676,000	1,946,000	2,746,000	2,209,000	13,612,000	31,937,000	7,069,000
1840..	2,983,000	2,993,000	2,407,000	3,395,000	2,278,000	13,456,000	29,987,000	6,643,000

No. 30.—STATEMENT SHOWING THE QUANTITIES AND VALUES OF DOMESTIC WOOLEN YARNS AND CLOTHS EXPORTED FROM FRANCE, WITH THE AMOUNTS OF PREMIUMS PAID, FOR EACH YEAR FROM 1820 TO 1840, INCLUSIVE.

[From Macgregor's Commercial Statistics, Vol. I.]

Years.	Yarns.		Cloths, kerseymeres, merinoes, &c.		Premiums paid.
	Quantity.	Value.	Quantity.	Value.	
	Kilograms.	*Francs.*	*Kilograms.*	*Francs.*	*Francs.*
1820	36,000	647,000	1,458,000	42,737,000	48,000
1821	31,000	540,000	1,339,000	39,211,000	485,000
1822	20,000	372,000	1,082,000	40,156,000	413,000
1823	15,000	274,000	1,003,000	32,808,000	439,000
1824	17,000	320,000	1,124,000	36,117,000	1,336,000
1825	16,000	281,000	1,167,000	37,540,000	3,058,000
1826	17,000	306,000	966,000	29,542,000	1,892,000
1827	23,000	441,000	1,006,000	26,928,000	2,110,000
1828	28,000	520,000	1,031,000	29,508,000	2,022,000
1829	64,000	1,181,000	1,133,000	30,425,000	2,330,000
1830	58,000	1,005,000	971,000	26,625,000	1,974,000
1831	57,000	1,071,000	993,000	27,018,000	2,497,000
1832	119,000	2,255,000	1,349,000	34,052,000	2,082,000
1833	76,000	1,435,000	1,471,000	36,663,000	3,644,000
1834	74,000	2,392,000	1,542,000	39,446,000	4,125,000
1835	44,000	808,000	1,577,000	38,366,000	3,085,000
1836	33,000	993,000	2,018,000	49,188,000	3,736,000
1837	84,000	1,504,000	1,670,000	43,428,000	2,025,000
1838	79,000	1,485,000	2,298,000	64,401,000	4,061,000
1839	71,000	1,351,000	2,201,000	60,588,000	3,883,000
1840	107,000	1,996,000	2,325,000	61,100,000	3,897,000

No. 31.—STATEMEENT SHOWING, BY COUNTRIES, THE VALUE OF DOMESTIC WOOLEN CLOTHS EXPORTED FROM FRANCE DURING THE YEARS 1833 AND 1840.

[From Macgregor's Commercial Statistics, Vol. I.]

Countries of destination.	1833.	1840.
	Francs.	*Francs.*
United States	6,207,000	12,634,000
Spain	5,239,000	7,675,000
Sardinian States	4,093,000	5,943,000
Belgium	2,062,000	5,070,000
England	1,650,000	5,001,000
Turkey and China	4,819,000	3,899,000
Switzerland	3,093,000	3,752,000
Germany	1,390,000	2,906,000
Chili	281,000	2,384,000
French colonies	771,000	1,456,000
Algiers and Africa, comprising 19,000 francs in 1838 and 94,000 francs in 1840, exported to Mauritius	683,000	1,447,000
Tuscany and Roman States	506,000	1,192,000
States of Barbary	1,115,000	962,000
Holland	243,000	892,000
Buenos Ayres	169,000	720,000
Brazil	378,000	642,000
Mexico	279,000	493,000
Naples and Sicily	621,000	464,000
Prussia	104,000	423,000
Russia	171,000	422,000
Egypt	1,017,000	380,000
Antilles, foreign	84,000	339,000
Peru	971,000	322,000
Austria	128,000	199,000
Colombia	24,000	109,000
Hayti	150,000	101,000
Foreign India	46,000	85,000
Sweden and Norway	69,000	5,000
Other countries	200,000	1,183,000
Total	36,563,000	61,100,000

No. 32.—STATEMENT SHOWING, BY COUNTRIES, THE QUANTITIES OF MANUFACTURES OF WOOL IMPORTED INTO AND EXPORTED FROM GERMANY IN 1845.

Countries from which imported and to which exported.	Woolen wadding.		Woolen yarns of all kinds.		Listing.	
	Imports.	Exports.	Imports.	Exports.	Imports.	Exports.
	Pounds.	*Pounds.*	*Pounds.*	*Pounds.*	*Pounds.*	*Pounds.*
Austria-Hungary		220	2,275,809	3,209,417	41,447	72,972
Bremen (free port)				221,502	441	
Hamburg (free port)		441	1,358,455	1,731,715	2,425	5,730
Belgium			7,539,692	22,707		5,071
Denmark				130,733		3,307
France	220		2,562,898	689,619	4,850	46,076
Great Britain	441		27,052,627	346,343		11,214
Italy				86,420		5,723
Netherlands		3,527	8,157	260,808		10,141
Russia		1,102		4,031,552	3,307	15,873
Spain				48,722		
Sweden and Norway				748,684		13,889
Switzerland	2,425	1,102	1,569,655	415,560	1,323	29,101
Turkey				1,102		9,480
United States of America				216,933		
All other countries			244,550	358,959		6,834
Total	3,086	6,392	42,612,293	12,520,845	53,793	235,450

No. 32—Statement showing, by Countries, the Quantities of Manufactures of Wool Imported into and Exported from Germany in 1885—Continued.

Countries from which imported and to which exported.	Coarse felts.		Rugs and felts, printed, &c.		Hosiery.	
	Imports.	Exports.	Imports.	Exports.	Imports.	Exports.
	Pounds.	Pounds.	Pounds.	Pounds.	Pounds.	Pounds.
Austria-Hungary	26,455	104,719	74,956	378,969	20,728	358,092
Bremen (free port)	441	21,385	5,732	103,175	12,346	150,798
Hamburg (free port)	39,242	193,343	45,633	629,415	42,108	1,545,184
Belgium		9,480	38,951	236,758	3,748	158,511
Denmark	1,102	21,605		109,567	2,425	80,247
France		061	63,933	349,429	58,861	683,562
Great Britain	25,794	169,313	274,693	95,018	30,644	1,184,754
Italy		22,928		180,336		134,260
Netherlands		23,810	22,471	199,075	7,275	510,026
Russia	657,187	26,676	3,968	130,733	2,646	7,716
Spain				72,531		177,911
Sweden and Norway		26,235		88,184		259,044
Switzerland	5,291	20,002	5,291	240,522	9,700	256,619
Turkey				22,707		
Egypt				1,102		
United States of America						101,412
Mexico and Central American States				4,850		
West Indies				8,818		
Argentine Republic				46,076		62,170
Brazil				32,408		
Other South America				6,173		
Asia			14,330	14,550		
All other countries	10,362	10,362	11,905	102,097	4,630	393,373
Total	765,874	650,579	580,672	3,030,684	195,106	6,073,874

Countries from which imported and to which exported.	Cloths and dress-goods.		Woolen plush.		Woolen fringes and button materials.		Laces, tulles, embroideries, and woven shawls.	
	Imports.	Exports.	Imports.	Exports.	Imports.	Exports.	Imports.	Exports.
	Pounds.	Pounds.	Pounds.	Pounds.	Pounds.	Pounds.	Pounds.	Pounds.
Austria-Hungary	154,322	3,578,547	4,628	254,194	1,764	175,045	8,157	153,219
Bremen (free port)	7,055	1,352,967	882	425,504	220	36,597	220	6,393
Hamburg (free port)	324,513	10,911,407	7,497	180,557	3,086	427,268	3,748	463,190
Belgium	135,5·3	1,252,213	3,527	50,706	882	127,867	3,307	33,286
Denmark	2,425	1,875,654	1,323	43,651	441	69,8·6		39,242
France	551,811	2,242,960	12,346	381,614	12,125	170,455	116,182	100,750
Great Britain	1,572,545	3,518,564	19,621	316,577	5,071	984,791	2,425	751,085
Italy		2,759,698		36,506	220	93,053		53,351
Netherlands	81,129	2,407,423	5,732	136,905	2,425	244,935		304,016
Portugal						77,822		
Russia		703,712	1,323	71,429	1,323	40,505		90,389
Spain		30,424				114,859		69,666
Sweden and Norway		1,994,281		31,084		112,436		7,037
Switzerland	46,736	3,145,263	1,102	30,203	882	118,208	2,646	120,501
Turkey		15,658						25,794
Egypt								10,362
United States of America		3,431,460		92,986		302,694		15,212
All other countries	61,971	3,018,389	661	52,237		146,386	3,307	91,710
Total	2,938,090	42,268,615	58,642	2,110,243	28,439	3,242,927	139,902	2,337,096

No. 33.—STATEMENT SHOWING THE QUANTITIES AND VALUES OF WOOL AND MANU-
FACTURES OF WOOL IMPORTED INTO AND EXPORTED FROM GERMANY FOR EACH
YEAR FROM 1875 to 1884, INCLUSIVE.

IMPORTS.

[One kilogram equals 2.20462 pounds. One mark equals 23.8 cents.]

Year.	Wool, raw.		Manufactures of wool.			
			Woolen yarn.		Cloth.	
	Quantities.	Values.	Quantities.	Values.	Quantities.	Values.
	100 *kilogs.*	*Marks.*	100 *kilogs.*	*Marks.*	100 *kilogs.*	*Marks.*
1875	565, 000	203, 000, 000	163, 000	103, 000, 000	70, 338	80, 350, 000
1876	650, 000	208, 000, 000	152, 000	89, 200, 000	67, 299	74, 430, 000
1877	685, 000	212, 000, 000	136, 000	74, 900, 000	57, 237	60, 352, 000
1878	680, 000	211, 000, 000	152, 000	79, 800, 000	50, 000	49, 000, 000
1879	925, 000	268, 000, 000	187, 000	94, 800, 000	69, 750	66, 204, 000
1880	677, 500	206, 267, 000	149, 000	93, 110, 000	23, 350	21, 339, 000
1881	773, 700	193, 430, 000	157, 000	84, 988, 000	21, 300	19, 972, 000
1882	885, 000	203, 555, 000	161, 000	83, 584, 000	14, 800	14, 342, 000
1883	909, 693	200, 133, 000	167, 000	80, 479, 000	12, 918	12, 439, 000
1884	1, 056, 602	221, 899, 000	190, 000	93, 396, 000	12, 722	11, 882, 000

EXPORTS.

Year.	Wool, raw.		Manufactures of wool.				Total value manufactures.
			Woolen yarn.		Other manufactures.		
	Quantities.	Values.	Quantities.	Values.	Quantities.	Values.	
	100 *kilogs.*	*Marks.*	100 *kilogs.*	*Marks.*	100 *kilogs.*	*Marks.*	*Marks.*
1875	199, 500		38, 700	29, 400, 000	129, 000		29, 400, 000
1876	199, 000		33, 700	23, 600, 000	117, 150		23, 600, 000
1877	222, 500		41, 400	27, 300, 000	169, 300		27, 300, 000
1878	213, 000		50, 500	30, 300, 000	124, 800		30, 300, 000
1879	225, 000		42, 000	24, 400, 000	123, 300		24, 400, 000
1880	143, 250	50, 139, 900	50, 000	32, 648, 000	167, 150	171, 161, 000	203, 809, 000
1881	120, 850	48, 340, 000	45, 000	29, 599, 000	184, 200	187, 086, 000	216, 685, 000
1882	134, 500	49, 698, 000	50, 000	34, 027, 000	192, 500	177, 579, 000	211, 606, 000
1883	127, 216	45, 796, 000	48, 000	30, 693, 000	198, 622	180, 146, 000	210, 839, 000
1884	113, 140	39, 316, 000	52, 000	32, 130, 000	214, 100	185, 102, 000	217, 232, 000

No. 34.—STATEMENT SHOWING, BY COUNTRIES, THE QUANTITIES OF MANUFACTURES
OF WOOL, AND THEIR TOTAL VALUES, IMPORTED INTO AND EXPORTED FROM ITALY
IN 1885.

Countries from which imported and to which exported.	Yarns.		Tissues of wool and mixed materials.		Felt.	
	Imports.	Exports.	Imports.	Exports.	Imports.	Exports.
	Pounds.	*Pounds.*	*Pounds.*	*Pounds.*	*Pounds.*	*Pounds.*
Austria-Hungary	65, 017	10, 141	1, 378, 316	96, 341	36, 817	5, 291
Belgium	26, 235		119, 269			
France	260, 363	73, 854	4, 430, 623	36, 596	111, 993	1, 102
Germany	127, 426	4, 850	1, 769, 192	4, 850	93, 475	
Great Britain and Ireland	131, 615		5, 254, 632	1, 543	287, 480	
Greece and Malta			1, 543	9, 921		
Switzerland	78, 484	13, 448	304, 896	48, 501	7, 937	1, 543
Turkey				25, 573		
Egypt				3, 307		
Tunis and Tripoli		2, 205	2, 205	2, 425		
United States of America and Canada.		13, 608		26, 014		

No. 34.—STATEMENT SHOWING, BY COUNTRIES, THE QUANTITIES OF MANUFACTURES OF WOOL, AND THEIR TOTAL VALUES, IMPORTED INTO AND EXPORTED FROM ITALY IN 1885.

Countries from which imported and to which exported.	Yarn.		Tissues of wool and mixed materials.		Felt.	
	Imports.	Exports.	Imports.	Exports.	Imports.	Exports.
	Pounds.	*Pounds.*	*Pounds.*	*Pounds.*	*Pounds.*	*Pounds.*
Argentine Republic				19,180		
Uruguay				11,164		
Paraguay				4,189		
Other countries		5,291	11,023	7,055		
Total	690,040	123,437	13,284,690	296,959	537,702	7,936
Total value	$472,543	$37,504	$10,311,125	$195,482	$154,338	$3,698

Countries from which imported and to which exported.	Woolen knitted goods and braids.		Ribbons and galloons.	Button materials.		Laces and tulles.
	Imports.	Exports.	Imports.	Imports.	Exports.	Imports.
	Pounds.	*Pounds.*	*Pounds.*	*Pounds.*	*Pounds.*	*Pounds.*
Austria-Hungary	23,369	27,998	1,543			3,527
France	47,840	3,086	3,307	1,102		52,029
Germany	47,840		2,424			14,771
Great Britain and Ireland	6,393	882				5,291
Greece and Malta		1,764				
Switzerland	14,330	5,512	882			10,802
Turkey		9,039				
Egypt		9,700				
Tunis and Tripoli		1,102				
United States of America and Canada		8,818				
Argentine Republic		13,226				
Uruguay		7,275				
Paraguay		2,425				
Other countries					*a*221	
Total	139,772	90,829	8,137	1,102	221	86,420
Total value	$195,779	$127,226	$9,283	$807	$179	$325,321

Countries from which imported and to which exported.	Covers made of list.		Carpets.		Wearing apparel.	
	Imports.	Exports.	Imports.	Exports.	Imports.	Exports.
	Pounds.	*Pounds.*	*Pounds.*	*Pounds.*	*Pounds.*	*Pounds.*
Austria-Hungary	2,205	882	40,505	0,834	176,148	
Belgium			3,527			
France	8,818		207,894	87,964	282,850	29,542
Germany			94,798		153,220	
Great Britain and Ireland	12,787		402,559	882	199,510	2,205
Greece and Malta						1,102
Switzerland	3,748	1,764	28,219	13,448	45,635	3,096
Turkey			8,598		2,425	21,385
Egypt						27,337
Tunis and Tripoli						4,189
United States of America and Canada		1,984		2,866	882	5,511
Argentine Republic		1,763				13,448
Uruguay						19,400
Paraguay						3,527
Peru						5,732
Other countries				3,527		7,055
Total	27,558	6,393	786,160	115,521	860,670	143,519
Total value	$6,096	$1,623	$317,493	$35,124	$1,431,597	$238,722

a Spain and Gibraltar.

No. 35.—STATEMENT SHOWING THE QUANTITIES AND VALUES OF WOOL AND MANUFACTURES OF WOOL IMPORTED INTO ITALY FOR EACH YEAR FROM 1874 TO 1884, INCLUSIVE.

[One kilogram equals 2.20462 pounds. One lire equals 19.3 cents.]

Year.	Wool, raw.		Manufactures of pure wool.		Manufactures of wool mixed with cotton.	
	Quantities.	Values.	Quantities.	Value.	Quantities.	Values.
	Kilograms.	*Lire.*	*Quintals.*	*Lire.*	*Quintals.*	*Lire.*
1874	6,051,000	27,232,000	a42,012	41,471,000	b	
1875	6,500,000	27,952,000	a50,088	45,962,000	b	
1876	8,065,000	34,681,000	a50,072	45,197,000	b	
1877	8,010,000	34,445,000	a46,748	41,982,000	b	
1878	6,539,000	28,116,000	a39,987.	51,983,000	b	
1879	8,530,000	34,155,000	21,607	29,737,000	12,717	12,112,000
1880	7,328,000	30,780,000	23,922	33,895,000	16,139	14,760,000
1881	9,536,000	38,143,000	36,701	43,331,000	19,499	15,017,000
1882	7,508,000	30,034,000	31,642	37,890,000	15,237	12,101,000
1883	9,540,000	31,974,000	36,398	41,730,000	16,036	12,038,000
1884	10,071,000	29,416,000	42,467	45,120,000	19,023	12,915,000

a Includes manufactures of wool and cotton.   b Included in manufacture of pure wool.

No. 36.—STATEMENT SHOWING, BY COUNTRIES, THE QUANTITIES AND VALUES OF MANUFACTURES OF WOOL IMPORTED INTO AND EXPORTED FROM THE NETHERLANDS IN 1883.

Countries from which imported and to which exported.	Yarns.		Felt for hats, for hats of all kinds.		Cloth, doeskins, and cassimeres.	
	Imports.	Exports.	Imports.	Exports.	Imports.	Exports.
	Dollars.	*Dollars.*	*Dollars.*	*Dollars.*	*Dollars.*	*Dollars.*
Denmark					40	11,976
Belgium	83,952	30,131	79,554	5,525	238,389	47,256
France		2,641	772		16	
Germany	175,004	3,687,263	223,994	11,404	549,726	67,800
Hamburg	652				786	
Great Britain and Ireland	4,543,765	53,184	87,222	287	274,692	10,510
Norway		1,111			442	
Russia					16	
Sweden		1,164			3	
Java		267,311	217	3,123	10	9,568
Curaçoa						64
All other countries	289			2,703	60	
Total	4,803,662	4,042,805	391,759	23,042	1,064,180	147,174

Countries from which imported and to which exported.	All other stuffs not elsewhere specified.			Blankets.		
	Imports.	Exports.		Imports.	Exports.	
	Dollars.	*Pounds.*	*Dollars.*	*Dollars.*	*Pounds.*	*Dollars.*
Denmark	489	141,557	258,125			
Belgium	1,005,267	68,738	125,339	1,483	1,376	1,003
France		1,338	2,440			
Germany	633,183	200,398	365,419	8,865	1,160	846
Hamburg	184	59,098	107,764			
Great Britain and Ireland	925,062	86,501	157,841	7,502	3,215	2,344
Norway	2	127,077	231,721			
Russia	8					
Sweden		52,203	95,189			
United States of America	9				452	330
Dutch Guiana		18,689	34,078			
Java		33,647	61,853		1,607	1,216
Curaçoa	2					
All other countries	3	331	603	1	132	96
Total	2,564,208	789,637	1,439,872	12,851	8,002	5,855

No. 36.—Statement showing, by Countries, the Quantities and Values of Manufactures of Wool Imported into and Exported from the Netherlands in 1883—Continued.

Countries from which imported and to which exported.	Flannels and baize.			Hosiery.			Tape.
	Imports.	Exports.		Imports.	Exports.		Imports.
	Dollars.	Pounds.	Dollars.	Dollars.	Pounds.	Dollars.	Dollars.
Belgium	1,848	678,487	494,788	132,445	2,400	1,570	476
France				12			
Germany	26,742	6,302	4,506	329,481	15,695	10,015	33,190
Great Britain and Ireland	4,649			43,413			2,904
Dutch Guiana		772	563				
Java		3,695	2,693		243	155	
Total	33,239	689,250	502,640	505,351	18,398	11,740	36,570

No. 37.—Statement showing the Quantities and Values of Wool and Manufactures of Wool Imported into and Exported from the Netherlands for each year from 1874 to 1884, inclusive.

[One kilogram equals 2.20462 pounds. One gulden equals 39.7 cents.]

Year.	Imports.				Exports.			
	Wool, raw.		Value of wool manufactures.		Wool, raw.		Value of wool manufactures.	
	Quantities.	Values.	Yarn.	Other manufactures.	Quantities.	Values.	Yarn.	Other manufactures.
	Kilos.	Gulden.	Gulden.	Gulden.	Kilos.	Gulden.	Gulden.	Gulden.
1874	8,007,000	9,608,000	17,436,000	11,604,000	6,835,000	8,201,000	10,936,000	4,503,000
1875	8,951,000	10,742,000	14,493,000	11,653,000	7,520,000	9,024,000	9,477,000	4,520,000
1876	10,744,000	10,430,000	14,490,000	11,325,000	8,869,000	10,406,000	10,572,000	4,268,000
1877	9,783,000	8,363,000	12,521,000	11,480,000	7,760,000	7,543,000	5,601,000	4,296,000
1878	8,562,000	8,116,000	13,012,000	10,855,000	7,616,000	7,060,000	6,488,000	4,581,000
1879	9,114,000	8,872,000	15,549,000	10,037,000	7,525,000	7,344,000	7,116,000	3,754,000
1880	9,698,000	8,730,000	10,810,000	10,284,000	9,239,000	9,125,000	6,085,000	5,882,000
1881	11,453,000	11,050,000	12,000,000	10,014,000	8,911,000	10,197,000	6,640,000	5,634,000
1882	11,912,000	11,888,000	13,423,000	9,943,000	8,462,000	9,475,000	8,151,000	5,601,000
1883	16,059,000	17,007,000	11,903,000	9,140,000	12,465,000	14,710,000	9,258,000	5,213,000
1884	20,172,000	21,555,000	12,814,000	7,842,000	17,203,000	20,495,000	7,120,000	4,913,000

No. 38.—Statement showing the Quantities and Values of Wool and Manufactures of Wool Imported into Norway for each year from 1874 to 1884, inclusive.

[One kilogram equals 2.20462 pounds. One krone equals 26.8 cents.]

Year.	Wool, raw.		Manufactures of wool.	
	Quantities.	Values.	Quantities.	Values.
	Kilograms.	Kroner.	Kilograms.	Kroner.
1874		1,014,000		14,488,000
1875	367,000	1,018,000	1,171,000	12,713,000
1876	303,000	1,002,000	962,000	9,465,000
1877	425,000	1,221,000	1,244,000	11,038,000
1878	270,000	767,000	986,000	8,324,000
1879	240,000	632,000	902,000	7,370,000
1880	360,000	1,080,000	1,140,000	10,482,000
1881	440,000	1,171,000	1,273,000	11,340,000
1882	415,000	1,107,000	1,362,000	12,860,000
1883	433,000	1,149,000	1,380,000	10,871,000
1884	455,000	1,136,000	1,483,000	11,734,000

No. 39.—STATEMENT SHOWING THE QUANTITIES AND VALUES OF WOOL AND MANU-FACTURES OF WOOL IMPORTED INTO AND EXPORTED FROM PORTUGAL FOR EACH YEAR FROM 1874 TO 1884, INCLUSIVE.

[One kilogram equals 2.20462 pounds. One milreis equals $1.08.]

Year.	Imports.				Exports.	
	Wool, raw.		Manufactures of wool.		Wool, raw.	
	Quantities.	Values.	Quantities.	Values.	Quantities.	Values.
	Kilograms.	*Milreis.*	*Kilograms.*	*Milreis.*	*Kilograms.*	*Milreis.*
1874	1,902,000	671,000	632,000	1,654,000	652,400	217,000
1875	2,024,000	836,000	806,000	2,148,000	728,800	224,900
1876	1,559,000	601,000	678,000	1,797,000	752,400	201,500
1877	1,629,000	814,000	728,000	1,853,000	987,600	251,000
1878	2,538,000	763,300	615,000	1,410,000	879,600	222,400
1879	2,092,000	582,000	461,000	1,038,000	722,300	167,100
1880	2,333,000	610,000	493,000	1,188,000	1,211,700	381,200
1881	2,889,000	778,000	556,000	1,496,000	609,000	198,000
1882	2,447,000	621,000	543,000	1,350,000	767,000	221,000
1883	2,743,000	686,000	735,000	1,479,000	800,000	203,000
1884	2,875,000	758,000	707,000	1,564,000	582,000	134,000

No. 40.—STATEMENT SHOWING THE QUANTITIES AND VALUES OF WOOL AND MANU-FACTURES OF WOOL IMPORTED INTO AND EXPORTED FROM RUSSIA IN EUROPE FOR EACH YEAR FROM 1874 TO 1884, INCLUSIVE.

[One pood equals 36.0676 pounds. One silver rouble equals 58.2 cents.]

Years.	Imports.		Value of wool manufactures	Exports.	
	Wool, raw.			Wool, raw.	
	Quantities.	Values.		Quantities.	Values.
	Poods.	*Silver roubles.*	*Silver roubles.*	*Poods.*	*Silver roubles.*
1874	536,057	16,468,323	13,329,402	1,053,036	11,357,254
1875	648,532	19,775,260	10,120,057	879,598	8,648,636
1876	443,367	12,725,406	12,635,500	1,179,688	11,954,458
1877	355,182	11,526,607	6,536,367	1,339,682	22,374,598
1878	794,561	24,487,205	10,536,940	1,093,939	11,961,230
1879	979,127	29,694,183	12,321,290	953,468	10,937,206
1880	821,754	24,405,000	12,103,000	1,441,466	13,659,000
1881	747,658	24,052,000	7,711,000	1,015,862	11,189,400
1882	807,916	28,717,000	8,964,000	1,208,984	12,323,000
1883	610,000	22,431,000	6,520,000	(a)	(a)
1884	503,000	18,607,000	5,467,000	(a)	(a)

a No data.

No. 41.—STATEMENT SHOWING, BY COUNTRIES, THE QUANTITIES, AND THEIR TOTAL VALUES, OF MANUFACTURES OF WOOL IMPORTED INTO AND EXPORTED FROM SPAIN IN 1885.

IMPORTS.

Countries from which imported.	Yarns.	Carpets.	Felts.	Blankets.	Hosiery.	Cloths.	Tissues.
	Pounds.	*Pounds.*	*Pounds.*	*Pounds.*	*Pounds.*	*Pounds.*	*Pounds.*
Austria-Hungary				38	432	3,817	27,630
Belgium	8,757	8,199	167		189	72,306	70,140
France	145,217	57,192	90,292	9,058	211,792	514,192	1,957,043
Germany	42,152	38,534	37,055	858	276,408	231,324	443,709
Great Britain	8,944	605,381	333,433	8,362	26,607	69,183	67,582
Portugal	584	708	167	71	454	20	868
Switzerland	123		756		3,224	114	14,950
Other countries		414	33	24	44	22	73
Total	200,777	710,428	461,903	18,391	519,150	890,978	2,581,995
Total value	$173,780	$236,337	$131,422	$12,695	$727,281	$1,191,208	$3,306,722

No. 41.—STATEMENT SHOWING, BY COUNTIES, THE QUANTITIES, AND THEIR TOTAL VALUES, OF MANUFACTURES OF WOOL IMPORTED INTO AND EXPORTED FROM SPAIN IN 1885—Continued.

EXPORTS.

Countries to which exported.	Yarns.	Blankets.	Hosiery.	Cloth.	Flannels.
	Pounds.	*Pounds.*	*Pounds.*	*Pounds.*	*Pounds.*
France	362	223	1,157	12,341	7,767
Germany			57		128
Great Britain and Ireland	1,517	1,982		357	1,230
Portugal		225	5	18,675	7,842
Canary Islands			388	1,883	6,585
Ceuta					40
Mexico					1,001
Cuba	476	1,021	84	13,975	13,245
Porto Rico		1,065	77	2,485	6,638
Argentine Republic		2,608			5,778
Uruguay		185		1,545	3,318
United States of Colombia			57	900	701
Philippine Islands		1,371	66	917	4,286
Total	2,355	8,680	1,891	53,174	58,649
Total value	$1,443	$6,079	$2,649	$92,339	$64,360

No. 42.—STATEMENT SHOWING THE QUANTITIES AND VALUES OF WOOL AND MANUFACTURES OF WOOL IMPORTED INTO AND EXPORTED FROM SPAIN FOR EACH YEAR FROM 1874 TO 1884, INCLUSIVE.

[One kilogram equals 2.20462 pounds. One peseta equals 19.3 cents.]

Year.	Imports.		Exports.	
	Manufactures of wool.		Wool, raw.	
	Quantities.	Values.	Quantities.	Values.
	Kilograms.	*Pesetas.*	*Kilograms.*	*Pesetas.*
1874	995,000	10,193,000	1,960,000	3,995,000
1875	794,000	9,948,000	4,225,000	8,141,000
1876	1,363,000	18,938,000	1,831,000	3,460,000
1877	1,521,000	18,965,000	4,044,000	7,529,000
1878	1,833,445	26,536,000	3,581,000	5,917,000
1879	1,810,000	22,812,000	3,840,000	6,148,000
1880	1,818,000	23,107,000	6,242,000	11,762,000
1881	2,081,000	26,454,000	3,877,000	6,472,000
1882	2,262,000	29,831,000	2,677,000	5,903,000
1883	2,096,000	26,643,000	3,931,000	8,011,000
1884	2,354,000	30,858,000	3,637,000	7,485,000

No. 43.—STATEMENT SHOWING THE QUANTITIES AND VALUES OF WOOL AND MANUFACTURES OF WOOL IMPORTED INTO SPAIN FOR EACH YEAR FROM 1873 TO 1883, INCLUSIVE.

[One kilogram equals 2.20462 pounds. One krona equals 26.8 cents.]

Year.	Wool, raw.		Manufactures of wool.				Total values.
			Woolen yarn.		Other manufactures.		
	Quantities.	Values.	Quantities.	Values.	Quantities.	Values.	
	Kilograms.	*Kronor.*	*Kilograms.*	*Kronor.*	*Kilograms.*	*Kronor.*	*Kronor.*
1873	1,691,724	5,969,000	490,803	4,303,000	1,672,545	16,858,000	21,101,000
1874	1,579,551	5,573,000	580,118	3,110,000	2,038,938	20,610,000	23,720,000
1875	1,394,515	4,592,000	517,776	3,647,000	1,568,548	15,760,000	19,407,000
1876	1,861,739	6,569,000	607,264	8,942,000	1,750,746	17,539,000	26,481,000
1877	1,848,788	6,876,000	603,196	3,128,000	1,980,543	19,887,000	23,015,000
1878	857,170	2,520,000	489,343	2,597,000	1,360,807	13,655,000	16,252,000
1879	911,053	2,670,000	547,194	2,635,000	1,280,993	12,883,000	15,538,000
1880	1,286,888	3,784,000	551,530	2,836,000	2,016,103	20,653,000	23,489,000
1881	1,620,327	4,861,000	635,582	2,463,000	2,163,024	21,093,000	23,556,000
1882	1,567,946	4,705,000	801,834	3,084,000	2,088,075	20,277,000	23,361,000
1883	1,840,733	5,524,000	918,461	3,423,000	2,353,616	23,196,000	26,619,000

No. 44.—Statement showing, by Countries, the Quantities and Values of Manufactures of Wool Imported into and Exported from Switzerland in 1885.

Countries from which imported and to which exported.	Wadding.				Yarns of all kinds.			
	Imports.		Exports.		Imports.		Exports.	
	Pounds.	Dollars.	Pounds.	Dollars.	Pounds.	Dollars.	Pounds.	Dollars.
Germany	6,173	1,621	441	139	572,955	487,711	1,447,139	1,100,611
Austria-Hungary			(*)	2	1,984	1,631	189,154	130,056
France	441	116	221	20	188,714	158,974	6,834	4,664
Italy					1,764	1,544	143,520	86,848
Belgium	221	58		5	231,302	197,294	2,866	1,668
Netherlands					11,023	9,544	441	286
Great Britain and Ireland					271,647	229,824	37,037	32,762
Denmark							882	978
Turkey in Europe							(*)	5
Algiers							(*)	141
Turkey, Asiatic							(*)	19
Total	6,835	1,795	662	226	1,279,389	1,086,522	1,827,873	1,358,038

Countries from which imported and to which exported.	Listing.				Tissues.			
	Imports.		Exports.		Imports.		Exports.	
	Pounds.	Dollars.	Pounds.	Dollars.	Pounds.	Dollars.	Pounds.	Dollars.
Germany	30,644	5,365	1,323	54	3,028,459	3,627,975	31,967	33,811
Austria-Hungary	661	116	221	355	21,605	25,515	5,952	6,105
France	11,905	2,084	221	20	1,179,682	1,408,012	73,193	81,403
Italy	23,148	4,053	221	154	29,542	36,207	31,305	33,188
Belgium	221	39			111,773	136,605	2,425	1,941
Netherlands					20,262	24,858	441	489
Great Britain and Ireland	1,102	193			1,121,260	1,371,149	2,425	3,144
Russia							1,323	1,347
Sweden and Norway							6,614	6,285
Denmark							2,866	3,284
Portugal								5
Spain							1,543	3,278
Greece							661	1,698
Danubian countries							2,205	1,900
Turkey in Europe							661	811
Egypt							2,205	3,477
Algiers							4,409	6,167
Other Africa							221	483
Turkey, Asiatic							1,102	1,830
British East Indies							221	550
Dutch East Indies							882	1,428
China, Japan, and French East Indies							1,323	1,234
British North America							441	212
United States of America						881	1,080	221	390
Argentine Republic							660	657
Australasia							1,984	1,525
Total	67,681	11,850	1,986	583	5,513,484	6,631,403	177,250	196,642

Countries from which imported and to which exported.	Blankets.				Ribbons, fringes, and hosiery.			
	Imports.		Exports.		Imports.		Exports.	
	Pounds.	Dollars.	Pounds.	Dollars.	Pounds.	Dollars.	Pounds.	Dollars.
Germany	119,710	104,799	1,984	777	217,193	331,863	7,496	14,959
Austria-Hungary	17,196	1,544	2,866	786	16,975	22,292	2,205	3,428
France	113,356	99,202	7,717	1,637	63,713	100,746	15,653	46,772
Italy	4,189	3,667	7,716	2,172	3,086	5,211	13,228	22,141
Belgium	661	579	441	147			1,323	2,232
Netherlands	441	386	(*)	19			1,984	3,059
Great Britain and Ireland	14,771	12,931	52,460	7,960	6,614	9,554	1,323	3,494
Russia							221	131
Denmark							(*)	15
Portugal							221	479
Spain							661	1,332

No. 44.—Statement showing, by Countries, the Quantities and Values of Manufactures of Wool Imported into and Exported from Switzerland in 1885—Continued.

Countries from which imported and to which exported.	Blankets.		Ribbons, fringes, and hosiery.	
	Imports.	Exports.	Imports.	Exports.
	Pounds.	Dollars.	Pounds.	Dollars.	Pounds.	Dollars.	Pounds.	Dollars.

Countries from which imported and to which exported.	Blankets. Imports. Pounds.	Blankets. Imports. Dollars.	Blankets. Exports. Pounds.	Blankets. Exports. Dollars.	Ribbons. Imports. Pounds.	Ribbons. Imports. Dollars.	Ribbons. Exports. Pounds.	Ribbons. Exports. Dollars.
Greece							(*)	91
Danubian countries			(*)	0			221	604
Turkey in Europe			661	135			221	550
Egypt			1,321	186			221	560
Algiers							1,984	2,344
Other Africa			2,205	295				
Turkey, Asiatic							661	1,271
British East Indies			882	104			(*)	9
China, Japan, and French East Indies							221	395
United States of America							882	2,841
Mexico			221	26			(*)	53
Chili and Peru			12,787	1,496			(*)	25
Brazil			112,020	18,056				100
Argentine Republic			31,967	4,026			1,102	1,806
Australasia							1,984	1,525
Total	270,324	223,108	236,153	37,851	307,581	469,666	51,812	110,243

Countries from which imported and to which exported.	Embroideries, laces, shawls, and scarfs. Imports. Pounds.	Embroideries. Imports. Dollars.	Embroideries. Exports. Pounds.	Embroideries. Exports. Dollars.	Carpets. Imports. Pounds.	Carpets. Imports. Dollars.	Carpets. Exports. Pounds.	Carpets. Exports. Dollars.
Germany	50,045	108,582	35	13,253	128,779	135,254	4,188	2,027
Austria-Hungary	1,102	1,737	9	3,518	1,984	2,084	660	610
France	17,857	45,934	46	29,653	61,077	64,153	2,645	2,873
Italy	3,748	6,330	18	6,050	3,068	4,169	4,328	1,527
Belgium				447	14,990	15,749		
Netherlands			2	612	4,189	4,400		12
Great Britain and Ireland	2,425	3,821	29	7,676	156,306	164,204	220	829
Russia				104	1,984	2,084		
Spain			(*)	164				
Danubian countries			(*)	418				
Turkey in Europe			(*)	39	1,764	1,853		
Egypt			(*)	9	221	232		
Algiers							(*)	5
Turkey, Asiatic					1,323	1,390		
British East Indies					2,866	3,011		
China, Japan, and French East Indies					441	463		
United States of America			(*)	690				
Mexico							(*)	10
Total	75,177	166,404		62,651	379,892	399,046	9,041	7,884

Countries from which imported and to which exported.	Felt, and partly manufactured felt. Imports. Pounds.	Imports. Dollars.	Exports. Pounds.	Exports. Dollars.
Belgium	1,543	1,158	1,984	1,282
Netherlands	662	579	(*)	31
Great Britain and Ireland	4,409	6,774	5,732	4,290
Russia			5,512	4,511
Sweden and Norway			882	687
Denmark			882	870
Portugal			441	309
Spain			441	372
Danubian countries			221	588
Algeria			(*)	62
Turkey, Asiatic			(*)	40
British East Indies			(*)	10
British North America			(*)	40
United States of America			(*)	19
Australasia			661	695
Total	6,614	8,511		13,606

* Quantities less than one quintal omitted.

No. 45.—STATEMENT SHOWING, BY COUNTRIES, THE QUANTITIES AND VALUES OF MANUFACTURES OF WOOL IMPORTED INTO AND EXPORTED FROM THE UNITED KINGDOM IN 1885.

Countries from which imported.	Imports. Woolen yarn.					
	For fancy purposes.		For weaving.		Other.	
	Pounds.	Dollars.	Pounds.	Dollars.	Pounds.	Dollars.
Belgium	20,734	15,840	11,010,630	6,108,027	....	....
France	79,707	54,695	2,736,767	2,047,293	....	....
Germany	1,115,812	975,833	847,007	462,600	16,525	6,079
Netherlands	37,920	27,987	28,457	16,794	9,544	4,973
United States of America	112	97	....	....	....	....
Other foreign countries	....	....	783	389	9,889	3,874
Total from foreign countries	1,255,285	1,077,452	14,632,653	8,635,112	35,058	15,826
Australasia	140	49	....	....	....	....
British East Indies	....	....	....	....	500	243
British West Indies	....	....	....	....	20	24
Total from British Possessions	140	49	....	....	520	267
Total imports	1,255,425	1,077,501	14,632,653	8,635,112	36,478	16,093

Countries from which imported.	Imports. Manufactures of goats' hair or wool.	Cloths.		Stuffs.		Other.
	Dollars.	Yards.	Dollars.	Yards.	Dollars.	Dollars.
Belgium	....	461,080	389,508	761,024	320,673	404,338
France	8,793	194,059	102,470	50,440,434	22,810,913	2,501,740
Germany	....	311,115	267,210	1,351,979	590,082	1,281,228
Netherlands	385,662	608,919	522,336	2,548,143	1,134,362	4,621,126
Turkey	....	....	....	....	....	561,196
Egypt	....	....	....	....	....	19,296
Persia	....	....	....	....	....	25,778
United States of America	....	18,200	18,268	....	....	21,109
Other foreign countries	1,824	1,765	1,129	16,310	4,341	24,630
Total from foreign countries	396,279	1,686,137	1,301,019	55,117,890	24,890,371	9,483,519
Australasia	....	....	....	....	....	4,920
British East Indies	7,377	1,512	1,353	....	....	201,030
Other British Possessions	....	508	527	2,999	798	5,966
Total from British Possessions	7,377	2,110	1,880	2,999	798	211,916
Total imports	403,656	1,688,247	1,302,899	55,120,889	24,891,169	9,695,435

No. 45.—IMPORTS AND EXPORTS OF MANUFACTURES OF WOOL INTO

Countries to which exported.	Exports.			
	Woolen yarn.		Worsted yarn.	
	Pounds.	Dollars.	Pounds.	Dollars.
Russia			1, 600. 500	824, 152
Sweden and Norway			1, 943, 900	807, 971
Denmark			1, 007, 300	453, 130
Germany	766, 600	385, 602	17, 951, 200	8, 391, 540
Holland	104, 700	45, 108	9, 733, 700	4, 861, 378
Belgium	640, 800	272, 972	1, 776, 500	880, 102
France	1, 263, 400	854, 300	4, 215, 400	2, 228, 920
Portugal, Azores, and Madeira				
Spain and Canaries				
Italy			387, 800	182, 854
Austrian territories				
Greece				
Turkey				
Java				
China				
Japan				
United States of America:				
Atlantic			993, 200	495, 181
Pacific				
Foreign West Indies				
Mexico				
United States of Colombia				
Peru				
Venezuela				
Chili				
Brazil				
Uruguay				
Argentine Republic				
Other foreign countries	145, 200	71, 323	189, 500	97, 371
Total to foreign countries	2, 920, 700	1, 629, 314	39, 798, 800	19, 222, 587
Malta				
British Possessions in South Africa				
British India:				
Bombay and Scinde				
Bengal and Burmah				
Straits Settlements				
Hong-Kong			100, 800	59, 089
Australasia	54, 000	26, 187		
South Australia				
Victoria			168, 300	106, 902
New South Wales				
Queensland				
New Zealand			111, 900	72, 676
Other colonies			93, 400	51, 926
British North America	85, 400	58, 437	104, 100	67, 250
British West India Islands and British Guiana				
Other British Possessions	14, 600	8, 380	39, 600	26, 025
Total to British Possessions	154, 000	93, 004	618, 100	384, 468
Total exports	3, 074, 700	1, 722, 318	40, 416, 900	19, 607, 055

AND FROM THE UNITED KINGDOM, BY COUNTRIES, 1885—Continued.

Exports.

Woolen fabrics.						Worsted fabrics.			
Coatings, duffels, &c., all wool.		Coatings, duffels, &c., of wool mixed with other materials.		Stuffs.		Coatings, duffels, &c.		Stuffs.	
Yards.	Dollars.	Yards.	Dollars.	Yards.	Dollars.	Yards.	Dollars.	Yards.	Dollars.
36,200	76,993								
80,000	104.119	438,600	289,245	458,200	82,526			2,290,500	331,292
63,300	84,521	362,400	233,631	100,500	46,636			624,400	104,868
1,203,600	1,675,740	1,785,400	1,003,564	1,133,800	190,081	132,000	140,768	3,872,500	575,838
351,100	422,123	1,391,000	861,079	615,400	151,134	58,000	42,313	8,072,200	1,263,017
1,061,800	1,414,774	3,388,000	2,678,910	1,590,000	443,703	164,000	140,073	9,609,400	1,536,179
4,051,900	3,703,636	7,563,400	3,841,119	4,818,900	1,282,785	343,800	336,737	20,563,600	4,048,388
107,200	159,899			189,900	48,534			1,506,800	197,667
43,300	73,397			155,700	77,961			541,900	71,104
582,900	726,043	987,200	480,309	2,383,200	657,415	337,100	315,208	11,179,800	1,414,059
43,600	74,423								
		53,500	43,823	325,700	91,982			569,900	89,188
96,900	113,638	563,000	312,517	1,329,800	412,420	159,400	102,167	3,650,700	543,734
								625,100	102,289
699,600	890,990	125,600	64,082	1,712,800	506,316			12,943,900	2,670,935
174,700	169,417	189,700	89,520	390,000	84,341			4,506,200	808,335
1,007,900	1,509,909	1,791,400	2,173,982	1,745,300	509,294	3,451,700	3,614,817	31,624,900	5,274,848
								251,800	55,342
				450,600	112,489			535,700	68,199
34,900	60,809			1,247,300	192,563			972,200	108,187
				208,100	79,898				
77,400	66,053			942,700	425,152			621,400	114,329
				177,200	63,357				
146,900	202,729	96,600	68,107	755,200	217,693			2,489,700	203,706
96,900	90,230	134,500	91,271	2,375,400	577,750			3,264,300	455,641
64,300	107,802	125,400	122,417	800,000	269,302			1,430,200	186,051
431,800	565,536	548,900	452,740	1,954,600	708,256			3,596,600	426,475
225,200	253,000	326,200	233,407	1,059,200	280,252	260,200	230,838	1,581,400	241,677
10,741,400	12,043,001	19,870,800	12,499,732	27,069,500	7,511,852	4,906,200	4,922,951	127,000,100	20,951,348
				182,000	54,276			218,800	84,956
199,900	167,456			1,152,100	219,367			416,000	61,235
403,500	304,278	741,500	250,087	1,279,100	292,452	55,500	44,859	418,200	75,703
237,900	188,582	321,200	138,058	1,349,000	364,292			982,800	191,643
				131,200	37,998			839,200	155,027
267,000	157,246	292,900	131,288	1,237,700	588,443			5,201,500	956,219
236,400	190,716			1,060,900	213,308				
833,000	800,330	550,200	281,255	4,166,600	865,789	359,800	342,105	1,926,500	378,224
746,500	739,328			3,019,700	632,932	261,900	248,839	1,768,100	323,394
142,100	127,444			776,400	142,564				
240,700	242,965			1,292,500	279,004			1,876,900	335,801
40,200	41,769	398,100	179,078	386,500	75,173	155,900	149,903	885,300	160,025
975,200	1,025,128	1,570,400	1,090,118	3,461,600	1,001,063	729,300	667,952	8,936,300	1,598,962
131,100	98,483	125,000	55,590	451,800	117,555			434,700	81,489
164,000	167,025	187,100	96,804	398,400	104,527	69,900	60,656	425,200	67,571
4,617,500	4,259,750	4,186,300	2,241,494	20,345,000	4,788,743	1,632,300	1,514,314	24,349,500	4,420,330
15,358,900	16,305,051	24,057,100	14,741,226	47,414,500	12,300,595	6,538,500	6,437,265	151,349,600	25,371,687

No. 45.—IMPORTS AND EXPORTS OF MANUFACTURES OF WOOL INTO

Countries to which exported.	Exports.			
	Flannels.		Carpets not being rugs.	
	Yards.	Dollars.	Yards.	Dollars.
Russia				
Sweden and Norway			204,900	116,183
Denmark			94,400	63,985
Germany			223,300	166,176
Holland			456,800	270,680
Belgium	70,500	10,792	522,300	285,907
France			1,660,900	679,363
Portugal, Azores, and Madeira			95,000	48,480
Spain and Canaries			549,900	250,406
Italy			163,100	81,032
Greece				
Turkey			264,000	101,564
Egypt			201,300	84,073
West Africa (foreign)	80,000	17,325		
China				
Japan				
United States of America	100,900	24,688		
Atlantic	72,800	17,334	1,107,300	850,854
Central America				
Mexico			111,300	54,656
Peru			121,500	55,142
Chili			305,300	141,479
Brazil				
Uruguay			78,900	49,410
Argentine Republic			487,100	296,238
Other foreign countries	373,600	83,227	364,900	153,397
Total to foreign countries	697,800	162,366	7,012,200	3,749,934
British Possessions in South Africa	532,700	103,608		
British India:				
Bombay and Scinde	483,200	84,478	69,300	37,117
Bengal and Burmah	548,600	109,102		
Straits Settlements				
Hong-Kong	120,500	24,819		
Australasia				
South Australia	895,700	158,000		
Victoria	1,981,700	399,442	760,600	398,800
New South Wales	1,977,800	399,866	586,500	314,425
Queensland	554,000	122,811		
New Zealand	1,066,200	196,237	340,000	168,016
Other colonies	156,700	31,623	304,700	156,229
British North America	1,324,200	203,322	1,861,100	895,334
British West India Islands and British Guiana	408,200	77,158		
Other British Possessions	278,000	57,862	128,100	63,892
Total to British Possessions	10,398,500	1,968,334	4,070,300	2,033,813
Total exports	11,096,300	2,130,700	11,082,500	5,783,747

AND FROM THE UNITED KINGDOM, BY COUNTRIES, 1885—Continued.

Exports.

Blankets.		Shawls.		Rugs, coverlets, or wrappers.		Hosiery.	Small wares and manufactures of wool or worsted unenumerated.	Yarn, alpaca, mohair, and other sorts unenumerated.	
Pairs.	Dollars.	Number.	Dollars.	Number.	Dollars.	Dollars.	Dollars.	Pounds.	Dollars.
......	......	......	......	......	......	......	28,940	113,700	72,087
.	......	......	......	......	......	54,695	41,161	......	......
15,319	26,610	......	......	15,822	31,946	39,050	......	......	......
......	......	......	......	45,387	92,843	140,287	89,033	4,863,700	2,437,012
......	......	......	......	25,545	31,326	41,969	27,982	4,613,300	1,535,050
......	......	......	......	63,912	87,144	87,378	58,544	748,700	358,466
......	......	......	......	171,812	286,009	223,950	45,692	1,187,700	1,143,525
......	......	......	......	49,194	35,715	......	......	......	......
......	......	......	......	43,518	46,495	54,247	28,080	103,300	67,552
36,743	115,467	......	......	......	......	107,740	......	......	......
10,685	32,844								
124,679	227,626								
......	......	141,244	231,601	50,217	88,249	531,339	125,818	471,100	190,645
16,358	31,150								
26,043	30,498								
89,048	102,878	......	......	115,704	81,820				
29,384	52,777	14,407	39,341	39,812	55,702				
93,959	159,339	31,438	67,708	110,155	108,148	30,757			
79,806	146,487	154,434	124,247	102,007	168,190	151,256	117,006	83,000	19,753
522,084	925,676	311,523	462,807	841,595	1,113,587	1,468,686	562,256	12,184,500	5,824,090
100,169	242,337	21,834	21,773	121,101	174,488	72,005			
27,460	43,005	70,784	29,987	61,945	65,186	79,431			
20,630	29,457	424,705	247,306				155,183		
40,488	76,959								
49,371	152,774	......	......	16,046	31,436				
......	......	46,738	30,239	131,820	200,456	......	89,203		
						110,713			
99,504	205,673					230,594			
134,601	289,177					141,756			
57,696	124,573								
64,518	144,136					133,595			
48,565	96,078					60,564			
28,426	61,337	51,199	66,253			357,434	132,812		
23,568	35,740	44,887	31,480	10,150	14,999	48,310	73,100	8,800	4,862
694,900	1,501,846	660,147	436,038	341,062	492,615	1,234,402	450,307	8,800	4,862
1,217,080	2,427,522	1,001,670	898,935	1,182,647	1,606,202	2,703,088	1,012,563	12,193,300	5,828,952

No. 46.—STATEMENT SHOWING, BY COUNTRIES, THE QUANTITIES OF WOOL (SHEEP, LAMB, AND ALPACA) IMPORTED INTO THE UNITED KINGDOM DURING EACH YEAR FROM 1844 TO 1860, INCLUSIVE.

[From McCullough's Commercial Dictionary.]

Years.	Spain,	Germany, viz. Mecklenburg, Hanover, Oldenburg, and Hanse Towns.	Other countries of Europe.	British Possessions in South Africa.	British Possessions in the East Indies.
	Pounds.	Pounds.	Pounds.	Pounds.	Pounds.
1844	018,853	21,847,684	15,313,087	2,197,143	2,765,853
1845	1,074,540	18,484,736	17,606,515	3,512,924	3,975,866
1846	1,020,476	15,888,705	11,733,601	2,958,457	4,570,581
1847	424,408	12,672,814	7,935,697	3,477,392	3,063,142
1848	106,638	14,429,161	7,024,098	3,497,250	5,997,433
1849	127,559	12,750,011	11,432,354	5,377,405	4,182,853
1850	440,757	9,166,731	8,703,252	5,700,529	3,473,252
1851	383,150	8,219,236	14,263,156	5,816,591	4,549,520
1852	233,413	12,765,253	13,382,140	6,368,796	7,680,784
1853	154,146	11,584,860	26,801,166	7,921,448	12,400,860
1854	424,300	11,418,518	14,481,483	8,223,508	14,965,101
1855	68,750	6,128,626	8,119,408	11,075,965	14,283,535
1856	55,090	8,687,781	14,480,869	14,305,188	15,386,578
1857	397,238	6,088,002	23,802,520	14,287,828	19,370,741
1858	110,510	10,395,186	17,926,859	16,597,504	17,333,507
1859	153,874	19,820,557	18,659,275	14,269,343	14,303,403
1860	1,000,227	18,438,488	17,454,604	16,574,345	20,214,173

Years.	British settlements in Australia.	South America.	Other countries.	Total.
	Pounds.	Pounds.	Pounds.	Pounds.
1844	17,602,247	3,760,063	1,308,831	65,713,761
1845	24,177,317	6,468,338	1,513,619	76,813,855
1846	21,789,346	4,890,273	2,404,023	65,255,462
1847	26,056,815	7,295,550	1,665,780	62,592,598
1848	30,034,567	8,851,211	924,487	70,804,847
1849	35,879,171	6,014,525	1,004,679	76,768,647
1850	39,018,221	5,296,618	2,518,304	74,320,778
1851	41,810,117	4,850,048	3,420,157	83,311,975
1852	43,197,301	6,252,680	3,661,082	93,761,458
1853	47,076,010	9,740,032	4,357,978	119,306,440
1854	47,480,650	6,134,334	2,954,921	106,121,995
1855	49,142,306	7,106,708	3,375,148	99,300,446
1856	52,052,130	8,076,317	3,167,430	116,211,392
1857	49,200,655	9,306,886	7,287,028	120,740,698
1858	51,104,560	10,046,381	3,024,216	126,738,723
1859	53,700,481	9,711,172	2,606,531	133,284,634
1860	50,165,930	8,890,940	6,657,861	148,396,577

No. 47.—STATEMENT SHOWING, BY COUNTRIES, THE QUANTITIES OF WOOL, WITH THEIR TOTAL VALUES, IMPORTED INTO THE UNITED KINGDOM, AND THE TOTAL QUANTITIES OF FOREIGN WOOL EXPORTED AND OF THE NET IMPORTS FOR EACH YEAR FROM 1861 TO 1885, INCLUSIVE.

[The wool included in this table is that of the sheep, lamb, alpaca, and the llama tribe. One pound sterling equals $4.8665.]

Years	Imported from—											Total imported		Total exported (foreign and colonial).	Net imports.
	Russia.	Germany.	France.	Holland and Belgium.	Turkey in Europe and Asia.	Egypt.	British possessions in South Africa.	British East Indies.	Australasia.	South America.	All other countries.	Quantities.	Values.		
	Pounds.	Pounds.	Pounds.	Pounds.	Pounds.	Pounds.	Pounds.	Pounds.	Pounds.	Pounds.	Pounds.	Pounds.	£	Pounds.	Pounds.
1861	20,790,004	3,617,933	......	......	......	......	12,676,286	19,161,004	68,560,222	12,351,777	7,069,565	147,172,841	9,717,686	54,377,104	92,795,737
1862	24,776,271	8,753,130	......	......	......	......	12,930,886	17,959,404	77,339,842	12,664,915	7,518,974	171,043,472	11,773,943	48,076,409	123,866,973
1863	25,530,838	8,801,162	......	......	......	......	20,106,617	20,070,111	77,173,440	18,248,181	6,787,309	177,377,661	11,684,572	63,932,929	113,444,735
1864	32,352,762	9,755,610	......	......	......	......	21,860,805	20,435,355	99,593,261	19,302,932	6,710,122	206,473,045	15,503,483	55,933,739	150,539,306
1865	32,529,844	7,138,340	......	......	......	......	29,220,623	17,105,617	109,734,261	17,867,853	3,610,209	212,206,747	14,910,430	82,444,945	129,761,817
1866	31,268,180	11,402,480	......	......	......	......	29,240,000	25,679,960	113,774,694	21,152,277	6,893,089	239,358,689	17,550,871	66,573,488	172,785,201
1867	17,288,086	4,197,777	......	......	......	......	36,126,750	15,234,620	183,108,170	21,381,241	6,366,404	233,704,184	16,178,034	90,832,584	142,677,600
1868	16,455,713	5,811,923	......	......	......	......	35,093,572	17,602,442	155,745,490	21,025,719	6,100,286	252,744,155	16,120,178	108,105,070	144,673,844
1869	17,500,863	7,308,802	......	......	......	......	35,307,882	18,796,579	158,477,900	16,117,931	5,561,652	258,441,689	14,696,746	116,608,305	141,853,384
1870	19,305,704	4,405,897	......	......	......	......	32,785,271	11,143,148	175,081,427	12,603,777	7,835,275	263,250,499	17,812,508	92,542,384	170,708,115
1871	15,381,831	8,132,120	6,663,689	4,600,456	16,322,734	7,048,677	32,972,735	14,217,460	182,710,567	19,229,406	11,610,136	325,030,299	17,936,689	137,511,247	188,169,095
1872	12,723,656	5,759,062	5,240,016	3,623,407	11,038,144	5,645,379	35,619,566	18,493,860	173,201,712	22,914,868	12,766,448	306,370,064	18,523,350	138,806,417	168,868,417
1873	11,166,563	8,294,628	1,557,165	2,240,868	8,323,442	4,588,323	35,018,187	19,302,908	225,365,631	21,099,262	12,766,418	318,030,779	18,541,678	123,246,123	194,790,607
1874	11,930,451	7,163,605	1,518,206	4,802,486	4,232,672	1,900,072	44,232,672	19,127,534	225,385,860	14,878,918	9,723,696	344,470,897	21,116,181	144,294,663	200,176,234
1875	15,084,641	7,320,700	1,675,527	3,915,251	5,564,694	2,247,769	42,158,317	22,819,289	238,869,631	15,711,954	11,967,308	365,578,223	22,437,413	172,075,439	193,990,139
1876	12,918,451	8,971,549	2,355,810	4,060,206	6,959,116	3,560,808	42,158,317	24,453,817	263,860,157	15,543,559	8,446,222	390,653,759	23,637,809	173,020,372	217,633,387
1877	12,939,038	9,517,489	2,054,159	4,205,246	7,213,634	4,434,143	41,566,778	27,039,247	276,566,074	11,543,301	9,425,544	409,949,198	24,312,418	187,627,222	222,530,871
1878	8,628,750	4,564,485	1,970,063	6,345,561	11,245,667	2,569,859	40,955,945	27,039,725	300,172,172	13,259,754	9,974,622	449,415,233	23,128,234	199,286,544	200,162,891
1879	15,924,991	4,225,051	6,384,605	6,345,501	6,436,514	2,725,506	45,385,839	29,202,554	276,831,804	12,867,657	6,039,691	441,117,110	24,009,243	243,386,008	173,724,091
1880	20,082,310	4,177,932	9,057,016	7,438,971	12,431,011	2,817,342	51,385,839	29,190,049	300,626,454	16,262,206	12,623,004	463,508,903	26,375,407	237,408,589	226,100,374
1881	15,704,057	2,263,651	3,011,131	5,143,277	6,718,782	1,986,796	54,839,239	22,215,855	345,783,796	15,853,192	9,948,303	478,150,141	24,365,011	220,305,583	157,844,557
1882	15,337,760	2,727,703	4,830,483	5,919,277	6,399,075	1,494,819	53,876,065	26,923,704	345,783,786	10,672,521	9,627,014	488,085,057	24,995,674	263,263,965	224,022,019
1883	28,148,121	4,315,436	3,337,906	5,716,131	6,669,070	1,638,842	43,876,981	24,822,110	351,085,906	7,664,219	8,577,346	495,946,779	24,953,132	277,234,064	218,712,695
1884	22,939,967	1,630,331	5,585,672	5,268,013	8,669,970	2,087,360	51,334,652	24,709,208	361,403,669	16,302,670	6,230,620	526,536,661	26,517,920	276,910,073	249,007,588
1885	29,649,386	1,886,954	7,621,322	5,268,013	11,112,489	2,375,614	47,013,467	25,697,174	356,035,791	12,868,622	6,138,758	505,687,550	21,177,088	207,501,675	238,185,915

No. 48.—STATEMENT SHOWING THE TOTAL QUANTITIES AND VALUES OF MANUFACT-
URES OF WOOL IMPORTED INTO THE UNITED KINGDOM EACH YEAR FROM 1861 TO
1885, INCLUSIVE.

[One pound sterling equals $4.8665.]

Years.	Woolen rags.		Woolen and worsted yarn.				All other manufactures of wool.	Total value of the imports of manufactures of wool.
			Berlin wool and yarn used for fancy purposes.		For weaving.			
	Tons.	£	Pounds.	£	Pounds.	£	£	£
1861....	10, 653	336, 107	214, 217	58, 910	1, 362, 874	306, 648	1, 419, 336	2, 121, 801
1862....	13, 109	437, 056	193, 098	53, 103	2, 051, 603	461, 611	1, 574, 281	2, 526, 051
1863....	15, 417	551, 824	218, 528	58, 723	4, 312, 857	970, 394	1, 813, 894	3, 394, 835
1864....	15, 642	642, 907	174, 653	48, 031	4, 479, 984	1, 008, 004	1, 849, 550	3, 548, 492
1865....	14, 585	565, 861	211, 244	58, 092	4, 180, 846	940, 692	1, 891, 104	3, 455, 749
1866....	15, 797	530, 947	287, 367	79, 028	8, 997, 889	1, 574, 527	2, 036, 671	4, 221, 173
1867....	14, 542	395, 801	303, 918	73, 902	5, 514, 947	1, 089, 350	2, 405, 600	3, 964, 653
1868....	15, 922	370, 412	387, 255	87, 133	8, 950, 693	1, 566, 371	2, 373, 366	4, 397, 282
1869....	16, 699	373, 322	434, 897	97, 855	9, 587, 631	1, 677, 834	2, 534, 523	4, 683, 534
1870....	17, 210	400, 326	611, 013	123, 984	9, 683, 402	1, 511, 170	3, 362, 656	5, 398, 136
1871....	24, 219	498, 754	464, 058	81, 883	11, 665, 465	1, 097, 289	4, 637, 025	6, 315, 561
1872....	29, 302	534, 329	423, 563	83, 010	11, 706, 427	1, 382, 064	4, 038, 660	6, 038, 000
1873....	24, 827	468, 556	325, 250	59, 194	15, 169, 662	1, 496, 463	3, 810, 662	5, 870, 575
1874....	25, 581	547, 399	533, 320	107, 471	13, 131, 850	1, 494, 945	3, 973, 811	6, 128, 626
1875....	25, 415	599, 402	727, 214	145, 049	11, 700, 928	1, 327, 887	4, 308, 357	6, 380, 695
1876....	28, 847	660, 960	841, 878	162, 387	12, 909, 902	1, 538, 496	4, 920, 711	7, 281, 854
1877....	33, 408	760, 256	976, 044	190, 369	12, 948, 662	1, 540, 239	5, 235, 948	7, 720, 812
1878....	32, 376	739, 137	1, 028, 550	204, 428	11, 343, 339	1, 365, 431	5, 934, 748	8, 243, 744
1879....	33, 309	660, 046	887, 233	167, 719	10, 022, 139	1, 233, 402	5, 637, 675	7, 698, 642
1880...	41, 266	820, 366	752, 700	128, 176	14, 194, 979	1, 713, 959	7, 649, 778	10, 312, 279
1881....	35, 265	761, 501	663, 922	117, 080	10, 068, 329	1, 206, 797	5, 985, 863	8, 101, 271
1882....	37, 511	820, 616	938, 819	106, 373	12, 731, 339	1, 585, 325	5, 982, 449	8, 554, 763
1883....	35, 767	757, 277	951, 221	170, 593	14, 558, 567	1, 831, 010	6, 251, 281	9, 010, 161
1884....	31, 022	678, 525	1, 094, 620	200, 440	13, 341, 685	1, 675, 019	6, 831, 737	9, 385, 721
1885....	32, 642	681, 995	1, 255, 425	221, 412	14, 632, 658	1, 774, 399	7, 374, 808	10, 052, 614

No. 49.—STATEMENT SHOWING THE QUANTITIES AND VALUES OF DOMESTIC WOOL AND MANUFACTURES OF WOOL EXPORTED FROM THE UNITED KINGDOM EACH YEAR FROM 1861 TO 1885, INCLUSIVE.

[One pound sterling equals $4.8665.]

Year.	Wool (sheep's and lambs.)		Yarns, woolen and worsted.		Manufactures of wool.								All other.	Total value of the exports of manufactures of wool.	Total value of the exports of wool and manufactures of wool.
					Cloths, coatings, &c., unmixed and mixed.		Flannels, blankets, carpeting, and baizes.		Stuffs, unmixed and mixed.		Carpets and druggets.				
	Pounds.	£	Pounds.	£	Yards.	£	Yards.	£	Yards.	£	Yards.	£	£	£	£
1861	15,715,288	1,143,358	20,492,256	3,325,088	21,371,840	2,998,465	13,403,982	1,031,455	122,555,608	6,121,616	4,067,351	508,052	458,898	14,444,774	15,688,122
1862	10,290,544	730,310	27,067,837	3,662,553	21,972,056	2,425,122	17,674,264	1,388,502	106,775,408	5,881,789	5,378,303	071,215	805,228	16,834,501	17,590,811
1863	8,230,214	688,330	31,660,220	4,870,393	27,762,256	3,064,010	17,311,400	1,414,399	103,835,142	8,330,937	5,257,092	810,783	905,908	19,310,440	21,078,740
1864	7,320,290	673,446	30,806,793	5,183,220	29,762,536	4,533,034	18,128,421	1,504,384	187,305,448	10,800,521	5,982,832	861,459	800,166	23,752,318	24,425,764
1865	9,656,042	601,660	30,425,731	5,110,474	29,015,680	4,023,034	14,700,397	1,203,127	223,078,142	13,000,537	5,743,000	861,453	692,364	25,251,889	26,158,540
1866	9,732,666	805,356	20,577,694	4,547,043	32,514,958	5,303,602	14,468,240	1,161,615	227,275,414	13,294,059	7,640,511	1,217,082	853,223	26,377,224	27,272,580
1867	8,862,197	775,831	30,052,474	5,730,310	31,189,209	5,327,375	11,120,055	830,519	200,462,996	12,144,996	7,673,951	1,101,986	724,039	25,800,257	26,672,001
1868	9,510,881	7,6,035	42,799,410	6,283,171	24,622,230	3,760,961	12,727,805	963,866	224,307,464	13,075,773	7,417,009	1,099,882	680,906	25,781,562	26,520,507
1869	12,410,225	922,150	37,185,740	5,538,205	28,218,489	4,275,686	14,925,710	1,009,209	250,062,034	15,130,340	9,656,401	1,466,758	604,078	28,207,528	20,120,687
1870	9,191,405	560,570	35,596,848	3,694,240	32,404,719	4,749,165	14,985,389	1,078,833	235,936,061	13,784,708	9,374,173	1,303,279	654,726	26,650,202	27,539,772
1871	11,957,282	828,799	41,225,577	4,100,725	33,583,497	5,563,037	14,091,283	1,030,502	307,235,042	17,053,200	10,057,454	1,648,411	987,436	33,283,112	34,111,911
1872	7,605,140	629,215	39,734,924	4,110,138	40,731,221	6,991,718	15,022,122	1,104,835	341,968,030	20,005,163	11,815,774	910,774	461,783	34,493,411	39,122,086
1873	7,034,735	620,848	34,744,307	6,393,493	58,354	6,563,014	447,313	864,282	834,692	21,277,382	1,000,597	1,001,302	783,014	30,749,371	30,749,371
1874	10,077,619	920,413	34,081,008	6,558,560	40,331,686	6,642,222	16,004,436	1,318,007	361,195,081	11,886,072	9,208,271	480,692	471,759	28,359,512	29,270,927
1875	9,536,521	924,264	31,723,627	5,039,307	42,058,354	6,830,203	10,129,301	1,203,637	251,815,549	11,159,014	7,522,660	1,159,079	249,592	29,758,632	27,690,896
1876	9,817,246	757,832	30,654,160	4,417,241	40,470,373	6,151,410	13,902,301	1,014,896	221,561,090	9,141,605	6,298,479	911,873	1,083,704	23,020,710	23,778,651
1877	0,548,099	705,610	20,972,530	3,608,322	43,520,800	0,203,107	17,036,601	1,567,800	209,102,462	7,225,414	9,454,449	847,763	1,025,843	20,932,659	21,638,260
1878	0,618,200	517,823	31,169,610	3,908,321	43,614,173	6,203,107	15,277,700	1,176,377	104,771,064	7,443,283	9,626,200	410,410	1,110,267	20,635,587	21,183,410
1879	15,700,000	841,278	33,374,500	3,714,210	46,238,900	0,145,773	11,663,700	806,003	186,646,100	7,921,532	6,000	803,223	1,184,535	10,515,306	20,516,674
1880	13,187,000	113,264	20,461,300	3,344,711	40,000,200	0,736,721	13,980,500	807,088	169,000,100	7,241,156	9,328,300	133,545	1,256,667	22,107,279	21,707,030
1881	14,068,800	694,366	20,731,400	3,225,636	55,679,400	0,552,654	15,378,200	072,439	192,100,100	7,237,501	9,711,200	1,164,438	1,201,701	21,354,452	22,246,818
1882	17,107,100	670,014	31,832,700	3,398,645	54,129,000	0,708,706	17,317,700	1,001,718	184,444,500	7,352,089	11,318,700	1,320,975	309,611	22,107,279	23,044,223
1883	10,413,100	1,029,099	33,488,500	3,890,425	40,068,500	7,151,483	13,372,000	837,824	185,565,400	7,687,834	10,099,300	1,258,892	1,179,542	21,582,063	2?,612,062
1884	18,128,800	825,185	39,272,100	3,890,425	5,039,100	7,931,839	15,659,000	911,711	217,121,200	8,718,320	11,540,800	1,109,511	1,316,576	21,036,989	21,853,171
1885	23,459,500	033,612	43,491,600	4,382,698	45,954,500	7,702,485	17,182,300	936,653	108,704,100	7,741,145	11,092,500	1,188,482	1,278,288	23,229,951	24,103,563

No. 50.—STATEMENT SHOWING THE TOTAL VALUES OF WOOLEN AND WORSTED GOODS AND YARN EXPORTED FROM THE UNITED KINGDOM IN DIFFERENT YEARS FROM 1718 TO 1860.

[From McCulloch's Commercial Dictionary.]

Years.	Woolen and worsted yarn.	Other manufactures.	Total.
		Official value.	*Official value.*
1718 to 1724, yearly average		£2,962,000	£2,962,000
1740		3,056,000	3,056,000
1750		4,320,000	4,320,000
1760		5,453,300	5,453,300
1770		4,113,000	4,113,000
1780		2,589,000	2,589,000
1790		5,190,000	5,190,000
1800		6,917,000	6,917,000
1810		5,773,000	5,773,000
		Declared value.	*Declared value.*
1820		5,580,000	5,580,000
1830	£122,430	4,728,000	4,851,000
1840	452,000	5,327,000	5,780,000
1850	1,451,000	8,588,000	10,040,000
1860	3,843,450	12,156,998	16,000,448

No. 51.—STATEMENT SHOWING THE QUANTITIES AND VALUES OF IMPORTED WOOL AND MANUFACTURES OF WOOL. ENTERED FOR CONSUMPTION IN, AND OF DOMESTIC WOOL AND WOOLENS EXPORTED FROM, THE DOMINION OF CANADA DURING THE YEARS ENDING JUNE 30, 1884, 1885, AND 1886.

IMPORTS.

Articles	Countries	Unit of quantity	1884.		1885.		1886.	
				Dollars.		Dollars.		Dollars.
Wool, raw	Great Britain	Pounds	1,688,978	389,006	1,524,996	320,995	5,268,216	911,266
	United States	do	2,061,423	551,051	4,785,521	815,839	4,160,805	592,681
	France	do	......	......	4,438	182	91,763	18,364
	Germany	do	1,183,656	183,177	173,118	28,308	25,000	7,085
	British Africa	do	......	......	1,194,144	149,675	2,285,114	246,839
	All other countries	do	360,039	46,238	89,952	25,413	146,211	20,015
Total		do	6,189,096	1,174,472	7,768,171	1,346,612	11,063,111	1,796,850
Woolen rags	Great Britain	Pounds	154,585	18,965	149,439	14,435	250,309	18,187
	United States	do	20,962	1,907	598,866	44,567	932,522	51,200
	Danish West Indies	do	3,500	52	......	......	......	......
Total		do	179,047	21,024	748,305	59,002	1,182,831	69,387
Blankets	Great Britain	Pounds	361,044	119,920	266,617	89,484	206,260	60,609
	United States	do	3,058	2,229	2,219	1,824	2,735	1,971
	All other countries	do	169	29	180	63	6	4
Total		do	360,271	122,178	269,016	91,371	209,021	68,674
Cassimeres, cloths, coatings, doeskins, tweeds, &c	Great Britain	Pounds	4,040,210	3,192,121	4,151,803	3,318,311	4,815,577	3,232,198
	United States	do	12,687	12,388	20,050	23,518	29,924	31,445
	France	do	3,877	4,191	8,048	13,550	7,500	9,345
	Germany	do	30,838	27,455	32,703	30,289	56,851	43,617
	All other countries	do	2,153	3,230	3,070	4,241	2,478	2,748
Total		do	4,089,165	3,239,397	4,215,674	3,389,859	4,412,330	3,319,353
Flannels, plain and checked	Great Britain	Pounds	299,635	231,180	312,009	236,456	*291,859	217,004
	United States	do	6,085	5,887	6,992	7,321	8,270	9,286
	All other countries	do	3,320	2,606	6,669	6,734	766	1,279
Total		do	309,040	239,733	325,780	250,511	300,904	227,569

*Unit of quantity, yards.

No. 51.—QUANTITIES AND VALUES OF IMPORTED WOOL ENTERED FOR CONSUMPTION IN THE DOMINION OF CANADA, &c.—Continued.

Articles.	Countries.	Unit of quantity.	1884.		1885.		1886.	
				Dollars.		*Dollars.*		*Dollars.*
Hosiery, shirts, drawers, &c	Great Britain	Pounds	326,488	415,027	303,902	410,784	320,043	422,940
	United States	do	4,714	8,965	5,903	10,131	7,298	12,291
	Germany	do	30,355	55,790	25,801	37,990	33,751	44,896
	All other countries	do	9,421	11,262	1,028	2,305	4,152	4,018
Total		do	370,978	510,950	336,724	470,300	365,244	465,045
Shawls	Great Britain			223,374		213,469		169,671
	Unite l States			1,478		1,828		1,979
	Germany			12,907		25,231		19,935
	All other countrie			494		1,079		1,508
Total				238,253		241,097		213,183
Yarn, knitting, &c	Great Britain	Pounds	246,516	186,575	216,423	166,910	212,050	166,107
	United States	do	3,280	2,717	2,598	984	2,181	1,912
	Germany	do	5,091	5,035	12,890	11,082	22,130	18,514
	All other countries	do	116	100	2,852	1,585	4,701	3,504
Total		do	255,003	195,327	234,682	181,661	241,161	190,127
Wool, all other manufactures of, composed wholly or in part of wool.	Great Britain			2,901,267		2,340,289		2,844,000
	United States			40,673		70,042		60,027
	France			35,859		87,323		143,336
	Germany			37,232		45,070		61,516
	All other countries			1,360		2,633		3,733
Total				2,122,390		2,515,357		3,113,592
Clothing, ready-made, &c	Great Britain	Pounds	390,392	470,238	308,376	462,062	472,121	613,518
	United States	do	15,965	32,336	10,242	21,330	14,844	22,533
	France	do	221	407	1,163	1,503	1,694	2,803
	Germany	do	5,352	0,437	11,016	18,852	19,991	32,619
	All other countries	do	411	403	1,415	1,292	1,301	1,367
Total		do	412,341	562,851	396,813	505,120	510,011	672,839
Carpets, Brussels and tapestry	Great Britain	Yards	1,807,580	739,066	1,911,280	831,580	2,010,789	822,562
	United States	do	8,884	6,080	8,093	4,933	8,447	5,052
	All other countries	do	533	151	767	560	4,109	2,450
Total		do	1,617,097	745,297	1,920,140	837,118	2,029,343	830,044

Article	Country	Unit						
Carpets, two and three ply, treble ingrain, composed wholly of wool.	Great Britain	Square yards	37,085	64,727	46,648	81,863	59,964	103,547
	United States	do	1,343	2,065	364	480	648	840
	All other countries	do			44	10		
Total		do	38,427	68,702	47,250	82,379	50,712	104,387
Carpets, two and three ply ingrain, of which the warp is wholly of other material than wool.	Great Britain	Square yards	12,908	31,571	22,200	55,944	29,316	73,890
	United States	do	442	820	1,763	3,329	988	4,397
Total		do	13,350	32,400	23,963	59,273	30,284	78,287
Felt, for boots, shoes, &c., imported for use in factories.	Great Britain	Pounds			45,564	64,797	35,691	48,998
	United States	do			881	2,649	1,904	6,100
	All other countries	do			211	478	579	796
Total		do		*a*	46,656	67,924	38,174	55,954
Felt, for glove linings, and endless felt, imported for use in factories.	Great Britain	do			9,618			20,862
	United States	do			11,037			8,506
	All other countries	do						60
Total		do			20,655			20,288
Felt, pressed, of all kinds, not filled or covered by or with any woven fabric.	Great Britain	Yards	52,636	*a*	*a*			
	United States	do	6,280		*a*			
	France	do	9,639		*a*			
	All other countries	do			*a*			
Total		do	68,505	*a*				
Dress or costume cloths, serges, and similar fabrics, &c.	Great Britain	Yards	11,035	707,007	370,143	2,402,960	292,917	1,643,854
	United States	do	4,521	7,223	3,225	10,746	2,740	11,210
	France	do		1,535	6,463	37,660	2,987	12,163
	All other countries	do			2,476	12,026	824	5,571
Total		do	16,450	715,825	382,307	2,473,007	298,474	1,672,804
Woolen netting for boots, shoes, and gloves	Great Britain				3,762		10,820	
	United States				12,400		6,515	
Total					16,108		17,335	
Manufactures of winceys of all kinds.	Great Britain	Yards	61,564		4,007	31,380	8,221	11,256
	United States	do	2,224		251	2,127		
	All other countries	do	418					
Total		do	64,200		4,318	33,513	8,221	11,250
Total value of wool and manufactures of wool.			11,187,007			10,430,240		9,604,260

a Not enumerated.

No. 51.—Quantities and Values of Imported Wool Entered for Consumption in the Dominion of Canada, &c.—Continued.

DOMESTIC EXPORTS.

Articles.	Countries.	Unit of quantity.	1884.	Dollars.	1885.	Dollars.	1886.	Dollars.
Wool, raw	Great Britain	Pounds	114,252	24,451	78,129	9,253	207,053	45,254
	United States	do	1,380,639	285,563	911,796	180,925	1,316,228	271,424
	All other countries	do	140	26	....	....	903	259
Total		do	1,501,031	310,000	989,925	190,178	1,524,184	316,937
Manufactures of woolens	Great Britain		....	15,843	....	27,057	....	5,608
	United States		....	2,821	....	2,849	....	5,739
	All other countries		....	23,391	....	25,827	....	10,936
Total			....	41,060	....	55,733	....	22,283

No. 52.—STATEMENT SHOWING THE VALUES OF MANUFACTURES OF WOOL IMPORTED
INTO AND THE QUANTITIES AND VALUES OF WOOL AND MANUFACTURES OF WOOL
EXPORTED FROM BRITISH INDIA FOR EACH YEAR FROM 1876 TO 1885, INCLUSIVE.

Years.	Imports.	Exports.	
	Manufact-ures of wool.	Wool, raw.	Manufact-ures of wool.
	£	*Pounds.* £	£
1876	869,760	24,138,636 1,109,740	217,202
1877	811,052	24,588,131 1,102,913	232,274
1878	782,781	23,612,983 966,845	225,324
1879	878,042	27,791,684 1,109,702	202,289
1880	927,876	28,666,852 1,187,799	162,229
1881	1,290,130	25,748,121 1,170,624	230,601
1882	1,121,232	26,757,352 1,042,246	227,692
1883	984,870	26,380,327 1,002,833	183,348
1884	1,217,053	25,229,180 983,002	156,509
1885	1,234,428	25,540,253 994,319	150,823

No. 53.—STATEMENT SHOWING THE QUANTITIES AND VALUES OF WOOL IMPORTED
INTO AND EXPORTED FROM NEW SOUTH WALES FOR EACH YEAR FROM 1875 TO
1884, INCLUSIVE.

Years.	Imports.		Exports.	
	Wool, raw.		Wool, raw.	
	Pounds.	£	*Pounds.*	£
1875	8,357,279	441,856	47,628,810	3,193,320
1876	6,765,905	331,606	54,872,771	3,299,738
1877	4,646,262	368,049	107,897,141	5,626,602
1878	5,449,582	285,393	116,005,930	5,960,206
1879	6,454,370	312,496	129,123,573	6,769,294
1880	10,945,936	519,608	162,486,322	8,437,534
1881	8,096,141	355,626	147,183,687	7,530,792
1882	8,316,114	389,806	153,351,354	7,773,704
1883	16,705,446	665,649	190,638,895	10,136,244
1884	11,404,239	486,946	183,016,518	9,382,499

No. 54.—STATEMENT SHOWING THE QUANTITIES AND VALUES OF WOOL AND MANU-
FACTURES OF WOOL IMPORTED INTO AND OF WOOL EXPORTED FROM VICTORIA
FOR EACH YEAR FROM 1875 TO 1884, INCLUSIVE.

Years.	Imports.			Exports.	
	Wool, raw.		Manufact-ures of wool.	Wool, raw.	
	Pounds.	£	£	*Pounds.*	£
1875	41,417,925	2,310,477	898,070	85,004,952	6,096,958
1876	46,831,787	2,179,184	789,183	106,265,877	6,413,754
1877	45,631,322	2,030,129	917,793	98,468,208	5,670,871
1878	49,170,516	2,362,697	866,179	101,809,800	5,810,148
1879	50,046,396	2,494,573	701,292	95,628,281	5,209,034
1880	60,723,152	2,977,264	645,543	112,486,206	6,417,466
1881	59,345,348	2,887,260	663,397	103,449,800	5,450,066
1882	53,839,210	2,734,738	924,905	108,028,601	5,902,624
1883	45,520,395	2,043,588	793,015	109,616,610	6,054,613
1884	59,075,280	2,575,905	923,072	119,542,407	6,342,887

No. 55.—STATEMENT SHOWING THE QUANTITIES AND VALUES OF WOOL IMPORTED INTO AND EXPORTED FROM SOUTH AUSTRALIA FOR EACH YEAR FROM 1875 TO 1884, INCLUSIVE.

Years.	Imports.		Exports.	
	Wool, raw.		Wool, raw.	
	Pounds.	£	Pounds.	£
1875	7,165,355	377,699	44,508,674	2,066,227
1876	9,086,734	438,079	43,068,705	1,838,299
1877	3,386,827	143,340	50,610,902	2,189,418
1878	13,414,375	667,891	67,982,463	2,417,397
1879	9,693,650	437,190	49,402,149	1,984,879
1880	10,009,719	508,397	51,544,118	2,065,176
1881	8,160,235	338,650	50,336,040	1,911,927
1882	17,775,666	863,874	57,926,306	2,400,563
1883	13,209,299	661,178	55,463,920	2,406,768
1884	16,816,068	793,206	64,112,240	2,616,626

No. 56.—STATEMENT SHOWING THE QUANTITIES AND VALUES OF WOOL EXPORTED FROM TASMANIA FOR EACH YEAR FROM 1875 TO 1884, INCLUSIVE.

Years.	Wool, raw.		Years.	Wool, raw.	
	Pounds.	£		Pounds.	£
1875	8,199,248	433,550	1880	9,025,228	542,244
1876	6,848,517	439,603	1881	8,269,724	498,400
1877	8,016,396	522,885	1882	7,748,542	432,768
1878	7,512,662	479,165	1883	8,257,765	450,367
1879	7,385,002	407,227	1884	8,215,101	453,567

No. 57.—STATEMENT SHOWING THE VALUES OF MANUFACTURES OF WOOL IMPORTED INTO AND THE QUANTITIES AND VALUES OF WOOL EXPORTED FROM NEW ZEALAND FOR EACH YEAR FROM 1875 TO 1884, INCLUSIVE.

Years.	Imports.	Exports.	
	Manufactures of wool.	Wool, raw.	
	£	Pounds.	£
1875	216,116	54,401,540	3,398,155
1876	137,763	59,853,454	3,305,816
1877	107,594	64,481,324	3,658,938
1878	137,207	59,270,256	3,292,807
1879	174,138	62,220,810	3,126,439
1880	103,103	66,860,150	3,160,300
1881	97,245	59,521,564	214,046
1882	155,314	65,356,867	3,119,837
1883	130,242	68,182,450	3,015,461
1884	100,521	81,130,028	3,267,527

No. 58.—STATEMENT SHOWING THE QUANTITIES AND VALUES OF WOOL EXPORTED FROM QUEENSLAND FOR EACH YEAR FROM 1875 TO 1884, INCLUSIVE.

Years.	Wool, raw.		Years.	Wool, raw.	
	Pounds.	£		Pounds.	£
1875	20,145,914	1,366,030	1880	24,360,723	1,387,530
1876	22,918,560	1,409,576	1881	25,388,013	1,331,869
1877	23,980,483	1,409,082	1882	24,763,149	1,329,019
1878	21,068,122	1,185,659	1883	43,231,606	2,277,878
1879	22,582,834	1,238,518	1884	35,525,977	1,889,504

No. 59.—STATEMENT SHOWING THE QUANTITIES AND VALUES OF MANUFACTURES OF WOOL IMPORTED INTO AND OF WOOL EXPORTED FROM NATAL FOR EACH YEAR FROM 1875 TO 1884, INCLUSIVE.

Years.	Imports.				Exports.	
	Manufactures of wool.				Wool, raw.	
	Blankets.		Other manufactures.			
	Pounds.	£	Yards.	£	Pounds.	£
1875	42,852	27,664	270,456	19,961	8,105,447	369,285
1876	63,261	38,481	98,164	9,632	8,550,177	366,280
1877	32,252	16,818	152,063	13,418	10,012,356	383,019
1878	72,858	37,101	207,515	16,368	12,077,966	429,057
1879	119,872	61,902	389,702	19,972	12,029,216	415,890
1880	176,116	106,461	356,035	23,310	15,283,049	529,321
1881	86,974	43,949	152,697	10,842	12,578,781	450,938
1882	131,212	73,183	361,103	21,011	14,056,126	481,449
1883	74,390	43,031	217,654	19,345	15,826,915	519,161
1884	74,660	35,147	428,164	21,863	17,330,981	523,377

No. 60.—STATEMENT SHOWING THE VALUES OF MANUFACTURES OF WOOL IMPORTED INTO, AND THE QUANTITIES AND VALUES OF WOOL EXPORTED FROM, THE CAPE OF GOOD HOPE FOR EACH YEAR FROM 1875 TO 1884, INCLUSIVE.

Years.	Imports.	Exports.	
	Manufactures of wool.	Wool, raw.	
	£	Pounds.	£
1875	266,867	40,339,674	2,855,899
1876	225,563	34,861,339	2,278,942
1877	163,813	36,020,571	2,232,755
1878	198,521	32,127,167	1,883,928
1879	279,456	40,087,593	2,156,609
1880	308,627	42,467,962	2,429,360
1881	312,090	42,770,244	2,181,937
1882	394,657	41,689,119	2,062,180
1883	181,850	38,029,495	1,992,745
1884	140,722	37,270,615	1,745,193

No. 61.—STATEMENT SHOWING THE VALUES OF MANUFACTURES OF WOOL IMPORTED INTO, AND OF WOOL EXPORTED FROM, EGYPT FOR EACH YEAR FROM 1875 TO 1884, INCLUSIVE.

[One piaster equals 4.943 cents.]

Years.	Imports.	Exports.	Years.	Imports.	Exports.
	Manufactures of wool.	Wool, raw.		Manufactures of wool.	Wool, raw.
	Piasters.	Piasters.		Piasters.	Piasters.
1875	19,416,000	7,380,000	1880	30,004,000	5,328,000
1876	22,705,000	10,535,000	1881	25,241,000	5,049,000
1877	13,814,000	8,756,000	1882	14,253,000	4,538,000
1878	16,052,000	5,173,000	1883	24,750,000	7,974,000
1879	18,746,000	4,762,000	1884	30,418,000	5,186,000

No. 62.—STATEMENT SHOWING THE VALUES OF MANUFACTURES OF WOOL IMPORTED INTO CHINA (EXCLUSIVE OF HONG-KONG) FOR EACH YEAR FROM 1874 TO 1884, INCLUSIVE.

[One H. tael equals $1.022.]

Years.	Manufactures of wool.	Years.	Manufactures of wool.
	H. taels.		H. taels.
1874	4,510,000	1880	5,811,000
1875	4,561,000	1881	5,854,000
1876	4,250,000	1882	4,496,000
1877	4,831,000	1883	3,893,000
1878	4,876,000	1884	3,710,000
1879	4,954,000		

No. 63.—STATEMENT SHOWING THE QUANTITIES AND VALUES OF WOOL AND MANUFACTURES OF WOOL IMPORTED INTO JAPAN FOR EACH YEAR FROM 1868 TO 1885, INCLUSIVE.

[One catty equals 1.333 pounds. One yen equals 99.7 cents.]

Years.	Wool.		Woolen yarn.		Alpacas.		Balzarine.	
	Catties.	Yen.	Catties.	Yen.	Yards.	Yen.	Yards.	Yen.
1868								
1869								
1870								
1871								
1872								
1873								
1874			427	497.79	44,162	8,931.72		
1875			84	149.48	92,136	15,774.07		
1876			3,892	4,790.25	65,339	11,745.30		
1877			560	878.75	38,321	7,098.41		
1878			1,384	1,448.08	112,913	26,840.56		
1879			1,203	1,231.45	71,857	12,643.61		
1880			5,866	3,639.15	205,002	26,551.18		
1881			1,345	2,022.30	2,374	598.32		
1882			7,581	4,043.06	801	217.00		
1883	273,163	89,845.48	5,212	2,993.94	10,083	1,516.79	68,265	7,364.12
1884	153,691	42,516.58	2,601	2,322.58	11,700	2,531.22	130,942	12,555.22
1885	255,238	75,385.18	16,154	10,218.37	14,553	2,167.68	30,190	1,900.81

Years.	Blankets.		Buntings.		Camlets.		Camlet cords.	
	Catties.	Yen.	Yards.	Yen.	Yards.	Yen.	Yards.	Yen.
1868	328,453	172,258.52	......	1,138.80	1,348,990	403,924.42		
1869	837,856	557,853.12	2,376	171.30	1,845,688	546,039.86		
1870	225,283	91,447.10	20,545	2,886.00	525,788	151,100.14		
1871	251,307	117,560.57	50,800	14,223.00	107,882	53,489.62		
1872	636,108	272,679.48	49,012	18,131.55	174,953	48,123.93		
1873	672,402	414,149.45	55,720	8,903.52	132,603	40,599.09		
1874	183,135	90,392.69	70,282	11,805.76	133,939	34,863.43		
1875	740,137	359,004.56	20,177	5,319.17	205,610	56,807.46	146,875	32,636.93
1876	247,701	127,611.86	53,965	6,775.95	52,873	13,719.45	3,586	780.00
1877	900,727	460,206.94	35,776	4,356.53	90,283	24,827.25	19,543	3,238.24
1878	758,152	339,682.69	96,924	10,498.24	101,061	25,942.99	40,352	7,118.08
1879	379,754	175,413.49	19,701	2,089.74	23,217	6,181.06	30,596	4,182.57
1880	593,502	264,775.74	37,006	4,016.77	65,090	18,066.48		
1881	523,079	231,861.06	46,740	4,495.05	58,807	13,793.78	23,477	2,994.50
1882	462,436	210,136.92	46,333	4,443.06	36,808	7,790.31	39,701	5,080.07
1883	620,140	278,868.55	33,758	3,202.07	29,768	5,872.25	93,216	11,996.07
1884	633,003	279,824.64	21,881	2,217.65	18,687	3,365.48	7,502	1,180.45
1885	484,337	207,871.42	20,709	1,880.75	18,631	3,637.85	29,102	3,812.32

No. 63.—Statement showing the Quantities and Values of Wool and Manu-factures of Wool imported into Japan for each Year from 1868 to 1885, inclusive—Continued.

Years.	China figures.		Flannels.		Italian cloths.		Lastings.	
	Yards.	Yen.	Yards.	Yen.	Yards.	Yen.	Yards.	Yen.
1868			39,551	10.745.45	13,820	2,785.61	22.062	7,738.02
1809			14,260	5,408.01				
1870			28,223	8,098.62	106,542	42,616.65		
1871			30,163	8,513.66	24,758	17,759.48		
1872			317,670	165,324.24				
1873			731,465	224,031.09	585,435	155,508.88	665,714	109,839.23
1874			108,072	30,220.04	205,448	50,615.62	13,720	4,646.00
1875			180,372	45,604.70	818,881	214,694.81		
1876			13J,315	39,896.11	774,676	188,480.04	303,835	59,684.52
1877			459,897	130,578.04	2,097,966	496,081.29	384,496	90,306.75
1878			622,320	170,982.50	1,520,397	339,813.66	653,882	137,109.63
1879			126,071	34,357.53	3,089,258	651,929.16	527,417	103,024.83
1880			100,489	28,348.03	4,355,706	891,429.02	541,579	89,153.36
1881			216,426	60,316.77	2,671,966	531,827.08	646,681	122,433.74
1882			375,017	105,784.93	2,676,351	573,494.60	201,747	46,949.26
1883	255,694	24,284.05	343,645	94,582.61	4,749,706	995,091.05	220,540	47,732.12
1884	83,013	7,915 91	633,775	172,587.69	2,480,938	450,337.77	56,986	12,336.32
1885	5,930	639.03	1,079,351	287,181.72	4,453,409	828,055.26	9,159	2,557.01

Years.	Long ells.		Lusters.		Mousseline de Laine.		Orleans.	
	Yards.	Yen.	Yards.	Yen.	Yards.	Yen.	Yards.	Yen.
1868	54,560	14,880.50			347,460	73,278.40	831,210	142,525.60
1869	55,081	19,176.65						
1870	102,707	63,530.55						
1871	126,180	46,435.80						
1872	172,931	53,202.13					4,495,344	887,932.05
1873	63,733	20,108.04	705,302	127,671.20	9,053,427	1,076,443.86	224,565	37,774.10
1874	61,576	19,819.61	114,918	19,540.11	4,752,524	981,237.17	1,010,404	338,525.02
1875	53,736	16,116.20	398,029	67,219.28	10,197,172	2,393,157.56	3,988,434	671,925.34
1876	72,138	25,549.71	361,518	55,567.70	10,819,785	2,263,273.43	1,553,662	244,634.14
1877	78,219	27,917.21	444,428	69,326.06	11,901,189	2,373,621.20	1,297,829	196,118.15
1878	63,564	22,872.96	274,339	39,349.06	13,626,117	2,693,766.90	2,086,376	277,062.31
1879	85,599	25,010.86	242,893	30,488.89	17,301,218	3,126,042.55	2,974,302	369,859.45
1880	63,358	21,291.44	176,362	18,884.42	20,946,299	3,478,056.83	1,448,032	173,337.90
1881	82,955	26,940.86	348,885	41,679.19	15,863,102	2,700,341.11	1,382,183	145,671.93
1882	56,493	15,983.78	38,418	3,953.98	8,873,846	1,221,784.80	746,908	75,297.32
1883	36,615	9,604.58	54,352	5,397.60	11,297,560	1,618,072.40	358,932	34,820.13
1884	59,158	15,600.46	101,427	10,271.33	14,607,355	1,839,997.61	338,362	33,658.76
1885	36,951	9,765.61	151,852	14,958.67	7,802,765	900,616.92	341,703	32,650.36

Years.	Serges.		Spanish stripes.		Woolen cloths.		Woolen cloths, in part of wool.	
	Yards.	Yen.	Yards.	Yen.	Yards.	Yen.	Yards.	Yen.
1868			10,657	4,200.88	194,049	235,344.93		
1869			3,473	2,778.66	461,156	606,171.25		
1870			8,038	18,690.14	437,237	640,306.18		
1871			10,136	29,660.73	436,574	840,039.02		
1872			7,036	6,148.14	1,261,868	3,036,480.47		
1873			3,163	2,467.70	1,038,158	1,320,895.77		
1874		13,912.75	9,484	6,622.81	84,102	112,886.79		
1875	662	128.70	10,161	7,387.79	1,845,247	530,868.19		
1876	1,412	750.49	22,521	15,365.04	1,970,407	594,600.90		
1877	31,791	14,830.73	12,287	9,645.60	490,738	684,936.13		
1878	64,325	26,388.85	25,604	18,974.74	503,393	702,653.31		
1879	66,065	34,007.34	3,112	2,742.35	157,447	212,109.05		
1880	52,837	27,036.39	10,450	7,705.18	143,224	188,484.03		
1881	32,217	12,825.12	8,807	5,879.22	75,329	89,234.63		
1882	34,711	19,291.88	7,248	5,748.09	157,469	181,881.34		
1883	85,137	40,176.04	5,025	3,997.70	169,834	192,120.09	197,339	80,577.99
1884	59,047	23,415.12	2,582	1,866.59	377,171	467,641.79	170,131	68,072.03
1885	60,571	26,143.86	6,371	3,814.72	364,763	391,904.64	192,858	82,439.61

No. 63.—STATEMENT SHOWING THE QUANTITIES AND VALUES OF WOOL AND MANU-
FACTURES OF WOOL IMPORTED INTO JAPAN FOR EACH YEAR FROM 1868 TO 1885,
INCLUSIVE—Continued.

Years.	Woolen damasks.		Woolen piece goods, un-enumerated.		Woolen and cotton mixtures, unenumerated.		Total.
	Yards.	*Yen.*	*Yards.*	*Yen.*	*Yards.*	*Yen.*	*Yen.*
1868			418,778	127,723.04	4,172,822	923,834.47	2,120,379.60
1869			656,413	478,558.56	2,135,797	690,611.32	2,912,858.73
1870			2,218,176	628,144.48	5,302,766	1,132,707.72	2,787,596.58
1871			3,190,117	952,096.88	6,507,729	1,920,297.28	4,002,976.10
1872			3,092,804	1,768,766.72	5,332,921	1,292,364.99	7,480,218.75
1873			841,192	322,822.67	10,726,032	3,608,041.16	7,475,353.66
1874			791,146	191,513.68	5,145,320	1,304,379.90	3,220,410.89
1875	162	158.57	1,312,759	319,518.71	6,504,681	1,390,857.97	6,136,009.49
1876	78	20.00	033,817	103,061.17	2,179,061	472,480.23	4,228,805.29
1877			318,640	81,553.04	1,907,493	631,923.43	5,307,443.75
1878	20	25.02	134,662	47,587.32	3,064,153	873,484.05	5,761,601.64
1879	72	11.47	284,127	42,643.07	2,486,776	639,550.06	5,476,518.53
1880	198	120.60	239,251	38,231.21	2,789,814	774,639.38	6,030,767.11
1881	153	88.46	378,053	61,071.96	2,493,992	511,225.07	4,576,312.15
1882	1,721	1,132.65	53,435	9,119.58	1,725,486	353,891.01	2,846,020.54
1883	1,113	701.34	31,114	7,287.56	212,925	65,659.99	3,622,045.12
1884	1,452	981.29	15,154	9,765.88	127,306	40,043.15	3,501,010.52
1885	1,339	698.07	29,655	7,955.20	253,513	75,872.78	2,978,147.81

Recapitulation of the total values of imports and exports of raw wool and manufactures of wool into and from the following foreign countries during the years named.

Countries.	Years.	Imports.		Exports.	
		Wool.	Manufactures of wool.	Wool.	Manufactures of wool.
		Dollars.	*Dollars.*	*Dollars.*	*Dollars.*
Austria-Hungary	1885	*a*18,633,700	10,819,033	*a*10,632,655	19,935,541
Belgium	1884	14,057,755	4,057,625		15,381,328
France	1885	54,792,129	19,209,283	17,530,755	71,702,919
Germany	1884	52,811,962	25,044,264	9,357,208	51,701,216
Italy	1885	*a*5,677,288	13,225,372		639,558
Netherlands	1884	8,557,335	3,113,274	8,136,515	1,950,401
Norway	1884	304,448	3,144,712		
Portugal	1884	818,640	1,689,120	144,720	
Russia in Europe	1884	10,829,274	3,181,794	*b*7,171,986	
Spain	1885		5,770,445	*a*1,444,605	166,870
Sweden	1883	1,460,432	7,133,892		
Switzerland	1885		8,098,305		1,787,924
United Kingdom	1885	103,064,219	48,921,046	4,543,423	113,048,557
British Possessions:					
Dominion of Canada	1886	1,796,850	9,390,757	316,937	28,283
British India	1885		6,007,344	4,838,853	733,980
New South Wales	1884	2,369,723		45,659,931	
Victoria	1884	12,535,642	4,492,130	30,867,060	
South Australia	1884	3,860,137		12,733,810	
Tasmania	1884			2,207,284	
New Zealand	1884		489,185	15,901,421	
Queensland	1884			9,195,272	
Natal	1884		277,439	2,547,014	
Cape of Good Hope	1884		684,824	8,492,062	
Egypt	1884		1,503,502	256,344	
China (exclusive of Hong-Kong)	1884		6,017,620		
Japan	1885	75,159	2,969,213		

a 1884.   *b* 1882.

No. 64.—INFORMATION IN REGARD TO WOOL AND WOOLEN INDUSTRIES OF THE
UNITED KINGDOM, FRANCE, GERMANY, AND RUSSIA.

The following statistics in regard to the wool industries, manufactures, &c., of the United Kingdom, France, and Germany are derived
from the official report of a royal commission appointed to inquire into
the depression of trade and industry of Great Britain, and from other
official data.

According to the report of the royal commission the number of persons employed in the United Kingdom in the worsted and woolen manufactures was as follows:

Years.	Number employed.	Percentage of population employed.
1856	166,885	.596
1862	173,046	.592
1868	249,930	.814
1874	276,702	.851
1885	277,546	.764

The following exhibits the decrease of the value of exports and the concurrent increase of the value of imports of worsted and woolen yarns and manufactures:

5-year periods.	Imports.	Exports.
1870 to 1874	£25,896,913	£157,538,261
1875 to 1879	33,912,846	110,942,983
1880 to 1884	41,525,820	109,740,697

Proportion of imported and home-grown wool retained for manufacture in the United Kingdom in the five years 1880-'84, as compared with the five years 1865-'69.

[Of the total supply.]

	1865-'69.		1880-'84.	
	Pounds.	*Per cent.*	*Pounds.*	*Per cent.*
Imported	236,300,000		481,200,000	
Of which re-exported	92,300,000		264,200,000	
Retained for manufacture	144,000,000	60.9	217,100,000	45.1
Domestic clip	161,000,000		135,000,000	
Of which exported	9,900,000		16,500,000	
Retained for manufacture	151,100,000	93.8	118,500,000	87.8
Total of imported and home-grown wool retained for manufacture	295,100,000	74.3	335,600,000	54.5
Exported for manufacture abroad	102,200,000	25.7	280,700,000	45.5

Wool retained for manufacture in the United Kingdom, the United States, France, and Germany, respectively, in the years 1866, 1876, and 1884.

	1866.	1876.	1884.
	Pounds.	*Pounds.*	*Pounds.*
United Kingdom (imported and home-grown)	313,000,000	360,000,000	381,000,000
United States (imported and home-grown)	229,707,000	235,020,000	376,036,000
France (home-grown not included, amount unknown)	190,119,000	271,484,000	365,767,000
Germany (home-grown not included, amount unknown)	No returns.	143,260,000	232,962,000

NOTE.—The domestic production of wool in France decreased from 43,434,300 kilograms in 1876 to 36,351,200 kilograms in 1882. The domestic production in Germany has decreased from about 62,273,000 pounds in 1873 to about 47,974,000 pounds in 1883.

The commissioners, in their report, commenting on the foregoing tables, state:

The seriously diminished value of our exports of woolens * * * during the years 1880 to 1884, as compared with the years 1870 to 1874, must be accepted as a clear proof that foreign tariffs are the great cause at work to prevent the natural and healthy growth of this important industry in this country. How rapidly they must have been growing in France, Germany, and the United States, whilst comparatively languishing here, is strikingly shown in the tables on the preceding page. In the eight years from 1876 to 1884, France, Germany, and the United States increased their annual consumption of wool by 325,000,000 pounds, or, allowing for the estimated diminution of the home production of France and Germany, 295,000,000 pounds, that is, 45 per cent., while ours increased only by 12,000,000 pounds, or 3¾ per cent. * * *

This is illustrated by the extraordinary fact that whilst the value of our exports of worsted and woolen manufactures in the five years from 1880 to 1884 exhibited, as compared with the five years from 1865 to 1869, a decrease of 43.1 per cent., the value of our imports, comparing with the same period, showed an increase of no less than 214.9 per cent.

This fact confirms the evidence given before us by witnesses connected with the various industries that in the case of countries like Germany, possessing in ample measure the population and other resources required for successful manufacturing enterprise, the adoption of a system of import duties on manufactures and even on primary articles of food, has not disqualified them from successful and growing competition with us in the home and colonial as well as in the neutral markets.

UNITED KINGDOM.

The woolen and worsted industries.

[From " Deutsches Handels-Archiv," March, 1887.]

	Establishments.	Spindles.	Doubling spindles.	Power looms.	Employés.
Woolen industries:					
1885	1,918	3,054,144	230,941	57,990	139,316
1874	1,800	3,165,569	158,312	57,090	134,605
1868	1,658	4,190,670	167,248	46,204	118,104
1862	1,679	2,182,609	....	21,770	86,983
1856	1,505	1,786,972	....	14,453	79,091
Worsted industries:					
1885	725	2,227,192	536,329	79,971	138,230
1874	602	2,182,792	399,658	81,747	142,007
1868	703	2,193,210	348,363	71,660	131,896
1862	532	1,269,172	....	43,048	86,063
1856	525	1,324,540	....	38,956	87,794
Shoddy, mungo, &c.:					
1885	108	93,766	2,222	1,981	4,709
1874	125	101,134	946	1,437	3,431

FRANCE.

State of the wool manufacturing industry December 1, 1875.

Articles.	Number of factories.	Number of persons. employed.
Wool and hair spinning and tissue making:		
Carded yarns and vicuna spinning..	1,037	4,196
Worsted yarn spinning..	2,350	28,772
Shoddy spinning...	129	4,776
Woolen tissue making..	20,677	65,138
Dyeing, printing, &c...	2,602	12,007

State of textile industries June 5, 1882.

Articles.	Number of factories.	Number of persons employed.
Wool and hair spinning and tissue making:		
Preparing wool	1,354	5,798
Wool spinning	5,859	47,347
Vicuna wool spinning	105	6,158
Shoddy spinning	179	8,354
Woolen tissues	28,201	108,007
Wool dyeing, printing, and dressing	2,678	20,611

There appear to have been other industries, such as weaving, knitting, crocheting, embroidering, and tissue making (stuffs not distinguished), which may largely include manufactures of wool, but the proportion thereof cannot be determined from the meager information accessible.

Progress of the wool industry of France.

[From the "Annuaire de Statistique de la France."]

Years.	Factories.	Persons employed.	Spindles.	Looms.		Quantity of raw wool imported and entered for home consumption.
				Machine.	Hand.	
						Pounds.
1872			2,899,894			237,727,848
1873			2,898,929	23,725		265,661,180
1874			2,955,139	27,557		258,646,012
1875	2,270	95,779	2,969,522	30,114	56,895	282,124,040
1876	2,090	110,954	2,946,632	38,267	62,230	271,454,312
1877	2,198	108,049	3,007,351	28,188	54,434	295,853,940
1878	2,300	105,839	2,995,400	30,139	41,603	317,596,400
1879	2,200	108,086	3,022,777	35,271	42,031	295,807,656
1880	1,926	110,904	3,037,837	41,044	37,632	332,951,668
1881	1,915	111,523	3,067,450	41,466	37,140	304,683,728
1882	1,915	113,220	3,063,961	44,516	37,127	310,726,532

GERMANY.

Factories employing power and the kind of power used.

[From the "Statistik des Deutschen Reichs," neue Folge, Bände 6 und 7, Berlin, 1886.]

Industries.	Establishments.	Employés.	Machines moved by—				Boilers.	Other local power.
			Wind.	Water.	Steam.	Gas or hot air.		
Wool cleaning	150	4,261	2	42	128	2	7	1
Yarns	1,182	42,294	3	504	846	17	4	11
Shoddy, mungo, &c	135	8,243		62	99		1	
Weaving	1,209	64,708		276	1,059	8	12	4
Dyeing, printing, &c	1,155	17,950	2	293	796	10	126	13
Total	3,831	137,456	7	1,177	2,928	37	150	29

Ownership, number, and employés of the woolen manufactures in 1882.

[From the "Statistik des Deutschen Reichs," neue Folge, Bände 6 und 7, Berlin, 1886.]

Ownership.	Wool cleaning.		Yarns.		Shoddy, mungo, &c.		Weaving.		Dyeing, printing, &c.	
	Establishments.	Employés.	Establishments.	Employés.	Establishments.	Employés.	Establishments.	Employés.	Establishments.	Employés.
Individuals	173	1,489	927	13,980	89	3,571	7,199	44,588	1,149	9,602
Associates	72	2,330	443	19,093	48	4,165	758	43,206	462	9,729
Corporations	8	1,150	45	10,402	4	586	19	1,880	38	476
Municipalities	1	2	3	61					1	16
State or national	2	49	4	52			5	228	1	15
Total	256	5,029	1,422	43,583	141	8,322	7,981	89,902	1,631	19,838

WOOLEN MANUFACTURES IN RUSSIA.

[From report of the French consul at Warsaw in "Bulletin Consulaire Français," July, 1887, p. 30.]

The following information in regard to manufactures of wool in Russia is derived from official data published by the Department of Commerce and Manufactures of Russia, from which it appears that the value of manufactures of wool in Russia were, in 1885, 104,498,000 rubles, and in 1886, 115,075,000 rubles.

Of the 68 wool-spinning mills, employing 4,789 workmen and producing goods to the value of 5,173,000 rubles, 32 mills, with 3,637 operatives and a production of 3,638,000 rubles, are located in the province of Moscow. The St. Petersburg district occupies the second rank, with a production of 805,000 rubles of thread and 700 operatives, distributed in 7 factories. The production of other provinces is of no importance.

The carpet weavers are concentrated exclusively in the Moscow province. Of the 9 factories, with 323 looms, employing 802 operatives, with an annual product of 550,000 rubles, the old capital contains 7 run by steam, the product of which exceeds half a million rubles.

In the manufacture of felt—of little consequence elsewhere—the district of Nijni-Novogorod holds the first place, with 10 factories, employing 315 operatives, and with a product of 195,000 rubles. Besides these, there are 3 factories, with a production of 36,000 rubles, belonging to the province of Tver, 2 with a product of 25,000 in that of St. Petersburg, 2 with a product of 18,000 in Livonia, and several insignificant factories in the provinces of Moscow, Kazan, Kalooga, Yaraslaw, Kharkow, Pskow, and in Courland.

In the production of cloths the Moscow province holds the first rank. Of the 390 factories, employing 48,000 hands, with a production of 40,769,000 rubles (25,916,000 arsheens* of cloth), in European Russia, the Moscowvite province contains 48 factories, with 18,880 hands and a

* 1 arsheen = 28 inches.

production of 18,407,000 rubles. The province of Grodno holds the second place, with 162 factories, employing 6,200 hands, and with an annual product of 5,884,000 rubles. Then come the provinces of St. Petersburg with a production of 3,789,000 rubles (5 factories and 2,226 hands), Tchernigow with 2,130,000 rubles (12 factories and 2,452 hands), Penza with 1,364,000 rubles (4 factories and 1,600 hands), Tambow with 1,246,000 rubles (8 factories and 2,795 hands), Esthonia with 750,000 rubles (1 factory and 557 hands), the province of Saratow with 594,000 rubles (6 factories, 898 hands), Perm with 553,000 rubles (3 factories and 1,202 hands), and Podolia with a production of 366,000 rubles (42 factories, 259 hands). Other manufactories of cloth of some importance are found in the province of Koursk (1 factory, 500 hands, with a product of 171,000 rubles), Yaraslaw (1 factory with a production of 180,000 rubles, 176 hands), Samara (2 factories with a product of 211,000 rubles, 455 hands), in Volhynia (37 factories with a product of 192,000 rubles), and in the province of Kiew (16 factories with a product of 175,000 rubles).

Beside these manufactures, there are in European Russia 190 factories of light goods of pure wool and of wool mixed with cotton or silk. These factories run 14,500 looms, employing 19,000 hands, their product amounting to 21,125,000 rubles; 169 of these establishments, with 13,882 looms and a product of 20,500,000 of rubles, are found in the province of Moscow. Yarns are produced in 67 factories with a force of 1,500 operatives and a product of 1,051,000 rubles. Here again the province of Moscow occupies the first place, with 39 factories, 1,043 hands, and a product of 701,000 rubles. The St. Petersburg province follows with 14 factories and a product of 195,000 rubles. Other factories are scattered through the provinces of Livonia (4 establishments with a product of 78,000 rubles), Grodno (4 establishments with a product of 49,000 rubles), Tchernigow (2 factories, product 14,000 rubles), and Novogorod (1 factory, product 10,000 rubles).

The wadding factories number 53 and their product amounts to about 160,000 poods, worth 854,000 rubles. This manufacture centers principally in the province of Riazan—17 establishments with 285 hands. Beside these there are 3 in St. Petersburg (with a product of 190,000 rubles), 6 in the province of Moscow (product 69,000 rubles), 5 in Astrakhan (50,000 rubles), 7 in Catherinoslow (52,000 rubles), 1, producing 37,000 rubles, in the province of Perm, and various small factories in the provinces of Kazan, Saratow, Tver, and Kherson. Gimps, braids, &c., occupy but an insignificant place in the national production. The number of factories is 53, employing 1,900 hands, with an annual production of 1,797,000 roubles. The principal places of their operation are St. Petersburg and Moscow. Ninety-three small, scattered factories have not been included in the preceding figures, which, in various localities, reach a product of about 1,000 rubles each annually.

RECAPITULATION.

Designation.	Establish-ments.	Employed.	Product.	Looms.
Spinning mills	68	4,789	5,173,000	....
Factories:				
Carpet	9	802	550,000	323
Felt	41	637	310,000	....
Light goods	190	19,072	21,125,000	14,500
Cloth	390	48,003	40,769,000	....
Yarn	67	1,487	1,052,000	....
Wadding	53	648	854,000	....

No. 65.—STATEMENT SHOWING THE PRESENT TARIFF RATES OF FOREIGN COUNTRIES ON IMPORTATIONS OF WOOL AND MANUFACTURES OF WOOL.

[Compiled from the United States Consular Reports.]

Countries.	Rates of duty.
EUROPE.	
Austria-Hungary:	*Per 100 kilograms.*
Wool, raw, washed, combed, colored, bleached, milled, and as refuse.	Free.
Manufactures of wool:	
Wool and hair tablets, hat-felts and hat-wadding	$3 34
Woolen yarns (of wool or animal hair) and vicuna yarns:	
a. Raw	2 97
NOTE.—Weft yarn, raw, or entry by way of custom-houses specially designated	58
b. Bleached, colored, printed, three or more twisted threads	4 45
Woolen goods (of wool or animal hair):	
Shaggy cloths, Halina cloths, pressed cloths, sieve-bottoms, ropes, cables made of horse hair, trellis and tied nets, both uncolored, hat clipping, cloth cuttings	4 45
Carpets:	
a. Of dog's, calf's or cow's hair; also with slight mixture of wool	4 45
b. Other, also printed	14 84
Girths	14 84
Woolen-woven goods not specially named:	
a. Weighing over 500 grams per square meter	18 55
b. Weighing 500 grams and less per square meter	29 68
NOTE.—Entirely woven with cotton warp, of one color, not figured, dressed like cloth, weighing more than 300 grams per square meter	18 55
Velvets and velvet-like fabrics (cut or uncut), fringes, buttons, ribbons, and knit goods (except those under carpets, other)	29 68
Light woolen and woven goods	37 10
Shawls and shawl-like textures, laces (lace shawls), embroidered woven goods, goods with metallic threads	55 65
Felt and felt goods (except carpets):	
a. Coarse felts of animal hair; also cut out, tarred, or varnished	4 45
b. Felt, other, and felt goods, both not printed	14 84
c. Printed	29 68
Belgium:	
Wool, raw	Free.
Manufactures of wool:	
Shawls and scarfs of India cashmere	5 per cent. ad valorem.
All others, including mixed tissues, where wool predominates in weight	10 per cent. ad valorem.
(On the last named the importer has the option to pay 200 francs, or $50.18, per 100 kilograms.)	
Denmark:	*Per hundred-weight.*
Wool, raw	Free.
Manufactures of—	
Coarse	$3 40
Others	6 80
Printed	18 13
Printed, fine	26 80
Woolen yarn:	
Fancy, colored	13 60
Uncolored	1 70
Colored	4 53

No. 65.—Statement showing the Present Tariff Rates of Foreign Countries on Importations of Wool and Manufactures of Wool—Continued.

Countries.	Conventional tariff.	General tariff.
EUROPE—continued.		
France:	*Per 100 kilograms.*	*Per 100 kilos.*
Wool, raw, of all kinds:		
Combed or carded............................	$4 63	Free.
Dyed	4 83	Free.
Manufactures of wool :		
Woolen yarn, pure :		
Single thread, bleached or unbleached, combed, measuring to the kilogram :		
10,000 meters or less	1 93	$5 98
More than 10,000 meters to 15,000........	2 90	5 98
15,000 meters to 20,000........	3 86	5 98
20,000 meters to 30,500........	4 83	5 98
30,500 meters to 40,500........	6 76	8 30
40,500 meters to 50,500........	8 69	10 81
50,500 meters to 60,500........	10 62	13 12
60,500 meters to 70,500........	12 55	15 63
70,500 meters to 80,500........	14 48	17 95
80,500 meters to 90,500........	16 41	20 27
90,500 meters to 100,500........	18 34	22 77
100,500 meters....................	19 30	23 93
Single thread, bleached or unbleached, carded, measuring to the kilogram :		
10,000 meters or less		3 57
More than 10,000 meters to 15,000.......	Same duty as yarn, single thread, bleached or unbleached, combed........	5 40
15,000 meters to 20,000........		7 14
20,000 meters to 30,500........		8 88
30,500 meters		10 81
Single thread, colored, combed, measuring to the kilogram :		
30,500 meters or less	9 65	11 97
More than 30,500 meters to 40,500........	11 58	14 28
40,500 meters to 50,500........	13 51	16 79
50,500 meters to 60,500........	15 44	19 11
60,500 meters to 70,500........	17 37	21 62
70,500 meters to 80,500........	19 30	23 93
80,500 meters to 90,500........	21 23	26 25
90,500 meters to 100,500........	23 16	28 76
100,500 meters	24 13	24 92
Single thread, colored, carded, measuring to the kilogram :		
10,000 meters or less.........		9 65
More than 10,000 meters to 15,000.......	Same duty as yarn, single thread, colored, combed.	11 39
15,000 meters to 20,000........		13 12
20,000 meters to 30,500.......		14 86
30,500 meters		16 79
Woolen yarn, pure, for weaving:		
Twisted, bleached or unbleached, combed, measuring in the kilogram, and in single thread:		
30,500 meters or less	6 28	7 72
More than 30,500 meters to 40,500........	8 79	10 81
40,500 meters to 50,500........	11 29	13 90
50,500 meters to 60,500........	13 80	16 98
60,500 meters to 70,500........	16 31	20 07
70,500 meters to 80,500........	18 82	23 16
80,500 meters to 90,500........	21 33	26 25
90,500 meters to 100,500........	23 84	29 34
100,500 meters	25 09	31 07
Twisted, bleached or unbleached, carded, measuring in the kilogram and in single thread—		
10,000 meters or less		5 40
More than 10,000 meters to 15,000.......	Same duty as woolen yarn, pure, twisted, bleached or unbleached, combed.	7 14
15,000 meters to 20,000.......		8 88
20,000 meters to 30,500.......		10 81
30,500 meters....................		12 55
Twisted, colored, combed, measuring in the kilogram and in single thread—		
30,500 meters or less	11 10	13 70
30,500 meters to 40,500	13 61	16 79
More than 40,500 meters to 50,500	16 12	19 11
50,500 meters to 60,500	18 63	21 62
60,500 meters to 70,500	21 14	23 93
70,500 meters to 80,500	23 65	26 63
80,500 meters to 90,500	26 16	29 34
90,500 meters to 100,500	28 66	32 04
100,500 meters	30 01	33 58

No. 65.—STATEMENT SHOWING THE PRESENT TARIFF RATES OF FOREIGN COUNTRIES ON IMPORTATIONS OF WOOL AND MANUFACTURES OF WOOL—Continued.

Countries.	Conventional tariff.	General tariff.
EUROPE—continued.		
France—Continued.		
Manufactures of wool:		
Woolen yarn, pure, for weaving:		
Twisted, colored, carded, measuring in the kilogram and in the single thread—	*Per 100 kilograms.*	*Per 100 kilos.*
10,000 meters or less		$11 39
More than 10,000 meters to 15,000	Same duty as woolen yarn,	13 12
15,000 meters to 20,000	pure twisted, colored,	14 86
20,000 meters to 30,500	combed.	16 79
30,500 meters		18 53
Woolen yarn, pure, for tapestry work:		
Twisted, combed, bleached or unbleached, measuring in the kilogram and in single thread—		
30,500 meters or less	$9 65	8 88
More than 30,500 meters to 40,500	13 51	12 55
40,500 meters to 50,500	17 37	16 21
50,500 meters to 60,500	21 23	19 69
60,500 meters to 70,500	25 09	23 35
70,500 meters to 80,500	28 95	26 83
80,500 meters to 90,500	32 81	30 49
90,500 meters to 100,500	36 67	34 16
100,500 meters	38 60	35 90
Twisted, combed, colored, measuring in the kilogram and in single thread—		
30,500 meters or less	14 48	14 86
More than 30,500 meters to 40,500	18 34	18 53
40,500 meters to 50,500	22 20	22 20
50,500 meters to 60,500	26 06	25 67
60,500 meters to 70,500	29 92	29 34
70,500 meters to 80,500	33 78	32 81
80,500 meters to 90,500	37 06	36 48
90,500 meters to 100,500	41 52	40 14
100,500 meters	43 45	41 83
Yarn, alpaca, llama, vicuna, or camel's hair, pure or mixed with wool, whatever shall be the proportion of mixture, or mixed with other filaments, wool of alpaca, &c., predominating in weight.	Same duty as woolen yarn, pure.	....
Yarns (mohair) made from the hair of goat, pure or mixed, the hair of the goat predominating in weight.	4 63	5 79
Yarn of other hair	Free.	Free.
Tissues of pure wool:		
Woolen cloth, cassimeres, and other tissues fulled, and tissues sheared, not fulled:		
Stuffs for upholstery, weighing more than 400 grams to the meter, square.	10 per cent. ad valorem ...	23 93
Moire	......do	14 48
Other stuffs:		
Weighing 400 grams or more to the meter, square.	......do	40 72
Weighing 401 to 550 grams, inclusive	......do	35 90
Weighing more than 550 grams	......do	31 07
Carpets, Axminster:		
Looped, uncut	......do	14 28
Velvet, finished	......do	19 11
Carpets:		
Persian	......do	35 90
Jacquard, chenille, and others	......do	23 93
Hosiery, pure wool and mixed wool:		
Gloves and garments, not fitted....	......do	125 45
Other, cut and seamless	......do	28 95
Other, fitted and finished	......do	57 90
Trimmings, ribbons	......do	47 86
Tapestry	......do	119 66
Shawls, broché or fancy figured, other than India cashmere.	......do	76 62
Laces	......do	71 80
Velvets of wool for upholstery	......do	43 04
Bolting cloth, seamless	......do ....*......	38 21
Blankets	......do	16 70
List slippers	......do	16 70
List of cloth	Free.	Free.
Tissues of wool, mixed:		{ 9.65 to 40.72 according to
Woolen cloth, cassimeres, and other tissues, fulled, warp cotton, tissues sheared, not fulled, the wool predominating.	10 per cent. ad valorem ...	the weight to the meter square.

No. 65.—STATEMENT SHOWING THE PRESENT TARIFF RATES OF FOREIGN COUNTRIES ON IMPORTATIONS OF WOOL AND MANUFACTURES OF WOOL—Continued.

Countries.	Conventional tariff.	General tariff.
EUROPE—continued.		
France—Continued.		
Manufacture of wool:	*Per 100 kilograms.*	*Per 100 kilos.*
Tissues wool warp, being silk waste, wool predominating.	10 per cent. ad valorem....	$57 32
Carpets:		
Wool mixed with cotton	......do	⎫ Same duty as
Wool mixed with other materials	......do	⎬ tissues or
Other tissues, the wool predominating in weight.	......do	⎭ pure wool.
Tissues, alpaca, llama, vicuna, sheep, yak, or of camel's hair, pure or mixed with other filaments, the wool of the alpaca, llama, vicuna, yak, or camel's hair predominating in weight.	Same duty as tissues of pure wool.	Same duty as tissues of pure wool.
Tissues of goat's hair, pure or mixed, the goat's hair predominating in weight:		
Cashmere shawls, long, made by hand:.......	5.20 per cent. ad valorem..	5 79
Cashmere shawls, square, made by hand......	......do	3 86
Scarfs, trimmings, fringes, &c., made by hand.	......do	193 00
Plain tissues, made by hand	......do	193 00
Other tissues of hair, pure or mixed, with other filaments, the hair predominating in weight.	Prohibited	7 14

	Rate of duty.
Germany:	*Per 100 kilos.*
Wool, raw	Free.
Combed..	$0 47
Manufactures, also mixed with cotton, linen, or metallic threads—	
1. Cloth selvedge	Free.
2. Coarse felts, not printed, not dyed	71
3. Good rugs, containing heads of cattle hair	5 71
5. Not printed felts; not belonging under No. 2; not printed felt goods and hosiery; good rugs. &c	23 80
4. Unprinted cloths and stuffs, not included under Nos. 7 and 8—	
If weighing more than 200 grams to the square meter of woven surface ...	32 13
If weighing less than 200 grams	52 36
6. *Printed articles,* as far as they do not belong to foot-rugs, weighing more than 200 grams to the square meter of woven surface; also, trimmings and buttonmakers' ware, plushes, weaving combined with metallic threads	35 70
Printed articles, not foot rugs, weighing 200 grams, or less than 200 grams, to the square meter of woven surface......................	52 36
7. Laces, tulles, or embroidered woven shawls, with three or more colors.....	71 40
8. Woven shawls, with five or more colors	107 10
Greece (a municipal tax of 2 per cent. is to be added to the duties in this schedule):	*Per oke.**
Wool, raw	Free.
Manufactures of wool:	
Woolen yarn, unbleached, and felt for men's hats....................	Free.
Yarn, bleached or dyed...........................	1 04
Coarse cloth, serge, belts, blankets....................	10
Carpets:	
Rugs, printed felt..............................	23
Rugs, woven or dyed.............................	58
Persian or Georgian	1 16
For hangings	1 93
Flannels in colors:	
Coarsely woven stockings, shawls, haversacks, sailors' caps, bedcovers, &c.	31
Finely woven...................................	97½
Trimmings, fringes, traveling rugs	1 16
Shawls, cashmere or merino	2 32
Tissues, to weight of—	
100 grams per square millimeter....................	2 32
200 grams per square millimeter....................	1 54
350 grams per square millimeter	96½
Above 350 grams per square millimeter.............	58
Part cotton up to 200 grams per square millimeter....	34
Above 200 grams per square millimeter	19¹⁵/₁₆
Clothing for men and boys:	
Light, for summer	25
Heavy, for winter..............................	87
Part cotton	48
For women and girls	2 90
Felt hats for women	19¹⁵/₁₆

* Oke—43.3 ounces avoirdupois; roughly, 2¾ lbs.

No. 65.—Statement showing the Present Tariff Rates of Foreign Countries on Importations of Wool and Manufactures of Wool—Continued.

Countries.	Rate of duty.
EUROPE—continued.	
Italy:	*Per 100 kilos.*
Wool, natural, washed, carded, dyed, waste wool, and refuse wool	Free.
Manufactures of wool:	
Woolen yarn—	
Untwisted, bleached or unbleached	$9 60
Untwisted and dyed	14 47
Twisted, bleached or unbleached	11 58
Twisted and dyed	17 37
Woolen textures (in textures composed in part of wool the duty is levied on that material which dominates in weight; if, however, the threads of the warp are of cotton, the duty is smaller)—	
Carded	27 02
Carded, with warps entirely of cotton yarn	18 10½
Combed	32 81
Combed, with warps composed entirely of cotton yarn	25 09
Embroidered	77 20
Felt—	
For hats	3 47
Tarred, pressed for soles, &c	1 85 1/10
For clothing	11 58
Woolen knitted goods and braids	38 60
Ribbons and galloons	42 46
Buttons	42 46
Laces and tulles	57 90
Covers made of waste strips of woolen cloth	11 58
Carpets made of waste strips of woolen cloth	11 58
Carpets	21 23
Sewed woolen goods of different materials are classed and taxed according to the predominating material.	
The Netherlands:	
Wool, raw	Free.
Manufactures of wool:	
Blankets	5 p. c. ad val.
Flannels	Do.
Knitted or woven cloths	Do.
All others, not stipulated	Do.
Cloth, doeskins	Do.
Norway:	*Per kilogram.*
Wool, raw	Free.
Manufactures of wool:	
Woolen yarn—	
a. Not dyed *	03 4/10
b. Dyed; also yarn of all descriptions, combined with metal threads †	05 3/10
Felts for machines, felts for paper machines, cloth lists	Free.
Other felts	21 4/10
Carpets, and material for carpets, bed quilts, saddle girths, and woven girths ‡	12 6/10
Hats and caps of all kinds of felt, or of woolen materials, &c	10 7/10
Knit goods, knitted, crocheted, netted, or woven:	
a. Stockings, undershirts, gloves, coarse §	07½
b. Other, including woolen scarfs of all kinds ‖	20 9/10
NOTE.—Stockings are reckoned as coarse when they have a length of 60 centimeters from the heel and weigh 160 grams or more per pair, and other lengths in the same proportion. Gloves are reckoned coarse when they have not more than one or two fingers. Shirts are considered coarse when each one with a length of 60 centimeters or more weighs 300 grams, and other lengths in the same proportion.	
Ribbons and textile goods interwoven with india-rubber, gutta-percha, and the like, and belts thereof	20 9/10
Blonde, bobbinet, lace, and gauze	67
Other open or clear goods, if either embroidered or woven in patterns, figures, stripes, or squares (embroidery on canvas excepted)	47 1/10
NOTE.—Goods shall be dutiable as open or clear, if intervals of a minimum thickness of one thread can be distinguished between the single threads outside the embroidery, or the interwoven close figures, stripes, &c., or, if this be impossible, when a piece of one-half meter square only 20 grams or less.	
Other woolen goods:	
a. Embroidered with silk or thread of metal	62⅓
b. Otherwise ¶	21 4/10
NOTE.—Woolen goods in combination with silk, or in combination with hair (provided they are not rated under "silk" or "hair"), or other spinning materials, shall be rated as woolen goods.	
Portugal:	
Wool, raw	Free.
Dyed	02¼

* In bond, 450 kilograms.
† In bond, 300 kilograms.
‡ In bond, 200 kilograms.
§ In bond, 225 kilograms.
‖ In bond, 70 kilograms.
¶ In bond, 75 kilograms.

No. 65.—STATEMENT SHOWING THE PRESENT TARIFF RATES OF FOREIGN COUNTRIES
ON IMPORTATIONS OF WOOL AND MANUFACTURES OF WOOL—Continued.

Countries.	Conventional tariff.	General tariff.
EUROPE—continued.		
Roumania:		
Wool, raw :	*Per 100 kilos.*	*Per 100 kilos.*
Of all kinds, unwashed	$1 93	$2 22
Of all kinds, not carded or combed.............................	3 86	4 44
Of all kinds, carded or combed, natural or dyed...............	9 65	11 10
Woolen yarns of all kinds......................................	13 51	15 54
Manufactures of wool:		
Woolen tissues—		
Ordinary, viz, rough blankets with long hairs, rough cloth, woolen carpets in the piece or by the meter. (Stuffs of wool or of cotton mixed with any other product than silk pay the duty of woolen or cotton tissues, according to whether the predominant material is wool or cotton. Ordinary stuffs called "cziak" are also included in this category.)	5 79	6 66
Cloths and other analogous tissues, not printed, flannel of all kinds, white or colored, Turkish caps or "fez," and "moultous" .... (All the fashionable stuffs for men's clothing, such as are manufactured at Brünn and Reichenberg, are included under "tissues analogous to cloths".)	11 19	12 87
All other woolen tissues not included in the above articles, excepting shawls and laces ; also all woolen hosier's and haberdasher's goods............................ (Are included also in this category the woolen stuffs called Thibets, merino lastings, Scotch cashmere, orleans, barege, lastings, reps (stuff for furniture), mousselines, gros-grains, damask, plush, velvet, &c.)	17 37	19 98
Woolen hosiery articles of all kinds, even trimmed with other tissues..	28 95	33 29
Knitted and worked shawls (imitation of Indian and Turkish shawls)...	30 88	35 51
Indian and Turkish shawls..................................	5 per cent. ad valorem.	5. 75 per cent. ad valorem.
Woolen lace	7 per cent. ad valorem.	8. 05 per cent. ad valorem.
Felt of all kinds ; also the following felt articles : Soles, boots and shoes (even with leather soles), with or without soles, and felt hats for soldiers and peasants (including Kronstadt caps, made of sheep's wool)	3 86	5 55
Felt objects other than those mentioned in the preceding article, including felt hats, mounted but not trimmed.	33 78	38 84
	Rate of duty.	
Russia:		
Wool and down—	*Per pood.* *	
Raw, washed, and not washed, not dyed ; also flock wool and cloth shearings..	$0 60	
Wool, not spun, of every kind, dyed ; also artificial wool (shoddy mungo), cloth rags, and wool waste dyed.....................	1 20	
Wool, worked into strips :		
a. Not dyed...	1 80	
b. Dyed...	2 70	
Wool yarn, pure or mixed with cotton, flax or hemp :		
a. Not dyed...	4 51	
b. Dyed...	5 41	
Manufactures of wool:	*Per pound.*	
Sec. 201. Woolen blankets and horse cloths...................	26	
Sec. 202. Woolen stuffs of combed wool or goat's hair, plain, woven of various colors and embroidered, with or without admixture of cotton .	54	
Note to sections 202 and 203.—(1) Unmilled stuffs of combed wool or goat's hair having a woof or warp of silk or silk waste, pay as silk goods ; but if the admixture of silk consists only of patterns or stripes woven in or embroidered, such goods pay 20 per cent. in addition to the duty in sections 202 and 203. (2) Handkerchiefs, scarfs, counterpanes, plaids. &c., of unmilled textures of combed wool or goat's hair, except those specially mentioned in section 205, pay the same duty as the material of which they are made.		
Sec. 203. The same printed, with 30 per cent. additional.		
Sec. 204. Bunting, white woolen stuffs for miller's seives, and sashes of wool of every kind, without admixture of silk.....................	15	

* 1 pood = 36.11 pounds.

No .65.—Statement showing the Present Tariff Rates of Foreign Countries on Importations of Wool and Manufactures of Wool—Continued.

Countries.	Rate of duty.
EUROPE—continued.	Per pood.
Russia—Continued.	
Wool and down—Continued.	
Manufactures of wool—Continued.	
Sec. 205. Shawls, handkerchiefs, sashes, and scarfs, Turkish or cashmere, also French terno and half-terno, as well as detached borders, edges, and other similar stuffs of pure wool, or mixed with cotton, silk, or bourre de soie......	1 98
Sec. 206. Unmilled woolen stuffs for use in manufactories, bags for oil-pressings, for sugar-bakers, &c.; cloths of peculiar make for factories, cloth list and all kinds of felt, not dyed, dyed and printed..........	67
Sec. 209. Woolen galloon or braid, plaited and knitted goods of every kind (hosiery), gloves, stockings, tapes, and ribbons of pure wool or mixed with hemp, flax, or cotton, except buttons and lace.........	33
	Per dozen.
Sec. 208. Fezes or Turkish caps of wool, embroidered or not with spangles..	1 20
	Per pound.
Dresses of cloth or woolen stuffs......................	1 20
Sec. 207. Woolen carpets of every kind...................	21
Servia :	Per 100 kilos.
Wool tissues—	
Rough blankets (for horses and for beds), ordinary carpets of goats' and other animals' hair, and rough wool (even cut into soles, &c., as well as tarred and varnished), cloth list	3 09
Rough cloths, such as cloth called halina coarse cloth (Loden), aba, chaisk, azur..	3 86
(Tare in percentage of the gross weights: 16 in cases or barrels, 8 in baskets, 5 in bales or sacks.)	
Tissues, even mixed with a small quantity of silk, or with metallic threads, viz :	
Cloths and tissues analogous to cloths for men's clothes and other strong-garments, flannels, washroll, long-piled cloths, teaseled, for linings, fine felt, and fine felt articles.............	11 19
(Tare percentage of the gross weight: 18 in cases or barrels, 10 in baskets, 5 in bales or sacks.)	
REMARK.—Under "tissues analogous to cloths" are included also all the fashion stuffs for men's clothing, such as are manufactured at Brünn and Reichenberg (Herrensock, Hosenstoffe, Modestoffe, "Nouveautés".)	
Thin, light stuffs, serving generally for women's garments, ("orleans, cashmere, mohair and the like), stuffs for furniture, table cloths, handkerchiefs, scarfs, shawls, and analogous tissues, with or without fringes or tassels, shag and woolen velvet	17 37
(Tare in percentage of gross weights: 18 in cases or barrels, 10 in baskets, 5 in bales or sacks.)	
REMARK.—The following stuffs are included under the above: Alpaca, mohair, Orleans, Thibet, lustring, cashmere, serge, llama, goat's hair, satin, Italia cloth, merino, damask, rep and stuffs for furniture, and fashionable stuffs for women. Handkerchiefs, shawls, and scarfs may be trimmed with simple embroidery.	

	Without treaty.	With treaty.
	Per 100 kilos.	Per 100 kilos.
Spain :		
Wool, common, unclean	$5 40	$ 69
NOTE.—Wool which, after being washed with sulphate of carbon, loses more than 10 per cent. of its weight will be considered as unclean wool.		
Wool, common, washed	10 81	9 28
Wool, common, unclean, of other classes, and long wool for worsteds	2 41	1 47
NOTE.—Wool more than 10 centimeters long shall be considered long wool.		
Wool, common, clean	4 83	2 93
Wool, combed or carded, and waste from carding	6 41	6 41
Manufactures of wool:		
Spun ("hilados ")—	Per kilo.	Per kilo.
Worsted, spun and twisted, crude or with oil...............	30	21
Same, clean or bleached	50	32
Worsted, dyed.................	58	38
Woven—	Per 100 kilos.	Per 100 kilos.
Carpetings of pure wool or mixed with other materials......	26 94	19 24
	Per kilo.	Per kilo.
Feltings mixed with other materials.......................	14	12
Blanketings mixed with other materials.................	43	34
NOTE.—Blankets called "plaids," or similar thereto, which pay according to the class of textile of which they may be composed, are not included in this item.		

No. 65.—STATEMENT SHOWING THE PRESENT TARIFF RATES OF FOREIGN COUNTRIES ON IMPORTATIONS OF WOOL AND MANUFACTURES OF WOOL—Continued.

Countries.	Without treaty.	With treaty.
EUROPE—continued.	Per 100 kilos.	Per 100 kilos.
Spain—Continued.		
Manufactures of wool—Continued.		
Woven—Continued.		
Hosiery ("cejidos de punto") whether mixed or not with cotton or other vegetable fiber	$0 77	$0 67
Cloths and all other fabrics of the cloth line, of pure wool, flock wool, hair, or mixed with these materials	1 54	84
The same cloths, when they have all the warp of cotton or other vegetable fibers, and the astrakans and plush of the same materials	1 54	50
All the other textiles of pure wool, flock wool, hair, or mixtures of these materials	97	71
The same textiles, when all the warps is of cotton or of other vegetable fibers	97	4

	Rates of duty.
Sweden:	Per 100 kilos.
Wool, dyed or undyed	Free.
Manufactures of wool:	
(Webs of wool or mixed with cotton, flax, &c., silk excepted.)	
Machine felt to use in manufactories	Free.
Felts and carpets	$8 16
Press cloths	22 73
Other kinds	23 82
Mixed with silk	31 09
Yarn, undyed and unbleached	2 72
Yarn, dyed or bleached	4 76
Switzerland:	Per quintal.
Wool, raw	
Washed colored	06
	12
Manufactures of wool:	
Yarn—	
Raw, single or double	97
Bleached, three times or more twisted	1 54
Colored	1 74
Bobbinet (according to nature).	
Cloth ends	77
Webbings—	
Raw	2 32
Bleached colored, printed	4 83
Blankets of all kinds—	
Not sewed	5 79
Sewed	3 09
Laces	5 79
Lace-makers' goods	4 83
Hosiery	4 83
Embroidery	5 79
Shawls	5 79
Carpets—	
Ordinary, not sewed	2 32
Others	5 79
Shoes from cloth ends	3 09
Felt stuffs	3 09
Felt articles—	
Not finished, raw	1 35
Colored, printed	3 09
Felt hats	5 79
Felt hats unfinished	1 35
Turkey:	Per 100 kilos.
Wool: All kinds, including alpaca, llama, vicuna, Angora, and other goat's hair and other camel's hair:	
Combed or carded	3 52
Dyed	4 40
Raw, washed or unwashed	1 58
Shoddy and other waste	70
United Kingdom of Great Britain and Ireland:	
Wool and manufactures of	Free.

NORTH AMERICA.

Canada:	
Wool, raw, hair of the alpaca and other like animals	Free.
Woolen rugs	Free.

No. 65.—STATEMENT SHOWING THE PRESENT TARIFF RATES OF FOREIGN COUNTRIES
ON IMPORTATIONS OF WOOL AND MANUFACTURES OF WOOL—Continued.

Countries.	Rates of duty.
NORTH AMERICA—continued.	
Canada—Continued.	
Wool, raw, class 1, viz: Leicester, Cotswold, Lincolnshire, Southdown combing wools, or wools known as luster wools, and other like combing wools, such as are grown in Canada	3 cents per pound.
Manufactures of wool:	
All fabrics composed wholly or in part of wool, worsted, the hair of the alpaca, goat, and other like animals, n. e. s.	22½ per cent.
Manufactures, composed wholly or in part of wool, worsted, the hair of the alpaca, goat and other like animals, viz: Blankets and flannels of every description, cloths, doeskins, cassimeres, tweeds, coatings, overcoatings, felt cloth of every description, n. e. s.; horse-collar cloth, yarn, knitting yarn, fingering yarn, worsted yarn, knitted goods, viz: shirts, drawers, and hosiery, n. e. s.	7½ cts. per lb. and 20 pr. ct.
Clothing, ready-made, and wearing apparel of every description, including socks and stockings, cloth caps, and horse clothing, shaped, composed wholly or in part of wool, worsted, the hair of the alpaca, goat, or other like animals, made up or manufactured wholly or in part by the tailor, seamstress, or manufacturer, except knit goods	10 cts. per lb and 25 pr. ct.
All manufactures composed wholly or in part of wool, worsted, the hair of the alpaca, goat, and other like animals, not herein otherwise provided for	20 per cent.
Treble ingrain, three-ply and two-ply carpets, composed wholly of wool	10 cents per square yard and 20 per cent.
Two-ply and three-ply ingrain carpets, of which the warp is composed wholly of cotton and other material than wool, worsted, the hair of the alpaca, goat, and other like animals	5 cents per square yard and 20 per cent.
Felt for boots and shoes and skirts, when imported by the manufacturers for use in their factories	15 per cent.
Felt for glove linings and endless felt for paper-makers, when imported by the manufacturers for use in their factories	10 per cent.
Winceys, plain, of all widths, when the material is not over one-fourth wool	20 per cent.
Checked, striped or fancy, not over 25 inches wide	20 per cent.
Checked, striped or fancy dress winceys over 25 inches wide, and not over 30 inches, when the material is not over one-fourth wool	2 cents per square yard and 15 per cent.
(But all checked, striped, or fancy winceys over 30 inches wide shall be subject to duty as woolen goods when the material is partly wool.)	
Mexico:	
Wool, in the fleece, net weight	$0.10 per kilogram.
Wool, carded, net weight	$0.16 per kilogram.
Manufactures of wool:	
Bandas and scarfs of wool, of all textures, without embroidery, including those of stockinet, net weight	$2.12 per kilogram.
Bandas of wool, of all textures, embroidered with wool, net weight	$2.86 per kilogram.
Bandas of wool of all textures embroidered with silk, net weight	$3.47 per kilogram.
Carpets of coarse frieze, of plain or cross texture, or of beaten wool	$0.61 per square meter.
Carpets and rugs of short-nap wool, uncut, warp of hemp or any other material	$0.89 per square meter.
Carpets and rugs of Brussels, cut or velvet finish, with warp of hemp or any other material	$1.30 per square meter.
Carpets of wool, corded, with hemp or cotton warp	$0.73 per square meter.
Clothing, ready-made, and separate parts of the same that come sewed, of wool of all classes, of textures with or without trimmings of any other material and with exception of those specified, net weight	$4.48 per kilogram.
Coverlets and counterpanes of wool	$1.38 per square meter.
Cravats of woolen goods, net weight	$2.61 per kilogram.
Drawers and shirts for under or outer wear, of flannel or any texture analogous to wool, with or without adornments of silk, net weight	$1.71 per kilogram.
Dress patterns partly made, of wool of all classes, with or without borders of wool, or of wool and cotton, and with or without trimmings of silk ribbon and cotton, linen or woolen lace, for women and girls, net weight	$2.04 per kilogram.
Dress patterns of woolen textures of all kinds, partly made with trimmings or embroideries of silk and with or without ornaments of wool and silk, or of silk, for women and girls, net weight	$3.10 per kilogram.

No. 65.—Statement showing the Present Tariff Rates of Foreign Countries on Importations of Wool and Manufactures of Wool—Continued.

Countries.	Rates of duty.
NORTH AMERICA—continued.	
Mexico—Continued.	
Manufactures of wool—Continued.	
Elastic of wool and rubber, of more than four centimeters in width, net weight..	$0.73 per kilogram.
Elastic braid, cord, and tape, of wool with india-rubber which measures up to four centimeters in width, net weight.	$1.71 per kilogram.
Felt of wool in pieces, net weight............................	$0.20 per kilogram.
Felt of wool (belting) in pieces, without beginning or end, for machinery, when it does not come united to the latter, net weight	$0.05 per kilogram.
Fringe, galloon, passementerie, edging, tape, cord and mesh of wool, with or without glass beads (bugles), or beads of metal, not gold or silver, net weight	$2.60 per kilogram.
Garters and suspenders of wool, with or without adornments or buckles, &c., legal weight....................	$1.05 per kilogram.
Gloves of wool, of all sizes and colors, unlined, net weight	$3.66 per kilogram.
Gloves of wool of all sizes and colors, lined, net weight	$1.63 per kilogram.
"Gusanillo" (a kind of frill), of wool, net weight.................	$2.60 per kilogram.
Jackets, buskins (gaiters), and all kinds of articles made of woolen yarn which are not specified even though they have some ornaments of silk or metal, not gold or silver, net weight	$1.87 per kilogram.
Lace and net of wool, and all manufactures of these materials, even when the have some adornment of silk or metal, not gold or silver, legal weight	$7.01 per kilogram.
Linings (covers) of wool, sewed or in patterns for umbrellas, sunshades, and parasols, net weight	$2.85 per kilogram.
Ponchos (a) of wool, net weight....	$1.22 per kilogram.
Rebozos (long shawls) of wool, and those textures stamped, marbled, striped with figures or designs which imitate rebozos, up to 26 threads of warp and woof in a square of one-half centimeter...	$1.18 per square meter.
Rebozos (long shawls) of wool, and those textures of wool, stamped, marbled, striped with figures and designs, which imitate rebozos, of more than 26 and to 38 threads of warp and woof, in a square of one-half centimeter	$1.79 per square meter.
Ruching (fluting) of woolen muslin, with or without woolen lace, net weight.............	$5.54 per kilogram.
Sarapes (b) tilmas and blankets, without openings for the arms, plain	$0.89 per square meter.
Sarapes and tilmas of wool, shaped for the arms to be free, with borders marked or stamped......................	$1.71 per square meter.
Sarapes of wool, imitation of those of Saltillo, marked or stamped	$7.17 per square meter.
Shawls (of various sorts) of wool, of all classes of texture not of net, with or without woolen embroidery, and with or without fringe of wool, or of wool and silk, or of silk and cotton, net weight	$3.20 per kilogram.
Shawls of various sorts, of wool of all classes of texture not of net, with trimmings, squares or embroideries of silk and fringe of any material, net weight	$4.80 per kilogram.
Skirt patterns of all textures of wool, net weight.............	$2.28 per kilogram.
Socks, stockings, underdrawers, and undershirts of woolen stockinet, and all manufactures of woolen stockinet not specified, net weight...............................	$1.79 per kilogram.
Tassels of wool, even when their insides are of another material, net weight	$1.05 per kilogram.
Umbrellas, sunshades, and parasols	$0.82 each.
Vests, and jackets of woolen stockinet, net weight	$1.14 per kilogram.
Woolen goods cut in dress patterns, of all classes and textures, with exception of those specified, net weight	$3.20 per kilogram.
Woolen goods of plain texture, a square meter of which weighs up to 150 grams, net weight............................	$1.03 per kilogram.
Woolen goods of plain texture, a square meter of which weighs more than 150 up to 200 grams, net weight	$1.14 per kilogram.
Woolen goods of plain texture, a square meter of which weighs more than 200 and up to 290 grams, net weight........	$0.86 per kilogram.
Woolen goods of plain texture, a square meter of which weighs more than 290 grams, net weight..........................	$3.92 per kilogram.
Woolen goods of texture not plain, a square meter of which weighs up to 100 grams, net weight.................	$3.06 per kilogram.
Woolen goods of texture not plain, a square meter of which weighs more than 100 up to 150 grams, net weight	$2.16 per kilogram.
Woolen goods, not plain texture, a square meter of which weighs more than 150 up to 200 grams, net weight........	$1.46 per kilogram.
Woolen goods, not plain texture, a square meter of which weighs more than 200 to 300 grams, net weight	$1.14 per kilogram.
Woolen goods, not plain texture, a square meter of which weighs more than 300 to 350 grams, net weight	$2.03 per kilogram.

No. 65.—STATEMENT SHOWING THE PRESENT TARIFF RATES OF FOREIGN COUNTRIES ON IMPORTATIONS OF WOOL AND MANUFACTURES OF WOOL—Continued.

Countries.	Rates of duty.
NORTH AMERICA—continued.	
Mexico—Continued.	
Manufactures of wool—Continued.	
Woolen goods, not plain texture, a square meter of which weighs more than 350 up to 500 grams, net weight	$2.73 per kilogram.
Woolen goods, not plain texture, a square meter of which weighs more than 500 up to 600 grams, net weight	$2.36 per kilogram.
Woolen goods, not plain texture, a square meter of which weighs more than 600 grams, net weight	$2.00 per kilogram.
Woolen goods, strips or separate pieces of, embroidered in wool, net weight	$3.10 per kilogram.
Woolen goods, strips or separate pieces of, embroidered in silk, net weight	$4.56 per kilogram.
Yarn of wool, with or without mixture of metal not gold or silver, net weight	$1.54 per kilogram.
Yarn, woolen, of all classes and colors, net weight	$1.54 per kilogram.
CENTRAL AMERICA.	
Honduras :	
Wool, raw	$0.03½ per pound.
Nicaragua:	
Wool, manufactures of :	
Alpaca, merino, or any other light fabric of wool, gloves, hose of all kinds, and shirts of all kinds	$0 41 per Spanish pound.
Rugs, and dyed sheepskins with wool on	$0.41 per Spanish pound.
Cassimeres, broadcloth, serge and flannels	$0.52 per Spanish pound.
Carpets, tablecloths, and curtains	$0.29 per Spanish pound.
Blankets, rugs, pouches	$0.17 per Spanish pound.
Saddlecloths	$0 21 per Spanish pound.
Common wool stuffs, homespuns	$0.29 per Spanish pound.
Thread for sewing and embroidering hats for ladies, of all kinds, and wool hats for men	$0.50 per Spanish pound.
Brocaded stuff in pieces, fringes, laces, handkerchiefs, ladies scarfs, and shawls	$0.83 per Spanish pound.
Tape, ribbons, and braid	$0.51 per Spanish pound.
Pants and clothing for men, ready-made	$0.62 per Spanish pound.
Lawns, nets, muslins, and any other fine stuffs for ladies	$1.24 per Spanish pound.
Ladies' dresses made up, or in fancy cuts	$2.07 per Spanish pound.
NOTE.—Goods mixed with wool, cotton or linen, pay duties as woolen goods.	
Ivador :	
Wool :	
Sheep, gross weight	$0.06 per pound.
Alpaca, gross weight	$0.12 per pound.
WEST INDIES.	
Hayti :	
Wool, raw	$0.04 per pound.
Manufactures of wool :	
Blankets	$0.25 each.
Caps, of wool or cotton	$0.25 per dozen.
Cloth :	
Fine, ordinary, of 4-4 and over	$0.60 per ell.
Common, over 4-4 wide	$0.30 per ell.
Common, 4-4 and under	$0.18 per ell.
Of serge, or wool and silk, and colored material for vests	$0.16 per ell.
Drawers, woolen	$0.25 each.
Gloves, of wool, thread, or cotton	$0 40 per dozen.
Gaiters, of cloth	$1 per dozen.
Garments :	
Of fine cloth, ready-made	$3 each.
Ordinary cloth	$2.50 each.
Of divers cloth, for children	$2 each.
Embroidered in fine gold	$5 each.
Of fine cloth embroidered in fine silver	$3 each.
Of divers cloth, cut and not sewed	$2.50 each.
Ready-made for children	$1 each.
Hats :	
Turned up, woolen, for soldiers	$2.75 per dozen.
Round, fine, of felt or silk, for men or women	$5 per dozen.
Round, ordinary, of felt, silk, or cotton, for men or women	$3 per dozen.
Round, common, wool or cotton, for men or women	$2 per dozen.
Round, for adults, fine, felt or silk	$4 per dozen.
Round, for adults, ordinary, felt, silk, or cotton	$2 per dozen.
Round, for adults, common, wool or cotton	$1.50 per dozen.
Kerseymere :	
Of pure wool, twilled, over 4-4	$0.25 per ell.
Of pure wool, twilled, under 4-4	$0.15 per ell.
Of wool and cotton, twilled, above 4-4	$0.20 per ell.
Of wool and cotton, twilled, under 4-4	$0.12 per ell.

No. 65.—STATEMENT SHOWING THE PRESENT TARIFF RATES OF FOREIGN COUNTRIES ON IMPORTATIONS OF WOOL AND MANUFACTURES OF WOOL—Continued.

Countries.	Rates of duty.

WEST INDIES—continued.

Hayti—Continued.
  Manufactures of wool—Continued.
    Merino:

Small width	$0.08 per ell.
Large width	$0.15 per ell.
Overcoats, of cloth or kerseymere	$2.50 each.
Ribbons, of wool, for mattresses	$0.01 per piece of 12 ells.
Rugs:	
Over 3 feet in length by 1 foot in width	$1 each.
Under 3 feet in length by 1 foot in width	$0.50 each.
Stockings:	
Woolen, for men	$0.50 per dozen pair.
For children, cotton and woolen	$0.20 per dozen pair.
Socks, of woolen	$0.50 per dozen.
Shirts:	
For men, with stomacher of wool	$0.25 each.
For soldiers and sailors, of wool, common linen, or ticking	$1 each.
Slippers:	
Of wool, common	$0.75 per dozen.
Of wool, fine, ordinary	$1 per dozen.
Shawls, of merino, of wool, and cotton	$3 per dozen.
Shoes, of knitted wool, called socks, for children	$0.25 per dozen.
Trousers, of fine cloth, knitted kerseymere, silk	$1.50 each.
Tufts, of wool	$0.25 each.
Woven stuffs:	
Woolen, for trousers, thread or cotton, 4-4	$0.12 per ell.
Woolen, for trousers, thread or cotton, under 4-4	$0.08 per ell.
Woolen thread or cotton, or pure cotton, plain or striped, 4-4	$0.06 per ell.
Woolen, for trousers, same as above, under 4-4	$0.05 per ell.
Woolen, for trousers, of 26 inches and under	$0.04 per ell.
Woolen lace:	
Wide	$0.05 per ell.
Narrow	$0.03 per ell.
Umbrellas, of woolen stuffs	$0.30 per ell.
Bombazine, or mourning, of silk and wool, alpaca or other material of like kind, of 30 inches and under	$0.08 per ell.
Bombazine, of pure wool or goat's hair, of 30 inches and under	$0.06 per ell.

	Spanish flag.	Foreign flag.
Porto Rico:		
Wools, bristles, horse-hair, and their manufactures:		
Raw, spun:	*Per 100 kilos.*	*Per kilo.*
Bristles, horse-hair, hair, and wools of all kinds and their refuse	$13 12	$18 86
Yarn of all kinds	48	69
Textiles:		
Textiles of felt in carpetings, horse blankets, and other uses, with or without hand work	10	14
Carpetings, Brussels, with or without hand work	27	39
Textiles, plain or twilled, of wool only or mixed with other materials, with hair on one or both sides, which have not been cleansed, as coating, balze, blankets, and similar goods	12	17
Cloths, cassimeres, ladies' cloth (elasticotines), lawns, and similar goods of wool only	1 00	1 45
Same, mixed with cotton	40	58
Textiles, worked, crossed, twilled, or damasked, of wool only, as merino, damask, rep, alpaca, serge, and similar goods.	1 00	1 45
Same, mixed with cotton	54	68
Textiles, smooth and plain, of pure wool or mixed with cotton, as alpaca, Orleans, fine woolen stuffs, fetaila, flannel, and similar goods up to 14 threads	37	53
Same, from 15 to 20 threads	54	78
Same, from 21 threads and upwards	90	1 29
Textiles, knit, of pure wool or mixed with cotton	76	1 10
NOTES.—(1) On all the above rates 6 per cent. additional duty. (2) Duties are payable in Spanish gold, but the treasury admits payments at present in Mexican silver at $1.05263 for $1 Spanish.		

SOUTH AMERICA.

	Rates of duty.
Argentine Republic:	

Export duties.

Wool:	
Unwashed	6 per cent. per 100 kilos.
Washed	Free.

No. 65.—Statement showing the Present Tariff Rates of Foreign Countries on Importations of Wool and Manufactures of Wool—Continued.

Countries.	Rates of duty.
SOUTH AMERICA—continued.	
Import duties.	
Argentine Republic—Continued.	
Wool—Continued.	
Wool, raw..	25 per cent. per 100 kilos.
Manufactures of wool:	
Flannel:	
Mixed, to 75 centimeters, ordinary	25 per cent. per meter.
Mixed, to 75 centimeters, medium...................	Do.
Mixed goods:	
Cotton, wool, and silk for clothing, common	Do.
Cotton, wool, and silk for clothing, fine	Do.
Merinos, cotton and wool, 100 centimeters...........	Do.
Muslins, wool, black or colored	Do.
Cloth...	Do.
Undershirts.......................................	Do.
Suits for men, wool...............................	Do.
Brazil:	
Wool:	
In the rough, carded, tinted, or prepared in any manner	$0.02 per pound.
In thread:	
Simple, for weaving	$0.05 per pound.
For silk throwing	$0.28 per pound.
Loose, for embroidery.............................	$0.31 per pound.
NOTE.—Under the tariff system of Brazil certain rates of duty are established called "duties of consumption," to each and every one of which 60 per cent. is added. It is to be noted also that under the recent emancipation law a further duty of 5 per cent. has been collected on all general imposts. This additional duty of 65 per cent. has been added in the above rates.	
Chili.	
Wool of sheep:	
Soiled	Free.
Washed	Do.
Of vicuna	Do.
Manufactures of wool:	
Articles which pay a duty of 35 per cent.:	
Boots and shoes, stamped cloth, wool, plush, or felt	
Babies' gaiters, wool or mixed goods	
Same of merino cashmere	
Carpeting	
Clothing, ready-made—	
Drawers, wool, woolen flannel, or cotton mixture	
Men's and boys' shirts of flannel wool, or with cotton mixture	
Sailors' shirts of woolen baize....................	
Body shirts of woolen point or woolen flannel with cotton mixture	
Ladies' capes, cloaks, or mantillas of cloth, cashmere, or any woolen goods	
Men's or boys' vests, silk, cloth, cashmere, or wool, with or without cotton mixture.....................	
Workmen's jackets of ordinary cloth or baize, with or without cotton mixture........................	
Men's and boys' short jackets of woolen point, with or without cotton	
Ladies' or misses' skirts of wool or cotton mixture, plain or ornamented..................................	
Coats of cassimere or woolen cloth	
Men's or boys' frock coats of cassimere or woolen cloth....	
Mantos of merino or woolen cashmere, bordered, with or without braid, &c...............................	
Men's and boys' trousers, cassimere or woolen cloth	
Men's and boys' raglans, cassimere or cloth	
Men's and boys' sacks or blouses, cassimere or cloth	
Men's and boys' overcoats, cassimere or cloth	
Children's suits (2 or 3 pieces) cassimere, wool or cotton mixed goods; trousers not more than 85 centimeters long	
Ladies' bath dresses, wool or linen, 2 pieces	
Fringes of wool for dress-trimming, with or without beads or other material	
Gloves of wool, with or without nap	
Gloves, woolen point	
Handkerchiefs, cassimere	
Caps of cloth or any kind of wool, silk, or mixture...........	

No. 65.—STATEMENT SHOWING THE PRESENT TARIFF RATES OF FOREIGN COUNTRIES
ON IMPORTATIONS OF WOOL AND MANUFACTURES OF WOOL—Continued.

Countries.	Rates of duty.
SOUTH AMERICA—continued.	
Import duties—Continued.	
Chili—Continued.	
Manufactures of wool—Continued.	
Articles which pay a duty of 35 per cent—Continued.	
Caps for babes, linen, wool, or silk, resembling hats	
Hats for men or boys of cloth or any kind of wool or silk......	
Hats of wool, or silk, or fur, not trimmed or adorned, for children and ladies...	
Articles which pay a duty of 25 per cent. :	
Blankets	
Bunting	
Dry-goods, woolen...	
Epaulets, woolen stuff..	
Felt, of wool...	
Flannel, of wool	
Fringes or ribbons of wool, with cotton or silk mixture, for upholstering carriages, worked, to 8 centimeters wide ...	
Hair cloth of wool serge, with nap, &c........................	
Hat-forms of floss wool	
Hats of floss-wool for men and boys	
Hats, woolen cloths for forming, cut...........................	
Jerga, of wool............	
Jerga, of wool with cotton, hemp, or jute mixture.............	
Handkerchiefs of coarse wool, in cases and in packages........	
Laces of wool or mixed goods, with or without beads...........	
Mantos or ponchos of wool....................................	
Plaitings of woolen gauze or tulle for ornaments, with or without woolen laces or silk threads, up to 8 centimeters wide	
Ribbons	
Satin...	
Serge...	
Stockings, wool, mixed, for men and boys	
Umbrellas, parasols, or hat covers	
Woolen or cotton-satin stuff for shoes	
Woolen or silk or cotton-mixed goods for shoes	
Ecuador :	
Wool..	$0 13
All kind of woolen goods	50 per kilogram.
Peru :	
Wool:	
Unwashed, 40 per cent ..,....................................	$0 09 per kilogram.
Washed, 40 per cent......'....................................	12 per kilogram.
United States of Colombia:	
Wool, raw...	05 per kilogram.
Manufactures of wool:	
Blankets	50
Thread for knitting, &c	60
Carpets for floor, or rugs	70
Baize, heavy coarse cloth, serge..............................	80
Transparent fabrics, all kinds of embroidered or meshed fabrics and its imitations, including laces, embroidery, and the like articles, and ready-made clothing..............	1 20
All other fabrics not mentioned in this tariff	1 00
Venezuela :	
Manufactures of wool :	
Blankets..	11 08 per 100 pounds.
Wool, manufactured	6 63 per 100 pounds.
Counterpanes, umbrellas	22 12 per 100 pounds.
Alpaca, braid, belts, caps, cravats, cassimere, cassinette, cambron, cord, damask, epaulettes, fancy trimmings, fringes, gloves, galloons, lace, nubias, ribbons, stocks, socks, saddle-cloths, shawls, serge, tassels, table-cloths, undershirts	44 23 per 100 pounds.
Curtains, hangings, shirts, shawls, and table-cloths with silk border or trimmings	88 46 per 100 pounds.
Adornments and clothing for women and children, cloaks, paletots, overcoats, ready-made clothes....................	176 92 per 100 pounds.
ASIA.	
China :	
Wool, raw (import duties)	48 per 133. 33 pounds.
Manufactures of wool:	
Blankets..	27 per pair.
Broadcloth and Spanish stripes, habit and medium cloth, 51 to 64 inches wide	16 per chang.*
Long ells, 31 inches wide....................................	06 per chang.
Camlets, English, 31 inches wide	07 per chang.
Camlets, Dutch, 33 inches wide	13 per chang.

* The length of a chang of 10 Chinese feet equals 142 English inches.

No. 65.—STATEMENT SHOWING THE PRESENT TARIFF RATES OF FOREIGN COUNTRIES ON IMPORTATIONS OF WOOL AND MANUFACTURES OF WOOL—Continued.

Countries.	Rates of duty.
ASIA—continued.	
Import duties—Continued.	
China—Continued.	
Manufactures of wool—Continued.	
Camlets, imitation and bombazettes	$0 05 per chang.
Cassimeres, flannel and narrow cloth	05 per chang.
Lastings, 31 inches wide	07 per chang.
Lastings, imitation, and Orleans, 34 inches wide	05 per chang.
Buntings, not exceeding 24 inches wide, 40 yards long	20 per piece.
Woolen and cotton mixtures: Lusters, plain and brocaded, not exceeding 31 yards long	20 per piece.
Woolen inferior Spanish stripes	13 per chang.
Woolen yarn	3 90 per 100 catties.
Corea:	
Wool, sheep, and other animals	8 per cent. ad valorem.
Woolens:	
Alpaca	Do.
Blankets	Do.
Camlets	Do.
Flannels	Do.
Lastings	Do.
Lastings, crape	Do.
Long ells	Do.
Merino	Do.
Mousseline de laine	Do.
Serges	Do.
Spanish stripes	Do.
Thibets	Do.
Damasks	Do.
Mixtures	Do.
Japan:	
Woolen manufactures:	
Broad, habit, medium, and narrow cloth—	
Not exceeding 34 inches	$0 20 per 10 yards.
Not exceeding 55 inches	33 per 10 yards.
Exceeding 55 inches	41 per 10 yards.
Spanish stripes	24 per 10 yards.
Cassimeres, flannel, long ells, and serges	15 per 10 yards.
Bunting	06 per 10 yards.
Camlets:	
Dutch	24 per 10 yards.
English	13 per 10 yards.
Lastings, crape lastings and worsted crapes, merinos, and all other woolen goods not classed under No. 76:	
a Not exceeding 34 inches	10 per 10 yards.
b Exceeding 34 inches	15 per 10 yards.
Woolen and cotton mixtures as imitations, camlet imitation, lastings, Orleans (plain and figured), lusters (plain and figured), alpacas, baratheas, damasks, Italian cloth, taffachelass, russell cords, cassandras, woolen fancies, camlet cords, and all other cotton and woolen mixtures—	
a Not exceeding 34 inches	10 per 10 yards.
b Exceeding 34 inches	15 per 10 yards.
Blankets and horse-cloths	16 per 10 catties.
Traveling rugs, plaids, and shawls	16 each.
Figured woolen table-cloths	24 each.
Woolen singlets and drawers	26 per dozen.
Woolen and cotton singlets and drawers	16 per dozen.
Woolen yarn, plain and dyed	3 25 per 100 catties
Siam:	
The treaty of 1856, between the United States and Siam, regulates the tariff, and fixes it at a uniform rate of 3 per cent. on the marked value of goods, payable either in kind or in money, at the option of the importer.	
British India:	
Wool	Free.
AUSTRALASIA.	
New South Wales:	
Wool	Do.
Wool packs	$0 06 each.
Victoria:	
Wool, greasy, washed, scoured, and Angora	Free.
New Zealand:	
Wool, manufactures	15 per cent. ad valorem.

No. 66.—Statement showing the Tariff Rates on Foreign and Colonial Wool Imported into the United Kingdom from 1818 down to their Abolition, the Quantities Imported and the Prices of Southdown and Kent Long Wool, in each Year from 1818 to 1845.

[From McCullough's Commercial Dictionary.]

Years.	Rates of duty.	Foreign wool imported.	Colonial wool imported.	Price of—			
				Southdown, per pound.		Kent long, per pound.	
		Pounds.	Pounds.	s.	d.	s.	d.
1818	¾d. per pound	24, 720, 139	....	2	6	2	0
1819	6d. per pound	6, 094, 990	....	1	7	1	3
1820	......do	9, 653, 366	122, 239	1	5	1	4
1821	......do	16, 416, 806	205, 761	1	3	1	1
1822	......do	18, 859, 265	198, 815	1	3	1	11
1823	......do	18, 863, 886	502, 839	1	3½	1	0
1824	December, 1824, 1d. per pound of 1s. value; ½d. per pound under 1s. value.	22, 147, 540	416, 945	1	2	1	1
1825	Colonial free	43, 465, 282	351, 684	1	4	1	4
1826	......do	14, 747, 103	1, 24², 009	0	10	0	11
1827	......do	28, 552, 742	562, 502	0	9	0	10½
1828	......do	28, 628, 121	1, 607, 938	0	8	1	0
1829	......do	19, 639, 629	1, 877, 020	0	6	0	9
1830	......do	30, 303, 173	2, 002, 141	0	10	0	10½
1831	......do	29, 110, 073	2, 541, 956	1	1	0	10½
1832	......do	25, 081, 298	2, 461, 191	1	0	1	0½
1833	......do	34, 461, 527	3, 614, 886	1	5	0	10½
1834	......do	42, 684, 932	3, 770, 300	1	7	1	7½
1835	......do	37, 472, 032	4, 702, 500	1	6	1	6
1836	......do	57, 814, 771	6, 425, 206	1	8	1	8½
1837	......do	38, 945, 575	9, 434, 133	1	3	1	3
1838	......do	42, 430, 102	10, 104, 253	1	4	1	5
1839	......do	44, 504, 811	12, 875, 112	1	4	1	5½
1840	......do	36, 498, 108	12, 938, 116	1	3	1	2½
1841	......do	39, 672, 153	16, 498, 821	1	0	0	11
1842	......do	27, 394, 920	18, 486, 719	0	11½	0	10
1843	......do	26, 633, 913	21, 151, 148	0	11½	0	11
1844	From June 6, free	42, 473, 228	22, 606, 296	1	2	1	2
1845	......do	44, 970, 793	31, 843, 762	1	4	1	3

No. 67.—Statement showing the Quantity of Raw Wool Produced in each of the Principal and all other Wool-producing Countries of the World.

[From the Uebersichten der Welt-Wirthschaft, by Dr. F. X. von Neumann-Spallart, Stuttgart, 1887.]

Countries of production.	Quantities produced.
Europe:	Pounds.
Russia (1884)	262, 966, 000
Great Britain and Ireland * (1885)	135, 936, 000
France (1882)	80, 138, 000
Spain † (1878)	66, 138, 000
Germany ‡ (1881)	54, 894, 000
Hungary § (1885)	43, 146, 000
Italy (1874)	21, 365, 000
Austria (1883)	11, 155, 000
Portugal (?)	10, 362, 000
Belgium (?)	4, 409, 000
Sweden (1884)	3, 307, 000
All other Europe	8, 818, 000
Total Europe	702, 654, 000

* Estimate by the "Bradford Observer."
† An estimate of 3.9 pounds of wool per head of 17,000,000 sheep.
‡ Estimated from the export accounts.
§ Estimate of 3.9 pounds of wool per head on the whole number of sheep in Hungary, Croatia, and Slavonia.

No. 67.—Statement showing the Quantities of Raw Wool Produced in each
of the Principal and all other Wool-producing Countries of the World—
Continued.

Countries of production.	Quantities produced.
	Pounds.
North America:	
United States (1884)	307,588,000
British North American Provinces (1884)	4,409,000
South America:	
Argentine Republic (exports 1885)	283,047,000
Uruguay (exports 1884)	59,084,000
Asia and Australasia:	
Australasia * (exports 1885-'86)	455,470,000
British East Indies (exports 1885-'86)	23,126,000
Turkey, Asiatic and Persia (estimated)	13,228,000
Africa:	
Cape Colony (exports 1885)	28,299,000
Natal (exports 1885)	17,306,000
All other countries †	88,185,000
Total production ‡	1,983,396,000

* From the estimates of "The Export," 1886.
† Estimate, by Jacoms, Son & Co. Includes wools from Brazil, Chili, Algiers, Egypt, Tunis, &c.
‡ Only a few countries have attempted to collect statistics of the actual production of raw (unwashed) wool. The usual method of arriving at the annual production is a valuation based on the
average yield of wool per head of the whole number of sheep in the country. This table must therefore
only be regarded as a "general view" and does not claim to be accurate as to the several amounts of
wool produced.

No. 68.—Statement showing the Number of Sheep and Lambs of the various
Countries of the World at the dates named.

[From Report of the Department of Agriculture No. 37, January and February, 1887.]

Countries.	Years.	Sheep and lambs.	Goats.
North America:			
United States	1887	44,759,314	
Canada:			
Ontario and Quebec	1881	2,249,011	
Nova Scotia	1881	377,801	
New Brunswick	1881	221,183	
Manitoba	1881	6,073	
Prince Edward Island	1881	166,496	
British Columbia	1881	27,788	
The Territories	1881	346	
Total	1881	3,048,678	
Ontario	1886	1,610,949	
Manitoba	1885	10,337	
Newfoundland	1875	28,766	
Jamaica	1885	13,390	
Guadaloupe	1880	13,690	14,709
Guatemala	1884	417,577	
South America:			
Argentine Republic	1883		3,000,000
Do	1885	75,000,000	
Falkland Islands	1885	516,975	
Uruguay	1884	15,921,069	5,656
Venezuela	1883	*3,490,563	(*)
Europe:			
Austria-Hungary:			
Austria	1880	3,841,340	1,008,675
Hungary †	1880	9,818,133	333,233
Do	1884	10,594,831	270,192
Belgium	1880	365,400	248,755
Denmark	1881	1,548,613	9,331
France	1885	22,616,547	1,483,342
Germany	1883	19,189,715	2,639,994
Great Britain and Ireland	1886	28,955,240	
Great Britain	1886	25,520,718	
Ireland	1886	3,367,722	
Isle of Man, &c	1886	66,800	

* Goats are included with sheep.
† In the figures for 1880, Croatia and Slavonia are included with Hungary.

No. 68.—STATEMENT SHOWING THE NUMBER OF SHEEP AND LAMBS OF THE VARIOUS COUNTRIES OF THE WORLD AT THE DATES NAMED—Continued.

Countries.	Years.	Sheep and lambs.	Goats.
Europe—Continued.			
Greece[1]	1877	2, 921, 917	1, 836, 663
Italy	1881	8, 596, 108	2, 016, 307
Netherlands	1884	752, 949	156, 255
Portugal	1870	2, 977, 454	936, 863
Roumania	1884	4, 654, 776	
Russia in Europe[2]	1882	47, 508, 906	1, 374. 805
Servia	1882	3, 620, 750	725, 700
Spain	1878	16, 939, 288	3, 813, 000
Sweden and Norway:			
Sweden	1884	1, 410, 177	101, 496
Norway	1875	1, 686, 306	322, 861
Switzerland	1886	337, 905	414, 584
Turkey in Europe:[3]			
Eastern Roumelia	1883	1, 858, 839	425, 569
Asia:			
Russia:[4]			
Caucasia	(5)	4, 544, 300	1, 227, 000
Transcaucasia[6]	(5)	5, 067, 500	
India:[7]			
Madras	1877-'78	4, 600, 000	2, 700, 000
Bombay and Sind	1877-'78	8 3, 300, 000	
Punjab	1877-'78	8 3, 850, 000	
Central Provinces	1877-'78	8 641, 000	(8)
British Burmah	1877-'78	8 20, 000	
Mysore	1877-'78	8 1, 500, 000	
Berar	1877-'78	8 386, 000	
Ceylon	1884	53, 757	
Africa:			
Algeria	1880	6, 992, 218	3, 293, 033
Do	1884	6, 056, 683	3, 618, 392
Cape of Good Hope[9]	1875	11, 279, 743	
Natal	1885	535, 482	
Mauritius[10]	1884	8 30, 000	(8)
Orange Free State	1881	11 5, 056, 301	673, 924
Australasia:			
Australia:			
New South Wales	1885	34, 551, 622	
Victoria	18e5	10, 664, 598	
South Australia	1804	6, 606, 406	
Western Australia	1885	1, 702, 719	
Queensland	1885	8, 994, 322	
New Zealand	1885	14, 624, 547	
Tasmania	1885	1, 648, 627	
Fiji Islands	1884	5, 869	12 11, 429
Oceania:			
Tahiti and Moorea	1883	3, 000	1, 300

[1] Thessaly, which has become a part of the Greek Kingdom since 1877, is not included in these figures. The number of live-stock in this province has been estimated to include 2,000,000 oxen, 1,500,000 sheep, and 1,000,000 goats.
[2] Exclusive of Poland.
[3] There are no returns available for Turkey proper, and none for any of her tributary States except Eastern Roumelia.
[4] There are no returns for Asiatic Russia except from Caucasia and a part of Transcaucasia.
[5] These figures are not of uniform date, but were gathered from 1874 to 1883.
[6] These figures embrace statistics from the provinces of Bakou, Tiflis, Elizabethpol, Erivan, and Koutais.
[7] This statement is exclusive of the Northwest Provinces and Oudh and Bengal, with several minor provinces and all the native States except Mysore.
[8] Goats are included with sheep.
[9] Including 217,732 cattle, 35,357 horses, 303,080 sheep, and 15,635 swine in Basutoland.
[10] Approximate statement.
[11] Merinos.
[12] Angora goats.

No. 69.—Statement showing Prices of Different Kinds of Wool at Boston for Each Month from January, 1882, to December 1886, inclusive, with Average Prices and Range of Prices of the Same for Each Six and Twelve Months Ending December 31, 1882, to 1886, inclusive.

[Compiled by Messrs. George W. Bond & Co.]

Periods.	Ohio and Pennsylvania, X and above.	Michigan X.	Ohio No. 1.	Michigan No. 1.	Fleece No. 2 and coarse.	Combing and delaine.	Low and coarse combing.	Territory.	Texas.	Fall California.	Spring California.
1882.											
January	43 to 47.2	40 to 43	46.2 to 49	46 to 47	33 to 43	44 to 52	35 to 42	15 to 33.2	18 to 30.2	13 to 27.2	22.2 to 35
February	42.2 to 49	39.2 to 43	44 to 48	45 to 47	35 to 38.2	44.2 to 52.2	38 to 45	15 to 32	15 to 32	14 to 28	17 to 35
March	41 to 48	40 to 42	46.2 to 48	40 to 44	33.2 to 43	43 to 48	40 to 40	17 to 32	18 to 29	14 to 27	17.2 to 35
April	40 to 45	39 to 41	42 to 46.2	40 to 45	30 to 42	40 to 48	34 to 40	17 to 30	22.2 to 33	13.1 to 28	20 to 30
May	40 to 45	38.2 to 41	44 to 46	40 to 45	32.2 to 37.2	42.2 to 46	30 to 38	18 to 30	23 to 33.2	10 to 22	16 to 33
June	40 to 45	38 to 41	44 to 46	40 to 45	30 to 37.2	42.2 to 48		15 to 30	18 to 33	10 to 24	17 to 33
July	38 to 45	38 to 40	43 to 46	43.2 to 45	30 to 38	42.2 to 49	32 to 40	18 to 30	15 to 32	15 to 15	15 to 36
August	40 to 45.2	38 to 40	42 to 45	43 to 44	30 to 37.2	42.2 to 49	33 to 42.2	18 to 30	14 to 30	17.2 to 32	25 to 38
September	40 to 45	38 to 40	43 to 47	43 to 45	31 to 41	41 to 50	33 to 42.2	14 to 32	18 to 30	11 to 17.1	21 to 33
October	40 to 45	38.2 to 40	43 to 47	45 to 46	30 to 40	40 to 50	32 to 41	14 to 30	17 to 30	17 to 24	20 to 32
November	40 to 45	37 to 39	42 to 46	45 to 46	30 to 40	40 to 50	32 to 40	13.2 to 30	20 to 30	14.2 to 21	18 to 32
December	37 to 45	37 to 39	42 to 46		30 to 38	42 to 48	to 40	17 to 30.2			22 to 31
Twelve months: Average range	40 to 45.6	38.5 to 41	43.3 to 47	42.8 to 45.5	31.3 to 39.6	42.1 to 49.3	34.1 to 41	15.8 to 31.5	18 to 31	13.3 to 23.4	19.2 to 33
Average price	42.8	39.8	45.1	44.2	35.5	45.7	37.5	23.7	24.5	18.4	26.1
Six months: Average range	39.2 to 44.8	37.9 to 39.8	42 to 46	43.3 to 45	30.2 to 38.7	41.8 to 49.2	33.7 to 41.4	15.4 to 31.8	16.8 to 30.6	14.4 to 20.3	29.2 to 32.7
Average price	42	38.9	44	44.1	34.4	45.5	37.6	23.6	23.8	17.3	26.4
1883.											
January	38.3 to 44	36.2 to 38.1	42.2 to 44	42 to 44	30 to 35	40 to 48	32 to 37	16 to 30	19 to 30	11 to 25	16 to 30
February	41 to 46	37.2 to 41.2	42 to 45.2	to 42.2	30 to 39.2	41 to 50	34 to 35	16 to 30	20 to 30	12 to 18	10.2 to 33
March	42.1 to 44	40 to 42	44 to 46.2	to 46	33.2 to 40	42.2 to 50	31 to 40	15 to 30	25 to 30	11 to 22	16 to 33
April	40.2 to 44	38.2 to 40.1	42 to 44.2	to 45	33 to 40	42 to 48	36 to 40	15 to 25	16.2 to 31	10 to 21	14 to 24
May	40 to 44	37.2 to 38	42 to 43.2	to 39	34 to 42	42 to 45			20 to 30	12 to 21	16 to 30
June	37 to 41.2	36 to 37.2	to 42			39 to 44		14.2 to 30	15 to 30		16 to 29
July	35.2 to 39.2	35 to 37	to 40.2	37 to 38	30 to 35	38 to 44	35 to 37	16 to 28	11.2 to 30		20 to 30
August	33.3 to 40.2	34 to 35	38 to 40	to 42	32 to 34	38 to 43	31 to 35.2	14 to 28.2	14 to 28		17 to 30
September	35.2 to 40.2	34 to 35	38.2 to 41.1	to 38.2	30 to 34	37.2 to 43	31 to 37.2	14 to 32	14 to 26	15 to 20.2	16 to 30
October	37 to 41.2	34 to 35	40 to 42	36 to 39.2	31 to 37	35 to 46	33 to 39	10 to 28	16 to 25	11 to 18	16 to 30
November	36.1 to 41.2	34 to 35	39 to 40		32 to 35	36 to 45	30 to 37	15.2 to 25	14 to 18	10 to 21.2	16 to 30
December	38.2 to 41.2	34 to 35	40 to 41		32 to 34		31 to 36		16 to 25		18 to 27.2
Twelve months: Average range	38 to 42.5	35.8 to 37.4	40.8 to 42.6	40.4 to 41.6	32 to 36.6	38.0 to 46.5	32.7 to 37.4	15.3 to 28.7	18.2 to 28.8	11.5 to 21.3	17.2 to 30.6
Average price	40.3	36.6	41.7	41	34.3	42.7	35.1	22.2	21.5	16.4	23.9
Six months: Average range	36.1 to 40.6	34 to 35.3	39.3 to 40.8	37.4 to 39.5	32.8 to 31.8	41	31.5 to 36.0	15.1 to 28.3	14.9 to 27.8	12 to 20	16.5 to 29.6
Average price	35.9	34.7	40.1	38.5	33.8		34.2	21.7	21.4	16	23.1

1884.											
January	37 to 42	33.5 to 35	39 to 40	37 to 40	31 to 33	36 to 45	32 to 33	13 to 26.2	15 to 24.2	9 to 15	20 to 28
February	36 to 42	34 to 35	34 to 39	39.5	29 to 33	36 to 45	29 to 33	15 to 25	14 to 24	12.2 to 18	15 to 29
March	36.6 to 40.8	33.4 to 34.8	36 to 38.7	37.5	28.7 to 32.4	37.8 to 42.2	30 to 33	15.4 to 23.2	15.5 to 21.1	12.3	17 to 26.4
April	36.6 to 40	32.3 to 34	33 to 36.3	36 to 37	33	37.7 to 41.7	33.2	17.5 to 23.1	15 to 19	12 to 15.5	18 to 24.2
May	34.7 to 38.7	31.6 to 33.2	35 to 35.2	34.2 to 36	33.5	36 to 37	....	17.8 to 22.4	16.4 to 22.4	16 to 17	16.2 to 21.4
June	33 to 36.8	31 to 32.2	35.5	....	30	35 to 38	32	15.2 to 23	16.7 to 24.4	14	15.7 to 24.5
July	32.2 to 36.6	29.5 to 30.7	....	33 to 34.5	28 to 30	33.3 to 37.2	....	14 to 22.7	13.2 to 24.2	11 to 15.2	15.7 to 20.8
August	31.8 to 35.6	29.8 to 31.5	32.5 to 34.1	....	....	32.6 to 37.1	27 to 29.2	14.8 to 24	14.8 to 24.3	8	15.4 to 25.1
September	33 to 36.5	30 to 31.2	33.5	32 to 32.7	....	34.7 to 37.6	29.8	15 to 24	14.7 to 23.1	....	15.5 to 24.7
October	32.2 to 36.1	29.3 to 30.5	33 to 34	33 to 33.2	....	33.7 to 37.6	....	13.8 to 23.5	14.2 to 20.2	....	14.7 to 24.7
November	32.7 to 35.6	29 to 30	34.2	31	27 to 33.5	33.7 to 36.4	....	12.8 to 23.8	13 to 20	9 to 18	14.2 to 23.1
December	32 to 35.1	29.5 to 30.2	....	....	28	32.6 to 36.8	30	13.2 to 23.6	14.5 to 19.5	9 to 12	14.3 to 24.8
Twelve months:											
Average range	33.9 to 37.9	31.1 to 32.3	34.6 to 36.9	35 to 35.2	28.7 to 31.8	34.9 to 39.3	29 to 31.7	14.8 to 23.8	14.8 to 22.2	10.8 to 15.1	16 to 24.7
Average price	35.9	31.7	35.8	35.1	30.3	37.1	30.4	19.3	18.5	13	20.4
Six months:											
Average range	32.3 to 35.9	29.5 to 30.7	32.8 to 34	32.7 to 32.9	27.5 to 30.5	33.4 to 37.1	27 to 29.7	13.9 to 23.6	14.1 to 20.2	9.3 to 15.1	15 to 23.9
Average price	34.1	30.1	33.4	32.8	29	35.3	28.4	18.8	17.2	12.2	19.5
1885.											
January	32 to 35.4	29.7 to 30.4	31 to 33.8	....	27 to 28	31.8 to 36.5	....	13.6 to 22.8	14.6 to 21.4	10.2 to 13.1	16 to 20.8
February	31.2 to 35	29 to 30	31 to 32	29 to 32	27 to 29.3	32.3 to 36.6	....	12.1 to 22.6	16.2 to 19.5	12 to 15	12.7 to 24.7
March	31 to 35.3	29.5 to 30	30 to 32	30.5 to 32.5	....	31.2 to 36.5	....	15.2 to 23.9	13.6 to 20	11 to 14	15.8 to 25
April	30 to 35	28.5 to 29.5	30.5 to 32	30 to 31	26.5 to 28	31.3 to 35.6	....	15.9 to 20.9	15 to 17.3	11 to 17	15.8 to 18.8
May	30 to 34.4	28 to 29	30 to 31	30 to 34	29	27.5 to 35.8	....	15.8 to 20.6	17 to 20	10 to 14	15 to 20.6
June	30 to 33.5	27.5 to 29	30 to 31.3	30 to 32	26	38.3 to 33.25	....	17 to 21.1	23 to 22.6	10 to 14	12.7 to 18.5
July	30 to 32.6	27.2 to 28	29.5 to 30.7	29.5	26 to 27	29.8 to 34	....	15.7 to 23	16.5 to 22.8	11 to 14	18.3 to 22.2
August	30.2 to 33.2	28.2 to 29.4	31.5 to 32.3	30 to 31	27 to 30	33.2 to 35.4	....	16.1 to 22.8	16.5 to 21.7	....	15.6 to 21.6
September	31.5 to 35.6	30.3 to 32.2	32.5 to 33.5	32 to 35	27.5 to 30	32.5 to 37.2	....	15.5 to 25	19.3 to 23.8	11	14 to 22.0
October	32 to 37	30.6 to 31.2	34.2 to 35.4	33 to 35	30 to 33.5	33.7 to 38	....	16.6 to 24.5	21.3 to 22.5	....	15.4 to 25
November	33 to 36.6	31 to 31.6	30.3 to 34.7	33.5	30 to 32	32 to 36.6	....	18.8 to 24.8	20 to 23.8	10 to 14	17 to 21
December	33 to 37.5	30 to 31.2	36	34 to 36	29 to 32	33.5 to 36.2	....	19 to 24.4	24.2	11 to 14	17.7 to 21.5
Twelve months:											
Average range	31.1 to 34.7	28.8 to 29.9	28.1 to 32.6	23.2 to 29.7	20.7 to 27	31 to 35.0	....	15.5 to 22.5	15.2 to 21.2	8 to 11.6	15.1 to 21.4
Average price	32.9	29.4	30.4	26.5	23.9	35.8	....	19	18.2	9.8	18.3
Six months:											
Average range	31.6 to 35.4	29.6 to 30.6	31.6 to 33.8	32.3 to 33.8	28.3 to 30.8	32.5 to 36.2	....	16.9 to 24.1	18.7 to 23.2	10.7 to 13.3	16.3 to 22.3
Average price	33.5	30.1	32.7	32.8	30	34.4	....	20.5	21	12	19.3
1886.											
January	32.8 to 36.3	30.4 to 32	35.2 to 37.2	34.5 to 36	....	33.3 to 30.7	....	18.5 to 25.3	19 to 24	....	15 to 24.8
February	32 to 36	31 to 32	35.5 to 37.2	35 to 35.5	....	34.3 to 36.5	....	18 to 24.4	19 to 24	....	18.2 to 24
March	31.6 to 35.1	30.5 to 31.2	....	....	....	34.2 to 36.1	....	19 to 25.2	19 to 24	....	17 to 22
April	30.6 to 34.2	28.0 to 30	33 to 35	....	....	33.2 to 34.6	....	19 to 25.2	18	....	17 to 22
May	30.2 to 34.2	27.5 to 28.5	33.5	....	....	28 to 31	....	18 to 23.5	17 to 21.2	....	10 to 18.2
June	30.2 to 33	30 to 32	33 to 35	....	....	30.5 to 32.3	....	19.2 to 23.0	20 to 24.5	11 to 15	15.5 to 20.4
July	32.5 to 35.2	30.7 to 32.1	....	35.5 to 36.5	....	34.5 to 37.8	....	19.5 to 26.2	21.3 to 26.2	12 to 13	16.2 to 23.7
August	32 to 35.1	30.5 to 31.8	....	36	....	35 to 38.6	....	19 to 27.7	21.5 to 26	....	18.8 to 24.2
September	32.4 to 35.7	31 to 32	....	35.9 to 36.7	....	34 to 38.2	....	19.5 to 27.8	20.7 to 25	....	18.7 to 24.5

No. 69.—STATEMENT SHOWING PRICES OF DIFFERENT KINDS OF WOOL AT BOSTON FOR EACH MONTH FROM JANUARY, 1882, TO DECEMBER, 1886, INCLUSIVE, &c.—Continued.

Periods.	Ohio and Pennsylvania. X and above.	Michigan. X.	Ohio. No. 1.	Michigan. No. 1.	Fleece No. 2 and coarse.	Combing and delaine.	Low and coarse combing.	Territory.	Texas.	Fall. California.	Spring. California.
1886.											
October	34 to 37.5	32.1 to 32.9		37 to 37.8		34.8 to 40.8		19.5 to 28.2	20 to 24	14 to 20	19.6 to 24.6
November	34.5 to 37.5	32.2 to 37		37		34.6 to 40		19.5 to 26.2	20.3 to 20.6	15 to 18	20.2 to 23.5
December	34 to 37.2	32 to 32.5		36 to 37		35 to 38.5		21 to 27.1	19 to 22.2	17 to 18	19.2 to 24
Twelve months:											
Average range	32.2 to 33.6	30.5 to 31.6	34 to 36.5	35.6 to 36.8	27 to 32.5	33.4 to 37.1	27 to 32	22.5 to 25.9	19.6 to 24.1	12.4 to 15.9	17.6 to 23
Average price	33.9	31.1	35.3	36.2	29.8	35.3	29.5	24.2	21.9	14.2	20.3
Six months:											
Average range	33.2 to 36.4	31.4 to 33.1		36.1 to 36.8		34.7 to 39.0		19.7 to 27.2	20.5 to 24.0	14.5 to 17.3	18.8 to 20.8
Average price	34.8	32.3		36.5		36.9		23.5	22.3	15.9	19.8

No. 70.—Statement showing the Price, or Cost, in the Foreign Markets of Imported Wools Entered for Consumption in the United States, for Each Year Ending June 30, from 1867 to 1887, inclusive.

Years ending June 30—	Class 1, clothing wools.			Class 2, combing wools.			Class 3, carpet and similar wools.		
	Value, 32 cents or less per pound.	Value, over 32 cents per pound.	Total clothing wools.	Value, 32 cents or less per pound.	Value, over 32 cents per pound.	Total combing wools.	Value, 12 cents or less per pound.	Value, over 12 cents per pound.	Total carpet wools.
	Cents.	Cents.	Cents.	Cents.	Cents.	Cents.	Cents.	Cents.	Cents.
1867	.265	.376	.327	.211		.211	.103	.175	.147
1868	.147	.390	.163		.121	.121	.107	.192	.150
1869	.197	.371	.202	.227	.345	.241	.107	.187	.132
1870	.170	.362	.191	.243	.367	.278	.105	.165	.116
1871	.198	.374	.201	.176	.367	.179	.105	.183	.126
1872	.227	.400	.247	.185	.436	.218	.108	.245	.177
1873	.250	.482	.279	.227	.591	.229	.119	.245	.209
1874	.286	.397	.338	.218	.391	.262	.120	.225	.169
1875	.257	.335	.274	.226	.399	.277	.124	.197	.145
1876	.241	.368	.253	.296	.380	.366	.122	.210	.161
1877	.235	.444	.236	.312	.356	.331	.115	.198	.140
1878	.237	.378	.244	.305	.353	.320	.112	.194	.134
1879	.211	.395	.213	.234	.388	.242	.113	.181	.117
1880	.227	.374	.229	.268	.373	.287	.112	.218	.137
1881	.225	.380	.230	.281	.362	.288	.117	.197	.141
1882	.220	.411	.224	.277	.371	.280	.118	.192	.141
1883	.220	.452	.221	.241	.446	.251	.121	.184	.139
1884	.222	.313	.225	.229	.402	.237	.110	.169	.125
1885	.221	.427	.221	.221	.428	.217	.101	.173	.109
1886	.160	.492	.181	.221	.395	.228	.097	.172	.105
1887	.183	.334	.184	.231	.417	.234	.100	.181	.120

Notes.—Washed and scoured wools not included in the above table.

During the years 1864 to 1867 inclusive the classification, according to value of classes 1 and 2, was 30 cents or less, and over 30 cents, per pound, respectively.

The rates of duty on imports of raw wool during the above period were as follows:

On wools of classes 1 and 2, if valued at 32 cents or less per pound, 10 cents per pound and 11 per cent. to include 1863, and 10 cents per pound after 1883; if valued over 32 cents per pound, 12 cents per pound and 10 per cent. to include 1863, and 12 cents per pound after 1883.

On wools of class 3, if valued at 12 cents or less per pound, 3 cents per pound to include 1863, and 2½ cents per pound after 1883: if valued over 12 cents per pound, 6 cents per pound to include 1863, and 5 cents per pound after 1883.

The only exception from the above rates was in 1867 on combing wools, being on wools valued at 32 cents or less per pound, 10 cents per pound and 10 per cent.; and on wools valued over 32 cents per pound, 12 cents and 22 per centum.

A reduction of 10 per centum was provided for from the regular rates of duty on all classes of wool from August 1, 1872, to March 3, 1875.

O

TREASURY DEPARTMENT.

WOOL AND MANUFACTURES OF WOOL.

SPECIAL REPORT

RELATING TO

THE IMPORTS AND EXPORTS OF WOOL AND ITS MANUFACTURES IN
THE UNITED STATES AND THE PRINCIPAL FOREIGN COUNTRIES;
ALSO ITS PRODUCTION, CONSUMPTION, AND MANUFACTURE;
ALSO THE TARIFF DUTIES IMPOSED ON THE IMPORTS
OF WOOL AND THE MANUFACTURES OF WOOL,
FROM 1789 TO THE PRESENT TIME,
ETC., ETC., ETC.

PREPARED BY THE
OHIEF OF THE BUREAU OF STATISTICS,
TREASURY DEPARTMENT.

WASHINGTON:
GOVERNMENT PRINTING OFFICE.
1887.